The Styles of
EUROPEAN ART

The Styles of
EUROPEAN ART

Introduction by Sir Herbert Read

with 873 illustrations

HARRY N. ABRAMS, INC., *Publishers*

NEW YORK

GENERAL EDITOR: URSULA HATJE

Translated from the German by
Wayne Dynes and Richard Waterhouse

Printed and bound in Great Britain

CONTENTS

Contents

I   A cast-gold ornament of a panther twisted into a circle. The eye, nostril, ear, claws, and tail were originally filled with inlay. Found in Siberia. Seventh or sixth century BC. Leningrad, Hermitage Museum.

II   The Sutton Hoo great buckle, gold. First half of seventh century AD. London, British Museum.

These two objects, separated by 1,300 years, illustrate the similarity of style that may persist over many centuries, a similarity that is to be ascribed to function and to methods of working the same kind of material rather than to any ethnic or cultural community of feeling.

STYLE is one of the most elusive concepts in the history of culture and it is one which English-speaking art historians have been content to leave ambiguous. (That the bibliography of the subject to be found at the end of this volume contains few works by English authors is no oversight.) The derivation of the word from the Latin *stilus* indicates that originally the connotation was personal: it meant the peculiarities of the marks made by an individual using a *stilus* or pen, and we sometimes revert to this meaning when we speak of style as the *handwriting* of a painter. The famous definition of Buffon, always quoted out of its context, equates style with *the man himself*; and Goethe, in a less well-known but finer definition, affirmed that style, far from being a superficial characteristic of art, belongs to the deepest foundations of cognition, or the inner essence of things. At the opposite extreme we speak of a style of hairdressing, a style of clothing, a boxer's or a skater's style. But always, in these popular usages, we refer to a personal idiosyncrasy, or, at most, an idiosyncrasy copied or adopted by a restricted group of people.

It may be that there is an imperceptible gradation of meaning between such uses of the word and the use of the same word in the classification of those phases of the history of art which are the concern of this volume. It is also possible that a difference of degree constitutes in this case a difference of kind. If we shift from the person to the period, from the individual work of art to the works of a school or of a generation or of a city or a country or a race, do we not lose sight of the original meaning of the word? In what sense is the 'Englishness' of English art, so obvious to the objective eye of a scholar like Dr Nikolaus Pevsner, a style in the sense that we also speak of the Turneresque, meaning a personal characteristic of the style of an individual artist, a style which may indeed be generalized and imitated by other artists.

Nevertheless some styles are less personal than others, and we still call them a style. We speak, for example, of the 'animal style' characteristic of the Scythian hunting people of Eastern Europe and Southern Russia, a style reflected in the art of the

III   Page from the Utrecht Psalter, illustrating Psalm LXIV (detail). School of Reims, ninth century. Utrecht, University Library, MS. 32.

IV   The Prophet Amos. From the Bury Bible, 1121–48. Cambridge, Corpus Christi College.
Two contrasted styles in the same kind of artifact. The style of the Utrecht Psalter is nervous, linear, highly individualistic (as is the style of the Winchester school in England about two centuries later). The twelfth-century Bible from Bury St Edmunds Abbey is by comparison stiff and conventional, the style of a school rather than of an individual.

Migration period in Central Europe and Gaul (see pages 119 to 129). Consisting for the most part of metal harness ornaments, this art is remarkable for its consistent vitality, a vitality in which it is not possible, however, to detect the 'handwriting' of any individual artist. Some other forms of art bordering on industry, for example, the illuminated manuscripts produced during the Middle Ages – such as the Utrecht Psalter (ninth century) or the Bury St Edmunds Bible (early twelfth century) – are so distinct and personal in their style that we can trace the work of one particular artist in manuscripts that are now widely distributed throughout the Christian world. These facts suggest that technique controls style, and that some techniques, such as painting and sculpture, take the personal impress of the artist more easily than others (metal-work or mosaics).

As a matter of fact we have a word to indicate the transition from a personal style to an impersonal style – we then call the result *stylization*. By this word we mean a style that has lost its personal touch, has become generalized and adaptable to a large number of artifacts. The stylized products of the Art Nouveau period are a relatively recent example of this process. It may still be possible to find a personal element in the style of artists like Toulouse-Lautrec and Aubrey Beardsley, and architects like Charles Rennie Mackintosh had a personal idiom that was then copied or imitated by other architects. But the general style that spread throughout Europe in the latter part of the nineteenth century was a fashion, a mannerism, that is only remotely related to the personal styles of the great artists of the past, or period styles such as the Gothic or the Renaissance.

V   Aubrey Beardsley, 'J'ai baisé ta bouche, Iokanaan'. Illustration to 'Salome', by Oscar Wilde, 1894.

VI   Wilhelm Wolz, Salome. Colour lithograph, 1896.
These two illustrations of the same subject show the conformity of separate artists to a common period style. It is possible that Wolz may have been directly influenced by Beardsley, but there are too many similarities of style among the artifacts of this period for the style itself to be attributed to any particular artists.

Heinrich Wölfflin, in the Introduction to a fundamental work on this subject,[1] considered the whole subject of the history of art as a problem of 'the development of style'. He began with the realization that all the elements of a work of art – form, subject-matter, tonality, motive – fuse into a unity which remains the expression of a certain temperament. But it is also obvious that an individual's temperament is formed, or at least strongly influenced, by his environment. It is not too fanciful to suppose, as Wölfflin did, that the general impression of tranquillity given by Dutch art is directly related to the flat meadows round Antwerp, whereas the vigour and movement and massiveness with which an individual like Rubens handles similar themes is the expression of a temperament that rises superior to its environment. The interrelations of individual temperament, physical and social environment, training and opportunity can be (and have been) discussed endlessly, and it is not within the scope of this introduction to review or summarize such an immense and complex subject. It is sufficient to defend the anomaly by which, in a volume of this kind, the concept of style is held to apply with equal rightness to individuals, periods, and peoples.

It will be found that the contributors to this volume follow the example of Wölfflin (and of other German writers such as Semper, Riegl, and Worringer) in treating style as essentially a 'problem', and by a problem they mean above all a problem of psychology. Form itself is a problem (the title of one of Worringer's books is, literally translated, 'Form-problems of Gothic'). There is no style without form, and though we speak of 'pure form', meaning a form devoid of stylistic idiosyncrasies, it is still possible to regard purity itself as a style (Raphael's style has sometimes been described as 'pure'). Style is always a mode in which form exists. The concepts used by Wölfflin to indicate the development of style in the

[1] *Kunstgeschichtliche Grundbegriffe*, translated as *Principles of Art History*, London, G. Bell & Sons, 1932.

VII   Chaïm Soutine, Portrait of a Boy, 1928. Washington, National Gallery of Art (Chester Dale Collection).

VIII   Amadeo Modigliani, Portrait of Madame G. van Muyden, 1917. São Paulo, Museum of Art.
At first sight no style might seem so individualistic as Modigliani's but it has an obvious affinity to that of Soutine. Both artists were part of the stylistic development that led from Jugendstil (Art Nouveau) through Munch and Van Gogh to the German Expressionists (and even to French painters like Rouault and Matisse) but both artists could also give an individualistic accent to a prevailing mannerism.

A psychology of perception should include a psychology of the creative process, a subject altogether too large for this brief introduction. But it must be affirmed, as against all attempts to categorize style by means of formal analysis, that the work of art, as Paul Klee said, is first of all 'genesis'; 'it is never experienced purely as a result'. Perception is the most vital process in living matter, in man in particular, and it is controlled by instinct rather than by the will. It is multi-directional, arbitrary, and when it comes to rest on a particular object, of which we then become 'conscious', it is already 'forming' a picture out of the amorphous confusion of visual sensations. There is a primordial element of style in each 'good Gestalt', as the psychologists of perception name this primitive act of awareness. The originative artist begins to work at this primitive level, as Klee again will witness – I quote an entry from his diary, written in 1902 at the age of twenty-three:

To have to begin by what is smallest is as precarious as it is necessary. I will be like a newborn child, knowing nothing about Europe, nothing at all. To be ignorant of poets, wholly without verve, almost primordial. Then I will do something very modest, think of something very, very small, totally formal. My pencil will be able to put it down, without any technique. All that is needed is an auspicious moment; the concise is easily represented. And soon it is done. It was a tiny, but real act, and from the repetition of acts that are small, but my own, eventually a work will come, on which I can build. The nude body is an entirely suitable object. In the academies I have caught it little by little from all sides. But now I will no longer project a shadow of it but rather proceed in such a way that everything essential, even though hidden by optical perspective, appears on the plane. And soon a small, incontestable possession is discovered, *a style is created*.[1]

[1] Quoted from *Art and Visual Perception: a psychology of the creative eye*. By Rudolf Arnheim, University of California Press, 1954. My italics.

art of the high Renaissance during the sixteenth and seventeenth centuries all reduce to formal contrasts – linear versus painterly, plane versus recession, closedness versus openness, multiplicity versus unity, absolute versus relative clarity of the subject. These are all *ex post facto* analytical terms. It is not to be supposed that Dürer, for example, deliberately chose a linear style while Rembrandt deliberately chose a painterly style. But it is no less difficult to suppose that these artists merely followed a prevailing fashion. Such academicism (as we call it) prevails in periods of decadence when, for want of an original style, artists resort to the deliberate revival of the style of an earlier period – a process which can excuse if not justify the moralistic attitude of a painter like William Blake, who condemned all painterly styles as the work of the Devil. By contrast this very deliberateness of styles in decadent periods confirms the unconscious roots of style in periods that are originative. In other words, we are brought back to the psychology of the process, which is a psychology of perception.

Between the creation of an individual style and the diffusion of a common style throughout a group of artists or the art of a country or a period there takes place a process of diffusion and assimilation that is the main theme of the contributions to this volume. It is not always, perhaps not often, possible to trace the origins of a style to the work of one artist, but there are artists like Giotto, Michelangelo, and Poussin whose names can be associated with a style that irradiates from a centre, that centre being a small, incontestable discovery and possession of one individual.

What is the nature of that unique discovery? Is it something that the artist has seen, some hitherto unobserved aspect of nature, or is it an invention, an arrangement of line, form, and colour that never existed before? Does the artist within the physiological limits of his reflecting eye, see an eidetic image of the object he has chosen to depict (let us ignore the all-important question of what leads him in the first place to make the choice of a particular subject), or is his version of the object, however seemingly exact, none the less determined by directives he has unconsciously absorbed from his environment?

It has been maintained, notably by Professor E. H. Gombrich, that the artist is always influenced by a pre-determined way of seeing – in other words, that he is always the victim of a prevailing style. Professor Gombrich suggests that the artist interprets what he sees according to the visual conventions of his age; if he looks at the object, at 'Nature', it is merely to correct a formula, or a *schema* already existing in his mind or imagination. The artist approaches Nature with a question – what do I see? – and the answer he receives must conform to what he considers reasonable or coherent – it must satisfy his visual judgment. The standard of his visual judgment is likely to be one that he has acquired by training or by imitation; it belongs to the visual conventions of the period. The artist's choice of a mode of expression is therefore restricted to certain formulas that readily appeal to (or are understood by) his contemporaries. This leads to a rejection of any theory of art as an expression of personal feeling – style has lost all its association with the *stilus*, with 'the man himself'. Equally, Gombrich rejects the other extreme which would see style as the expression of some supra-individual spirit, the 'spirit of the age' or 'the spirit of the race'.

The German art historians whom Gombrich criticizes – Riegl, Worringer, Sedlmayr – might object that the conventions that are said to determine what and how the artist paints are concepts of an equally supra-individual and intangible kind. It is necessary in all this discussion of the problem of style to bear in mind Mr T. S. Eliot's distinction between style and individual talent. To identify style with a convention whether of a school, a country, or a period, is to give it a body but to deprive it of its life-blood, which always comes from the sensibility of the individual artist. Art would have no history but for the individual artist's determined effort to invent a significant form – a form signifying his unique visual experience. Our basic psychological activity (whether or not we are artists) is one of integration, of seeking an equilibrium between the mind or psyche and the external world. Style represents such a moment of achieved equilibrium. To quote an art historian who has made a profound contribution to our subject, Henri Focillon in *The Life of Forms in Art*:

> Human consciousness is in perpetual pursuit of a language and a style. To assume consciousness is at once to assume form. Even at levels far below the zone of definition and clarity, forms, measures, and relationships exist. The chief characteristic of the mind is to be constantly describing *itself*. The mind is a design that is in a state of ceaseless flux, of ceaseless weaving and then unweaving, and its activity, in this sense, is an artistic activity. Like the artist, the mind works upon nature. This it does with the premises that are so carelessly and so copiously offered it by physical life, and upon these premises the mind never ceases to labour. It seeks to make them its very own, to give them mind, to give them *form*.[1]

To this quotation I would add another from a critic of literature who has been all too unjustly forgotten, J. Middleton Murry in a book devoted to *The Problem of Style*:

> For the highest style is that wherein the two current meanings of the word blend: it is a combination of the maximum of personality with the maximum of impersonality; on the one hand it is a concentration of peculiar and personal emotion, on the other it is a complete projection of this personal emotion into the created thing. The manifest dangers of talking about style are two: the danger of talking about the accidents and not the essentials; and, in the endeavour to avoid this, the danger of vague generalization. Style is many things; but the more definable these are, the more capable of being pointed at with the finger, the more remote are they from the central meaning hidden in the word: the expression that is

[1] Trans. C. B. Hogan and G. Kubler. New York (Wittenborn), 1948, p. 44.

inevitable and organic to an individual mode of experience, an expression which, even when this exact relation has been achieved, rises or falls in the scale of absolute perfection according as the mode of experience expressed is more or less significant and universal – more or less completely embraces, is more or less adequate to, the whole of our human universe. In comparison with this meaning of the word Style, others seem to fade away almost into triviality; for this is the style that is the very pinnacle of the pyramid of art, the end that is the greatest of all as Aristotle would say, at once the supreme achievement and the vital principle of all that is enduring in literature, the surpassing virtue that makes for many of us some few dozen lines in Shakespeare the most splendid conquest of the human mind.'[1]

In the end, therefore, the problem of style remains a personal problem, and however ingeniously the historian may weave together the strands that were individual and vital at the time of their temporal existence, his generalized pattern is essentially deceptive. Just as a word like *foliage* is a dead concept unless we remember that it indicates a multiplicity of particular forms, each unique not only as a species among other species, but also as an individual leaf of a particular size and shape, a leaf moreover with vivid colour ceaselessly vibrating in the adventitious winds, absorbing the rays of a common sun and receiving sap from a common soil, so the word *style* is a dead concept unless we remember that it indicates (in so far as it constitutes style) a passionate intention on the part of the artist to represent a moment of vision that is unique. We may forget, as we look through the many illustrations in this volume to which no artist's name is attached, that nevertheless the work of art is a product of human hands, and that to the degree these hands worked with an infallible instinct and matched the work, not merely with the work of other artists, some of whom they may have acknowledged as masters, but also with the subtlest apprehension and affirmation of their own nervous sensibility, to that degree these works of art achieved a combination of vitality and beauty we call style. Style is not imitation; style is not the matching of making to any bloodless concept; style, to repeat Goethe's definition once more, 'rests on the deepest foundations of cognition, on the inner essence of things, in so far as this is given to us to comprehend in visible and tangible forms'.

[1] Oxford University Press, 1925, pp. 35–6.

HERBERT READ

The art of the Greeks

The problem of art in early times

Art, in its beginnings, has little to do with ability or communication. It is more an instrument to bring the world under control, to make the unintelligible clear, the unreal real and present. It makes what is strange close and familiar, and expresses joy at the richness of life.

The first works of art are not art as we understand the word, but rather functional works, for domestic or religious use. The world is full of hostile and friendly spirits, of beasts and spectres, of gods claiming worship and demanding representation. Only through representation in its fullest sense of image and invocation, dance and song, are beings of different natures brought together. Only in this way can spirits and gods be made tame, well-disposed towards man and ready to have dealings with him. In the ecstasy of the ritual dance man himself becomes god and the god so near that he seizes the dancer and manifests himself through him.

A few works bear eloquent witness to this closeness of the gods in early times [3]. It is hard to say whether they represent deities or human beings, for god and man appear indistinguishable.

The role of time in the work of art

Every object made by human hand is the product of a process in time. Man needs time to mould clay into shape, to carve a figure, or a stone. During the early periods of history, the gods were often imagined as personified by or residing in a stone that had fallen from the sky, or a sharp piece of wood or a striking rock foundation. Such matters belong more to the history of religion than to the history of art. For the most part, the object that can be worshipped or used is brought into existence only through effort.

Through the temporal process of effort, the substance of the work gains a new quality. Both functional and cult objects are there 'for something else':

1 Bronze statue of Poseidon, found in the sea off Cape Artemisium (Euboea) in 1926 and 1928, c. 460 BC. Athens, National Museum. The torso is the fulcrum of movement here. Slight relief emphasizes the extension of the body.

the work serves a purpose. What we call a work of art, however, exists not for something else, but simply for and by itself. This modern conception was unknown to antiquity until the Hellenistic age. Yet every antique work of handicraft has such a modern heightened quality that, while not originally intended as a work of art, it has become one for us. The more strongly the time process seems to express itself in the work, the more intensely this exists as a work of art.

The stylistic problem of mimesis and abstraction

The first creations of man that are recognized as works of art show an amazing closeness to nature, a sympathetic understanding of reality (*mimesis*: imitation), which we meet for example in Ice age cave paintings. On the other hand, an abstracting and geometrizing tendency appears early on, that separates these works of man from the flourishing life of nature. In a sense, these opposite approaches have behind them opposite outlooks on human life. The empathic mode of representation resembles the outlook of those who hunt and gather, whereas the abstract tendency, which is evident from about the sixth and fifth millennia BC, can be linked with the activity of settled farmers and town dwellers.

These two approaches do, of course, interpenetrate as the ages pass, and one of the most remarkable experiences is to watch the gradual change of a naturalistic into an abstract trend, and the breaking up of a solidly built geometric system through the intrusion of realist pictorial concepts. Like Worringer, one can even view the whole of art history as a dialectic between two principles of style: abstraction and empathy.

What does 'style' mean?

Human beings always experience time as history. In specific situations and under similar conditions history raises the same questions, which are answered in different yet essentially analogous ways. Related conditions lead to similar works, which betray the historical character of their origin. The particular historical context marks the form of every creation, from dress and footwear to temple, from ritual dance to poem or theatre.

This common formal language in every aspect of life is what we generally mean by 'style' (in the sense of 'period style'). During these early periods it has such force that one can speak of 'stylistic pressure' which affects many quite differently intended attempts at expression. The process resembles the development of speech, where the child's experiment is absorbed by the pre-existing pattern, the personal intent by the accepted word. All private ventures thus end in a pre-established form, which can only occur in a given historical situation. 'Not everything is possible in every era.'

The problem of style becomes more complex in self-conscious ages, because the individuality of a particular artist can then be distinguished from the general style of a period, and up to a point may even contrast with it. Answers of a more or less personal character are given to questions raised by the particular historical situation. The artist achieves his own style through coming to terms with predecessors and fellow combatants. In Greek art from the archaic period on there was much scope for individuality, but even during classical times it never found such frequent expression as in art since the Renaissance.

The determinants of Greek art

The art of the Greeks, like that of every people, was formed by the basic factors of geography and climate, as well as by the special conditions of the Bronze age culture of the second millennium BC and the Iron age culture of the first. But in Greece a wholly distinctive contribution was made by religion and myth, which provided art with its subject-matter and problems. Even today, a visitor can see an amazing richness and plasticity of structure in the Greek countryside. Everyone knows what sharp contours the bright light produces. Under such conditions it was almost to be expected that the clearly articulated, firmly outlined sculptural form should become the special vehicle of expression in Greek art.

With its rugged mountains, fertile plains, twisting bays and girdle of sea, the variously shaped and structured landscape favoured a division and fragmentation of Greek tribal life into states that were quite literally city-states (*polis*). It was mainly this that gave rise to the many-sidedness of Greek life and the exceptional urge for freedom and independence. Art in the great civilizations of the ancient Orient preserved almost the same forms for thousands of years and was historical only in the mechanical sense of rise and decline. Greek art, open to all stimuli, has an inner history following a logical course that belongs to it alone. Since it is in Greek art that man was first revealed and represented as a free being before a free and humane god, Greek form underlies the development of Roman and hence also of European art.

Contrary to Oriental religions, religion in Greece was not upheld by a priestly caste. Any free man could become a priest, and anyone inspired by the Muses could extol the gods and their deeds in song. True, there were privileged families from which the priests at the large sanctuaries often came; but their power was never such as to allow them to dominate religious life.

The freedom enjoyed by the Greeks accords with the freedom of the Greek idea of a god. Though Zeus (Jupiter), the father of the gods, directs and guides the history of the world, he himself is subject to a final destiny behind him, embodied in the Moirae (Parcae). Alongside rule his brothers Poseidon (Neptune), god of the seas, and Hades (Pluto), lord of the underworld. Hera (Juno), the sister and wife of Zeus, is a powerful and high-handed Olympian, as are Aphrodite (Venus) and her child companion Eros (Amor), the goddess of love and god of amorous desire. No less mighty are Apollo with his golden bow, the far-striking son of Leto (Latonia), and his sister Artemis (Diana), the chaste mistress of the hunt. Hera's lame and ugly son Hephaestus (Vulcan) is the god of smiths and weapons, lawful husband of the beautiful love goddess. Another powerful and independent goddess is the virgin Athena (Minerva), who sprang from the head of Zeus. She holds sway over Attica, protecting wisdom, learning, handicrafts, and all kinds of work. But just like Ares (Mars), the fierce god of battle, she delights in warfare and combat. Hermes, Zeus' son by Maie, appears as the god of flocks and herds, of trade, deceit, and lucky finds or discoveries. He is the messenger to the gods and guide of souls, who leads the dead to the abode of Hades. Dionysus is the lord of wine, who with his band of frenzied maenads and satyrs ecstatically breaks laws and regulations. Hestia (Vesta) watches over hearth and home, guarding social life in house and city.

To the Greeks, Mother Earth (Gaea, Ge; lat. Tellus) was the oldest deity, who with Uranus – Heaven – was the progenitor of every god and human being. Later, the cult of the Earth Mother merged with that of Demeter (Ceres), who was worshipped with her daughter Kore chiefly at Eleusis. Demeter protects the earth's fruits, but Kore was carried off by Hades, and as Persephone (Proserpine) now spends a third of the year with him in the underworld.

The gods conceived by the Indo-Germanic Greeks originally had no images. They were worshipped under the open sky in sacred groves, the focus of worship being the altar, at which sacrifices were made. Not until the Greeks encountered the statues of the Mediterranean world did their gods receive cult figures and temples. Temples always remained the homes of the gods, who were thought of as dwelling there. Zeus first acquired a temple and cult statue at Olympia during the fifth century BC. Despite the many votive offerings of the archaic period that portray him, he had been worshipped under the open sky, without a real cult image. A Greek temple is the house of the divinity, not the congregation's meeting-place, like a church in Christian times.

All these figures from the Olympian family – which has many other members, such as Asclepius (Asculapius), god of healing and son of Apollo, or Nike (Victoria), goddess of victory – were clearly individualized from the start, appearing as free, independent, and often autocratic beings. The Greeks were able to develop into free men with their own personalities, after the model of their free gods. It is therefore wrong to hold, with Marxist historians, that the distinguishing mark of Greek culture is that of a slave-owning people. No doubt most artists of the heroic age of the second millennium BC came from Crete or the Orient to sell their skill to the princes; but from the geometric period (tenth to end of eighth century BC) onward, Greeks as well practised handicrafts and art, and besides this improved their status. During the Greek classical age the artist was no longer a philistine looked down on contemptuously, but someone honoured and respected who could mix with the great. His self-confidence was already considerable in archaic times. His work appears unconstrained, and was praised down the ages. Whereas only one person – the god-king – was really free in the Orient, a Greek city-state consisted of many freemen, all of them strongly differentiated. Christianity first brought the message that all human beings are free. But the foundations of this doctrine lie in Greek antiquity; for the Greeks made the idea of freedom fundamental to our lives.

THE PREHISTORIC PERIOD OF THE SECOND MILLENNIUM

This period is characterized by middle and late Helladic (Mycenaean) culture in the mainland and middle and late Minoan culture on Crete, both of which used bronze and therefore belong to the

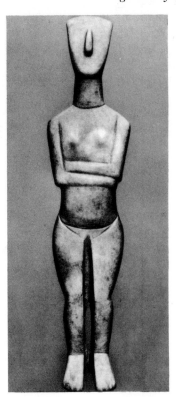

2 *Statuette of a goddess, a so-called Cycladic idol, third millennium BC. Berlin, Staatliche Museen. Starkly abstract rendering of the body and head; little plasticity (these figures found in graves must have been laid flat, not erected).*

Bronze age. The first Greek immigrants had already settled on the mainland, and through intermarrying with the native Aegean population (Pelasgians, Carians, Leleges) their civilization, determined by the superior Minoan culture of Crete, reached its peak. In the fifteenth century BC, the heyday of Minoan art was ended by invading Greeks (Achaeans). From the late thirteenth century BC, civilization on the mainland was destroyed through the incursion of the Dorians and West Greeks, who razed the strongholds of the Mycenaean rulers and conquered the Peloponnese. Citadel VIIA at Troy – Homer's citadel – fell during the late thirteenth century BC.

In the middle of the second millennium BC, Crete had complete maritime supremacy in the Mediterranean, as is proved by the absence of fortifications to the palace buildings. A king such as the legendary Minos plays a great part in Greek myth, and the fact that Athens was under tribute to Crete is shown by the story of Theseus and the Minotaur. Greek myth originates in this age of territorial conquest, of mighty

3   *Faïence statuette of a priestess (goddess?), from the Palace of Knossos, seventeenth century* BC. *Heraclion, National Museum. Typical Minoan female costume: a flounced skirt, leaving the chest free. Clearly articulated structure: the lower part bell-shaped; the upper part of a refined yet natural physicality.*

royal families and of great upheavals. About 1100 BC iron weapons began to come into use. This was a fundamental change in the pattern of culture. The victorious advance of the Dorians was probably due in part to these new weapons and to the increased mobility brought by the now general use of the horse ridden in battle. The chief 'sacred' animal of Minoan civilization was the bull, which was largely supplanted by the horse in geometric times. As early as the sixteenth century BC the Minoans possessed a type of picture-writing (Linear A) that has yet to be deciphered and was used principally for documents and archive records. From the fifteenth century, Linear B developed out of it.

Our oldest representation here of art on Greek soil is an *idol from the Cyclades*, belonging to the early Bronze age culture of the third millennium BC [2]. The feminine forms of the body have been abstracted in an amazing simplification. On the cone-shaped neck rests a head of which only the nose is a defining

feature. The breasts have been schematized as round swellings, the forearms rest horizontally before the body, and the genitals are represented as a triangle. This is a coldly abstract formal language. The figure has no pedestal, being half-sitting and half-standing. These Cycladic female idols, mostly found lying in graves or houses, presumably represent the Great Goddess. Ours, too, can be taken to represent a fertility goddess, the mother of all generation, growth, and ripening.

Seen against the abstraction in Cycladic sculpture of the third and early second millennium BC, the faience *statuette from Knossos [3]*, now at Heraclion, takes us into a different world. Here we have ripe, plump corporality, a gaily coloured figure magnificently captured. With apron and corseted waspwaist, the goddess stands in a big flounced skirt, grasping snakes in her raised hands. A predatory beast perches on her head, which is adorned with a kind of diadem. Her wide-open eyes stare intently. Her breasts have been left bare, following the fashion of the times. As other examples show, the figure is imagined as though seized by ecstasy and only its size forces it round to a frontal view. It remains an open question whether the figure represents a queen or priestess in a divine form, or a goddess herself, so completely fused are appearance and conception, image and divinity. The style indicates at once a naïve and a refined closeness to nature. It is clear from the complicated dress that this is a decidedly courtly art. At its peak, it combines stylization and natural form in a manner quite different from that of the Greek classical age. This emphasis on the female element in Cretan art indicates the strong matriarchal impulses still shaping society in the second millennium BC.

The bull was the 'sacred' animal of Minoan art. In the milieu of refined court society, ritual bull games took place, and were depicted in frescoes at the palace of Knossos. In one of the frescoes of the palace, a religious dancer is shown performing a kind of somersault on the back of a bull stretched out as it leaps. A girl seizes the bull by a horn, perhaps in order to swing herself over it in the same way. Behind the animal another female figure stands lightly poised with raised arms: she is probably meant to catch the dancer on the bull's back. Such an instantaneous seizing of a complex and lively movement appears just as naïve and, at the same time, sophisticated as the above-mentioned statuette. Time and again Cretan art seeks to capture the intoxication of movement, and in so doing achieves astonishing results. It shrinks from nothing, for the artist has as yet no conscious limits. The event takes place spontaneously within its colourful frame of stone, and finds its

centre in the whirl of the dancer spinning over the
bull's back. For all the naturalism, the figure of the
bull has been lengthened casually, and out of all
proportion.

The fresco just described comes from the east wing
of the earlier *Palace of Knossos [4]*. The rooms, grouped
in profusion about a central courtyard, make it clear
what the Greeks had in mind when they called this
palace the Labyrinth. The multitude of interlocking
chambers prevent the visitor from forming a general
picture, particularly if one visualizes the actual
chambers and walls, instead of simply looking at the
remains of masonry that survive. On the outside
there are storerooms. Next to the courtyard itself lie
the throne room and grand apartments, those on the
east side probably belonging to the women. Large
stairways make up for the once considerable differences in height: the western part was certainly two-
storied, the eastern probably three. Even bathrooms
and flushing lavatories were included. To the north-
west lies a great flight of steps used for religious
ceremonies. Inside the palace is a small chapel for the
palace deity, the snake-taming goddess.

The ground-plan of the *Citadel of Tiryns* looks quite
different *[5]*. The rooms of the citadel are much more
clearly arranged, and were defended against possible
attack by a colossal wall. From the entrance protected by a bastion on the east, the visitor proceeded
through a gateway into one courtyard, from which a
propylaeum (entrance gateway) gave access to
another. Then, through a further propylaeum, he
entered the main courtyard surrounded by columns.
In its axis lay the men's house, consisting of a porch,
an ante-room, and a throne room (megaron) containing the hearth. This style of house is typical of the
Mediterranean lands and can be traced back to the
later Stone age. Here again there was a bathroom. The
Greek character of the layout emerges clearly in its
limitation to essential features, and in the axial
emphasis. We come across the same relationships at
Mycenae and Pylos, as well as other palaces of
Mycenaean times. Along with the two bastions, the
magnificent *Lion Gate at Mycenae [6]* focuses attention on the entrance to the citadel. The mighty walls
are made of huge irregular blocks, the building
method thought to have been used by those primeval
giants the Cyclopes – hence the term 'Cyclopean
masonry'. Above the vast lintel weighing over
twenty tons two lions stretch upwards, their fore-
paws resting on the base of a column. Their heads
were of a different material, and turned towards
whoever entered. This heraldically fashioned pair
flank a typically Cretan column which broadens
upwards and supports an entablature. The column

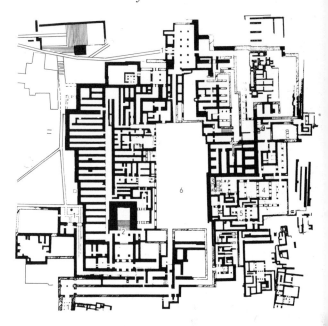

4 Plan of the earlier palace of Knossos, before its destruction at
the end of the fifteenth century BC. Laid out like a labyrinth
around a rectangular courtyard; walls asymmetrical; staircases
with walls join the several stories together; living rooms in the
shape of columned halls. 1 entrances; 2 steps to the upper storey;
3 staircase to the 'underground' of the eastern side; 4 hall; 5 the
queen's apartment; 6 courtyard.

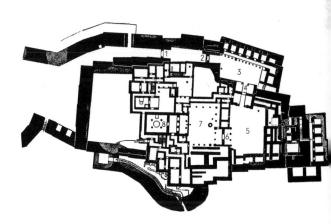

5 Plan of the citadel of Tiryns at the end of the thirteenth
century BC. Cretan influence in the broken contours and architectural shape, but a new and simpler principle of arrangement
through the clear succession of gateways and courtyards; the
megaron is in the axis of the courtyard. 1 first gate; 2 second gate;
3 forecourt; 4 first propylaeum; 5 first inner courtyard; 6 second
propylaeum; 7 second inner courtyard; 8 megaron.

The dead kings of antiquity were honoured as heroes by later generations in this way, and had their own cults, as is proved by the finds.

Stelae [7] glorifying the exploits of these dead stood on the graves. The reliefs show combats between warriors in war-chariots or on foot, as well as fights between animals. Spiral patterns deriving from Cretan models are carved over the relief area. The grave stelae, related to Egyptian stelae in type, differ from them in standing free over the tombs. The ornaments and images have proved to be imitations of Cretan motifs, while the abundant grave goods consist in part of things actually imported from Crete. The dependence of the mainland civilization on its superior Minoan model is thus more than clear. Minoan goldsmiths and other craftsmen doubtless found work and commissions at the courts of the mainland kings, though for subject-matter they had to conform to the taste of the Mycenaean lords. So instead of Cretan religious scenes, dances, and acrobatic games, we find animals and hunts on the richly inlaid *ceremonial daggers [8]* from the shaft

7 *Limestone stele from the ring of shaft graves at Mycenae, sixteenth century BC. Athens, National Museum. Shallow relief; style and composition dependent on Minoan images, although the subject of battle is not Minoan.*

6 *Lion Gate of the city of Mycenae, c. 1300 BC. The first example of monumental sculpture on European soil; composition derived from Cretan models of smaller works, e.g. seals, but independent mastery of the large scale, particularly in the bodies of the lions.*

is a religious object symbolizing the mistress of the animals. Thus the meaning of the relief above the lintel is that the deity and her two primordial beasts protect the gate and with it the whole palace. This relief from the second half of the fourteenth century BC is the oldest piece of monumental stone sculpture on European soil, and in its own way bears witness to the imposing achievements of Megalithic mainland art.

Near the mighty citadel stand citadels of the dead that are just as impressive statements in their own fashion: the beehive or tholos tombs. Up to the present day they remain known by such names as the 'Treasury of Atreus', and still stand erect at Mycenae and many other places in the Mycenaean world. Older, however, than the tholos tombs are the shaft graves. At Mycenae, these were surrounded with a magnificent ring of stones. The shaft graves date from the sixteenth century BC, whereas the great circle of slabs belongs to the fourteenth or thirteenth.

graves. On the other hand, the *gold seal-rings [9, 10]* from chamber tombs in the lower city of Mycenae are Minoan works. Winged griffins are represented, and cult scenes taking place round sacred trees.

Just as unique as the stelae over the shaft graves are the *gold masks [11]* found on the skulls of interred princes. These also belong to the second half of the sixteenth century BC. Though not yet portraits in our modern sense, they clearly differ from each other in appearance. Characterization has certainly been achieved. The artist was probably a local man, and despite his observation of the originals the stylization is extremely forceful. In the mask shown here, the basic Greek traits are unmistakable. Mighty deeds and severe grandeur can be felt in the silence and stiffness of death on this face. Perhaps it was less a desire for protection against evil powers than a wish for the living to be preserved, that gave rise to these disciplined forms.

The closer link of Minoan art and nature appears also in *painted ceramics*. This is evident from the example reproduced *[12]*, dating from the time of the palace style (fifteenth century BC), and already showing a marked hardening. Flower and marine animal motifs still flourish, twined around the spreading bulk of the pots. During the late Mycenenaean period of the twelfth century, however, vessels contract in volume, and the repetitive frieze of soldiers *[13]* is merely an application onto the body. A model has been taken from wall-painting. These warriors with spear and round shield, marching out to do battle, already belong to the period after the Dorian Invasion.

The importance to Greek myth of the Mycenaean age cannot be overrated. Numerous myths are connected with the Mycenaean citadels of Argolis,

8 Detail of a ceremonial dagger from the shaft graves at Mycenae, sixteenth century BC. Athens, National Museum. Minoan in style and technique (metal inlay, gold, silver, copper); but the lion hunt is a Mycenaean theme. (Above)

9, 10 Golden seal-rings from graves in Mycenae, c. 1500 BC. Athens, National Museum. Minoan in theme (griffins, ritual) and style (waist-bands).

11   Gold mask from a shaft grave at Mycenae, possible that of Agamemnon, sixteenth century BC. Athens, National Museum. Clear structure of the face, anticipating later Greek portraits; first attempt at characterization, but much ornamentation (ears).

12   Coloured vessel from Palaecastro, East Crete, c. 1500 BC. Heraclion, National Museum. Decorated with plant motifs, which help emphasize the contours of the vessel.

13   Crater from the end of the Mycenaean period, twelfth century BC. Athens, National Museum. A typically Mycenaean theme: warriors leaving for battle. The vessel is clearly articulated with the frieze in the broadest area; firm drawing.

Boeotia (Thebes), and Sparta, including those of Perseus and the Atreids, as well as the Trojan and Theban legends. Although Homer did not give these orally transmitted tales their final form until the eighth century BC, the events themselves belong entirely to the thirteenth and twelfth. Even such a truly Greek figure as the goddess Athena can be traced back to the Mycenaean palace goddess. Since the cult of the hearth before the throne is met with universally in the throne rooms of Mycenaean palaces, it is not too bold to conjecture that the hearth fire was under the protection of a goddess like Hestia. Cult marks for earth goddesses have also been found. The essentials of Greek religion and Greek myth go right back to the heroic 'prehistorical' age of the second millennium BC.

Stylistic movement in the second millennium can be summarized as follows. From an abstracting, geometric tendency at the start, there developed the mature, vital, naturalistic art of the mid millennium, when Crete had taken over the chief role in civilization. While adopting Cretan models, mainland art always kept a certain stiffness of line and hardness of form, which at the end of late Mycenaean art found full expression, and in a way made easier the development of the style of the new, geometric period. At its height in the fourteenth and early thirteenth century BC, the Mycenaean civilization boasted no less than sixty-eight types of vessel; at the close of the twelfth there remained only ten – an indication of the cultural break and the scale of the catastrophe brought by the territorial conquests of the Dorians.

THE PERIOD OF THE GEOMETRIC STYLE (TENTH TO EIGHTH CENTURY BC)

Here, as with preceding ages, the dates that have come down to us are rather uncertain. From archaeological finds and ancient accounts, we may conclude that the Ionians settled on the western coast of Asia Minor (the so-called Ionian colonization) as late as the second millennium BC, in consequence of the Dorian invasion of Greece. Then the Dorians themselves advanced across the Peloponnese to Crete, to the southern Cyclades and Sporades, and right on to Caria and Pamphylia in south-western Asia Minor. In Greece, there took place at this period the transition from monarchy to rule by a newly self-confident aristocracy. Athens alone seems to have been spared the Dorians' incursions, for the Athenians always regarded themselves as aboriginal.

The great migrations of late Mycenaean times brought poverty, a discontinuance of natural trade with the Near East, and the spiritual and artistic isolation of the Aegean. Greece seemed to languish in a new dark age, with no great architecture, sculpture, or painting, and at first even without valuable jewellery. Yet the exclusively geometric decoration of implements and vessels should not be interpreted as a reversion to a primitive kind of vase ornament. Geometric art is rather a new beginning on ancient cultural ground. Athens, with its distinguished Mycenaean past, now became the focus of artistic creation for all Greece. The skill in handicrafts of Mycenaean times had continued there uninterrupted, and it now possessed the simplicity, the force, and the spirit of a new age.

At the close of the geometric period, about the mid-eighth century BC, began the great westward colonization of the Greeks. Lower Italy and Sicily, North Africa and the southern coasts of France and Spain, were covered with Greek towns and settlements. The spiritual centre of these movements was Delphi, with its sanctuary of Apollo.

When Phoenician lettering was adopted, probably early in the tenth or ninth century BC, the Greek alphabet took shape. Thus the foundations were laid of Latin script and our present-day writing system. Homer's century was probably the eighth BC, while Hesiod lived and wrote at the juncture of the eighth and seventh.

Reference points for dating are rather more accurate from the eighth century. The Olympiads, which began in 776, were later regularly used by Greeks to reckon time. In addition, of special importance for chronology are the years when Greek colonies were established in Lower Italy and Sicily. 753 or 751 BC is the official date of the founding of Rome.

The geometric style, which Alexander Conze showed in 1870 to be that of the implements and vessels of the post-Mycenaean Greeks, differs fundamentally from all other geometrizing modes of decoration since Neolithic times. Geometry – line, circle and point – is the essence of this art. From these elements of geometry grew an imposing abstract artistic language. The geometric principle was abandoned as development proceeded, and only a few patterns, such as the fret [15] were absorbed into later ornamentations. But the power of a geometric art directed towards precision, proportion, and rhythm remained active as Greek art evolved. The geometric period was the first independent phase of Greek art after a Mycenaean age under alien influence.

14 Amphora in the proto-geometric style, tenth century BC. Athens, Ceramics Museum. Strengthening of the structure of the vessel; instead of free-hand painting the beginning of the 'mastery of circle and line'. Abstract, geometric decoration.

15   *Amphora in the early geometric style, ninth century BC. Athens, National Museum. Emergence of the meander, the most important ornament of the geometric period; austere distribution of ornament on the body of the vessel.*

At the beginning of the new age comes the *proto-geometric* style (tenth century BC) which occupies a middle place between the period of latest Mycenaean and early geometric pottery *[14]*. The chief decorative motif succeeding the Mycenaean spiral is made up of concentric circles or semicircles drawn with compasses. The elongated bubble form of Minoan and Mycenaean vases is no longer used. Variation in the proportions of foot, body, shoulder, and neck becomes the guide to comprehension. In contrast with the Mycenaean principle of sheer bulkiness, vases are structured on corporal, sculptural and anthropomorphous lines. Identical or similar patterns are used on the same parts of vessels.

The fret or key pattern on a band encircling the vase first appears in the *early geometric* period. The ornaments themselves are abstract and not, as in late Mycenaean and still to some extent in proto-geometric art, produced by making natural forms geometric. Indeed, the whole system of decoration is abstract, since in principle it can be transferred to any

surface *[15]*. Already a dynamic tension between the ornament and the body of a vase has been attained.

Unlike Mycenaean and proto-geometric vessels, always clay-grounded, the early and severe geometric vases (ninth to early eighth century BC) have black grounds. The light, clay ground does not appear again until the start of the eighth century, when it is more amenable to receive the greater quantity of ornaments and images.

An *Attic amphora at Munich [16]* typifies the *severe geometric* style of the early eighth century BC. It is clearly organized in structure from the slight contraction at the foot and expansion of the body to the contraction at the shoulder where the handles start, and from the neck division to the projecting lip. These ear-like handles give the vessel a front and a back view. The decoration of encircling bands is an exciting contrast to the corporeal form. A frieze of birds reduced to strict profile is shown above the simple rings of the foot zone. Repetition of form is stressed by the small filling pattern between them. The first fret, together with the broad chequer, a lozenge, and another fret, occupies the vase's body

16   *Attic amphora in the severe geometric style, beginning of the eighth century BC. Munich, Museum für antike Kleinkunst. Figurative frieze subordinated to abstract ornament.*

zone above the triangle and lozenge bands. A frieze of reclining ibexes, their heads turned back, defines the important area where the handles begin. The appearance of the neck is emphasized by a big double fret, while a frieze of grazing deer extends below the lip. Although the figured bands are already stressed by a lighter ground effect, a convincing unity of abstract ornamental form and animal figure has been established, but it could only be achieved by radically simplifying the natural shapes. The tension between image and ornament, encircling bands and vase structure, has been controlled in a masterly way.

It was the need to recount and represent that finally burst the bonds of geometric abstraction. During the eighth century BC, the big vases such as amphorae and craters increasingly became supports for pictures centring on the dead and burial rites. The sculptural frame of the funeral urns, which stood on graves as monuments and had a hole in the bottom for drink offerings, was given monumental proportions (height up to 5¾ feet). A perfectly preserved *crater* from the period after the middle of the eighth century BC *[17]* clearly illustrates the profusion of images. The huge bowl rises above a tall foot adorned with simple rings and a fret. Its lower picture frieze shows armed warriors on chariots drawn by two horses: they are the noble comrades of the dead man who ride around the grave mound. Bands separate this from the larger frieze, which represents the lying in state of the deceased and the chorus of mourning men and women. Its importance is stressed by the double handle on either side. The dead man, seen from above, lies on the bier. A chequer-patterned cover is depicted separately, although it is supposed to be draped over him. Below the bier stands the horse-drawn chariot that will take him on his last journey and, in his honour, be buried with him.

The geometric picture structure is governed by an urge for clarity. All figures and objects are spread out on the surface in an 'abstract' way that makes them unambiguous. Human figures appear together in a silhouette taken from different angles; the head is in strict profile; the upper part of the body is shown from the front, and the lower part from the side profile. The eyes are already left blank, and the woman's breasts are briefly indicated. Compared with the wealth of figures represented here ornament, formerly the main decoration of a vessel, seems insignificant. Only the large rings above the handles and the fret at the top recall it. The figures stand out against the ornaments filling the space between them and appear to be interwoven as in a tapestry.

The development of the late geometric style stems from this crater. Two styles emerge, one in which the

17 *Attic crater, beginning of the late geometric style, middle of the eighth century BC. Athens, National Museum. Figurative pictures displace the ornamentation. The vessel served as a grave monument.*

precision of ornamental drawing is completely lost, and the other an open style in which the figures drift forlornly in the ground and such orientalizing motifs as the lion and the antelope make their appearance. In late geometric art we also find the first signs of mythical representation. Except for a few definite examples, however, geometric art depicts general situations rather than particular scenes from myths.

The figure style of small sculptural works of the mature geometric period is best represented by a few *ivory statuettes* from a grave near the Dipylon at Athens *[18]*. They are images of naked goddesses wearing the divine crown, or polos, adorned with a large fret. Though each is flat and almost board-like in shape, the proportions are remarkably sure, due, no doubt, to the influence of Oriental art. The closed outline has a defining effect. Deftly poised, the legs are close together, and the knees slightly bent. The arms frame the upper part of the body, while the palms lie flat against the thighs. In the clearly wrought face the eyes have a distinct message. There is no

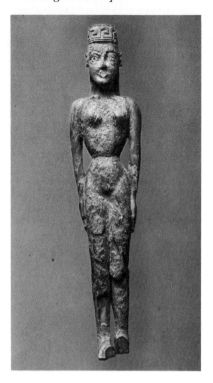

18   Ivory statuette in the mature geometric style, second quarter of the eighth century BC. Athens, National Museum. Little plasticity of volume despite the slight contours; firm vertical and horizontal relationships.

19   Attic bronze statue of a warrior brandishing a spear, ritual offering for the Acropolis, end of the eighth century BC. Athens, National Museum. The geometric formal shape gives way to a more organic structure.

mistaking the geometric nature, the firm structure of vertical and horizontal relationships.

The *Warrior brandishing a Spear [19]* from the Acropolis at Athens is a later work than these goddesses carved during the second quarter of the eighth century BC. He already belongs to the last phase of geometric art. Except for his cone-shaped helmet he is quite naked. In his raised right hand, which is pierced, he once held a spear. With its elongated proportions, the figure is strained to the utmost and reduced to essentials. The head juts out vigorously, expressing strength and primitive force. Here again, the huge eyes dominate the face. It is as if the whole figure depended on its gaze, so intensely does life flash from the eyes. The geometric style is finally shattered by this eruption of vital energy. It is the force of life itself that protests against abstraction.

The oldest identified cult buildings – not yet, of course, very sizeable – belong to geometric times. These temples were derived entirely from the dwelling-house, from the simple rectangular (or oval or apse-ended) hut and the elongated Mycenaean megaron. Supports in front of the actual room or between the projecting side walls formed a porch: both types survived throughout antiquity as the *Anta Temple [20]* and the *Prostyle Temple [21, 23]*. However, the original plan of the peripteral, the noblest kind of Greek temple, may be detected as early as geometric times – towards the end of the eighth century, according to the investigations carried out so far. Every Greek temple was simply a house for a deity and a shrine for the cult statue, public worship always being conducted in front of it at the altar. So the addition of a surrounding ambulatory, or peridrome, bounded by a range of columns (peristyle), meant another enlargement of a building which, considering the size of its contents, was already extravagantly big. The peristyle not only distinguished it from secular architecture, but also gave it a consistent appearance from all sides, made it something 'in the round' and thus a plastic structure. Though the source of this invention was probably the Greek homeland, the earliest known temple of the kind is one discovered on *Samos [22]*. It was already a considerable size, with its length of 98½ feet, or 100 Samian feet – the traditional length measurement used for so many

Greek temples. Divided longitudinally by a row of supports, the interior was less a moulded space than a room focused on the cult statue. The central colonnade, which took into account the axial position of the statue, was later replaced by two rows of columns. The superstructure of the temple at this time, and in the following decades as well, consisted of perishable materials: sun-dried brick over a stone foundation for the walls, wood for the columns and roof framework. We therefore know very little about the appearance of the elevation. During the next hundred years, the wood building technique was converted into a stone one, in which the elements of wood construction can still be identified. Columns and capitals have turned shapes; the ends of the ceiling beams are matched in Doric buildings by the triglyphs, in Ionic by the dentils; mutules and regulae with their guttae correspond to wooden blocks with nails. In the same period, the *Doric Order [24]* was fully developed by the end of the seventh century BC, and the *Ionic [25]* by the beginning of the sixth. Both derived from the late geometric wooden structure.

The column, the wall, and the horizontal entablature, whose form was in each case first developed in the temple building, remained the basic elements of Greek architecture until the end of antiquity. All other architectural complexes were derived from them: stoas, propylaea (gate buildings), gymnasia, palaestrae, and houses with a peristyle round their

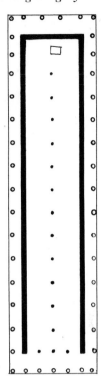

22 Ground-plan of the Temple of Hera at Samos. The cella building with a central row of wooden columns, dating from the first half of the eighth century BC, became during the second half of the century a rounded hall with wooden columns.

20 Ground-plan of an anta temple: two pillars forming a porch (pronaos) stand between the walls.

21 Ground-plan of a prostyle temple; a row of four pillars stands before the cella.

23 Model of a clay temple, ritual offering for the Heraion of Argos, end of the eighth century BC. Ground-plan of a simple prostyle temple with two columns before the cella, which supports the flat roof of the porch. The roof of the cella is a pointed gable (after G. Oikonomos).

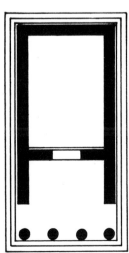

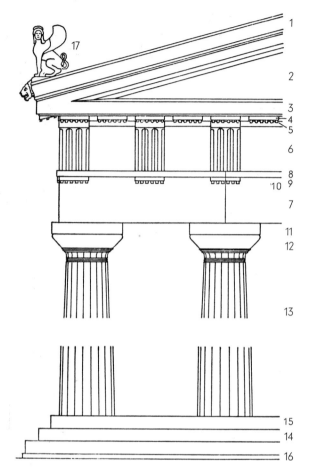

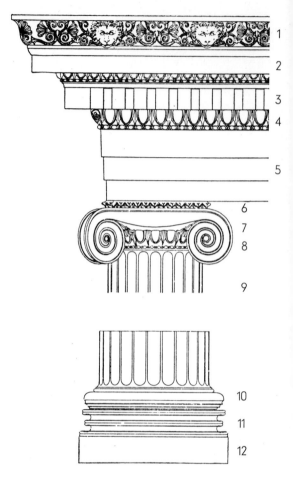

24 *The Doric order. 1 cyma (pediment moulding); 2 tympanon; 3 geison (cornice) with 4 mutulus; 5 guttae (gutter); epistyle with 6 frieze of metopes and triglyphs (slab with three slots); 7 architrave; 8 taenia; 9 regula; 10 guttae; capital with 11 abacus; 12 echinus; 13 shafts (fluted); 14 crepis (the basis of three steps) with 15 stylobate (upper step); 16 euthynteria (upper ground surface); 17 acroterium.*

25 *The Ionic order. 1 cyma (pediment moulding); 2 geison (cornice); epistyle with 3 dentils 4 Ionic cyma; 5 architrave of three fascine; capital with 6 abacus; 7 volutes; 8 echinus; 9 fluted shafts with 10 torus (roll); 11 trochilus (grooved channel); 12 plinth (foot of column).*

central courtyard. The evolution of these types ran parallel to that of the Greek temple.

The geometric style is the conscious formula of an artist, not an imitation of nature. Its ornamental vocabulary is conditioned by handicrafts and applied science. Without assistance from the textile crafts, especially weaving, the fret, among other things, could hardly have been produced. The Greeks alone made geometric form a true vessel of reality. Behind the beginnings of Greek art in the geometric style lies an intuition of the geometric and mathematical structure of the cosmos – 'cosmos' being a word with three meanings: ornament, order, and universe. By virtue of its very limitations, geometric art made

visible the laws of existence behind the images presented by the senses.

The geometric world foundered on this one-sidedness. Because images of a myth needed to be unique and unmistakable, the course of art was bound to lead from general sign-like symbols to specific outward forms. Because symbolic signs no longer sufficed to contain artistic energy, the world of abstract forms split open, and the way was clear for the development of archaic and classical art. It is certainly no accident that geometric art started to disintegrate at the time when Greek colonization began. The richness of a newly discovered reality and the influence of an Orient that rejoiced in images forced the Greeks to abandon the geometric style; but, as the foundation of Greek art, it had ordained severity and established law for all succeeding periods.

THE PERIOD OF THE ARCHAIC STYLE (LATE EIGHTH TO LATE SIXTH CENTURY BC)

During this age the Greek city-states constantly increased in power, mainly due to the activities of the aristocratic classes. Greek colonization in the Mediterranean extended to Egypt (Naucratis), France (Massalia), and Spain. In the late eighth century BC a brisk trade began with the Orient, chiefly through the agency of the Phoenicians. From the end of the seventh century on, this trade was simplified by the minting of money in Asia Minor (Lydia), an innovation soon adopted in Greece (Aegina). Greek coins had a guaranteed weight of precious metal and are often artistic masterpieces.

Sparta consolidated its position in long-drawn wars by subjugating Messenia. In the mid-seventh century BC a Peloponnesian alliance against Sparta was centralized at Argos, under King Pheidon. The whole of Attica coalesced into a unified state led by Athens. During the seventh century, the phalanx of hoplites (heavy-armed infantry) which Sparta had developed won general acceptance in military tactics.

From the mid-seventh century, the reins of government were seized by tyrants, who backed the people against the powerful nobility. They included Cypselus and Periander at Corinth, Polycrates on Samos (overthrown 522), and Peisistratus at Athens (died 527). After its liberation from tyranny (Hipparchus, one of the sons of Peisistratus, was murdered by Harmodius and Aristogeiton in 514; Hippius, the other, was expelled in 510), Cleisthenes gave Athens the first truly democratic system of government, which lay behind the city's dominating role in the ancient world from the fifth century on, and survived in essence until Athens lost its independence.

Eminent legislators were active at the close of the seventh century: Dracon and later Solon in Athens, Lycurgus in Sparta. Poets stand out as distinct personalities: Archilochus of Paros (mid-seventh century), as well as Alcaeus and Sappho, both of whose works show the first flights of the lyrical muse. At the same period, Ionian nature philosophy was in its prime.

The archaic style I: the orientalizing phase
(Late eighth century to c. 650 BC)

The forces that disrupted the archaic style were a combination of discontent at the rendering of reality in geometric art, and an increased contact with the Orient, with its love of images. In the last quarter of the eighth century BC, images were possessed by a turbulent vitality that found expression in such daemonic beings as sphinxes and griffins. The restless force of the age next stabilized itself in the great representations of myth that dominated the seventh century. This was a second founding of Greek art, characterized now by imposing size and receptiveness to foreign stimuli.

An *Early Attic amphora from Eleusis* [26] may be

26 Early Attic amphora from Eleusis, second quarter of the seventh century BC. Eleusis, Museum. The geometric arrangement is obscured by figures and plant-like ornaments that cover the surface of the vessel.

regarded as typical of the new, varied, and dynamic style. The vigorous life of the time is already apparent in its taut form, yet the paintings on it are even more forceful. The scene is dominated on the neck by the blinding of the Cyclops Polyphemus, whom Odysseus and his companions have made drunk. The enormous one-eyed giant sits hunched up on the right with a drinking cup of an unusual shape in his hand. Odysseus, drawn in white, adroitly guides the red-hot pole that will be thrust into the Cyclops's eye with all the force of his men. Only a few ornaments fill in the ground, so that the size and power of the figures are all the more conspicuous. Despite the general formal massiveness the limbs – especially the arms – are strikingly small, and contribute quite considerably to the vivid and energetic portrayal of the event. A powerful group of fighting animals, lion against wild boar, adorns the vessel's shoulder, while the big frieze round its belly shows a no less remarkable scene: the beheading of Medusa by Perseus. Not the actual deed itself, but what followed it, has been represented here. The other two Gorgons are pursuing Perseus, but the goddess Athena confronts them, covering the hero's hasty retreat. Only the lower part of Perseus's body has survived.

The heads of the Gorgons, whose hurried pace is shown by the way their bare legs emerge from their skirts, have a strange, quite unhuman appearance. Basically, they are shaped like griffin bowls, but snake heads stretch outward instead of griffin heads. The bestial mouths are rendered as broad bands set with enormous tusks, while the eyes are menacing dots placed wide apart.

27   *A Rhodian plate, the so-called Euphorbus Plate, second half of the seventh century BC. London, British Museum. This gives the impression of tapestry through the interweaving of plant-like ornaments with the battle scene.*

28   *Late proto-Corinthian jug, the so-called Chigi Jug, third quarter of the seventh century BC. Rome, Villa Giulia. Style of Corinthian miniatures; clearly drawn figures, sparing disposition of ornaments.*

The archaic style II: the Daedalid phase (c. 650–620 BC)

The fierce energy apparent in the scenes on the early Attic amphora of about 670 BC was replaced in the second half of the seventh century by a new, severe, and additive mode of composition, which is best exemplified in Corinthian painting. Eastern Greece remained rather firmly in the grip of Oriental influences and blended its figures, carpet-like, with the many filling ornaments, as on the *Euphorbus Plate [27]*, a Rhodian piece showing Menelaus and Hector in single combat over the body of Euphorbus. Corinthian painting, on the other hand, achieved an unexpected lucidity and precision in the *Chigi Jug [28]*. Groups of human beings are particularly clearly arranged on this object. The clash of the phalanxes, roused by the music of flutes, has been accurately portrayed in a miniature-like painting technique. A great many other scenes are spread over the jug,

which is only 10¼ inches in height. They include a Judgment of Paris, a lion hunt, a hare hunt with huntsmen holding back the dogs, and a procession of riders and chariots. The profusion of images is at the same time most carefully organized, each figure being a part of this pictorial cosmos made up of legend, battle, and the essence of the hunt.

This new consolidation of the formal language in the middle and the second half of the seventh century BC has long been known as the Daedalid style, in allusion to the mythical sculptor Daedalus. It found its purest embodiment in sculpture, especially on Crete. There is a lintel imposingly adorned with reliefs that comes from a small *Anta Temple in Prinias* [29]. Over a frieze of panthers two goddesses are enthroned against the jambs, commanding the entrance to the inner room, or naos, of the temple. The additive structure is especially clear in these enthroned deities, who are composed of a vertical shank, a horizontal thigh, and a vertical upper part of the body. Their forcefully controlled faces are dominated by wide-open eyes.

The same Daedalid formal language also governs the style of a *Female Statuette from Auxerre*, now in the

Louvre [30], and of a *Bronze Youth* at Delphi [31]. The Auxerre figure (probably a goddess) stands in a strictly frontal pose. She is wearing a dress adorned with frets, belted above the hips, and a cape covers her shoulders. Her large right hand is held in a peculiar gesture against the bosom, whereas the left lies firmly along the thigh. Her strongly expressive face is framed by hair curled into ringlets above the forehead and descending to the breast in four boldly plaited tresses on either side. Despite the pillar-like stiffness of build, there is a typically Greek energy in the compelling eyes and the wide, vivacious mouth. Like the goddess from Auxerre, the magnificent Daedalid statuette of a youth preserved at Delphi was made after the middle of the seventh century BC. Proud and free in his nakedness, and wearing only a mitra (waist-belt), the youth confronts his god – unless indeed he represents Apollo himself. This nakedness of Greek figures of youths is characteristic of the Greek attitude towards religion. The Orient never dared represent a god or his votary unclothed, or a marble or bronze figure as free-standing and unsupported. Here, the hands are clenched and rest against the thighs on a level with the genitals, thus expressing the amassed energy of the quietly standing adolescent. Stretched into a triangular shape, the face seems to look boldly and breathe easily. Long hair arranged in horizontal layers frame it on both sides. This youth from Delphi anticipates the main genre of archaic art, the great race of kouroi (youths), who

29 *Two enthroned goddesses on a lintel of a temple in Prinias (Crete), middle of the seventh century BC. Limestone. Heraclion, National Museum. Daedalid style; return to vertical and horizontal shaping of the figures which are here half life-size.*

30   Limestone half life-size female statuette from Auxerre, shortly after middle of the seventh century BC, found probably in Crete. Paris, Louvre. Daedalid style; typical triangular form of face.

31   Bronze statuette of a youth, shortly after middle of the seventh century BC. Delphi, Museum. Daedalid in form and body structure, this anticipates the kouroi in the arrangement of arms and legs.

32   Zeus and Hera, wooden group from a piece of furniture in the destroyed Heraion of Samos. East Ionian variant of the Daedalid style, third quarter of the seventh century BC. Oriental type of representation (sacred wedding) but Greek in design and expression.

were erected in sacred precincts or over graves and form the main genre of archaic art.

The plump form of Oriental models was echoed more strongly in eastern Greece: a *Wooden Group from Samos*, now destroyed, may be taken as an example of this *[32]*. It probably belongs to the third quarter of the seventh century BC and represents the sacred marriage of Zeus and Hera. The youthful-looking Zeus in a short doublet grasps Hera's breast with his right hand, having put his left around her shoulder. A mighty eagle, simplified like a symbol, clasps the heads of the two figures in a frontal pose. Although this relief follows the Oriental pattern for divine couples, it already appears entirely Greek in the coherent representation of the incident. The group was probably on Hera's kline (couch) for the sacred wedding. The Daedalid style is here fully evident.

The archaic style III: early, mature, and late archaic phases (Late seventh century to 500 BC)

The imposing consolidation of form in the seventh century BC – the Daedalid period – achieved a new coherence at the close of the century. In Athenian vase decoration, the gay, polychrome proto-Attic style developed into black-figure painting. The silhouettes of figures are here uniformly black, inner details being shown by scratches and an occasional touch of red. An *amphora by the Nessus Painter*, so called after the scene on the neck of this vessel, provides the best illustration *[33]*. Heracles has caught up with this mixture of man and horse, and planting his foot on the small of the centaur's back in an enormous stride, now pulls him by the hair, about to kill him with his drawn sword. Nessus raises his arms, beseeching help; but Heracles is going to kill the creature who tried to assault his wife Deianera. The names of the figures have been added in early Attic letters ('Netos' instead of 'Nessos') which along with the filling ornaments serve to enrich the background.

Some notable pieces of large-scale Attic sculpture have survived from the last quarter of the seventh century BC. The marble *Head of a Kouros* from the Dipylon gate by the Kerameikos, or Potters' Quarter *[34]* captures all the force and splendour of this period. It is clear from the source of excavation that the head belonged to a statue standing on the grave of an Attic youth of those times. The presence of the statue represented an image of abounding life on the tomb of the noble youth. The stone came from Naxos or Paros, two islands of the utmost importance in the development of larger Greek sculpture on account of their rich marble quarries. This head is built up of spherical shapes. Crucial to the impression made by the long, oval face are the slightly protruding eyeballs below the wide, curving brow. The elongated eyes

33 Heracles and Nessus, scene on the neck of an Attic amphora by the Nessus Painter, end of the seventh century BC. Athens, National Museum. Beginning of the black-figured vase style; less filling ornaments.

34 Head of a kouros, over life-size, from the Dipylon (one of the gates in the Athenian Wall). Part of a marble grave statue, end of the seventh century BC. Athens, National Museum. Spherically moulded surfaces; ornamental composition of the various parts (eyes, ears).

are surrounded by thin, yet heavy, lashes. The bone structure, hidden by the full curves of the flesh, can only be guessed at. The ears, and the hair, divided up into so many identical nodules, are still purely decorative elements. A fillet extending above the forehead is elaborately knotted at the back.

Rather later than the Dipylon kouros head is the *Kouros from the Sanctuary of Poseidon at Cape Sunium [35]* about 9¾ feet tall. Monumental and powerful in its erect pose, this free-standing figure has its left leg forward as if stepping out, and its hands clenched against its thighs. The stiffness of the frontal posture is broken by a slight turning towards the right, an effect produced by setting the statue at an angle to the front of its base. The components of its bodily structure are still additive: the joints, especially the knees, are formed like hinges. The groin, the edge of the thorax, and the medial line are also ornamentally styled. But movement and energy are expressed in the powerful chest, thighs, calfs, and arm muscles.

35   Marble kouros, over life-size, an offering for the consecration of the Sanctuary of Poseidon at Cape Sunium, c. 600 BC. Athens, National Museum. Tectonic coincidence of the various parts; emphasis of joints by ornamental composition.

36   Marble statue of Cleobis, by the Argive artist Polymedes, an offering for the consecration of the Sanctuary of Apollo at Delphi, c. 600 BC. Delphi, Museum. Powerful vitality expressing the Doric ideal of the body. Emphasis on the limbs as the source of energy.

Once again, the head dominates. The eyes, the source of mental life, rivet one's attention. Above the forehead, the hair is curled in a curious spiral arrangement held firm by bands. For all the monumentality, size, and power of this figure, its individual forms are articulated purely as decorative shapes. Each member has been represented singly, expressing itself alone. The aim is to show not the interaction of these parts but their rich sequence, their ordering with equal status.

Together with Attic, Cycladic, and Cretan art, it was above all the Peloponnesian region that made a decisive contribution to the early Greek image of man. The statues of the Peloponnese, and especially Argolis, emphasize the power and strength of the body. Executed about 600 BC by the Argive artist Polymedes, the figures of the two brothers *Cleobis and Biton [36]* appear as primitive heroes when compared with Attic kouroi. The decorative rendering of the form is almost shattered by the primeval energy of the physical development. The pulse of

life beats fiercely in limbs, eyes, and wide-stretched mouths. The statues of the youths probably relate to a votive offering from their mother, who was a priestess of Hera at Argos. Once, when she had to ride to offer sacrifice at the Argive Heraeum, no draught animals were available, so Cleobis and Biton stepped in, and pulled her chariot the distance of about 9½ miles. Having reached the sanctuary, the mother gave thanks for her sons' feat and begged Hera to make them a present. The goddess could think of no better gift than a quick and easy death. One of the fundamental beliefs of the Greeks was that it is best not to be born, or, once born, to die soon (Sophocles, *Oedipus Coloneus*, 1124 ff.); and that it is better to be a day-labourer on earth than a lord among the shades (*Odyssey*, II, 488 ff.). It is characteristic of the archaic attitude, however, that Cleobis and Biton are shown not peacefully asleep, but rejoicing in their youthful energy, standing upright and reminding us of their deed and death.

From the period of the earliest large sculpture, when cult images of life-size and larger than life were produced, comes the first definite evidence of imposing stone temples. Among the best preserved is the *Temple of Hera at Olympia [37, 38]*, from the late seventh century BC. The Doric order is fully developed here, the long, squatly proportioned structure being largely built of stone (foundation, footing of cella walls). Two steps (later three) raised it as on a pedestal above its surroundings, to form a continuous whole. Originally of wood, the sturdy columns and their capitals were from the early sixth century on gradually replaced by stone ones, each representing the style of its period, as is clearly apparent from the capitals; but there was still one wooden column as late as the second century AD. The archaic columns had a strongly swelling outline (entasis), and the echinus of each capital was compressed like a cushion, as if to give plastic expression to the load they supported. In later times, the columns became increasingly taut and erect, their echinus steeper and less curved. The symmetry of the peristyle was reflected by the cella (enclosed 'core' of a temple): to the naos and its vestibule (pronaos) a

39 Limestone pediment of the Temple of Artemis on Corfù, c. 600 BC. The figures are not yet fully plastic: they are part of the relief formed by the tympanon wall. The forms are arbitrarily arranged; the composition not as yet subordinate to a definite subject.

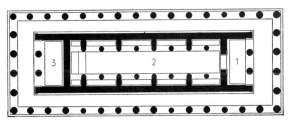

37, 38 Ground-plan and present condition of the Temple of Hera at Olympia, end of the seventh century BC. The first peristyle temple to be built mostly of stone. Symmetrical arrangement of the cella in the pronaos (1), naos (2) and opisthodomus (3). The peristyle gives the building an overall plasticity.

rear room (opisthodomus) similar to the vestibule was now added, to round off the symmetry of the cella. All purely Doric temples are characterized by this arrangement. The naos ceiling was supported by two rows of columns between spur walls, a special Peloponnesian form of the tripartite naos. The tiled saddle-roof now formed two pediments, each crowned by a disk acroterium, apparently but actually not in conflict with the plastic conception of the main body of the building.

While the Heraeum had no architectural decoration apart from these acroteria, the huge, roughly contemporary *Artemis temple on Corfù [39]* possessed two sculptured pediments, as well as metopes with reliefs. Moreover, it was already built completely of stone. On one of the Corfù pediments the central place is taken by a running Gorgon. She appears as mistress of the two animals lying at her side, with her children Chrysaor and the winged horse Pegasus. Unlike the Gorgons on the *Early Attic amphora from Eleusis [26]*, Medusa is conceived here entirely as the demonic mistress of life and the underworld. The mythical scenes that are later to fill the main area are still pressed into the corners, legends of gods and of heroes being juxtaposed with equal emphasis. This Corfù pediment remains in all respects a product of the early archaic additive approach to image-making. Perhaps Artemis, goddess of the temple, sheltered here behind the mighty Gorgon.

40   *Crater by the painter Cleitias and the potter Ergotimus, the so-called François Vase, between 570 and 560 BC. Florence, Museo Archaeologico. The frieze emphasizes the structure of the vessel. Centralized composition; figure positioning; precise painting; development of an Attic miniature style.*

stimulated the artistic imagination of the Greeks. Such images seem to declare that man can feel at ease in the world in spite of its monsters, because he meets and conquers them in battle.

The big frieze around the shoulder represents, in the wedding procession of Peleus and Thetis, the union of gods and divine beings with a mortal. All the immortals come to bring gifts to Peleus and wish him happiness in his marriage to the nereid Thetis. Peleus receives them without fear, and gives them hospitality at his palace. The presence of gods does not, as so often, cause death, but allows the union of Peleus and Thetis to bring forth the hero Achilles, that resplendent figure who has come to embody Greek civilization. On the back of the crater are represented Achilles' surprise attack on Troilus, the horse-race held in the presence of Achilles to honour the dead Patroclus, and the hunting of the Calydonian boar. On the two handles Ajax is seen carrying

41   *Achilles and Ajax at a board-game, amphora by the painter and potter Exekias, c. 530 BC. The Vatican, Museums and Galleries. A high point in Attic black-figured vase-painting. Extremely precise drawing; composition in a single picture; harmonious relationship between the plasticity of the figures and the curved shape of the vase.*

The pictorial richness of the story-loving archaic period can be admired almost at its full, in Attic vase-painting of about 570/560 BC, on a crater at Florence called the *François Vase [40]*. This large crater with voluted handles, which has come down to us as the joint work of the painter Cleitias and the potter Ergotimus, served to mix wine and water. A veritable cosmos, a whole universe of images is spread around its five bands. Round the brim are displayed a scene of the arrival at Delos of Theseus' ship after his rescue of the Attic youths and maidens by slaying the Cretan Minotaur, and in memory of the mythical event, a performance of the festive dance in honour of Apollo that the Athenians repeated every four years.

The frieze round the neck shows Theseus and Pirithoüs leading the Greeks in battle against the centaurs, brutish monsters who use tree-trunks and boulders for weapons, so that the invulnerable Caeneus is driven into the ground with rocks. This fight between centaurs and Greek heroes was represented from late geometric times onward, and grew increasingly important in the archaic period. It is represented most powerfully in the magnificent west pediment of the Zeus temple at Olympia and the wonderful south metopes of the Parthenon. From early times onward, the trial of strength with these creatures, a cross between man and beast, greatly

the body of Achilles from the battle. The divine
wedding is thus linked indirectly with the deeds and
death of Achilles, by way of numerous other scenes.
Many more scenes fill the frieze surrounding the
belly, and additional groups of figures surround the
foot of the vase.

Despite the almost immeasurable richness of the
pictorial bands, the style is incredibly precise. Even
where individuals are arranged together, each figure
is most carefully defined. Along with the incised
details of the black silhouetted figures, white has been
used for the women's bodies, white and red for the
clothing. Every form is clearly outlined and perfectly
developed both in itself and as part of the whole.
Differentiation and overlapping produces an effect
of simplicity. Space, without perspective, appears
marvellously fresh and capacious. A functional
article has become a work of art that one can con-
template time after time, reflecting on the stories
and incidents.

A generation later, the pictorial frieze is concentrated into a single picture with large figures, the
work of one of the greatest vase painters of archaic
times. On an amphora now in the Vatican, the artist
Exekias depicted nothing on the main field except
the two heroes *Ajax and Achilles* peacefully playing a
board-game *[41]*. But this scene also suggests the
scale of the war and the immense armoury of the
Greeks before Troy. Though bending forward close
to their game, the heroes are ready for battle. They
carry armour and jambs, and Achilles wears his
helmet with the tall plume. Both hold spears in their
left hand, so that the figures lean towards each
other as in a piece of architecture. Behind the men
stand their ornamented shields, on one of which Ajax
rests his helmet. The composition is wonderfully
regular, rigid symmetry being avoided through
slight imbalance: only Achilles wears helmet and
rerebrace. Both figures are rendered plastically, a few
strokes rounding out their limbs. With their richly
embellished, carpet-like cloaks and the pure profile
of their bearded heads, they still remain imprisoned
by the surface. The inscriptions in elegant lettering
divide up the ground in a masterly fashion.

The intense concentration of the heroes on their
game is captured in an almost lyrical way. One
forgets that the unified image of the figures is still
entirely derived from the composite richness of
separate forms. A freedom of expression has been
achieved that through its beauty, precision and
delicacy conceals the fact that it is not yet a truly
classical freedom. The conflict between a figure's
adherence to the surface and its plastic construction
is resolved by Exekias in an image that cannot be

*42 Over life-size marble kore from the Athenian Acropolis, the
so-called Peplos Kore, c. 530 BC. Athens, Acropolis Museum.
The figure is still shown in frontal pose and is built up from the
various parts, but the contours give it an overall shape. There is
a noticeable symmetry in both upper and lower halves of the
body; animation is emphasized by colour applications.*

detached from the curved body of the vessel without losing its beauty. At the zenith of late archaic art, around 530 BC, Exekias arrived at an intimate union of picture and vase that was never again achieved in the same way.

These vase pictures make it clear that all Greek painting of the archaic period is extremely 'unpainterly' in the modern sense. What it represents is always a firmly contoured, clearly articulated outward form determined essentially by sculpture and drawing. That is why Greek sculpture is the purest expression of Greek art. The *Kore wearing a Peplos* from the Acropolis [42] is the finest of a series of sculptural works belonging to the period of the Exekias amphora. The girl stands as slender as a pillar. In her outstretched left hand she once held a votive offering for the citadel goddess, Athena, and she herself is an attractive gift to the deity. The massiveness and primitive strength of the statues dating from about 600 BC is entirely missing in this figure. For all the strict adherence to surface and frontal pose, she still appears lightly built. The smile on her lips seems to spread across the whole figure. A close-fitting garment made of a single piece of material is girdled at the waist and folded over on the chest. The breasts stand out roundly, and one can imagine the posture of the legs beneath the material. Hair, eyebrows, eyes, mouth, and edges of the robe are all defined by colour applications. Radiant confidence is expressed by the steady eyes and the figure's slim erectness. The connexion between the body and the material from which it was made resembles Exekias' work. The Peplos Kore achieves such a freedom of construction in its glowing vitality that one forgets it is still wholly governed by the principle of an accumulation of separate forms, and of a decorative correspondence evident, for example, in the similar arrangement of the plaits on each shoulder, and in the flute-like folds of the chiton above the feet.

To a large extent, the style of late archaic times was determined by east Ionian Greek art. The great wealth of the trading cities of Asia Minor, the close contact with the civilizations of the ancient Orient, and the brilliant mode of keeping court favoured by such Ionian tyrants as Polycrates on Samos and the Lydian king Croesus, gave rise to a luxuriant, more sensuous art, of a painterly trend. During the first half of the sixth century BC the architects Rhoekos and Theodoros built a new temple 344½ feet long [43] to replace the old 100-foot (Samian) *Temple of Hera on Samos*. Burned down soon after completion, it was rebuilt by Polycrates. A double peristyle surrounded its tripartite naos and deep pronaos like a wood, to form a dipteros. Shortly afterwards appeared the even

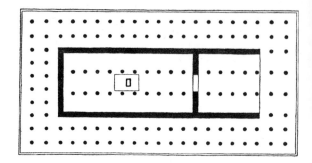

43 *Ground-plan of the Temple of Hera on Samos, built by the architects Rhoekos and Theodoros before the mid sixth century* BC. *The first large temple to be built in the Ionic style: double peristyle (dipteros); axial relationship; the entrance and direction of cella stressed. The building originated from the late geometric peristyle temple, but the rational Ionic design detracts from plasticity.*

44 *Reconstruction of the temple of Artemis at Ephesus, after the mid-sixth century* BC. *A painterly effect created by the many columns rising like plants, thereby concealing their supporting function.*

bigger *Temple of Artemis at Ephesus [44].* Here, as in the contemporary Apollo temple at Didyma near Miletus, the naos formed an open court, which contained a little temple (naiskos) for the cult image so that the peristyle, in this instance triple at the front, only accentuated the monumental character of the sanctuary walls. The slender columns soared up from richly moulded bases to a height of about $65\frac{1}{2}$ feet, ending in Ionic capitals, with their strongly curving volutes between an echinus adorned with an egg-and-dart motif and a shallow abacus. Above lay the three-stage architrave, the dentil course bordered by ovolo mouldings, the corona, and a sima (gutter-parapet) decorated in relief. Doric temples support and weigh down; the Ionic stretch upwards, plant-like. In the Doric, equal emphasis is given to all sides; in the Ionic the main end was stressed. Columns were set farther apart, and at Ephesus, their feet were adorned with reliefs. The front colonnade was tripled and the opisthodomus dispensed with. Unlike the rounded Doric capital, the Ionic has a front view, being planar. The ground-plan shows that the relating cella walls and axes of the external and internal columns seems to lack tension beside a Doric structure.

A similar temple was begun at Athens for Olympian Zeus by the sons of the Athenian tyrant Peisistratus, but it remained unfinished (cf. p. 65).

Among the many korai of the Attic Acropolis, the Peplos Kore stands apart. All the others are dressed as Ionians, in a thin fine chiton and slanting mantlet. An example of this may be found in the sculptures of the porch of the *Siphnian Treasury at Delphi*, built in the form of an anta temple *[45]*. Two korai supported the entablature as caryatids, their bodies in harmony with the archaic and structural restraint of the architecture.

It was usual for the Greeks to equate the Ionic column with the slender form of woman and the Doric with the powerful build of man. The other elements of this building were also Ionic in type. Above the architrave lay a frieze bordered by Ionic decorative members: an egg-and-dart on an ovolo moulding below, a leaf-and-dart on a cyma reverse above. The frieze here ran right round the building, instead of the usual dentil course. On the east end of the reconstruction we see, to the left, a meeting of the gods to discuss the Trojan battles, while, to the right, two quadrigas hurry away from each other, framing the battle before Troy over the corpse of Sarpedon. Particularly important is the north frieze, not shown here, where the battle of the gods and giants is represented in a bold arrangement of groups well ahead of its time. The pediment is reserved for a local Delphic legend: Heracles, the Dorian hero, who attempted to

45 *Plaster reconstruction of the Siphnian treasury at Delphi (a typical anta temple), erected shortly after 525 BC. Delphi, Museum. Caryatids take the place of pillars; the walls are adapted to the figures, thereby emphasizing their corporality. The building is richly decorated in Ionic style, which stresses the surface qualities while reducing structural clarity.*

carry off the sacred tripod of the Delphic sanctuary but was prevented by Apollo, who seizes his property. On the ridge and at the lower corners of the roof are placed acroteria, which subdue the force of the organic and sculptural structure of the Greek temple.

The treasury founded at Delphi shortly before 525 BC by the inhabitants of the Cycladic island of Siphnos is just one of many such buildings raised by Greek cities at the main Greek sanctuaries, chiefly in archaic times. They sheltered the costly votive offerings of the cities to a god, and thus became imposing evidence of the architectural competition between these city-states.

In Attic grave sculpture of the late archaic period the slender stele is the dominant form. The deceased was represented as an armed warrior, as on the stele that Aristocles executed in about 510 BC for the *Tomb of Aristion [46].* Aristion is wearing helmet, body

armour, and greaves. Carved in strict profile, the body almost seems to burst the narrow frame of the relief. Once again, the strength and harmony of the figure depend on the composite richness of separate forms, though these are already more organically united. The hair style, beard, and folds of the short chiton visible on the upper arm and thigh, are exquisitely refined work. Their graphic quality animates the large, slightly concave surface. Here, too, colour emphasizes the individual forms. The deceased is shown standing peacefully, rather than as victorious or about to die in battle. Armed and deep in thought, the figure recalls the living Aristion in his prime.

Late archaic art produced some bold results in sculptures for pediments. About 520 BC pediment sculptures showing Attic influence were made for the *Temple of Apollo at Eretria [47]*. The Attic hero Theseus is represented lifting up Antiope, Queen of the Amazons, and is about to make away with his precious burden in his chariot. The interlacing movement is clear even from the fragment. But in a purely archaic manner, the sense of action is absent from these heads. Theseus and the Queen smile nonchalantly. Nevertheless, a certain mystery surrounds the group, a conflict between the organically unified movement and the elegantly wrought individual forms. Perhaps the art of Antenor, the greatest Attic sculptor of late archaic times, lies behind this work. It was Antenor who after Hippias' expulsion fashioned the group of the tyrannicides Harmodius and Aristogeiton. He himself could not take the step to the severe style of early classical art; but the two masters most prominent in the new age came from his workshop.

Roughly comparable to a late work by Antenor is the *Grave statue of Aristodicus*, discovered in 1944 near Keratea *[48]*. This youthful figure still follows the old kouros pattern: the hands once clenched before the thighs, and the left leg advanced, as if to take a step. The head, growing straight out of the sturdy trunk, tilts slightly forward. The break with archaic practice is made evident by the short curly hair and plastically rendered genitals. During the period around or soon after 500 BC archaic form, still built up compositely, achieved such a powerful fusion that one could already take it for the new organic classical form. But Aristodicus has not yet achieved true freedom: for all its strength and vitality, the structure of the figure is still governed by archaic constraint.

46 *Marble grave stele of Aristion, executed by Aristocles about 510 BC. Athens, National Museum. The surface is unified by delicately layered relief. The 'engraving' of dress and legs shows archaic elements.*

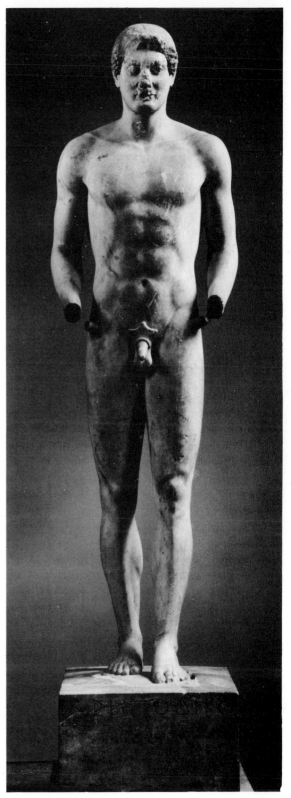

47 Theseus and Antiope, marble group from the pediment of the Temple of Apollo at Eretria, c. 520 BC. Chalcis, Museum. The crossing of the figures from the front is a bold stroke. The various parts of the lower body are hidden by Antiope's dress.

CLASSICAL ART

The fifth century BC was dominated first by the struggle of all Greece against the great powers, such as the Persians in the East and the Carthaginians in the West, and then by the subsequent rise of Athens to become the leading political and military power until its total collapse at the end of the century. Athens' ascent was founded on the prominent role Athenians played in the Persian Wars. At Marathon in 490 under Miltiades they beat the Persian army sent to punish them for supporting the revolt of the Ionian cities. Through the programme of naval construction hurried on by Themistocles, Athens won

48 Marble grave statue of Aristodicus, c. 500 BC. Athens, National Museum. The last development of the kouroi type; the earlier pattern of frontality is maintained, but the arms are slacker and the chest has volume. The single parts are fused together, but are still not subordinate to functional unity.

the sea battles off Salamis in 480 and Mycale in 479, in which the Persian fleet was destroyed, while on land the Persian army was defeated near Plataea in 479 by a force under the Spartan general Pausanias. At the same period, the united West Greeks under Theron and Gelon beat the Carthaginians at Himera in 480 and the Etruscans at Cumae in 474. The defensive war against the Persians developed into a war of attack (Cimon's victory on the Eurymedon 469 and the one near Salamis on Cyprus in 450), which only ended with the Callias Peace of 449. In the Attic maritime league founded in 478, Athens had hegemony on account of the fleet. During the years 480–430 (pentecontaetia) the city reached the absolute peak of its power and splendour, under the eminent statesmen Cimon and Pericles. This situation led to constant disputes with Sparta, though at first these seemed settled in 446/445 by a thirty-year peace. But in 431 trade disputes between Corinth and Athens finally led to the outbreak of the Peloponnesian War which lasted nearly thirty years. In 430 Athens was visited by a terrible plague, whose victims included Pericles. With the changing fortunes of war, the Peace of Nicias was concluded in 421, then broken through the Attic expedition to Sicily of 415. The dubious game of the resourceful Alcibiades brought about the final defeat of Athens, sealed in 415 by capitulation and the razing of the walls.

This period saw the flowering of Attic tragedy and literature in the works of Aeschylus, Sophocles, and Euripides. It was also that of the historians Herodotus and Thucydides, of the Dorian poet Pindar, and of the philosophers Anaxagoras and Socrates at Athens.

Early classical art: the severe style (c. 500/490–450 BC)

The Persians had twice captured Athens before the battles of Salamis and Plataea, completely destroying both town and citadel. All the well-preserved Attic works of archaic times come from the so-called Persian rubble; for when the Athenians were reconstructing the Acropolis, they 'interred' them there, where they lay untouched until the excavations. On returning home, the Persian king took with him to Persepolis the epitome of the young Attic democracy, Antenor's group of the tyrannicides. This work returned from Persepolis after Alexander the Great had conquered the Persian empire. Shortly before 476 BC Critius and Nesiotes, the city's leading artists and both pupils of Antenor, were commissioned to replace these statues of *Harmodius and Aristogeiton*, and in 476 their group *[49]* was ceremonially displayed

49　*Marble group of the tyrannicides Harmodius and Aristogeiton, Roman copy of the bronze original by Critius and Nesiotes, erected in the agora (market-place) at Athens, 476 BC. Naples, National Museum. The first large work of Greek classicism: subordination of all parts to an overall rhythm. The torso is accentuated as the centre of energy.*

in the agora (market-place) at Athens. How far Critius and Nesiotes followed their teacher's example is not known. Nevertheless, their work springs from the spirit of the generation that fought at Marathon and Salamis. Shoulder to shoulder, like a team, the heroes charge to the attack. Harmodius lifts his sword to strike the fatal blow. The bearded Aristogeiton shields his comrade with his outstretched arm, over which lies his cloak. Both are represented nude, as heroes. It is not the historical event – the murdered Hipparchus has been left out – but the readiness to do the deed that is shown in the powerful onslaught. The figures are seized by an impetus that binds each member of the body into an active, rhythmic whole. The organic form of classical art here achieves its first free and true manifestation. Only a fragment of the inscription on the marble base survives from the original group, which was cast in bronze, the material used for large-scale classical sculpture. For the great, unitary organic movement could be caught better in a bronze cast of the modelled form than in hard, unyielding marble. The group by Critius and Nesiotes has come down to us through one Roman marble copy, made for a Roman connoisseur. With a few exceptions, the masterpieces of Greek classical times are now known only through such copies.

At least one piece from the workshop of Critius, even if not by his own hand, remains to us in a marble *Statue of a Youth* from the Persian rubble [50]. The right leg is slightly advanced, in contrast to the archaic kouros. A clear distinction is already made between the leg supporting the weight of the body, and the unburdened free leg. The supporting leg presses into the hip, and the left groin is consequently higher than the right. The whole body truly lives, as a functional whole. Soaring and

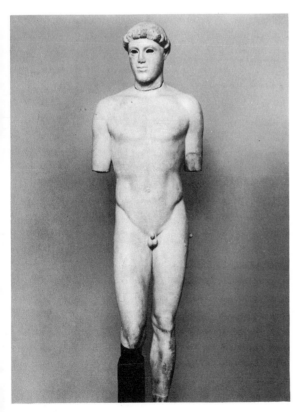

50 *Marble statue of a youth, from the Persian rubble on the Athenian Acropolis, the so-called Critius Youth (perhaps the work of Critius), before 480 BC. Athens, Acropolis Museum. Departure from archaic frontality: the head is turned aside; a relaxed position through separation of free and supporting legs, and an inter-relationship between the various parts of the body by contraction and relief of the hips. The face is an early example of the severe style.*

downward-pressing forces counterbalance in the easy play of joints and muscles, forming a classical equilibrium of rest in movement and movement in rest. With its firm chin and short hair rolled round a circlet, the head turns slightly to the right and stresses the opening of the free-leg side. Eyeballs, irises, and pupils of other coloured substances were once fixed into the eye-sockets, giving the work a lively impression. The left hand must have rested loosely along the thigh, while the right, drawn farther away, perhaps held a drinking-cup towards which the head is turned. The figure offers the libation and itself as a gift to the goddess. The late archaic richness of the separate forms has yielded to an austere, grave, masculine harmony of them all. The massiveness of Aristodicus is abolished by the easy play of a new freedom.

It is no accident that Attic artists at Athens were the first to achieve this unprecedented freedom of the male form. One prerequisite was the political freedom won by Athens through the overthrow of the tyrant Hippias. Another was the new self-awareness of the individual, who had learnt to see himself as a separate personality with autonomous value. The idea of a free man before a free god lay behind this new outlook, which opposed the human form as a microcosm to the macrocosm of the world. Only the generation that fought the Persians could have dared, and did dare, to take this step into the new territory of freedom.

A landslide during the fourth century BC saved at least the remains of one masterpiece of what is known as the severe style: the *Charioteer from Delphi [51]*. Only fragments have survived of the accompanying chariot and team of four horses, but the figure of the charioteer gives us a good idea of the whole group. Erected to commemorate the chariot victory of Polyzalus, tyrant of Gela, at the Delphic Games of 474, the team and their driver stood at rest. The author of this work, unparalleled in the intensity of its restraint, is thought to have been Pythagoras of Regium, who had reason to emigrate from Samos to the mainland at the beginning of the fifth century. Hollow cast, the charioteer statue is made up of several parts. The close placing of the legs and the strange costume with its high-belted chiton are both remarkable. Head and upper body are distinctly turned to the right, although the movement of the body remains hidden beneath the long, descending folds of the garment. The right hand still holds the reins. Matchless calm and confidence are expressed by the head upon the powerful neck. The forehead is adorned with a perforated band, under which the hair passes to form curls at the temples. The firm

nose, the horizontal line of the brows, the resolute eyes, and the big strong mouth above the forceful chin determine the structure of the oval face. 'Noble simplicity and calm grandeur': these words of Winckelmann seem closest to the spirit of the figure, when one contemplates it objectively. Considering that Winckelmann knew not a single genuine example of classical Greek sculpture, this characterization is remarkably accurate. The artist, who usually represented the culmination of movements, has here given the figure a maximum of absolute freedom through a minimum of movement. If the spirit and mobile quality of Attic art are missing from this work, its tension built up of slight displacements and asymmetries radiates such dignity that it fully holds its own beside Attic sculptures of the period.

During the latest excavations at Olympia it was possible to recover many fragments of a masterpiece of terracotta sculpture in the severe style. This group, which shows *Zeus abducting Ganymede [52]*, was executed about 470 BC at Corinth by an unknown

52   Zeus abducting Ganymede, half life-size terracotta group from the Zeus Sanctuary on Olympia, Corinthian work, c. 470 BC. Olympia, Museum. Despite plastic modelling the surface is extended as in a relief. Typical shape of a group composition.

51   Bronze statue of a charioteer of a quadriga, an offering of the tyrant Polyzalus of Gela (Sicily), for his victory in the chariot races, 474 BC. Delphi, Museum. Plain frontality is replaced by a body turned from top to toe and deliberate optical corrections.

only slightly earlier. He represents a young victor at the very moment of putting on the crown he has won. Probably a votive relief, this work expresses the youth's gratefulness to the deity who has helped him to victory. Quietly and modestly the champion bows his head, shown in strict profile. Through a discreet use of perspective (foreshortening of the right shoulder and part of the chest), the plasticity of the young body unfolds before us, admirable in the rise and dip of the chest, the depressions of the muscling. It is characteristic of early and mature classical art that the attainment of freedom in the rendering of the human form no longer led to an aboundingly energetic archaic self-confidence but to a proud humility and voluntary self-effacement. Not man, but the gods were the measure of all things.

The gods alone had a truly radiant appearance. On the *West Pediment of the Temple of Zeus at Olympia [54]* Apollo is shown in the midst of the turmoil of the battling centaurs and Lapiths. He halts the wild antics of the brutish centaurs with a triumphant gesture of his right arm, and in the struggle between demonic monsters and human power, unmistakably awards victory to man.

The Temple of Zeus was built between 470 and 457 BC after plans by the local architect Libon, and in its structure represents the classical form of the Doric temple *[55, 56]*. Every member derived its dimensions from a basic measurement, the interaxial (the distance between two column axes). The fully symmetrical cella, comprising pronaos, naos, and

53 Marble relief, effigy of a young victor from the Athena Sanctuary at Sunium, towards 470 BC. Athens, National Museum. The figure is connected to the ground through subtle graduations of relief and abbreviations of perspective.

master who may have come from the Aegina school. The action is represented on a pediment-shaped base. The bearded Zeus carries his light burden under his right arm, while Ganymede holds the love-gift, a cock, with his left hand. In its early form, the myth does not yet involve the eagle abducting the son of the Trojan king. Instead, Zeus himself in travelling dress and cloak and knotted stick has come to take his cup-bearer to Olympus. The god's hurried pace is indicated by his great stride, with the left leg emerging from the cloak. Encircled by the arm of Zeus, the boy hangs at the god's side. His head, miraculously still, is slightly turned towards his own right side, to form a balancing contrast to the vigorous leftward movement of the head of Zeus. Full of tensions and enclosed by a clear outline, the magnificent counterpoise of the structure points to the period after the Persian Wars.

The most charming image of a boy of this period may well be the Ganymede of the Olympia group. The youth on an Attic stele found at Sunium *[53]* is

54 Battle of the Lapiths and Centaurs, middle of the west pediment of the Temple of Zeus at Olympia, before 456 BC. Olympia, Museum. Relaxed position through balanced and opposing composition (contraction of the right, supporting side). Emphasis on centre of pediment through the raised position of Apollo.

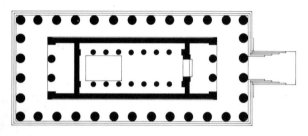

55, 56   Ground-plan and elevation of the east side of the temple of Zeus at Olympia, between 470 and 459 BC, erected by the local architect Libon. The classical version of the Doric temple. Every member is planned on a basic measurement: the interaxial.

opisthodomus, fitted into the classically proportioned peristyle of six by thirteen columns in such a way that the cella walls were aligned with the axes of the second and fifth end columns, and the antae with the middle of the second and eleventh side intercolumniation (the space or distance between two columns). Two double-storied rows of columns divided the naos into a nave and aisles, an arrangement that can still be seen in the slightly later *Temple of Hera at Paestum [57]*. About thirty years after the building had been completed, Phidias' colossal cult image of Zeus was set up in the nave, and galleries were installed over the aisles at the level of the upper storey so that it could be seen properly. Huge columns supported the entablature, their shafts slightly swelling, and the echinus already in fairly taut profile. The angle columns were drawn inward, so that the outermost metopes did not need to be enlarged. They would have been enlarged had the intercolumniation remained equal, since the angle triglyph had to lie not over the middle of the column, but at the end of the entablature (angle triglyph conflict). The six metopes above the pronaos and six above the opisthodomus bore reliefs showing the

deeds of Heracles, and this number of twelve subsequently became the rule. But the metopes of the peristyle were left unornamented, the sculptural decoration being concentrated on the vast pediments and acroteria, which have not survived.

The east pediment shows the preparations for the chariot-race between Pelops and Oenomaus for the hand of Oenomaus' daughter Hippodamia. In a typically classical way it is the tense moment of quiet before the start that is represented, not the race itself or the death of Oenomaus.

At the centre of the pediment, Zeus dominates the conflict between the old and new royal lines. Invisible to Pelops and Oenomaus, he is all the more present to the spectator, who knows that Zeus, like Apollo on the west pediment, has already decided the issue. Unfortunately, there are big gaps in what has survived of the pediment figures. Most of all one misses the head of Zeus, which can be visualized only very roughly in terms of the splendid head of an original bronze *Statue of Poseidon* from the sea off Cape Artemisium *[1]*. Nearly seven feet tall, this shows Poseidon in a striding posture with his left arm extended forward as he swings the right arm back to hurl his trident at an enemy. The authorship of this figure, created round about 460, is still uncertain. The likeliest artists are the Boeotian Calamis and the Aeginetan Onatas. A long, thick beard dominates the bottom part of the head. Eyes of a coloured material were once inset beneath the sharply drawn-out brows. The head is covered with thick waves of hair, parted in the centre, and falling low over the brow in long locks. A powerful moral atmosphere of vigorous masculinity and implacable sternness is expressed by the head and the mighty body.

In Attic vase-painting, the transition from the black-figure to the red-figure technique had already been effected during the last quarter of the sixth century BC. Through body perspective and concise rendering of detail the clay-coloured figure could now acquire a plasticity quite beyond the reach of the black-figure silhouetted form. This revolutionary change took place about 525 in the workshop of the potter Andocides. The major works of the fifth-century Attic vase-painting were executed accordingly in red-figure. Much more so than in archaic times, vase pictures were now influenced by wall-painting, all traces of which have since completely disappeared apart from this reflection in applied art.

57   The temple of Hera at Paestum, after 450 BC. The interior of the cella is divided into three by two tiers of columns. A narrow central range: as in every Greek temple, the door is the only source of light.

Produced during the fifties of the fifth century BC
a *calyx-crater* decorated by the Niobid Painter *[58]*
owes a debt to the works of the great painter
Polygnotus of Thasos. On the front is shown a
meeting of heroes, among whom we can name with
certainty the goddess Athena on the right and
Heracles in the middle. The figures are distributed
over the ground on strips of land, apparently introduced into wall-painting by Polygnotus. Space is not
unified; each figure in this meeting is self-contained
in its own space, through body perspective. The laws
of sculpture and plastic modelling applied to all
classical painting.

The known works of Myron are already on the
threshold of the mature classical period, though it is
true that they also have only come down to us in
Roman copies. His *Discobolus [59]*, which represents
a champion on the point of throwing a discus, must
have been made shortly before the middle of the
century. The intricately entwined movement of the
turning athlete, who swings the discus for the throw
while already taking aim, is, in the last analysis, still
modelled in the severe style. Despite the effort to

*58   Attic red-figured calyx-crater by the Niobid Painter, 460–
450 BC. Paris, Louvre. Assumed to be a product of the style of
Polygnotus. The frieze-like isocephalous composition is abandoned for a free disposition of figures over the surface.*

*59   Discobolus of Myron, Roman marble copy (the Lancelotti
version) after the bronze original from the mid-fifth century BC.
Rome, Museo delle Terme. Functional unity of members; completely plastic shape; the artist has captured the 'ideal' moment
that includes past and future movement.*

achieve a sense of space, the figure remains imprisoned
in a very narrow spatial box and is still fixed, like a
relief, to the front. The sense of momentum has been
captured in a taut network of structure. Wholly
subordinate to this great continuum of motion, each
member is strained to the utmost. The toes claw into
the ground, the veins and sinews of the tensed body
stand out, the depiction of the muscles is exact and
sure. The face, precisely modelled, has an air almost
of indifference: here, too, the old heritage is apparent.

Mature classical art (450–400 BC)

After the Persians destroyed the Acropolis at Athens in 480 and 479, the Athenians were faced with the task of rebuilding their holy places. In Mycenaean times the Acropolis, like the citadels at Tiryns and Mycenae, had been the king's residence, but in Hellenic times it became the residence of the gods. Athena was mistress of the citadel as well as guardian of all Attica. She won the land in a contest with Poseidon through her gift of the olive tree, Poseidon being able to offer only the salt-spring on the Acropolis. Since the archaic buildings were almost completely burnt down, Cimon had already set about raising a new version of the big temple of Athena Parthenos. But the realization of his plans did not get much further than the huge substructure and lowest column drums, so that Ictinus, who in 448/447 began to replan the building under Pericles, had only this substructure to incorporate. One can still see the original column drums in the north wall of the citadel.

The *Parthenon [60, 61]* is the most perfect Greek temple. In a typically Attic fashion, its Doric style has an admixture of Ionic elements (certain small decorative parts and above all the frieze round the cella). Despite its huge dimensions (101½ by 228 feet, i.e. slightly bigger than the temple of Zeus at Olympia; columns 34¼ feet tall), the building seems not heavy and bulky, but perfectly light and completely harmonious. Itself hexastyle amphiprostyle, the cella fits into the classically proportioned peristyle of eight by seventeen columns (n by $2n+1$) in a similar manner to the Zeus temple. But it was given a novel internal arrangement: instead of simply dividing the naos in three, the double-storied rows of columns were linked up to form an ambulatory, and the space with a clear width of 34¾ feet that was thus created allowed room for the gold-and-ivory statue of Athena by Pheidon. With this, an interior space as such had been realized for the first time in Greek art. The virgin servants of the goddess sat in the west room of the cella, which gave the name 'Parthenon' to the whole building. Four Ionic columns supported the wooden coffered ceiling – another brilliant innovation producing a high, light space. The details are incredibly refined: no two stones are alike. In accordance with the optical corrections (all horizontals from substructure to entablature are convexly arched, all verticals tilted slightly inward, so that the – elliptic – angle columns lean diagonally), each stone was treated individually, but nevertheless formed part of the whole. The temple appears as a plastic, living growth. This plastic effect is increased by the close column spacing

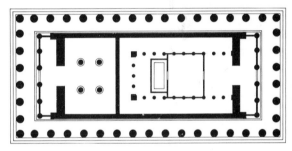

60, 61 View from the west and ground-plan of the Parthenon on the Acropolis, erected from the design of Ictinus, 447–432 BC. Slender pillars with light timber-work. The corners are strongly emphasized by the corner columns. Optical corrections through convexity of horizontals and concavity of verticals (pillars and walls). Narrow round hall: relationship between corner columns emphasized; broad cella to create an interior space; instead of a divided naos, the cult image can be seen from all sides. Ionic pillars on the western side of the cella.

and by the drawing in of the angle columns (angle contraction). As this goes beyond what is needed (so that in the frieze of metopes and triglyphs new conflicts arise, to be resolved by a barely perceptible narrowing of the outer metopes), the corners gain in strength. Thus, through the rich orchestration of the means, a complex refinement has been achieved in the harmony of the parts, yet it still gives an impression of inevitable simplicity and simple inevitability.

The vigorous, soaring harmony of the structure is most clearly expressed, however, in the sculptural decoration that crowned and concentrated the organic energy of the building. In only fifteen years of work at the Parthenon a consistent language was developed,

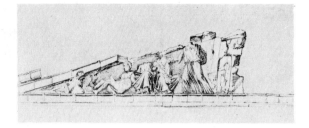

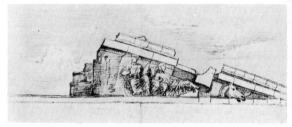

62   *Drawings by Jacques Carrey, 1674, showing the condition of the Parthenon pediments before the Venetian siege of 1687. Paris, Bibliothèque Nationale. Rough sketches of Phidias' figures, executed 438–432 BC. Above: the east pediment – birth of Athena (lost) in presence of the gods with Helios and Selene at the sides. Closed form; the triangular pediment gives the separate groups a sense of overall composition. Below: the west pediment – quarrel between Athena and Poseidon over Attica. Mature classical form gives way to Baroque; late work of Phidias.*

63   *Lapith and centaur, south metope XXVII of the Parthenon, after Phidias' design, 447–442 BC. London, British Museum. The centifrugal movement is unified by the circular form. The figures are freely developed in relief.*

behind which there must have been a directing will and a guiding hand. The new, mature classical style was created by the sculptural genius of Phidias, a friend of Pericles. The world-mastering and world-creating greatness of his mind is apparent even in the programme. Athena's birth in the presence of the gods was represented on the east pediment, the quarrel between Athena and Poseidon over Attica on the west one. The ninety-two metopes of the peristyle showed, on the east, the battle of the gods and giants, on the west, the Greeks fighting the Amazons, on the north, the battles before Troy, and on the south, the struggle between the Lapiths and the centaurs. All the battle scenes were split up, mostly into groups of two figures, but these reached out over the triglyphs and thus formed larger unities. Finally, on the 525-foot-long frieze round the cella, there was represented the solemn procession of the Panathenaea, which ended with the newly woven peplos for the city goddess being handed over in the presence of the gods. All the brilliance and splendour that the citizens of Periclean Athens had to offer were here displayed in honour of the gods in a manner at once free and submissive, proud and humble.

Precious fragments of the wonderful pediments have survived *[69]*, though they cannot be studied in detail here. Instead, we reproduce the drawings *[62]* made by the Frenchman Jacques Carrey in 1674, before the Turkish powder-magazine exploded in the Parthenon during the Venetian siege of 1687. Even here, unfortunately, the central group of the east pediment is missing. It showed Zeus enthroned, his head already split open with an axe by Hephaestus, and the new-born Athena crowned by Victory. The gods take part in the glorious event as spectators. The whole scene is framed by the ascending team of Helios in the left corner of the pediment and the descending team of the moon goddess Selene in the right. Goethe developed his idea of the primal horse from the head belonging to Selene's team. Phidias' art indeed seizes the essential nature of the animal. For one of the secrets of mature classical form is its ability to render the ideal form of the primitive being uncluttered by incidentals. On the powerful west pediment Athena and Poseidon meet in contest over the land of Attica. The clash and recoil become almost a rending apart under the pressure of the rearing teams of horses. It is an anticipation of the Hellenistic formal idiom. Only certain static elements, such as the grouping into one circular composition of the two violently agitated gods, holds back classical dynamism from breaking-point.

We find the same principle of composition in the remarkable metopes of the south row: the centrifugal movement of the *Lapith and Centaur Fighting* on south metope XXVII [63] is tied to a circle made out of the two bodies straining away from each other. The enormous tension of these bodies gives rise to the bold amalgamation of static and dynamic form. The harmony of mature classical form is hard won despite its apparent simplicity, and has an extremely complex basis.

Poseidon, Apollo, and Artemis [64] may serve here as a detail on the frieze of the magnificent band of figures descended from Olympus. Visibly present at the solemn handing-over of the peplos, they themselves take no part in the event; two of them seem to be completely engaged in a private conversation. Apollo turns round towards the dignified Poseidon, who has been made to look curiously stiff and rather obdurate – as if he had not yet recovered from the humiliation he suffered in the dispute over Attica. It is almost as though Apollo were persuading him not to look so sullen. The face of Artemis radiates ease, and her body shows delicately beneath the copious folds of her chiton and cloak. The plastic fullness of the figures on this 3½-feet-tall frieze seems all the more astonishing if one reflects that the depth of relief comes to hardly more than two inches. This freedom in the modelling is achieved through body perspective and slight foreshortenings. A harmonious blending of body and rich drapery determines the appearance of the figures. Apollo and Poseidon wear only a mantle (himation) that leaves the upper part of their bodies free. The physical forms are roundly modelled under the many taut and bunched folds. Descriptive rendering of materials is carried so far that even the weave of the cloth is indicated through closely spaced notches. A laurel wreath made of

64   *Poseidon, Apollo, and Artemis; part of the east frieze of the Parthenon, after Phidias' designs, 442–438 BC. Athens, Acropolis Museum. Mature classical relief style; unified relief space; interplay between garment and bodies.*

precious metal was once fixed into the small holes in Apollo's hair. He and Poseidon probably held a bow and trident in their respective left hands. Here again colour was used to emphasize the figures, which stood out against a darker, probably blue, background. The representation of these gods is utterly unforced. The strong expressive faces with big, eloquent eyes hardly differ from the faces of the human beings in the procession, which are just as remarkably rendered. They seem only a shade more majestic and introspective. The youths of the frieze are self-absorbed like Apollo and Artemis. The humanity of gods and men is represented superlatively, and at the same time itself becomes a mystery in the mature classical form created by Phidias. His most famous works, the two huge cult statues of Athena Parthenos (for the Parthenon) and Zeus (for the temple of Zeus at Olympia), which were many times life-size, have both been lost, and cannot be reconstructed even through Roman copies.

The principal achievement of the other leading master of the Greek classical period, Polycleitus from Dorian Argos, was to create the classical image of the athlete and hero. His chief works are now known only from Roman copies. In the Doryphorus, which was probably meant to represent the hero Achilles, he established what became known as the 'Canon', the ideal proportions of the male figure. About 420 BC he created the *Diadumenus* [65], so

65 *Diadumenus (tying the fillet of victory around his head),
Roman marble copy from a private house in Delos, after the
bronze original of Polycleitus, c. 420 BC. Athens, National
Museum. The high point of classical Doric-Argive athlete
statuary. The purest contrapposto arrangement of crosswise
rhythm. Single parts are in proportion to the whole; the figure is
self-absorbed; fulfilment of plastic composition in frontal view.*

figure seems to have been developed from the positions of standing and stepping, and just as this theme
can be understood both as a pause in stepping and a
ceasing to stand, so each part of the body, every
muscle and joint, is captured as it moves, yet seems to
be held in suspense. Despite the body's massiveness
and weight, an impression of curiously agile mobility
is thus produced. The growth of the heavy robust
frame is stressed by the bent arms, which, despite
the figure's spatial development, are extended in a
viewing surface. Even if one walks round the statue
and inspects it from all sides, the front view remains
the chief one. The head has a grave and masculine
appearance. The short curly hair is pressed together
by the fillet in such a way that the loosening up of
the mass of hair still seems strongly marked. In
Polycleitus' works the organic character of classical
form is realized, all parts being subordinated to a
great rhythm and a consistent idea. The classical law
of structure may be found not only in the microcosm
of the human image, but just as much in the structural
principle of the Parthenon and even in the order of
the Attic polis. Although each form is created distinct,
each serves as part of the whole.

A coherent scheme seems to underlie the new
arrangement of the *Athenian Acropolis*, which began
with the building of the Parthenon. While it preserves the autonomy of individual structures, it still
seeks for a deliberate co-ordination *[66]*. In 437 BC,
even before the Parthenon was finished, Mnesicles
began the *Propylaea [67]*, the gateway leading to
the sacred precincts of the Acropolis. However,
partly because of the Peloponnesian War, which
began in 431, but mainly because of opposition to
the project from reactionaries and conservatives, it
remained incomplete. The simple propylaeum of

called on account of the subject: a strongly built
athlete tying the fillet of victory round his head.
The right leg carries the weight of the body, whereas
the left foot is set back, only touching the ground
with the ball and tips of the toes. The supporting
leg presses vigorously into the hip, while the shoulder
above drops. The head is turned towards the side of
the supporting leg and is slightly tilted. In contrast,
the left shoulder is raised, so that an opening on the
side of the free leg answers the contraction on the
side of the supporting leg. The muscles of the supporting leg are tensed, but those of the upper body
on that side are relaxed; the muscles of the free leg
are relaxed, but those of the upper body on that side
are tensed. This crosswise rhythm is an example of
classical equilibrium, of contrapposto. It signified both
rest in movement and movement in rest. Just as the

66 *Ground-plan of the Acropolis, after the new arrangement of
448 BC. Preservation of the autonomy of each structure, but anticipation of late classical and Hellenistic effects in the Propylae.
1 Propylae with 2 north-west wing (Pinacotheca), 3 south-west
wing, 4 projected east wing, 5 Nike temple, 6 Parthenon, 7
Erectheion.*

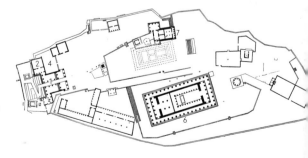

67 *Propylaea of the Athenian Acropolis, 337–332 BC, constructed after the plans of Mnesicles. View from the north-east wing (Pinacotheca). Many-membered wing structure, subordination of parts to the whole.*

archaic times, with its columns between antae, became here an enormous construction. The hexastyle prostyle west and east porticoes, which along with the five-door gate wall form the actual gate building, look like temple fronts. Behind the west colonnade two rows of slender Ionic columns supported beams with a wide span, the five front bays being followed here by a spacious hall with a central passage and two broad side aisles. Doric and Ionic were welded into a magnificent integrated whole. It was intended that wing buildings should link up with the gate structure, but only the north-west one (the subsequent Pinacotheca) was entirely finished; the south-west building was partly erected, while the two east ones (long halls) got no farther than their foundations. The west buildings, projecting on tall substructures, open up with rows of columns towards the ascent to the citadel and as it were embrace it. This ascent consisted of a wide ramp filling the whole space between the west wings, and was probably planned as a flight of steps. If the Parthenon represented the perfection of the Greek temple, Mnesicles' building had a totally new, revolutionary spirit. The union of originally independent types of structure and their axial arrangement pointed ahead, anticipating Hellenistic times.

On the western extension of the Propylaea's south substructure, the Nikepyrgos, a temple of Athena Nike (Victory) was built during the Peace of Nicias (421–415 BC) after plans by Callicrates. A graceful structure in the Ionic style, it stood opposite the powerful Doric architecture of the Propylaea. Its

tiny cella, almost square, is enclosed at either pediment end by four prostyle columns (amphiprostyle). The architrave, with its three fascias and the sculptured frieze above (instead of a dentil course; cf. 45), binds the walls and rows of columns together. The temple used to be surrounded on three sides by a 'balustrade' adorned in relief with Victories sacrificing bulls. This was erected during 410–409, under the impact of the last siege of Athens.

At the same period as the Nike temple, and again in the Ionic style, the Erechtheion was begun. Like the Propylaea, however, it remained unfinished. The cella of the hexastyle prostyle temple, broken up into many partitions, had to accommodate a great many tokens and cults (image of the city goddess, mark of Poseidon's trident, grave of Cecrops, Athena's olive tree, citadel serpent). On the north, a spacious open porch and on the south, the famous Caryatid porch [73] is attached to its flanks. Here also, a winged structure was probably intended, with its centre taken up by the two porches. Thus the building now only impresses through the elegant splendour of its separate parts.

The burial of the dead of the first year of the war (431 BC) must have occurred with special pomp at the beginning of winter. The largest and most remarkable of classical Attic grave reliefs, that of the *Horseman of the Villa Albani* which had already been carried off from Athens to Rome in ancient times, perhaps refers to the fallen of this first year, since its battles were fought only by mounted units on the Athenian side. Found at Rome in Winckelmann's day, the relief shows a cavalry engagement [68]. The Attic rider has just leapt from his steed and like

68 *Attic marble relief of a rider from a public grave, c. 430 BC. Rome, Villa Albani. Unified centrifugal and circular composition.*

69   *Figure of Iris, from the right half of the west pediment of the Parthenon. London, British Museum. Extremely close interplay between body and garment.*

Harmodius raises his sword-arm to strike his enemy lying on the ground a mortal blow. At the same time, he restrains the prancing horse with his left hand. The opponent vainly tries to protect himself with his arm enwound in a cloak, as if it were a shield. Helplessly his eyes implore the victor, whose garment flutters round him in the storm of excitement. Yet this heated incident takes place within an incredible stillness, and one senses a hesitation before the blow. The fight occurs in rough and rocky land. The powerful rearing movement of the horse is wholly in the Parthenon style, and the victor's exomis (short-belted chiton) recalls, in the rich and resonant language of its folds, statues from the Parthenon's west pediment. One example is the running figure of *Iris [69]*, messenger of the gods, whose torso is among the finest sculptures from that pediment. The idea of combining dynamic, centrifugal forces with a static, circular pattern seems entirely Phidian in spirit in the Albani relief. The deceased could be portrayed as a victor only on the

public tomb. This is the daring innovation of Periclean art when compared with archaic sepulchral monuments. The image of the deceased was intended to live on in memory as the heroic image of a conqueror. In this noble view of destiny, the Albani horseman relief may serve as a symbol for the classical greatness of Periclean Athens, of the city that in the course of a few years was cast down from a summit of power and splendour to a chasm of doom. For it is not Attica's distress or Sparta's victory but the vigour and potency of the surviving fragments of Periclean Athens that have impressed and shaped the mind of man.

In vase-painting, pictures appeared that fully accord with the spirit of the Parthenon. On a *Stamnos by the Kleophon Painter* from about 430 BC *[70]*, now at Munich, the warrior's farewell is represented, as it is on many white-ground lekythoi (oil-jugs) that were put in graves. A young woman stands with bowed head, profoundly moved, before a youthful warrior leaving for the field. In her right hand she holds the jug from which she has poured the parting

70   *Red-figured stamnos by the Kleophon Painter, c. 430 BC. Munich, Staatliche Antikensammlungen. The Parthenon style is transferred to smaller works of art.*

cat sits on a pillar, against which leans a boy who probably held a small oil-bottle and a scraper, utensils that would characterize the deceased as an athlete. Behind the hand raised in greeting is a bird-cage belonging to the bird in the youth's lowered left hand. A stately band of open palmettes and lotus blossom enriches the straight upper border of the stele. The deceased appears in his prime, surrounded by the things he loved in life. Only the face of the little servant conveys a sense of grief. He faces towards the front and no longer has any palpable relationship to the dead youth. Turning away, he makes evident the narrow frontier between life and death. The calm portrayals of life in its beauty and sadness on fifth-century Attic grave stelae are among the most moving products of Greek classical art.

One man, through his far-sightedness and human greatness, laid the political foundations of the Attic classical period: Pericles. His image has come down

72 Head of Pericles, Roman copy after Cresilas' memorial statue for the Acropolis, after 429 BC. Berlin-Dahlem, Pergamum Museum. This is not a portrait but an idealized picture of a strategist and statesman, with no interpretation of personal features, modelled after the images of Athenian citizens on the Parthenon frieze.

71 Marble grave stele from the island of Aegina, c. 425 BC. Athens, National Museum. Garments and figures are in the Parthenon style.

libation into the young man's bowl. The warrior, perhaps her husband or her brother, has raised this phiale, and looks intently at the woman. He carries his shield on his left arm; spear, helmet, and sword, together with a short chiton, complete his equipment. At the sides, a white-haired old man and a woman with hand raised in salutation round off a scene of departure moving in its tranquillity. Greek classical art used its newly won freedom to create such quietly introspective images, apparent also in works of handicraft.

From the outbreak of the Peloponnesian War, stelae with portraits of the dead were again to be found on the graves of Attic citizens. An exceptionally complete *stele from Aegina [71]*, datable around 425 BC, shows the deceased as a young man of quality wearing the himation, a mantle-like wrap, and lifting his right hand in salutation. The after-effect of the Parthenon style (cf. the Apollo on the frieze slab from the east end: *64*) is unmistakable in the pose, the movingly refined shape of the head, and the drapery. In the background below the youth's raised hand a

the same time they developed them to the full. The workshop of Alcamenes may perhaps have given us the *Korai of the Erechtheion Caryatid porch [73]*, where they serve as light and graceful supports for the entablature. Despite the structural constraint, full freedom has been achieved for the 'servant' figures here, in contrast to archaic caryatids *[45]*.

Round about 410 BC the further development of the Parthenon form led to a decidedly rich style typified in the Victories from the Nikepyrgos 'balustrade'. With the *Nike adjusting her sandal [74]* the extravagant play of folds in the transparent drapery cleverly stresses the body's exposure. But the drapery also has a life of its own. The unity of body and dress in Parthenon art has crumbled into its component parts, while the destruction is covered over and hidden by a brilliant level of artistry. In mature classical art, the figure relief seems to grow from, and be bound to, its background. The bond is now burst by the bold movement of the figure, which steps out into a space before the surface.

74   *Nike adjusting her sandal, slab from the marble 'balustrade' of the Nikepyrgos, c. 406 BC. Athens, Acropolis Museum. The dress is independent of the body, which seems almost naked, and moves with great refinement. A high point of the mature style.*

73   *The Caryatid porch of the Erechtheion, built between 421 and 415 BC. Tectonic composition of bodies (pillar-like shape of garments over the supporting feet; upper part of figure square; the head already superimposed) – an effect softened by contours on the side of the free leg, and intensified relationship between garment and body.*

to us in Roman copies of a *Memorial statue* carved by the sculptor Cresilas after Pericles' death *[72]*. No attempt has been made to render incidental traits. Pericles' bulbous head is covered by the helmet he wears as a general. The excessive height of the head is apparent only through the eye-holes of the helmet that has been pushed back. Pericles is shown not as an old man, but in the very prime of life, with an elegant short manly beard. All his features are treated boldly: the eyes are striking, the strong nose and full mouth refined. It is not the personal peculiarities but the very nature of this statesman who gave his name to a whole age that has been captured here in an idealized way.

Even after Phidias had left Athens, the mature classical Attic style remained under his formal influence. His pupils Alcamenes and Agoracritus simply varied the forms he had created, while at

Late classical art (400–c. 330 BC)

The fourth century BC is marked by the decline of the Greek city-state. Sparta's hegemony over Greece, exercised after the Peloponnesian War and a series of attendant conflicts, was finally broken by Thebes under the leadership of Epaminondas (battle of Leucrta 371 BC, battle of Mantinea 362). Thanks to the wise political guidance first of Conon (founding of the second Attic maritime league 378/377) and later of Lycurgus, Athens enjoyed a political and economic revival. Under a series of energetic kings, the Macedonians had built up a strong state which owed its systematic military and territorial expansion above all to Philip II (reigned 359–336). In the middle of the century they began to exert influence on events inside Greece. Philip's enrolment as a member of the Amphictionic Council provided the legitimate means. Quarrels within the Amphictionic League led to a war between Philip and the allied Athenians and Boeotians; it ended with the battle of Chaeronea on 2 August 338, which signified the end of the independent Greek polis. General peace in Hellas resulted from the founding of the Panhellenic Rates under Macedonian leadership at Corinth. There, Philip was entrusted with the campaign of revenge against the Persians, although its realization had to await his son.

The great poetry of the fifth century was succeeded by philosophy: Socrates, whose ideals were taught by his pupil Plato, died in 399. Plato and Aristotle taught and wrote at Athens. The Attic orators Demosthenes, Isocrates, and Aeschines championed the two opposing political concepts of the autonomous city-state and a united Greece.

The beautiful linear effects of the late fifth century are fully manifest in the Victory 'balustrade' and the work of the Meidias Painter. Form was less agitated at the beginning of the fourth century, although conventionalized calligraphic flourishes are still evident. During the years around 400 the transition occurred from mature classical objective form to the more subjective variety of late classical times. Out of the plastically oriented mature classical world of forms developed the painterly late classical approach. Statues in bronze, the favourite material of the previous period, were replaced by marble, which, unlike the earlier objective coloration, was now lightly and impressionistically painted. Figures changed their proportions: bodies were slimmer, heads smaller. Space, which in the classical period was used to express form, was now used to form expression. The mature classical ethos of the figure turned into pathos. One can discern a restriction of

75 *Marble grave stele of Dexileus, who fell before Corinth in 394 BC. Athens, Ceramics Museum. Sober, realistic composition and survival of elements from the mature style.*

public life, counterbalanced by a withdrawal into private life and philosophy. The cults of new deities, such as Asclepius, the god of healing, gained ground.

Graves of Attic warriors of the fourth century still faithfully follow the mature classical pattern. The *Stele of Dexileus [75]*, who died in the cavalry before Corinth in 394, is of a much older, mature classical type. One can recognize the distinct character of early fourth-century composition only in the compact foreshortening of horse and fallen enemy. The foreshortening also contributes to the form, which for all the movement is calm in its effect, and to a new realism in the representation of physical qualities. Once again the fallen rider is portrayed as a victor, and the boldly rendered faces are still entirely in the mature classical spirit. This stele stood over an empty grave in the burial place of Dexileus' family, since according to the law the dead man was interred in the public tomb. From its erection it is clear that Dexileus was revered by his family as a hero.

76   Marble acroterium figure, the so-called Aura, from the west pediment of the Asclepius temple at Epidaurus, worked by Timotheus 380–370 BC. Athens, National Museum. Survival of the mature style in the dress; melancholy expression of the face.

The leading master of the transition period was probably Timotheus, whom we may include in the Attic school. He designed the models for the pediments of the Asclepius temple at Epidaurus, as well as making the western acroteria. It was still the great mythic subjects of the fifth century that were represented on the pediments: at the east end the fall of Troy, at the west the battle with the Amazons. The *Acroterium figures* are Victories and on the corners, girls on horseback representing perhaps nereids or wind goddesses. These graceful girls *[76]* seem to be slipping lightly from their mounts. Although the drapery is richly profuse, the body stands out quite clearly under the material. The harmony of the groups still draws its strength from the mature classical form, overtaken only in the warmly human rendering of the face with its melancholy expression. Compared to that of the 'balustrade' Victories *[74]*, the garments have become still more independent. The structure has also hardened, and one feels that the idiom of the rich style is being used in a formalistic way.

The favourite conformation of the head is already observable with Timotheus. It culminated in openly dramatic and vigorous expression with Scopas of Paros, who together with Praxiteles and Lysippus reflects most clearly the stylistic trend of late classical art. Scopas was a sculptor of much spontaneous talent who broke the self-imposed law of the mature classical figure and boldly incorporated the surrounding space in the plastic form. In his statues he gives prominence to the suffering and hardship of heroic action. Half-way through the century he and his workshop created the pediment sculptures for the temple of Athena Alea at Tegea, considered the finest temple in the Peloponnese. The Calydonian Hunt and a local Tegean myth were represented on the east and west pediments. The wild boar was killed near Calydon, all the really important Greek heroes taking part. Among them Meleager and the huntress Atalanta specially distinguished themselves. Only fragments of the *pediment sculptures* have survived, though even as shop products these can tell us about the style of Scopas. The vigorous head reproduced here *[77]*, abruptly turning on a thick neck, has a

77   Marble head from a pediment of the Athena temple at Tegea, by Scopas, c. 350 BC. Athens, National Museum. Active form replaces the classical serenity; pathos and painterly effect.

base, while a third showing quadriga races has been assigned to the cella. Statues were placed between the peristyle columns. The well-known *Sarcophagus with Mourning Women* from the royal necropolis of Sidon [79], now at Istanbul, is fully comparable in the arrangement between columns of statues almost in the round and indeed even as regards the general conception of a tomb temple. A quadriga crowned the pyramid roof of the Mausoleum, which lent its name to all subsequent large sepulchral buildings. The portrait statues of *Mausolus* and his wife Artemisia, who had the structure continued after his death, were created by the local sculptor Bryaxis [80]. Powerful thrusting movement characterizes the image of Mausolus, who perhaps stood next to Artemisia in the chariot with its team of four horses. The body has almost completely vanished under the exceedingly rich development of the drapery. Only the knee of the free leg pushes forward. A restless contour, broken by the folds, stands out along the side of the supporting leg. Mausolus' face has some exotic traits, which are emphasized by the un-Greek style of his long hair. The whole statue is founded on an agitated massiveness expressed in its turbulence and insistent thrusting movement. A painterly surface effect makes the volumes indistinct. With these figures Bryaxis was already showing late classical art

78 *Reconstruction of the Mausoleum, tomb of King Mausolus in Halicarnassus, Asia Minor, designed by Pythius in the mid-fourth century BC. Type of tower grave in Asia Minor, combined with the Greek Ionic temple.*

79 *Sarcophagus from the royal necropolis of Sidon, the so-called Sarcophagus with Mourning Women, mid fourth century BC. Istanbul, Archaeological Museum. Transference of Ionic temple structure to the sarcophagus. The female figures are in the Praxitelean tradition of clothed statues; their style of arrangement between the columns is customary for Asia Minor.*

short lower face, with broad cheek-bones and deep-set eyes whose lids disappear under the bulge of the brows. The short hair is only sketchily treated. Extreme tension and naked passion have been drawn out of the marble, with the natural form exaggerated and altered for effect. The reticent calm of the mature classical cast of features is converted into a vehemently strained expressive form of elemental plastic force.

For the spectacular *Tomb of Mausolus*, ruler of Caria who died at Halicarnassus in 352 BC, the most eminent artists of the day were summoned to prepare the sculptural decoration. This tomb [78] was one of the Seven Wonders of the World, and counts among the greatest architectural achievements of the times. Its arrangement as a temple on a huge base is derived from types native to Asia Minor. Pythius was its architect. Scopas, being the most distinguished of the sculptors, was given the east side, Timotheus the south, Bryaxis the north, and Leochares of Athens the west. Two friezes representing the battles with the centaurs and the Amazons probably adorned the

80 Marble statue of Mausolus, perhaps from the quadriga on the roof of the pyramid, made by Bryaxis about the middle of the fourth century BC. London, British Museum. The structure of the body is concealed by the mass of garments, now fully independent; painterly effect; the features are un-Greek.

81 Ground-plan of the Athena temple at Priene (Asia Minor), built by Pythius after the mid-fourth century BC. The Ionic rounded hall temple is adjusted to the Doric though introducing an opisthodomus (back hall) and similar composition of all the sides; the ground-plan is abstract and rational.

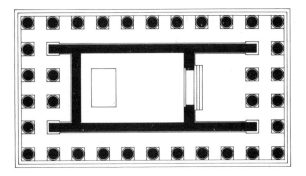

the way to Hellenistic form, a form he himself used in his cult image of Sarapis, the Ptolemies' strange god of healing and the underworld, for the city of Alexandria.

After the turn of the century, the same architect Pythius built an Ionic *Temple of Athena* for the city of Priene, near the river Maeander. It represents the classical interpretation of this order *[81]*. The rational arrangement already evident in archaic Ionic temples was carried out here with admirable clarity. Underlying the ground-plan is a network of squares within which all the parts – peristyle columns, antae, columns between the antae – were axially related to each other. A mass of simple proportions gave the building a crystalline form that was saved from academic coldness by the plant-like, organic quality of the Ionic style. The regular conformation of all sides, and the addition of an opisthodomus (although a small one), made this structure resemble the Doric temple with its sculptural character and all-sidedness.

Older than Bryaxis was the Attic sculptor Praxiteles, whose early works dated back even to before the middle of the century. In accord with the late classical conception of the Olympian gods, he portrayed them no longer in their grandeur and majesty but in their playful self-enjoyment and their happy, untroubled aloofness. Praxiteles many times modelled Aphrodite in the full beauty of her half-draped or naked body. These statues of his are characterized by a painter-like, pictorial composition. Only the painter Nikias of Athens was allowed to colour them. Those that have come down to us have done so only as Roman copies, with one exception. This mature, if not actually late, product of his own hand is the famous *Hermes with the infant Dionysus*, at Olympia *[82]*. Hermes grows slenderly out of the long-legged stance. His bodily forms are softly blended and modelled, their calm glow concentrated in the gentle head of the god. The interflowing of forms is particularly emphasized by the delicate transitions of the face which, blissfully content, rests self-absorbed in its action. A mass of short curly hair surrounds the head. In this Hermes the messenger of the gods and the carrier of the little Dionysus have been fused into an image of a sweetness that seems almost unearthly. For all its lyrical immediacy, Praxiteles' figure is nothing else but a token of the remoteness of the gods. Despite the magic of his presence, he remains inaccessible to prayer or invocation. The group is composed

82 Marble statue of Hermes with the infant Dionysus from the Hera temple in Olympia, the work of Praxiteles, c. 330 BC. Olympia, Museum. A picture-like composition of figures. Light plays on the surfaces; the forms are slurred.

83   Statue of the Belvedere Apollo, Roman copy after the original of Leochares c. 330 BC. The Vatican, Museums and Galleries. Elegant movement; the figure is open to space; its form contrasted to the dress: Alexandrian style of presentation.

in an entirely pictorial way. Hermes' left arm, which bears the child, is supported by a tree-trunk over which the god has thrown his cloak. Its soft material is also spread across his arm, so as not to hurt Dionysus. The Hermes figure makes it effect only when viewed from the front. Its back is not fully chiselled, since it was never intended to be seen. This precedence of a pictorial conception over sculptural modelling in the round is typical of the late classical idiom in which Praxiteles worked.

In his *Belvedere Apollo [83]*, the Attic sculptor Leochares, who had already collaborated on the Mausoleum, gave expression to the late classical idea of this god. The slim figure steps lightly, a bow in his once extended left hand. The vigorously turned

head stares at a possible enemy in the distance. The plastic thrust of the outstretched arm is underlined by the drapery, against which the body stands out resplendent, its weight poised undecidedly on both feet. Through its arrangement in ringlets, the hair enhances the sublime, avenging expression of the face, with its parted lips. This celebrated work has been a frequent influence since the Renaissance. In the slender rise of the figure and the hovering composition focused on a single direction, the sheer majesty of the god who wards off harm again displays itself. At the height of the late classical style, this work dating from about 330 BC signifies the preparation for the sudden change to Hellenistic form, which culminates in agitation for its own sake.

Leochares also created the statues of the Macedonian royal family to be housed in the Philippeum at Olympia. He made them of gold and silver, and thus used a technique previously kept for images of the gods. The appearance of the Alexander in this group can perhaps be recovered from a mature Hellenistic statue found at Magnesia on the Maeander and now at Istanbul *[84]*. Alexander has been made to look like a Zeus. He wears the himation, which leaves the upper part of his body exposed. In his lowered left hand he held the sword of the ruler of the world, and with his right probably leant on the sceptre. Although the pushing and shifting of forms, at its climax in the magnificent head, is exaggerated in the mature Hellenistic recast, it can still be associated with the Baroque attitude of the Alexandrian age. Out of the mature classical figure standing in repose developed this imposing, self-displaying, effect-seeking portrait of the god-like conqueror.

The sculptor Lysippus undoubtedly contributed most to the perfecting of late classical form and its conversion into the active form of Hellenistic times. Lysippus helped give the creative activity of the period from 360 BC to the end of the century its particular stamp. Shortly after the mid-century appeared his portrait *Head of Socrates [85]*, made for the Pompeion at Athens (the storehouse for equipment used during the Panathenaea). The ugly philosopher has been brilliantly rendered by Lysippus. His head, with its wide, stubby nose, could be mistaken for that of a Silenus. In the concentrated structure of the broad face with its small, ironic eyes beneath the high forehead, encircling hair and beard play an important part. One can discern the penetrating force of Socratic thought in this work. Over half a century after his death, the philosopher's appearance was conjured up as if in expiation. It is an ideal portrait, free from the pros and cons of current political opinion.

84 *Mature Hellenistic statue of Alexander the Great, from Magnesia on the Maeander. Istanbul, Archaeological Museum. Remodel of a statue by Leochares, c. 330 BC. Baroque presentation; characteristic display.*

85 *Head of Socrates, Roman copy after a statue by Lysippus shortly after 350 BC. Rome, Museo delle Terme. Idealized portrait of the philosopher; individual features (the nose) are united to an overall representation of the essential philosophical nature. (Left.)*

86 *Statue of Apoxyomenus (scraping off the dust from the palaestra), Roman marble copy after the bronze original by Lysippus, c. 320 BC. The Vatican, Museums and Galleries. The surrounding space is included in the plasticity; the figure no longer realizes itself in frontal view but only in its surround; the athlete is portrayed not as victor, but in the exhaustion after the struggle. New proportions: long legs and smaller head.*

87   The battle between Alexander and Darius, mosaic floor from Pompeii, copied from the picture by Philoxenus of Eretria, c. 320 BC. Naples, Museo Nazionale. Baroque pathos of the *Alexandrian period; spatial disposition through overlapping and bold foreshortening; plasticity of figures through shadow effects.*

Created about 320 BC in honour of an Olympic champion who was perhaps Cheilon of Elis, the *Apoxyomenus*, a young man scraping himself, may be regarded as a late Lysippus *[86]*. Even the theme is indicative of the late classical and early Hellenistic conception of the victor statue. The athlete is no longer shown at the moment of his feat, like Myron's Discobolus, or before the god who gave him victory. Instead, the efforts and exertions of the contest are expressed, with the exhausted champion cleaning off the dusty oil of the palaestra. The eyes stare out listless and weary. The left arm reaches obliquely across the upper body to scrape off the dirt from under the outstretched right arm. Out of the broad, long-legged standing pose an unstable, vacillating equilibrium has been developed, in which the thrill and strain of the contest is still reflected. The functioning of the body is vigorously rendered. In the bold jut of the extended right arm another dimension of space has been conquered. The Apoxyomenus embodies two conflicting effects: the melancholic outlook of late classicism and the spatial activity of the Hellenistic period. We owe a new, realistic conception of the human image to Lysippus. A saying of his has come down to us: 'one should copy nature, not a master'. But on the other hand he had a keen artistic intel-

ligence and wanted to systematize his knowledge like Polycleitus, whom he admired. Being an artist of repute, he did many portraits of Alexander, who employed him as court sculptor along with, and perhaps in preference to, Leochares.

Only a few years after Lysippus modelled his Apoxyomenus, Philoxenus of Eretria painted for Cassander, a successor of Alexander on the Macedonian throne, a glorification of the *Battle between Alexander and Darius*. This painting has probably come down to us in a mosaic copy from Pompeii *[87]*, which shows the Macedonian cavalry engaged against the Persians, and the flight of Darius in his chariot. Alexander, whose helmet has slipped from his head in the heat of the battle, is riding his horse Bucephalus, and has just run a Persian nobleman through with his couched lance. Darius, filled with terror, stretches out his hand. Impotent and helpless, he has to witness the inability of his loyal troops to stand firm against the charge of the new Achilles. This tremendous action takes place upon a narrow stage of landscape. A dead tree with mutilated branches and the bristling lances in the background form the setting for the climax of the savage drama, in which the battles on the Granicus, at Issus, and at Gaugamela have probably been combined as a single scene. Shortly before his death Goethe saw one more drawing of the Alexander mosaic: 'This age and those to come will not suffice to comment properly on such a miracle of art. After enlightening scrutiny and contemplation we shall be obliged to return, time after time, to pure and simple admiration.'

HELLENISTIC ART

The Hellenistic age is characterized by the spread of Greek civilization as far as Asia and Egypt, and by a shift of political and cultural gravity away from the centres to the regions bordering the Mediterranean. This extension was brought about by the campaigns of Alexander the Great (356–323 BC), who in a few years conquered the Persian empire and thrust on to India. When Alexander died his huge empire, after brief, fruitless attempts to maintain it under central control, broke up into many separate kingdoms, among which Egypt under the Ptolemies, Syria under the Seleucids, and Pergamum under the Attalids and Macedonians were the most prominent. In 279 Gallic tribes invaded Greece and crossed over to Asia Minor, where they were defeated by the Attalids. Rome made its entry in the West as a new power, first annexing Magna Graecia and Sicily (a province from 227). During the second century BC Macedonia became a Roman province (battle of Pydnia in 168, won by L. Aemilius Paulus), followed by the rest of Greece in 146, the year when L. Mummius destroyed Corinth. In 133 the childless Attalus III willed his kingdom to the Romans. Most Asian territories were in Roman hands by 63 BC, Egypt being the last Hellenized state absorbed into the empire in 30 BC.

The formation of large Greek states ruled by kings ran parallel to the growth of middle-class societies, which had begun as early as the fourth century. Hand in hand with this development went a progressive disintegration of the old religion, a trend revealed in the comedies of Menander (343–293). The philosophical doctrines of Epicurus (342/341–271/270) and the Stoic Zeno (at Athens from 315), were already showing cosmopolitan traits in the great centres of Alexandria and Antioch.

Early Hellenistic form (Late fourth to mid-third century BC)

The age of Alexander signifies at once the perfecting of the late classical formal idiom and the breakthrough to Hellenistic art. The new stimuli were not received everywhere in equal strength. The school of Praxiteles, for example, continued to develop the delicate Praxitelean form. In Athens, too, the Baroque trends met with during Alexandrian times were not followed up. At the start of the third century BC a plain style asserted itself in Attic art, concentrating on heavy physical realism and firmly defined plastic cubes. The chief example of this is the *Statue of the Attic orator Demosthenes* – known from Roman copies – which Polyeuctus created about 280, almost forty years after the statesman's death [88]. Simply posed, with his hands probably once clasped before him, the patriot stands in grief at the loss of freedom. The horizontal and vertical lines of the drapery folds meet each other stiffly, lying like bonds around the thin, scrawny body. In the gaunt face, wrinkled and furrowed, burns an impotent desire for liberty. The formal language is dry, terse, and angular. Polyeuctus was consciously seeking the antithesis to the harmony and graceful linear effects of classical form.

88 Statue portraying Demosthenes, Roman copy after the original by Polyeuctus, c. 280 BC. The Vatican, Museums and Galleries. Plain, dry style; the figure is more confined in its space through harder plasticity. The portrait has realistic features.

Mature Hellenistic form (*Mid-third century to c. 160 BC*)

From the mid-third century BC Hellenistic art became increasingly Baroque, an approach that culminated in agitated crowd scenes. At the same time there began a realistic approach to the real world. New fields were opened up to the figurative artist: genre and the still life. A typical big-city art developed, which found fulfilment in glorifications of the pastoral idyll (cf. the poet Theocritus) and scenes from street life. Although myth did survive, the gods had lost something of their power. Tyche, the Roman Fortuna, determined the world's fate as a capricious goddess of chance. Oriental mystery religions such as the Egyptian cult of Isis and Osiris increased their importance.

In sculpture, new themes were found, such as that of the suspended body, so familiar to us from Christian art. Large figures to be seen from all sides were now shown sitting on the ground. The famous marble statue of a *Drunken Old Woman* [89] dates from the middle of the century. Sitting on the ground,

89　*Statue of the Drunken Old Woman, Roman copy after an original of the mid-third century BC. Munich, Staatliche Antikensammlungen. Realistic genre picture; pyramidal composition of the figure.*

90　*Girl of Antium, marble Greek original of the period c. 240 BC. Rome, Museo delle Terme. The figure composition is closed; contrast of dress with the smooth surface.*

the emaciated figure holds between her knees a wine-bottle whose shape points to Alexandria. Her veined and wrinkled head is thrown back in blissful intoxication. The clothing has fallen away from her shoulder and reveals the worn body, while on the ground it spreads out in crumpled folds. This realistic genre image is inscribed within a severe, cubic pyramidal form. Realism and formalism are combined, heightening the tension.

Mature Hellenistic art went to extremes: alongside the *Drunken Old Woman* a figure as touching as the *Antium Girl* could be produced [90]. This represents a cult servant deep in thought as she holds a tray with food offerings. An original of high quality, this belongs to the period around 240 BC. Through being placed obliquely and well to the side, the free leg imparts a strong momentum to the whole self-contained figure. Girlishly delicate in its modelling, the head gazes towards the sacrificial tray. The crêpe-like folds of the chiton and rich complex of mantle folds play round the slender body without losing any of their independence. This image of youthful service and peaceful meditation has been achieved, in its unpretentious grandeur, from countless little rhythms, out of whose unrest a stillness has been masterfully built. Not simple classical, but inherently complex repose is presented. Even where it aims to 'be', and not to produce an effect, Hellenistic active form is composed of oppositions that are always strained to the utmost. The girl's bare shoulder contrasts subtly, in its smoothness, with the animation of the clothing, as does the simply treated head with the rich drapery.

The powerful and easy movement of Hellenistic active form is magnificently realized in the *Victory of Samothrace*, a work possibly created about 190 BC as a votive offering for a naval success [91]. The winged goddess, bringing victory, glides down on to the ship's prow, her vigorous descent expressed in the mighty flourishes of the robe. Blown back by the wind, the thin chiton presses against her body and stretches over the breasts in sharp ridges. The girdling just below the chest emphasizes the forms of the subtly turning body. This triumph of movement must have reached its climax in the head, whose loss is thus especially regrettable.

At Pergamum, the struggles of the Attalids against the Gauls found visible expression in votive offerings. Around 230 BC the famous group of a Gallic prince killing his wife and himself was created. The *Dying Gaul*, too, numbers among these offerings [92]. Even the subject-matter of the groups is typically Hellenistic. It is the moment of dying or suicide that is represented now, rather than the trial of strength in battle. The victorious Pergamenians are not portrayed at all. Only the pride and suffering of the enemy are realistically shown – not without pathos – in a vivid characterization. Bracing himself as he stubbornly fights off death, the Gaul is not merely a brilliant psychological study; anatomically, too, he has been rendered with complete truth. The sword wound under his right breast is shown in relief; muscles, veins, and sinews are both tensed and relaxed in the moment before the final stiffening. Round his neck he wears a torque, the twisted necklace of the Gauls. His shaggy hair marks him as a barbarian, yet his death is seen not contemptuously, but as something almost grand and noble. On the base lie the shield and trumpet that have slipped from his hands. Perhaps created by the sculptor and art theorist Epigonus of Carystos, this work has reached us only in a Roman copy of the Antonine period.

Pergamene art culminated in the colossal structure of the great *Altar of Zeus*, raised under Eumenes II between 180 and 160 BC. This was the most immense friezed altar of antiquity [93]. On an almost square

91 Marble statue of the Nike of Samothrace, c. 190 BC. Paris, Louvre. Painterly effect of dress; subtly turning body providing a view from all sides.

92 Statue of the Dying Gaul, Roman copy after the original by Epigonus of Carystos, from the period c. 230 BC. Rome, Museo Capitolino. Spatial composition of figure, realistically anatomical body; characterization of the Gallic type.

93   *Altar of Zeus from Pergamum, between 180 and 160 BC, set up by Eumenes II. Berlin-Dahlem, Pergamum Museum. The altar is monumentalized – extended by a podium and enclosed by a hall of pillars. The sculpture on the podium frieze is an integral part of the architecture.*

94   *Athena in battle with the Giants, slab from the east frieze of the Pergamon altar. Berlin-Dahlem, Pergamum Museum. 'Quotation' from mature classical art (west pediment of the Parthenon); Baroque pathos of figures; complete obscurance of relief ground.*

95   *Pillars of the temple of Olympian Zeus in Athens, part of the structure erected by Cossutius under Antiochus IV (175–164 BC). The Corinthian capital is used in place of the Ionic in the exterior structure.*

platform, up which led a broad flight of steps between side walls, lay the actual altar surrounded by colonnades like the squares of the period. Round the whole base, including the side walls, extended a frieze about 655 feet long showing the battle of the gods and giants. A second, smaller frieze, with scenes from the tales concerning the founding of Pergamum, ran along inside the colonnades. Magnificent acroterium figures crowned the huge construction, in which architecture and large sculpture were combined as an indissoluble whole in a manner undreamt of before. A frenzy of movement pervades the figures of the big frieze, whose forms are dramatically larger than life. Though, formally, the gods of the Parthenon's Pheidian west pediment are evoked on the east frieze slab showing *Athena in Battle with the Giants [94]*, they have been worked quite naturally into the new high baroque form. Athena, rushing towards the right, has grabbed her winged opponent by the hair, and is about to strike him down pitilessly. From the right, Victory hastens with outspread wings to crown the triumphant goddess. Gaea emerges wailing from the depths, the earth mother mourning the death of her sons. Naked emotion, vividly heightened forms and turbulent, almost recklessly compassed, movement govern the composition of the entwining, meeting, and parting bodies. In a sort of colossal *horror vacui*, the ground of the high relief is so overspread with figures that it almost vanishes. It becomes a rear wall before which occur the sculptural explosions of the huge, interlinking bodies. This is the highest point of a Baroque stylistic trend in antiquity.

In the vast frieze with the battle of the gods and giants all the deities and divine beings then recognized were brought together. A cosmic pantheism became visible, a world full of gods and spirits. The primitive Greek experience culminated in this mighty baroque theogony, consciously linked to its beginnings in Hesiod.

At the same period work was resumed, with money from the Seleucid king Antiochus IV (175–164 BC), on the huge *Temple of Olympian Zeus* begun at Athens under Peisistratus *[95]*. The Roman architect Cossutius was in charge. The building followed the ground-plan of the archaic structure as a dipteros, with the axial relation customary since the Athena temple at Priene. What was really new and fruitful was the use of the *Corinthian capital*. This type – a bell-shaped core surrounded by a double wreath of acanthus leaves, from which spiralling tendrils shoot out, topped by an abacus with four concave sides – was evolved in Attica for interior decoration, for example at Phigalia, Tegea, and Epidaurus *[96]*. The articulating wall (Lysicrates monument) was developed and first came into use externally for architecture in Asia Minor. It combines the plastic Doric form with the organic, plant-like Ionic. Thanks to the Olympieion at Athens, this capital now became 'acceptable', and after Sulla had taken a few columns from the still unfinished building for the Jupiter temple on the Capitol, began its triumphant progress through the history of Roman art.

The love of Hellenistic princes and rich trading cities for pomp and show was not satisfied simply by raising magnificent temples. Great squares came into being, enclosed by multi-storied stoas, which already displayed what later became the usual sequence of the Doric and Ionic orders in Rome. At the centre stood the temple and altar, to which mighty gate buildings gave access.

This tendency towards the organization of larger groups of buildings had announced itself in Ionia as early as the fifth century BC, above all in the laying out of regular lines of streets crossing at right angles, with which the name of Hippodamos of Miletus is associated *[97]*. During Hellenistic times older sanctuaries, too, underwent such modifications. This did not accord with the archaic and classical feeling, since it meant a reduction of the plastic value of the individual building. One such layout has survived on the narrow *Acropolis at Lindus on Rhodes [98]*. Through a long stoa with projecting wings, a broad stairway led between column-crowned bastions to the propylaeum, whose gate wall had five openings.

96 Corinthian capital from Epidaurus, second half of fourth century BC. Epidaurus, Museum. The capital was now used in interior decoration.

97 Plan of the city of Priene on the Maeander (Asia Minor), new design of the fourth century BC. The town is planned in 'insulae' through streets running parallel and around the slope and cross-streets at right angles (partly raised as steps). In the central 'island' the public buildings are laid out: market, city hall, other halls, temples and altars. Clearly rational planning in place of organic growth.

98 Reconstruction of the sanctuary of Athena at Lindus on Rhodes. Fourth century BC. The temple is incorporated in an axial terrace plan of mature Hellenistic style. The whole complex has a characteristically painterly effect.

Beyond this lay a colonnaded court, in one corner of which stood the temple of Athena, a Doric amphiprostyle building that dated back to the fourth century. An effective sequence and gradation of the component structures was here achieved in a very small space by exploiting the natural step of the terrain.

Late Hellenistic form (Mid-second to late first century BC)

After the big Pergamum frieze there emerged a basic uncertainty with regard to style, which explains the search for the classical prototypes that finally ended in a slavish copying of classical originals. Already in the smaller frieze of the Pergamum altar, dating between 180 and 160 BC, the Baroque effect is breached by classicist influences and the adoption of pictorial motifs.

The Aphrodite of Melos *[99]*, known the world over as the *Venus de Milo*, belongs to the same century. Although the idea derives from a fourth-century model, this has been elaborated in a purely late Hellenistic way through the cramped standing pose and disalignment of the fully draped lower part of the figure. The restless play of the vigorous drapery folds is subtly contrasted with the delicate curves of a body in full flower. With its dreamy harmony and melancholy air, Aphrodite's head is almost the literal copy of a Praxitelean model, both in the shape of the face and form of the hair.

Aphrodite, represented so often in the fourth century, was also now a special favourite. In a group of *Aphrodite, Eros, and Pan*, her naked beauty is contrasted with the sturdy, lascivious figure of the goat-legged god *[100]*. Aphrodite holds a sandle in her right hand ready for a blow she hardly means to strike, judging by her coquettish glances and the playful movement of the little Eros. Her hair is partly covered by a cap, which suggests that Pan has surprised the goddess after her bathe. Despite Pan's twist and his envelopment in space, the group makes its effect only when viewed from the front. The classicist planar tendency also reveals itself in the figure of Aphrodite. Only the opposition between the lovely female body and the ugly little god conveys the spiritual attitude of the period around 100 BC when the work was produced.

99 Venus de Milo, marble original from the period shortly before the middle of the second century BC. Paris, Louvre. Classicistic pattern of a statue of the fourth century BC. The garments and naked body are differentiated and contrasted; the frontal view emphasized.

100 Aphrodite, Eros and Pan, a marble statuary group from the period c. 100 BC. Athens, National Museum. Eclectic composition: Aphrodite is dependent on late classical models; Pan is in the Hellenistic tradition. This sets up a contrast between surface qualities and more spatial arrangement.

Probably the last work of independent Greek art is the famous *Laocoön* group *[101]*, created by the Rhodian sculptors Agesander, Polydorus, and Athanadorus in the first century BC. This sculptural group shows the fate of a priest of Apollo and his sons as if it were a painting. Laocoön, while offering a sacrifice at the altar, is being put to death with his sons for his disobedience to a god's command. The death struggle of a father and his children against demonic serpents is the true theme. Discovered in 1506, this work had a powerful effect on the Renaissance and what followed, but it was already famous in antiquity. Emperor Titus owned it, and it was praised by the elder Pliny as being superior to all other works of sculpture and painting.

The father and his younger son have been forced back on to the altar by the pressure of the serpents' bodies, while the elder son is held tight in their coils. Laocoön has received in his flank the deadly bite of one serpent, and the other is about to sink its fangs

into the breast of the smaller boy. Helplessly, with fading eyes, the child seeks protection from his father, who himself rears up in the throes of death. The elder son, trying to free himself from the tangle of coils, looks across with horror at his father, whose suffering is mirrored in the youth's face. The restoration of Laocoön's right arm, which until recently raised a coil of snake as if in triumph, was incorrect. A few years ago it was possible to attach the original arm, which only came to light long after the rest. It is bent back towards the head, in an effort to tear the serpent away from the neck. Whereas the Baroque approach is unmistakably active in Laocoön's body and face, those of the two boys are classicist in their recourse to the Lysippian formal idiom. This return to classical models is especially characteristic of Athenian art. In the mid-second century BC the Hellenistic rulers were already ordering copies of classical works. A leading part was played in this activity by the neo-Attic studios of Athens, which later also passed on the classical forms to Rome.

101 Marble group of Laocoön, work of the sculptors Agesander, Polydorus and Athanadorus, first century BC. The Vatican, Museums and Galleries. Mature Hellenistic pathos is unified with classicist posture: the surface contains both centrifugal and centripetal movement.

The art of the Etruscans

The origin and language of the Etruscans is unknown to us. They would seem to have migrated from the eastern Mediterranean to the heart of central Italy (Tuscany) before 800 BC. With them 'vault' and chamber tombs (tumuli) entered the urnfield area of the Italic peoples, who cremated their dead. From the mid-eighth century on, the Etruscans extended the region under their control northwards (eastern Alps, Rhaetia) and southwards (Latium, Campania). They also won naval supremacy in the Tyrrhenian Sea (victory over the Greeks off Alalia in 540 BC: Corsica became Etruscan). Etruscan kings ruled Rome, exerting a strong religious influence that revealed itself in the later Roman state cult. It is said that the Etruscan terracotta sculptor Vulca created the statues of gods for the Capitol at Rome about 500 BC. But in 509 the Tarquins were expelled by the Romans. During the fifth century Etruscan predominance began to diminish, and the fourth century brought a struggle for survival against the Gauls to the north (in 387 the Gauls took Rome) and the Romans to the south (Veii, Rome's mortal enemy, fell in 396). By 280 they had finally acknowledged Roman supremacy and in the first century at last received Roman franchise. But the same period saw a last flicker of political opposition: between 82 and 79 BC Sulla waged a war of extermination in Etruria. Of the distinguished Romans of Etruscan descent we shall mention Maecenas, who immortalized his name through his generous fostering of young talent.

Since archaic times Etruscan art had been only a peculiar dialect of the Greek formal language, often developed to the point of unintelligibility. Appreciation of the exemplary and superior Hellenic art is apparent from two facts. Greek artists were summoned to the courts of Etruscan princes and, more important, Greek vases were placed in Etruscan tombs. The majority of well-preserved Greek vessels of archaic and classical times come from Etruscan cemeteries.

Likewise, the Greek temple seems to have formed the model for the Etruscan, though with fundamental differences. The Etruscan temple had no peristyle round its cella, developing only the columns at the front. The cella was usually divided into three rooms, and was substantially wider than its Greek equivalent. Stressing the broad front gave the architecture a pronounced façade, an effect that continued to play a decisive part in Roman building. The roof framework of the Etruscan temple was left open, with the ridge-pole given special emphasis. Instead of being arranged in the pediment fields, terracotta figures were set arbitrarily on the slopes of the pediment or along the ridge.

Sculpture of the archaic period

The well-known terracotta statue of the *Apollo of Veii* [102] belonged to a group dating from about 500 BC that adorned the ridge of the temple at Veii, and perhaps represented Heracles bringing down the hind in the presence of Artemis, Apollo, and Hermes. Exactly what meaning the Greek myth had taken on in its Etruscan interpretation can no longer be determined. Apollo is shown stepping foward. The mass of the figure is partly upheld by a volute-shaped support. Apollo's body is soft and doughy in the modelling. With its delicately terraced folds, the clinging garment seems almost a second, ornamental skin. This bulky, unarticulated body is crowned by a head that, in comparison, looks curiously small. A

102 *Terracotta statue of Apollo, figure from the acroterium of the temple at Veii, c. 500 BC. Rome, Villa Giulia. Dependent on Ionic art in the rich folds of the garment, but at the same time ornamented in the two levels of the body. The archaic facial expression is over-refined.*

103 Bronze statue of the Capitoline She-Wolf, mid-fifth century BC. Rome, Museo dei Conservatori. Archaic frontality is relaxed (the head is turned obliquely); the body is presented organically, but details are ornamental (neck, head and backbone).

wide, wolfish smile and the almond eyes beneath the sharply drawn bulges of the brows determine the appearance of the face. The Greek feeling for clearly arranged proportions is not evident in this work, which seems heavy and earthbound in its expression as compared with contemporary Greek kouroi *[48]*. Even the choice of material is typical of Etruscan sculpture. Contrary to Greek practice, no marbles were produced, but only statues in terracotta, nenfro, and limestone, along with the bronzes common to both civilizations.

In metal casting and goldsmith's work the Etruscans had been achieving excellent results since the seventh century BC. The famous *She-Wolf of Rome [103]* is an Etruscan work from the mid-fifth century, and to some extent is influenced by Greek models in the vivid rendering of the animal. But the heraldic, ornamental quality of the quietly standing wolf, who sniffs uneasily as she suckles the twins Romulus and Remus, is essentially Etruscan. Though the children were there originally, they are modern replacements in their present form.

Etruscan sarcophagi, which stood in the burial chambers, are also often of terracotta. In late archaic times a type was established that showed the dead man and his wife taking their meal together on a couch *[104]*. The picture of a happy after-life governed the conception of death held by the superstitious Etruscans, whose funeral cult was especially highly developed. The custom of having the man share the couch with his wife at a meal was quite un-Greek. On the other hand, the wooden

framework of the couch, on which a soft cushion lies, has a thoroughly Greek form. The remains of the deceased were laid to rest in the couch itself, and the reclining figures constitute a removable lid. The style of these late archaic figures created at the end of the sixth century again involves a disproportion between the small heads and the fleshy bulk of the upper bodies. In a curious piece of abstraction, no attempt has been made at a really plastic treatment of the lower bodies, which are hidden by a cover.

Painting of the archaic and classical periods

During the sixth and fifth centuries, images of a gay after-life in the other world formed the decoration of Etruscan burial chambers, which completely imitated the appearance of a house with its furniture. Dancing and feasting, hunting and fishing, sport and erotic scenes are the subjects of these wall-paintings. The frescoes, often remarkably well preserved, are particularly important in that they also allow us to make inferences about the lost Greek models, whose colouring and figure arrangement were doubtless similar. But the association of these figures with representations of plants is typically Etruscan. There is no example in Greek art of a figure rendered as ornamentally as in the Tomb of the Lionesses at Tarquinia, which dates from the late sixth century. An image of a reclining man, probably the deceased

104 Death-bed, coloured sarcophagus from Cerveteri, towards the end of the sixth century BC. Rome, Villa Giulia. The figure composition is archaic and additive; abstract rendering of lower parts of the bodies, thereby bringing forward the upper half and heads.

himself, occupies one of the side walls of the tomb. The man's reddish brown body stands out in strong contrast to the light green garment. In his extended right hand he holds an egg, which we may take to be the usual funeral offering. The figure is still built up in the archaic manner, with the lower body, head, and arms shown in profile, the upper body from the front. This rather violent construction is softened by the decorative impulse underlying the figure's appearance. The dead man lies watching the Dionysian scene on the end wall. There, dancing and music-making figures are grouped around a big crater in the middle of the picture area. An expressive frenzy of motion showing itself in curious angular movements has seized the dancers. In the pediment field above are represented the lionesses that gave the tomb its name. Below an ornamental border, the sea is indicated by means of leaping dolphins and gulls.

The development followed by Greek art in mature classical times was not shared by the Etruscans: late

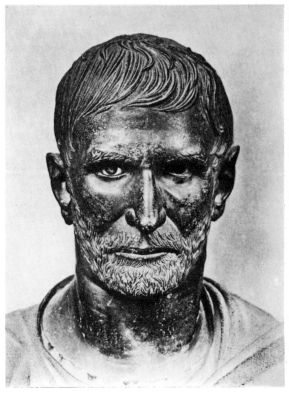

106 *Bronze portrait head of a man, so-called Brutus, beginning of the third century BC. Rome, Museo dei Conservatori. Geometric form of the head, built up of contrasting parts.*

105 *Head of Hades from a wall-painting of the Tomb of the Ogre at Tarquinia, first half of the fourth century BC. Closely related to late classical Greek painting; plasticity of the head through shadows.*

archaic forms survived well into the fifth century. Only the rich style at the end of the fifth and the late classical form of the fourth century were influential and assimilated. The *Head of Hades* from the Tomb of the Ogre at Tarquinia may serve to represent the Etruscan variant of late classical form *[105]*. Persephone accompanied the ruler of the dead, whose impressive face appears beneath the wolf-cap. The plasticity of his profiled features has been achieved by shading with parallel lines, a technique that must have begun to be adopted in Greek painting at the start of the fourth century.

Hellenistic form and Etruscan art

In Etrusco-Italic bronze sculpture of Hellenistic times one finds some excellent works that differ radically from contemporary Greek products, most of all in the treatment of the portrait. The bronze portrait head at Rome of a bearded man *[106]*, known as *Brutus*, is a remarkably forceful rendering of the sitter.

All the separate forms have been inscribed in the geometrically constructed head without any interposing transitions. Unyielding severity, bitter cynicism, and resignation are engraved in this cold face with its tight lips. Vigorous will and firm character are expressed in the deep-set eyes and short, jutting chin below thick, yet quite unplastically treated, sidewhiskers. Perhaps the subject was a Roman of the early third century, from the heroic age of the Republic, but we cannot identify him.

In Etruria, the dramatic, baroque Hellenistic formal idiom was combined with an expressive folk art to produce remarkable works in the countless cinerary urns of the late period. Whereas the ash-chests themselves usually have Etruscan versions of mythical scenes around them, on the lids of the urns the deceased are shown reclining. Their bodies are shortened or bent in an extraordinary way, only the heads being fully modelled in the round. A popular art arose that often achieved striking effects through its naïve expressive power. Turning to one another morosely yet at the same time tenderly, the married couple on the *Lid of a Cinerary Urn* at Volterra seem almost a caricature [107].

The significance of Etruscan art, in itself only a provincial variant of the Greek, lies in its having prepared the reception of Greek forms into Roman art. By and large, it was this process that made it possible for Greek art to acquire such importance.

107 Married couple, lid of a cinerary urn, mid-first century BC. Volterra, Museo. The last stage of Etruscan art; neglect of the body for the sake of the head; realistic caricature portraiture.

The art of the Romans

THE ART OF THE REPUBLIC

According to the calculations of the Roman Varro, the city of Rome was founded by Romulus in 753 BC, a date that tallies with the latest archaeological finds. The monarchy dominated by Etruscan influence was abolished, and a democratic political system at first wholly shaped by the aristocracy was established officially in 510 BC, no doubt to match the corresponding event at Athens. The next two centuries were occupied by social disputes, the levelling away of class differences, and the extension of the territory under the city's control, at first to Latium and southern Etruria. By 266 BC Rome, in many chequered conflicts, had united Italy as far as the southern edge of the Po plain. When this position was achieved the life and death struggle against Carthage began, from which Rome issued victorious after two wars (264–241 and 218–201 BC). Rome's ascendancy in the western Mediterranean brought clashes with the Eastern powers which led to the conquest of these lands as well (first Macedonia, then all Greece in 146 BC). The last century of the Republic, during which the entire Mediterranean came into Roman hands (large parts of Asia Minor became a Roman province in 63, Caesar conquered Gaul in 58–51, Egypt was annexed in 30 BC), was filled with unrest caused by social grievances. Attempts to redress them led to civil wars and the undermining of democracy by the rivals on each occasion: the Gracchi, Marius and Sulla, Caesar and Pompey, Octavian and Mark Antony. Octavian emerged triumphant from the arena (Battle of Actium in 31 BC), and, with the courtesy title of princeps, ushered in the imperial age as Augustus.

The conquest of Greek areas brought an increasing acceptance of Greek culture and art, vainly opposed by M. Porcius Cato (censor in 184 BC). Many works of art came to Rome when the cities of Tarentum (272 BC), Syracuse (212), and Corinth (146) were plundered. In 241 BC Livius Andronicus produced the first Greek tragedies and comedies in Latin; Plautus (254–184) and Terence (died 159) followed him. The focus of Greek humanism at Rome was the younger Scipio and his circle, which Cicero evokes in his dialogues. Panaetius taught Stoic moral philosophy, and the historian Polybius analysed the reasons for the rise of Rome. The first flowering of Roman literature came at the end of the Republic: Caesar (100–44 BC), Cicero (106–43), the lyric poet Catullus (87–54), and the historian Sallust (86–34).

108   *Relief with representation of a censor, the so-called Altar of Domitius, a Roman historical relief, between 80 and 70 BC. Paris, Louvre. Realistic representation of the past: exactitude; continuation of Greek and Hellenistic relief art in the obscurance of the relief ground.*

The beginnings of Roman art were under Etruscan influence, as is already shown by the fact that the Etruscan sculptor Vulca, from Veii, did the terracotta figures for the Capitol at Rome. Greek vases of the sixth and fifth centuries have also been found there repeatedly. Then, from the late fourth century on, Hellenistic art exerted a growing influence, which became dominant in the late Republican period round about 100 BC. Roman art was late to discover itself: the creative force was not a basic drive for the Romans, unlike the Greeks. If the Greeks had already made for themselves an artistic world of the spirit before proceeding under Alexander to conquer the then-known physical world, Roman art only developed after Rome's conquests. Rome took over the formal vocabulary of Greek art. While Greek form was being made practicable, a remarkable thing happened, as in the case of all spiritual assimilation: under the artist's hand the adopted form grew into something with a meaning quite different from its original one. In the second century BC the Romans were still wholly pupils of the Greeks, even summoning them to work at Rome (round about 140 the first Greek-style marble temple was built there by Hermodorus). But during the first century a Roman taste asserted itself, and works of art came to express the Roman attitude to life. Even though the artists in this and the following ages were mostly of Greek origin, the objective static form of classical Greece and the Hellenistic active form was now grounded in reality and history, to become an active display form or a simply functional one. A state and later court art arose that represented the power of the *respublica*, both decorating and serving a purpose. The typical Roman view was that no art form existed for its own sake, but had to adorn something and do something. Horace put it into words: 'Aut prodesse volunt aut delectare poetae' (Poets aim either to be useful or to delight).

With their sense of reality, the Romans acknowledged the exemplary character of Greek art. The masterpieces of Greek sculpture were repeatedly copied and reproduced, and it is only through this that we can form any idea of sculptors such as Polycleitus, Myron, Scopas, and Lysippus. But these copies were torn from their original context and used now for decorative purposes, to adorn a house or garden. There was a brisk art market in Roman times. This is where the modern conception of art has its roots.

Alongside the upper-class Hellenizing art, though, a popular art existed in which the vivid sense of reality could find direct expression. The belief that art was a class matter and the different social strata had different ideas of taste was also characteristic of Rome.

In two categories of visual art the Romans were quite independent. First we have the portrait, in which the sitter's likeness was caught with a fidelity almost unknown till then. Greek portraiture always aimed at the subject's essential nature and ideal form, whereas in the Roman portrait there developed an extreme, unsparing realism, whose efforts reached their climax in life-like representation. Had photography been possible in ancient times, the Romans, not the Greeks, would have invented it. The Greeks portrait is a product of the heroic treatment of the subject, while the Roman derives from the death-mask and ancestral image. Whereas Greek portrait statues were a public matter and restricted to distinguished men, Roman portraits were something private, and served to recall one's forebears, who were thus preserved in the ancestral gallery of every house.

The other category devised by the Romans is the historical relief, which originated in the pictures that were carried during the triumphal processions of victorious generals, and that showed the different phases of the war. Here again the Romans' active sense of reality was responsible for the mode of representation.

The new world is manifest in a historical relief that

used to be connected with the *Altar of Domitius Ahenobarbus [108]*. It dates from the decade between 80 and 70 BC and represents the census of an as yet unidentified censor. In the middle of the scene stands the altar of Mars between the god in armour and the censor about to offer a sacrifice. On the right, the sacrificial animals are being led up for this *suovetaurilia* of a bull, a ram, and a boar. The musicians taking part in the ceremony approach the altar from the left. This is the lustrum sacrifice that followed the conscription of soldiers for the citizen army. The left half of the scene shows officials engaged in making entries on the rolls. Armed soldiers stand near by, one with his hand raised in greeting. Gravity and sternness characterize the frieze, in which the war god Mars, like an official, sees that duty is done. The religious function is being performed with a pedantic solemnity. In this plain, unpretentious work, the Roman taste for impersonal dignity, strict formality, and well-defined ceremonial is fully apparent. It is typical of the Romans' eclectic approach that the historical relief is accompanied on the other sides of the altar by mythological scenes (Poseidon's marriage) after Greek models.

The remarkable technical ability of the Romans is best revealed in architecture. The temple, for a start, underwent a significant recast. Following the old Italic custom, it always rose on a high podium, as opposed to the plain three-step substructure of the Greek temple, and its front was always made prominent and specially emphasized, as against the Greek temple's in-the-round, corporeal conception *[109]*. Moreover, the Roman temple was oriented, always lying in a particular axis of the sanctuary. This links up with the old tradition of having a space marked out for the taking of auspices (omens drawn from observing birds) by the augurs.

The monumental sanctuaries inspired by the Greek Orient were similarly reshaped, as for example in the case of the magnificent *Sanctuary of Fortuna at Praeneste*, south-east of Rome *[110]*. Built under Sulla after 82 BC, it climbed the steep slope in seven strictly axial terraces. Two enclosed ramps led from the third to the fourth terrace, so that one could look out over the landscape only on emerging from them. Steep flights of steps obscured two more terraces, whose stoa façades hid their substructures. Then a wide square bordered by stoas gave a view of the countryside again and for the first time one could see the actual holy place, a small round temple rising above a stoa-crowned theatre. Seclusion from and opening towards the landscape were impressively combined. Just as impressive is the mastering of the technical problems. Behind the terrace façades were

109 Roman temple at Nîmes, the so-called Maison Carrée, built in the last decade of the first century BC. Despite the Greek style of individual parts (Ionic columns with Corinthian capitals, architrave, decorated frieze, cornice), orientation and the effect of the façade are Roman.

110 Reconstruction of the terraced sanctuary of Fortuna at Praeneste, built under Sulla after 82 BC. The symmetrical, axial plan is here raised on a colossal scale. Technically perfect application of mortar in the substructures. The row of arcades becomes a compositional principle.

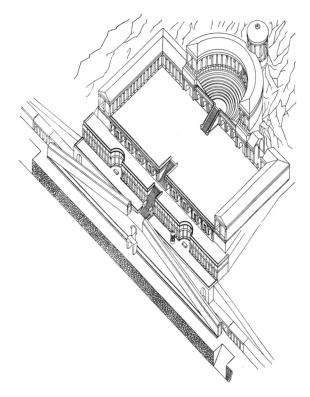

111 *Pont du Gard, aqueduct across the Gard for the city of Nîmes, last quarter of the first century* BC. *Conscious application of vaulting in three tiers.*

placed semi-vault structures that also bear the weight of the next terrace; the stoas received barrel-vaults. The Greek architectural principle of a vertical-and-horizontal construction was also infringed by joining the colonnaded stoa of Hellenistic type by arcading. Each arch was set in an arrangement of half-columns and architraves that formed a facing and served no structural purpose. This union of Roman structure and Greek tectonic principle, which was accomplished here for the first time in Roman architecture, remained a dominant motif [cf. 120], and eventually flourished again during the Renaissance. It was made possible by the systematic use of a new building material: mortar. Not unknown to the Greeks, but conflicting with their idea of the sculptural nature of architecture, it gave the Romans a chance to realize their ideas in space.

This is particularly clear in functional architecture. Their huge vaulted structures, their monumental street layouts, their mighty bridges spanning rivers in bold arches, and the equally impressive aqueducts advancing straight as an arrow through the country, like their roads, without regard for or relation to the landscape – all these have survived to this day as evidence of Rome's greatness.

Everything Rome did expressed a relentless urge for power; and everything done was subservient to use and purpose. Although Greek architecture of the Hellenistic age knew about the rational arched construction, it employed it only in substructures. Roman architects stretched arches over the country-side, and thereby marked it unmistakably and for all time.

The energetic thrust of movement exerted by a row of arches crossing the landscape like the march of the legions is best shown by that magnificent feat of engineering the *Pont du Gard,* near Nîmes, which it supplied with fresh water [111]. The conduit is raised on small arches over two tiers of large ones, and thus spans the valley of the Gard. This huge structure probably belongs to the last quarter of the first century BC but the boldness of the purely functional work, which achieves a grand rhythm and enormous power from the practical form, is still characteristic of the late Republican period, of the men who created the *imperium Romanum.*

The *Portrait of Caesar* can serve here to represent the vigorous generations of the late Republic [112]. It was probably done after his death. Sorrow and gloom overspread these features, incised in the landscape of the face. Behind the high, furrowed brow the lively mind is hidden; sarcasm and a bitter contempt for life play about the tight lips; the bone structure is very prominent. The big, overshaded eyes already announce Caesar's deification. A whole life's fate and history, with all its contingencies and grandeur, is recorded in the realistic face, the converse of Greek ideal portraiture. This survey of a brilliant personality seizes and transports us by the immediacy of its presence. The Romans' new, dynamic conception of the portrait was at the back of Western portraiture in the Renaissance.

To the late Republican period also belong important wall-paintings, which have survived chiefly at the Vesuvian towns of Pompeii and Herculaneum. Here, pictorial friezes with large figures – so-called megalographs – make an appearance, more or less dependent on Hellenistic models. In the *Frieze of the Tablinum* (dining-room) in the Villa of the Mysteries, Pompeii, the initiation of a woman into the Dionysian mysteries is represented *[113]*. At the centre, Dionysus is lying in Ariadne's lap. To the right, a kneeling maidservant unveils the phallus on a winnow, near which a sturdy winged goddess (Nemesis?) prepares to strike a blow with her rod at a woman kneeling with bared upper body, in the frieze round the corner of the room. On the left of Dionysus, an old Silenus holds up a kantharos, from which a boy is going to read the future. Behind, a youthful satyr raises a big Silenus mask. The figures are disposed in interlocking groups before an articulated wall. In the formation of the group itself, there is no mistaking the centripetal and centrifugal tendencies of Hellenistic art. The solemn air and the reference to the owners of the villa are, however, Roman elements. In Greece, this frieze in the tablinum of a private house would hardly have been possible.

As foreshadowed in the mystery frieze, the dissolution of the wall by painting sham architecture on

113 *Wall-painting from the tablinum of the Villa of the Mysteries, Pompeii, mid-first century* BC. *Incorporation of a large figure frieze into perspective painting, which acts as a three-dimensional cover for the wall. Dependent on classical and Hellenistic Greek models; eclectic choice of motifs.*

112 *Head of Caesar, portrait executed after his death. Rome, Museo Torlonia. Idealizing tendencies of the incipient Augustan age after the introduction of Republican portraiture; a classicist reaction to the realism of the preceding period.*

114 *Wall from the bedroom in the villa of Boscoreale near Pompeii, last quarter of the first century* BC. *New York, Metropolitan Museum. A high point of illusionist painting; the wall vanishes under breaks in perspective, landscape and architectural prospects.*

it reached a climax towards the end of the Republic. The *Walls of the Bedroom at the Villa of Boscoreale [114]*, near Pompeii, are covered with architectural landscapes and views into gardens that breach the solid walling and enlarge the space with a painted illusory world.

THE ART OF THE EARLY AND MID-IMPERIAL AGE

From 31 BC to AD 193 Rome's power was at its height. The Julio-Claudian imperial family ruled till AD 66 (Augustus 31 BC–AD 14, Tiberius, Caligula, Claudius, Nero). Augustus was extolled as the Prince of Peace of the *pax Romana*. Classicism in poetry (Virgil, Horace, Tibullus, Ovid) and visual art had the strength to find a style of its own. In the religious field, the period saw the adoption of Oriental cults, such as those of Isis and Mithras, as well as a deification of the emperor (state religion, along with Roma). After the rule of the Flavians (AD 69–96; Vespasian, Titus, Domitian), the empire reached its greatest extent under Trajan (98–117) and its highest efflorescence under Hadrian (117–38), Antoninus Pius (138–61), and Marcus Aurelius (161–80). Septimius Severus (193–211) and Caracalla (211–17) followed.

The main borrowing from Greek form and the development of Roman engineering had already taken place in late Republican times. Already then, too, the realistic tendency in portraiture and the historical relief was accompanying the formalistic tendency that made use of Greek models. A synthesis of these two opposing trends was not achieved until the Augustan age. Greek classicism formed the idealistic basis of Augustan art, but this found its own character and acquired its political and historical stateliness through its realism, whereas the formalistic trend of Republican art had to remain apart in the private sphere of decoration.

Augustan classicism

The *Statue of Augustus* in armour, from the Villa of Livia near Prima Porta, is the marble copy of a bronze original erected officially soon after 17 BC *[115]*. Augustus is shown as a general delivering the *allocutio*, the address to his army. He has on his general's cloak and relief-adorned breastplate. In the bronze original, to which belonged the dolphin support and Cupid (an allusion to his family's descent from Venus), Augustus was represented not barefoot as *divus* – the deified emperor – but wearing a general's shoes. The marble copy must therefore have

115 *Marble statue of Augustus, from Prima Porta, made after AD 14 as a copy of a bronze statue after 17 BC. The Vatican, Museums and Galleries. Reformulation of a classical Greek model. The beginning of a division between image and meaning: the imagery of the armour represents a political programme.*

been made for Livia after his death. Although the Doryphorus of Polycleitus is used for the statue's motif, this converts the mature classical form with its inwardly balanced quality into that of the gesture of address and thus into a dynamic display form. Here for the first time a breastplate has been decorated in relief with a whole programme of images. On high, beneath the sky god's mantle, the sun god drives his chariot, ahead of which fly Aurora with her pot of dew and Venus, the morning star. In the middle, Phraates, King of Parthia, is giving back the Roman standards to Tiberius. Personifications of the provinces and the gods Apollo and Artemis frame the scene, which is closed below by mother Italia with her two children and the cornucopia. Heaven and earth have been ransacked to provide a setting for the historic occasion, so strong was the self-confidence of Roman power.

Between 13 and 9 BC the *Ara Pacis*, the altar of peace glorifying Rome's greatness and the building up of the Roman state, was erected by Augustus on the Campus Martius. The actual altar stands within a large enclosure, which is adorned outside with magnificent acanthus spirals and remarkable reliefs, and inside with rich festoons. On the decorated side walls of the altar there are small friezes with sacrifices. The big friezes on the outside of the·flank walls represent the processions of the Imperial family and the 'senatus populusque Romanus'. In this dichotomy, the princeps's new conception of the state is apparent from the contrast. The band of closely packed figures rises in front of the ground *[116]*: a Roman counterpart of the Panathenaea frieze on the Parthenon has been created in the stern solemnity and severe dignity of these processions. The four reliefs on the outside of the end walls show figures of the earth goddess Tellus (a personification of the pacified globe) and of Roma, the sacrifice made by Aeneas on his arrival, and the Roman She-Wolf with Romulus and Remus. Wrought as a sumptuous treasure almost of applied art, the altar enclosure stands for the civil pretensions and reflects the socio-historical reality of the Augustan age.

Augustan mural painting checked the painter-like, Baroque dissolution of late Republican times, and returned to a planar treatment of the walls. These were now adorned with scenes intended to be real individual pictures, and which entered into competition with their Greek models. The picture of the *Punishment of Cupid [117]*, from Pompeii, shows the

117   The Punishment of Cupid, wall-painting from Pompeii, Augustan. Naples, Museo Nazionale. A genre scene in mythological form. Atmospheric landscape representation; in contrast classicist interpretation of figures; subdued and refined colouring.

116   The Imperial family on the frieze of the Ara Pacis, built between 13 and 9 BC on the Via Flaminia (Corso), Rome; now rebuilt on the Tiber. Surface markings of rich ornament and frieze; despite the two levels and frontality of many heads the figures remain tied to the surface; Roman counterpart to the Parthenon frieze; historical frieze that achieves ideality through being bound up with myth and allegory.

tearful little figure from back view. He is being consoled by a woman, while Venus, with another cupid on her shoulder, looks sadly across at the wrongdoer. The charming genre scene takes place in an airy landscape of rocks and trees. It is late Hellenistic in conception, though the figures have the mark of a refined classicist taste. The reference to everyday happenings is also clear in this mythological picture.

The Flavian period

In the development from the Augustan to the Flavian style, a preference for painter-like effects grew increasingly prominent. With murals, this led to a revival of Republican-type painting, to a renewed dissolution of the wall by means of sham architecture and prospects recalling theatre façades. The *Arch of Titus*, raised after AD 80 by the senate and Roman people for his victory in the Jewish war (AD 71), is adorned inside its opening with a relief of

118 The Spoils from the Temple of Jerusalem, frieze around the Arch of Titus in the Forum Romanum, Rome, erected after the death of Titus in AD 81. The effect of space in the relief is given by sharp differentiation between the figures and the height above them. Baroque quality of Flavian art; imitation of the art of the late Republic.

119 Tomb temple, relief from the Tomb of the Haterii, towards the end of the first century AD. Rome, Lateran Museum. Naïve delight in narrative, love of realistic detail at the cost of artistic form.

the procession in which the spoils from the Temple of Jerusalem, the seven-branched candelabrum and the shewbread table, were carried *[118]*. These precious utensils and the boards that name them tower high above the close-packed, laurel-crowned heads of the soldiers, who are grouped pictorially in the triumphal procession as it marches through the Porta Triumphalis. The arch of triumph and honour was a typically Roman innovation. It preserved the memory of an historic occasion in monumental form, and had a strong influence on the Renaissance.

Along with the classicist and Baroque currents in Roman relief sculpture, which are a manifestation of the courtly, official art, a third can be followed from Republican times on. At first more or less influenced by one of the two prestige-reflecting trends, it gained in importance during the imperial age. This is a popular art, to which belong, for example, reliefs from the *Tomb of the Haterii [119]*. Here, in the pictorial manner of late Flavian times, are represented a richly adorned temple-shaped tomb, a building crane (no doubt a reference to the trade of the tomb's occupant), and above the temple, the dead woman on her couch. Not artistic penetration of the theme, but delight in rendering precisely observed reality, characterize this *ars humilis*.

During Imperial times Rome took on the appearance still revealed today in the mighty ruins. Under the Flavians, in particular Vespasian, the *Colosseum* was built *[120]*. This great stone amphitheatre owes its name to a colossal statue of Nero set up near by. The huge structure was used for animal-baiting and gladiatorial combats, and Christians were burned there too. It is completely free-standing, unlike Greek theatres, which always rest against a slope. Bold arch constructions support the tremendous weight of the auditorium, which had room for about 50,000 people. Three tiers of arcaded openings articulate the outer wall. The arches are set in a vertical-and-horizontal framework of half-columns and architraves: the purest embodiment of the system evolved in Sulla's times. On the model of Hellenistic stoas, the three lower stories have been individualized, from bottom to top, by the Tuscan (Doric), Ionic, and Corinthian orders. A fourth, with a smooth wall divided up by pilasters, was added later under Titus and Domitian.

Continuing the embellishment of Rome begun by Augustus, Trajan laid out the forum that bears his name. This *Forum of Trajan* was completed in AD 113, after the plans of Apollodorus of Damascus *[121]*. Through a triumphal arch one entered a square, in the middle of which stood only the equestrian statue of the emperor. Stoas on either side hid two great apses. A building set transversely and left almost plain

on the outside closed the square towards the north: this was the gigantic Basilica Ulpia. Within it, double colonnades comprising ninety-six columns enclosed a space that had a clear width of about 82 feet and was covered by a wooden ceiling. Yet this forest of columns recalling a Greek Ionic dipteros did not contribute to the plastic effect of the exterior, but only to the structure of the internal space. Buildings such as this served as models for the early Christian basilicas of Constantine's period. Taking up the apse motif of the square, the Basilica Ulpia also had two apses, which again were cut off from the main space by a 'fence' of columns. Two libraries (for Greek and Roman texts) stood opposite each other, adjoining the basilica. Between them rose Trajan's Column, whose figure band describes the emperor's martial exploits like a scroll. In another apsidal court, placed against the rear wall in a typically Roman way, stood the temple of the deified emperor.

This union of Greek Hellenistic design with purely Roman ideas of space, also characteristic of the

120   The Colosseum in Rome, amphitheatre erected under Vespasian (AD 69–79), the fourth tier added under Titus and Domitian (AD 79–96). Structure in three rows of arcades. The spacing of arches is formed by half-columns and architrave arrangement; the mortar-work is hidden behind the façade.

122   Marble head of Trajan, portrait made probably shortly after his death (AD 117). Ostia, Museo. Dependent on portraits of the late Republic and early Empire. Painterly relation of the tightly geometric facial structure.

121   Ground-plan of Trajan's Forum in Rome, completed in AD 113 after the plans of Apollodorus of Damascus. Axial and symmetrical design in the tradition of Hellenistic and Augustan buildings. 1 entrance, 2 square with the equestrian statue, 3 Basilica Ulpia, 4 libraries, 5 Trajan's Column, 6 Trajan's Temple.

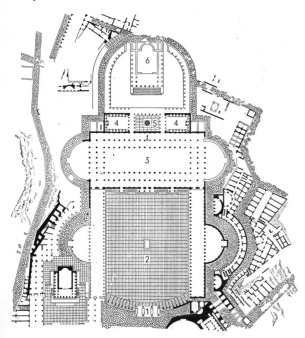

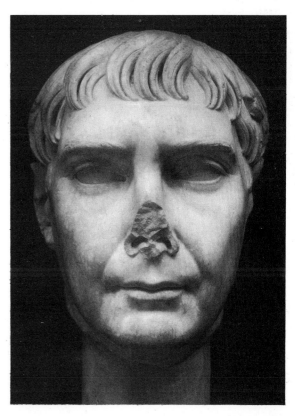

Augustan age, can likewise be observed in the portraiture of this period. The personality of the Emperor Hadrian is best shown in his *Marble portrait statue [122]*, which combines the revived late Republican form with the expansive force and relentless dynamism of this ruler. His strong will is very evident from his face. During Trajan's reign Roman form achieved its greatest dynamism.

The Hadrianic period

Under Hadrian the influence of Greek forms increased. A new, classicist type of statue was created for Hadrian's divinified favourite, the handsome Pythian youth *Antinoüs*. The beautiful body, imitated from severe style forms *[123]*, has been plaintively softened, and is attuned to the tender, melancholy head, with its sensual mouth and rich parure of curls. An ideal of beauty has been established here that springs from a romantic nostalgia for the vanished

123   *Marble statue of Antinoüs, portrait executed after his death (AD 130). Naples, Museo Nazionale. The body echoes the work of Greek classicism. Hadrianic classicism: sentimentality and idealizing of facial features.*

past of Greek classical times. These statues of a youth drowned in the Nile, who had his own cult all over the Roman world, contain an almost dream-like quality. Compared to the energetic, vital images of classical Greece, a strangely unreal figure has been created here that, for all its show of sensuousness, conveys, not physical presence, but a yearning aspiration for the beyond. The dualism of embodied form and disembodied spirit that ruled over late antiquity is manifest in this figure, the last to convey the ecstatic Greek love of beauty.

The striving for reality found what is no doubt its grandest expression in the *Pantheon*, which Hadrian ordered to be rebuilt about AD 120. It replaced a rectangular construction of Agrippa's, and its portico stands on the Agrippan podium. The Pantheon was dedicated to all the gods, and being a domed rotunda, resembled the vault of heaven. It is the first monumental structure of ancient times that to such a marked degree no longer makes its effect outwards as a body, but serves purely as a shell for the interior space *[124]*. A classicist Corinthian portico has been set before the plain three-membered cylinder, without any organic connexion. Despite the specially light building materials this cylinder carries a dome with

124   *Interior of the Roman Pantheon, erected between AD 120 and 126, engraving by Antonio Sarti in 1829. The clearest formulation of a Roman interior through abstract and mathematical form (the sphere): the wall is the shell of space, without actual plastic value; Greek architectural design is incorporated.*

125   *Bronze equestrian statue of Marcus Aurelius, c. AD 173. Rome, Capitol. Characteristic representation of the 'Imperator Mundi' over the (now lost) fallen barbarian. On the head, a contrast between the tangled hair and smooth surfaces of the face.*

an enormous thrust, which is discharged by a carefully thought-out system of relieving arches. In typical Roman fashion, the attachment of the dome is masked externally by the third ring of the cylinder. The interior corresponds to a sphere (dome and cylindrical substructure match each other in height). A round opening in the crown of the dome, with diameter of 29½ feet, gives the space a calm, even light. This harmony of space is answered by the clean and clear arrangement of the wall. The substructure has been divided into two zones conforming to the golden section, the lower articulated by alternately round and rectangular niches, the upper by delicate inlaid work (now, alas, destroyed). In addition, the stones used for wall and pavement are of a subdued colour. The ceiling is coffered with panels that grow smaller towards the dome aperture. They were once stuccoed and perhaps adorned with (golden) stars. The total effect is quite miraculous. Such achievements by the Romans in vault construction were first made possible by new means, such as brick ribs with a concrete filling: new architectural ideas found new building material. The Pantheon, together with the Parthenon and Santa Sophia, has become one of the landmarks of architectural history.

Like Hadrian, the first emperor with the style of beard of the Greek philosophers, Marcus Aurelius wore a philosopher's beard and lived as a philosopher. Like Hadrian, too, he was an emperor of peace, although he as well had a big triumphal column raised to him. Trajan's Column, standing in his forum at Rome, commemorates his successes in the Dacian wars, while that of Marcus Aurelius commemorates his victories over the Marcomanni and Sarmatae. It was set up before the temple of the deified emperor. In a large relief band, which winds round the column, preparations for battle and the battles themselves are realistically represented. *Marcus Aurelius* also had a triumphal arch. Perhaps the *Equestrian statue* of him *[125]* which since 1538 has stood at the centre of Michelangelo's Capitol, should be connected with his entry into Rome. The emperor is wearing a military cloak over his belted tunic, and has raised his right arm in salutation. Under the horse's right hoof there was once a tiny barbarian king. This superlative example of the equestrian figure is in a long tradition reaching back to archaic times. Marcus Aurelius has been treated wholly as a lofty philosopher and ruler of the world: with its powerful frame, the broadly built horse carries his proud dignity aloft, stressing the unapproachable aloofness of the *imperator mundi*. The mighty statue greatly furthered the development of the equestrian figure of the Quattrocento and even the Middle Ages.

The Antonine period

The splendidly Baroque attitude of Antonine art, which rediscovered the mature Hellenistic art of Pergamum, still survived in the days of Septimius Severus and Caracalla. On the *Arch of Septimius Severus*, which glorifies his victories over the Parthians and Arabs *[126]*, the relief decoration seems almost wild in its profusion. Set on separate pedestals before the framing fluted pilasters, the Corinthian columns are topped by the jutting entablature. The Baroque idea of a projecting and receding wall has been realized here with the aid of the columns. Erected about 203, this triumphal arch dates from the late phase of Roman Baroque, and its steeply rising structure is characterized by a soaring verticality.

Because of its architectural enrichments, the *Round Temple at Baalbek [127]* is also to be placed at the juncture of the second and third centuries AD. The free-standing Corinthian columns are again crowned by a powerful jutting and receding entablature. A

126 *Arch of Septimius Severus in Rome, Forum Romanum, built c. AD 203. Baroque façade design through cropped pillars. Mastery of popular art in the relief: rhythmic arrangement and naïve, non-perspective representation.*

127 *Round Temple (of Tyche?) at Baalbek (Heliopolis, Lebanon), from the turn of the second and third centuries* AD. *A Roman podium temple. Baroque movement through the podium and architrave swinging towards the centre, so that the surrounding pillars seem cut short. The plant-like ornament is from the late period.*

bold, space-moulding piece of architecture has sprung from the Baroque imagination of its' unknown designer, a work whose ancestor can be traced back to the spatial solutions of Hadrian's Villa near Tivoli. Space here is determined by a pictorial view of architecture, which in contrast to Greek treatment models the interior as well as the exterior and enables one to experience both of them as sheltered and sheltering hollow spaces. Since the Antonine period, free-standing sculpture also had been hidden away in niches and shell-shaped cavities, as it were: the human being feels himself encased, seeking refuge in the enveloping space.

The gigantic thermae also must have given their visitors an impression of fantasy, of abduction into an enchanted world. As in a nineteenth-century railway station, one would have felt at once crushed and swallowed up in these outsized halls. The thermae were centres for the exceptionally developed bathing activities of ancient times, but they were much more than just public baths, for they served also as club-houses and cultural meeting-places. Despite its strictly symmetrical ground-plan, the vast complex of the *Thermae of Caracalla [128]* – where even now important operatic performances take place in summer, and these only in a small part of the baths –

must have offered the eye impressions unimaginably great and varied. No longer buildings on a human scale, these thermae had as it were to be measured against the infinite and eternal. The greatest possible earthly splendour nullified itself and prepared for the invasion of a beyond that, with Christianity, would revolutionize the aspect of the ancient world. Among the many mystery and otherworldly religions of this age, which strove after the salvation of the individual, Christianity was only one that occupied an important, but not a unique, position. Plotinus said he was ashamed to have a body and, in so doing, expressed the then prevailing view; despite these huge establishments for physical culture, people no longer felt at home with their own bodies.

THE ART OF THE LATE IMPERIAL AGE

After the Severi came the long line of soldier-emperors, prominent among whom were Gallienus (260–8) and Aurelian (270–5), who built the Roman city wall. Internal unrest, external enemies, and a declining belief in the old gods determined the pattern of the third century AD. At the same time, Christianity was gaining a vast number of adherents, and this led to repeated persecutions. After the soldier-emperors, the empire was once again made secure within and without by strong, authoritative personalities, among them Diocletian (284–305), who replaced the principate by the dominate – by an absolute monarchy. With Constantine the Great

128 *Ground-plan of the complex of Thermae of Caracalla in Rome, built from* AD 206 *to* 215. *Closed outline, but many divisions in the interior: space is arranged with strict symmetry.* 1 *Frigidarium (cold bath),* 2 *Tepidarium (lukewarm bath),* 3 *Caldarium (warm bath),* 4 *Palaestra (sports ground).*

129   Sarcophagus of the emperor's son Hostilianus (died AD 251), the so-called Ludovisi Battle Sarcophagus. Rome, Museo delle Terme; Ludovisi Collection. Baroque interpretation of the tradition of Hellenistic battle scenes.

130   Tepidarium of Thermae of Diocletian in Rome, consecrated AD 306, from which Michelangelo built his S. Maria degli Angeli. A gigantic space for profane use covered over by the domed ceiling; rich adornment with gaily coloured marbles and figures in the niches; shortened pillars.

(323–37), the recognition of Christianity, and the removal of the imperial capital to Constantinople (Byzantium; from 330), a new era began, although antique forms did not immediately fade away, but remained active in repeated revivals.

Notable among the soldier-emperors is *Gallienus*, who brought about some sort of renaissance of Greek taste. The Hellenistic formal groundwork is unmistakable in his portrait *[131]*; yet, with the intent gaze of the eyes, the brooding air of the fastidious lips, and the nervously crisped beard, it no longer has the effect of a living Greek face, but almost of a mask that reveals rather than hides the soul's nostalgic quest for beauty. The portrait was probably done after AD 260.

To the period of joint rule by Gallienus and his father Valerian (253–60) belongs the relief slab of the big *Ludovisi Battle Sarcophagus*, which shows a general and his army in victorious combat with barbarians *[129]*. The mass of interlocking bodies is dominated by the general, who encourages his troops from his horse, urging them into the fray with his extended right arm. Even though the relief, whose ground has completely vanished under the strongly plastic bodies, derives from Hellenistic models in its individual figure groups, the swarming crowd scene of the battle is typically Roman and, in the last analysis, wholly determined by the revival of Baroque tendencies in Gallienic art.

Art in the age of Diocletian and his fellow-rulers the tetrarchs was shaped entirely by the power of the

131 *Marble portrait of the Emperor Gallienus, after AD 260. Rome, Museo delle Terme. Formal definition through a return to Greek portraiture, but late antiquity is evident in the eye-sockets and the typical upward gaze of the eyes.*

spirit, for all the size and almost challenging earth-liness of such huge architectural complexes as his palace at Spalato and his thermae at Rome. People wanted to capture the pomp of this world in mighty buildings so as to be able to withdraw from the world inside them. Inaugurated during 305/6, the *Thermae of Diocletian* took up the colossal area of 389½ by 345½ yards. The present-day Piazza dell'Esedra, with its diameter of 157½ yards, is simply the thermae's former exedra for gymnastic games. In the tepidar-ium, the hall with warm water, Michelangelo built his S. Maria degli Angeli *[130]*. The church's un-decorated façade is formed from an old brick wall of the thermae installations. Vast architectural piles were laid out for great crowds of people, as is shown by a glance at the surviving halls of the thermae, whose bare brick walls were once richly adorned. Gilt stucco, costly coverings of marble, and sumptuous mosaics were introduced everywhere, along with many statues. The inner wall surfaces of the halls must have given an impression of luxurious tapestries in many colours, made to seem quite unreal by the different sources of light.

After his victory at the Milvian Bridge in 312, *Constantine the Great* became sole ruler of the Western empire. In his honour, a colossal seated statue of him, its head alone over 8½ feet tall *[132]*, was set up in the Basilica of Maxentius by the Forum Romanum. The treatment of Roman portraiture, once so forceful and realistic, is absent from this face. In the monu-mentality of its forms, and with its dominant eyes staring fixedly into the beyond, it now merely typified the ruler. The powerful forms are only a body for the transcendent spirit. With Constantine, Roman art as such came to an end. He himself transferred the capital of Rome's empire to Byzantium, which was called Constantinople in his honour. Christianity became the state religion. The old gods had lost their power, though they long continued to live out a shadowy existence in popular belief. Despite a few works of the Hellenic revival, antique form had reached its fulfilment.

132 *Colossal marble head of the Emperor Constantine from a seated statue of the type of a divine statue, formerly placed in the Basilica of Maxentius. Rome, Museo dei Conservatori. Despite the clear plasticity of the face, the gaze is spiritual and transcen-dental, embodying the final separation of soul and body, which becomes merely a frame.*

Just as Christianity grew from the soil of many late antique cults and older religions, so too the beginnings of its art were fed by the stock of late antique forms and types from the whole Mediterranean area. The first centuries of Christian art are characterized by a processing and recasting of the antique models into new patterns, which, in the second half of the millennium, furnished the Christianized lands of Europe with their first artistic starting-points.

The current view is that Rome, Asia Minor, Syria, and Egypt all contributed to the genesis of Christian art which originated in the period about 200, when the Christian doctrine was swiftly spreading through a Roman empire threatened by internal decay and external dangers. The earliest art is a sepulchral or tomb art limited to symbols and a few figures and scenes from both Testaments that express the faithful's hope of a life to come. Constantine's recognition of Christianity in 313 created the legal prerequisite to a public Christian art, his continuing of Diocletian's centralist reorganization of the empire its material basis. Hitherto only modest rooms – mostly in the homes of well-to-do believers – had been available for the cult. But now monumental church buildings began to appear, their spread accelerated by the growing cult of martyrs. At almost the same time the Church started to use the visual arts for didactic purposes. As regards iconography – that is, the meaning of the images – many ceremonial themes were adapted from Roman Imperial art: e.g. Christ giving the Law and the Homage of the Apostles. Beside these, pagan subjects survived, especially at Rome and in the Hellenistic cities of the East.

During the fourth and fifth centuries, the advance of the Germanic tribes led to the loss of the Western provinces, the conquest of Italy, and the destruction of the Western Roman empire (476). Ravenna succeeded Milan as the political and cultural capital of the West, while Rome only kept its importance through the power of the Church. The East, on the other hand, was able to survive despite internal crises and external threats from the Persians and Germans,

thanks to its wealth and able emperors. It was in the East, too, that the great councils were called together which defined, after long religious conflicts, the basic dogmas of Christianity. Constantine founded the Eastern capital Constantinople in 324–30. Particularly after Theodosius had divided the Empire in 395, Constantinople quickly came to surpass all other cities as the political, economic, intellectual, and ecclesiastical focus of the Eastern Roman empire, which also had a very strong fertilizing influence on the West for a thousand years. During this period the foundations of all later iconographical developments were laid, and here the East (Palestine, Syria) played a leading part, along with Rome. The extensive cycles of illustrations to the Scriptures, the Apocrypha, and legends of the saints, were produced, in part now linking up with Jewish traditions. For the holy figures distinct types were established – e.g. Christ as a mature, bearded man – and theological programmes increasingly determined the choice of scenes.

ARCHITECTURE

The main types of church structures

Unlike the ancient temple, the Christian church is at the same time the house of God, a place for the cult, and the assembly room of the congregation. The different sacred rites govern the form of their own rooms and buildings. It was the numerous tasks to be performed and the influence of pagan architecture that brought about the diversity and the swift, regionally varied development of early Christian architecture. The monumental church building originated with Constantine's foundations in Rome, Constantinople, and the Holy Land. The basilica and the centrally planned structure were the two main themes which were to occupy Christian architecture for centuries. In the first Roman basilicas – the cathedral adjoining the Lateran Palace, *S. Giovanni in Laterano* (AD 313), and *St Peter's* (AD 324) – the type was at once brilliantly realized *[134, 139]*. A five-part main body, with a rather wide nave surmounted by a clerestory, led into a high transept. This opened, in the extension of the nave, into a semicircular apse containing altar, priests' benches, and bishop's throne.

133 Ivory diptych of five parts. Upper Italy, late fifth century. Milan, Cathedral Treasury. This, the left wing, shows the Lamb of God, scenes from the life of Christ and the Virgin Mary, and the Evangelists with their symbolic beasts. The expressive effect is built up of contrasts in size and colour (inset of almandine).

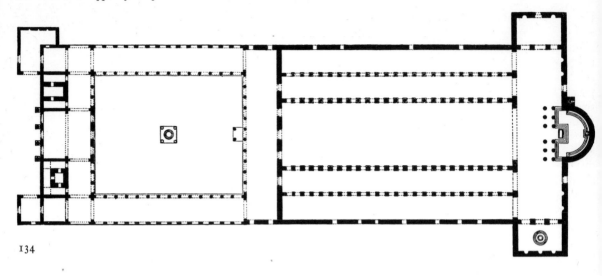

134

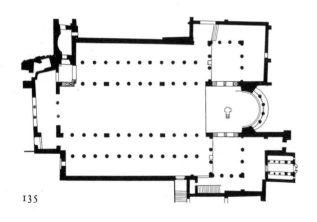

135

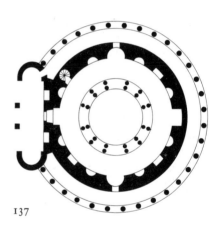

137

136

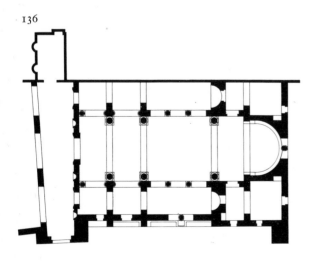

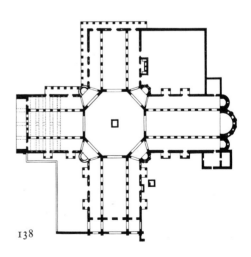

138

Colonnades, or columned arcades, separated the nave and aisles from each other, while a great 'arch of triumph' framed the entrance to the transept. Only the apse was vaulted, the other spaces having open-roof frames. This huge interior was governed by the principle of subordinating all its spatial divisions and their orienting and gradation towards the apse, the focus of the cult, the stepping in height and width of the aisles, the stately avenue of the nave, and not least the light, which entered only from above, distinguishing nave and transept from the darker subsidiary spaces. No spatial division was self-sufficing, no architectural member of value in itself. The arcades were subordinated to the wall as part of the principle, and the adherence of the columns to the plane made them look less plastic. Supported by these very light members, the wall too seemed thin and weightless. Its costly facings of marble and mosaic made an essential contribution to the transcendental-izing of the space. If here, too, important hints were taken from antique architecture (commercial and palace basilicas), the synthesis of these elements and the concentration of artistic shaping on the sacral interior were both entirely new. The outside was unornamented, and articulated only by the rhythm of the windows and the stepping of the nave and aisles. In its rise towards the apse, the succession was reinforced at the entrance end by a vestibule (narthex) and a court (atrium) framed by arcaded passages.

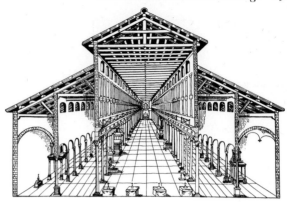

139 Reconstructed interior view of the basilica of S. Peter, Rome, 324. The walls are diaphanous; the colonnades have become arcades, and are faced with marble and mosaic. Open rafter-work roof; orientation focused on the altar and bishop's seat in the apse.

134 Ground-plan of the basilica of S. Peter, Rome, founded by Constantine in 324. Five-part main body, leading into a transept with a semicircular apse; at the west, a vestibule (narthex) and court (atrium).

135 Ground-plan of the basilica of S. Demetrius, Salonica, fifth to seventh centuries. A galleried basilica. The five-part main body and tripartite transept are placed directly over a crypt.

136 Ground-plan of the basilica at Kodja Kalessi, Meriamlik, c. 450. A domed basilica, with the middle bay extended to support the quadratic domed space and columns between the piers. At either side of the apse is a subsidiary space (pastophoria).

137 S. Costanza, Rome, tomb of Constantina (died 354). Ground-plan of a circular central structure with an inner passage-way and twelve arches with coupled columns and (now destroyed) exterior pillared passageway. The niches in the walls were for altars and sarcophagi.

138 Ground-plan of the basilica at Kalat Seman near Aleppo, fifth century. Cruciform layout with tripartite arms round a central octagon. The apse is on the east, a portico and peristyle on the west.

The basilican church with a nave and two aisles which made its appearance a little later was of crucial importance for the future. Nave and apse, often unaccompanied by a transept, entered into a closer unity, so that the spatial pattern was simplified without changing its spiritual character (S. Pudenziana, Rome). For baptistries and monumental tombs, among other works, the most varied types of cen-trally planned buildings were derived from pagan models such as round, cruciform, or octagonal structures, with niches in the inner face of the wall and often with a dome. Centralized buildings, in which a circular or polygonal walk extended round an internal ring of columns, were, however, original. In *S. Costanza at Rome* [137, 140], twelve arches with coupled columns support the drum, whose large windows distinguish the middle space from the sur-rounding passageway. The pure centralizing tendency has, however, been infringed, in so far as the main axes are given a cruciform stress through a wider intercolumniation and an enlargement and vaulting-over of the corresponding wall niches. In other places only the axis towards the altar was emphasized.

Liturgical requirements and a desire to give the church precinct an imposing appearance often led to the grouping together of different structures as a whole complex of buildings: for example, two basilicas with baptistries between them (Trier), two aisleless churches (Aquileia), chapels and mausoleums alongside of a basilica (St Peter's, Rome). The increase in height where the cult had its focus was provided by attaching a centralized structure to a basilica in place of the apse (octagon over the Nativity Grotto, Bethlehem).

galleries (tribunes) extended above the aisles, opening in arches towards the nave. These basilicas are mostly shorter, and more balanced in the relationship of length, breadth, and height. Also, the light is evenly distributed, since the windows are in the outer wall at both aisle and gallery level (S. John of Studion, Constantinople). The most impressive building of this kind is the basilica of *S. Demetrius at Salonica [135, 141]*. It has a nave and four aisles in the main body, a nave and two aisles in the transept, galleries over all aisles, and a clerestory above the nave. Spaciousness, the diaphanous structure of a wall resolved into arcades and windows, and harmony in the proportions and the fall of light jointly determine the spatial effect.

Quite different principles of style underlie Syria's architecture, in which important preparations for Romanesque were made. Here, basilicas were built in massive ashlar, with pillared arcades of wide span (e.g. Rusafa, Ruweiha). Their eastern part (bema) is characteristic. For liturgical reasons, the externally polygonal apse is flanked by two subsidiary spaces

141   Basilica of S. Demetrius, Salonica, fifth to seventh century. View across the nave to the east (a restoration after the fire of 1917). Galleries above the aisles, two rows of arcades, with wide arcade and window openings.

140   S. Costanza, Rome, tomb of Constantina (died 354). A view, taken in the ambulatory, of the wall and ceiling mosaics; double-columned arcades open on to the central domed space.

Regional church structures

In the second half of the fourth century and during the fifth, a remarkably varied development of constructional and spatial types followed. Though the principles of space and surface organization already established continued to set the standard, highly diversified provincial styles arose in connexion with regional building traditions. A west–east alignment of the church now became the rule. In the Western Roman empire, the basilica with a nave and two aisles remained the dominant type of structure. It grew elongated and more slender in its proportions, with a narrower window zone and taller arcades. Since the nave was made wider and the windows bigger at the same time, the contrast in the main space between the openwork wall and dark spatial backing of the aisles became even stronger (S. Sabina, S. Maria Maggiore, Rome). On the other hand, in the East, which led in architecture, the galleried basilica was preferred. Instead of the clerestory,

142 Reconstruction of a three-aisled and pillared basilica at Turmanin (Syria), fifth century. The entrance is emphasized by two flanking tower-like structures at the corners, between them a balcony (perhaps influenced by Roman buildings).

143 Main façade of the basilica at Kalat Seman near Aleppo, fifth century. Ashlar walls, tectonic and plastic construction with pediments and pillars, and a purely decorative arrangement of arches.

(pastophoria) and somewhat raised. The interior looks heavy and stony, owing to the unfaced walls with their small windows, the barrel-vaults, and the flat stone ceilings. Even the outside is a bulky cube-like structure. A two-tower façade pairs off with the three components of the east end, as at *Turmanin [142]*. The heavy ashlar walls are articulated by plastic motifs – cornices, arched mouldings, colonnettes – and occasionally also by tectonic elements – pillars, pediments – in a relief-like, decorative way, as in *Kalb Lauzeh at Kalat Seman [143]*.

The coastal areas of the eastern Mediterranean, Asia Minor, and Constantinople among them, were the focus of a trend leading to a synthesis of the longitudinal and centralized buildings. Here, also, new forms were devised (dosseret capitals), as well as a new style of architectural ornament: fine-structured patterns overspread the capitals, friezes, etc., with a play of lines, light, and shade. In a few basilicas, the focus of the cult has been emphasized by covering the last bay before the apse with a dome. Other churches have a big dome extending over the whole central area, which is surrounded on three sides by subsidiary spaces, as in *Meriamlik at Kodja Kalessi [136, 144]*. Basilican traits are mostly confined to the arcades and galleries set between the dome piers. The vertical of the dome and the horizontal flow towards the altar interpenetrate in these compact

and precipitous buildings (domed basilica, the first step towards the Byzantine cruciform domed church). An important development was undergone by the cruciform church, at first a plain structure with aisleless (e.g. Mausoleum of Galla Placidia, Ravenna) and later also tripartite arms (e.g. Salona), its central space picked out by piers and a dome.

144 Cross-section of the basilica at Kodja Kalessi, Meriamlik, c. 450. Interpenetration of the vertical and horizontal flows; the dome is raised (and built of wood); barrel-vaults in the bays, galleries and plastic wall arrangement.

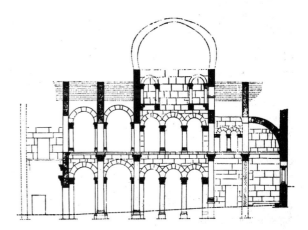

One of the most imposing compositions of this type is offered by the church of *S. Simeon Stylites at Kalat Seman* near Aleppo *[138, 143]*. Four basilican arms with nave and two aisles lead as a cross to a large octagonal space (originally with a wooden dome?), at the centre of which the column once stood. In addition, there are vestibules and, in some cases, forecourts at the entrance ends of the arms. The east arm is concluded by three apses, while small apses are set in the diagonals of the octagon. A richly varied group of spaces and bodies has been produced, culminating in the middle of the symbolic cross. With fully centralized buildings, too, extremely complex spatial patterns are found, either where an octagon containing supports has been given a square exterior (Esra), or where several rings of columns are penetrated by a cross-shape, due to niches or column groups in the main axes (S. Stefano Rotondo, Rome). The development of early Christian architecture thus tended towards a more marked external grouping, towards a complication of the space and wall forms, towards a centralizing of the space accompanied by a stressing of the altar direction, and towards a diversifying of the light effects.

SCULPTURE

The recognition of Christianity did not mean a completely fresh start for the figurative arts. Christian painting and sculpture developed on a foundation of late antique art, which as early as the third century had changed radically, above all at Rome. In the course of this change painting increased in importance, while sculpture, especially monumental free-standing work, passed further and further into the background. The relief was preferred to forms modelled in the round, particularly since early Christian sculpture was mainly concerned with the decoration of sarcophagi and the outsides of ivory diptychs (their insides served as writing surfaces). Stylistically, there is a departure from the classical idea of the organically constructed figure and its natural relation to setting and space. Instead of this, figures are placed for the most part frontally before the relief surface, in an abstract spatial zone without clearly distinguishable depth. They are planar, inorganic, and chiefly determined by their outline. Composition follows the principles of an abstract and decorative surface arrangement: symmetry, rhythmic succession, isocephaly (all heads on the same level), etc. Scenic treatment is often replaced by a dignified grouping firmly pointed at the spectator. These figures are bearers of meaning, their gestures and poses suggest associations of ideas. On the one hand, there is an increase in material reality, and on the other, a heightened spiritualization. By the age of Diocletian and Constantine the new style was fully developed, and in an extremely inorganic, stark, and often also technically crude manner.

Of course, this trend by no means implied a complete exhaustion of antique formal resources, which long continued to exist particularly in the Hellenistic cities of the East. Above all, classical principles of representation were several times revived in deliberate renaissances, of pagan as well as sacred works. Out of this constant interpenetration, this 'interlacement of the Middle Ages with antiquity' (Garger), arose the exceptionally varied, richly nuanced pattern of early Christian art.

The first renaissance began as early as late Constantinian times. Characteristic of it are youthful, idealized figures with softly modelled bodies and drapery, and relaxed movements. On sarcophagi, friezes of closely aligned figures are succeeded by a distribution through arcading and trees, which create narrow space-stages where almost fully rounded figures play their parts, e.g. the *Sarcophagus of Junius Bassus*, AD 359 *[145]*. During the last phase of Roman sarcophagus sculpture (till about 400), the composition is unified before a rich architectural background, or else made rhythmical with the aid of columns or town walls. A special type is represented by the imperial porphyry sarcophagi at the Vatican. They have ornaments and figures of a block-like inorganic kind that stresses the hardness of the stone.

145   Sarcophagus of Junius Bassus (died 359) in the crypt of S. Peter's, Rome. Scenes from the Old and New Testaments. Box spaces between the pillars; a delicate, idealizing style with almost complete plasticity. The movement of the figures resembles antique models.

The fourth-century renaissance

The most important renaissance movement occurred in the age of Theodosius (about 400). All works from this period are distinguished by their elegance, their strong aesthetic appeal, and their technical refinement. Especially in the Eastern court art now dominant, dignified images of antique models are marked by the new formal principles of frontality, firm outline, and reduced organic quality together with a delicate, agitated relief treatment of the folds (e.g. portrait statues of emperors and high officials from Ephesus). In ceremonial reliefs (pedestal of the obelisk in the hippodrome at Constantinople, AD 390), the hieratic effect is further increased by the isocephalic alignment of similar, frontally disposed figures, and by a 'status perspective' that graduates the figures by their rank, and not according to optical perspective. These works have close Western relations above all in the products of Milanese court art, such as the *Stilicho Diptych* (AD 400), with its superlative display of solemn dignity, harmony of composition, elegance of line, and extremely delicate gradation of relief [147]. Rome and upper Italy also were creating works in ivory and metal, of a purely Hellenistic stamp with both mythological and Christian subjects. Notwithstanding the great variety in the products of the different workshops, Western art was for the most part less hieratic and intense, but correspondingly more plastic and more realistic than that of the East.

The fifth-century styles

Soon after 400 began another change of style, whose fruitful consequences led during the fifth century to a violation of antique idea of form in the West even more so than in the East. Figures are now heavily concentrated in a solid cube, to which the details, the straight or curved parallel folds, provide a contrast (statues of officials from Aphrodisias, 410/20; still more block-like, more abrupt, the colossal statue of an emperor from Barletta, 450). Relief figures, too, become broad, squat, compact, or planar in construction, the folds being less modelled than engraved. Chiaroscuro values replace those of modelling, and there is a decline in the firmness of the composition. At the same time, however, the narrative achieves a plain incisiveness which is at its most eloquent in the large expressive head. During the second half of the century, these tendencies were carried to the extreme. The plastic volume wastes away. Exceedingly long or exceedingly broad figures are applied to the surface untectonically and without space, divided by

146 *Sarcophagus of Rinaldus, 420/30. Ravenna Cathedral. On the front: Peter and Paul paying homage to Christ in Heaven. On the other sides: the monogram of Christ, cross, lambs, vessels. The vaulted cover is decorated in a scale pattern. Symbolic characterization; strengthening of the relief surface and simplification of lines.*

147 *Ivory diptych, c. 400. Monza, Cathedral Treasure. Left: Stilicho; right: Serena and Eucherius. Typical Milanese court art, showing the elegance of shallow, delicately graded relief.*

dry, angular lines. They are wholly transcendental, and often ecstatic and visionary, as in the case of a head from Ephesus now at Vienna or an *Ivory diptych* at Milan *[133]*, which is based on contrasts of size and colour, discreetly yet with Mannerist effects.

This stylistic trend can also be followed on Ravenna sarcophagi, of which there are a considerable number. They offer a good survey of sculpture in the Eastern empire and its further development in the West, since the earliest works were still produced in Byzantium itself, and those that followed remained in close stylistic dependence. All these sarcophagi consist of an oblong box closed by a gabled or vaulted lid. They are tectonically structured (e.g. pilasters at the corners), and worked on all four sides, each of which present only one scene with a few figures or symbols. The earliest examples (Sarcophagi of Liberius and Pignatta, both about 400) have figures carved almost plastically on narrow space-stages, with soft modelling and Hellenistic folds. Soon space and organic proportioning diminish, and the figures are simplified as bodies and contours; but sweeping gestures now reach out over the smooth ground, which contributes as a field of spiritual tension to the scenic effect, as for example on the *Sarcophagus of Rinaldus,* 420/30 *[146]*. With time, the relief grows increasingly flat and dry, the movement stiffens, till at length only symbols are presented, and even these lose their tectonic firmness, to become planar, barely modelled signs.

After the fifth century the production of sculpture diminished very rapidly in the West, while in the East sculpture followed the developing classicism of Justinian's Byzantium.

PAINTING

In early Christian times, painting was of prime importance among the figurative arts. Third-century evidence is mostly confined to catacomb decorations, but after Christianity had been recognized under Constantine, its increasing imagery soon came to be used for adorning monumental churches. This gave painting a completely new importance, not only from the decorative standpoint, but above all as the elucidator in pictorial terms of the Christian doctrine of salvation. New decorative systems had to be evolved that would suit the spatial conditions of early Christian types of building, and a new style was needed for representing Christian messages either symbolically or by narrative. Manuscript illumination, another major field of painting, also gained important possibilities of development, through the new tasks

of the Christian books used by the Church. During the fourth century, the book underwent a crucial change in the transition from the late antique roll to the codex – that is, to a series of sheets of parchment between hard covers.

As regards form, the various late antique trends continued also in early Christian painting. Unfortunately, the number of surviving works is comparatively small, so that only the broad outlines of a stylistic development are discernible. The Hellenistic cities of the East kept their classical heritage almost undiminished until into the sixth century (e.g. floor mosaics at Antioch; Imperial palace, Constantinople). From Roman and Oriental traditions the Eastern provinces, such as Syria, evolved graphic, expressive, and vividly narrative pictorial idiom. The Coptic art of Egypt carried on local traditions in its themes (e.g. the reinterpretation of Isis as Mary) and in its severe linear compositions with their sign-like terseness. At Rome a change similar to that in sculpture can be observed: illusionistic depth of space was given up, the figure simplified, expressiveness increased.

148   Lucina crypt in the catacomb of S. Callixtus, Rome, mid-third century. The central medallion of a vault, showing the Good Shepherd. A light, painterly, illusionistic example of the late antique style.

Catacomb and early church painting

The oldest surviving Christian painting is to be found in the catacombs at Rome (early third century onwards). Following the system of late Roman decorations, the vaults and ceilings of the burial chambers are divided up by simple lines into geometrical fields, which contain figures, small scenes, and ornaments. A light, delicate painting technique and antique corporality are characteristic of the early period, as for example in the *Lucina Crypt in the Catacomb of S. Callixtus [148]*; both give way in the course of time to a broad drawing-in of contours and details, to a plane-and-line construction with colour contrasts. Faces and gestures are expressively intense.

The catacomb decorations are all frescoed. When, in the age of Constantine, painting rose from its more popular status to the rank of fine art, a more lasting and impressive material was sought. Mosaic offered itself, a Romano-Hellenistic technique whereby small coloured stones or bits of glass are set in damp cement. Although the mosaic decorations of the first Christian basilicas have been lost, their monumentality and stateliness are reflected in the catacomb art of that period.

At the same time, late antique traditions still lived on uninterrupted, in some cases mixing with Christian themes. Thus, in *S. Costanza at Rome*, the mausoleum of Constantine's daughter Constantina (died 354), Christian subjects are represented in the niches, whereas the twelve fields of the circular passageway show a wealth of profane, decorative, and symbolic motifs and scenes (grape-gathering). The style is characterized by the flatness of the ornament, by the plump plasticity and violent movement of the figures, and also by the strong colours against a white background *[149]*.

The fifth-century style

Round about AD 400 painting, for all its stylistic variety, seems to have acquired a uniformly Christian character, in which classical forms are reinterpreted according to the new representational and expressive values. As in sculpture, the rendering of the spatial setting, plastic volume, and organic proportion is dispensed with more and more; compositional balance, monumental figures, soft modelling, and flowing lines now predominate. Colour is light and resplendent, with the unreal luminosity of the gold background playing an ever increasing part in the process of spiritualization and withdrawal. At Rome, the classical tradition survives in the heavy three-

149 Vault mosaic at S. Costanza, Rome, mid-fourth century. A portrait bust (possibly of Constantina) between vine leaves and Bacchic scenes. The white ground appears in antique models.

dimensional quality and the realistic movement (S. Pudenziana, apse), more strongly than for instance at Milan which under Eastern influence is the champion of an elegant, impressionistic style more narrowly confined as regards composition (S. Aquilino, apse). The high quality of Theodosian painting in the Eastern empire is today attested only by the mosaics in the church of S. George at Salonica, where saints are shown before a frieze of palace architecture treated in perspective. The same style involving a spiritual and courtly modification of antique prototypes appears here as in Eastern sculpture of the period.

During the fifth century, a comprehensive decorative system was evolved for the main spaces of a church: theological subjects have their place in the apse, on the arch of triumph, and in the dome, while the cycles of the Old and New Testaments and figures of saints are placed in the nave, where they often claim several superimposed zones. With the various kinds of theme there are usually certain stylistic differences: for theological subjects, centralized compositions and an imposing monumentality in the figures; for New Testament scenes, a concentration on the dramatic or symbolic content while suppressing narrative detail. In Old Testament scenes, on the

150 *Mosaic in the nave of S. Maria Maggiore, Rome, second quarter of fifth century, showing the Jews rebelling against Moses. Hellenistic tradition: lively narrative and movement; spatial illusion; impressionistic colouring.*

other hand, the Hellenistic heritage from the more distant time of their origin maintains a stronger influence, to produce a rich narration, animated figures, and landscapes full of atmosphere. These differences are particularly clear in the *Mosaics of S. Maria Maggiore at Rome* (432–40). On the arch of triumph (Youth of Christ as a triumphal theophany, or manifestation of God) there is a ceremonial display of monumental figures, of boldly linear compositions and gorgeous colours. In the nave, with its Old Testament scenes, a painterly, narrative style, with small, active figures before a varied landscape background is evident *[150]*, the drawing being wholly subordinated to a gay, impressionistic colourfulness. Yet even though the subject-matter brings about two distinct ways of representation, both are held in check by a superordinate period style (discernible at Naples, too, among other places), which predominates because detail is reduced so that the figures gain in visionary expressive power, and the messages in direct effectiveness.

The Ravenna mosaics

A concise survey of the development and different facets of this age's style is again provided by Ravenna, with its many surviving mosaics. Ravenna mosaic-work is court art of the highest order and at the same time a pictorial expression of the most profound theological thought. The merging of these two worlds has produced a formal language that gives the images a supernatural quality as sensitive and brilliant as it is hieratic and solemn. Under the influence of Rome, Milan, and above all Byzantium, the first works – Mausoleum of Galla Placidia (died 450), Baptistry of the Orthodox (430–58) – display the post-Theo-dosian, still classical style, with lively, sometimes elongated, graceful figures that float rather than stand before the unreal domain of the blue background. The garments are fluidly draped, the heads expressive portraits. Especially effective is the elegant colour harmony of blue, gold, and white, with a little green and red (Baptistry, dome). The late antique tradition is also evident in the image of the Good Shepherd in the Mausoleum, though the free movement in the landscape has frozen in a strictly contrapposto composition. Above their marble plinth, both spaces are fully decked out with mosaics in a richly

151　*Mosaic from the nave of S. Apollinare Nuovo, Ravenna, c. 520. Christ foretells the denial of Peter. Illusionism is abandoned in favour of an expressive spirituality; the composition is symmetrical, with firm, strong lines and full colouring.*

interlinking system of figures and ornaments that, in the Baptistry, builds up in concentric zones to the Baptism of Christ at the crown of the dome.

Fifty years later, this Hellenistic manner had changed into a hard, dry linear style. In the Baptistry of the Arians (*c.* 500), the decorative scheme has been simplified, and the figures are presented almost frontally in a uniform rhythm (dull white against a gold background). Soon afterwards, stronger Byzantine influence becomes apparent. In *S. Apollinare Nuovo* (*c.* 520), once Theodoric's palace church, the Christological scenes (miracles and Passion) occupy small picture areas filled by a few large figures in severe, often symmetrical compositions [*151*]. There is an absence of narrative detail, as of pictorial illusionism: spreading across the surface, the frontally disposed figures with their boldly curved outlines stand out from the gold background. It is a relief without depth, whose grave, often dramatic intensity now reaches right out from the picture to the spectator, further heightened by a sonorous colour harmony in which the gold and Christ's purple are dominant. This terse, solemnly expressive style marks at once the end of early Christian and the start of Byzantine painting, which not long after would attain its first peak in the classical period of Justinian.

Byzantine art is the art of the empire that continued the *imperium Romanum* in the lands of the eastern Mediterranean on a foundation of Greek culture and Christian faith. Constantinople, the 'new Rome', was the capital of an autocratic emperor and a centralist administration, the focus of trade, industry, learning, art, and civilization. The patriarchate of Constantinople became the hub of Orthodox Christianity. Under Justinian (527–65), the Roman world empire was re-established once again; but soon after, with the conquests of the Lombards in Italy and the Persians in the East, and with the annexations of the Slavs and Avars in the Balkans, the empire began to shrink to its eastern heartlands (among them, Asia Minor and the coastal areas of Greece), whose defence and temporary enlargement in almost continuous wars dominated the whole of Byzantine history. Old enemies such as the Avars and Persians, finally overcome under Heraclius (610–41), were followed by the Bulgars and Islamic Arabs, who repeatedly threatened Constantinople.

A severe religious and political crisis arose with the Iconoclast Controversy (726–843). As a reaction against the excesses of image-worship and the associated increase in the power of the monasteries, and also under the influence of an Islam hostile to such representations, all religious images were officially banned and destroyed. These violent theological and political disputes ended in victory for Orthodoxy, and in a new clarification and strengthening of the two central hierarchic powers, Church and Empire.

Under the Macedonian dynasty (from 867), the empire started to expand again, reaching its greatest medieval extent during the late tenth century: in the East, as far as the Caucasus and Euphrates, in the West, after the destruction of the first Bulgar empire by Basil II (975–1025), as far as the Danube and the Adriatic. Already before this, the ecclesiastical and cultural dependency of the Slavs on Byzantium had begun when they were converted to Christianity in the ninth century (the Russians were converted in the tenth). During the eleventh century the disintegration of the empire proceeded apace, owing to external enemies such as the Seljuks in the East (they conquered Asia Minor), but above all to the decay of the tight military and administrative organization set up by Heraclius. Although the emperors of the Comnene dynasty (from 1081) managed for a short time to consolidate Byzantium's position of supremacy in the East, the empire suffered new threats and weakenings from the West through the crusades, the strong Norman kingdom in Sicily, and the rising Italian cities – especially Venice, which from 1082 had a monopoly of trade in the Mediterranean. The political, cultural, and religious antagonisms (Eastern Schism in 1054) culminated in the massacre of the Latins in 1182, as a result of which the Fourth Crusade was diverted by the Venetians to Byzantium, Constantinople was taken and a Latin empire established on the Bosphorus (1204–61). Beside this, many other states arose on formerly Byzantine territory, including Epirus, Morea, Trapezus (Trebizond), Serbia, and Bulgaria. From Nicaea, the exile capital of the Byzantines, Asia Minor, and Thrace, among other regions, were won back, and in 1261 Constantinople itself was regained. After an initial consolidation the empire, inwardly corrupt, succumbed to the pressure of the Serbs and Bulgars, then above all to the Osmanli Turks, who conquered Asia Minor around 1300 and the Balkans from about 1350 (battle of Kossovo Field in 1389; destruction of the Serbian and then the Bulgarian state). During its last fifty years Byzantium was a Turkish tributary and confined to the capital – until, when Sultan Mohammed II took this on 29 May 1453, the Byzantine empire perished. Byzantium as a state was dead, but its Orthodox faith, its civilization, and its political ideals lived on for centuries among the Greeks as well as the Balkan Slavs, and above all in the young Russian empire of the Tsars (Moscow, the 'third Rome'). It also had immeasurable importance for Western civilization in the Middle Ages and modern times, as the preserver of Roman law, of Greek science and philosophy, and of Hellenistic art and culture.

The periods of Byzantine art correspond to the broad phases of Byzantium's political history. After the gradual development from about 400 of an artistic language peculiar to the Eastern empire, the first specifically Byzantine period, that of early Byzantine art, commenced with the rule of Justinian and took in the sixth and seventh centuries. Following the artistically impoverished age of the Iconoclast

152 *Hagia Sophia at Constantinople, 532–7. View towards the east. The outstanding example of the spatial illusionism of the epoch of Justinian. The main dome is supported by semi-domes; the walls are resolved in arcades and windows. Light comes from the top.*

Controversy, a middle period Byzantine art began around 850, and continued till about 1200. Characteristic, one would say, of the nature, form, and spirit of Byzantine art, this period may be divided into two phases: the time of the Macedonian dynasty (*c.* 850–1050) and that of the Comnene (*c.* 1050–1204). Late Byzantine art developed during the years of Latin rule (1204–61), and it extended across the age of the Palaeologue emperors (1261–1453). Thereafter, Byzantine art survived in the Slavonic lands, and on Mount Athos it has come down to our own times.

ARCHITECTURE

The age of Justinian

Hagia Sophia at Constantinople [152, 153], the church of Divine Wisdom, is among the noblest buildings in the world and the most mature architectural creation of Justinian's age. For nearly a thousand years it was the spiritual centre of the Byzantine empire, the cathedral of the patriarchs, and the setting for important state occasions and a resplendent ceremonial in which the might and dignity of the theocratic empire were displayed. Justinian founded the

153   Ground-plan of Hagia Sophia at Constantinople, 532–7. A different dome was erected in 562 after the first had collapsed in 558. Commissioned by Justinian, the architects were Anthemius of Tralles and Isodorus of Miletus. The plan shows the synthesis of longitudinal and central structures. Dimensions in metres: length 81, breadth 70, height of dome 56, diameter of dome 33. The central oval space with niches is surrounded by independent side spaces, a narthex, and an atrium (destroyed). The buttresses are partly Turkish in origin.

154   S. Vitale at Ravenna, 538–47. View towards the northeast. The wall is now subordinate: the wall structure of the central domed space, with niches and pillared arcades, is broken up. Note the vertical emphasis and the longitudinal accent in the raised, illuminated altar in the apse.

155   Ground-plan of S. Vitale, Ravenna, 538–47. A passageway surrounds the octagon. Note the niches between the piers, the longitudinal flow broken by the central space, and the deep choir bays by the apse.

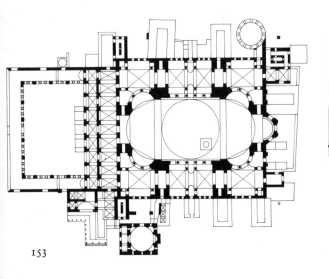

153

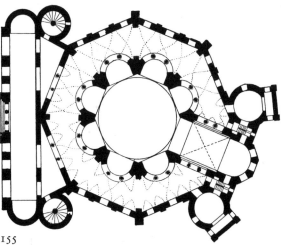

155

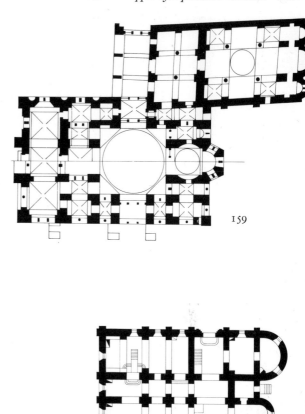

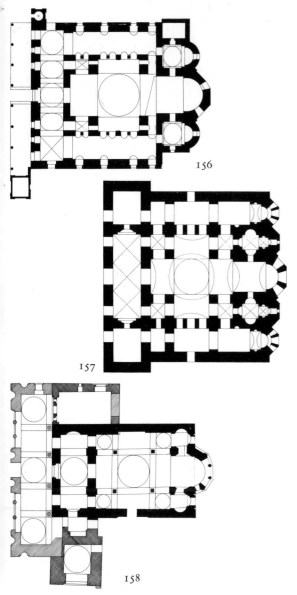

156 *Ground-plan of the church of S. Sophia, Salonica, first half of eighth century. The first step towards the Greek-cross domed church. The dome structure is broken up. Note the pastophoria (subsidiary spaces) alongside the apse.*

157 *Fenari-Issa Djami, Constantinople, early tenth century. Ground-plan of a five-part Greek-cross domed church (with side naves). The central barrel cross is domed and the corner spaces cross-vaulted.*

158 *Kilisse Djami (church of S. Theodore), Constantinople, tenth century. Ground-plan of a classical Greek-cross domed church (without side naves). The corner spaces are dome-vaulted with pillars. The outer narthex was added in the thirteenth century.*

159 *Ground-plan of Hosios Lukas, Phocis, last half of eleventh century. A subsidiary type of Greek-cross domed church. The domed space of the katholikon (main church) is extended across the arms of the cross. Eight piers support the dome, joined by arches and corner niches. The arms of the cross are placed in an outer ring of space. The subsidiary church is in the classical domed Greek-cross style.*

160 *Ground-plan of the cathedral of S. Sophia in Novgorod, eleventh century. A typical five-part Greek-cross domed church with a bay in the west and extended by subsidiary parts.*

'Great Church', and two brilliant architect-mathe-maticians, Anthemius of Tralles and Isidorus of Miletus, were its builders (532–7; second conse-cration in 562, after the dome had collapsed and been reconstructed on different lines). A massive edifice piled up out of huge cuboid blocks and held together by the dome, Hagia Sophia towers above the city. The interior effect is in complete contrast to the external. Spacious, open, and weightless, it seems to be exempt from all physical laws. A gigantic square dome space forms the centre of the building; the shallow dome floats above four wide arches on piers, and is bathed in a supernatural light from the forty windows at its foot. Its immense thrust is discharged east and west by semi-domes of equal diameter (36 yards), both carried on piers arranged octagonally and themselves buttressed by three niches opening in arcades between the piers. The great arches north and south extend over two rows of columned arches and windows. A mantle of subsidiary spaces surrounds this vast one with an optical foil, except on the east where the deepened central niche frames the altar: side aisles, with tribunes, that form a line of independent halls, and, in the west, a narthex also crowned by a gallery. These complex patterns of space and curva-ture produce exceptionally rich vistas. They contrast with the spaciousness, abundant light, and harmony of the main part, in which the enormous spans of the arches, the verticals (piers), and the horizontals (arcades and continuous cornice bands) are perfectly balanced. All the construction has been masked, not least by covering the walls with multicoloured slabs and inlays of marble, the vaults with mosaics con-taining much gold, and by drawing out the archi-tectural ornament into chiaroscuro web. Hagia Sophia represents the summit of a classic art in which Romano-Hellenistic building and decorative tradi-tions, along with early Christian ones from Asia Minor, were expressed to perfection. In the system of its space and wall arrangement, the ground was prepared for medieval architecture.

There are other buildings that show the high quality of Justinianic architecture. In SS. Sergius and Bacchus at Constantinople (527–36), the traditional type of octagonal centrally planned structure has been modified according to the new monumental style of hierarchically related spatial forms. Eight massive piers carry the dominant gored dome. The walls between the pier arches open up towards the quad-rate passageway in colonnades with an architrave and gallery arcades above. Niches are hollowed out at the corners but only the wider and deeper altar space opens to the full height. *S. Vitale at Ravenna* (538–47) is akin to this church, although instead of

the calm, broad proportioning, sheer verticals govern the central octagon *[154, 155]*. The tall piers rise with-out being crossed by horizontal mouldings, and the slender niches pierced by arcades are stretched between them like thin membranes. The arcade is heightened by the dome. In dynamic contrast, the real accent of the space is formed by the longitudinal axis towards the altar niche: before the apse a deep, fully open choir bay has been inserted. In S. Vitale basic stylistic features of Western archi-tecture, such as verticality, are prefigured. The pres-bytery mosaics of the church are discussed below.

As for the many demolished churches that once spread the system and style of metropolitan archi-tecture all over the empire, we will mention only the type represented by the Church of the Apostles at Constantinople and S. John at Ephesus. Large, light cells of space (five and six respectively), with domes over arches resting on piers, were arranged in the shape of a cross. Their side walls had a basilican articulation, and aisles crowned by galleries accom-panied them as darker stretches of space. This type was to be adopted for S. Marco at Venice *[311]* during the eleventh century, and in France *[287]* during the twelfth.

After this brief classic phase came a reaction against spatial illusionism, with a return to earlier building traditions. Through the general change in the con-ception of beauty and a growing conformity to the theological idea of the church structure, a decisive change in type and style took place. The *churches of the late sixth to the eighth century* seem heavy and block-like, bitty and ambiguous in the relation of their space and wall components *[156]*; the symbolic meaning of the forms has ousted their previous clarity and rational character. Their core is now a central dome space over four piers whose massy thickness is clearly reflected in the four barrel-vaults that bind them together. This spatial focus is overlapped by a longitudinal movement produced by the arcades dividing up the side walls of rubble and concrete, by the aisles with their galleries, and by the deep bay before the apse. Together with the subsidiary apses (pastophoria), this one forms a coherent transverse space-component, while a second cross-piece comes into existence at the west end with the narthex (vestibule). An important innovation is the piercing of the heavy dome piers, at first by narrow passages and later by small cross-vaulted spaces, with the mass of the pier thus eaten away and the dome's pressure distributed on the wall or on slender pillars towards the middle of the space. At the east end these corner spaces have apses of their own attached to them. The outer aisles were soon entirely discarded.

The Greek-cross domed church

With this the consistently developed pattern of the *Greek-cross domed church* was fully established in the second half of the ninth century [157]. The square central space (naos) is now dominated by the cross of barrel-vaults with the dome in the middle. To this primary spatial unit are subordinated the small cross-vaulted – later also domed – spaces between the arms of the cross, as are also the narthex (often double) to the west and the three eastern apses, of which the middle one gives the space a second accent through its greater width and height. This pattern remained binding for subsequent Byzantine church architecture. True, it was varied in ground-plan, elevation, proportions, style, and details; but the dominant feature is always the dome over the cross, a dome that does not appear to be a carried load, but descends from above as a self-supporting heavenly sphere over the heterogeneity of the lower spaces. The hierarchic arrangement of the church building, a symbol of the cosmic order, fully accords with Byzantine thought in all fields of life.

Early Greek-cross domed churches (the most notable was the once very famous New Church of Emperor Basil I, AD 881) are low, broad, and heavy; yet adopting the previous practice of lining the vaults with mosaics and the walls with slabs of coloured marble has brought about an optical desubstantiation of the fabric. From the tenth century on, a strong vertical impulse and a crystal-clear spatial structure prevailed in all churches. The spaces rise up high over a narrow ground-plan (diameter of dome $11\frac{1}{2}$ to 23 feet), while the four piers beneath the dome are extremely slender. These were replaced from the eleventh or twelfth century by columns, and as the proportions at the same time grew more balanced, such churches appear particularly harmonious: weightless and luminous in the roof zone, and with a hall-like expansion of the lower space, as for example at *S. Theodore* [158, 161], and S. Saviour Pantocrator, both in Constantinople; and Hosios Lukas, subsidiary church.

At first a heavy mass with little articulation, the outside of Byzantine churches was increasingly built up of plastic blocks, after the full development of the Greek-cross domed church. Through the gradation of substructure, narthex, apse, minor domes, barrel-vault cross, and main dome over a tall drum, the same hierarchic order was imposed on a compact architectural body as is found inside it. Neither façade nor towers provide additional accents. From the eleventh century onwards, but especially in late Byzantine times, the walls were given a rhythm by

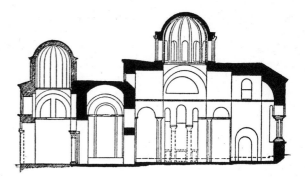

161 Longitudinal section of Kilisse Djami (church of S. Theodore) at Constantinople, tenth century. Dominated by the domed crossing space. Slender, delicate proportions. The outer narthex was added in the thirteenth century.

162 Hosios Lukas, Phocis, second quarter of eleventh century. Note the verticality and comparative width (8 metres) of the dome space; the round corners developed from the square; the raised, narrow altar space with a lower vault over the bay; and the marble facing of the walls.

163 *Hosios Lukas, Phocis, second quarter of eleventh century. View of the east exterior, with the katholikon on the left and the subsidiary church on the right. A closed block made up of plastic cubes, staggered by cross arms and a dome. Note the decorative use of stone and brick.*

164 *Fethiye Djami (S. Mary Pammakaristos), Constantinople, thirteenth century. View from the east to the main dome (right) and the added Greek-cross domed chapel (left). The wall structure is made plastic through raised niches, dentils, and blind arcades.*

means of plastic and coloured ornamentation. Pilaster strips, niches, graduated blind arcading, string-courses, and framing arches produce a lively wall relief whose pictorial effect is further enhanced by the various colours of the brick, stone, and plaster courses, and later also by coloured terracotta, as at S. Mary Pammakaristos [164].

Starting out from Constantinople, an important variation of the Greek-cross domed church spread through Greece. The dome space extends over the area where the arms of the cross used to be, and the four central supports are left out, so that a big square space comes into being, from which squinches producing corner 'niches' form a transition to the round dome. Cross arms are added to the aisles. In *Hosios Lukas*, dating from the second quarter of the eleventh century [159, 162, 163], which owing to its almost perfectly preserved lining of marble and mosaic is the most notable of the group, the aisles are spanned by encircling galleries. The wideness of the open dome space, the vertical drive reduced in strength by the horizontal lines of the stories and cornice bands, and the optically tenuous structure of the walls articulated by niches and graceful arches all give an impression of balanced monumentality.

The Slavonic lands are important areas of Byzantine architectural penetration. In the Balkan kingdoms the tradition of older, simpler types, such as the basilica and cruciform church, led to regional styles. Even the Greek-cross domed church was often modified. Alongside the dominant Byzantine influences, Romanesque and, later, Gothic forms also made an appearance.

But it was in Russia that the trends of Byzantine architecture were continued most impressively. The Russian church structure derives from the Greek-cross domed church, double-aisled in the two great cathedrals of S. Sophia and Kiev and *Novgorod [160, 165]*, of the first half of the eleventh century. Its

165 *Cathedral of S. Sophia in Novgorod, eleventh century. View from the east. Closed, steeped construction, with onion domes over a high drum.*

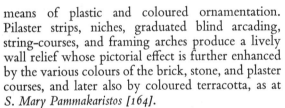

further development led to extremely steep buildings over narrow ground-plans. The inside is a simple domed hall, the outside a tall, compact cuboid block with vertical articulation, ending at the top in arches or gables. Out of this cuboid grows the high, tower-like central dome structure, often crowned by an onion dome (e.g. at Novgorod and Vladimir-Suzdal). This type, as also the Greek-cross domed church, was continued by Western architects in the fifteenth to sixteenth century, with early Renaissance forms now governing the articulation of the exterior, as in the case of the Dormition and Annunciation cathedrals at the Kremlin, Moscow.

PAINTING

The Byzantine pictorial world – its subjects, pro-grammes, and formal features – is quite distinct from that of Western art. It is based on a wholly different valuation of the picture. From the theological disputes of the Iconoclast Controversy emerged a theory of the image that, founded both on Christianity and Neoplatonic philosophy, raised the religious picture to the status of a hallowed object. Every image of sacred persons and events is a reflection of the depicted original, sharing in its holiness; and the worship offered to the image transmits itself to the imaged. All this presupposes an authentic portrayal with historical scenes faithful to the Holy Scriptures, as also to the Apocrypha and legends of the saints; and with sacred persons, one preserving the traditional facial traits and attributes. This theory meant the subjection of pictorial themes to theology and liturgy, as well as the retention down the ages of the same types, once they had been created and approved.

The pictorial decoration of churches also follows a great theological programme, which, evolved for the Greek-cross domed church, was realized in its purest form during the middle Byzantine period. Several systems of symbols are interwoven. The church is a reflection of the hierarchically disposed universe. Its highest, most open, and architecturally purest zone stands for heaven and is reserved for the timeless, supernatural, and holiest scenes: in the dome, the monumental vision of Christ as the almighty ruler (Pantocrator) above prophets and angels, or else the Ascension or Pentecost; in the apse, the Virgin either standing or enthroned. The second zone, that of the barrel-vaults, squinches, and upper wall fields, symbolizes spatially the Holy Land and temporally the calendar of feasts for the ecclesiastical year. It contains a cycle, based on the liturgy, of those events from the life of Christ most important to the story

of his sufferings and the Salvation, together with the Death of the Virgin. Each event is therefore present in image on its annual feast-day, and every holy place, such as Bethlehem or Golgotha, has by proxy its own site in the building. Forming a third zone closest to earthly things, the choir of the saints spreads over niches, arches, and piers, to represent the Church's strength of faith. These saints are arranged according to rank, from the Early Fathers in the sanctuary to the holy women in the narthex. Complementing and explaining each other, church space and pictorial array thus form a perfect unity as the symbol of a divine world order in which the beholder is spatially and spiritually included. This universal work of art is among the greatest of Byzantine artistic achievements. Not until the twelfth century was the strict, dogmatic programme enlarged with narrative cycles from the life of Christ, the Virgin, and individual saints, which were often joined by the Last Judgment, Old Testament cycles, and religious allegories.

Manuscript illumination was much less bound by programme. Extensive picture cycles, which often illustrate their subjects to the letter, scene by scene, were added to most books of the Old and New Testaments, including Genesis, Job, Psalms, and the Gospels. Legends, such as the apocryphal life of the Virgin, and calendars of saints' days (menologia) also came to be furnished with large sets of pictures. These illustrations, which in part go back to early Christian times, were copied from century to century. Through different choices and combinations, new types of image and new cycles were evolved to accompany the various texts as a pictorial commentary (lectionaries, collections of homilies, etc.). Book illumination thus developed and handed down the largest repertoire of scenes, on which the other figurative arts also relied.

The religious panel painting, or icon, has a special importance and role in Byzantine art. Known since the fourth century in the form of martyr portraits, the icons of holy and divine persons became during the seventh century the object of an image cult that was often abused, and which sparked off the Iconoclast Controversy. The Orthodox teaching on the image determined the range of subjects, the formal types, and the functions of the icon. Christ and the Virgin were most often represented, but there are also angels, saints (at times in calendar groupings or with scenes from their life), and festival images. Along with frontality and a visionary, spiritual quality, set types of face, pose, and gesture were preserved in icon painting with exceptional strictness and faithfulness, so as to achieve the required authenticity and magical relationship to the original. As sacred objects, icons played an important part both in the liturgy and in private devotion. During late Byzantine times there evolved the big image screen (iconostasis) cutting off the sanctuary from the space for the congregation. It reached enormous dimensions, particularly in Russia, with up to five rows of pictures.

The tasks and nature of Byzantine imagery made painting by far the most important of the arts. Sculpture in the round and the monumental relief both disappeared, especially after the Iconoclast Controversy. Only the small-scale relief of ivory or metal remained in use for religious or secular purposes (small domestic altars, caskets; altar fitments). Among the different kinds of painting, mosaic-work rated highest. Its richness and gem-like luminance reflected most clearly the supramundane sacred character of the religious truths portrayed. Thanks to exceedingly refined technical methods, mosaic was best suited to achieve a maximum of luminance, coloured reflexions, and liveliness of surface in the vaulting of a church interior. It made possible a clear firmness of outline and modelling, and thereby the purest embodiment of the formal principles. Closest to the mosaic in its aesthetic qualities is the enamel, with its bright and translucent coloured glass pastes between cloisons and frames of gold. Wall-painting and manuscript illumination aimed at the splendour and firm chromatic and formal structure of architecture and painting proper, but owing to their less rigid technique they mostly tended to give greater freedom to the detailed narration and to more strongly linear and abstract, or painterly and illusionistic, form.

The formal character of Byzantine painting, independent of all stylistic peculiarities and developments, is governed by two essential features. Unlike that of the Western Middle Ages, Byzantine art never lost its link with antiquity. From its own Hellenistic past, it kept the primary importance of the human figure for a message and form; an understanding, even with incorrect anatomy, of natural bodily movement; a clarity of action; a sure sense of proportion and harmony, from which extreme drama is usually as remote as extreme abstraction; and an unexampled refinement in the composition, colouring, and technique. Though sometimes reduced, influence from antiquity made possible repeated revivals of ancient modes of figuration in so-called 'renaissances', such as those of Justinian, Macedonian, and Palaeologue art. The second component of Byzantine painting effected during late antique and early Christian times stems from the alteration of ancient form in the interest of a symbolic and transcendental valuation of the image. Direct relationship with the beholder, concentration on thematic importance, and a severe dignity reflecting a sacred original beyond common understanding was of the essence of Byzantine pictorial art. Its formal means are frontality and symmetry, a three-quarter view in scenic representations, an enlargement and isolation of the main figure, and a clearly legible, vivid language of gesture. Another result of the figures being turned towards the spectator is the image's planarity, the surrender of an illusionistic space with its own inherent value. The monumental painting in Greek-cross domed churches achieves a peculiar, specifically Byzantine kind of tridimensionality: through their positions on the curved surfaces of the dome, squinches, and niches, the figures confront each other 'across the physical space' (O. Demus). Architectural space thus becomes a picture space, the whole church one single spatial icon enclosing the beholder.

Byzantine art's formal manifestations are inseparably united with the spiritual contents, the theological programmes they present in visual terms. Both express the didactic and propagandist aims, the need for prestigious display, and the humanist taste of the patrons: emperor and court, Church and higher clergy. It was not until the late Byzantine period that popular and monastic influence, too, exerted upon fine art a formative direction, and that the artist's personal share in evolving new forms increased. The centre of artistic activity, with numerous workshops passing on their special character for generations, the meeting-place of older traditions, and the latest trends in style, was Constantinople. From here, whether intact, or reduced, or reinterpreted, Byzantine art radiated over all the territory of the empire. It penetrated into the Slavonic lands, which based on it formal achievements of their own, and, with many fruitful stimuli, reached even into Western Europe (Carolingian and Ottonian art, the whole of Europe in Romanesque times, the Italian *maniera greca* in the twelfth and thirteenth centuries, etc.).

The age of Justinian

As in architecture, the age of Justinian marked a classic phase in the figurative arts, bringing earlier stylistic trends to maturity, setting fresh ones, and blending regional peculiarities into a single empire style. Works from the second quarter of the sixth century represent the style in every species of art (among ivories, the throne of Bishop Maximian at Ravenna, for example), above all in the splendid ensemble of *Mosaic scenes* and decorations in the

166 Mosaic above the altar of S. Vitale, Ravenna, 538–47. Sacrificial procession of Emperor Justinian with Bishop Maximian and their followers. A courtly ceremonial image of a religious rite. The ambiguous effect is gained by symmetrical, flat frontality and spatial arrangement, individual portraiture, and ornamentation and representative symbolism.

Presbytery of S. Vitale at Ravenna [166]. All works from this period are distinguished by a severe monumentality and powerful harmony hitherto unknown, and by exceptional refinement in the aesthetic effects and technical means. Figures are solid-looking, broad, and, through renewed antique influence, often to a large extent organic. Yet they stand in thin layers of space and remain bound into a strict, usually symmetric, composition that articulates the picture surface in a clear, bold rhythm of forms and lines. The heads look like expressive portraits, but through the regularity of their modelling and the firm lines of their contours and inner details, they point beyond the individual to the timeless world of symbols. An orchestration of exceedingly sumptuous and richly nuanced colours combines with the subtle play of light to create a harmony of celestial splendour.

At this period manuscript illumination, a typically medieval type of art, came to the fore with some works of outstanding quality. Miniatures are still more rigorously subordinated to the book they adorn than is monumental painting to architecture: in content, as illustrations of a usually religious text, and in form, as part of the aesthetic whole of writing, picture, and ornament. The period style and a long tradition of workshop practices set the stylistic key. But this is frequently varied, even within a single book, by using different, often much older models, by the separate kinds of decorations, such as preliminary pictures at the start of a book or illustrations

167 The Vienna Genesis, purple vellum, sixth century. Vienna, Österreichische Nationalbibliothek. Jacob crosses over to Jabbok and wrestles with the Angel. The bridge here forms the spatial unification of various parts of the scene. Hellenistic, painterly, and illusionistic style.

168 Gospel book, purple vellum, sixth century. Rossano, Archiepiscopal Museum. Christ and Barabbas before Pilate. Representative and dramatic rendering in strong surface composition; division into two layers. The lines are emphasized through isolating the figures.

inserted in the text, by adapting the mode of representation to the subject, and so on. Manuscript illumination is thus a many-sided, formally rich, and, despite its anonymity, personal art. Its diversity is already apparent in the surviving manuscripts from the sixth century. Of the three luxurious books with purple vellum and silver writing, the *Vienna Genesis [167]* retains from its Hellenistic models a narration of genre-like richness with scenes often in continuous succession; an illusionist embedding of animated, softly plastic figures in landscape and atmospheric space; an impressionistic way of painting; and strong light colours. In the two *Gospel fragments* at Paris and Rossano *[168]* related to it, the severe planar composition, the dramatic isolating and grouping of the figures, their bold gestures, and the local colour full of contrasts are all wholly subservient to the religious, liturgical message. Another recast of late antique models is to be met in the Syrian Rabula Gospels of

586. Its expressive and realistic style combines antique pictorial means (foreshortening, coloured light-perspective) with symmetrical compositions, violent gestures, broad brushwork, and forceful, sharply accented colouring.

In the stylistic course of post-Justinian art two currents are discernible. One expresses itself in an uninterrupted continuation of Hellenistic formal ideas, given new impetus through conscious evocations (silver utensils with Christian and mythological themes; frescoes in, for example, S. Maria Antiqua at Rome). The other leads by way of a growing reduction and dissolution of organic formal coherence to an abstract linear style that opens up new spiritual dimensions of the image (*Mosaics in the Basilica of S. Demetrius at Salonica*). Strictly frontal and quite unplastic, the figures have here been captured in the surface and fitted immovably into the frame of the background *[169]*. Precise lines contour them and divide up their garments into almost geometric portions of the surface. The monumentality

169   Mosaic on a column from the basilica of S. Demetrius, Salonica, after 629. S. Demetrius between the City Prefect and Bishop. The mosaic has the spiritual quality of an icon through its severely geometric and linear abstraction and surface frontality.

of the figures and the visionary detachment of their expressions rest on the firmness of this linear frame that gives coherence to the entire picture area. These images extending over the church walls and piers in no general decorative order, are mostly votive works, and therefore offerings of private piety. Type, style, and message were moulded by a new kind of cult relationship to the image: through its form and content, the picture became an icon. This change of style and character is closely linked with the intensive spread of icon worship, as well as with the spread of the portable icons themselves, that took place during the seventh century.

Almost no work of art has survived from the iconoclast period. Though artistic activity was not completely interrupted, it was confined to representations of the Cross, to ornament, including plants and animals, and themes connected with the emperor cult. Besides an abstract trend partly inspired by Persian forms and motifs, classical traditions apparently continued to be fostered, as shown for example in early Islamic art, which was influenced by Byzantium.

After a break of almost a century in figure representation, art was bound to look back towards the past. During the second half of the ninth century, style changed from one work to the next, governed by the different traditions of the sixth- and seventh-century models, as well as by technical uncertainty and the quest for a formal language appropriate to the new sacral conception of the image. In church mosaics, which still include no scenes, the figures stand frontally posed before the expanse of the gold background, seldom united as a rhythmical ensemble.

The Macedonian renaissance

With manuscript illumination, whose golden age now began, the divergencies of style grew still more marked, often in a single book. Thus, among the forty-six whole-page miniatures of a manuscript produced for Basil I in 880/6, there are large, compact compositions borrowed from monumental painting, with single figures and figure groups of iconic frontality. Another type [170] has frieze-like picture areas and simple narratives. Squat figures with big heads, eloquent hands, and crumpled garments are juxtaposed among coulisses and views of towns without any compositional order, the accents being given by strong, fresh colour rich in contrasts. A different kind of illustration is represented by the marginal psalters (e.g. Chludov Psalter, Moscow): many small, unframed pictures stand in the margin beside the text

170 Homily of S. Gregory of Nazianzus, made for Emperor Basil I, 880–6. Paris, Bibliothèque Nationale. Raising of Lazarus, Entry into Jerusalem. Additive image and figure composition, strong colour contrasts. The details of individual forms are antique in style.

panel, which they illustrate either literally or as a commentary, and are done in a loose, soft, sketchy painting style, with a vivid rendering of types.

Towards the middle of the tenth century the so-called Macedonian renaissance reached its height. A leading part was played by the scholarly emperor Constantine VII Porphyrogenitus (913–59), in whose scriptoria scientific and literary works were copied, along with their illustrations. Far more than before, classical subjects were given contemporary meaning, and with them the Hellenistic style of the models (e.g. theriaca of Nicander, Paris; ivory caskets with mythological scenes). These themes and their style now left their stamp on Christian art as well. Personifications and antique architectural and landscape motifs were inserted in established scenes, and, above all, antique modes of representation were adopted. A painterly illusionism with colour modelling replaced the linear

brush in only four colours, which none the less determine with ultra-fine graduations the plastic modelling of the figures, their embedding in space, and the delicate tonings of the background landscapes and architecture. Representations of ancient philosophers are the forebears of the evangelist images, which are placed before the Gospels as portraits of their authors. Meditating, listening to inspiration, writing, they stand or sit before stage coulisses or the gold background – powerful, block-like figures of dignified aloofness.

Religious and imperial ivories also shared in this classicist turn towards the past. Besides works with lively scenes at times carved in the round and enclosed by space-holding canopies, there is a somewhat later group in which the figures are lined up frontally in shallow boxes of space. With a most delicate surface modelling, the curvature of the relief

172 Ivory, c. 950. Paris, Cabinet des Médailles. Christ crowning Romanos II and Eudocia. Symbolical and ceremonial representation; slightly painterly treatment of body and clothing in a boxed space.

171 The Paris Psalter, second quarter of tenth century. Paris, Bibliothèque Nationale. David as a Shepherd, with Melody, Echo, and Mount Bethlehem. High Macedonian renaissance work showing painterly illusionism; organic and plastic figure composition in an atmospheric landscape. The idyllic quality derives from Hellenistic models.

organization of figure and picture area; solid-looking, statuesque figures, comparatively organic in their structure and movement, are active within an open field of space and at times a coherent landscape panorama, for example the *David as a Shepherd, with Melody, Echo, and Mount Bethlehem,* in what is probably the most famous Byzantine manuscript, the *Paris Psalter [171].* Much is very close to the classical prototypes: the idealized heads of a painterly softness, the mountains and coulisses fading away in the distance in tender light tones, the splendour of a colour orchestration that combines bright local colours with daring and delicate intermediate hues and sparkling highlights, the framing like that of panel paintings. True, there are many discordances even to the point of harshness in the composition, faults in the figure construction (e.g. where there is foreshortening), sharp folds that are often unfunctionally autonomous, and other points that show how far were the later copyists from their models. The Hellenistic tradition is approached most closely by the unique Joshua Roll (Vatican Library), a work of outstanding quality. Here, the long frieze of pictures is drawn with the

becomes slighter, the fold structure rectilinear and thinly layered, the proportions slender and elongated, as in the *Christ crowning Romanos II and Eudocia, c. 950 [172]*.

Towards the end of the tenth century, a new style evolved. Although it was based on the earlier phases of Macedonian art, it transformed them in a way that continued to point a course throughout the next two centuries. This style is linear both with regard to the severe, compact, and thoroughly co-ordinated arrangement of the relief surface, and to the more graphic build of the figures. Colour is an important means of achieving this linear structure. Applied in thin hatchings and held between firm contours, pure and mixed hues of many sorts (e.g. greyish violet, greeny blue) are combined to form a model of colouring. On its metallically polished surface, gold, too, is incorporated as a background and as the colour of light on the fold ridges. The most important example of this style is the *Menologion of Basil II (c. 985)*. It contains over four hundred miniatures (festival pictures, saints, martyrs, etc.), which are signed by eight different painters, although these vary only slightly in period and workshop style. Pictorial compactness is here complete *[173]*: a secure frame of orthogonals and diagonals binds the composition together and gives it a rhythm. Outlines of mountains enclose the figures or contrast with their movements. Space has been consolidated as a plastic relief layered into depth, with a narrow stage of foreground. The figures appear weightless, often elongated and twisted in a mannerist way. Their garments are composed of intricate, calligraphic, splinter-like patterns

174 *Mosaic lunette in the narthex of the main church at Hosios Lukas, Phocis, c. 1050. Christ washing the Disciples' feet. Monumental, expressive linear style, clearly accented composition, with contrasts modelled in chiaroscuro.*

173 Menologion of Emperor Basil II, c. 985. Vatican, Library. The Baptism of Christ. Late Macedonian classicism; linear and rhythmical organization of picture surface and figures; note the academic compositional scheme and the relief space and graphic colour structure.

with comb-shaped lights, and their faces reflect the ideal of spirituality and asceticism that was characteristic of the entire Byzantine Middle Ages.

Eleventh-century art presents a very complex aspect where style is concerned. Numerous workshops were founded alongside the imperial one, each with its own stylistic traits, developments, and reliance on tradition. As well as *de luxe* editions, less costly works appeared. Products of art as well as artists themselves were exported; the style of the capital met with changes in the provinces, the Slavonic lands and Italy.

Today, only a few surviving works give evidence of the former richness of monumental painting. In them, the various stylistic trends of metropolitan art and their diffusion throughout the whole empire may by discerned. Competing with the brilliant classicism of court art at Hagia Sophia, Nea Moni on Chios, for example, represents an illusionism working through the impact of colour on the eye, with geometric tracks of colour rich in contrasts; while S. Sophia at Ochrida (Serbia) represents a lively style characterized by small components and parallel lines. The ascetic, visually expressive ideal of the age was embodied above all in the art of the great monasteries, which now increased in importance compared to court art, and of which there is a monumental sample dating from about 1050 at the monastery church of *Hosios Lukas* in Greece *[174]*. In this notable cycle of

lettering, and the text itself together constitute a single decorative whole. The image loses its independence and becomes a picture writing, the local detail and lively little figures (often only two to three centimetres tall) forming a very legible narrative or a rhythmic, frontally orientated frieze [175]. These figures are thin, slender, graceful, flatly modelled, with typical faces, and eloquent gestures. They are made up of a network of delicate coloured lines that sometimes imitate the gold cloisons and coloured fillings of enamels. The evangelist figures are often distinguished from this harmonious preciosity by firmer, more plastic forms on a larger scale.

This period's taste for rich calligraphic effects can also be discerned in enamelling (reliquaries, book-covers, etc.), a technique that in the second half of the tenth and the eleventh century reached a supreme level of quality [176].

176　Book-cover, silvergilt embossed work with filigree and cloisonné enamel, first half of eleventh century. Venice, Treasure of S. Marco. Archangel Michael. The image is magically heightened by the preciousness of the material and its effects of light and colour.

175　Gospel book, third quarter of eleventh century. Parma, Biblioteca Palatina. Christ in Glory and Saints. The ornamental field is unified in a decorative manner with the symbolic scenes and surrounding figures and script. Calligraphic figural and ornamental style ('style mignon'); refined, metallic colouring.

mosaics, which is among the best examples of the middle Byzantine system of decoration, the scenes dispense with all narrative detail, and are entirely confined to the heart of the action, so that the compositions have been tersely simplified. The broad, heavy figures form a relief in which particular parts of the body are singled out plastically. Reduced to parallel straight and curved lines, their garments link up across the picture area into a severe, geometrically linear structure. These mosaics lack the aesthetic subtlety of the court art, replacing it by religious emphasis and a powerful inner and outer monumentality.

In manuscript illumination, the great number of surviving works itself reflects the amplitude of a production rich in stylistic variants. Broadly, the trend towards the small, delicate, and calligraphic persists. Framed pictures, scenes in the margins and between the lines of writing, ornamental panels and borders, initials that are sometimes figural, ornate

The Comnene renaissance

With the Comnene renaissance, there began in the late eleventh century a stylistic phase that again looked to works of antiquity for a guide. It was less interested in impressionistic, painterly illusionism than in sculpturesque qualities and a sensitive humanism with its roots in Hellenistic art. The principal work is the mosaic decoration, carried out by artists from Constantinople, of the *monastery church at Daphni*, near Athens. Restrained spirituality joins a lyrical mood of individual humanity to form the keynote of these figures and scenes [*177*]. The compositions fit into the picture areas without geometric rigidity. Their monumental and harmonious structure is based on flowing movements and on the apparently informal distribution of the figures within the tangible relief space, figures that are organically conceived and loosely balanced. Continuous modelling and beautifully curved lines produce a varied surface. This elegance is matched by the colouring,

177 Mosaic in the nave of the main church at Daphni near Athens, end of eleventh century. Anastasis (Descent into Hell, the Byzantine representation of the Resurrection). Comnene renaissance. Humanistically ideal figures and statuesque postures after classical Greek models.

178 Mosaic in the apse of Cefalù Cathedral (Sicily), second quarter of twelfth century. Pantocrator (Christ as Lord of the World), with the Virgin, Angels, Apostles. A Byzantine theme used for domes of churches and used here in a basilica. Clear, statuesque features with spiritually ascetic expressions.

which, in an optical illusion, turns luminous and dark tones into values of light and shade.

The surviving manuscripts again bear witness to many divergencies of style. Seldom fully apprehensible, the renaissance movement acted in miniature painting rather as a liberation from the pleasantly calligraphic systems of lines, giving images in books more plastic, spatial, and painterly values. In the expressive autonomy of the lines, the sharp contrasts of light and shade, and swift tempo of the pictorial narrative, typical features of late Comnene art were being prepared.

The stylistic course of the remainder of the twelfth century can be followed only in works done mostly by Greek artists in Norman Sicily, Serbia, and Russia. In its main phases, which were always accompanied by local trends and variants, it first led to an exceedingly rich linear style, in which the statuesque figures

179 Mosaic from the dome of the south transept of Monreale Cathedral (Sicily), third quarter of twelfth century. Gethsemane. Late Comnene mannerism; line, form, and colour all dynamically cohesive; decorative overall structure; and dramatic expressiveness.

take the form of a relief modelled into small parts and covered with streams and cascades of lines *[178]*. About 1160 the style changed considerably. Extremely slender figures with a delicate, graphic structure were woven together into a tight pattern. The flexions of the bodies, the broad gestures, the fluid drapery curves, even the contours of the landscape, all adapt themselves to the impulses of movement (Nerez, Serbia; executed under Comnene patronage, 1164). The lyrical, intimate expressive power of these works changed soon after, at *Monreale [179]*, into eloquent and dramatic vitality. All figures and movements are now dynamically integrated. A web of animated, swiftly repeated and contrasted lines with sparkling lights clothes every figure, linking it with the next and knotting figure groups into a decorative ensemble. No form is self-contained, for even the contours of the hills and the architecture are attuned to the composition and silhouettes of the figures. Currents of line and movement reach from one picture to another, thereby bringing composi-

tional and decorative unity to the whole extensive array of mosaics.

Strong influences from this late Comnene style are also detectable in St Mark's at Venice. In the late twelfth and the thirteenth century several workshops were busy on the mosaics, first of the interior and then of the vestibules. They followed a general programme that was Western but with diverse Byzantine models. The Byzantine stylistic elements were variously and increasingly modified towards Romanesque, until finally, in the last vestibule domes, the early Palaeologue style was again adopted in a purer form.

Far from marking a break in artistic activity, the period of the Latin empire (1204–61) saw the ripening of a completely new formal language, which first flourished round about 1260–80. Its manifestations and phases of development are indicated by many examples of wall-painting in Serbia, Macedonia, and Bulgaria, as well as by icon and manuscript painting. Here, Greek artists from Constantinople and from the empire's second art centre, Salonica, were active side by side with local painters. The style first changed towards compositions clearly and calmly balanced within the picture area, towards a new monumentality and less organically articulated plumpness in the figures, and towards a delicately

180 Fresco on the west wall of the monastery church of Sopočani (Serbia), c. 1265. Death of the Virgin. Early Palaeologue renaissance; severe spatially plastic figures and buildings; illusionistic light effects; painterly modelling.

linear or a fine-structure plastic rendering of the drapery. Also new are the quiet or hypnotic intensity of expression and a fresh, natural animation in the expressive, often softly modelled faces (frescoes in Serbia: Studenica, Mileševa, Morača, etc.).

The Palaeologue renaissance

What may be seen as a start and a tendency led soon after to the classic maturity of an art whose major works, the frescoes by Greek masters at *Sopočani [180]* and the Deesis mosaic in Hagia Sophia, count among the most remarkable and finest of Byzantine paintings. Once again we have a renaissance – the early Palaeologue – although not in the sense of careful imitation but, for the first time, of a creative struggle that uses Hellenistic means of representation to produce new forms and contents.

Fully modelled, heavy, heroic, the figures stand and move in a field of space, grouped into depth on the picture stage by means of foreshortening and overlapping. Broad hill and terrace landscapes form a background, with massive architectures reaching out with plastic limbs into the space. This atmospheric picture space is created chiefly through a painterly, illusionistic use of colour and light. Luminous or tender, the colours are related to each other by means of the most delicate admixtures, contrasts, and reflexions, while soft lights and shadows model the bodies of figures and architecture. For the first time, an illusion is given of light pouring in diffusely. The harmony, perfection, and monumentality of this classic style are founded not only on the flowing rhythm of the gestures and of the boldly and freely draped garments, but also on the intensity of all relationships, heightened in the heads to a restrained fervour and a lyrical sensibility.

These stylistic phenomena and changes can again be seen in the works of every subdivision of painting. Icons grew in number and importance, both as large panels on iconostases and as small ones for private devotion. A luxury art product of Palaeologue Constantinople is the sumptuous and technically brilliant *Mosaic Icon* made up of tiny studs of metal and precious stone *[181]*. Even when very small, these works retain the monumentality and painterly illusion of space and light encountered in wall-painting, which they often surpass through their refinement and intimate power of expression. Apart from the activity of Greek artists, it was above all these products of the minor arts that, looted by the crusaders, determined the pronounced Byzantine

181 Mosaic icon, second half of fourteenth century. Florence, Opera del Duomo. Left wing. One half of a complete picture cycle (Annunciation, Nativity, Presentation, Baptism, Transfiguration, Raising of Lazarus). Delicate, subdued mannerism; intimate feeling for atmosphere.

character of Western painting in the thirteenth and to some extent even in the fourteenth century (*maniera greca* in Italy).

During the last quarter of the thirteenth century, the classic unity of style broke up, and true Palaeologue art began. This age's supreme masterpiece is the array of mosaics and frescoes dating from about 1315–20 in S. Saviour in Chora (Kariye Cami) at Constantinople. The very mode of décor oversteps, both in iconography and form, the hierarchically strict bounds of earlier ensembles. Vaults and wall fields are covered in richly anecdotal sets of scenes – among them, the *Life of the Virgin [182]* and the youth and miracles of Christ – that contain many genre-like features based on antique models or actual observation (e.g. contemporary costumes) and never before

182 Mosaic lunette in the interior narthex of Kariye Cami (S. Saviour in Chora) at Constantinople, c. 315–20. A high point of Palaeologue painting. Illusionistic picture stage, spatial movements in fantastic architecture; graceful and over-enlarged figures; colour and light effects; individual scale of expression.

icons. Its further development led, probably under the influence of the mystical and ascetic Hesychast movement, to an expressive sense of mood and atmosphere, such as that of a devotional image. Picture and figure structure became simpler, graceful figures are distributed over broad, rugged landscapes, and a finely articulated lineation associates with rich but muted colours to form a loose, painterly ensemble (e.g. Mistra). At times, the expressive qualities of this style are heightened into mystic ecstasy or visionary drama. In the *Transfiguration* [183] from a manuscript of Emperor John VI Cantacuzene (1370–5), diagonals burst out of the floating calm of the glory, and prostrate the figures

183 Theological manuscript of Emperor John VI Cantacuzene, 1370–5. Paris, Bibliothèque Nationale. The Transfiguration. Dramatic vision, baroque energy of forms, mysterious light symbolism (aureole).

encountered in monumental painting. Each representation is a separate whole, due both to illusionistic picture space and a mode of composition, gesture, and mime adapted to that particular subject. The intellectual and spiritual message is extremely varied, linking up from figure to figure so that the individual scene becomes a pictorial drama that, with an extensive range of expression reaching from the heroic to the idyllic, speaks directly to the beholder. This art has an exceedingly rich formal vocabulary charged with dramatic force. Though the illusion of space is carried further, there is still no exact perspective: different zones of space and landscape interlock. Space-creating impulses issue in particular from the fanciful, diagonally placed or bent architecture. The figures are now smaller in relation to the picture area and move freely in space. Mostly, they are either extremely slim, mannered, and graceful, with small heads, or else blown out to become extremely broad. Distortions of the bodily structure, caricatured features, and tranquil or violently impulsive gestures reveal a leaning towards surprise effects, as do the firm, full modelling, the sharp-edged, splintery fold lines, the flashing highlights and comb-patterns, and an exceedingly wide range of colours contrasting light, delicate hues with sombre or harsh ones.

This Palaeologue style spread outwards from Constantinople across the whole domain of Byzantine art (e.g. church of the Holy Apostles, Salonica; local variants in Serbia at, e.g. Studenica, Staro Nagoričino) and is also represented by some notable on the ground. The colour-and-light painting, with its delicate transitions from white to blue, is of the utmost refinement.

In the late fourteenth century, the style became more subdued, with clearly disposed, firm and rather dry forms. The creative energy of Byzantine art was exhausted, and Western influence increased, reaching Constantinople itself towards 1450. At the same time, there began a regimentation of programmes, types, and techniques on the lines of the Mount Athos Painter's Book (produced in the sixteenth century, partly after earlier sources), so that it was possible for the old pictorial formulae to continue being copied right into the nineteenth century (frescoes at the Athos monastery; icons).

A strong popular and provincial element modified and diluted the late Byzantine style in the art of the Balkan lands. But only in Russia did an independent encounter with Byzantine painting give rise to an important national art diversified into local schools whose character was often moulded by an out-standing artistic personality. The chief centres of art, where mural paintings and above all many icons were produced, included Kiev in the eleventh century and from the twelfth Novgorod, which held the lead during the late fourteenth and the fifteenth century. Other focuses were Pskov, Vladimir-Suzdal, and Tver. Then, with the fifteenth and sixteenth centuries, the importance of Moscow steadily grew. The special concern of Russian painting is a concordant and decorative organization of the picture surface. Line and colour are its chief means of giving form. Precise, boldly curved contour and structural lines fit the slim, planar figures and coulisses into a supple two-dimensional rhythm; delicate, clear, transparent hues fill broad expanses, complementing one another in harmonious balance. Compositions are calm and easy to read. The noble or folk-type quality of the figures is always directly and vividly expressive. Byzantine ingredients of the mature and late Palaeologue styles were absorbed into this artistic language. A large contribution to its develop-ment was actually made by Greek artists, such as the important fresco and icon painter Theophanes, who was active at Novgorod before 1400 and later at Moscow. Within this common idiom each school had its own distinct character and evolution. Nov-gorod painting, for example, is vigorous in its com-position, its figure construction, and its pure, strong

184 Andrei Rublev. Icon, beginning of the fifteenth century. Moscow, Tretjakov Gallery. The Holy Trinity (symbolized by the Three Angels with Abraham in Mamre). A high point in Russian icon art; classical circular composition, linear rhythm; light and delicate colouring.

hues. Moscow preferred lighter colouring and more delicate linear rhythm. The outstanding artist there in the early fifteenth century was Andrei Rublev. Solemnly monumental, his icons *[184]* are dis-tinguished by their classic, finely balanced unity, their harmony of line, their soft, glowing colour-fulness, and their lyrical depth of feeling. They mark the zenith of Russian icon painting. In the second half of the fifteenth century there began, with the decline in size of icons, the taste for precious forms and colours, and with the diminishing spiritual tension, a development towards canonic picture formulae which were handed down for centuries and made icons appear less as works of art than as pure objects of devotion.

Perhaps the clearest starting-point of that age we call the Germanic migration period is the invasion of the northern Black Sea area by the Huns round about AD 375. This historic event led to the extinction, rise, and disappearance again of a whole series of Germanic kingdoms both within and beyond the borders of the Roman empire. Among them, only the Lombard kingdom in Italy, that of the Visigoths in Spain, and the Frankish kingdom of the Merovingians in central and western Europe still existed at the end of the sixth century. Across the North Sea, Angles, Jutes, and Saxons had settled round about 450 in what had once been Roman Britain. Far away from the general political upheavals of the Continent, the Scandinavian North alone provided the stable conditions in which the crucial step was taken towards the birth of an autonomous Germanic art.

The various Germanic and Latin peoples, along with many foreigners who had meanwhile settled on their eastern borders (Avars, Slavs), were only welded into that coherent whole which formed the true basis of future development once the Carolingian empire was formed. This may be taken to be the end of the period, a demarcation justified, moreover, by the supply of relics. For broadly speaking, the old Germanic custom of providing the dead with weapons, ornaments, and vessels for food and drink was abandoned under Christian influence, even in the Frankish empire at about the start of the eighth century, which means that our main source of archaeological knowledge ends here. The artistic activity of the migration and Merovingian period was by and large confined to the adornment of those things that men and women prized in life and which when made for the leaders of society have given us samples, often of really high quality, revealing the age's specific bent in art.

The Swedish scholar Holmqvist has pointed out that in so far as they did not come into permanent contact with the urban forms of life of the Mediterranean area, the Germans at that time probably had no need or real opportunities to develop higher types

of art such as architecture, sculpture, and painting; and that this must have helped to intensify their own decorative artistic activity and to increase their capacity for outstanding achievements in this field. What little exists in the way of stone figure carving, as on Frankish gravestones from the Rhine and Moselle region, is quite unheralded and unrelated, except for the general iconographic dependence on antique imagery. It cannot be linked up with what had come before, since it did not have any predecessors in its own area, or with what came after, such as the masterpieces of court ivory-carving from Carolingian times. These beginnings of a popular stone sculpture must therefore be left right out of any investigation of the stylistic course of early Germanic art. Things are rather better in the case of figurative metal-work, which is more amply represented. To form a picture of European art in pre-Carolingian times, one has to rely almost entirely on a special study of the ornamentation of metal objects.

Before we turn to these finds, there are still a few qualifications to be made, since the stylistic development of the early Middle Ages until far into the Ottonian period was by no means governed solely by the contribution of Germano-Latin culture. We shall have to leave out of our portrait the rich decorative art of the horse-riding inhabitants of the Steppes, who at that time under the collective name of Huns, Avars, and Old Hungarians, repeatedly shared in Western history as rulers in southern Russia or the Carpathian basin. Instead, we shall confine our study mostly to the regions of Northern Europe and Lombardy.

The first Germanic animal style

Ornamental art between the North and Black Seas was at first quite clearly dependent for technique, style, and subject on contemporary late antique work. Although they had lived for centuries in contact with the Roman empire, as neighbours on its military frontier along the Rhine and Danube, the Germans had over a long period acquired many products of Roman handicraft, in the form of merchandise, plunder, or gifts, without being noticeably inspired even to imitate these models. Things did not change until the fourth century, when late

185 The Tassilo Chalice, c. 777. Kremsmünster, Monastery. A bronzegilt vessel with a chip-carved surface of interlaced animal and foliate motifs, and portraiture showing Mediterranean influence. Made probably by an English craftsman working in Rome.

ornament, whose original home was among the North Sea Germans. *Belt ornaments* were mass-produced in the Western Roman empire, with spiral, rosette, or zigzag patterns filed into them. As illustration, we give just one example *[186]*, which also has a fauna of crouching quadrupeds that form the indispensable border decoration to these enrichments. The animals are mostly heraldic pairs of lions looking forwards or backwards, from which a variety of smaller creatures, perhaps hares, seem to be fleeing. In the fifth century, surface-filling spiral ornamentation was adopted on decorative forms of their own by the Rhineland Germans on both sides of the Gallic diocese, as well as by the Goths in the lower Roman Danube provinces. But only among the Rhenish Germans did the border animals and biting lion heads encounter that spontaneous response which gave the impetus for all future animal decoration in

186   *Late Roman belt-clasp, c. 400. Found in a grave in the Aisne region. St-Quentin, Musée Antoine Lécuyer. Typical stylization of the animal border.*

187   *Bronze belt-buckle of second century date. Found at Hontheim (Moselle). Bonn, Rheinisches Landesmuseum. The representation of Neptune between two dolphins shows the unhampered naturalism of the early Roman period.*

Roman ornamental work itself had reached the degree of illusionistic reinterpretation that is marked in particular, according to the pioneering researches of Riegl, by a gradual breaking up of the ground surface through excessive and 'painterly' adornment.

How did this change manifest itself in actual artistic creation? Among its most typical expressions are chip-carving ornament and coloured pseudo-cloisonné (cold inlay), both of which were to gain decisive influence over the decoration of the migration and Merovingian period. We begin with chip-carving work, since it is most closely related to early animal

188   *Part of a silvergilt brooch from Galsted (Jutland). End of fifth century. Copenhagen, Nationalmuseet. The three-piece antique group is re-arranged here in a most striking manner: the animals' bodies are skeletons, and individual features are abnormally enlarged. Early phase of Animal Style I (North Sea German).*

189   *Silvergilt metal brooch from Vedstrup (Seeland), beginning of sixth century. Copenhagen, Nationalmuseet. A tectonic composition in Animal Style I, with a pair of two 'biting' heads, border animals and broadly spaced animal patchwork.*

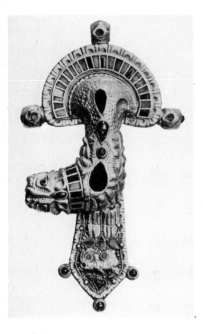

the Nordic, Anglo-Saxon, and Frankish area. Decorative antique animal figures had occasionally been imitated in embossed work by the Germans at other times as well, but such cases remained without more widespread effects. What antiquity had to offer in the way of naturalistic types, as in the masterly *Neptune and Dolphins group [187]*, was now drastically changed as on a *brooch from Jutland [188]*. Here, two skeletal quadrupeds, their bodies bent almost timidly in the narrow step spaces, cling with their front paws to the upper corners of the brooch-head, which also serves as a support for their own monstrous heads, with gaping jaws and jet of water. Their hind-legs are turned through 180 degrees away from the axis, and on their necks lie three-stranded tufts of hair. It cannot be denied that, in the animal heads, the later representation surpasses that of the Roman model.

All the same, it was distinct figures that were still being modelled here. The early, uninhibited phase of the first Germanic animal style was marked by a disintegration of figures. On a classic *South Scandinavian brooch [189]*, we can follow every stage of the change in style. If the large 'biting' heads and the border creatures scurrying down to the lower edge still resemble their live counterparts, the paired animals that now fill up the rhombic foot-plate cannot really be regarded as such any longer: two creatures like grasshoppers are arranged about the central inlay, with bent, pointed legs and heads up. Yet even the pair of beasts is not enough to fill the large brooch-head, which is crammed with an animal patchwork bereft of all natural coherency.

190 Silver brooch with gold foil, from Szilágy-Somlyó (Rumania), mid-fourth century. Budapest, Hungarian National Museum. Combination of earlier elements of the coloured style with the repoussé lion figure. Late Greek work of the Black Sea region, commissioned for Germany.

191 Sword fitting of the Frankish king Childeric, made in a Danube workshop or at the royal court in Tournai (Belgium), c. 460–70. Paris, Cabinet des Médailles. Coloured inlay work of Pontic origin; note the contrast between the finely wrought cell walls and the thick garnet mosaic.

192 Golden eagle brooch from an Ostrogothic grave or treasure, found near Domagno (San Marino), c. 500. Nuremberg, Germanisches Nationalmuseum. Abstract cloisonné mosaic is here included in the stylized naturalistic form of a clasp.

It is obvious that decoration of this kind hardly offered starting-points for further development. Which path Northern artists took to find their way out of this predicament will be shown in a moment. First, on chronological grounds, we must have a look at the other event so important for the formation of style, namely the adoption of polychrome gemming by south German goldsmiths. Of the two main types – garnet inlay in a continuous cell mosaic of vertically soldered sheet-metal cloisons; and gems applied separately, either flat or *en cabochon*, and distributed over the surface in variously shaped cellular collars – the second seems to have been adopted in antique art since Hellenistic times, while the first made its entry during late antiquity, perhaps *via* the Sassanid Persian empire. Both techniques were then further developed in goldsmiths' workshops already under strong Persian influence in the ancient Greek colonial cities by the Black Sea. An idea of the masterly skill is given by a *silver brooch from Transylvania [190]*, whose most striking parts display continuous bands of cells along with stones mounted separately as in the case of the repoussé lion protome that forms its chief adornment. Although buried round about AD 400 in the Transylvanian Carpathians as part of a rich royal or tribal hoard, this unique pair of brooches leaves no doubt about its late Greek derivation both in regard to the naturalistic animal figure and to the encircling decorative band. If the piece therefore still represents an alien product, though one already somewhat forcibly adapted to the Gothic brooch form, the examples of goldsmith's work that follow will illustrate the gradual absorption of garnet inlay into purely native artistic products.

When the Frankish king Childeric I died in 482 at his capital of Tournai, his swords with their garnet-adorned gold *hilt and scabbard fittings* were buried with him *[191]*. In them one may perhaps see the greatest refinement of south Russian colourism by German masters at the royal court. Among the finest Ostrogothic works of Theodoric's times must be counted the *Eagle brooches* found south of Rimini *[192]*, again paired. Harmoniously grouped around the convex breast shield inlaid like a rosette, the 'feathered' parts of the royal bird show a positive obscurance of the basic form by the richly patterned cloisonné-like work. The animal motif of the lion brooch, deriving from antiquity, apparently left no mark on Germanic art. But the eagle brooch, an animal symbol probably deriving from the more distant (Iranian) east, had become the lawful artistic property of the Goths. In this varying attitude towards foreign motifs the age-old Germanic familiarity with the eagle may have played a part, whereas the image of the lion would have been less immediate. Moreover, plastic works with the naturalistic assurance of form shown by our lion protome *[190]* may have daunted at first meeting rather than encouraged imitation. The deeper cause of this bias, however, should probably be sought in the historical moment of the encounter with the motifs. After the middle of the fourth century, the Black Sea Gothic kingdom, then reaching the height of its political consolidation, began to be receptive to Graeco-Persian late antique art; but soon afterwards the catastrophic invasion by the Huns left it in a condition which long prevented any higher development of life. Thus late Ionian repoussé imagery could not be taken up there spontaneously by Germanic craftsmen and remodelled according to their own sense of style. Not until

Theodoric's conquest of Italy were the conditions established for a brief efflorescence of the Gothic goldsmith's art; and it is very instructive to form a clear idea, through the contrast with barbaric prototypes such as the unshapely eagle brooches from the gold treasure of Petrossa in Rumania, of how Ostrogothic masters at the close of the fifth century succeeded, with a refined cloisonné technique and discipline, in giving their own expression to the Persian eagle symbol.

The second Germanic animal style

As we saw from the south Scandinavian brooch *[189]*, north Germanic animal ornament had reached an impasse. An escape only seemed possible through introducing, or perhaps reviving, another element, namely the completely flexible, multi-linear ribbon-work. Ribbon ornament had existed in the eastern Mediterranean area from time immemorial and in many different patterns. Thrusting deep into France

193   *Bronze-covered iron helmet from boat-grave V, Välsgarde (East Sweden), towards 650. Uppsala, University Museum. First experiment of a rhythmical arrangement with the application of animal motifs.*

194 Animal-decorated gold cross from Zanica (Bergamo), beginning of seventh century. Bergamo, Biblioteca Civica. Interpenetration of northern and Mediterranean influences.

195 Silvergilt dress brooch from the grave district of Nocera Umbra (Perugia), mid-seventh century. Rome, Museo Nazionale. Balanced arrangement of the surface through strictly symmetrical animal composition.

by the Rhone route, in the sixth century, it superseded the dying Roman chip-carving and scroll decoration. But even animal ornament of north Germanic character was originally alien to the Frankish brooch. On imported insular works it now penetrated sparsely in the stiffly articulated style – that, say, of the south Scandinavian brooch [189] – which here again needed the loosening, relaxing ribbon interlace to rouse the imagination of continental masters. The fermentative process also seized the more distant, central Swedish North, where, in the meantime, the regions about Lake Mälar had taken the political lead under the kings of the Svear. From a boat-grave field of the Uppland aristocracy comes an *Iron helmet [193]* whose gilt decorative plating shows an ornamental 'chaos' of animal style and ribbon interlace.

That these were the expressions of a common Germanic bent in art is quite obvious from Lombard goldsmith's work in Italy, where the most varied ornamental currents were heading for a real crisis. If we disregard their Danubian heritage of scroll-work and zigzag, the Lombards were already well acquainted with the older form of the north Germanic animal style [189] when, in 568, they occupied Italian territory. In their new home, the harmonious

Mediterranean ribbon ornament was developed chiefly as a beaded variant imitating filigree, while the free, zoomorphic striped interlace entered as a third component, perhaps of Rhineland Frankish origin. The clash of these elements is expressed in a remarkable *gold cross [194]* from the Bergamo district. Like bubbling lava, beaded ribbons have become entangled with heads, clutching hands with clawed feet. There is no beginning or end, and one cannot extricate a complete 'animal'. But Lombardic art managed to convert what looked like a final period into a new sequence, whose phases are more strikingly indicated by one of the classic *Lombard brooches [195]*. In the head- and foot-plates are fitted interlaced pairs of animals, roughly S-shaped and mirroring each other, with angular eye frames, attenuated snouts biting around their own bodies, and clearly recognizable hind-legs placed over the indistinct lower head. Yet it is not the perfect symmetry of the parts that is the great achievement here, but the tectonic harmony between the decorative form inherited from earlier times and the new planar interpretation. Here in the South the climax had been reached of the so-called second Germanic animal style, with its classical insistence on symmetric forms of composition and its return to the perceptible animal figure.

196   The Kingston Brooch, seventh century. Liverpool, City Museum. Found in grave 205, Kingston Down, Kent. The surface is decorated with gold filigree ornament, cuttle-fish shell, garnets, and lapis lazuli.

197   Jewelled purse lid from the Sutton Hoo ship burial. Early seventh century. London, British Museum. The border is made up of twisted wire filigrees; the panels are inlaid with garnet and coloured glass which once enclosed a piece of ivory or leather in place of the modern white background. Note the combination of abstract decoration, Animal Style I, and quasi-realistic representation.

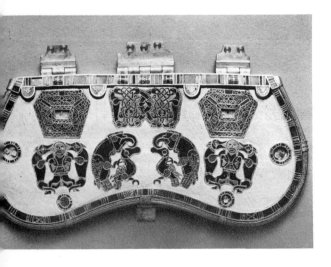

English and Irish art

From Southern and Eastern England, the Anglo-Saxons, in close connexion with the south Scandinavian trend, made a basic contribution to the two first Germanic animal styles. As in Germany, Celtic artists of Britain took over from the Romans the chip-carving technique, and made exciting innovations in metal-work with such non-geometrical motifs as spirals and leaves. During the fifth and sixth centuries much of this art was based on animal forms executed in the same technique. 'The creature loses its zoological reality and is converted into mere pattern. Heads and legs, tails and teeth, are mixed together into an attractive pot-pourri of confusion which covers every square inch of the surface of the object' (Kendrick). This, the agitated and disjointed 'helmet and hand' style, was succeeded towards the seventh century by the 'ribbon' style, where animals are interlaced in quieter ornamentation.

The other Anglo-Saxon contribution to the art of this period lies in the rich polychrome jewellery of Kent and East Anglia, produced between *c.* 550 and AD 700, and which shows a technical proficiency unrivalled elsewhere in Europe. One of the most luxurious examples of the Kentish school is the *disc brooch from Kingston [196]*. The Suffolk school differs from Kentish work in the various shapes of individual garnets, sometimes mushroom-shaped, as on the Wilton Cross, sometimes curved to make boars' heads, as on the epaulettes and *purse lid from the Sutton Hoo burial [197]*. The boar is only one of the number of motifs derived from the pre-Roman Celts. The escutcheons of bronze hanging-bowls from this period are decorated in a curvilinear spiral style directly connected with native British ornament.

The East Anglian royal cenotaph at Sutton Hoo was deposited more than fifty years after Augustine's mission to England. Pagan work survived, as shown in the ivory Gandersheim casket decorated in late ribbon style, while at the same time the jeweller adapted his craft to Christianity with such success that in the eighth century Anglo-Saxon craftsmen were making objects for the altar of St Peter's itself. The *chalice* presented by Duke Tassilo of Austria at the foundation of the monastery of Kremsmünster in 777 *[186]* was almost certainly made by a craftsman trained in England or in the *Schola Saxonum* at Rome. The portraits of Christ and the Apostles on its chip-carved surface are of Mediterranean influence; the interlaced animals and foliate motifs, of English origin, are in the mainstream of European art. Space does not permit us to include illustrations of other Anglo-Saxon masterpieces of Christian art, such as the pectoral cross of St Cuthbert, the seventh-century Ixworth Cross, and the ninth-century Fuller Brooch. When during the ninth century Viking invasions reduced the supply of gold available for works of art, the chip-carved bronzegilt technique was replaced by carved silver. This indeed was the 'Silver Age' of Anglo-Saxon art.

In Ireland, on inherited Celtic foundations and through close, direct contact with the monasteries and art of Coptic Egypt, a focal art industry had been evolving since the fifth century. When the monasteries had grown in size and wealth, the demand arose for liturgical vessels, reliquaries, and Gospel books, and a masterly art style in book-painting, metal- and enamel-working came into being to meet the demand. With the rapid increase in communications between Ireland, Britain, and Europe after the mid-sixth century, Irish craftsmen were provided with numerous motifs to choose from. The most fruitful contact was provided by the foundation of the monasteries of Iona and Lindisfarne. Here, two eclectic art styles originated, the Irish and Northumbrian, both of them deriving from Columban roots. The Book of Durrow, dating from *c.* 675, is the earliest example of these Irish and Northumbrian styles. Its text is the Vulgate of Jerome, copied probably from one of the manuscripts brought back from Italy by Benedict Biscop. But the evangelical symbols illustrated follow the order of the Gospels in the old Latin version used by Irish Gospel books, while the interlacing animal ornamentation on one 'carpet' page seem to have been copied directly from seventh-century Anglo-Saxon metal-work of the ribbon style. The new and distinctive feature of the Book of Durrow is the plain or broad-ribbon interlace, a regularized version of the early ribbon style but without zoomorphic characteristics, and derived probably from Coptic sources. Other manuscripts from Irish and Northumbrian scriptoria will be discussed in a later chapter; it is sufficient to say here that during the eighth century Irish influence was strong not only on the Continent [cf. *238*] but can be traced as far as eastern Sweden.

Much of the metal-work produced in Ireland between the period AD 700–825 was plundered by the Vikings, and its chronology is provided by dated Viking graves in Norway. Most of this work, cast in bronze, consists of reliquaries. The pins and brooches of earlier date were embellished with millefiori and enamel during the late seventh century, although it was more normal to cover the surface of the bronze with unenamelled ornament engraved in the spiral patterns evident on both Irish and Anglo-Saxon hanging-bowl escutcheons. During the early eighth

198 *Head of the Tara Brooch, c. 700. Dublin, National Museum of Ireland. Cast in bronzegilt, the panels are filled with gold filigreed animals and gold wire interlace. Interlaced ribbon animals or birds alternate with panels of chip-carved trumpet spirals on the ring. A high point of elaborate ornamentation.*

century the Irish metal-worker learnt from Anglo-Saxon examples of wax-casting the technique of chip-carving. Spiral patterns were zoomorphized in the elaborate brooches of this period. Anglo-Saxon garnet or polychrome cloisonné inlay techniques were imitated by the Irish and developed through making glass studs with an angular metal grille set in the surface. The old type of penannular brooch now became fully annular; enlarged terminals were closed up or joined together by small bridges of metal. The *Tara Brooch* [*198*] is one of the earliest pieces where the terminals are brought together. Cast in bronze, it is decorated with a super-abundance of minutely fine ornament on front and back. Long panels of chip-carved spirals alternate with panels of interlaced ribbon-style animals and birds. The Ardagh Chalice, the other outstanding achievement of eighth-century Irish metal-work, shows a more restrained design, and perhaps more skilful ornament, than the Tara Brooch. During the ninth century craftsmen relied heavily on rectilinear interlace, a somewhat monotonous design produced too often.

The art of ornamentation

That wavily proliferous and again mirrored motifs
could also be used, if required, for the pressed S- and
8-groups is made clear, on the northern side of the
Alps, by showy *belt trimmings* of chased cast bronze
[200] from the Burgundian and Alemanic area.
This wavy, tendril-like movement has been used
quite inexhaustibly, moreover, on a profiled *bridle
fitting* [199] by an inventive Uppland master. Real
plant models underlie the motif when, in particular,
the animal's feet are bipartite or fan-shaped, with
single curled-up toes, as exemplified on the framed
inner part and animal-adorned border strips of the
well-preserved counterplate [200]. The fact that this
foreign element could only be adopted in the South
is due to the privileged role of the palmette motif in
early Byzantine goldsmith's work. Its use on stamped
strap ornaments can be represented by a small *belt
mount* [201] found not far from Istanbul, while a fine
Gold-leaf cross from Stabio [202] illustrates the important part played by the Lombards as mediators. In the
bisected trefoils, one can recognize the direct prototype of the pinnate feet of the advanced second style.
The dominant role of beaded ribbon interlace also
began with Lombard mediation, whereby the earlier
striped interlace of the first animal style was over-
powered in the seventh century.

We leave the continental Frankish kingdom at a
time when, on the threshold of the eighth century,
animal ornament was rapidly disintegrating, along
with most other branches of decorative metal-work,
into thread-like figure-of-eight loops, while, in the
Lombard kingdom, Byzantine taste was gaining the
upper hand and thus preparing the end of the last

199   *Bronzegilt bridle fitting, with five ribbon animals placed
opposite each other and looking backwards, from boat-grave XII,
Vendel (Uppland), c. 650. Stockholm, National History
Museum. Here the play of movement typical of the northern
Animal Style II is changed into plant-like forms.*

200   *Counterplate of a triangular belt-clasp, from Wurmlingen
near Tuttlingen (Württemberg), later seventh century. Stuttgart,
Württembergisches Landesmuseum. Mature example of the
continental Animal Style II from the Burgundian–Alemanic
zone.*

201   *Golden belt ornament from the Istanbul region, second half
of seventh century. Sofia, Archaeological Museum. The decoration consists of Byzantine palmettes of the period after Justinian.*

202   *Gold-leaf cross from a Lombard warrior's grave at Stabio
(Ticino), second half of seventh century. Zürich, Schweizerisches
Landesmuseum. The Byzantine palmettes appear ambiguous in
this example of the south German Animal Style II.*

203   Mouth fitting of a scabbard mount with two mirrored interlaced animal patterns of Style III, from a horseman's grave in Gotland. Mid-eighth century. Stockholm, National Historical Museum. 'Pantomimic expressive movement' dating from the end of the north German pre-Viking animal style. These highly imaginative creatures show a remarkable elasticity.

204, 205   Bronzegilt detail of a scabbard mount from boat-grave V, Välsgarde (East Sweden), c. 700. Uppsala, University Museum. Representation of a horse-shaped animal figure amid finely spun lines. This is clearly seen in close detail, but not apparent when the hunting 'belt' is seen as a whole.

Germanic ornamental forms and also of the animal style. It was quite another story in the North. If the second animal style had as yet shown no features there [193, 199] diverging essentially from those of its Southern manifestations, now a series of new stages with different evolutionary trends began in the Swedish and Gotland art province, partly as a turbulent development and partly growing more organically. Of the two *scabbard mounts* [203, 204] from chieftains' graves containing many weapons in this centre, the earlier type displays the broad outline of a horse stepping out vigorously amid a tangle of sharp-edged lines, its head and feet alone still governed by the animal and half-palmette style with which we are acquainted. Detached from its ground [205], the figure is not only in complete formal accord with the contemporary pony brooches of the North, but also suggests links between the horse motif and the

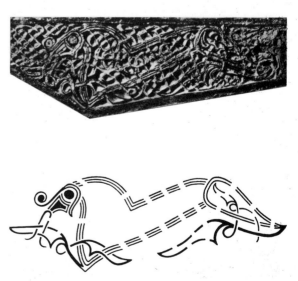

flourishing religion of Odin and Valhalla. It has long been realized that reverting from comparatively naturalistic animal motifs to varying degrees of abstraction is a law of the animal style's Northern phases. Only because of this can such a non-physical, non-corporeal enrichment as the *mouth fitting* of the latter scabbard *[203, 206]* still be recognized as belonging historically to early Germanic animal ornament; and it was the sharp eye of the Swedish art historian Bernhard Salin that first revealed, in the composition possessing rich tonal graduations, two pairs of animals rearing diagonally in opposite directions, with snake heads and menacing tentacles. In the 'organically conceived waxing and waning of the bodies, and in the unbroken flow of movement right into the finest branchings of the limbs-creeper' (Jenny), we thus have before us the logical end link of a long chain of decorative north Germanic animal figures, and one that at the same time represents a culmination of its kind.

It is clear that, from the point reached here, the only path left open to ornamentation led to true 'crypto-grams', or else, in a sort of anticipated rococo, to cleverly fugitive plays of curves. During the ninth century a fresh impetus roused the creative forces once more to new and great achievements when, in the encounter with Oriental animal and plant ornament and with corresponding trends of insular and continental Carolingian art, there unfolded the stylistic phases of what is known after famous Nor-wegian works as Viking art. Here we leave the separate Nordic pagan development, which ran on till about 1100, and make another brief survey of

207, 208 Detail of a two-sided sword hilt decorated with gold leaf, from the grave of a Norwegian chieftain, at Snartemo (West Agder), early sixth century. Oslo, University Collections. The beginnings of a German figural representation developed from copies of late Roman medallions and elements of the early Nordic animal ornamentation.

206 Mouth fitting of a scabbard mount with two mirrored interlaced animal patterns of Style III, from a horseman's grave in Gotland. Drawing of [203].

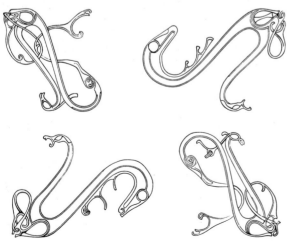

figure representation on earlier Germanic works in metal.

In recent years art historians have observed the deep impression that must have been made on the imagination of north Germanic goldsmiths since the fourth century by the profile busts of emperors, their right hand expressively raised, from late Roman gold medallions. Iconographically, this gesture characterizes the pair of fierce crouching men on a *sword hilt [207, 208]*; and prisoner groups from Roman triumphal art may be at the back of the symbolic 'shackling'. In this context, the indigenous creative principle of the early animal style speaks out with even more force, especially in the motif of the magnificently striped hair. This, like the crossing of arms and hands, probably indicates that the formidable group concerns a sacred and magical blood-brotherhood – something entirely appropriate to the gold-hilted sword of a south Norwegian nobleman. From here it certainly took a long course of development to reach the mature, free style of the *gold-plate bracteate [209, 210]*. This lancer also depends historically on antique types, whether of Christian mounted saints or from military memorial art, although they did not, of course, in any way prevent the foreign scheme being supplemented by material from the faith bound up with battle and death of Wodan's Alemanic worshippers. Compared to earlier prototypes, the detaching of the group from the ground, the more confident figure style, and the garment details are a conspicuous advance. For the present, though, it remains uncertain how much of this is due to the south German find-place – far away from the North – as a distinct art area, or how far the stylistic release is to be seen as a natural outcome of the roughly 150-year gap between these two repoussé works. The focus of this later figurative art, which embraced the Continent in a wide arc, seems to have lain in those regions of east Sweden where the second animal style came into full bloom at the same period.

We have deliberately refrained here from opening for the reader a picture-book of Germanic antiquities of the migration period. Glass and clay vessels and in particular the beautiful grave pottery all have their own style that, changing by century and people, could no doubt have helped to give a broader picture of stylistic trends; but as a gauge of talent for artistic creation they would have been out of place. What in this sense the Northern peoples achieved of value is neatly summarized in Steingräber's judgment: 'Their creative sense of form expressed itself most tellingly in dynamic abstract ornament.' It has been shown how, with the adoption of late Roman chip-carving, the process of converting natural shapes began, and

how the basis of future animal ornamentation was thereby established. And even the human image, drawn on various occasions from the ample late antique stock of types, was adapted to the same strict principles of style.

209, 210 Gold-plate bracteate, with a lancer above his fallen enemy and protecting war-demons (see drawing). Found in a grave at Pliezhausen near Tübingen, seventh century. Stuttgart, Württembergisches Landesmuseum. This shows the further development of north German figural art from the previous technical and stylistic principles, supported by iconographic independence from antique models.

Most periods of art history are given names that, for all the arbitrariness and fortuity of their origin, still individuate these periods conceptually and localize them geographically. But the term 'early medieval' simply places in time an age that is among the most obscure in the history of Western civilization. This is the most convenient way to do justice to the highly inconsistent impression that art presents from the eighth to the start of the eleventh century.

The evolution of early medieval art was directed by strong political impulses, so that one may speak of a Carolingian and an Ottonian art inside the period. With Charlemagne, a new chapter of Western history began. Not only did he greatly extend the sphere of Frankish power, but, by reviving the imperium, established a model for politics and thought. The imperial coronation at Rome in 800 sanctioned the claims of the new empire to be the lawful successor to the Roman one, and, beyond that, also confirmed this empire's unity with Church and pope. The new imperium was conscious of being linked by tradition to its late antique ideal, and from this there issued the emperor's policy of a directed culture. Intentional references to late antique and early Christian models can be detected everywhere, in architecture just as in painting and sculpture. Art, also, was intended to make plain the unity of empire and Church, which meant that it was in the first place courtly and ecclesiastic. The mainstays of its development were the emperor, his learned advisers, and in particular the now flourishing or newly founded Benedictine monasteries, which increasingly came to be independent centres of culture.

The Christian Church unified the West beyond the boundaries of the different spheres of power, and in this sense Carolingian civilization was universal and supra-national. Obviously, cultural community fostered a brisk exchange of ideas across wide areas, which led to the complexity of Carolingian art as is particularly apparent in book illumination. Alongside the ornamental forms of the highly developed Irish illumination handed on by missionary monks, there was the strongly illusionistic painting style

taken over from early Christian and Byzantine models. At times these different trends combined, although never in a final transforming synthesis, so that all such experiments have something provisional about them. Neither the north European stylistic modes nor the deliberate 'revival' of a misunderstood antiquity could do full justice to the new range of Christian themes.

The most notable feats of Carolingian art come within the sphere of architecture. The first monumental stone buildings north of the Alps were produced at this time: vast imperial palaces modelled on those of the Roman emperors; centrally planned structures and basilicas closely following early Christian ones. New solutions were found that pointed to the future, as in the westwork – the mighty west end of churches. On the other hand, the products of book illumination and ivory carving, despite their quality, were backward-looking. But in this very attempt to appropriate the antique style, the human figure began to be released from those ornamental bonds so characteristic of the North.

Though the tendencies of Carolingian art remained active even after the emperor's death and the division of his empire (843), there was a perceptible decline in quality and monumental proportions. Until into the tenth century the raids of the Saracens, Hungarians, and Normans disrupted the West. It was the Saxon dynasty that first managed to stabilize the situation. Around the middle of the tenth century the Ottos returned to the political ideals of Charlemagne. The Ottonian empire also wanted to be universal, and professed its unity with the Church. Nevertheless, its centre of gravity clearly lay in the German sphere, since the western part of the old Carolingian empire, later France, had increasingly gone its own way since the division. Independent national developments now grew more conspicuous, and the first differences appeared between the separate historical regions, such as the German tribal areas or the various French centres of culture. Important influences on the church structure came from Burgundy, in connexion with the Cluniac reform of the Benedictine order that began there. New ideas for building were also developed on both sides of the Pyrenees, though more significant are the first beginnings, linked up with this, of a monumental sculpture. By comparison, Italy and northern Europe were less productive.

211   The Evangelist Luke, from the so-called Gospel Book of Ada, c. 800. Trier, Stadtbibliothek. The Evangelist is enthroned in a niche filled with pillars, as in late antique portraits of authors. The spatial and corporeal representation has become linear.

Under the Saxon emperors, German art reached a peak unequalled elsewhere in the West. Carolingian, late antique, and Byzantine models were referred to, but an overriding principle is much more evident. The dimensions of churches became generally bigger, the interiors clearly articulated in rhythmic order, and the first signs appeared of a systematic treatment of the whole fabric. Manuscript illumination saw its various models fully converted into a formal language of aristocratic dignity and stylized otherworldliness. Such an exceptional work as the bronze doors of Hildesheim Cathedral represents, in its figure scenes, a 'new start in the conquest of the human form' (Jantzen). The turn of the millennium meant at once an end and a beginning: the end of the 'early Middle Ages' and the beginning of Romanesque art, whose characteristics were already emerging.

ARCHITECTURE

Ever since the spread of Christianity, the most important task of Western architecture had been to raise churches. The basic types were established as early as pre-Carolingian times: cathedrals, monastery churches and the structures belonging to them, pilgrimage churches, baptistries, and tomb churches. All these types had their roots in the Mediterranean area, but they soon showed certain changes. The number of monuments that bear witness to pre-Carolingian building activity is indeed extremely small, and when describing them we have to rely on what are mostly quite inadequate remains and restorations. A few buildings in Visigothic northern Spain, in France, Germany, Ireland, and England give us a rough idea of this early stage. The native tradition, which Carolingian architecture in many ways linked on to, can therefore only be discerned with difficulty. The late antique and early Christian elements are far more evident – most immediately in those buildings that rose in close dependency on Charlemagne himself, like the chapel of the imperial palace at Aachen and the churches of monasteries founded or promoted by the emperor.

Centrally planned Carolingian buildings

Consecrated in 805, the *Palatine Chapel at Aachen* is a centrally planned building, and so belongs to the type that already in early Christian times was often used

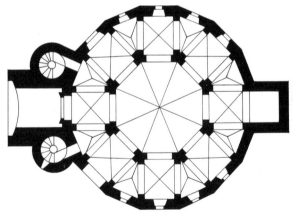

212, 213 Palatine chapel of Charlemagne at Aachen, consecrated 805. View of the interior and ground-plan. A central building with galleries after Italo–Byzantine models such as S. Vitale, Ravenna [155], but harsher and more massive than these. The eight corners of the interior walls are doubled by the alternate square and triangular vaulted bays in the ambulatory.

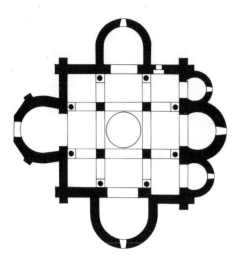

214, 215 Church of Germigny-des-Prés near Orléans, con-
secrated 806. Ground-plan and view of the exterior. A tiered
structure of apses, subsidiary portions, and cross arms, culminating
in the high, tower-like central dome. The ground-plan is in the
Greek-cross form, with square subsidiary spaces after Byzantine
models. The apses are built to some extent in the west Gothic
horseshoe form.

for baptistries and tomb churches. It once stood within the great complex of the palace, and was originally connected to a large hall by colonnades about 130 yards long. An equestrian statue of Theodoric brought from Ravenna is said to have been placed in the colonnaded forecourt, no doubt with deliberate reference to the emperor. Many columns in the chapel itself [212] also came from Italy, so it is not surprising that the architect, whose name has come down to us as Odo of Metz, based his general conception on an Italian work. His model was probably *S. Vitale at Ravenna [155]*, a building of Byzantine origin. Yet for all the details they have in common, these interiors, when compared, reveal two different ideas of space. Whereas in S. Vitale the niches of the central octagon curve out into the surrounding passageway and give the space an effect of air and light, at Aachen a heavy lower story with powerful piers forms a base for the gallery zone reserved for the emperor and his court. Here, instead of the semicircular niches that at Ravenna blur the space, arches running straight from pier to pier separate the central space clearly and distinctly from the passageway. The detail is of a perfection and elegance previously unknown in the North, and even the ground-plan [213] has a richness that is

ultra-refined in the transition from the central octagon to the sixteen-sided external casing. Nevertheless, the impression of space is dominated by a taut steepness and massive monumentality. The Palatine Chapel is among the best preserved and choicest examples of Carolingian architecture, a model that would be turned to repeatedly in the following centuries.

Quite another type of centralized structure is represented by the *Church of Germigny-des-Prés near Orléans*. Its builder, Bishop Theodulf of Orléans, belonged to the inner circle of the imperial court. He came from Visigothic Spain, a fact that may perhaps account for certain peculiarities of this edifice consecrated about 806. Though it now exists only as a nineteenth-century restoration, the church has the Byzantine ground-plan of a Greek cross inscribed in a square [214]. The space opens into a big apse on three sides, and eastwards into three smaller ones. These apses are shaped like horseshoes, a form also taken by the arches that subdivide and articulate the interior; it undoubtedly points back to the Visigothic homeland of the bishop. Only fragments of the rich stucco decoration have survived. Also Byzantine in character is the build-up of the various space compartments towards the central dome, an ascent that can be clearly seen from the outside as well [215].

The Carolingian basilica and westwork

For the monumental church building of the West, the centrally planned structure was less important and indicative of the future than the basilica. It is true that the centralizing principle, with its tendency towards a vertical arrangement of wall masses, seems to have been fruitful for the basilican scheme as well, since both at times united to produce new, pioneering forms. The earliest basilicas built under imperial patronage can now only be reconstructed from documentary sources and excavations. St-Denis near Paris (begun 760) and Fulda (begun 802) were flat-ceilinged basilicas with transepts, on the model of St Peter's at Rome. The *Church of the monastery at Centula in Normandy*, on the other hand, reveals a new conception. It was built from 790 to 799 for Angilbert, a son-in-law of Charlemagne, and can be reconstructed fairly accurately from old prints made after a twelfth-century drawing, and from contemporary accounts. This restoration *[216]* shows that the eastern transept was opposed by a similar structure to the west, and that these two groups, with their pair of flanking stair towers and big middle tower, were almost mirror-images of one another. Only the apse at the east end stressed the building's alignment from west to east. The western structure must have been among the first examples of something very characteristic of Carolingian architecture: the westwork. It had a

217   *Westwork of the monastery church of Corvey, 873–85 (the upper, steepled stories of the central structure and towers were first added in the twelfth century). The two square flanking towers are united to the central structure to form a compact building block.*

216   *Monastery church of St-Riquier at Centula near Abbeville, completed 799. Reconstruction. Early Christian basilicas were arranged on a simple west–east axis, and their exteriors left undecorated. Here, in contrast, both ends of the building are of equal significance, with similar heights and structures.*

vaulted entrance hall containing the font at ground-floor level, and above was a chapel, with an altar, that opened on to the nave. This room not only served as a parish church – later it often came to be dedicated to S. Michael – but was reserved for the emperor when he attended divine service on his visits to the monastery. The nave was unvaulted and probably had an open-roof framework, as may be assumed to be the case in most large Carolingian basilicas where they did not have a flat ceiling. Put together out of mighty blocks, this architectural body went far beyond what were presumably its models in the Mediterranean area *[142]*, and, especially in Germany, continued to set the pattern for centuries.

With its well-preserved late Carolingian westwork *[217]*, the *Monastery Church of Corvey* can give us an impression of the lost prototypes (873–85). The middle part was heightened round about 1150 by the two windowed stories, so that the original effect of a compact main body between two towers has been somewhat altered. Inside, above the entrance hall, is the baptistry, at once a chapel of S. Michael and a 'box' for the reigning family.

When, about 820, the abbot of St Gall wanted to rebuild his monastery, a bishop close to the imperial circle sent him an 'exemplar', an ideal layout for a Benedictine monastery. This original sketch made on parchment still exists [218], and gives us most valuable information, even though it cannot be interpreted down to the last detail. Especially noteworthy is the ground-plan of the church, which clearly provides for a second apse at the west end, with a semicircular paradise and two round towers to counterbalance the eastern parts. The rest of the plan shows the general structure of such a monastic community with its various economic undertakings. Beyond this the arrangement of the so-called clausura, the area within the monastery reserved for the monks alone, gives an indication of the basic form that was the rule throughout the rest of the Middle Ages.

None of these monasteries has survived. Only the *Gateway of Lorsch Monastery* (c. 770), which preserves almost completely its original appearance [219] remains as witness to what must have been most impressive buildings. With its three archways and hall above, it probably derives from a similar construction

at Old St Peter's in Rome. If the arrangement of the ground-floor, with arches between half-columns topped by stylized antique capitals, reflects quite strongly the influence of this Roman model, the upper story, with fragile pilasters and a steep gabled roof, almost recalls the forms of wooden buildings, in spite of the antique details. Its tile patterning can be compared to a number of tendencies in contemporary book illumination.

From the period of late Carolingian architecture let us mention the church of *S. Georg at Oberzell* on the island of Reichenau. An important monastic centre had already been formed at an early date here, though it did not reach its prime until Ottonian times. Even if this small building lacks monumentality, its basilican body from the late ninth century still gives

218   Plan of the monastery of St Gall, c. 820; after the original sketch made on parchment. St Gall, Stiftsbibliothek. The early Christian T-form of the church is altered with the extension of the eastern choir. At the west is another choir, surrounded with a semi-circular atrium. The monastic living quarters are grouped at the south around the cloister. Note the many other buildings (schools, infirmary, centres for rural industry and manual craft); and the spiritual and social unity of the medieval monastery.

219   Gateway of Lorsch Monastery, c. 770. Erected perhaps as a hall for reception and royalty for the former monastery church to the west. Entrance to the first story is by way of staircases in the semicircular towers. The decoration of the façade shows antique motifs applied to a surface.

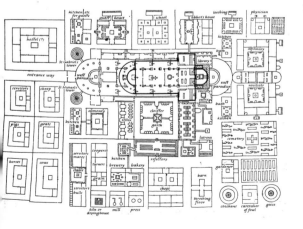

Spain

Architecture outside the sphere of Carolingian power did not have the same monumentality or richness of form, since it lacked a promoting and directing central authority. But for this very reason native traditions could at times be continued. Thus there still exists in the Asturias, in northern Spain, a series of buildings based on the early churches of the Visigoths, who had settled there and were converted to Christianity from the end of the sixth century. Developed under the influence of antiquity, their refined stone building technique made it possible for them to cover important parts of a church, such as chancel and transept arms, with barrel- or groined-vaults, and even to put a barrel-vault over the entire nave.

A comparatively well-preserved example is the small eighth-century cruciform basilica of S. Pedro de la Nave near Zamora [221]. Its outer walls are built of large squared stones, and where nave and transept intersect there rises the once domed crossing-tower, a feature native to Byzantine architecture that was also adopted in the North [cf. 216]. Inside [222], the barrel-vaulted nave is separated from the aisles by heavy masses of masonry. The arcade arches have the typically Visigothic horseshoe form, represented in Carolingian architecture by the church of Bishop Theodulf at *Germigny-des-Prés* [215] mentioned above. But this shape became the actual hall-mark of Islamic art, which helped to mould Spanish art and civilization for many centuries after the Arabs

220 S. Georg at Oberzell, on the island of Reichenau, begun at the end of ninth century. Gothic choir. Despite later additions the effect is that of a simple Carolingian basilica, with simple pillared arcades and walls like panes. The naves are all flat-ceiled. The orientation towards the choir is obvious.

221, 222 Visigothic church of S. Pedro de la Nave near Zamora, eighth century. The basilical cross-section and Latin-cross form are clearly visible from the exterior. A square tower is raised on top of the transept crossing. Note the shaft-like effect of the barrel-vaulted nave; the horseshoe-shaped arcades; and the early examples of figural ornament on the columns.

us an impression of a Carolingian interior [220]. The arcaded nave, whose remarkable fresco decorations belong to the tenth century, is lit by small round-headed windows in the clerestory, and, like the aisles, it has a flat ceiling. What is now a Gothic choir rises over the ninth-century crypt, another important part of the building to be found in many Carolingian churches. In these small underground passages and rooms reliquaries were kept, or the bones of saints and clerical dignitaries were laid to rest. Later on, especially in Romanesque times, crypts were developed into complete lower churches whose layout then affected the entire ground-plan of the chancel [cf. 262].

had conquered the Iberian peninsula at the start of the eighth century. Thanks to the close proximity of Christians and Arabs there evolved in the early Middle Ages a hybrid style known as 'Mozarabic', which comprises the artistic statements of the Christians in those areas controlled by Islam. The tendencies of the highly developed Islamic architecture, which now set the example for the greater part of Spain, are particularly easy to recognize in the *Mosque of Cordova [223]*. Unlike the plastic modelling and accenting of the fabric that was then emerging in the North, the space here has been put together from a basic form that can be endlessly repeated. What is characteristic here is the absence of any definite direction in the spatial structure, which is developed all round and only articulated by the many columns and arches.

If in Spain an autonomous evolution can be followed, Italy, which had once been among the original homelands of Christian art, held fast to the early Christian types of building until into Romanesque times, without making any essential changes. Where new elements brought into the country by the Goths or Lombards did appear, one can hardly say that they contributed substantially to the pattern of development during the first millennium.

223 *The mosque of Cordova, begun 786. The forest of pillars with double-arched arcades creates a centrifugal spatial effect with a lack of clear definition.*

England

In north-west Europe, in England and Ireland, the church building remained of modest dimensions during early medieval times. It tended towards narrow, elongated, aisleless spaces. The Germanic mode of building in wood seems to have held its own for a long time beside stone construction, as for example at the *Church at Greenstead*, 1013 *[224]*, and indeed, it even affected the latter: the well-preserved west tower of *Earl's Barton* of the tenth or eleventh centuries *[225]* shows a typical conversion of wooden-structure forms into 'stone half-timbering'. The 'Celtic' churches, some of which, according to Bede, were built by masons from Gaul at the time of Benedict Biscop, are of rough-coursed stone and rubble, with small chancels. Perhaps the most outstanding monument of pre-Norman English architecture is the church of All Saints at Brixworth. It was originally basilican, with a western narthex and outer atrium, and a wide, two-aisled nave. But even in this ambitious structure, the Roman brick arches are crudely built and are not centred or turned radially.

Even if the architecture of the tenth and early eleventh centuries, in fact of the period directly preceding Romanesque, is mainly distinguished by

224   *Greenstead Church, Essex, 1013. Anglo-Saxon wooden structure of oak beams as perpendicular supports.*

225   *West tower of Earl's Barton church, c. 1000. The framework is used to decorate and articulate the stories of the stone tower.*

the emergence of national and regional peculiarities, an effort to achieve ordering principles can be observed almost everywhere, notwithstanding the difference between the individual forms and ideas. The conditions for the development of a single style were beginning to take shape on all sides. A series of demands on the church building that made their appearance during the period were certainly not without an effect on this evolution. Thus the increasing size of the Christian congregations called for bigger spaces for the laity, which meant that naves had to be enlarged. New problems regarding the form of the chancel were posed not only by the growth of the clergy and changes in the liturgy but also by the great crowds of pilgrims who had to be able to pass by the venerated relics that until then had usually been kept in the very limited space of the crypt.

Of much importance in connexion with the working out of new chancel solutions is the reformed Benedictine order of the Cluniacs, which had been active since the early tenth century and quickly spread from its original Burgundian home. Major prerequisites to a systematization of the building as a whole were realized in German Ottonian architecture. These preparations were weakest in Italy, rent in the south by the clashes of the Byzantines, the Saracens, and the ultimately victorious Normans. Only in the north, in Lombardy, did native beginnings born of the late antique tradition appear, alongside French and German influences. They concerned not so much the ground-plan and structural grouping as the plastic and decorative articulation of the exterior. Early attempts at vaulting, too, are traceable here.

Burgundy

At this period what was later to be France was still broken up into a number of independent regions of varying artistic importance and activity. Among them Burgundy has a special place, since it was here that the Cluniac monastic reform movement, of such weight for the entire West, had its source. From the mother house at Cluny the new order soon extended to the other French regions, to Spain and northern Italy, and during the eleventh century to Germany as well. In so doing, it passed on the forms evolved in Burgundian territory, while also absorbing foreign influences.

During the late tenth century two solutions to the problem of the east end were found, which provided the model and pointed the way for their times: the

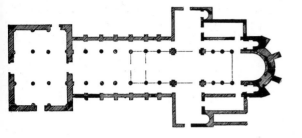

226 *Ground-plan of monastery church of Cluny II, consecrated 981. Burgundian staggered apse. Further altar space is gained by the staggering of the eastern end. The side aisles of the choir bridge the gap between apse and nave.*

arrangement was taken over, though with one essential difference: instead of the massive ring wall of the crypt ambulatory, the upper building received columns linked together by arches. In layout and function, this east-end solution was undoubtedly dependent on the further development of the early Christian crypt that had already begun during Carolingian times; but only above ground could it arrive at its ultimate form.

227, 228 *St-Philibert at Tournus, c. 950 to 1120. Ground-plan and view of the nave towards the east. The ground-plan shows the surrounding choir crowned with three chapels: the three rectangular chapels are arranged around the ambulatory. A new feeling for mass and monumentality is evident in the great circular piers and steep proportions of the nave.*

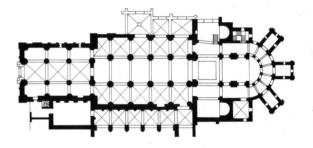

staggered apse (apse echelon) and the apse with an ambulatory and radiating chapels (chevet). The staggered plan first appeared in the *second Monastery Church at Cluny [226]*, consecrated in 981, and which was subsequently replaced by a third, larger building in the eleventh century. Each priest had to say Mass daily, and the requirements of this liturgical usage were met by staggering the eastern parts. The aisles were continued beyond the transept into the chancel, where they ended in small chapels beside the main apse. Further altars could be set into the east walls of the transept wings. The east end thus acquired a rich and varied conformation, and through the continuing of the aisles into the chancel it was organically united with the western part. This type of church not only spread across Burgundy and Normandy but in the late eleventh century became of particular importance in respect to German buildings of the so-called Hirsau school *[268, 269]*.

The second Burgundian form of east end, the chevet, was more forward-looking. Among the earliest examples of this type, which still determined the basic pattern of the great Gothic cathedral chancels, is the church of *St-Philibert at Tournus*. Building activity started round about 950 and did not end until 1120, although the shape of the ground-plan *[227]* had probably been fixed by the beginning of the eleventh century. Between the two towers at the west end is a two-storied vestibule whose upper floor, like Carolingian ones, is dedicated to S. Michael. In the nave *[228]* with its mighty round wall-work piers, the bold and austere formal language of the early eleventh century is expressed with exceptional clarity. The building's oldest parts are at the east end, in the crypt, which has a round ambulatory that opens into three oblong radiating chapels. When the chancel came to be erected, this

As regards the shaping of the chancel chapels, the rather inorganic rectangle soon gave way to the semicircular apse. With the eastern part of the church at *Vignory*, completed about 1050, this new solution becomes clearly visible *[229]*. To the nave end, which should have a pair of lateral towers (one of them never built), is attached a lower-lying apse accompanied by the still lower ambulatory and its semicircular chapels. In the interior *[230]*, two more significant trends of this age are apparent, namely the emphasis on the thickness of the wall by using pillars rather than columns, and the opening up of the wall, now realized to be heavy and bulky, by means of galleries.

With Carolingian architecture, too, we hear of basilicas where instead of the columns usual in early Christian churches rectangular pillars were employed. Even if we can hardly picture their spatial effect, it may be assumed that for all their massive monumentality, they still lacked a sense of the stony material quality of the wall. Above the arcades carried on columns, the clerestory must almost have seemed to lack any weight of its own, as for example in *S. Georg* at *Oberzell* *[220]*. At Vignory, the openings bore deep into the thickness of the masonry. The pillars seem like bits of this thick wall left standing there, an impression strengthened by

229 Priory church at Vignory, begun at the end of the tenth century; consecrated 1050. This view from the south-east shows how the typical staggering of the structure around the eastern end (gabled nave, high choir, ambulatory, and chapels) here achieves a differentiated, organic unity.

230 View of the nave towards the east. Galleries break up the massive interior walls. A large arch separates the nave from the choir.

the capitals reduced to a narrow impost. For the chancel, however, it remained the general rule to use the column, which was regarded as a superior element and often kept for parts of the building to be given special emphasis. For the most part, galleries were installed only in those Carolingian buildings with centrally planned structures and westwork, so their use for the nave probably goes back to early Christian models *[cf. 141]*. Already then the nave galleries were set apart for the women during divine service, and this is also the original purpose of some of the first medieval examples. Beyond this, they made it possible to accommodate a larger number of the faithful inside the church. But above all, they seem to suggest a new stylistic inclination, the urge to shape and articulate the wall masses plastically.

This is where Romanesque, with its tendency to open out the substances of the wall, got under way, and in so doing prepared the structural skeleton of Gothic.

A richer development of the chancel, its organic attachment to the nave, and a new feeling for the substance of the structural body are the essential features of Burgundian architecture during this last early medieval phase. Similar tendencies can also be observed in the region on either side of the Pyrenees which around the turn of the millennium became an important centre of resistance to the Moors in Spain, and from which the reconquest of the Iberian peninsula was launched. Round about AD 1000 a series of big churches was raised in Catalonia, which included the first fully vaulted buildings. The *Castle Church at Cardona [231]*, consecrated in 1040, has a barrel-vault supported on transverse arches over its nave and groined vaults over its aisles. There is also a clear, taut articulation of the powerful wall masses, which in their austere grandeur are in no way inferior to the Northern examples.

231 Castle church at Cardona (Catalonia), consecrated 1040. View of the northern transept. Nave and aisles are vaulted. Note the steep and narrow proportions and the strict arrangement of wall masses.

Germany

In the course of the political reorganization of the empire under its Saxon rulers (919–1024), and above all under Otto I, there was a tremendous upsurge in building activity. The new status of the bishops had much to do with this development. As princes of the Church on a level with the princes of the empire they came to be mainstays in the emperor's struggle against the temporal princes and in their efforts to obtain hereditary power for their families. Thus the bishops' churches – the cathedrals – whose importance in Carolingian times we know almost nothing about, now came into the picture far more, being on the same footing as the great monastery churches. These first cathedrals of the empire subsequently underwent such changes and renovations that at most only a few basic features and the measurements can still be inferred. These were taken over almost unaltered in the later buildings, as has been proved by excavations and the remains of such substructures in the cathedrals of Magdeburg, Worms, and Mainz. Not just the dimensions but also the essential form of the old plans has frequently survived, and it appears that there was a general preference for the two-chancel arrangement already in the Ottonian imperial cathedrals. With this, the tendency initiated in Carolingian times towards a disposition of two equivalent vertically ascending structural groups at the west and east ends of the church became a characteristic peculiarity of German architecture. There may have been liturgical reasons for such an arrangement of chancels at both ends, and the tradition existing in the German area may also have played a part *[cf. 216, 218]*, but beyond all this, it seems to have particularly suited German architectural thought at that time. For nowhere else saw the rise of these huge, mutually corresponding groups, whose unmistakable pattern contrasts fundamentally with the clear one-way flow of contemporary French buildings.

If, in accordance with the political trends, Ottonian architecture turned back to the Carolingian heritage, it made a deliberate selection from the many models then still to hand and refashioned them. Less important in this connexion are the various, and at times quite remarkable, centralized buildings descended from the Palatine Chapel at Aachen (Ottmarsheim in Alsace, chapel of the Valkhof at Nijmegen, western part of Essen Minster). More interesting is the further development of the westwork. A huge one *[232]* was built at the church of *S. Pantaleon at Cologne* (956–80), the city's first sizable ecclesiastic structure raised by Archbishop Bruno, brother of Otto I. The basic Carolingian model has been observed *[cf.*

232 Westwork of S. Pàntaleon, Cologne, consecrated 980. The structural elements are more differentiated than in the Carolingian period. Cornices, a frieze of rounded arches, and pilasters join together the separate forms and underline the tectonic unity.

216], but not only the richness of form (the towers, for example, are square at the base, then octagonal, and circular at the top) and the decorative articulation (pilasters and small round arches) are new, but also the firmer, clearly ordered composition and interrelation of these individual parts.

The territory of the Saxon dynasty achieved at this time a special importance comparable to that of Burgundy for France. It is here that the new architectural ideas seem to have crystallized. Essential parts of the church of *S. Cyriakus at Gernrode*, belonging to a nunnery founded in 961 by Margrave Gero, have survived unchanged, including the nave *[233]*. The tribunes, which in fact had no following on German soil at this period, are striking and novel. Their presence here can probably be accounted for by the use, Byzantine in origin, of this part of the building as a gallery for nuns or for women generally. The urge to rhythmize the nave walls makes itself felt, especially in the alternation of pillars and columns in the lower arcade.

What at Gernrode is still just hinted at appears fully developed in the most mature work of Ottonian architecture *[234–6]*, the church of the Benedictine monastery of *S. Michael at Hildesheim* (1001–33). The man who had it built was the extremely active Bishop Bernward, a champion of classical culture and well versed in all the arts. Despite some alterations and severe damage in the Second World War, the structure can still give us an idea of the feeling at the turn of the millennium. The systematic arrangement of the whole edifice was carried out even more logically here than in France, and the principle of the double chancel applied with a consistency hitherto unknown. This gave rise to a scheme which provided the model for the next two centuries. Its features can already be discerned in the ground-plan, where the squares produced by the intersection of an equally wide nave and transept at either crossing are not only the same size as each other but form the unit of measure for the pillar spacing in the nave. The new significance of the

233 Nunnery church of S. Cyriakus at Gernrode, c. 975 (the square arches are nineteenth century). View towards the east. The nave walls are harmonized by the alternation of pillars and columns in the lower arcade stories.

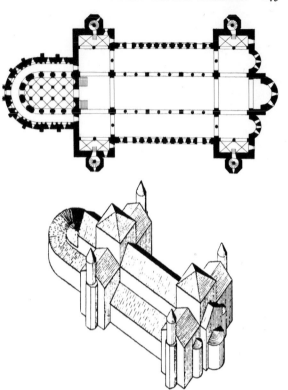

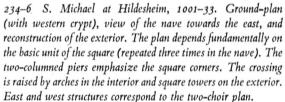

234-6 S. Michael at Hildesheim, 1001-33. Ground-plan (with western crypt), view of the nave towards the east, and reconstruction of the exterior. The plan depends fundamentally on the basic unit of the square (repeated three times in the nave). The two-columned piers emphasize the square corners. The crossing is raised by arches in the interior and square towers on the exterior. East and west structures correspond to the two-choir plan.

crossing is reflected within the space, as it is cut off evenly on all sides from nave and transept by great arches. This liturgically important part of the building is thus made to catch the eye. The square basic unit even affects the elevation of the nave wall, since the corners of the square are marked by heavy rectangular pillars, between which stand two columns.

When the crossing-square was taken as a basis for moulding ground-plan and elevation, the edifice at last acquired those exactly definable proportions that are a vital prerequisite in particular to the division of Romanesque vaulted buildings into bays. At Hildesheim itself, the principle of this so-called metrical system was not yet fully applied. The eastern extension of the chancel is too short, while the transept arms are oblong. But the rhythmic organization is clearly apparent, and the same effort to achieve an orderly combination of the structural parts also

governs the exterior with its richly articulated groups at the east and west ends. At Hildesheim, German architecture is on the threshold of Romanesque.

PAINTING

There is no doubt that early medieval churches, like their early Christian and Byzantine models, were adorned with extensive cycles of paintings. The themes of frescoes and mosaics, including the profane ones, have come down to us in the so-called *tituli* – verse or prose explanations of the picture subjects. Chroniclers tell us that along with Biblical scenes, the palaces contained representations of the emperor's campaigns. Of this early monumental painting only a few, widely scattered remains have survived, and they hardly permit of a stylistic classification. Only at Rome are there still a number of mosaics and frescoes, though they no more enable us to reach a final conclusion about the formal language of the court centres than the wall-paintings in the southern Tyrol (Mals, Naturns), Switzerland (Müstair in the Grisons), or France (Germigny-des-Prés) from Carolingian times. On the other hand the products of book illumination do acquaint us with this formal language and its evolution, and constitute the fullest

generatio

evidence of early medieval art. From the various monastery scriptoria in which the manuscripts were prepared, there have survived not just single volumes, but often whole sets, so that here one is less dependent on restorations and hypotheses than in the case of contemporary architecture.

The change from papyrus rolls to bound codices with parchment pages had occurred in early Christian times [167, 168]. Even the two basic patterns for representing Christian themes were already to hand: the narrative approach, with religious scenes illustrated often in a continuous sequence, and the more hieratically severe one, usually centring about Evangelist images modelled on the late antique author portraits. In its deliberate recourse to earlier examples, Carolingian illumination could draw stylistically on the whole range of late antique, early Christian, and Byzantine art, from the illusionistic conception realized by painterly means to stylizing abstraction. At the same time, the northern European elements became far more clearly apparent than in architecture. While Frankish book illumination from Merovingian times, with its fish and bird ornament, could still have an effect now and then, a more lasting influence was exerted by insular models, which were already much employed on the Continent in the early eighth century, thanks to the Irish and Anglo-Saxon mission. Ireland had been converted to Christianity by Coptic monks from Egypt as far back as the fifth century. Since there was no direct link with antiquity, the island never having been occupied by the Romans, the groundwork of the book art that flourished there from the seventh century lay in the native Celtic tradition, with its interlace, bird, and fish ornament, and in Syrian and Coptic forms. It was in Irish manuscripts that the opening letters at the start of the chapters were first developed into richly adorned whole-page initials, with twining, knotting, and often whorled ornaments, as in the *Book of Kells*, from the beginning of the eighth century [237]. Even the human figure was redeveloped as a decorative and planar object, and a movement of endless ribbon interlace became the dominant feature as in the Crucifixion from a *Gospel book* at *St Gall* [238]. Made at about 750, this was probably brought by Irish monks from their homeland to the monastery they had founded.

238 Crucifixion, from an Irish Gospel book in St Gall, c. 750. St Gall, Stiftsbibliothek. Even the human form is seen as a surface ornament. Christ is clothed in a long robe, after Syrian models, which is transformed into border ornament.

237 First page of the Book of Kells, beginning of eighth century. Dublin, Trinity College. A masterpiece of Irish manuscript illumination. Letters and ornament are developed together into a closed surface. Note the richness of form of the animal interlace motifs.

Carolingian illumination

It was these insular tendencies that first prevailed in Carolingian book illumination; but early Christian and Byzantine models soon came to the fore, affecting the work of the different scriptoria more and more strongly. The scriptoria cannot always be precisely located, and we must make do with the designation 'school'. One of the most important schools, which probably had its home at Trier and worked mainly for the court, is grouped about the so-called Ada Manuscript, a Gospel book presented by a certain Ada – probably a sister of the emperor – to the monastery of St Maximin at Trier shortly before 800. At the heart of the figure scenes are the Evangelist pictures [211]. The style is resplendent and radiantly colourful, but linear and ornamental in its general

239   The Four Evangelists, from the Aachen Gospels, Reims school, beginning of ninth century. Aachen, Cathedral Treasure. Strongly antiquitizing style. The landscape, full of atmosphere, is briefly sketched. Note the painterly modelling and differentiation of forms, and the expressiveness of clothing and posture.

240   Psalm illustration from the Utrecht Psalter, Reims school, c. 820. Utrecht, University Library. Pen drawing sketched in a spontaneous narrative style. The animated figures are held together in a dynamic grouping.

effect. A rich stock of decorative forms not only overspreads the throne and framing architecture, but also governs the very stylized rendering of the drapery. The expressive face has been defined by means of a few sure lines, and the hand raised with the quill is portrayed likewise in a confident gesture. This bold, monumental picture style occupies a correspondingly ample format ($14\frac{1}{8}$ by $9\frac{1}{2}$ inches).

In the strongest contrast to the hieratic appearance of the Ada school Evangelists and to their more linear and planar conception are the works of the Reims school, active round about 800. From Reims come the Purple Gospels of the Vienna Treasury, on which the German kings swore their coronation oath, as well as the *Aachen Gospels [239]*. The Evangelists are not enthroned separately in a richly fashioned architectural setting here. Instead, all four of them have been placed in a painterly, almost impressionistic manner within one tersely suggested landscape, which may bring to mind late antique representations conceived wholly in terms of atmosphere. Luminance and shadow, light and dark bring the forms into being. Yet an inner restlessness is apparent, especially noticeable in the agitated treatment of the drapery and the striking poses of the Evangelists. The tendency towards an expressive exaggeration in the figure may be regarded as a distinguishing feature of the Reims school. In the *Utrecht Psalter [240]*, written about 820, the exaggeration almost becomes edginess. This codex contains the richest surviving picture cycle of its times. An extremely spontaneous calligraphy, which only makes use of pen drawing here, furnishes the Psalms with illustrations in an enthusiastically narrative manner that follows the text word for word. The episodes are strung out like a frieze, with the animated figures held together in a rhythmic grouping.

Though further stylistic elements can be seen in each of the other Carolingian schools – at Tours, St-Denis, Metz, and St Gall – we have characterized the two most important trends in the Ada group and the Reims school which also provided the models for subsequent developments in the ninth century.

Ottonian illumination

As with architecture, the late ninth and early tenth centuries brought a certain decline in the vigour of book illumination. Only from 950 onwards were there outstanding achievements again, especially in Germany. But in England, too, one can observe a new flowering of pictorial creation, represented by among others, the manuscripts of the Winchester school. Its masterpieces include a liturgical service

Cologne, Regensburg, and the island of Reichenau richly adorned manuscripts were produced, especially the Gospel books of the Ottonian rulers and bishops. The choicest and most important works come from the monasteries on Reichenau, where one of the few remaining, and probably most informative, examples of tenth-century German monumental painting is to be found. Although the nave frescoes of S. Georg at Oberzell *[220]*, with their representation of Christ's miracles, are highly instructive in their present state when viewed in the original, only the broad features of the composition can be seen when they are reproduced. Moreover, they, too, are clearly dependent on book illumination, whose surviving statements are thus better able to reveal the trends of the period.

Ottonian illumination also turned to foreign models, for at the time of its heyday – during the second half of the tenth century – the native tradition was almost exhausted. Late antique examples were

242 The Evangelist Luke, from the Bamberg Gospel book of Otto III, end of tenth century. Munich, Staatsbibliothek. One of the finest works of the Reichenau school. A strict composition in circular and oval shapes, with emphasis on gestures and features (widely opened eyes). A remarkable visualization of divine inspiration.

241 Ascension, from the Benedictional of Bishop Aethelwold, c. 980. London, British Museum. English miniature work of the Winchester school. The many figures fill the whole picture surface with their swirling, entangled forms.

book containing benedictions for episcopal use, the *Benedictional of Aethelwold* (*c.* 980). In the many-figured scene of the Ascension *[241]*, the dependence on Carolingian examples, such as the agitated drawing style of the Reims school, is unmistakable, and the classicizing acanthus foliage of the frame also points back to continental models. Nevertheless the Irish Celtic heritage speaks out clearly in the inter-flowing composition and in the exuberant entangle-ment of figural and decorative motifs.

Compared with this swirling imagery, which for all the expressiveness of its figures is still at bottom pre-dominantly ornamental, German Ottonian illumina-tion developed into a no less eloquent but extremely restrained language of gesture. The Ottonian flower-ing of art is also referred to as a renaissance, but it differs in essential respects from the Carolingian one for instead of being centrally directed, it grew spontaneously and at the same time from different centres. In the monastery schools of Echternach,

243   The Angel throwing the Millstone into the Sea, from the Bamberg Apocalypse of Henry II, Reichenau school, c. 1020. Bamberg, Staatliches Bibliothek. Expressively heightened but severely disciplined forms. Colours are used symbolically to distinguish the three areas: earth, air, and firmament.

surrounded by an almond-shaped glory (mandorla). With his raised arms he holds up more glories, which contain his special sign as well as prophets and angels. Tongues of flame symbolizing divine power and inspiration dart out of these mandorlas. At the Evangelist's feet animals drink from the fountain of life. The Carolingian prototype, whose monumentality in the last analysis is based more on formal qualities, has been heightened to an intensely expressive inward grandeur. With its image of the emperor and twenty-nine scenes from the life of Christ, this work produced at the end of the tenth century contains one of the largest and artistically most significant Christian picture cycles of its times.

Given this formal language, it was now possible to render such an abstract and visionary theme as the Revelation of St John. In the *Bamberg Apocalypse* of Henry II (*c.* 1020), and with extreme conciseness and the utmost restraint of gesture, the hereafter is presented in the strictest sense of the word 'present'. The

244   Jesus calming the Storm on the Sea of Galilee, from a Cologne Gospel book (the so-called Hitda Codex), first quarter of eleventh century. Darmstadt, Landesbibliothek. An example of the painterly and expressive style of the Cologne school, showing the strongly marked delineation and spontaneous approach.

used less frequently than Carolingian or Byzantine works. What is unique in Ottonian illustration is the conversion of these into a disciplined yet expressive formal language endowed with the utmost spirituality, this being a trait that certainly relates Ottonian to Byzantine art. The Evangelist pictures of the *Bamberg Gospels [242]* rightly count among the grandest pictorial embodiments of divine inspiration in the whole of Western art. When they are compared with those of the Carolingian Ada group *[211]*, on which the Reichenau school partly depends, the fundamental change becomes apparent. The framing, with its arch on columns, has been taken over, as have the fine-structured and still more minutely observed decorative motifs, down to the two birds in the upper corners of the picture. The Bamberg Evangelist himself is no longer set in an elaborate throne construction, but floats in a transcendental region. His form, highly expressive despite its rigour, with eloquent face and wide-open visionary eyes, is special status of the book during the early Middle Ages, its holiness as the bearer of God's word, is nowhere else more clearly evident. The religious visions are fully supernaturalized, while the suggestion of space in the picture is correspondingly reduced to a minimum. In the image of the Angel with the millstone *[243]*, three horizontal, differently coloured zones indicate the division into earth, air, and celestial region. This means that the colour hardly serves any longer to represent material qualities, being now of a mainly symbolic character. The detail, especially in the figure, is closely determined by the line, which fixes the contours and articulates the surface; but surface and line are always subordinated to the will to make the theme still more expressive.

In the works of the Cologne school, which have livelier compositions that link up more closely with the Carolingian book illumination of Reims, the colour values are given an entirely planar and expressive interpretation. The scene of the Storm on the Sea of Galilee *[244]* from the *Hitda Codex* (first quarter of eleventh century) is undoubtedly more spontaneous than the Reichenau paintings in the energetic, bird-like form of the ship with its fluttering sail, in the broadly painted crests of the waves, and in the more folkish characterizing of the heads. But for all its animation it does not attain to the same majesty and grandeur. The severe Reichenau style contains far more points of departure for Romanesque painting.

245 *Bronze equestrian statue (perhaps of Charlemagne), c. 870. Paris, Louvre. Modelled after the examples of antique equestrian statues, this is a symbol of imperial power and dignity rather than a portrait.*

SCULPTURE

Carolingian ivory and gold work

Although the Iconoclastic Controversy (cf. p. 109) which had such important consequences for Byzantine art during the eighth century, was settled for a while in favour of image worship by the Second Council of Nicaea in 787, it was not without effect on Carolingian art. Charlemagne, in the *Libri Carolini*, took the view that while the worship of images should indeed be condemned as idolatry, their destruction was just as reprehensible. The cult image was thus rejected, but the representation of Biblical events continued to find approval, especially for its educational value. This meant that the development of sculpture, particularly free-standing sculpture, was severely limited from the outset. When sculpture did appear, it was either in church buildings, on for example bordering friezes and capitals, or else to such church furnishings as pulpits, altar-rails, and altars with their columned superstructures (ciboria). It could also be used on movable objects such as candlesticks, chalices, or the increasingly common reliquaries, and not least on the covers of manuscripts. The technique that offered itself here was relief, which had more and more overshadowed free-standing sculpture even in late antique times. Free-standing sculpture still remained a possibility under Charlemagne, for a gilt equestrian statue of Theodoric from Ravenna is said to have stood in the court of Aachen Minster. This is generally thought to have been the model for the small *bronze equestrian statue* in the Louvre *[245]*, whose rider may be Charlemagne. But the date (*c.* 870), well after the emperor's death, and also the particular attitude of the age towards the individual, stop us from looking for portrait elements in the figure. It is not a likeness but an antique-type symbol of the ruler, stressing in particular his office and dignity. This kind of representation appeared only infrequently during the early Middle Ages.

In the Carolingian period, the trends of sculpture were expressed almost exclusively through the small ivory or metal bas-reliefs, and both these techniques served chiefly to adorn the richly ornamented book-cover. Ivory-carving not only enjoyed great popularity during Roman times but was widespread in early Christian and Byzantine art also [cf. *133*]. It was from the Byzantine region that important stimuli now came, and one often meets on bindings from still later periods Byzantine originals set in the decorative

246   Christ, centre part of an ivory diptych from Lorsch, Ada school, first half of ninth century. The Vatican, Museums and Galleries. Antiquitizing, linear style on a shallow relief. Note the solemnly hieratic frontality of the figure.

forms of an artistic language that is partly foreign. Broadly speaking, the style of Carolingian reliefs corresponds to the tendencies of the different schools of painting, since they probably came from the same workshops as the manuscripts.

The earliest works have been associated with the Ada school [*211*], and the cover of the *Lorsch Gospels* [*246*] is able to confirm this link. In both cases we find a measured sculptural style that creates a solemn and impressive effect; and the close relationship is conveyed especially clearly by the planar composition of lines in the drapery, thanks to which the ivory panel seems almost like a painting converted into an extremely shallow relief.

From this hieratic, rather stiff trend, that of a west Frankish group depending on the lively figure style of the Reims school can be distinguished. It includes one of the most outstanding examples of Carolingian goldsmith's work, the binding of the *Codex Aureus* (*c.* 870) *from S. Emmeram, Regensburg*, which was probably written at Reims for Charles the Bald [*247*]. Embossed in thin plate of gold, the reliefs are surrounded by an extremely sumptuous frame adorned with gems of many colours and with pearls. Germanic affection and talent for works of this kind in precious metal are undoubtedly operative here, but they are

the oldest surviving examples, the early eleventh-century *Madonna* from the Treasury of Essen Minster *[249]*, the link with decorative art is still clear, since the fascination of gold as a precious material, apart from its symbolic significance, obviously contributes to the effect. The thin, gleaming skin of the metal has

249 Madonna, beginning of eleventh century. Essen, Cathedral Treasury. Wooden core with gilded silver-leaf (crown and orb are twelfth/thirteenth century additions). One of the earliest examples of a three-dimensional image of the Mother of God. The simple bodily forms are in strong contrast to Carolingian models. The precious material has the effect of distancing the spectator.

247, 248 Christ enthroned with the Evangelists and scenes from the life of Christ, cover binding of the Codex Aureus from St Emmeram, embossed in gold-leaf, set with precious stones; Reims school, c. 870. Munich, Staatsbibliothek. An outstanding example of Carolingian goldsmith's work. Clearly articulated structure in decorated spaces and raised picture field. The scenes show the agitated, expressive figural style of the Reims school [240]; our example [248] is of Christ and the Woman Taken in Adultery. The figure of Christ is rendered in high-arched relief, with large, weak forms.

joined by a new feeling for clear, almost architectural organization. Generally still alien to the Germans, the figural element now comes strongly to the fore. In the *Codex Aureus [248]* there are distinct echoes of the little figures from the Utrecht Psalter, with their agitated movements. Nevertheless the Christ of the central field, solemnly enthroned within two glories, already suggests the formal idiom of Ottonian art. The only indications of the body are a few large, roughly oval, forms in a flat, soft modelling, washed by the drapery's play of lines.

Ottonian sculpture

Ivory and gold are also among the principal materials of Ottonian decorative art. By the beginning of the eleventh century the views on the significance of the religious image set forth in the *Libri Carolini* had altered so much that free-standing works could now be executed. The widespread cult of relics certainly helped to bring about this change, for the earliest sculptures done in the round, which were placed over the altars or carried in processions, contained relics. They were therefore consecrated statues and not just devotional images as in later periods. Along with carvings of Christ on the Cross, figures of the Virgin increasingly became objects of adoration. In one of

been laid over a wooden core, and the eyes are picked out colourfully in cloisonné enamel. The bearing of the figure is majestic and the distance of the divine image from the spectator underlined. The delicate crimping of the drapery follows the body's large, soft forms, and resembles that of the enthroned Christ on the St Emmeram book-cover, or a three-dimensional translation of a bas-relief. Sculpture with the naturalistic quality of antique works could not appear in an age whose highest aim was the fully spiritualized portrayal of divine and supernatural figures or events.

In the *Gero Cross* (*c.* 970), Cologne Cathedral possesses one of the oldest representations of the crucified Christ visible from all sides *[250]*. The figure has been carved life-size in oak and is painted, although no longer now as at first. This immensely expressive work marks a trend towards a more 'passionately dramatic characterization' in the portrayal of Christ on the Cross, as against that of an 'aristocratic composure' (Hamann). 'Passionately

250 *The Gero Cross, crucifix in Cologne Cathedral, c. 970. Wood (the figure restored). Early example of a three-dimensional life-size crucifix. A strongly emotional representation (features of suffering shown on the face, and position of the head and body). Despite realistic details the form is predominantly abstract.*

dramatic', however, implies, not restless, nervous movement but controlled emotion. While the head of the dead Saviour is tilted to the side and conveys extreme suffering, his trunk hangs limply on the Cross, hardly supported by his bent legs. The forms of the body are broadly conceived and softly modelled, but with sinewy transitions on the knees and arms that make the painful stretching clear. In the more abstract and linear treatment of the flowing locks and elaborately knotted loin-cloth, the decorative element comes into play, though here it is entirely devoted to heightening the expression.

German bronze doors

This desire to let the body become the vehicle of expression is apparent throughout Ottonian art, and it has been embodied in an almost unique way in the bronze doors of Hildesheim Cathedral. The antique technique of bronze-casting was already practised during Carolingian times, and from the Aachen foundry came among other works the screens and doors of the Palatine Chapel. These, it is true, were still entirely without figure decoration. Besides these two doors, the richly figured casts of a column of Christ with a spiral frieze modelled after Trajan's Column were produced in the early eleventh century in the bronze workshop started at Hildesheim by Bishop Bernward, who was also very active as a builder. Originally meant for the church of *S. Michael at Hildesheim*, the casts were completed in 1015, according to the inscription *[251]*. Both were cast in one piece, and on eight superimposed fields they tell the Creation story as far as the murder of Abel to the left, and to the right, that of Christ's life and Passion. There is a deliberate antithesis, with the Fall, say, opposed by the Crucifixion as the deliverance from sin. Beyond this, the portrayals on the individual doors have been arranged as regards theme in groups of four, so that there is a rich, numerically expressible interrelating of scenes that has its counterpart in the clearly thought-out system of proportions at S. Michael's. Whereas the border images and also the compositions within the relief panels go back to Carolingian illustrated Bibles, this systematic arrangement is something new. So also is the relief style, especially with regard to the figures. Instead of what until now have been the two principal ways of representing the human form in relief – the planar, linear conception of the Ada school on the one hand and the agitated figure style of west Frankish workshops on the other – a clear concentration on moulding the figures plastically and forming their eloquent

251 Bronze doors of Hildesheim Cathedral (once intended for church of St Michael there), 1015. Both doors were cast in one piece. The eight fields on each, with representations of the Old Testament (left) and New (right) respectively, are related to one another in theme. The forms are in part three-dimensional (heads) on the shallow relief of the picture space.

252 Adam and Eve, detail from one of the picture fields of the Hildesheim bronze doors. The features display a new corporality in their sharply defined form, though they serve to express gestures rather than to portray reality.

gestures is evident here. Everything secondary, like vegetation and architecture, has its proper place in the composition, but remains imprisoned by the relief ground. The figures, on the contrary, are almost in the round, and their heads, completely freed from the surface, seem to lunge out of the panel. The germ of true plasticity is apparent, but the relation between ground and figure remains undefined, the scenes still occurring in a transcendental pictorial field. Even though the rendering of the bodily forms [252], akin to those of the Gero Cross,

may seem awkward, it reveals an independent power of invention and expression that is less concerned with the naturalistic detail than with the terse, eloquent, and gripping pictorialization of the Bible scenes.

The style of the Hildesheim doors stands almost alone in its period. Only Italy and Spain, during the late eleventh century, can show similar new creations. Despite its efforts to achieve overriding principles, the style of Ottonian art was still heterogeneous. Besides the realistic and strongly expressive trend there was a hieratic, solemn one and a third that

253   Old Testament and allegorical representations from the bronze doors of Augsburg Cathedral, c. 1015. Detail. The panels were separately cast and placed together. Close dependence on antique style and themes (Hercules; centaurs). Decorative effect of the motifs in the picture spaces.

kept especially firmly to antique forms and subjects. The latter appears on *Augsburg Cathedral's bronze doors [253]*, almost contemporary to those at Hildesheim. At Augsburg, separate rectangular panels of greater height than width were attached to a wooden core, though today they are no longer in the right order. Notwithstanding the high quality of the detail, the general effect is strongly decorative and lacks the vitality of the Hildesheim work. In low relief, the panels show representations of the months, antique motifs (Hercules, centaurs), and Bible figures. The style has a *mouvementé* elegance, and, as at Hildesheim, there is no real contemporary parallel in the North.

Late Ottonian works are generally more inclined to follow the trend represented by the Reichenau school. The *Basle Antependium*, a gold altar frontal produced about 1020 and given by Henry II to Basle Cathedral *[254]*, shows a strengthening of the hieratic severity of form and attitude, perhaps under renewed influence from Byzantine models. Surrounded by three Archangels and St Benedict, Christ appears in the central, heightened arch, with the orbis terrarum in his left hand. According to the 'significance criterion', the imperial donors who kneel at his feet are tiny. The heads and bodies of the large figures

254   Christ between Archangels and St Benedict, the so-called Basle Antependium (altar frontal), probably Reichenau work, c. 1020. Paris, Musée de Cluny. Gold-leaf applied to cedar wood. Solemn figures in strengthened forms and powerfully defined relief.

swell out from the surface, an extremely restrained and orderly play of lines flowing over their forms. This solemn and severe sculptural idiom signifies the point of departure for Romanesque statuary.

Architectural sculpture

Even if works of decorative art and bronze-casting, together with the few surviving individual statues, throw most light on the tendencies of early medieval sculpture, new possibilities foreshadowing Romanesque are more than once hinted at in architectural sculpture also. Already early on, capital ornament came to adopt elaborate forms, in which stylized antique foliage was sometimes combined with Germanic interlace motifs. A special place is taken by the Ottonian cushion (block) capital, whose oldest examples can be seen in the church of *S. Michael at Hildesheim [234]*. As a blending of sphere and cube, it forms the transition from round column to rectangular impost with a tectonic clarity that corresponds to the rational organization of the building as a whole, and was also active as a model in Romanesque architecture.

255 Christ enthroned between Apostles on the lintel of St-Genis-des-Fontaines (Pyrenees), c. 1020. The earliest example of figural decoration on a church portal. Antique chip-carving technique.

In Visigothic Spain and the Pyrenees, and in central France as well, the first attempts were made at decorating the capital with figure scenes. From here it was only a step, though a huge one, to putting representations from the Bible on the church exterior. The lintel *[255]* over the portal of *St-Genis-des-Fontaines* (Pyrenees) is the oldest surviving example of this (*c.* 1020). Christ appears enthroned in a mandorla held by angels, while to his left and right groups of three Apostles stand within the arches of an arcade. Compared, say, to the extremely high-quality work of the *Basle Antependium*, the treatment of this stone relief, with its planar, ornamental chip-carving technique, may seem old-fashioned. More significant here than the planar style is the setting of this relief above a portal, and thus in the place that was to have particular importance in the development of French Romanesque sculpture.

Until the start of the nineteenth century, it was usual to designate Western art of the centuries preceding Gothic as pre-Gothic, early German, or even Byzantine and neo-Greek. The term 'Romanesque' first appeared round about 1820 in French art literature in connexion with the architecture of this art period that gradually impressed itself on the historian's mind. In virtue of the correct observation that several of its features (e.g. round arch and column) are traceable to Roman building, and under the inspiration of the term 'Romanesque languages', which was then already current in philology, 'Romanesque architecture' was used to denote a stylistic concept that quickly spread and was finally extended to the other categories of art also. Today, however, historical restrictions are imposed, for it is no longer applied to the whole of the first phase of Western art, whose beginning coincided with the rise of the Carolingian empire and whose end was marked by the emergence of Gothic. True, this age's unity is still recognized as regards historical development; but the signs of a common 'Romanesque' style embracing all Europe did not appear until about 1050.

The Romanesque meant a new beginning for Western art. It united the different starts of the early Middle Ages and, drawing on inner strength, found a compelling language of its own in every field. Nevertheless its style remained complex, being made up of many regional components and therein reflecting the political dismemberment of the various countries, which only slowly welded themselves into an integrated whole. The normative power of the Gothic cathedral, which gave European art a supranational cast, was still denied to the Romanesque church. Its outward features can be comprehended no more in one universal basic type than those of sculpture and painting. Whereas the forms of later styles – Gothic, Renaissance, Baroque – evolved within the limits of a region, indeed of a particular locality – the Île-de-France, Florence, Rome – Romanesque is only revealed by viewing all its diverse regional expressions together. To understand

it, one must always seek for the motives and forces that brought it into being; for no period is as clearly imbued as the Romanesque with pious and deeply felt conceptions of the other world.

At the time of the far-reaching monastic reform movements, of the great pilgrimages, and of the Crusades, the entire West was seized by a new, almost passionate outburst of religious activity that included all classes and conditions. Even if Church and temporal rulers, as the main supports of the development, were increasingly led by considerations of power politics – as the conflict between pope and emperor that broke out after the mid-eleventh century clearly shows – this made little difference to what Romanesque art regarded as its main concern. Instead of being merely a meeting-place for clergy and congregation, the sacred building was to convey in all its parts the meaning of the Christian message of salvation and, as a whole, present the faithful in a concrete and vivid way with an image of that 'heavenly Jerusalem' which represents the kingdom of God. Every kind of art helped to produce this edifice, but architecture had the central role, with the other arts subservient to it. In keeping with the Church's firm resolve to hold its own, it now turned to the exterior, which early Christian art had mostly seen only as an undecorated shell for the richly adorned interior. Thus, combined with the preliminary works of the early Middle Ages, complex structures crowned with towers arose, their huge stone masses rising high above the small, usually wooden, secular buildings. Figure sculpture, which hitherto had played almost no part except in the minor arts and sporadically on capitals and friezes, now had the same status as painting – it seems indeed to have eclipsed the latter slightly. Figures reached life-size, while the range of subjects increased notably and gradually coalesced into a synopsis of medieval ideas about the beyond. More and more frequently, the representations, all of which were concerned with the redemption of man, centred round the Last Judgment. Besides divine and holy beings, the elaborately graded hierarchy of this world of figures included men, beasts, and a host of demons in numerous forms. Such portrayals of evil were not intended simply to warn the faithful of the Devil's might, but also to protect the sacred edifice, through exorcizing magic, from the onslaught of hostile powers. Even if the many layers of meaning in these

256   Monastery church of Murbach in Alsace, c. 1150. Only the eastern section remains. Romanesque characteristics are evident in the additive joining of single parts to the monumental group, and in the plastic effect of the heavy walls (frieze, blind arches, and galleries).

images only reveal themselves to close scholarly investigation, their formal aspect calls for sympathetic insight on the part of the modern spectator. It was the art of the Expressionists, with its particular emphasis, that first opened our eyes to the expressive power of Romanesque sculpture. Apart from those of the late phase, in which the trends leading to Gothic are already discernible, the figures should never be assessed by present criteria. Men's attitude then towards another world that, cut off by an unbridgeable gulf from this one, allowed no personal approach to it, ruled out realistic portrayal from the start. Thus it is hardly a question of inability but of inner necessity if the human images of this age confront us with block-like stiffness, or with bodily movements that are a frank negation of organic form. Behind every pictorial work lies the transcendentalizing power of abstraction.

The beginnings of what we oppose as typically 'Romanesque' to the various tendencies of the early Middle Ages can already be observed at about the turn of the millennium. Around that time there was an increase of activity in architecture almost without parallel before or after. The main sources of energy were the monastic movements, and above all that of the influential reformed Order of the Cluniacs, with its home in Burgundy. 'It was as if the world renewed itself, cast off the old, and spread a glittering robe of churches over everything', wrote the Cluniac monk Raoul Glaber in his chronicle for the year 1003. The architectural forms of early Romanesque found their purest expression in France and Germany. Here, towards 1050, there arose buildings characterized not only by their imposing dimensions, carefully thought-out ground-plan, and neat ashlar masonry, but also by their massive and severe overall effect. They are based on a clear interrelating of the different structural masses as well as on a discreet articulation of the surfaces. Inside, apart from the opening-up of the walls with tribunes and other galleries, it was in particular the vaulting over of the entire space that was embarked upon. In setting this technical problem a part may have been played by the thought that a rising vault seemed a more appropriate crowning terminal for the 'heavenly Jerusalem' than the hitherto usual flat ceiling.

As regards development, the other European regions are less important than the two countries that were the source of Romanesque, a fact that has a mainly political explanation. Spain held a central position between East and West. Its northern part had clear links with south-west France, with which it still formed a cultural whole. Although English art had been included in Western developments since the Norman Conquest, its long continuing stylistic dependence on Normandy cannot escape notice. In grappling with antique, Byzantine, and, in the south, Islamic and Norman influences, Italy arrived at very independent and protean forms of Romanesque, which in some ways seem rather backward, but in others already foreshadowed the Renaissance.

When by about 1100 all the regions of Europe had evolved their own local types of building with various spatial schemes, there began a second phase of Romanesque, which focused chiefly on the vaulting and on the plastic diversification of the structural body. The mighty wall masses were split up into courses, and within, were increasingly hollowed out with galleries, triforia, and tribunes. At every opening in the exterior, by widows, by doorways, and on façades, decorative forms were planted, seeming almost to grow out of the substance of the masonry. Now began the period of large-scale sculpture which in France, northern Spain, and upper Italy developed in direct connexion with the structure, whereas Germany produced mainly individual free-standing works. This second, high Romanesque phase brought forth abstracting and symbolic images in which the figures stiffen into blocks or are possessed by the supple movement of ultra-slender limbs.

In the mid-twelfth century, a fundamental change of style commenced in every field of Romanesque art. Architecturally, it took clear and unmistakable shape in the first buildings to introduce Gothic. They rose in the Île-de-France, which now also came to the fore politically. The efforts of other French areas leading towards the framework building were logically summarized in the Île-de-France. The rest of Europe still remained tied to the Romanesque mass building, which entered a late, chiefly decorative phase. Now that the hieratic severity of the early period had already been toned down with ornamental features in high Romanesque, a fondness for rich, sometimes almost showy, appearances was asserted. The motive forces behind these changes revealed themselves in imagery, which now often reflected an attempt to reduce the deep chasm between this and the other world by a portrayal of man based on more mundane models. This new picture of man had its origin in the system of knighthood, which gained in political importance at the time of the Crusades. The 'Christian knight' came to embody a Western attitude of mind, to be an ideal that seemed even worthy to represent all Christian figures. This radical change was a sign of the Gothic spirit, whose cultural expressions everywhere gave evidence of man's new approach to worldly and religious things.

Architecture

At the centre of Romanesque artistic activity stood the church. There were indeed corresponding achievements in the temporal sphere, but secular building still lacked the independence to create a style. This age's endeavours found their purest expression in the sacred building, and the visual arts were made subservient to it.

After the troubles of the 'dark' tenth century, a lively upsurge in building activity began round about the turn of the millennium in Germany and France, and during the eleventh century also seized England, Italy, and Spain. In every land people now set about the new architectural tasks, which meant that the same problems were posed almost universally: the house of God should not only accommodate a large congregation, but also the numerous clergy, and, on top of this, meet the requirements of the relic cult and the processions of pilgrims. These problems were solved differently in each particular art centre – with novel and progressive ideas or through a continuation of earlier traditions – but there was nevertheless a more or less clear expression of similar trends which for the first time gave the West a stylistic unity across the boundaries of the regional schools of architecture.

If one asks about the features of this common style limitations of time and place must be made; for these traits appeared earliest and at their most pure in Germany and France, whereas the other countries either stood in clear dependence on one of these areas – for instance England on Normandy and Spain on south-west France – or else evolved, like Italy – special forms in which the language of the style comes through greatly modified.

A time sequence has been indicated. Germany and France are the sources of early Romanesque, where the new trends had already become apparent just after the turn of the millennium. In Lower Saxony there was a consistent development of the ground-plan according to the metrical system and, linked up with this, the alternation of supports [cf. 234, 235]; in Burgundy, the east-end solution of an apse with ambulatory and the opening-up of the nave wall by means of tribunes [cf. 229, 230]. The appearance of the exterior was often determined by equivalent structural groups to east and west in Germany, and by an elaborate stepping of the chancel components in France. It was on these groundworks that Romanesque church buildings rose, now more firmly and plastically organized outside, with connective and embracing forms contributing to this effect [257].

257 Monastery church of Maria Laach, begun 1093. The western choir was consecrated 1156, the atrium 1220–30. View from the north–west. The two-choired completely vaulted structure foreshadows the principles of the German high Romanesque. Overall arrangement of clearly articulated forms.

258 East choir of Mainz Cathedral, completed c. 1135. Plastic definition of exterior structure. Steeped arches surround the apsidal windows; above them the dwarf gallery with its round-arched arcades in the hollows. Note the step-wise niches on the gable. The pilasters and round-arched frieze are the principal elements of the decorative formal vocabulary.

Embracement by means of round arches is an essential feature of Romanesque: in all parts of the building smaller arches, linked or ranged, are encompassed by bigger ones. Other such features are the breaking up of the wall through blind arcades and rows of columns reaching step-wise into depth, its excavation by large window openings and galleries, and the division of its thickness into separate layers, often through the use of little round-arch arcades known as dwarf galleries [258].

Apart from this thorough plastic structuring of the inner and outer walls, the main concern of Romanesque architecture was to vault the entire church. This is also its most notable achievement. It marks a second phase, which took up the first half of the twelfth century. The initial experiments, which can be shown to have occurred at about the same time

259   *Monastery church of Ste-Madeleine at Vézelay, 1120–40; the choir dates from the beginning of thirteenth century. View of the interior towards the east. A vaulted structure of the Burgundian high Romanesque. The nave consists of a row of separate bays with cross-ribbed vaults. The structurally important elements are emphasized: piers and their bases, on which the vaulted bands rest. The changing colours of the stone introduce a lively accent.*

but independently in France and Germany, date from as early as the closing years of the eleventh century. Then, after 1100, churches sprang up in every land with barrel-, groined-, and even rib-vaults. It should be clear that this innovation was not adopted just for practical reasons, such as reducing the risk of fire. The vaulting over the nave may be regarded as a form of embracement transferred to the realm of space, especially when a clear division of the vaulting into bays was aimed at. In the most progressive vaulted structures there is an evident determination to cut the nave up into a series of vertical sections, of like compartments clearly marked off on all sides by strong piers, by wall shafts, and by transverse arches in the vaulting [259]. This is an additive and at the same time space-clamping principle far removed from the unaccented flow of early Christian basilicas. Admittedly, flat ceilings were still often used; but the future belonged to the vaulted building, to the plastic emphasis of those parts of the wall that climb aloft as lines of force, and in whose structure their task of supporting the vault is plainly expressed. Beginning in Normandy, this development was completed in the first Gothic buildings of the Île-de-France, and therewith the Romanesque period came to an end in northern France. But the remainder of the West was held fast until into the thirteenth century by a late Romanesque style that produced no new spatial forms but aimed at decorative enrichment or carried further the modelling of the wall substance.

GERMANY

Until the collapse of Hohenstaufen rule in 1256 the German empire formed the centre of the West, its sphere of power including large parts of Italy and, to the east, reaching across the Elbe. Even afterwards it remained in principle the Holy Empire of the Ottonians, a unity of temporal power and Christian faith. There is evidence of the still enduring strength of this unity in the first big buildings of the Salian emperors, most notably Speyer Cathedral. The efforts at monastic reform which had been radiating from Cluny in Burgundy ever since the late tenth century were also approved and supported by the imperial authority in Germany. Not until the mid-eleventh century, when as a result of Cluniac reform the papacy confronted the secular rulers with a new claim to power, did the unity of Church and empire break. It was above all the emperor's right to appoint bishops that sparked off this struggle for power (Investiture Contest), which continued till the decline of both empire and Church.

Salian architecture

The Contest was not without effects on architecture, whose phases coincided with the reigns of the Salian and Hohenstaufen monarchs. In line with the Cluniac movement, the first large Salian buildings were of an austere and solemn monumentality, with the eastward flow more strongly emphasized again inside. From the late eleventh century, the development forked: beside the ascetically severe, unvaulted, and sternly ordered reformed churches imitating the Black Forest monastery of Hirsau, a daughterhouse of Cluny, there sprang up in deliberate contrast the great cathedrals and unreformed houses in an imposing 'empire' style, with bold vaulting, complex tower groups, and rich architectural decoration. In the Hohenstaufen buildings of the twelfth and thirteenth centuries tendencies towards intricate forms become apparent: there was a revival of the double-chancel scheme and of centralizing notions, but above all a huge delight in ornament, indulged with especial freedom on the exterior. During the ultimate phase of German Romanesque, in the first half of the thirteenth century, the big cathedrals – Speyer, Mainz, Worms, Bamberg, Naumburg – acquired their present appearance, partly through the continued use of considerable portions of older structures. Germany thus held fast to the Romanesque tradition at a time when France was already building Gothic cathedrals.

261 *Speyer Cathedral, 1030–61. Reconstruction of the nave of the early Salic foundation: the most important example of early German Romanesque. Arcades and windows are enclosed in narrow perpendicular arches that divide up the wall into components of equal space.*

260 *Monastery church of Hersfeld, 1037–1144, in ruins since 1761. View of the transept and choir. The monumental quality of early German Romanesque is evident in the skeleton of the main walls. The space surfaces are clearly articulated.*

Of the large edifices from early Salian times, two of the most important have survived only as ruins, namely the abbey churches at *Hersfeld*, built between 1037 and 1144 *[260]* and Limburg an der Hardt (1025–45). The plain, grave language, with its sense of proportion and dignity, can still be detected in the ruined walls. If one disregards the later alterations, this early Romanesque style is also clearly displayed by *Speyer Cathedral*, dating from 1030 to 1061 *[263]*. With the new imperially monumental scale is combined an execution of the highest quality, above all in the confidently formed ashlar masonry. The restoration *[261]* of this first building founded by Conrad II shows the new conception of the interior. Mighty pillared arcades lead towards the chancel, but the pulsing of the arches is not, as in earlier structures,

262   *Crypt of Speyer Cathedral, 1031–61. One feature of the Romanesque was to extend the crypt into a regularly spaced hall-like undercroft. Note the heavy, clear-cut details on pillars, capitals, and vaults.*

confined to the lower story, with an unarticulated, sheet-like wall surface rising above. Instead, it is this very upper zone that gives it its main accent. Pilasters climb aloft from the imposts, embracing each clerestory window with a round arch. From the ground ascend engaged shafts with cushion capitals, and they too carry round arches, set against the wall. Thus aisle opening and clerestory windows are united in a vertical accent beneath a single arch, the wall being at the same time plastically structured to become a sequence of perpendicular divisions, and this in a way as clear and elegant as it is logical. Still flat-ceiled, the nave stresses the movement towards the chancel. The aisles alone are vaulted, apart from the large crypt to the east. Only now were these lower churches developed into hall-like rooms [262], where soundly formed cross-vaults rise above columns with capitals. In comparison with this crypt, probably the finest and biggest of its age (it was intended as the mausoleum of the Salians), the earliest hall crypts from the tenth century seem like gloomy little cellars.

Under Henry IV, the task of vaulting the nave was begun at Speyer in 1082 [263]. One may regard this venture, which is among the boldest of its time, as a show of strength against the urge for power of a papacy under Cluniac influence. The shafts against every second pier were now strengthened to support the transverse arches that thrust themselves between the new groined-vaults. In this way almost square bays came into being down the nave, each accompanied on either side by two such vaulting compartments of the narrower aisles. It is thus an arrangement first intimated by the alternating supports of *S. Michael at Hildesheim* [234] and known as the 'metrical' system. But whereas at Hildesheim the squares based on the crossings separated off can only be deduced from the ground-plan and the four angle piers of the nave sections, at Speyer they are also indicated in the vault. Their centre is clearly and distinctly marked by the point at which the groins intersect. The embracement of the wall surfaces has been logically extended to the space, so that the nave now appears as a sequence of calm, vertical sections. In France, the same problem led simultaneously to

263   *Speyer Cathedral. The vaulting of the nave was begun in 1082. The alternate piers were strengthened to support the overarching vaults. Every bay forms part of a completely harmonized 'metrical' system.*

various solutions, but in Germany it had found its classic, exemplary answer at Speyer.

Mainz Cathedral, of which the nave and east end date from 1081 to 1137, the rib-vault and west end c. 1200–39 *[258, 264, 265]* largely followed the pattern of Speyer in its wall structure, its original vaulting, and its details. But it kept the double-chancel scheme bequeathed by an earlier, Ottonian building – now, amid the disorders of the Investiture Contest, probably even in pointed opposition to the trends of the monastic reform movement. Here, again, the arrangement of the blind arcading in the nave and of the dwarf galleries, niches, and round-arched corbelling on the outside bear witness to the elegant, sculpturesque character of late Salian architecture.

Cluniac reform affected by no means every Benedictine house. Founded in 1093 by a supporter of Henry IV, the monastery church of *Maria Laach [257]* was fully vaulted in the early twelfth century over a ground-plan that, while renouncing the metrical system, still adopted the two-chancel principle. Outside, the church is a typical group building. The idea of the westwork returns here, with an emphasized rectangular central tower accompanied by two round stair towers. At the east end, an octagonal tower rises above the crossing, and behind, in the angles between chancel and transept, there are again four-sided towers. The outcome is a rich opposition of different solid-geometrical forms. All parts of the exterior – window axes, stories, towers, and belfry openings – are stressed and embraced by articulating motifs, which include pilaster strips, round-arched corbelling, and blind arcading. Every separate feature, and every group, has thus been united with the others to form an integrated whole of the utmost power and tension. In late Hohenstaufen times the west chancel had an atrium set before it, a forecourt on early Christian lines chiefly intended as a meeting-place and for mustering processions. Once to be seen in front of numerous medieval churches, these atria (parvises) have rarely survived in their original form *[cf. 304]*.

Like Speyer, Mainz, and Maria Laach, the church of *S. Maria im Kapitol at Cologne*, consecrated in 1065, shows the tendencies of Salian architecture especially clearly. The important east parts fell victim to bombs during the last war, so that the layout can best be seen in the restoration *[266]*. To a basilican nave with a westwork-type façade was attached, in the east, a chancel of trefoil plan *[267]*. This form, once common in late antique and early Christian centralized buildings, appeared for the first time in the West here, and the most varied theories have been developed to connect it with native ancestors or Eastern models.

But more important than the derivation is undoubtedly its use to give the chancel areas a centralizing pattern. Mounting step-wise, the different structural

264, 265 *Mainz Cathedral, view of the nave looking west, and ground-plan. Nave and eastern parts built 1081 to 1137, nave vault and western parts c. 1200–39. The cathedral of the emperors of the high Romanesque period. The metrical system is evident in the ground-plan with its two choirs added to the earlier foundation. The shape of the square crossing determines the choir and transept arms. The square shape in the nave is altered to fit in with the rectangle; the bays of the nave are accompanied by aisle bays half their width.*

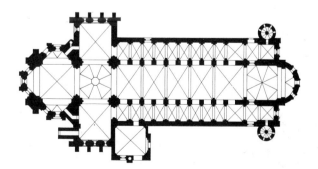

266, 267 S. Maria im Kapitol at Cologne, consecrated 1065. Ground-plan and reconstruction of the exterior (after Rahtgens). The eastern parts are symmetrically arranged: transept and choir are joined to the nave by a trefoil plan. On the exterior, the various sections of the eastern parts are joined together by a lower passage-way around the building.

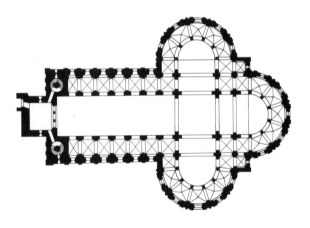

268 Monastery church of SS. Peter and Paul at Hirsau, 1082 to 1091, destroyed in the seventeenth century. Ground-plan, showing the typical German Cluniac church with slight variations (the choir takes the place of a semicircular apse); modelled on Cluny II [226]. Note the staggered chancel with its many altar niches. The last bay of the nave is marked off by piers as a 'minor choir'. The western vestibule is decorated with two towers.

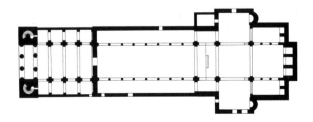

parts culminate in the crossing-tower, with the concentration of distinct elements surrounded and tied together, as it were, by the three lower semicircles. Embracing motifs, and ones that articulate the surface, cover the whole of the exterior. Within, the trend towards a unified spatial structure is revealed even more clearly. Today, alas, we have to rely for our description on the ground-plan. While the nave had a flat ceiling, the aisles received cross-vaults, as in the first Speyer edifice. But instead of ending at the transept arms, as was usual hitherto, the cross-vaults were carried round these and continued in the chancel, returning from there to their starting-point against the western turrets. The trefoil plan, traceable only in very isolated cases in other lands, subsequently became a characteristic of Cologne and Rhineland buildings, though mostly in a simplified form without an ambulatory *[273]*.

The Hirsau school

Compared to these rich, imaginative works that represent Salian imperial dignity, the other branch of German Romanesque architecture seems ascetic, severe, and reserved. From the monastery of Hirsau, in the Black Forest, the principles of the great Cluniac revival movement spread first to southern Germany and then to the entire German empire. Abbot Wilhelm of Hirsau's great new edifice, the church of *SS. Peter and Paul* (destroyed in the seventeenth century except for a few remains), was erected from 1082 to 1091 on the model of Cluny II, which had been built in the late tenth century *[cf. 226]*. This reversion to an already old-fashioned scheme was probably not just a protest against the architectural style of the Salians, with its delight in ornament, but a deliberate self-restriction, a return to the ideas of early Christianity. If a flat-ceiled basilica with columns was chosen at Hirsau, this is evidence of not wanting the new imperial splendour rather than of not being able to provide it. The ground-plan *[268]* shows a rigorously square-based system, which has been imposed in particular on the transept and chancel. At the west end an atrium-like galilee is set in front of the main structure, while to the east extends a staggered chancel with square-ended main and subsidiary presbyteries. The monks' choir is in the crossing, and the first nave bay to the west of this is marked off by piers as a 'minor choir' for unordained lay-brothers. These features are just as typical of Hirsau buildings as their rigid west–east direction, which is underlined by the firm rejection of a crypt thrusting up into the chancel. There is also the extremely clean finish of such architectural details as the ashlar blocks and the cushion capitals, these latter being of German origin and fully in keeping with the effort to achieve a simple effect. This plain style is characteristic of the buildings dependent on Hirsau, even though the basic scheme may be varied greatly; so it is permissible to talk of Hirsau architectural customs but not of hard and fast rules. In place of the destroyed Hirsau building, the churches of Kleinkomburg (1108), Paulinzella (1112; a ruin since the seventeenth century), Allerheiligen at Schaffhausen (early twelfth century), and *Alpirsbach*, begun in 1095 *[269]* can still give us a notion of the fastidious severity of this movement that in all respects deliberately opposed the richer forms of imperial edifices.

Hirsau ideas also influenced new buildings outside the actual monastic congregation. The Premonstratensian church of *Jerichow* (begun 1149) in the Brandenburg Marches has the same ascetic, reserved forms, and – probably the earliest instance of this – it

269 *Monastery church at Alpirsbach, founded 1095. View of the interior looking west. The pillared basilica is flat-ceiled, after the model of Hirsau. The space is bare and undecorated.*

270 *Premonstratensian church of Jerichow, begun 1149. The first important brick structure of the Brandenburg Marches takes over the ascetic forms of the Hirsau school.*

is also completely brick built *[270]*. In other German regions (Lower Saxony, Bavaria) too, naves long continued to be flat-ceiled, cross-vaults only being used occasionally in transept, chancel, or crypt.

Hohenstaufen architecture

Vaulting, one of the chief problems of Romanesque construction since the outset of the twelfth century, made only slow headway in Germany. The beginnings that had appeared so grandly at Speyer came to a halt as the Hirsau style gained ground. Indeed cross-ribs, which were already common in Normandy about 1100, did not gain acceptance until the mid-twelfth century, when they became one of the major constructional innovations of the Hohenstaufen age. Probably as a borrowing from adjacent France, the rib-vault would seem to have made its first German appearance in Alsace, the region where the imperial family had most property. Here, in the mid-twelfth century, began a period of extensive and, compared to work in the conservative south German area, very progressive building activity. Jutting up powerfully, the east end of *Murbach [256]*, all that remains of a once important monastery, gives an impressive picture of the still austere formal idiom of early Hohenstaufen architecture.

During the second half of the century, people started vaulting over entire churches in other regions also. In Lower Saxony Henry the Lion raised the first uniformly vaulted building in Brunswick Cathedral (1173–95), which, for all its monumental dignity and restrained severity, still seems rather old-fashioned, especially as regards the heavy, almost unarticulated mass of the exterior. Westphalia produced broadly spreading halls with rib-vaults that rise like domes [271] – ancestors of its great Gothic hall spaces.

The architecture of the Hohenstaufen age unfolded most richly in the Rhineland. Already heralded in Maria Laach, the tendency towards a greater plastic elaboration of the exterior was now continued, and it led to buildings like the two-storied chapel of *Schwarzrheindorf*, consecrated in 1151 [272], or like *S. Aposteln* [273] and Gross S. Martin at Cologne, both of whose chancels were erected round about 1200 over trefoil ground-plans on the model of S. Maria im Kapitol. Most of these edifices use the pointed rib-vault developed in France, together with

272   *Two-storied chapel at Schwarzrheindorf, consecrated 1151. The overall structure of Rhineland buildings became more plastic at this time. Much application of the round-arch frieze and blind arcades. The dwarf gallery, the dominating feature, encircles the whole building.*

271   *S. Maria zur Höhe at Soest, beginning of thirteenth century. View of the interior facing east. The hall space consists of single bays with rib-vaults that rise like domes. The ornate piers and pointed arches anticipate Gothic architecture.*

the native metrical system. The constructional advantages of the contemporary Gothic were thus fully recognized, yet the general fabric of German buildings continued to be Romanesque. There remained a feeling for the substance of the architectural masses, which interior and exterior were divided into layers with niches, blind arcading, and dwarf galleries, but not pierced and opened up structurally.

At the same period, the three middle Rhenish cathedrals underwent a more or less thorough revision. In Speyer this was mainly confined to renewing the nave vault while preserving the groin construction, but in Mainz rib-vaults were introduced and the sumptuous western structure added. *Worms Cathedral* rose on earlier remains as a new building, which was completed in 1224. Although the smallest and last to be finished of these three cathedrals, it is the most consistent, and can therefore best illustrate the trends of late Hohenstaufen architecture [274]. The interior, of pillared-basilican form with rib-vaulting, derives from Speyer and Mainz, but everything is more slender and wiry. Outside, too, the late western parts in particular rise up steep and straight. If one bears in mind that the classic Gothic west front of Notre-Dame at Paris *[369]* was then already complete, the fundamental difference between German and French architecture becomes especially clear: in the first, groups of plastically moulded structural bodies, with the walls broken up into niches or galleries and pierced by round-headed windows, yet still preserving their essence; in the second, a display wall extending relief-like in the plain and showing a perfect harmony of horizontal and vertical members, while the buttresses clearly indicate the Gothic 'skeleton'.

Hohenstaufen architecture could never evolve into Gothic, since its tremendously plastic character was in total contrast to that of the building whose framework broke up the wall. Only with the uncon-

274 *Western choir of Worms Cathedral, 1170–1224. An example of the late phase of German Romanesque. Built with the traditional two choirs, but with the additions of single structural elements. Although the impression of monumentality remains, the high arches that break the prismatic effect mark the beginnings of a new plasticity.*

ditional adoption of the whole Gothic system, as at Cologne *[405, 406]*, would the Romanesque be abandoned and the new age of Gothic introduced.

FRANCE

Unlike Germany, eleventh- and early twelfth-century France had no dominant, unifying power of a strong ruling house to help mould the style of an entire age. The land was split up into many duchies, counties, and other areas of political influence. Not until the late twelfth and the thirteenth century did a centralization of power begin, proceeding from the royal domain of the Île-de-France, and with it a political rise.

Too little has survived of the early Romanesque buildings of the eleventh century for us to be able to make out separate developments or common features. The most important novelties of this initial

273 *Choir of St Aposteln at Cologne, begun 1192. Revival of the trefoil ground-plan [267]. All the parts are brought together into a single compact building block. The strong emphasis on horizontals joins the wall spaces by the rise of round arches. Note the painterly effect of the shadowed hollows that rise from the bottom to the dwarf gallery of the wall.*

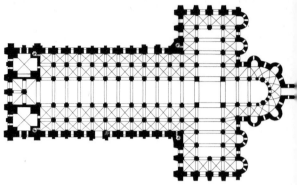

275–7   St-Sernin at Toulouse, begun c. 1080, consecrated 1096, upper tower beginning of thirteenth century. View of the eastern exterior, the nave leading towards the choir, and ground-plan. The type of the French vaulted pilgrimage church; the ground-plan is adapted to meet the needs of large crowds of pilgrims: a five-part main body, three-part transept, and choir with ambulatory. Clear east–west direction. A high barrel-vaulted nave with galleries; the space effect is opaque because of the indirect light from the aisles and galleries. The rich impression on the eastern exterior is due to the rising steepled members.

phase are the first large-scale attempts at vaulting, and the new east-end solution of the chevet, which from now on set the pattern for nearly all French churches. Towards the close of the eleventh century, however, art regions with distinctive stylistic traits apparent in sculpture as well as building develop in particular areas. We may therefore talk of schools of architecture, although this is not to say that forms from one school did not spread into neighbouring regions and produce a fruitful interaction. In Auvergne and Poitou hall-type churches arose with a nave and two aisles and sometimes with galleries. Their special features are barrel-vaults and a rich, decorative elaboration of the chancel parts and the façade. In Aquitaine aisleless dome-covered spaces were preferred, in Provence simple, often solid buildings. Burgundy evolved various basilican spatial forms: along with pointed barrel-vaults are to be found the first entirely cross-vaulted churches. Normandy is distinguished by its coherent structuring of the nave walls, above which the first rib-vaults were erected soon after 1100. But in spite of the differences between the various schools they were all endeavouring to solve the two main problems of Romanesque building, namely how to articulate and penetrate the wall mass plastically, and how to vault the whole church.

The pilgrimage churches

Meanwhile a supra-regional link between the diverse art areas had been established in France. A major role was played here by the great pilgrimage churches, which had grown very much in importance since the early eleventh century with the ever-increasing pilgrimages to the tomb of St James the Greater at Santiago de Compostela in north-west Spain. Starting out from various ecclesiastical centres, regular pilgrimage roads developed, their courses touching a series of important churches, in part reformed from powerful Cluny but also including canonical foundations. For these pilgrimage churches, the first big vaulted structures in France, an architectural scheme was evolved that, even though regional peculiarities did enter into it, may broadly be regarded as the earliest Romanesque type with a more general binding force.

The oldest and formally directive building, the church of St-Martin at Tours (begun *c.* 1000), was destroyed during the wars of religion and the Revolution, but two large followers, Ste-Foix at Conques (*c.* 1050–1140) and *St-Sernin at Toulouse*, begun *c.* 1080 *[275, 276]* have survived. To this group must also be added the goal of the pilgrims, the cathedral at Santiago de Compostela itself. Forms and tendencies that had emerged in the last pre-Romanesque phase and in early Romanesque – the chevet, the tighter clamping together of nave and chancel, the use of pillars, and breaching of the wall with galleries – were now consistently developed further.

St-Sernin's ground-plan *[277]* shows the rich and mature layout of this type. The basis of the system of proportions is the crossing-square. A nave with double aisles (in the other buildings they are mostly single) opens into the single-aisled transept from which four small apses curve out to the east. The chevet has five radiating chapels. Entering from the west, the stream of pilgrims could pour into the five spaces of the main limb, go round the transept wings, and be led past the venerated relics in the chancel. Within, the stepped-back arches on pillars and the tribunes above them are just as characteristic as the half-columns rising up from the floor to support the transverse arches of the barrel-vault. The result is a sequence of precipitous, plastically fashioned bays that lead at an even pace towards the chancel. Especially at the east end the exterior is of impressive magnitude, with its climax in the tall crossing-tower. There is a confidence apparent here that welds the different parts together, and articulates them by the embracement of sculpturally recessing and swelling motifs.

Burgundy

These big pilgrimage churches were surpassed, however, by the third version of the monastery church at *Cluny* in Burgundy (1088–*c.* 1130). It vied with Speyer Cathedral in being the largest church in Christendom after Old St Peter's, but the Revolution only spared one transept arm *[278]*. The layout included features shared with the pilgrimage churches, such as the chevet and double aisles. To the west, however, the nave had a galilee placed before it, and at the east end there was a second transept richly set with apses and towers. A clear orientation governed

278 Monastery church of Cluny, reconstruction of the third version, 1088 to c. 1130, mostly destroyed in eighteenth century. A Burgundian vaulted building with pointed barrel-vaults in the nave. The first-part nave with western galilee leads to the complex eastern structure with two transepts and doors with ambulatory. The composition of the varied elements is extremely assured, and culminates in the mighty tower of the crossing over the high altar.

antique manner and the small blind arcade inserted between the lower story and the window zone – a forerunner of the Gothic triforium. Both motifs were taken from antique gateways – one such still exists at Autun – but they have been transferred to the interior, where they help to loosen up the wall plastically.

Along with a few other buildings, Cluny and Autun formed a group within the Burgundian school that, owing to the paramount importance of Cluny III, won supra-regional authority. Another Burgundian type is represented by the church of *Ste-Madeleine at Vézelay*, 1120–40 *[259]*. Here the round arch has command (the chancel was renewed about 1200 in Gothic form), especially where the alternating colours of their stones accent the transverse arches that separate the individual cross-vaults from each other. There is no blind arcading between the

280, 281   Notre-Dame-du-Port in Clermont Ferrand, twelfth century. View of the nave towards the east and the transept crossing. The type of the Auvergne hall church, with barrel-vaulted nave, galleries and choir with ambulatory, related to the pilgrimage churches. The arcades of the arches joined to transept walls are repeated in the gallery lights [281]. A decorative inlay of coloured stones enlivens the structure. (Right.)

279   Cathedral of St-Lazare at Autun, erected 1120–40 in close dependence on Cluny III. The shape of the Romanesque doors is carried over on the interior walls: instead of the usual semi-circular pillars, fluted pilasters support the barrel arches. A round-arch blind gallery (precursor of the Gothic triforium) is placed between the pointed-arch arcades and the clerestory.

the structure, leading towards its complex eastern part, whose almost hierarchically ascending members culminated in the high crossing-tower. Not only was this chancel arrangement monumentalized at Cluny, in keeping with the fact that here was the most important bit of the church, but it gave the different groups in the monastic community their architecturally determined place. With the many apses and chapels, it provided enough room for side altars at which the monks could say their individual Masses. Inside, pointed arches appeared for the first time, both in the main arcades and in the barrel-vault over the nave. Their origin is disputed, and they should probably be interpreted less as an indication of Gothic architectural principles than as a formal motif reflecting the Burgundian bent in art. Descendant structures are more informative about such features, as is shown by the nave of the cathedral of *St-Lazare at Autun*, 1120–40 *[279]*. Especially notable, besides the pointed arches, are the pilasters fluted in the

lower arches and the window zone; instead, rich stepped effects and decorative features enliven and mould the wall surfaces, which are again split up into vertical section by tall half-columns.

Auvergne

The vault problem, which Burgundy solved in various ways, also occupied the other regional schools of France. Churches in Auvergne bear certain resemblances to the great pilgrimage churches, and the earliest Auvergnat buildings probably helped to determine their form. The hall-like main body, with single aisles, generally has galleries, and to its tall, barrel-vaulted nave is attached, at the east end, a chancel with an ambulatory round it [280]. Typical are the wall-work arches that divide off the crossing on all sides from nave, chancel, and transept wings. Their surface is pierced by arches and they have been given a mosaic-like enrichment with variously coloured stones that are found only in Auvergne [281]. Simple forms thus add up to a robust style that also marks the exterior [282]. With only two small towers to the west, the main accent here as well is at the east end. As the transept is stepped, the crossing-

282 *Monastery church of St-Austremoine at Issoire, beginning of twelfth century; the crossing-tower is restored. The eastern part of Auvergne churches is dominated by a socled storey with arcades rising from the transept. Coloured stone inlay is also applied to the exterior.*

tower rises from a separate story. The result is a graduated structure whose lively effect has been heightened by the very individual ornamentation and the stone inlays.

Poitou

For churches in Poitou, a hall interior is the distinguishing feature: narrow barrel- or cross-vaulted aisles that accompany the barrel-vaulted nave have the same, or almost the same, height as the latter [284]. This never possesses its own clerestory windows, and, externally, is united with the aisles under a single roof to form a coherent structural block. Although the steeply proportioned interior [283] seems as spacious as in a basilica, it is very much darker, since light only comes in through the aisle windows. The continuous row of tall columned arches leads to the chevet, this steady movement being stressed by a barrel-vault uninterrupted by

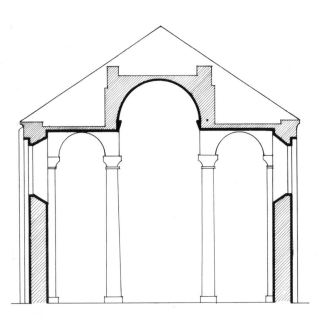

*283, 284 Monastery church of St-Savin-sur-Gartempe, c. 1080.
View of the nave towards the east and section of the main part.
A Poitou hall church; barrel-vaults in the nave and both aisles.
Light from the aisle windows illuminates the space. The direction
eastwards is emphasized by the long strips of roof painting [348].*

*285 Façade of Notre-Dame-la-Grande at Poitiers, c. 1150. An
outstanding example of a Poitevin west façade. The wall,
crowned with a gable, is completely covered with pictorial
decoration and flanked by two-towered bundles of pillars. The
surface is laid out in horizontal rows of arcades.*

transverse arches. Particularly overhead, later buildings developed more elaborate forms, such as
pointed barrels. The shape of the supports was also
varied, especially characteristic in this connexion
being the quatrefoil form. But the hall type always
remained dominant, and with it the problem of
opening out the nave wall plastically did not arise.
On the other hand, the exterior of Poitevin churches
is richly adorned with figure and ornamental motifs,
in particular the west front [285], which stands forth
as a gable-crowned display façade between two
lateral clustered piers with towers on them. The
almost luxuriant profusion of figure-work is disposed in horizontal stories, appearing as a pictorial
relief zone carved out of the wall's foremost layer.
This is balanced by the strongly emphasized vertical
features of the architecture – by the small lateral
towers swelling 'in the round' from the substance of
the wall and by the large apertures boring into the
middle axis.

Aquitaine

In old Aquitania, the region about Angoulême and
Périgueux, churches were raised that differ most of

all from those of other French areas. These Aquitanian domed churches probably go back to Byzantine models, a link that could certainly have been established during the Crusades. The basic element is a square compartment of space covered with a dome on pendentives. Multiplied, it can be combined in different ways: either by aligning several such compartments to form a nave without aisles *[286]*, or else by arranging them as a Greek cross, with a square on each side of the central one. This type has a particularly impressive representative in *St-Front at Périgueux*, 1120–50 *[287]*, a building related to *S. Marco at Venice [310]*. Both probably follow the pattern of the destroyed Justinianic church of the Holy Apostles at Constantinople. Although the centralizing spatial schemes are alike, in St-Front there is no illusionistic blurring of the space with mosaics, but just the monumental effect of the architectural form. Thus Aquitanian buildings diverge considerably from the Byzantine conception, all the more so since their supports were developed plastically in a Romanesque way. Here again distinctive

287 *Interior of the cathedral of St-Front at Périgueux. This building was begun in 1120–50, and like S. Marco [310] follows the pattern of the (now destroyed) church of the Apostles in Constantinople by Justinian: a centralized structure over a Greek cross and with five great domed spaces. The vaults rest on massive pierced piers.*

286 *Nave of the monastery church of Fontrevault, after 1120. An Aquitaine vaulted church. A single-part nave merging into a choir is developed out of consecutive single-vaulted spaces. The semicircular pillars give a plastic effect to the piers and walls.*

288 *Church of Les Saintes-Maries-de-la-Mer, c. 1150–80. An example of the unadorned Provence churches. The plain, barrel-vaulted space is surrounded by a monumental fortress-like exterior.*

forms subsequently emerged, most notably in the vaulting zone where the domes turned into bulbous groined-vaults with ribs applied to them. But on French soil the pure domed church was built only during a fairly brief period (till about 1150), and only in Aquitania.

Provence

In Provence, the southern part of the country, the simple form of an aisleless church terminated to the east by a chancel apse [288] was preferred. Only occasionally was it expanded into a basilica through adding narrow aisles. Within, underpinned by transverse arches, stretches a barrel-vault which from the mid-twelfth century also took the pointed form known from other regions. These churches have particularly impressive exteriors, characterized by their very careful ashlaring combined with a monumental arrangement of the mighty structural masses. One also finds classicizing enrichments and statuetype sculpture around the portal constructions [332], to which the Roman past of this region has made a large and evident contribution.

Normandy

From the French schools so far considered, northwestern architecture, that of Normandy, is distinguished by an especially taut articulation of the interior and the exterior. As early as the eleventh century a series of large buildings arose here, evidence of the Normans' growing power. Foreign ideas, especially Burgundian Cluniac ones, were methodically adopted and elaborated. Even in the first, flat-ceiled basilicas, with their two-tower fronts and Burgundian staggered chancels, the opening up of the wall through tribunes was carried further. In the church of *Mont-St-Michel*, begun *c.* 1060 [289] the half-columns soaring up from the floor divide the vigorously fashioned nave wall into clearly separated vertical sections. Round about the same time, William the Conqueror founded at Caen the abbeys of *St-Étienne* [290, 291] and *Ste-Trinité* [292], whose massive heaviness is considerably tempered by the vertical stress of the articulation. Inside St-Étienne, the walls have been opened up to the maximum and almost dissolved. The tribune arches are as wide as those of the lower arcade, and even the clerestory zone is split up by rows of arches, except for a few remains of walling. All the strength and energy seem to be concentrated in the vertical lines of force traced

289   Monastery church of Mont–St–Michel, begun c. 1060. View of the nave wall. A Norman basilica with galleries. The rising semicircular columns emphasize the particularly powerful effects of the wall dimensions.

290, 291   Monastery church of St-Étienne at Caen, founded by William the Conqueror, 1064–77, vault c. 1100. The nave walls below the vaulting are reconstructed (after Dehio and von Bezold); the eastern section of the nave also. In the first story and galleries the wall is completely open. The emphasis is on vertical lines which culminate in the rib-vaults. (Right.)

by the supports and engaged shafts; it is here, and no longer in the substance of the masonry, that the accent of the wall structure lies. When, about 1100, Norman churches received a nave vault in accordance with the general European trend, it was natural to use not the barrel- or groined-vault customary in other areas, but ribs that visibly continued the force lines of the supports into the roof zone. Thus the nave of St-Étienne was covered over with sexpartite vaulting whose heavy ribs were already developed as a supporting framework even though they are still rounded

292 *Monastery church of Ste-Trinité at Caen, begun 1054. View from the south-west. The mighty two-tower front with its decorative joining of the walls is typically Norman.*

and far from possessing the variability of the Gothic pointed-arch rib system.

With the introduction of the rib-vault, the individual nave bay finally became a spatially independent unit. One of the main problems of Romanesque architecture had thus found a logical, forward-looking solution that would be the basis of the first Gothic buildings.

ENGLAND

The Norman style

Chroniclers tell of big early medieval churches in the British Isles, but the oldest large structures to have survived were all raised after the Norman Conquest. Their descent from the buildings of Normandy is obvious; indeed, the Norman forms retained their power here until the end of the twelfth century, a time when Gothic already prevailed in Normandy itself. Of the many cathedrals and abbey churches founded in the thirty years before the close of the eleventh century, we may distinguish two main types, one of which followed the apse and ambulatory plan found so often in the French pilgrimage churches, and the other which has a tri-apsidal plan. Canterbury, Lincoln, St Albans, Ely, and Durham

geometric patterns on the round piers. Outside, one sees the characteristic two-tower façade and mighty crossing-tower of Normandy.

Durham certainly counts among England's most important Romanesque buildings, and at least in the vaulting it was ahead of its times, as afterwards there was a return to the open-roof framework, which went on being used for smaller churches till into late Gothic. In other places, capitals were of various types and shapes, the arches sometimes quite plain, sometimes decorated. The smaller church buildings conform to groups more easily, for instance in the Welsh Marches where Celtic influences survived, or in the Scots border country where the familiar interlace patterns recur. But in the more important buildings, no overall theme can be traced, other than a tendency towards massive, dignified simplicity, reminiscent perhaps of the Rhineland cathedrals rather than those

294–6   Durham Cathedral, 1093 to c. 1130. View of the nave facing east; ground-plan, and exterior from the north. The structure, based on the metrical system, is vaulted with cross-ribs. Note the alternation of piers and their rich decoration, with galleries and clerestories above. The exterior with its massive towers is typically Norman, though it looks forward to Gothic architecture.

293   St Albans Cathedral, c. 1080–1115. An example of the early Norman style in England with massive arcade piers and large galleries. Despite the vertical lines of the pilasters the main emphasis is on the horizontals of the wall openings.

belong to this latter group; Winchester, Gloucester, and Norwich to the first.

Within these two major divisions, English church architecture displays many differences of approach. Although the large gallery opening *[293]* at *St Albans*, the wall passage, and the attached shaft were all taken over from France, the general effect usually still remained one of horizontal succession, not least owing to the immoderate length of the nave. Norman rib-vaulting was also used here, and in *Durham Cathedral* (1093–c. 1130) it produced the first edifice to be consistently vaulted throughout in this manner *[294–6]*. Following the metrical system, hefty round piers alternate with powerful compound ones. Only before the latter do shafts climb up to cushion capitals on which rest the pointed transverse arches that span the nave and separate the oblong vaulting compartments. The total impression is of a primitive plastic and decorative force that also governs the details including the chevrons and billets on the tribune's containing arches and the ribs, but above all the

of France. At *Gloucester* the triforium above the huge piers appears tiny [*297*]; at *Southwell* it appears large in proportion to the shorter supports [*298*]. *Norwich* preserves a perfect balance between lower tier, triforium, and clerestory [*299*], while in the late Norman work at *Oxford Cathedral* [*300*], much of the triforium is made part of the main bay.

The English Cistercian foundations of the twelfth century revived a characteristic of Saxon architecture, namely the square east end. The austerity of these buildings foreshadows the rise of the Gothic, but not until the end of the century, with the adoption of the French cathedral system, did the native stylistic tradition succumb, and even then many of its tendencies were carried over.

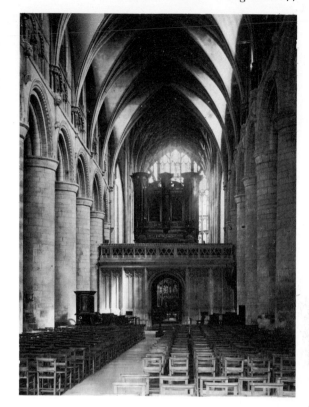

297 Gloucester Cathedral, begun 1089. View of the nave facing east. The early Gothic vault of 1240 cuts into the windows, which are unusually high. Note the absence of any ornamental connexions between pillars and arches; and the way the triforium disappears above the piers.

298 Southwell Minster, Nottinghamshire, begun before 1114. View of the nave, facing south-east. In this example, the triforium is almost as large as the lower story on which it rests. All the emphasis is on the horizontals, since the bays are unbroken by piers.

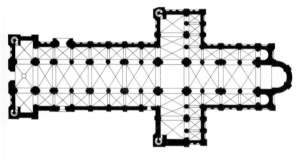

SPAIN

Like England, whose Romanesque architecture is in the last analysis inconceivable without the Norman achievements, Spain also constitutes a border area within the field of Western developments. Arabic and Jewish civilization began to make a strong impact there in the eleventh century. From about 1125 Toledo was the country's intellectual centre, where the important philosophical works of the Jews and Arabs were translated, thereafter to have a fruitful effect on the entire West. The ties of the Christian part of the land with its neighbours in France and Italy were firm enough, however, to hold fast against the East and to strengthen the attachment to the West. Spain thus occupied a central position between Orient and Occident – an often unsteady one reflected in its art, too, for many centuries. Along with the native early medieval and Christian tradition [cf. 221, 222, 231], it was above all Islamic civilization and, ultimately with persistence, French examples that shaped architecture during Romanesque times. The

301 Crossing-tower of the cathedral of Zamora, end of twelfth century. Byzantine, Islamic, and French elements are united in the bizarre form of this 'cimborio'.

299 Norwich Cathedral, begun 1096. View of the three stories of the nave, looking south-east. Triforium and arcade arches are of similar height. The major piers of the nave are unusually elaborate, with sixteen shafts.

300 Christ Church Cathedral, Oxford. View of the crossing, looking south-west. This is an example of late Norman work (1180) showing the triforium arcade enclosed within the arches of the main bay.

302 *Choir of the cathedral of Avila, begun c. 1200. The fortress-like choir is evidence of the wars and divisions that occupied Christian Spain for so many centuries. A surrounding choir with radiating chapels was added on to the massive walls.*

indigenous tradition, with its plain and severe forms, continued chiefly in Catalonia, while Islamic influence appeared chiefly in the decorative treatment of particular parts of a building, such as doorway surrounds or the intricate arcading of cloisters. Also typical is a rich internal and external elaboration of the crossing-tower or *cimborio [301]* with many openings, gables, and angle turrets, the whole being covered over with scale-shaped stone tiles.

As the pilgrimages to Santiago de Compostela grew in importance, so French architectural forms flowed into the country. The cathedral begun at Santiago about 1070 continued the series of the great pilgrimage churches, even if certain details may be more Spanish. Those buildings that accompany the pilgrimage road are also of mainly French descent, although French workmen will have been used very rarely indeed. Away from the big centres, however, there are numerous almost unknown churches in which old and new, native and foreign have coalesced into a distinctive regional type *[302]*. Thus in keeping with its disharmonious situation, Spanish Romanesque architecture presents a thoroughly inconsistent picture, and hardly a single work has overcome its provincial dialect, or has achieved a style of its own worked up from foreign patterns.

ITALY

During the early Middle Ages, Italy was politically dismembered as well as exhausted and impoverished by continual disturbances of war. The growing distress of every class affected the monks too, with the result that Cluniac reform, so influential in other lands, here only scored local successes. There were few rich men, whether temporal or ecclesiastical princes, to commission buildings, and it was not until the second half of the eleventh century that the situation had sufficiently improved for the first sizeable new works to be begun, all in the northern part of the country. It was here, especially in Lombardy, that architecture had remained most alive, not only because of the native antique and early Christian tradition, but also owing to the closer link with the German empire and to the nearness of southern France. At Venice and Rome, on the other hand, early Christian and Byzantine influences continued long and persistently, while the south and Sicily were to a great extent dominated by the forms of their Saracen and then their Norman conquerors. Only in Tuscany, and chiefly at Florence, did independent, almost classical solutions appear, although these did not concern the building's structure so much as the decorative articulation of its wall surfaces.

In its spatial forms Italian Romanesque architecture remained conservative, with transepts and staggered apses or chevets often absent, as were also the elaborate groups of towers. If towers were used, they mostly took the archaic form of a single, free-standing campanile. Here, too, it was sought to loosen up the substance of the wall, though not through the systematic structuring that in the North finally led to complete disintegration, but rather through a division into layers, whereby the outermost part often achieved the effect of an illusionistic, pictorial relief that seems to be purely applied to the body of the building.

The three most notable works of early Italian Romanesque were all begun in 1063: the church of the Benedictine abbey of S. Abbondio at Como, Pisa Cathedral, and S. Marco, the Dominican church at Venice. Profound differences resulting from the political situation in Italy mark these buildings erected not so very far apart. *S. Abbondio at Como*, dedicated in 1095, most clearly shows Lombardy's connexions with Northern Romanesque. It presents Cluniac features not merely in its ground-plan but also in its exterior and interior *[303, 304]*. The nave and double aisles are still flat-ceiled, and only the chancel and the spaces before the minor apses have been given vaults. In its unadorned simplicity, the nave with high arches on round piers may call to mind Hirsau buildings. Jutting up strongly and slenderly, the exterior with its two eastern towers also reveals the Romanesque feeling for mass and articulation. Only the richly ornamented window surrounds of the chancel may be regarded as a Lombard characteristic.

Northern Italy

Not until the twelfth century were largish churches of a relatively uniform character built in northern Italy. Their new spatial forms – metrical system, galleries, occasionally even vaults – can hardly be considered independent developments, and they probably go back to French and German sources. Typically north Italian, though, is the look of the façades, with their portals as show-pieces. Among the earliest of the series is *S. Zeno at Verona*, 1123–78 *[305, 306]*. A baldachin-like porch structure covers the entrance, its slender columns set on reclining lions, a motif that often recurs not only in connexion with portals but also with cloisters and pulpits. To left and right figure reliefs have been let into the wall, here still without clear anchorage in the general structure of the articulation. Powerful, angular engaged piers split up the façade wall into vertical sections, the intermediate fields being subdivided by pilasters. Round-arch corbel tables form or underline the horizontals and border the gable slopes, while a small gallery made up of coupled arches pierces the wall somewhat hesitantly. Although the nave was heightened during later building operations, this has scarcely impaired the interior's effect of cool monumentality. Heavy compound piers of squat yet exceptionally well-balanced proportions alternate with slender columns. Ascending shafts mark this alternation in the upper wall zone. Diaphragm arches span the space, thereby indicating the division into bays. The east end is raised higher than the western part, for there a 'stage' crypt thrusts upward, opening in arches towards the nave. A stairway connects it with the latter, whereas the chancel is reached by steps from the aisles. The spaces flow calmly into one another, dominated by the calm stride of the bays.

Begun about 1130, soon after S. Zeno, the new western limb of the old and famous church of *S. Ambrogio at Milan [307, 308]* displays quite a number of enrichments in the details, yet remains just as static. The building plan no doubt provided from the start for complete vaulting, though probably in the form of simple groined vaults and not of the slightly domed-up ribbed ones which were constructed somewhat later. These however in no way alter the effect

303, 304 Monastery church of S. Abbondio at Como, 1063–95. View of the nave facing east and exterior from the south-east. The pillared basilica, in five parts and lacking a transept, has a steepled eastern section with two flanking towers. The choir window surrounds show the richly decorative stone masonry characteristic of Lombardy.

305, 306   Monastery church of S. Zeno at Verona, begun 1123; the nave heightened and rose window of the façade added towards 1200; wooden roof fourteenth century. This mighty basilica, which possesses no transept, is the first of a series of converted upper Italian churches. Note the portico, typically roofed on the massive west façade. Clear vertical disposition through pilasters; the wall is enlivened by horizontal galleries. Piers and pillars alternate in the nave. The interior space, still unvaulted, is broader and well proportioned.

307, 308   S. Ambrogio at Milan, c. 1130 to c. 1160. View of the nave facing east, and west façade with atrium. The nave and richly decorated galleries are composed of a row of bays with domed vaults. The overall impression is dark, with indirect light in the nave. Vertical and horizontal accents complement each other in the interior space.

of sombre stateliness and broadly spreading, almost oppressive weight. Here again a strongly accented division into bays with alternating supports is in control. Each bay comprises two tribune and main arcade openings, but instead of an energetic upward movement as in Germany and France there is a peaceful recumbence of all parts – indeed the vaults appear to sink rather than to rise. The nave walls are almost fully opened up, yet the apertures have not been bored into the thickness of the masonry but cut out as from a panel. A similar appearance is presented by the imposing west front with its atrium and two-storied narthex: the wall has been opened out into two layers, one before the other, so that a rich play of light and shadow is produced.

At *Parma*, from about 1140 until into the thirteenth century, was raised one of those groups of buildings so characteristic of Italy that comprise a basilican church, a tall campanile, and a centrally planned baptistry *[309]*. The west end of this vaulted and galleried basilica presents the Lombardic façade in its mature form: broad rather than tall, with a gently rising gable, the integrated wall surface spreading out in harmonious balance. Three ranges of dwarf galleries open the wall and give a view of its deeper stratum resting in a play of shadows. The two-storied portal, of elegant forms, and the big window aperture above it stress the central axis without

309 *Parma Cathedral, c. 1140 to c. 1160, and Baptistry, 1196–1270. The west front of the cathedral is a classical example of the northern Italian façade. Note the elegant, two-storied portico; the layers of the wall; the dwarf galleries that break up the stone face and appear to make the back surface another continuous wall.*

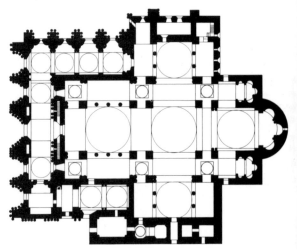

310, 311 *Cathedral of S. Marco, Venice, begun 1063. View of the interior facing east, and ground-plan. A centralized building with five domed spaces over a Greek cross, on Byzantine models. The effect of additional space is disguised by the spatial illusion of mosaic decoration. The predominating effect is painterly and diffuse despite the massive strength of architectonic members.*

disturbing the horizontal arrangement. In a slightly altered, even more opened-out form, this façade articulation of the display-wall type can also be seen on the prismatic body of the baptistry (1196–1270). There is a hint of the skeletal, of a framework character in the strong corner buttresses that reach right up to the topmost story, but it is lost in the overall impression of compactness.

Other important buildings from this group, such as the cathedrals of Modena, Ferrara, and Cremona, vary in a more or less similar way the features just described. They all have a north Italian articulation

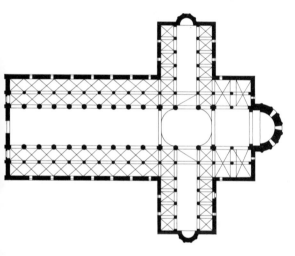

312–14 Pisa Cathedral, 1063–1270; 'Leaning Tower' 1137–50; Baptisterium, 1153 to end of fourteenth century. Aerial view, interior, and ground-plan. A splendidly monumental composition in design and execution, the cathedral is a five-part, cross-shaped, galleried basilica. Note the clear eastward orientation of the interior and the effects of light created by the decorated surfaces. The exterior walls are resolved in delicate multifold rib-work.

of the exterior, not only on their façades but also on their western limbs and chancels.

A special place in the Romanesque architecture of northern Italy is taken by *S. Marco at Venice*, begun in 1063 *[310, 311]*, for nowhere else is the assimilation of foreign patterns so evident. One can say with some certainty that this edifice is based on the no longer existent Justinianic church of the Apostles at Constantinople, from which S. Marco's relation St-Front at Périgueux probably also derives *[287]*. Not only was the Greek-cross ground-plan adopted at Venice, with four domed spaces grouped over it around a central space, but the building was adorned with mosaics – chiefly, moreover, by Byzantine artists, whom the victorious Venetians had brought to their city after the capture of Constantinople. The Greek-cross domed scheme demands the joining together, as aimed at in Romanesque architecture, of a number of equivalent space compartments, a goal

to which the Aquitanian churches come very close while dispensing with all decoration. At Venice, however, the accent was placed on an illusionistic dissolution of the walls and vaulting with mosaics. Thus the dominant impression is of a diffuse, dream-like, and floating effect of space, which even the massiveness of the breached piers and the wide sections of barrel-vault rising above them cannot hide. Venice remained an enclave open to the East in the north Italian area. In the thirteenth century the church of S. Antonio at near-by Padua followed the example of S. Marco, but used somewhat modified, already Gothicizing forms.

Tuscany, Rome, and Southern Italy

For Tuscan architecture the rebuilding of *Pisa Cathedral [312–14]*, begun in 1063, meant a crucial

turning-point. Known from documents, the original architect Busketos seems to have been a Greek, although his design cannot be traced back to Eastern models as clearly as S. Marco. If such models do exist – one thinks here of early Christian designs from Syria – then they have undergone a decisive change. Compared to the often dark and heavy Lombardic works, everything at Pisa is lighter, more graceful, and, despite the imposing dimensions, even rather more playful. This unique building complex seems to bear traces of an alien, Oriental world. Around the oblong crossing with a roughly oval dome, the cathedral's ground-plan groups a western limb with double aisles, two single-aisled, boldly jutting transept arms, and a comparatively long double-aisled chancel, which means that the whole displays slight centralizing tendencies (the nave was three bays shorter to start with). Inside, all the aisles were given groined-vaults, whereas the nave still has a flat ceiling. Above the columned main arcades are open galleries with pairs of arches contained by round ones. The two stories are divided by a forceful horizontal moulding – indeed the horizontal is dominant everywhere, thanks not least to the lively stripe pattern on the gallery piers and to the coloured stone inlays of the clerestory walls. One is conscious here of a strong decorative spirit, which has also fashioned the exterior. A filigree of open arcading spreads out in horizontal courses, its separate components architectonically structured and plastically shaped yet merging into a veil-like relief in their succession. Within and without there is thus a play of extremely refined and assured forms over the building, whose body as such remains intact but gives an impression of lightness and grace. This applies to all three structures belonging to this group set with amazing effect in the once quite unobstructed surrounds.

The confident, elegant forms of Pisa Cathedral, its sound execution, and the splendour of its materials must have made an enormous impression on contemporaries. Its style was imitated in particular at Pisa and neighbouring Lucca, though also in the rest of Tuscany. At Florence this decorative principle underwent a refined classical recast. Looking down towards the city from high ground, the magnificently sited

315, 316   S. Miniato al Monte at Florence, end of eleventh century to c. 1170. West façade and view of the nave facing east. The most important building of the 'Florentine Proto-Renaissance'. Spatial and surface proportions are classically balanced. The façade and interior walls are covered with a geometric surface decoration of marble, influenced by antique models. The form is still antique (no transept; open pulpit) despite alternating cross-arches that indicate the bays.

church of *S. Miniato al Monte*, begun in the late eleventh century, the façade about 1170 *[315, 316]* is among the finest examples of the Florentine 'veneer' style. The inner and outer wall surfaces have been covered with white marble and grey-green serpentine in an exceedingly elegant manner that is no less delicate than firm. Here, the sometimes rather ostentatiously heaped-on finery of Pisan buildings gives way to a discreet, purely geometric division of the surface. The antique flavour of the façade is unmistakable, not just in the details – cornice profiles, aedicule, fluted pilasters – but also in the general effect. These buildings, which form a small group confined to Florence and its more immediate neighbourhood, are accordingly regarded as precursors of the Renaissance, as achievements of a Florentine Proto-Renaissance. This seems the more justified inasmuch as it was from these very churches (cf. p. 275) that the first great Florentine architects of the Renaissance, beginning with Brunelleschi, drew inspiration. S. Miniato's interior is that of an open, airy basilica, with diaphragm arches spanning the nave at every third support. This division into bays in association with an open-roof framework is also common in northern Italy, where it appears at *S. Zeno* *[306]*, for example. As there, a 'stage' crypt rises at the east end well above the level of the nave floor. The decorative forms of the wall zone join up as horizontal bands that are interrupted rather than articulated into planes by the diaphragm arches. Altar rail, pulpit, and paving are all covered with rich inlays.

These finely structured stone inlays are characteristic of the architecture produced at Rome during this period. One can almost say that creative architectural activity there was limited to making only these inlays, since new church buildings, which were in any case comparatively rare and not so very big, generally kept to the basic forms of the early Christian basilica. A group of Roman artists, the Cosmati, began executing these skilfully contrived inlays during the twelfth century, and the richly adorned cloisters of *S. Paolo fuori le Mura [317]* and S. Giovanni in Laterano offer some of the best-known examples of Cosmati work.

In southern Italy architecture remained just as conservative in its spatial forms as at Rome. After its conquest by the Normans, large churches appeared in Apulia from the late eleventh century onwards, but they are evidence of their builders' forceful and impressive views on architecture rather than essential elements in the general pattern of architectural development. It was in Sicily, which passed to the Hohenstaufens in 1189, that the main focus of Norman building lay. The Norman conquerors

317 *Cloister of S. Paolo fuori le Mura at Rome, 1220–41. The richly decorative execution of the spindle-like pillars with inlays of cut, coloured stones is typical of the so-called 'Cosmati work'.*

318 *Cloister of Monreale Cathedral, end of twelfth century. Cosmati work. Norman, antique and Saracenic motifs give the building an Oriental character.*

319 *Eastern section of Palermo Cathedral, 1172–85. The massive, pinnacled masonry is completely covered with Saracenic decoration of the late Romanesque period.*

discovered there a broad layer of Saracenic art, whose decorative features they transferred to their own boldly towering edifices. Byzantine motifs flowed in as well, with the result that extremely rich hybrid forms arose. Built in several phases and by a number of workshops, the *Cloister of Monreale Cathedral*, of late twelfth-century date [318], has the greatest abundance of ornamental forms. Coupled columns sculptured or set with coloured stones bear capitals that have figural or non-figural decoration mixing classical with Eastern motifs, above which rise tall Saracenic pointed arches. The pointed arch likewise dominates the decorative system of the exterior: produced by the intersection of round arches, it covers the eastern apses of *Palermo Cathedral [319]*. The general tendency of late Romanesque towards fashioning a rich, ornamental exterior developed from the inherited forms of alien cultures is also apparent here.

Even though Italian architecture in the age of Romanesque may have contributed little to the two building problems that paved the way for the subsequent Gothic (opening up the walls; vaulting), it still clearly expressed the Romanesque approach in numerous works, and it is particularly impressive where, on a basis of the classical tradition, it already intimates the spirit of the Renaissance.

SECULAR ARCHITECTURE

The chief problems of medieval secular architecture include those of military and domestic building. Their monumental solutions are the castle and the fortified town, in both of which a combination of residence and defence has been sought. True, we know from early German history that the great once preferred unfortified halls, and that even the *Pfalz* – a German term deriving from the Latin 'palatium' – was at first an unfortified royal dwelling. In the course of the Middle Ages, however, even the imperial palaces became especially imposing castles [320] that resembled other castles in layout and mode of defence but had substantially larger main rooms.

The principal forms of the castle depend on regional factors. In southern and western Europe

320 *Imperial 'Pfalz' at Gelnhausen, end of twelfth century. A tower (on the left) flanks the two-part towered hall and remains of the chapel. The 'Palas' (lord's abode) on the right has a main central entrance and many window arcades.*

321 *Münzenberg Castle in the Wetterau, end of twelfth century. The massive 'Ringburg' lies on top of a broad hill-spur. Two 'Bergfriede' were necessary as look-outs from all quarters.*

people aimed at an overall pattern that was as regular as possible, while in the North, particularly on German soil, the castle grew out of the terrain, and even as regards defence methods adapted itself to its situation. In the process, two German basic types evolved. First there is the *Ringburg*, which with its *enceinte* composed of buildings and wall lies on a tract of ground equally protected on all sides, such as an island or a sugar-loaf hill *[321]*. The *Ringburg* generally has a free-standing main tower, or *Bergfried*, which served less for immediate purposes of defence than as a last refuge. These towers are sometimes built for habitation in their upper stories (fire-places, etc.), while their 'dungeons' are to be regarded as storage cellars. Another important part of every castle is the lord's abode (*Palas*), which contains the living-rooms, including the hall and a series of smaller heatable chambers. The castle chapel is also usually in the lord's dwelling, though it can often be found in or against the gate building, which as the exposed point of the *enceinte* gets special emphasis.

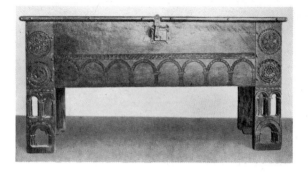

323 Romanesque chest from Nussholz, twelfth century. Sion, Musée de Valère. The light, transportable chest is the most important object of medieval furniture. Note the window-like supporting legs; and the arcades and rosettes, motifs in part taken over from architectural decoration.

322 Liebenzell Castle, end of twelfth century. 'Bergfried' and 'shield wall' defend the most exposed side of the 'Abschnittsburg'. Wall and tower remain undecorated, though the regular placing of the stonework is impressive.

324 Castle Hedingham (Essex), c. 1140. The English 'keep' grew out of the French 'donjon'. A rectangular, many-storied, fortified block. The steep vertical lines once culminated in four square towers at each corner.

325   *Castel del Monte, c. 1240. This hunting castle of Frederick II is the purest example of Hohenstaufen art in Apulia. An eight-cornered fortification with eight corner towers and an inner court. Note the antique motifs (main gate) beneath Gothic pointed arches (windows, interior vaults).*

326   *City fortification at Avila, twelfth century. The girdle of walls has semicircular towers consisting of massive quarry-stones. The effect of weight is enlivened by their irregular height and by the battlements.*

The second type, known as the *Abschnittsburg*, generally lies on a spur, and in such a way that a deep wide ditch cuts it off from the adjacent high ground. The defensive power here is concentrated on the ditch side, the *Bergfried* often being coupled with an especially high and thick wall *[322]* that stands as a shield before the other castle installations to protect them.

Hardly anything has survived of the interior fitments of castles from this period, except for a few fire-places and pieces of furniture – particularly chests *[323]*, although these may be of middle-class or ecclesiastical provenance. Castle rooms were kept plain, as they would still be in Gothic times, and apart from a few chapels and tower chambers, they remained unvaulted. The magnificent window arches of the bigger castles were closed with shutters in bad weather.

Related to the German *Bergfried* are the French *donjon* and British *keep [324]*. These mighty towers, the earliest of which date back to the tenth century, are probably of Norman origin, and were used for living in even during periods of peace. They constitute an exceptionally imposing union of military and domestic architecture.

In Italy, the *castello* offers the ideal form, a regular square of walls with strong angle towers. The residential buildings are pressed up against the defensive walls. Of these *castelli*, the finest were raised under Frederick II during the first half of the thirteenth century in Apulia, where the most impressive and best-preserved example is the *Castel del Monte [325]*.

Broadly speaking, towns did not start to flourish until the thirteenth century. In the German area, a few remains of town fortifications from late Hohenstaufen times have survived (Esslingen). The wall with strongly advancing towers *[326]* that still girds *Avila* in Spanish León is unique; it was built during the twelfth century to keep out the Moors. The tall, militantly sturdy towers that exist in certain Italian towns likewise date back to the twelfth century, for example at Bologna; S. Giminiano *[327]*, though something similar is also to be found in the south German region (Regensburg). These were the fortified homes of noble families, who apparently felt they needed to be well protected even against their neighbours. Of unfortified middle-class houses, only a few late Romanesque façades remain. In Italy there is a whole series of town halls of imposing form and size that belong to the late twelfth and the thirteenth century *[328]*. They are huge, sumptuous buildings, often with a great hall on the first floor above an open, vaulted loggia.

*327   View of S. Giminiano. These high defence towers of the
nobility were built in the twelfth century; they still form a
unique silhouette in this hill town.*

*328   Town hall of Piacenza, thirteenth century. The castellated
structure is a typical expression of the realistic Italian cities. Note
the richly decorated late Romanesque windows on the first story,
and the open ground story which already has Gothic arcades and
vaults.*

Sculpture

During Romanesque times the plastic arts were
exclusively in the service of the church buildings; and
just as the latter rose over an orderly ground-plan as
a richly articulated structure well developed in all its
parts, so Christian imagery had imposed on it an
order in which the various trends of the early Middle
Ages gradually coalesced into the synopsis of a
comprehensive theory of the world. This theory was
shaped to an especially large extent by ideas of the
beyond, with the Last Judgment and apocalyptic
visions playing the dominant part. The representations that express it have a medieval ambiguity about
them, and the boundaries between human, animal,
vegetable, and abstract forms are indistinct, so that
the meaning of these images often escapes us today.

We have seen how in Romanesque architecture,
far more than in that of earlier ages, plastic tendencies
emerged, doing so just as clearly in the joining
together of the different structural members as in the
elaboration of the walls. This makes the increased
importance now achieved by sculptural works all the
easier to understand, since it appears as a manifestation of the same artistic bent. Architectural sculpture
gave emphasis to certain important parts of the
building, such as portals, windows, and capitals. The
movable furnishings of the church already known in
the early Middle Ages were joined by individual
works including devotional images and tombs, along
with altar rails and the Crucifixion groups over the
rood-beams. It was in accomplishing this wide range
of tasks, as in organizing the pictorial programme and
making it fit meaningfully into the church building,
that Romanesque sculpture developed.

The large-scale statuary around the portals and in
the interior now came to have rather more importance than the products of the minor arts, although
these likewise revealed the general stylistic trends,
occasionally even earlier than big sculpture. Gold and
ivory thus gave way to bronze (tomb plaques, doors),
wood, and stone (architectural sculpture and
individual statues). This is evidence of a stylistic
change that made itself apparent in the often life-size
figures: the antique illusionism that during the early
Middle Ages had still lingered on in the delicate ivory
relief or the transfiguring glitter of gold was now
finally rejected, its place being taken by a symbolic
and austere portrayal of the after-world. This could
be rendered in different ways, finding just as valid
an embodiment in strongly convex and fully rounded
figures as in low and surface-filling relief. Side by
side with the calm, hieratic and severe conception of

German sculpture appeared the ecstatic visions on French tympana. But such regional variants always continued to be ruled by the same determination to achieve an aloof and, as it were, hypnotic type. This applies to every land whose sculptural activity became important in Romanesque times, to Germany, France, and Spain just as to Italy. Even the continuing influence of antique models, so much a feature of the South, had no effect on the abstractive power of transcendental representations.

Not until near the end of the twelfth century were there signs of a change, when new life suddenly seized the block-like and rigid figures. One is justified in connecting this with the renewed influx of antique and Byzantine forms. It seems, however, that for the first time then there was an inward readiness to adopt these forms, to assimilate them in a genuine meeting, and to make them serve the new indigenous ideas. Romanesque sculpture, which hitherto had only used a symbolic version of the human form for elucidating the contents of the Bible, gradually filled with earthly reality. A terrestrial model, the knightly ideal of beauty, appeared worthy to represent divine figures. With this, sculpture was on the threshold of Gothic, in which the balance between natural and supernatural, form and message, would enjoy a brief classic perfection.

France

The earliest examples of medieval figure sculpture on buildings are thought to have been found in the Pyrenean area [cf. 255]. They are thus in a region whose northern Spanish and southern French inhabitants then had close linguistic and cultural ties, and which with the pilgrimages to Santiago de Compostela acquired a fairly consistent artistic character. Half a century after these initial, still primitive, experiments, the first major centre of French Romanesque large-scale sculpture came into being around Toulouse. This was closely connected with almost contemporary and very similar ventures in north Spanish León, and it still cannot be finally settled which had priority. The most impressive of these early works are today attached to the inner ambulatory wall of the pilgrimage church of St-Sernin at Toulouse; they comprise a rather more than half life-size marble relief of *Christ Enthroned* [329] and a series of Apostles. These figures are distinguished by their austere and calmly majestic appearance, such ornamental details as the drapery lines or the hair being fully subordinated to the grand general composition. Even if the solemn frontality and softly

329   Christ enthroned in Glory; after 1096. This marble relief, now in the choir ambulatory of St-Sernin at Toulouse, stands at the beginning of large-scale French sculpture. A small-scale model is here extended to a representation of almost life-size. Frontality and hieratic solemnity combine with the ornamental detail to form a strict composition.

modelled fairly low relief style still reveal their descent from decorative art (ivories and book illumination), the Romanesque spirit is clearly expressed in the monumentalizing and simplifying of the forms.

Barely twenty-five years later, a new, substantially more advanced stage in the development of south-western French sculpture was reached at Moissac, somewhat farther to the north. The Cluniac priory church of *St-Pierre* was once a link in the chain of important pilgrimage buildings here, and the perfectly preserved *portal* [330] of its south porch can still make the overwhelming impression that pilgrims once received on entering the church. One's eye first alights on the tympanum, whose surface is entirely covered with multi-figured representations. The focus and dominant motif is a Christ surrounded by the Evangelist signs and two angels. On a considerably smaller scale, the Twenty-Four Elders of the Apocalypse are aligned in three superimposed bands. The actual entrance is divided by a richly adorned trumeau and closed to left and right by jagged arcs. In the figure style of the tympanum, the calm solemnity of Toulouse has yielded to an agitated, expressive formal idiom. The figures are greatly elongated, their thin, fragile limbs bent in complex standing and walking attitudes. Every detail – the heads turned as far as they will go, the jagged hems, the long, wispy beards – is seized by the inner excitement, which weaves it into a general fabric of lines that continues as far as the curves of the lateral entrance walls. Though at times almost modelling in the round, the relief style cannot hide the fact that a strongly planar and linear conception prevails here, one that is far from having the monumental grandeur of the early stage, but which, instead, has gained in expressive intensity.

This style, variants of which are to be found in other regions of south-western France and in Spain, also marks the sculpture of Burgundy. One of the

330 Portal of the south porch of St-Pierre at Moissac, c. 1120. An early example of an arch decorated with figural reliefs. The solemnity of the early style is evident in the representation of Christ enthroned and the Twenty-Four Elders of the Apocalypse. Note the ornamental stylization and agitated, elongated figures.

331 Portal of the west vestibule of Ste-Madeleine at Vézelay, c. 1130. Burgundian churches too had portals decorated in an abstract and visionary style of relief. The agitated figural composition of the miracle of the Pentecost is enclosed in a distinctly tectonic frame.

finest examples of this is offered by the central *portal* inside the galilee of *Ste-Madeleine at Vézelay [331]*, a church of equal importance architecturally. The way this portal has been fitted into the architecture has the same classic balance as the division of its tympanum into main part, framing fields, and surrounding decorative frieze. Yet the actual representation seems almost more agitated, palpitant, and ecstatic than the one at Moissac. It shows the miracle of the Pentecost with the Apostles being sent out to preach the Gospel to the peoples of the earth (these appear as fanciful figures on the lintel and framing fields). Perhaps Peter the Venerable, prior of Vézelay and a notable theologian, drew up the plan for this representation of a theme that must have had a particular significance at the time. It was at Vézelay that St Bernard of Clairvaux preached in 1149 and King Louis took up the Cross, and from Vézelay Richard

332, 333   West portals of St-Gilles-du-Gard, c. 1150. This, the most important three-porch design of southern French late Romanesque, is modelled on Roman triumphal arches. Attention is focused less on the tympanum decoration than on the large figures of the front and portal walls. The figures have some of the movement and life of antique statuary.

Cœur de Lion and Philip Augustus of France started for the Third Crusade.

Around the middle of the twelfth century French portal sculpture, like architecture, arrived at a number of exemplary solutions of a distinctive regional character. While in the west the richly adorned display wall of Notre-Dame-la-Grande at Poitiers was built with the important innovation of large figures under rows of arches in the middle story *[285]*, southern and northern France saw a further development of the three-arch portal decorated with statues. In Provence the Roman heritage could be a major source of inspiration, and the great portal arrangement of the abbey church of *St-Gilles-du-Gard [332]* is hardly conceivable without the example of Roman triumphal arches. Even the ornament – fret, acanthus, egg-and-dart, and so on – points back to the classical past. Set in shallow niches between fluted *pilasters [333]*, the large statues modelled in strong relief with an almost plastic fullness look calm and collected. Antique sculpture seems far closer than in the works previously considered.

This pacification of form, which also marks north Spanish sculpture, could lead to rigidity. The figures against the pillars in the cloister of the church of *St-Trophime at Arles [334]* are block-like creations. There is no crossing of the legs to make their calm standing pose indistinct, and even the drapery, with its parallel descending folds, contributes to their columnar appearance. One cannot help seeing them as tectonic members of the architecture – in this case, as it were, angle columns. Up to now, the evolution of Romanesque sculpture in France had appeared most clearly in the visionary reliefs on tympana. The shaping of figures in the round, as also their fitting into the portal structure, brought a new problem. This development heralds the Gothic. In the statue portal, whose over life-size column-like figures receive those who enter between its deep splayed jambs, the new form of a rich and plastic portal scheme had been discovered. The first solution of this kind was still strongly affected in its details by Romanesque otherworldliness, but its structure was already Gothic. It appeared at Chartres *[462]*, and thus in that north French region of the Île-de-France which may be regarded as the cradle of the Gothic style. The tendencies towards a relaxing of the stiffened Romanesque human image began in France round about 1200, which means that they belong here to the Gothic stylistic period *[cf. 464]*. Statues carved in the round had first to become regular components of the architecture in order to free themselves from the tectonic severity of the early forms and change into knightly figures with a living soul.

plinths, and capitals show how strongly influential the classical heritage remained during the Middle Ages in Italy itself. Even in the symbolic and severe recasting of the models, it is always perceptible. So, too, in northern Italy, which was almost the sole region to introduce figure sculpture consistently into its portal structures, one looks in vain for the ecstatic, otherworldly rendering of religious themes met on French tympana. The rich arrangements of sculpture that in south-west France often cover the whole façade can be seen here only in much abridged forms. Generally speaking, the effect of the west front is determined by the north Italian porch, to which the sculptural works are also clearly subordinated.

If one excepts the bronze reliefs on the doors of S. Zeno at Verona, still late eleventh century and related stylistically to Hildesheim rather than Italy, then the *figure scenes at Modena Cathedral* begin the development. A certain Master Wiligelmus and his assistants decorated the west front at Modena round

334   Pillar in the cloister of St-Trophime at Arles, second half of twelfth century. An example of the last phase of Romanesque sculpture in southern France. The pillared, block-like forms of the figures show the trend that led to the Gothic statue portals of northern France.

Italy

Since the early Middle Ages, a rich strain of architectural sculpture had spread from the Lombardic north as far as the Campagna. Its chiefly ornamental motifs – foliage, scroll-work, interlace, and occasionally animal and human forms as well – are of partly antique and partly Germanic origin. This decoration settled in bands largely on window and door frames, but above all on such internal church furnishings as pulpits, lecterns, screens, and candelabra. Except in the north, whose architecture likewise owed the biggest debt to northern and western Europe, Italy kept this strongly ornamental trend, which allowed the human figure only a subordinate position, even in the twelfth century. It reached its zenith in the colourful and most elaborate inlays of cut stones that are particularly common in the Campagna [335]. The few figure motifs that did get hidden away in the scroll-work of the carved friezes on cornices,

335   Pulpit in the cathedral of Sessa Aurunca, thirteenth century. A chief example of the 'pergamo' developed in the Campagna: here supported by lion pillars. Cosmati work is combined with sculptured decoration that shows a marked dependence on antique styles.

336   Master Wiligelmus: Genesis scenes on the west façade of Modena Cathedral, c. 1120. The beginning of figure sculpture on upper Italian portals. A deep-cut composition in verticals and horizontals. Note the block-like forms of the powerful relief.

337   Benedetto Antelami: Relief of the Deposition in Parma Cathedral, 1178. This example shows the persistence of the Modena style. The schematically aligned figures have a columnar stiffness. The upper surface is enlivened by the pleated clothing.

about 1120. One sees here how that initial stage of north and west European Romanesque prevails in the strip reliefs, full of severity and inner monumentality *[336]*. Beyond this, the figures show in the clock-like, clearly contoured, and strongly projecting forms of their bodies that they were fitted into the action as vehicles of expression, yet were subordinated to it without losing their independence.

The Modena style occurred again, sometimes greatly modified, on various north Italian portals. In the course of the development, foreign influences too became apparent, in particular from neighbouring

Provence. This applies to the sculptor Antelami, who was active at Parma and actually named himself on one of his works. Such an attitude is characteristic of Italian artists, who emerged from medieval anonymity much earlier than those in other lands. Antelami's first surviving work, a relief of the *Deposition [337]*, seems to continue the block-like conception of the Modena figures, even though more than half a century separates it from them. Yet the thick-set, rather monotonously aligned figures with their clothing gathered in many small folds already contained the seeds of new forms that would become evident round about 1200 in the two large *figures in the niches* on the cathedral of Borgo San Domino *[338]*. In view of the enormous advance, it may be of little consequence that one has to reckon here with influence from Provençal portal statues *[333]*, for the result is essentially different. The very placing in a niche of a work carved fully in the round gives the figure an entirely new intrinsic value, since it is freed

338   Benedetto Antelami: Statue of King David on the façade of Borgo San Domino Cathedral, c. 1200. Note the change in style due to the influence of antique statuary in southern French models [333]. Antelami takes the figure out of relief and leaves it as a completely plastic niche statue.

339 Marble fragment of an over life-size ruler figure, beginning of thirteenth century. Barletta, National Museum. An outstanding example of Hohenstaufen art in Apulia, based on Roman emperor statues.

ated, relics of this Apulian group, whose artistic and intellectual ideals centred on the Roman imperial age. Even so damaged a piece as the marble bust thought to represent *Frederick II [339]* reveals the outstanding quality of this art, and its determination to break the bonds of the medieval commitment to an abstractive rendering of man. These efforts, which may be considered to have foreshadowed the Renaissance, developed no further than the opening stages, just as the southern kingdom of the Hohenstaufens disappeared. The after-effects of this magnificent approach to sculpture appeared during the second half of the thirteenth century in the works of the Pisani, a sculptor family that moved from Apulia to Tuscany (cf. p. 249), and of their circle.

Germany

Whereas in other lands the evolution of larger Romanesque sculpture took place mainly on façades

340 Madonna of Bishop Imad, the so-called 'Imad Madonna', c. 1050. Paderborn, Diözesanmuseum. Wood, originally decorated with plate of gold. This work, strongly hieratic and far removed from reality, stands at the beginning of German Romanesque sculpture.

from the line that grows out of the building and given an individual life of its own. Admittedly this statue cannot be envisaged without its ties with the architecture, as it calls for the enframing hollow. Even the separate features of such a nearly life-like figure – the hint of contrapposto in the standing pose, the opposition of body and drapery, the carriage of the head and hands – are scarcely to be interpreted as reflexions of earthly reality but as an adopting of antique motifs still wholly governed by ornamental constraint. All the same, the inflow of these forms easing Romanesque stiffness announced the arrival of a new spirit, which was also blazing a trail in the North *[343]*.

A further art centre came into being at the outset of the thirteenth century in the southern part of the country, where architecture and sculpture enjoyed a brief, intensive flowering under Hohenstaufen rule. Nowhere else in contemporary Western sculpture is the closeness to the antique as directly perceptible as in the few remaining, and sometimes badly mutil-

and portals, in Germany it is most impressively shown by individual statues. This may be partly due to the fact that, with their preference for double chancels, German churches from the outset offered little in the way of starting-points for a richer development of the west front. Yet even with buildings that have an unmistakable direction there is no plastic figure decoration round the portals to be compared with French examples. There seems, in fact, to be a different attitude towards sculpture here: 'sculpture is not the daughter of architecture, but its younger sister' (Pindar). Thus, instead of on the exterior, German statuary evolved chiefly inside the church, whether as free-standing devotional images, as the splendid groups of the rood-crosses, or as reliefs on tombs, altar rails, and sumptuous pieces of goldsmith's work. Wood, stucco, and metal were often preferred to stone, the most important material in other countries. Unless they were products of decorative art, these works had to hold their own against the surrounding space, often without any architectural support, a fact that makes more comprehensible their severe and solemn monumentality, their block-like form, and their ornamental stylization.

Among the most remarkable devotional images that have come down to us from early Salian times is the so-called *Imad Madonna [340]*. Like the statue of the Essen Minster treasury *[249]* some thirty years earlier, this Virgin carved in wood was once covered with plate of gold. Not only has the scale increased (the *Imad Madonna* is over a metre tall and therefore bigger by a quarter than the Essen one), but the last traces of a delicacy still clinging to the earlier work have been completely eliminated. With their intense severity, the large forms, which are almost built rather than sculpted, assert themselves even without a covering of gold – indeed, one could perhaps say that they make a still more powerful and convincing impression. A clear, strict coherency welds the parts into a whole, relates them in a play of simple contrasts of direction. The decorative motifs are used to bind together all the individual forms. Sculpture now gained in immediate, concrete presence. Instead of remaining captive within an imaginary pictorial domain, the sacred image stepped out from it, to be set before the eye of the beholder in a physically tangible form.

This plastic form consolidated from within was also realized in relief, the technique most capable of leading to a painter-like, illusionistic interpretation of figure subjects. In the *bronze tomb plaque of Archbishop Friedrich of Wettin [341]* the effigy almost bursts from the metal surface, which is no longer a 'picture'

341   Bronze tomb plaque of Archbishop Friedrich of Wettin in Magdeburg Cathedral, c. 1150. Note the closed form of German high Romanesque. Even in relief the plaque raises itself block-like from the ground. Note the gesture of the hand raised in blessing and the fully plastic head.

342 Madonna, from the Crucifixion group at Sonnenburg Monastery (Tyrol), end of twelfth century. Cologne, Schnütgen-museum. The block-like, completely plastic high Romanesque figure is enlivened by the play of the dress, which becomes an important factor in shaping form.

space but a background. The raiment clings like foil to the body, which is clearly outlined as an integrated block-like mass. Only the head and hands have been individualized, not in the sense of portraiture which was not aimed at in an age concerned with the symbolic exemplar, but subserviently to the hieratic, emblematic total effect.

Under such circumstances it was possible for the first monumental free-standing figure of the Middle Ages to be produced in Germany: the cast-bronze *Brunswick Lion [344]*. True, its form was prefigured in works of artistic craftsmanship (lion-shaped water-jugs); but it is significant that this form could now be expressed in monumental terms, crystallizing into a real, plastically fashioned symbol.

Towards the end of the twelfth century, German sculpture reflected an endeavour to breathe new life into figures stiffened in transcendental stillness. If we compare the statues, with probably hardly a decade between them, of the *Madonna* belonging to a

343 Standing Madonna in S. Maria im Kapitol at Cologne, end of twelfth century. The late Romanesque is evident in the conception of the inner movement of the figure, in the natural, rounded fall of the garments, and above all in a new expressive capacity, which brings the work closer to reality.

antique forms passed on by them seem to accord with an artistic aim that makes possible an effective assimilation and recasting of these forms. The Apostle figures are characterized by a hitherto unknown beauty of appearance evident most of all in the nobly dignified attitude and the flowing, rounded cast of the drapery as well as the eloquent expression of the face. The strongly pictorial effect that this relief undoubtedly gives must not make us overlook the fact that it was achieved with predominantly sculptural means. Thus the bodily forms are really rounded and can be explored with the hand, while the strips of shadow that emphasize the fall of the drapery folds are produced by deep, hollowing channels. The figuration in the face is heightened to an almost passionate intensity. Between the large planes of the cheeks and brow are sunk shadowy eye-sockets whose gaze has a more compelling expressiveness than the drill-holes of the pupils can generate.

Looking back at the separate stages of development, from the solemn and hieratic linear style of

345   The Apostle Philip, stucco relief on the altar rails of the Liebfrauenkirche at Halberstadt, c. 1190. Under the influence of Byzantine forms the rigidity of the Romanesque gives way to a new, knightly ideal of humanity.

344   Monument to Henry the Lion in Brunswick: the so-called 'Brunswick Lion'. Life-size cast-bronze. In the first monumental piece of sculpture of the Middle Ages the figure of the lion becomes a splendid symbol, returning to craftsmanlike examples. Note the ornamental effect of the mane and the militant expression of the head.

Crucifixion group from Sonnenburg Monastery *[342]* and a standing *Madonna* in S. Maria im Kapitol at Cologne *[343]*, a development becomes apparent that resembles the one in Antelami's work *[337, 338]*. It leads from a block-like form whose severity is toned down a little by the play of folds applied from without, to a human figure stirred from within, its expression and attitude showing touches of earthly reality. Not only are Mother and Child close to each other in a display of spiritual affection, but the physical structure indicates a new feeling for corporality: the stiff pose relaxes into a contrapposto undulation, while the limbs become rounded beneath the drapery, which falls in lively lengths of material.

Shortly after, this more realistic conception led in Germany to works like the *stucco reliefs of the Halberstadt altar rails [345]*. Here again, as so often in the preceding century, one can point to direct links with Byzantine ivories. For the first time, however, the

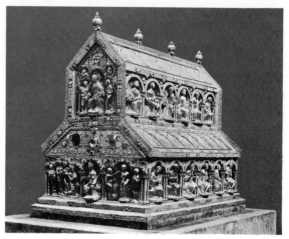

346, 347 Nicholas of Verdun, Shrine of the Magi in Cologne Cathedral, 1186–96. Silver, chased, and gilded. The new tendencies of the late Romanesque are summed up in this work. The shrine has a basilical form. In the round and trefoil arcades are seated figures (on the long sides) and representations of scenes (on the short sides). The figure of the Apostle James [346] shows the expressive strength of late Romanesque sculpture in the richness of falling draperies over a rounded, organic body.

Carolingian ivories [246] and the transcendental, rigid monumentality of the *Imad Madonna* [340] to this new acceptance of earthly beauty, one can judge how far German sculpture had come in almost four centuries. But even this last work, which already anticipates the Naumburg figures [469], would never be viewed as a naturalistic image of the present world, but as a realization of the wish to exalt an earthly ideal of man into an image of divine beings.

If we end our section on German sculpture with a glance at decorative art, this is not to round the subject off, which could only be done by mentioning many other things, but because it was in Germany that this branch had particular importance. Although the phases of development are exemplified by the individual statue, they were often prepared in church appurtenances – in candelabra, vessels, and shrines. The main centres of this extremely fertile goldsmith's art lay in the Rhine, Meuse, and Moselle areas, and

its products were distributed very widely in France as well as Germany. Among its greatest masters is Nicholas of Verdun, who came from Lorraine. His works, including the figures on the *Shrine of the Magi at Cologne* [346, 347], can be clearly associated with the tendencies of German sculpture. As regards form, these shrines are directly dependent on architecture, reflecting most exactly in their basilican and centralized arrangements the church buildings of the times. Their lavish ornamentation in embossed plate of gold, precious stones, and cloisonné enamel, combines with the sculptured figures to form an immensely rich and sumptuous whole. Rendered as seated figures in the round, Nicholas of Verdun's Apostles [346] may without hesitation be set beside the Halberstadt stucco reliefs. Despite their small size, they show the same plastic formative power that fashioned in idealized types a new image of man closer to earthly things.

Painting

To the modern age, it seems that Romanesque art has revealed itself most truly in its great church buildings and their sculptures. There may be something in this, for despite the ambiguity and other-worldliness of its forms Romanesque pressed towards a display of the concrete, tangible substance. Moreover with the progressive opening-up and piercing of the nave walls, which hitherto had often been entirely covered in Bible scenes, the contribution of fresco to the overall effect of the sacral space was reduced. If this meant that, purely as regards quantity, painting suffered an eclipse, it still remained a vital part of Romanesque artistic activity. In the union of the church, all the different categories were on the same level, and their statements made in the most varied techniques combined with the architecture to form that unbroken symbolic complex into which the religious edifice fused during Romanesque times.

Pictorial creation, which was extensive, manifested itself in diverse ways. There were the fresco cycles inside churches, the book illuminations turned out in quantity by numerous monastic schools, the stained-glass windows providing a new medium of expression that came slowly to the fore, and, not least, the sumptuous works of applied art in gold and enamel. From this profusion we will take just a few examples, with an emphasis on wall-paintings, as these are probably the most impressive revelations of the Romanesque desire to produce monumental symbolic form. We can dispense here with the division of the material by countries in favour of a choice comprising those specimens, drawn from the various European regions, that show different stylistic phases and pictorial types especially clearly.

High Romanesque wall-painting

Whereas the beginning of large-scale sculpture meant a fresh start with almost no medieval preparations, painting in all its spheres continued already existent formal traditions. One has to take into account the enduring influence of earlier stylistic trends, and allow for reversions and borrowings. Thus the repeated inflow of Byzantine forms often brought considerable changes in style. Of the two modes of rendering religious subjects already developed in early Christian times – the solemn and severe, mostly frontally posed figure or group for symbolic themes (e.g. Christ as judge of the world) and the more narrative and illustrative interpretation for Testament scenes – the second had largely lost its spontaneous narrative style as early as the Ottonian age, while gaining in intensity of expression instead. These trends, which probably also went back ultimately to Byzantium, were carried further in Romanesque art. Wall-painting showed them soon and vigorously in Italy, where the influence of Byzantine forms was particularly strong throughout the Middle Ages.

Probably painted during the second half of the eleventh century, the *fresco cycle in S. Angelo in Formis* near Capua is among the best-preserved examples of a pictorial programme involving the whole interior of a church. Scenes from the Old and New Testaments, typologically opposed, adorn the nave walls. In the apse Christ is enthroned in glory, while the west wall is entirely covered by a representation of the Last Judgment organized in five superimposed bands. This extensive series of pictures goes far beyond its early Christian models and presents an arrangement of the Christian themes that became the rule in the West and differs on essential points from Byzantine schemes. Nevertheless the style of the frescoes has a strongly Byzantine cast – indeed in some cases one must take it that specially summoned artists were at work, although in others certain changes are already apparent. In *The Healing of the Blind*, the antique feeling for the body is still discernible, albeit under garments whose fall is determined by hard, strongly linear forms. The expression centres on the eloquent bearing of the stocky figures and on their large faces with penetrating eyes. Natural movement has been stiffened into symbolic gesture, and organic form subjected to a severe, ornamental discipline. Even the landscape details are reduced to a minimum, with regularly repeated tufts of grass indicating the vegetation, while the background is formed solely by the abstract and symbolic horizontal articulation of the different colour zones (earth, air, firmament). The colouring is full of contrasts, but restrained. Apart from the strong brown of the outer garments, it is chiefly shades of delicate blue and green that prevail. Byzantine influence remained dominant in Italian painting until 1300. Only with Giotto did a new conception of man assert itself.

Round about 1100 the hall church of *St-Savin-sur-Gartempe [283]* acquired its ceiling decoration, which is likewise a unique specimen of Romanesque painting. The entire barrel-vault over the nave was covered in four longitudinal bands with Old Testament scenes after models that are thought to have been found in book illuminations from the same region. These connexions seem all the more plausible in that the rich stock of forms and picture types belonging to illuminated manuscripts is often

348 God the Father before the People, scene from the ceiling frescoes of St-Savin-sur-Gartempe, c. 1100. A greatly simplified composition of the French high Romanesque, whose effect was calculated to be seen from a distance. The accents are placed on the isolation and grouping of figures. Expressive gestures make the action intelligible.

arches. Solemn frontality prevails, in keeping with the subject. Only the big angel figures display the movement that we know from France. Despite the compelling quality of the hieratic gesture and the gaze the total impression is very largely determined by a planar and decorative nature. Strong colours rich in contrasts mould the composition, while graduated, shadowing nuances emphasize each line rather schematically. Every form is ornamented, the plump bodies and the large, flat, oval faces as well as the framing mandorla and the arcade. Yet the representation preserves its monumental and otherworldly character, and is not lost in decorative detail. The transcendentalizing power of abstraction can make itself felt just as convincingly in ornamental stylization as in expressive figure scenes.

Among the oldest surviving glass windows are the *Prophet windows* dating from the early twelfth century in *Augsburg Cathedral [350]*. The very technique of joining together different bits of glass makes ornamentalizing an obvious danger; but the over life-size figures assert themselves in an almost block-like severity and with an intensity of concentrated,

reflected in the large fresco cycles. An unquestionable success, the conversion into a monumental composition is suited to the effect made from a distance. The scenes are divided up into rectangular fields with contrasting colours. In the scene of *God the Father before the People [348]*, the single figure stands out against a dark background, the group against a light one. The solid mass of people has stiffened into a block that still shows a clear impulse of movement. Opposite this tight, compact form, the figure of God the Father spreads out frontally in a grand, spacious attitude. Its rich drapery, with calligraphic flourishes of creases applied in white, swirls out in fluttering folds. It is in the treatment of the drapery that details still recall earlier, ultimately antique, motifs. These seldom wholly disappeared in painting, which continually had to come to terms with late antique forms transmitted by Byzantine models. In its general effect, however, this figure already corresponds to the conception that disembodies the human form into the schematic image of a supernatural world, a conception that was expressed soon after in the tympana of Moissac and Vézelay *[330, 331]*.

Round about 1125, at roughly the same date as the sculptural works just mentioned, the apse of the Spanish church of *S. Clemente at Tahull* was frescoed with a representation of Christ enthroned in a mandorla *[349]*. He is surrounded by angels, while, below, Apostles and the Virgin are lined up under

349 Christ enthroned above the Apostles and Virgin Mary, fresco from the apse of S. Clemente at Tahull, c. 1125. Barcelona, Museo de Arte de Cataluña. Note the expressive height and transcendental quality of the hieratic representation.

hypnotic expression that put them on an equal footing with the creations of sculpture.

Late Romanesque painting

Shortly after the middle of the twelfth century the first signs appeared in painting of a new closeness to life. The seated figure of an *Ancestor of Christ [351]* seems, as other figures in the lower part of the double chapel at Schwarzrheindorf, much more like an image of a self-confident earthly ruler than an expres-

350   The Prophet Hosea, detail of a stained-glass window in Augsburg Cathedral, beginning of twelfth century. Stained-glass painting came to the fore when it was decided to brighten the nave walls. The rendering of the large figure is in the high Romanesque style: all organic and decorative details are subordinated to the ornamental rule.

351   An Ancestor of Christ as a king enthroned, in the lower part of the double chapel at Schwarzrheindorf, c. 1156. The hieratic stiffness weakens the life-like quality of the late Romanesque. Colour contrasts are abandoned in favour of a painterly style.

sion of hitherto existing ideas of the supernatural being of Bible characters. Terse and linear, the style largely dispenses with colour diversification, reflecting a tendency that had already made an early appearance in manuscript illumination. The vigorous face is indicated with a few confident lines, as are the strong, ample body and the robe gathered into many folds. This no longer leads its own decorative life in abstract flourishes and jags, but follows the bodily forms in a natural fall. The over life-size figure fills the narrow niche with amazing presence, though it still has a generalized, almost schematic appearance that neither can nor will show what is individual and unique.

This linear style appears in rich profusion on the *Klosterneuburg Altarpiece*, which the great goldsmith Nicholas of Verdun *[346]* created probably as a pulpit facing rather more than two decades later, in 1181. In fifty-one enamel-work panels – mostly gold against a blue background – scenes from the Old and

New Testaments are placed in opposition to each other. The Byzantine models that were also present here have been refashioned extremely independently in a way reflecting the readiness to accept and approve of earthly things that existed then all over Europe. In the scene of the *Circumcision of Samson [352]*, the figures are full of pulsing life. Realistic observations have been introduced, as in the frightened expressions of the parents, the helpless movement of the child, and the intent stooping attitude of the priest handling the knife. Beneath the rich, flowing garments the limbs fill out in natural proportions and easy movements. There is likewise a clear rendering of the architectural space, and even the oil-lamp has not been forgotten. The solid core of the figures is hewn out distinctly.

This new rendering of the human form, its seizure in the counterplay of body and dress, was not the

353 Jesse's Dream and two Prophets, detail of the ceiling painting in S. Michael at Hildesheim, c. 1220. The 'jagged style', a late phase of German Romanesque painting. The pleating is fully distinct, and determines the whole effect of the work.

352 Nicholas of Verdun: Circumcision of Samson, gold and enamel panel on the Klosterneuburg Altarpiece, 1181. Byzantine influences are evident in the late Romanesque. Realism, movement, and the finely drawn play of vestments are combined in an expressive unity.

only stylistic genre – alongside it the older, severe conception remained – but it is certainly the one most characteristic of the period around 1200. It was operative in Germany until the mid-thirteenth century, a time when the first Gothically curved figures were already being produced in France. During its late phase it intensified into an almost baroque jagged style, which appeared above all in book illumination, though also in monumental painting. S. Michael at Hildesheim possesses, in Germany, the sole surviving painted wooden ceiling from the Middle Ages (*c.* 1220). Divided up into separate pictures, the theme of the Jesse Tree – Christ's ancestors from Adam and Eve to the Virgin – covers the whole ceiling. The large central fields are accompanied by smaller lateral ones in an arrangement that may call to mind the metrical system of the ground-plan. *Jesse's Dream [353]* shows the figure lying asleep on a richly draped bed. Stretches of material wind round the naked body, following the limbs with their folds. Swirling waves appear to flow over every solid form and harden at the edges like icicles. Although the core survives, the husk grows increasingly independent. This incipient separation of body and raiment, substance and applied form, marks a final stage similar to the one that late Hohenstaufen architecture had reached: it permitted variations, but no further development. Only the Gothic spirit would finally surmount this phase.

'Gothic' is what the Italian Vasari in the sixteenth century called that dark age between the great past of antiquity and his own period of rebirth, the Renaissance. For him, as for his compatriots and contemporaries, 'Gothic' meant much the same as 'barbaric', and Vasari in fact still tried to make the Goths responsible for this medieval style that he detested. The same attitude survived until about 1800, with all medieval art deprecatingly classed as Gothic. Even the young Goethe approached Strasbourg Cathedral with this prejudice. Expecting to find a barbaric mixture of 'the disorderly, the unnatural, the pieced together, the botched up, and the over elaborate', he discovered, with astonished admiration for the splendid boldness of this edifice, the overwhelming power and originality of Gothic.

The romantics of the early nineteenth century dreamed of a rebirth of Gothic, and the once negative concept gradually took on new meaning. 'Gothic' became a positive designation for the art of the later Middle Ages, as against the Romanesque art of the earlier. From the mid-nineteenth century onward romantic enthusiasm and historicism led to extensive reconstruction and restoration of medieval works, undertakings on whose value opinion is now very much divided. Finally there came those mechanical copies of the period after the Franco-Prussian War (the German *Gründerzeit*), when neo-Gothic was just one among many possible kinds of arbitrary stylistic imitation. Through its own expressionistic vitality, the early twentieth century felt attracted by the expressive power of Gothic images, as also by the supposed dynamism of Gothic architecture. What most appeals to our age of creative engineering is the union of technical boldness and artistic form.

The stylistic period we now call Gothic stretched from the mid-twelfth century to the beginning of the sixteenth, involving various countries and regions at different times. Beyond this, there were such wide divergencies in style down the centuries and from place to place that there is only one feature which we may call distinctively Gothic: the pointed arch. The pointed arch is the basic element of Gothic architectural construction, of the coherently planned static

structure that now took the place of the heterogeneous wall masses of Romanesque. Even the most complex fifteenth-century vaulting and tracery forms grew out of the pointed arch. As the 'Gothic line', it dominates the formal language of the entire age.

Naturally, one cannot regard the pointed arch as merely a technically dictated or even an accidently discovered form, which is what the nineteenth century often did. It is a genuine stylistic feature that in all its varieties is always a means of expression and communication. This becomes especially clear if the parallels with some of the most important features of intellectual and spiritual history of the age are considered. Thus the attempt of Scholasticism to unite reason and faith, to prove the Christian doctrine of salvation by logic, reached its climax in France during the thirteenth century with St Thomas Aquinas, and this outlook found formal expression in the cathedral, the complete work of art. The deepening of early fourteenth-century German mysticism was echoed in the spiritualized forms of the visual art of this period. The courtly, chivalric elegance that flourished round about 1400 in Burgundy also appeared in the Gothic play of line. Thanks to the continuing effect of the Gothic tradition, the early middle-class realism of fifteenth-century Netherlandish and German painting seems closer to the heart and more profound than the contemporary work of the incipient Renaissance, influenced by antiquity. If one looks for a connexion between these different phenomena, one discovers a fundamental trait: the common endeavour at that time, particularly in and after the fourteenth century, to free the self from the supra-personal powers and institutions that had dominated the early Middle Ages, and to arrive at a new, independent knowledge of environment and the individual.

The Gothic was born in France. Here, since the late eleventh century, forms and constructional possibilities had been under development in the various regions that, from the mid-twelfth century, united with each other in the focal region of the Île-de-France. Out of this transitional stage there grew, around 1200, the pure Gothic of the classic cathedral [cf. 355, 380, 383].

The first half of the thirteenth century constitutes the main building period of these great French cathedrals. Not without reason they are often also called 'royal churches', since along with the bishops

354 Choir of Bourges Cathedral, begun 1190–1200. Light and wide steepled space. The tripartite structure of the nave wall corresponds to that in the side aisles.

it was the kings who were the real patrons and promoters. Supported by a similar God-given ruling power, the 'imperial cathedrals' of Germany were nearing completion at the same time, but in what still remained the forms of the late Romanesque Hohenstaufen tradition. Yet the sculptural decoration of these German cathedrals in particular shows that chivalry was now entering as a new force besides these older powers of king, emperor, and bishop.

Whereas in France creative vigour was already flagging towards the end of the thirteenth century, it was only around the middle of this century that other lands, including Germany and Spain, began to be concerned with Gothic. The new style had in general absolutely no native and independent preliminary development or transitional forms on which to build there. People largely began by taking over the entire formal apparatus from France, not just in architecture but also in the figurative arts, and sooner or later they permeated it with creative ideas of their own. It was different in England, which owing to the Norman element had its own background of Gothic. Nevertheless here too French influence held sway over the cathedrals of the first half of the thirteenth century. This initial phase, known as Early English *[356]*, was thus the result of many variations on the model of the French cathedral. The close of the phase and the transition to late Gothic cannot be clearly determined. About as early as 1250 a highly individual development took shape in England. For Germany, the completion of the chancel of Cologne Cathedral in 1322 put a visible end to the encounter with France. Special forms such as the German hall church appeared quite early on in different regions. Above all, architecture now lost its primacy, to which sculpture and painting, despite their splendid achievements, had been subordinate. The elaboration of the altar, with the development of the altar panel and the centre-piece to which wings were attached, brought increasing independence to the figurative arts. With this, the outward conditions were also established for a rise in the importance of artistic individuality, all early Gothic art having been the work of anonymous partnerships and associations. Where names are known from previous times – usually found in builders' statements of account – they cannot be linked with sharply defined creative personalities.

It is no accident that the first artists in the modern sense were active round about 1300 in Italy. They largely determined the aspect of Italian art at that period, and this partly explains why Italy adopted no more than certain features of north European Gothic – doing so, moreover, only in the late thirteenth century. Through the individuality of their work, Giotto and his contemporaries show that Italy had hurried on far ahead of other lands in freeing the individual from old ties. This process was sustained in Italy, as in the other countries, by the towns and their inhabitants, even though it took different stylistic paths. Usually established for the first time in the twelfth or thirteenth century, or else raised again on almost forgotten antique foundations, these towns grew into new centres during the fourteenth and fifteenth centuries. Crafts and trade took their place beside the previously dominant agriculture. Politically, too, quite a number of them gained full independence, particularly where, as in Germany and Italy, strong superior powers were absent. As free city-states or leagues, they became crucial elements in the pattern of political power. Thus it was worldly and realistic civic pride, but also deep medieval piety, that shaped fifteenth-century art, especially in the Netherlands and Germany.

During the last phase of Gothic development, round about 1500, the Gothic countries of the West were united once more by a complex style to which the French have given the name *flamboyant*. There appeared churches and palaces covered with flickering forms in France, intertwining vaults in open German hall churches and mighty Spanish cathedrals, fantastic tracery in windows, intricate fan-vaults in English chapels and halls. Meanwhile, in the works of Bramante, Leonardo, Raphael, and Michelangelo, Italy was approaching the climax of its Renaissance.

355   A classical French cathedral (Reims, choir, 1210–41; nave second half of thirteenth century). A strong, steep wall and space structure, with massive members. Every single bay is composed as a unit, whose succession makes up the entire space.

356   An 'Early English' cathedral (Wells, c. 1200–39). Note the emphasis on horizontals, the decorative features, and the linear aspects (profiles of arcades, triforium, and rib-vaulting).

357   Tuscan Gothic (Florence Cathedral, begun 1296). Gothic only in detail (pointed arches), this building shows features of the Italian tradition (midway between the early Christian basilica and the Renaissance church). Closed wall surface; rose-window vaulting over the corbel ledge; piers.

358   A South German late Gothic hall church (Dinkelsbühl, parish church of S. Georg, begun 1448). An example of German 'Sondergotik'. Note the three-part main body with nave and aisles the same height; the tall, broad windows, and the piers which rise to the netted vaulting uninterrupted by capitals or abutments.

355

357

356

358

Architecture

At the centre of Gothic art stands the religious building. Church architecture remained the principal
concern of artistic activity even into the fifteenth
century, and forms the most extensive and complete
body of surviving Gothic works. Figurative art was
produced in direct connexion with the church, which
also had a stylistic influence on the forms of secular
architecture. In the great associations of the masons'
lodges, which were often attached to the cathedral
buildings for generations, builders and stonemasons,
sculptors, glass artists, and the various kinds of skilled
craftsmen worked together and alongside each other.
Not only were the lodges of the cathedrals and other
major churches linked by regular exchanges, but the
smaller associations that moved from building to
building also ensured the constant spread of artistic
ideas and technical skill.

It was undoubtedly itinerant building workers who
early in the thirteenth century brought the new
Gothic forms from the French lodges to neighbouring countries. The reappearance of specific architectural ideas and features sometimes enables us to
trace their actual routes. Regional independence,
however, caused considerable delays in adopting the
Gothic style before the development of native architectural forms. These separate achievements of the
various lands [356–60] made their appearance at quite
different times: the English cathedrals in the thirteenth century, Tuscan Gothic around 1300, the
south German hall churches around 1400, the last
Spanish cathedrals towards 1500.

But in spite of all its variations imposed by time
and region, the Gothic building always kept to that
basic principle developed in the French transition
period of the second half of the twelfth century. The
heavy, block-like Romanesque wall building, which
could only be plastically moulded and decoratively
enriched, was succeeded by the statically planned
framework, the visible structure that seems in its
airiness to relieve the stone of its weight and
spiritualize the material.

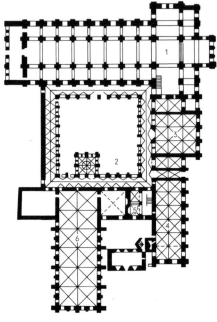

359, 360   Cistercian monastery church of Fontenay in Burgundy,
1139–47. The three-part church with basilical cross-section shows
typically Cistercian characteristics in its eastern parts: rectangular
choir and chapels on the chancel arms. 1 church; 2 cloister, with
chapel around a fountain; 3 main chamber; 4 lay refectory;
5 caldarium; 6 refectory; 7 smithy and mills.

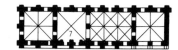

The reformed Order of the Cistercians, founded about 1100 in Burgundy, spread during the twelfth and thirteenth centuries into neighbouring regions and then throughout the West. More rigidly and centrally organized than earlier monastic Orders, the Cistercians passed on formal features belonging to the immediate preparations for Gothic architecture. The Order usually pushed out its foundations into backward areas, so that its buildings, the first large stone structures of any kind in those places, were especially influential. However one probably ought not to think in terms of regular lodges belonging to the Order but rather of certain architectural practices ensuing from the demand for simplicity and asceticism.

Next to nothing has survived unchanged of the mother-houses in Burgundy. *Fontenay* (1139–47), one of the oldest daughter-foundations of the mother-house Clairvaux, is best able to give us a notion of such an early Burgundian monastery layout *[359, 360]*. With its pointed-arch arcades and its pointed barrel-vault strengthened by transverse arches, the

361 *Cistercian church of Poblet in Spain, end of twelfth century.*

362 *Church of the Cistercian abbey of Lilienfeld in lower Austria, first half of thirteenth century. View from the transept to the two-part choir ambulatory. The pointed arches are combined with simple, forceful forms. The piers, without flanking shafts, support large horned capitals. Note the heavy rib-vaulting.*

church remains wholly in the tradition of Burgundian late Romanesque, as it was embodied in the famous third version of the monastery church at Cluny *[cf. 278]*. But because of Cistercian asceticism Fontenay abstained from several forward-looking motifs already prefigured in Cluny III.

Across Provence Cistercian architecture spread to Spain, where the monastery church of *Poblet*, of late twelfth-century date *[361]*, is an exceptionally well-preserved example. In Italy (Fossanova, 1179–1208) this architecture acquired importance not only through exemplifying an advanced vaulting technique, but in its simple forms also set the pattern for churches of the mendicant Orders there. A native, still wholly Romanesque tradition mixed with the new forms during the twelfth century in Germany (Eberbach and Maulbronn). The Cistercians were especially influential as regards the architecture of the eastern German territories: in Austria such early Gothic features as pointed arches and heavy rib-vaults go back to the effect they had there, as at

France

The pointed arch was probably first used and regarded as more static than the round one in Burgundy towards 1100. Other important features leading to Gothic made their entry in northern France, above all Normandy. Here, round about 1100, the separate vaulting compartments were covered over with quadripartite rib-vaults. In the case of the hitherto usual cross-vault the individual cells of a vaulting bay meet in diagonally arching groins. Already increased by the groins, the vault's stability was now reinforced by means of ribs. These were extended cross-wise over temporary supporting frameworks (centerings) as independent members, and the cells, which no longer needed to be stable in themselves, were laid over them as lightly as possible [364, 365]. Even before the introduction of the rib-vault, on constructional and aesthetic grounds the ribs required preparatory wall shafts of the sort that had been usual in Normandy as motifs articulating the wall. Perhaps recalling the wooden architecture of their north European home, the Normans showed a general tendency to articulate their buildings thoroughly with shafts, applied arcading, and galleries, thereby loosening up the solid mass of the wall as early as the eleventh century. The west porch with two towers was likewise known in Normandy towards the end of that century. Shortly after came the first buttresses and primitive flying-buttresses, which developed the building's form more richly outside, too, while at the same time gathering up in lines of force a concentration of the thrust exerted by its vaulting. From the eleventh century the big abbey and pilgrimage churches of the different French regions often had complicated chancel layouts, with an ambulatory and radiating chapels set round the apse.

Chevet, two-tower front, rib-vaulting, wall articulation, and buttressing are the most important architectural elements that, combined as a meaningful whole, constitute the outward formal apparatus of the Gothic cathedral. This union took place in the Île-de-France, the domain of the French royal house, which was now growing stronger. It started with the rebuilding of the eminent monastery church of *St-Denis*, a new version of which was begun on Abbot Suger's initiative in 1137 to take the place of a Carolingian edifice. Owing to later reconstructions, only the ambulatory and its wreath of chapels [367] along with parts of the two-tower front, which was altered in the nineteenth century, now tell us about the mid-twelfth-century work. Ambulatory and

363 *West façade of the monastery church of Chorin (Brandenburg), completed 1334. In the colonized areas of eastern Germany Cistercian architecture was built with a new material: brick. Powerful forms of great richness and harmony characterize the buttresses, blind niches, tracery windows, and triangular gables of this façade.*

Heiligenkreuz, 1136–60, and *Lilienfeld*, first half of the thirteenth century [362]. In the area east of the Elbe, which was opened up during the thirteenth century, Zinna, *Chorin [363]*, and Peplin are notable monastic foundations of the Order. At this time the importance of Cistercian architecture was already declining in the west. The few new buildings that were erected followed the formal tendencies of their milieu, as with Altenberg (begun 1255) in relation to Cologne Cathedral. For the German hall chancels, which began to appear in the second half of the fourteenth century, Cistercian architectural thought may once again have provided inspiration, as a simple treatment of the ground-plan even in the case of large chancel constructions (Pontigny, *c.* 1200; Zwettl, 1343) suited the development of the German hall church.

radiating chapels are no longer, as in older buildings, independent bodies joined to one another. Instead, they have been harmoniously drawn together in the construction of the vault, which, probably for the first time, combined rib-vaulting with the pointed arch. What still associates this building with the transition period is the sculptural roundness and multiplicity of its details, and the absence of that

364, 365 Diagram and view from below of an early Gothic cross-ribbed vault.

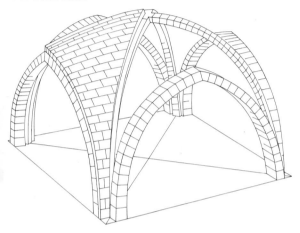

366   Choir of Laon Cathedral, begun c. 1155–60. Early Gothic, four-storied wall elevation: arcades between rounded piers, galleries, triforium, and clerestory; above, sexpartite rib-vaulting.

367   Choir of the abbey church of St-Denis, 1140–3. A double ambulatory and radiate chapels with, for the first time, a fully developed and unified system of cross-rib vaulting.

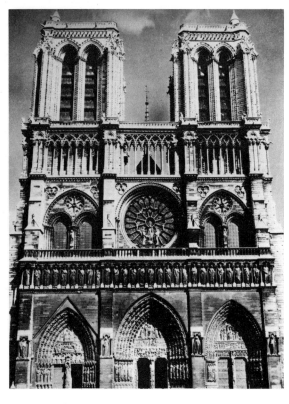

368　West façade of Laon Cathedral, begun c. 1190.

tautening structure that would first distinguish the cathedrals raised about 1200.

Many works that belong to the closing years of the twelfth century appear to have absorbed the new ideas issuing from St-Denis, or else to have arrived at similar solutions independently, as in the case of the *Cathedrals of Laon and Paris*, which were built at about the same time. Both have tribunes *[370, 371, 373, 376]*, a division of the vaulting bays that still recalls the Romanesque metrical system, and, before the thirteenth-century alterations, fairly simple

All these drawings are on the same scale. Upper row: façade formations. Middle row: wall systems of naves (in each case a vaulted bay). Lower row: cross-section of flying-buttresses and side aisles up to the apex of the nave.

370–2　Development of the west façade. The front wall and lower parts of two flanking towers are divided into three parts. The façade anticipates the interior structure – the arcade story corresponds in size to the porches, the triforium to the gallery, and the clerestory to the rose window. 370: Laon, west façade, begun c. 1190. An example that shows the transition to Gothic. 371: Paris, Notre-Dame, west façade begun c. 1200. Note the King's gallery above the porches and the balustrade over the rose window. 372: Reims, west façade, c. 1240. The verticals and horizontals here achieve a classic equipoise.

373–5　Wall system of the nave. 373: Laon, begun c. 1155–60. Four-part structure: arcades, galleries, triforia, clerestory. Sexpartite vaulting: a nave bay stretches over two arcades and corresponds to two aisle bays. Note the simple pointed arch of the windows. 374: Chartres, begun 1194. Three-part structure: arcades, triforia, clerestory (no gallery). Nave and aisle bays are the same width. 375: Reims, begun 1210. Three-part structure: of tauter proportions than Chartres.

376–9　Cross-sections. Basilical structure: the window area of the nave is higher than the aisles. The thrust of the nave vault is relieved by buttressing arches and piers. 376: Laon, begun c. 1155–60. Four-part wall structure in the Transitional style. Height of nave apex: 24 metres. 377: Chartres, begun 1194. A fully developed buttress system with opened arches. Height of nave apex: 36·5 metres. 378: Bourges, begun 1190–1200. Five-part arrangement [354]: the nave is accompanied by a lower outer and upper inner aisle. Height of nave apex: 37·5 metres. 379: Beauvais, begun 1247. A highly complicated system of buttresses. Even the wall behind the triforium is fenestrated. Height of nave apex: 47·5 metres.

369　West façade of Notre-Dame, Paris. Lower zone c. 1200; windows c. 1220; towers 1225–50.

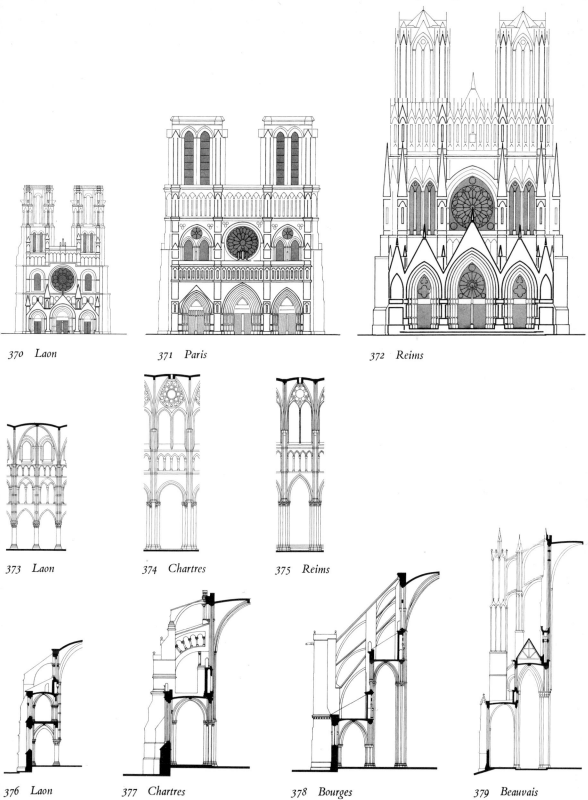

370 Laon

371 Paris

372 Reims

373 Laon

374 Chartres

375 Reims

376 Laon

377 Chartres

378 Bourges

379 Beauvais

380　Nave of Chartres Cathedral, begun 1194.

all cathedrals from the second half of the twelfth century, it was still a question of architecture belonging to a transition period. This is most apparent where the transitional style and mature Gothic are right next to each other in the same building, as is the case with *Chartres Cathedral*, for example. In 1194 a fire destroyed the cathedral begun in 1130 and probably still under construction. Begun directly after the fire, the new building steadily advanced – from west to east – towards the central part of the older towered front, the part in which the three portals are united *[462]*. At about the same time an organic connexion between façade and interior was already being achieved at St-Denis through the arrangement of the side porches in the towers, and this solution thereafter remained the general rule. Then, at Chartres itself, the Gothic longing for an appropriate fusion of all parts into the whole determined even the form of the transept ends.

The assurance shown by the details of these façades, as also of every other piece of Chartres Cathedral dating from after 1194, differs radically from the groping though most attractive uncertainty of the older west-end features. For the first time, main limb, transept, and chancel rise over a unified ground-plan with the cogent clarity of form and construction that

chancel layouts. But in spite of these common features, the Île-de-France building, the cathedral of Notre-Dame begun at Paris in 1163, is clearer and more modern. The difference is most apparent in a comparison of the towered fronts *[368–71]*, which were probably both raised about 1200. There is a pronounced contrast between the calm and severe clarity of the Paris façade and the hollowed-out, expressively *mouvementé* appearance of Laon's west end. As an art centre the Île-de-France had left the other French regions well behind, including the north that had first been so progressive. Yet here, as with

381, 382　Ground-plan and chancel of Reims Cathedral, 1210–41.

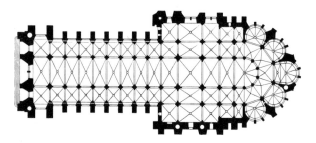

is understood as Gothic. The interior walls ascend in three zones: an *arcade* with shafted round or octagonal piers, a *triforium*, and a *clerestory* [374, 377, 380]. Outside, the heavy exposed flying-buttresses not only support the walls but look as if they brace the soaring nave with its low accompanying aisles and the chancel with its ambulatory and radiating chapels.

In its time and for its time the cathedral was the very centre of existence, embodying that integrated whole of faith, knowledge, and action taken for granted by the Middle Ages. Even its figurative decoration told contemporaries of all that was believed, known, and done. The cathedral no longer opposed men almost like a castle, as did its Romanesque predecessor, but instead led them through the rhythmic sequence of its arches to the altar and to God. Inspired by faith, the daring of natural reason attained the supernatural.

383   Nave and choir of Amiens Cathedral, 1220–69.

384   Choir of Beauvais Cathedral, 1247–72. View of the ambulatory vaulting and choir windows.

385   Ste-Chapelle in Paris, 1243–8.

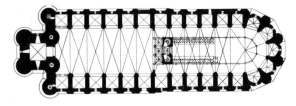

386, 387　Eastern section and ground-plan of Albi Cathedral, begun 1282. A simple-nave brick building with square chapels between piers receding into the wall. The fortified appearance is emphasized by the round towers.

French Gothic is with few exceptions a temperate style. Crossing-towers planned at Chartres, as also at Reims, never got beyond the initial stages – indeed at Reims not even the spires of the west towers were built. This desistance was probably not due to any practical inability. Begun in 1210 and finished in its essentials towards 1300, *Reims Cathedral* is considered the best proportioned among the large buildings of this group *[355, 372, 375, 381, 382]*. The formal language – tracery, buttressing, and so on – is still more precise and above all lighter than at Chartres, without, as in the case of later works, stiffening into formalism or dissolving as decoration.

Amiens is the third of these classic cathedrals.

Like a Greek temple of the fifth century BC, it was cast in an overall form possessing canonic, exemplary balance. Begun in 1220 and finished except for the towers with the completion of the chancel in 1269, *Amiens* appears steeper, narrower, and harder *[383]*. In this it pointed the way to the exaggeration of the vertical measurements risked at Beauvais, but also to the series of churches, in some instances left incomplete, that kept to the scheme of the classic cathedral till into the fourteenth and even the fifteenth century, spreading as far as southern France.

The chancel of *Beauvais [384]* was begun in 1247 and built so steeply upward that it had to be strengthened with intermediate piers after a collapse in 1284. At Beauvais even the back walls of the triforia were given windows, and this meant that the last strip of solid walling, to which the pent-roofs of the aisles and ambulatory had previously been attached, became open-work structure *[379]*. A similar tendency towards extreme transparency is shown by the *Ste-Chapelle [385]*, begun at almost the same time in Paris (1243). St Louis of France had it erected as his palace chapel.

Along with buildings that followed the rule of the classic cathedral there were a number of independent styles in which regional traditions often lived on. The cathedrals of *Bourges [354, 378]* and Le Mans comprise bold and individual staggered spaces, while that of Poitiers is an ample, lofty hall. *Albi Cathedral*, built between 1282 and 1390 *[386, 387]* sprang from the tradition of the southern French aisleless churches. The influence of the mendicant Orders during the second half of the thirteenth century is attested in southern France by the churches of the Jacobins. Their church at Toulouse, a double-naved hall consecrated in 1292, is the most imposing example.

England

Although conditions in England differed in various ways from those on the Continent, since the basis of an organic development of the state had been created very early on with the sealing of Magna Carta in 1215, here also the cathedrals remained the principal concern of architecture even into the fourteenth century. One must not of course forget the parish churches of England, even if they never gained the importance of German churches – this because English towns never acquired the autocratic freedom of German imperial and Hanseatic cities.

Two conditioning factors underlay Gothic architecture in England; the Norman element that had later typical of English buildings, namely a much elongated ground-plan and a layout involving two transepts.

The most outstanding example of the 'Early English' Gothic cathedral is *Salisbury*, built at one stretch from 1220 to 1258, and thus the contemporary of Amiens. The western limb, the two transepts, and the square-ended chancel are loosely strung together [389, 390]. The chancel was embellished by a Lady

388   *Choir of Canterbury Cathedral, 1175–84.*

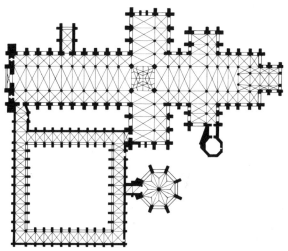

389, 390   *Ground-plan and aerial view of Salisbury Cathedral, 1220–58. The structure is crowned by the crossing-tower, which stands over the meeting-point of the nave and transept at the exact centre of the building.*

shaped the church building there since William the Conqueror's subjugation of the country, and the direct impact of French models during the last quarter of the twelfth century.

Individual proto-Gothic features such as the pointed arch, the rib, and the buttress appeared in England as early as the start of the twelfth century, thanks to Norman influence. Walls articulated into galleries and attached shafts were common [cf. 295]. Yet without the external impetus, without the reception of French stimuli, the first Gothic work, the chancel of Canterbury Cathedral [388], would be inconceivable. Begun in 1175, it represents the same stylistic stage as the cathedrals of Laon and Paris, and still properly belongs, with its rich, plastic forms, to the Transition period. But in spite of the French forms, neither at Canterbury nor in the subsequent Gothic cathedrals has the ground-plan that clear and concentrated arrangement nor the elevation those steep proportions characteristic of French churches. Nor does English Gothic have the chevet with its ambulatory and radiating chapels or the two-tower front with its portals and sculpture. On the other hand, the eastern part of Canterbury already showed some of the traits chapel, something just as characteristic of English cathedrals as the polygonally centralized chapter-house, here to the south of the western transept. *Lincoln's* west front *[391]* has been developed into a richly articulated decorative wall that bears no real relation to the complex of linked spaces behind it.

The details of English Gothic also lack a French incorporation into the whole. In place of deliberate constructional necessity, there appeared already at Canterbury a decorative succession of sharp, linear forms applied like fillets, a structure perhaps derived from Norman models. Loose co-ordination remained the basic idea of English architecture until the end of the Gothic period.

Ornamentation in England was developed with much imagination. The first phase, known as Early English, reached from 1175 to the mid-thirteenth century, from the still roundish Romanesque forms of the choir at Canterbury to the simple clarity of Salisbury. This stage was followed by that of the Decorated style, which lasted till about the mid-fourteenth century. As the name itself implies, the

392   Lincoln Cathedral, view of the nave looking east, vaulting completed 1233. This, the tierceron system of vaulting, marks a step towards the Decorated style.

391   West façade of Lincoln Cathedral. Late Norman style of the second quarter of twelfth century. The turrets on the face date from 1220 to 1230.

decorative element increased everywhere: in the window tracery, on the walls, in the vaulting. At a very early date the vaulting displayed, besides the usual cross-ribs, the first additional ones, forming star patterns as in the nave vault at Lincoln, completed in 1233 *[392]*. In the 'Angel Choir' of the same cathedral, built from 1265 to 1320, the first inter-lacing ribs are ranged like fans, and a rich play of lines covers the walls. Whereas the tracery forms of this period were still mainly geometric and severe during their early, thirteenth-century phase *[393, 394]*, the lines grew more sinuous in the fourteenth century, when the first mouchettes took shape in the windows. An especially fine example of the late Decorated style is the crossing of *Wells Cathedral*, built in 1338 *[395]*. We should also mention the naturalistic ornamentation to be seen at *Southwell Minster [396]* where the chapter-house and vestibule display foliage carving 'of a precision of surface to be compared only with the classic Greek art of the Parthenon' (Pevsner). The sculpture here has become almost illusionistic in a painterly way.

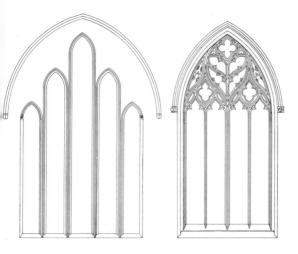

393, 394 English Gothic window shapes. In the early stages (thirteenth century) the strictly geometrical forms of the lancet windows would be enclosed by one pointed arch. Crossed lines characterize the Decorated style of fourteenth-century tracery windows.

395 Crossing of Wells Cathedral. The arch, added in 1338, and the panel ribs of the vault show the Decorated style at its most highly developed.

396 Southwell Minster, view of the chapter-house from the vestibule, c. 1300. The wall arcade of the chapter-house is decorated with naturalistic carved foliage of outstanding quality.

If one accepts the end of Early English to be that point when the French cathedrals lose their decisive influence and decorative elements become more important than structural, then one must regard the English Decorated style as already a transition to late Gothic. But its association, as here, with the first great phase of Gothic is more in accordance with the general European development, and it takes into account the innate leaning of English architecture towards the decorative.

Spain and Italy

Large parts of southern Spain were still in Moorish hands around 1200. Not until about the middle of the thirteenth century was the *Reconquista* vigorously resumed by Ferdinand of Castile. But after the period of foreign rule even the areas won back before (only the Asturias had always remained Christian) were at first culturally virgin soil and ready to receive Christian artistic forms, which streamed in chiefly from the regions north of the Pyrenees. In Catalonia,

397 Burgos Cathedral, begun 1221. The Spanish delight in decoration covers the whole building with exuberant ornament.

Cistercian abbeys of the Burgundian proto-Gothic type arose during the twelfth century at Poblet [361] and Santas Creus. These buildings were followed by Tarragona Cathedral, begun before 1200. Churches in the French transitional style were also raised during the twelfth century in north-west Spain (Salamanca, Avila).

In the early thirteenth century northern French cathedrals became the model. Léon Cathedral kept closest to the French style. Spain's most important early Gothic cathedrals, *Burgos*, begun in 1221 [397] and *Toledo*, begun in 1227 [398], took their cue from French stepped spaces such as the interior of *Bourges* [354] or Le Mans, and thus paved the way for the running together of spaces, that characterizes the late Gothic churches of Spain. A similar trend is shown by the chapels of Toledo's chancel, which are still essentially decorative additions. Building activity continued at both these cathedrals until the early sixteenth century, and not only on the originally planned main structure. In the course of time there were many additions within and without that obscured the spatial pattern of the interior and blurred the general effect of the exterior.

This is typical of Spanish developments. A fondness for proliferative spaces and a marked delight in ornamentation became basic traits of Spanish late Gothic. In many respects, sometimes even as regards particular features, this may be attributed to continuing Moorish influence. Catalonian architecture, on the contrary, remained clearer and more severe. Begun in 1298, Barcelona Cathedral has such tall narrow aisles that the space seems almost unified.

Unlike every other country that contributed to the art of this period, Italy remained virtually unaffected by French cathedral Gothic. We may distinguish the developments here of the thirteenth century from those of the fourteenth by pointing to the fact that during the early, thirteenth-century phase the Gothic style was used with few exceptions only on the buildings of the Cistercians and the mendicant Orders. Besides the Cistercian church at Fossanova already mentioned, others, like Casamari (1203–17), also display the heavy Burgundian transitional style. As in Spain, so here as well there were certain regions that adopted Cistercian architectural ideas.

398 Toledo Cathedral, begun 1227. Development and extension of French models: windows and triforia are joined together.

without amounting to architectural rules were shared by friars' churches in every country; large, capacious parts for the congregation; plain details conforming to the demand for absolute poverty, and in general already early Gothic in form as befitted the progressiveness of the Orders. It was this very attempt at simplicity that contributed to the fact that in Italy, as indeed also in Germany, the new Gothic forms were turned into an independent national style.

S. Francesco at Assisi (1228–53), the two-storied mother-church of the Franciscan Order, is at both levels a plain aisleless structure crossed by a transept [399, 400]. Some details may go back to southern France or to the Cistercians, but undoubtedly native elements are visible in the great wall surfaces that, broken only by small windows, here and in later Italian Gothic buildings positively challenged the painters to create their imposing fresco cycles.

Although a few churches directly descended from Assisi made do with the aisleless plan, as early as the second half of the thirteenth century at least the bigger Italian friars' churches received a nave and two aisles,

401 *Dominican church of S. Maria Novella at Florence, begun 1283. A hall-like nave with high, wide arcades and simple cross-vaulting.*

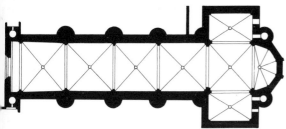

399, 400 *S. Francesco at Assisi, 1228–53. Ground-plan and view of the nave facing east. A single-nave hall church with transept. Simple cross-ribbed vaults over square bays. The ambulatory in the apse divides the wall structure into two parts. Giotto's frescoes of the life of S. Francis decorate the walls.*

Whereas the Cistercians, like the early medieval Orders, still regarded their monasteries as secluded communities and did not open their churches to the outside world, the mendicant Orders of the Franciscans and Dominicans had been in closest contact with the changing fabric of society ever since their early thirteenth-century beginning. They built their houses in the towns, devoted themselves to the sick and the poor, and allowed the people into their churches for divine service, in particular sermons. Accordingly there soon took shape a number of basic features that

402   Siena Cathedral, nave, c. 1230–59. Note the pointed arch windows above the Romanesque arcades. The alternate layers of black and white marble enliven the overall effect.

as in the case of the earliest with this layout, S. Francesco at Bologna (1236). In the older Florentine friars' churches, S. Trinità and *S. Maria Novella*, a late thirteenth-century building *[401]*, the space broadens out like a hall. The small windows rise to the tips of the nave's wall arches, and the clerestory almost disappears above the wide, high curves of the arcade arches. Light and graceful detail makes S. Maria Novella a particularly pure example of a native Italian early Gothic. A lucid humanism is already evident here.

The Italian cathedrals of the thirteenth century, *Siena*, begun *c.* 1230 *[402]*, Arezzo (1277), and even Orvieto (begun before 1285), adopted Gothic features such as the pointed arch but basically remained in the Romanesque tradition. On the other hand, the façades of Siena and Orvieto are already the work of those great masters and their schools who led into the late, fourteenth-century phase of Italian Gothic.

Germany

In Germany the invasion of the Gothic style was resisted until about the mid-thirteenth century by forces that stylistically represent the plastic fullness and decorative richness of late Romanesque. This phase cannot just be dismissed as backward-looking. The large cathedrals of *Mainz [268]*, Worms, Bamberg, and Naumburg, which all rose on old foundations around 1200, used the pointed arch, the rib-vault, and other structurally advantageous novelties from France quite as a matter of course, but these were fitted into a traditional system of construction that provided no basis for a transition to true Gothic. This form of architecture was continued by the Holy Roman Empire, then still very much alive, and also by resplendent Hohenstaufen rule, whose collapse about the middle of the century not only ended an historical age but at last opened the way in Germany for new developments, including artistic ones.

Even the Cistercians, who also paved the way for Gothic in Germany although they did not have much effect until the start of the thirteenth century, had to adapt themselves to the native forces in their first,

403   S. Elisabeth at Marburg, begun c. 1235, consecrated 1283. View from the south-east. The chancel is developed in three parts on a trefoil plan. Note the steep verticals of the buttresses, and the two windows between each, following French models.

churches at Esslingen and Erfurt arose in addition to simple aisleless buildings. Also common were flat-ceiled basilicas (Franciscan churches at Regensburg, Freiburg, and Rothenburg), and particularly in northern Germany, hall churches such as that of the

405, 406 Cologne Cathedral, begun 1248 on the model of Amiens and Beauvais. View from the south-east and cross-section through the nave and four aisles. The exterior decoration is combined with structural features (trusses).

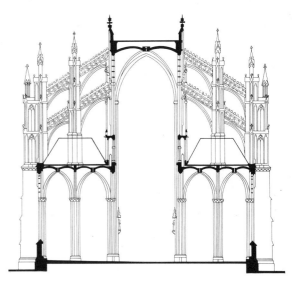

404 Choir of Magdeburg Cathedral, begun 1209. An example of German late Romanesque simplification of French models – note the heavy shapes (columns); emphasis on the wall surface (arcades) and round-arch vaulting in the galleries (the so-called 'Bischofsgang').

twelfth-century monastic buildings, Eberbach and Maulbronn. As in Italy, the friars' churches, especially during the second half of the thirteenth century, were more important in connexion with the spread of Gothic. The plain form of the barely articulated main body, out of which grows the long, narrow chancel, and the nave's often flat-ceiled interior with smooth walls above wide arches still recall in all respects various simple Romanesque churches, while at the same time they are filled down to their last detail with the new Gothic spirit of rigorous unity. It was in the friars' churches that German architecture first achieved a synthesis of its own tradition, intent on simplicity, and of the soaring Gothic formal organization. There was, however, no standard pattern in the architecture of the mendicant Orders, but only the force of spiritual bonds. Often the product of regional or local factors, vaulted basilicas like the Dominican

407   West façade of Strasbourg Minster, begun 1276. Top of tower 1399–1439. The storey above the rose window was completed despite Erwin von Steinbach's plan of 1275 for a two-towered structure.

Minorites at Münster. The earliest genuinely Gothic churches on German soil, both begun about 1235, are *S. Elisabeth at Marburg [403]* and the Liebfrauen-kirche at Trier. The Trier church, as a centrally planned building, is an exception, but S. Elisabeth, finished on completion of the nave in 1283, combines a number of interesting formal tendencies. The ground-plan of its eastern parts is particularly un-usual, with the transept arms ending polygonally and matching the chancel. This form had occurred shortly before in Champagne, but could also derive from late Romanesque trefoil plans of the Rhine-land. The nave, however, was raised as a hall over a long, narrow ground-plan, probably owing to a change of design. The route followed by this origin-ally north German architectural form led to the art regions of southern Germany by way of Marburg.

As for the big church buildings, the cathedrals and minsters, the course of their encounter with French cathedrals was more involved, except where they belonged to the imperial group. Whereas the imperial cathedrals were based on their Ottonian predecessors in their ground-plans, the spatial axis of the Ottonian structure that had been destroyed by fire was shifted when the new *Magdeburg Cathedral* was begun in 1209. The chancel *[404]* started by following the example of French cathedral east ends, but while the lowest story was still being built reductive tendencies set in. Instead of the planned buttresses the chapels received weak little angle columns. The arcade piers inside have a wall-like heaviness, and the vaulting of the ambulatory is groined. The nave, not finished until 1363, has a simple two-zone structure com-prising arcade and clerestory. This was customary for German basilicas during the second half of the thirteenth century, mostly due to the influence of friars' architecture.

Cologne Cathedral, in contrast, follows the French pattern very closely indeed as regards both plan and elevation *[405, 406]*. Begun in 1248, the chancel was dedicated in 1322. Already towards the end of the fourteenth century work on the rest of the building – transept, nave, towers – had reached a standstill, and the age of the great cathedrals was finally over. An attempt to complete the structure on the basis of the existing parts and original plans discovered for the

408   Single-tower front of Freiburg Minster, 1275 to c. 1340. The filigree-work of the perforated peak is characteristic of south German buildings.

towers was postponed until 1842. The fact that the first entrepreneur, Archbishop Konrad of Hochstaden, decided to adopt French forms so consistently may be interpreted as a deliberate counter to Hohenstaufen late Romanesque, perhaps on political grounds. Instead of mere imitation, the Cologne architects developed what they borrowed to the limits of the possible. Nowhere in France does the ground-plan link together the different parts of the building so completely. Nowhere else does the space ascend so effortlessly between walls where the supports have been resolved into clusters of shafts and triforia into windows. The buttressing of the exterior, its pinnacles, ornamental gables, and delicate tracery give the edifice a floating richness that far surpasses the simple clarity of French cathedral Gothic.

In this systematic extension of ideas from Western Europe, Cologne Cathedral had almost no imitators in Germany. Generally speaking, the development of big German churches of the thirteenth and fourteenth centuries followed the course already indicated in the building history of Magdeburg Cathedral. In the south-west, *Strasbourg Minster* is closest to the French pattern, even geographically. True, the Hohenstaufen late Romanesque eastern part dating from the first half of the thirteenth century largely determined the proportions of the nave, built sometime between 1260 and 1290; but the width of the nave, aisles, and arches expresses a new, indigenous sense of space that returned soon after in the western limb of Freiburg Minster. Whereas at Strasbourg triforia are still inserted between the arcades and the broad clerestory windows, at Freiburg this French intermediate motif gives way to plain wall. Around 1275 Erwin von Steinbach (*c.* 1244–1318) designed for Strasbourg the famous two-tower front *[407]* which, rising above three portals adorned with sculptures, is again of French descent in its basic features. But the way the tracery 'arcading' set independently before the stone almost etherializes the latter shows the consistency that already distinguished Cologne Cathedral as compared to the French pattern. Erwin von Steinbach's brilliant plan was only executed in the lower parts. The conflict between the two- and one-tower solutions that broke out in the fourteenth century was brought to a close early in the fifteenth by adding the late Gothic spire at the side. In the case of *Freiburg*, on the other hand, a dominant central

409, 410 The Marienkirche at Lübeck, mid-thirteenth to mid-fourteenth century. Aerial view from the south and view of the nave looking east, second half of thirteenth century. A three-part basilica with rectangular side chapels, and ambulatory and choir chapels enclosed by a single vault.

tower was raised at one attempt round about 1330, in accordance with the initial scheme *[408]*. Thereafter the single tower became one of the main features of big German town parish churches, such as the Frauenkirche at Esslingen and Ulm Minster.

French cathedral Gothic was also distinctively remodelled in the Baltic area of north Germany. The influential building here is the *Marienkirche at Lübeck*, begun in the mid-thirteenth century with a chancel and finished in the mid-fourteenth century *[409, 410]*. As the chief parish church of this centre of the German Hanseatic League, it far surpasses the town's cathedral in importance and quality. Its two-tower front, exposed buttress system, and chancel with ambulatory and radiating chapels undoubtedly have a western source; only the transept is missing. But the brick used and also the region's own formative trends led to radical simplifications. The towers have plain, cuboid bodies, the piers clear cross-sections, and the deep window embrasures are carried right down to the arcade arches. Together with the rather steep proportions of the interior, these embrasures reveal the studied boldness of Gothic particularly clearly.

At Wismar, Stralsund, and Rostock, the big ports along the coast, a series of notable brick basilicas followed the example of Lübeck. Apart from these, many hall churches were built throughout north Germany, and not only in the region of brick Gothic. In Westphalia, the actual source of this spatial form, the hall of *Minden Cathedral* (begun 1267) rises over slender clustered columns *[430]*.

LATE GOTHIC ARCHITECTURE

France and England

Around 1300 and in the early fourteenth century the change-over to the second great phase of Gothic occurred. The architects are no longer at most just names, like the heads of lodges in early Gothic times, but can be related to their works. Particularly in Italy, they began to move about freely from one building job to another, without being tied to a particular lodge.

Stylistically there was a growing stress on the decorative, though it was not a matter of a purely quantitative increase but rather of a change in the character of the separate features. In early Gothic the details – corbels, rib mouldings, window tracery – were all the product of constructional factors. They underlined functionally the articulation of the building as a whole, often at the crucial points in its structure. Fourteenth- and fifteenth-century forms

411　*Early Gothic tracery of thirteenth century date (these very simple designs first appeared at Reims Cathedral). The two-part lower window terminates in pointed arches, above them a circle with a sexpartite inset made up of three-quarter circles.*

412　*Late Gothic tracery of fourteenth and fifteenth centuries. An example of the French Flamboyant style, so called from the 'fish bubbles'. Similarly spaced ribs with narrow passages.*

strove increasingly to obscure or cover intersections and transitions. The round mouldings of shafts and ribs, eminently able to bear a load, became sharp-edged, indeed hollowed-out tracks *[358]*; the impost mouldings that stressed the point at which the ribs sprang from the shafts became plain bands that, like the shafts below them, could ultimately vanish altogether. Ribs and arches now grew straight out of piers and walls. As for vaulting, the development went

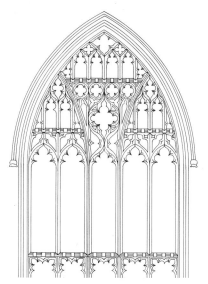

413 Late Gothic tracery of fourteenth and fifteenth centuries (known in England as the Perpendicular style, 1350–1550). Lattice-work with a preference for perpendicular bars, often in a drily rational overall arrangement and with harsh joinings.

414 West façade of La Trinité at Vendôme, beginning of sixteenth century. An example of the Flamboyant style with interwoven 'fish bubbles' (developed further than in the German late Gothic).

415 Gloucester Cathedral, view of choir facing east. The east wall was erected 1347–50. The essence of late Gothic tracery, a lattice-work of stone and stained glass. A thin stone trellis in front of the arcade and triforium veils both wall surfaces and openings.

from simple cross-ribs *via* the English tiercerons of the late thirteenth century *[392]* and the star-vaults *[440]* that were still quite structural in conception to the fans *[415]*, nets, ornamental stars, and loops *[433]* with which the fifteenth century ceiled its rooms in England, Germany, and Spain. Tracery began during the thirteenth century with simple round shapes *[411]*. In the early fourteenth these became curvilinear motifs that could already take a *mouvementé* form, like the so-called mouchettes *[412]*. Fifteenth-century tracery covered with lively and whirling or stiff and lattice-like lines *[413]* the big window areas that no longer ended in traditional pointed but in ogee or mixed arches.

Features of this kind served the endeavour already active in early Gothic to weld the entire building into a single structural whole. The architectural bodies and spatial forms of late Gothic favoured this tendency. Aisleless chapels and undivided hall rooms drove out the intricate fabrics of the basilican cathedrals. In France, however, the memory of the classic

416 *Norwich Cathedral, view of choir facing west. The side arcades are late Gothic; the two lower stories of the east wall date from 1119. The Romanesque clerestory was replaced by a Gothic one in 1362.*

cathedral remained alive into the sixteenth century. Over traditional ground-plans churches like *La Trinité at Vendôme* – the façade here dates from the beginning of the sixteenth century *[414]* – used only the late Gothic formal language of Flamboyant.

In contrast to the marked agitation of French Flamboyant, the contemporary English Perpendicular preferred lattice-like forms that thrust direct and hard against the surrounding arch mouldings. These forms first became fully active in the choir of *Gloucester Cathedral* (1331), where they overran the walls and continued in the network of the vault *[415]*. In 1362 the Romanesque clerestory of the choir at *Norwich Cathedral* was replaced by Gothic windows, and a century later a rich lierne-vault with 329 carved

bosses replaced the flat wooden roof of the centre aisle *[416]*. The fourteenth-century west front *[417]* of *York Cathedral* shows how successfully the architect here solved the problem of including within a two-towered structure the main traceried window of the west end. In King's College Chapel at Cambridge (1446–1515), the vaulting grows like fans from slender, sharp-edged clusters of shafts between the broad windows. At *Westminster Abbey*, the lattice-work of ribs in *Henry VII's Chapel* has at last freed itself from the surface of the ceiling and gathered around pendants *[419]*. The chapel's exterior, too, is covered with the stone panelling of the latest Gothic *[418]*.

Besides the stylistic traits, all these examples show another tendency of late Gothic building: at this period only extensions such as chapels and chancel parts were added to the big cathedrals and abbey churches, and in ground-plan they are simple rooms that in many ways resemble the secular halls. It is the bold formal fantasy of the decorative elaboration that gives these works their special charm.

417 *York Minster, view of the exterior from the south-west. The west façade was completed up to the roof of the nave in 1338. The three towers were built during the fifteenth century.*

418, 419 Henry VII's chapel in Westminster Abbey, 1503–19. Filigree panel-vault with hanging stone pendants. On the exteriors lattice rib-work of the Perpendicular style.

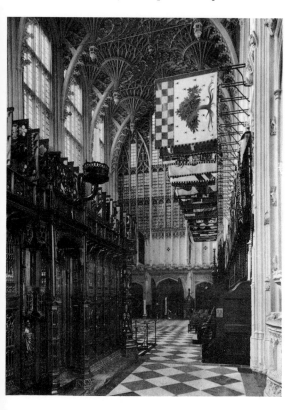

Spain and Italy

The north European late Gothic of France, England, and Germany preserved an inner unity of structure and ornament even with the greatest decorative enrichment. The very ribs of English and German vaults built about 1500, though detached from the ceiling, still grow out of the stone of the masonry. In Spain, on the other hand, there emerged towards the end of the fifteenth century a decorative tendency that could cover important surfaces, such as the façade, without any reference to the building's inward structure. It took form in the Plateresque style, a mode of ornamentation that, as its name indicates, was evolved by silversmiths. The Plateresque combines north European stylistic elements passed on by masters from the Netherlands and northern Germany with the Spanish partiality for surfaces smothered in decoration, this trait being undoubtedly a Moorish heritage. The earliest example of the style is to be found at *Valladolid* (*S. Gregorio*, late fifteenth century; *442*), but it reappeared soon after, already mixed with some Renaissance forms, at Salamanca (façade of the new cathedral). This decorative opulence was not concentrated on the façades alone, for as a general principle people loved to set accents alongside the calm wall surfaces, in which small windows were cut in the South. Thus the constructional buttressing of the thirteenth century turned into playful ornamentation, and even some of the older cathedrals, such as *Burgos*, were crowned with exaggerated crossing-towers *[397]* and surrounded with whole ranges of sumptuously adorned chapels.

The effort to simplify architectural space and body in Spain led during the fifteenth century to a preference for two spatial types: that of the aisleless church in the area influenced by Catalonia, and that of the broadly spreading stepped interior, particularly in the South. Often given double aisles, the main limbs are usually accompanied by rows of side chapels, and in ground-plan these churches approximate to a square as even their transept and chancel hardly protrude from the general outline. This unaccented effect of building and space was prefigured in Moorish works, and many of the cathedrals were, after all, raised in place of earlier mosques. Along with these stepped interiors, which already in Spanish early Gothic paved the way for a slurring of the true basilican build-up of space, there was no shortage in Spanish late Gothic of hall interiors, the most consistently unified spaces even from the standpoint of the Moorish heritage (Saragossa Cathedral, rebuilt as a hall in 1499–1559). Many of these churches (in the later works such as Granada

a strong horizontal feature above the very wide arches. Arnolfo di Cambio (*c.* 1250–*c.* 1300), who created this church, must be regarded as the first great European architect in the modern sense.

The basic design of *Florence Cathedral* also goes back to Arnolfo *[357, 423]*. Even the crowning dome was provided for in the initial plan, though it was not

421, 422 Franciscan church of S. Croce in Florence, ground-plan and view of the nave facing east, 1295–1442. At the ends and on the eastern parts of the transept rectangular chapels are arranged, whose walls are decorated with fresco cycles.

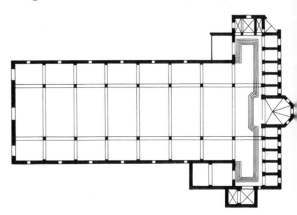

420 Burgos Cathedral, crossing, 1539–67. Fenestrated star-vault and rich decoration in the Plateresque style.

Cathedral, Renaissance forms were already super-seding Gothic, even though the basic approach remained the same) have been ceiled with rich ornamental vaults. Like Plateresque surface decora-tion, this vaulting combines the Spanish and Moorish with the north European and late Gothic, satisfying the penchant for a richly decorative cover through the introduction of intricate star forms, here some-times in a completely filigree version *[420]*.

Italian architecture of the fourteenth century fol-lowed in all respects the course discernible as early as the thirteenth. The new friars' churches (e.g. that of the Frari at Venice) were simply larger in size and more compact in structure than the older ones. At Florence the Franciscan church of *S. Croce* (1295–1442) received a nave that with its breadth of about 62½ feet surpasses almost every other medieval example *[421, 422]*. Even technical considerations here called for an open-roof frame, such as was used at that date by many German friars' churches as a sign of poverty. This mode of covering a space is in keeping with the Italian tradition, and at the same time it neutralizes the Gothic upward movement, which, at S. Croce, has already been slowed down by

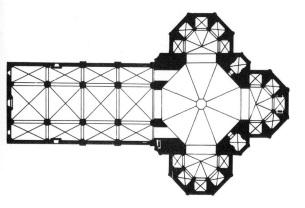

423 Ground-plan of Florence Cathedral, begun 1296 by Arnolfo di Cambio, consecrated 1436. The trefoil-shaped eastern part is joined to the nave by rectangular piers placed far apart. Low, square chapels are placed next to the five-cornered transept arms. Note the octangular dome space at the centre.

executed until the early fifteenth century, when Brunelleschi, by finishing the cathedral, prepared the way for the new age of the Renaissance. Before this, Arnolfo's design had undergone a revision in the mid-fourteenth century that for the most part just increased the overall dimensions and made the details suit the times. Only the pointed arches are Gothic in this building, and even they are not really necessary from the constructional or artistic point of view. Besides the influence of Florentine Proto-Renaissance buildings [cf. 316], the spirit was already active here that would lead to the final departure from Gothic. Florence Cathedral's façade, which in its present form dates from the nineteenth century, was planned by Arnolfo as a pure display front bearing no relation to the interior behind it. This conception also underlies the façades of the cathedrals at *Siena*, 1300 [424] and Orvieto (early fourteenth century).

First noticeable in Spain in the cathedrals built round about 1500, the desire for outward largeness governed Italian architecture as early as the fourteenth century. A number of projects were so extravagant that, having only been partly carried out in the four-teenth century, they were left unfinished, since by and large the fifteenth took no interest in continuing medieval schemes. Such is the case with the nave begun in the second half of the fourteenth century for Siena Cathedral: the building that exists today was intended to become only its transept. Begun in 1387, the construction of *Milan Cathedral [425]* dragged on until the eighteenth century. Figures and pinnacles make the façade extremely ornamental. Significantly, the plans for this most Gothic of Italian churches came from Germany, as did some of the master-builders.

424 Decorated west façade of Siena Cathedral, begun before 1300 by Giovanni Pisano.

425 Milan Cathedral, begun 1387. A five-aisled building with a pinnacled west façade decorated with Gothic forms.

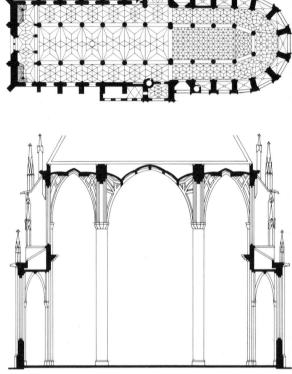

426 *Peter Parler, choir of S. Veit, Prague Cathedral, after 1353. Window zone and triforia are joined close together. In the vaulting, parallel ribs are the essential shapes of the network.*

Germany

In Germany late Gothic decorative enrichment generally concentrated on window tracery and on the development of ever more intricate forms of vaulting. Yet the stretches of wall did not become neutral planes, as in Spain or Italy, but kept a soaring animation, due mostly to the form of the windows. Inside, the vaults grew from the walls and from light piers, making the room seem almost impossibly weightless.

Rich in tradition and probably also thought to be particularly grand, the basilican spatial structure held

427-9 *Heiligkreuzkirche at Schwäbisch Gmünd, nave first half of fourteenth century, choir begun 1351. The Parler-style hall choir is joined to the lower nave with simple net-vaulting (1491-1521); the vaulting of the nave dates from c. 1500. The choir ambulatory and three-sided nave are of the same height, as the cross-section shows. The buttressed pillars are placed at the end of rectangular chapels, which take the form of niches. A profiled ledge divides the upper window wall and the chapels into two zones the same height.*

its own till into the fifteenth century, especially for big town parish churches, which gave architecture its most important tasks in Germany at this period.

In 1344 Charles IV had a Frenchman begin the cathedral at his capital Prague with a proper French cathedral chancel. Then in 1353 Peter Parler from Schwäbisch Gmünd took charge, the first German architect whose name can be associated with characteristic works. The upper part of his *Prague Cathedral*

430 Minden Cathedral, begun 1267. View of the nave facing east. An early Gothic Westphalian hall built on an almost square ground-plan, and with vaults rising dome-like over the individual bays.

431 Hans Stethaimer, choir of the Franciscan church in Salzburg, begun c. 1408. Further development of the Gmünd hall choir: the thin round supports remain only in the axis of the nave; the vaulting of the chapel is raised by buttressed pillars. The light, wide hall is experienced as a unified space despite its three sections.

432 Marienkirche at Danzig, nave built as a hall 1483–1502, choir 1379–1447, vaulting 1498–1502. The largest north German brick hall church. The proportions of space are steeper than in other north German buildings.

433 Church of S. Anne at Annaberg, 1499–1522. View of the nave facing east. A Saxon hall church from the latest phase of the Gothic. The space is highly unified, with vaults of looped and purely decorative (no longer constructive) curved ribs.

chancel [426] is an open lattice exhibiting an incredible unity. With its vaulting made up of parallel ribs the development of the net-vaults began.

What is evolutionally the most important structure to have issued from the circle of the Parler family, which included a whole series of architects, should probably be connected with the leading master, Peter Parler himself (1330–99). This, the hall chancel of the *Heiligkreuzkirche at Schwäbisch Gmünd [427–9]*, was begun in 1351 but not vaulted until about 1500. It is joined to a low western limb that counts among the earliest south German hall interiors [429]. The ground-plan of the chancel derives from that of the cathedral chevet although the ambulatory is as high as the apse it surrounds and the chapels, about half this height, are set between the buttresses in such a way that externally they are enclosed by a common line of wall.

In the boldly developed form of this Gmünd chancel the hall church, which was becoming more and more prevalent in Germany, gained a curving

eastern termination, even if the first of these structures, such as Gmünd itself or the chapel-less chancel of S. Sebaldus at Nuremburg (1361–72), attached themselves to older, lower western parts.

Two architects completed the Gmünd ideas round about 1400: Hans Stethaimer (1350/60–1432) in lower Bavaria and Hinrich Brunsberg (1350/60–1430?) in Pomerania and Brandenburg, both of whom built hall churches with the new chancel form as a single whole. In the case of Stethaimer's most mature work, the chancel begun in 1408 for the *Franciscan church at Salzburg [431]* the chapels reach to the full height of the hall space and weld the exterior together as one towering block. Similar in conception, Brunsberg's buildings such as *S. Katherine at Brandenburg* (begun in 1395) seem to have a north German squatness and heaviness in comparison with the tall, open interiors of the south. Especially on its gables, the block-like exterior is loosened up by the richest decorative forms that brick Gothic produced [434].

The hall western limb and hall chancel became the most common architectural forms of German late

434 Hinrich Brunsberg, church of S. Katherine at Brandenburg, begun 1395. The gable of the Corpus Christi chapel shows the richest decorative forms of brick architecture.

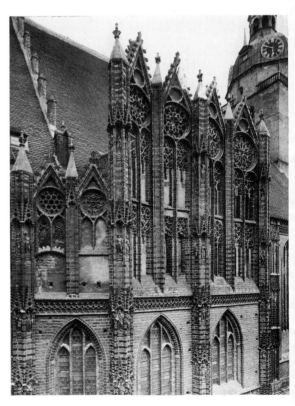

Gothic, and many varieties appeared. In south Germany the magnificent town churches bear witness to this, as at Nördlingen and *Dinkelsbühl [358]*, while in the north-east even cathedrals were built as halls (Frauenburg, Königsberg), though with simpler chancel layouts. The north German hall underwent an impressive development in the towering wall masses of the *Marienkirche at Danzig* (1379–1502). Unusually light for north Germany, the interior rises with slender piers to the web of the net- and cell-vault *[432]*. A last, especially graceful series of hall churches owes its existence to the discovery of silver in the Erzgebirge. *Annaberg*, 1499–1522 *[433]*; Pirna, 1502–46; and Schneeberg, 1515–26 are of this type. The trends of German late Gothic leading to a unification of the architectural space and body and to a decorative floating conclusion of the structure in the vaulting zone, are once more richly displayed in this group of buildings.

SECULAR ARCHITECTURE

Even though church construction, as its principal task, determined the course of Gothic architecture, our picture of it would be incomplete without a look at secular building. Not only did this produce works of notable quality in close stylistic dependence on the forms of church architecture, but it also brought forth new types of building, especially during the late Gothic period, which saw the rise of the middle class. The castles that had formed the most important secular group in the early Middle Ages were now joined by stately, palace-like edifices. But above all there were the towns with their fortifications and imposing gateways, their town halls and other public buildings, their hospitals, guildhalls, and market halls, as well as their dwelling-houses, although these have rarely survived.

Gothic castles often differ from Romanesque ones only in the changed (i.e. pointed) forms of such details as windows and gates, and in their more sophisticated defence arrangements – the latter chiefly in southern and western Europe. In Italy and Spain the castles distinguished by their regular wall formation and heavy angle towers grew larger *[435]*. In France and Britain it was those with an internal keep or *donjon* (Vincennes, late fourteenth century) or a towered enceinte *[436]* that predominated. German castles appeared livelier and more pleasant to live in *[437]* than the older, more clearly disposed ones. The desire for prestige and display that occurred now and then (Marburg, fourteenth century) was most monumentally realized in the castles of the

435   Castello di S. Giorgio, Mantua, end of fourteenth century. An Italian castle with heavy, projecting corner towers and great fortified walls, surrounded like the towers with fortified passageways.

436   Harlech Castle, Merionethshire, 1283–90. An English castle with projecting round towers. Inside the outer ring is a 'donjon', also with round towers.

437   *Burg Eltz on the Moselle. Thirteenth to sixteenth centuries. This irregular structure, built out of the land it stands on, is still complete today.*

439   *Palace of Jacques de Cœur at Bourges, 1442–53. An angular structure, with certain sections forming part of the town fortifications. This was the town residence of a wealthy merchant, with a court and seven towers.*

438   *Castle of the Teutonic Order at Marienburg; high castle (right) end of thirteenth century; middle castle (left) beginning of fourteenth century, seat of the Grand Master; Grand Master's Palace (centre), second half of fourteenth century.*

440   *Marienburg, the great 'Remtor' of the Grand Master's Palace, second half of fourteenth century. Banqueting-hall with Prussian star-vaults, which rise from narrow pillars. An example of the return to the columned rooms of monastery architecture.*

441 *The Alhambra in Granada, Court of Lions, completed 1377. A palace of the late Moorish period. The interior courts and spaces display decoration of the richest luxuriance.*

442 *Portal of the college of S. Gregorio at Valladolid, 1488–96. Gothic, Renaissance, and Moorish elements are combined in the Plateresque style ('platero'=silversmith) on this chiselled surface.*

443 *The Doge's Palace at Venice, first half of fourteenth up to the end of the fifteenth century. This, the largest city palace in the form of a nobleman's palace, serves as a town hall.*

Teutonic Order in its Prussian territory. Both creatively arranged and well able to resist attack, they embodied the very idea of the Order, an idea that combined monasticism with chivalry *[438]*. The great halls of these Teutonic castles count among the most powerful achievements of medieval architecture, just as the star-vault *[440]* developed in them at the beginning of the fourteenth century counts among the basic stylistic features of European late Gothic.

Gothic secular halls undoubtedly derived from the magnificent assembly rooms of the monasteries, from their chapter-houses and refectories, and from the cathedral closes that were developed particularly richly in England. Cloisters became the model for the arcades that now surrounded the courtyards of a good many town palaces, the homes of the nobility and upper middle class *[439]*. In Spanish secular architecture elements of the Moorish palace lived on *[441]*, as in the colleges at Valladolid *[442]* and Salamanca dating from about 1500.

The larger civic buildings, especially town halls, have various points in common with the religious

ones, though also with private town palaces *[443]*. Above all in Tuscany, as at Florence or *Siena [444]*, in Flanders, at *Ypres [446]*, and on the Baltic coast (Danzig), they often possess, besides magnificent halls and inner courtyards, huge, dominant towers, such as had already appeared on a number of town dwellings of the twelfth and thirteenth centuries (S. Giminiano, Regensburg).

Very little in the way of middle-class homes and their interiors has withstood the ravages of time: a few house façades in Italy, France, and Germany; a few rooms, mostly restored *[454]*, and a certain amount of furniture *[448–53]*. Nevertheless here too one can see how strongly the features of the Gothic style affected even the smallest detail.

Although there also exist a number of the great walls with towers and gates that surrounded medieval towns – whether these had grown up untidily *[445]* or been laid out evenly *[447]* in their street formation – they have as a rule been considerably renewed and restored. In the regular intersections of a town like Aigues Mortes, founded according to a pre-established plan and built within a short time, memories are preserved of Roman fortified camps with their square divisions.

444 *Palazzo Pubblico in Siena, 1289–1310, Torre del Mangia, 1338–48. The tower is the central point of a powerful city-state.*

445 *Carcassonne. A city with a double ring wall and plan of the later thirteenth century. The towers are placed according to the lie of the land.*

446   *Cloth Hall at Ypres, c. 1260–1380. This centre of Flemish trade, with a front measuring 132 metres, is one of the largest medieval secular structures. Its central axis is accentuated by a weighty, quadrangular tower.*

447   *Aigues Mortes. The city was fortified after 1272. Founded by St Louis, the layout is regular, with evenly spaced towers and gates.*

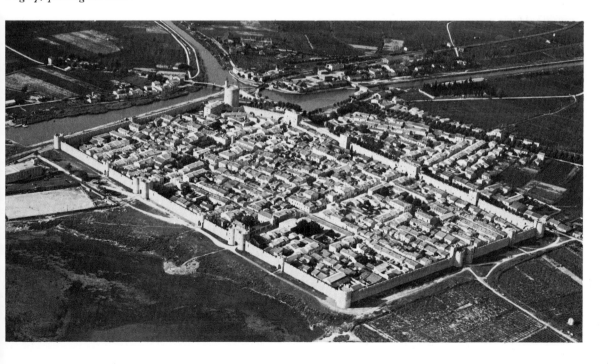

448   Gabled cupboard from Lower Saxony, thirteenth century. Hanover, Kestner Museum. The usual narrow early Gothic shape of a cupboard with simple iron hinges. (Above left.)

449   Cupboard from Swabia, 1465. Ulm, Museum. A broad, two-storied piece with rich late Gothic tendril ornamentation. A work of Jörg Syrlin the Elder, master of the choir stalls of Ulm Minster. (Left.)

450   Canopied bed from France, c. 1510. Paris, Musée des Arts Décoratifs. 'Heaven' is represented on the back and side walls (in south German Gothic work the bed has four posts). Note the pleated ornament. (Above.)

FACING PAGE

451   Chest from France, fifteenth century. Short feet, tracery on the front and a lid. The trunk is an important piece of furniture up to the Baroque. (Above left.)

452   Side-board from Flanders, fifteenth century. The wing doors and side panels have tracery decoration.

453   Armchair from the Netherlands, fifteenth century. A closed-box chest shape designed from boards, often with a tip-up seat as the stool. Panelled ornament. (Above right.)

454   Jacob Russ, Town-hall chamber in Überlingen, 1494. Slightly vaulted roof with carved balcony, wainscot panels topped with richly carved tracery, and between these figures of Imperial rank. (Right.)

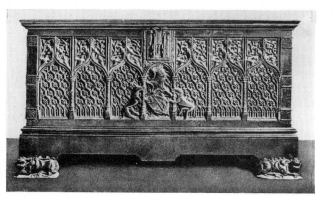

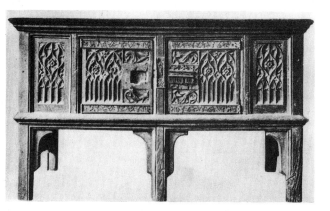

Sculpture

One of the principal factors underlying the development of Gothic stylistic traits was the growing effort to unite the Christian dogma of a world stretching between heaven and hell with the mortal world of experience whose reality was becoming increasingly important. The rise in human and terrestrial content is more directly apparent in the sculpture of the thirteenth century than in its architecture, even though figuration always remained idealized, combining the earthly with the transcendental. Despite the closeness to the human model, naturalistic, not to mention portrait elements were still excluded at that period.

We first meet this new conception of man in French cathedral sculpture. The development of statuary, too, is inconceivable without the impetus from France – indeed, one can say that it was directly dependent on the evolution of the French cathedral. Along with Gothic architecture, the forms of French sculpture then spread throughout the Christian West in the course of the thirteenth century, and, as with building, there were regional changes, adaptations, and simplifications. Nevertheless German sculpture of the period around 1250 was at bottom quite close to French works of the early thirteenth century, and even the great Italian sculptors of the second half of the century arrived at a comparable human and idealizing approach by their own route [456, 457]. Towards 1300 there began another withdrawal from the world, above all in German sculpture, which now grew increasingly important north of the Alps. This change first made itself apparent in a certain stiffening of the figures, and eventually attained a lyrical and exalted inwardness under the influence of mysticism. But for all the intended otherworldliness one is still aware in this sculpture of a strong human feeling, of a reduction in the distance between the earthly and the transcendental.

Round about the middle of the fourteenth century there issued from the architect and sculptor family of the Parlers tendencies towards a concise and sometimes vividly narrative realism. It was replaced by stylistic forms that arose in the courtly art centres of Bohemia and Burgundy. Around 1400 these forms became active as the international style that, owing to the full, rich curves of the strongly ornamental drapery folds, is often known as the Soft Style.

While Italy, in the fifteenth century, was already advancing towards the high Renaissance, Northern sculpture continued to be dominated by elements of the Gothic style, and, especially in the Netherlands and Germany, a growing secularization and also *embourgeoisement* of religious themes is discernible.

Amid the great output of this late Gothic phase, a number of remarkable and highly individual creative personalities stand out. A powerful, at times even crude realism and intricate fold flourishes that can be likened to the decorative forms of architecture are characteristic of this final stage.

Apart from smaller art works and a few individual statues, thirteenth-century sculpture was produced in the builders' workshops and closely bound up with religious architecture. Already in Romanesque times the stone-masons had tended increasingly to elaborate certain parts of the building, such as its capitals and window or door frames, with carved work. Bosses, ornamental gables, pinnacles, finials, and so on gave the decorative architectural sculpture of Gothic many more footholds. The scenes in relief on the tympana above the portals became deeper, as compared with

455 Sketch of the towers of Strasbourg Minster, end of fourteenth century. Note the very close relationship between architectural details (buttresses and traceried galleries).

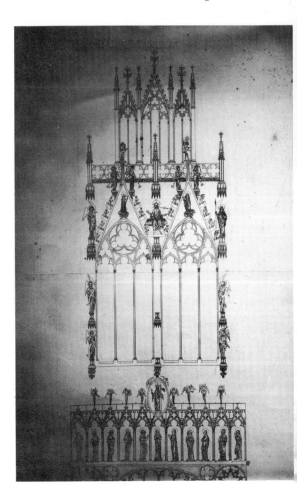

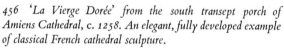

456 'La Vierge Dorée' from the south transept porch of Amiens Cathedral, c. 1258. An elegant, fully developed example of classical French cathedral sculpture.

457 Giovanni Pisano, marble statue in Prato Cathedral, c. 1315. This shows the influence of French cathedral sculpture combined with idealizing, antiquitizing influences.

458 Madonna in the cathedral of S. Stephan, Vienna, c. 1320. The relationship between Mother and Child is more intimate and inward than before, under the influence of mysticism.

their Romanesque forerunners, and the archivolts accompanying these tympana also received figure decoration now. Finally, the portal jambs were given special emphasis through monumental statues carved in the round. Large cathedrals generally had three portals grouped at their west end, and these were accompanied by similar tripartite arrangements at the ends of the transept. Additional sculptures had their place in the upper zones of the west front, on the towers *[455]* and buttresses, and even on the water-spouts of the roofs (gargoyles).

The iconography of sculptured works, that is to say their range of themes, was greatly extended in France during the thirteenth century. As a rule, the

portals of the west front were still reserved for the figure of Christ. The tympana were now no longer confined, as almost always in Romanesque times, to showing the Redeemer enthroned, but recounted the life of Christ in increasingly numerous figures and scenes. This was joined on an almost equal footing by scenes from the life of the Virgin, a group of subjects that had its first beginnings in late Romanesque art. A side portal was often devoted to it, if not actually the main western doorway. One of the lateral entrances not infrequently portrayed the life of saints, especially those connected with the place or the church. There were also representations of the virtues and vices, the rulers from the Bible, the sciences, and the months – in short, of all that this age's conception of the world included. It was a conception that had to be grasped in faith as an indivisible whole, and that found its image in the Gothic cathedral and its sculptures.

Producing architectural sculpture remained an important task of statuary until the end of Gothic, even if the accent was more on decoration during the fifteenth century. From the early fourteenth, though, new ranges of subject-matter and fields of duties were opened up and previously less important ones enlarged. Tombs grew increasingly grand and ostentatious. In England, for example, which made little contribution to the development of Gothic sculpture, the tomb became a central theme of statuary, and here as elsewhere it is these monuments that, through being securely dated, enable us to follow accurately the evolution of style.

Independent devotional images, very few of which have survived from Romanesque times and the thirteenth century, were produced particularly in Germany during the early fourteenth century, and some of them embodied completely new subjects:

459   Relief with representation of the months and zodiac, on the left western porch of Amiens Cathedral, c. 1230. March: Aries and tilling the fields; April: Taurus and hawking. A narrative figure style with garments rendered in a naturalistic way.

460   Niccolò and Giovanni Pisano, relief with the zodiac and months, from the great fountain in the market square of Perugia, c. 1275–8. Lively movement and realistic observation show French influences; the empty ground surface is stylistically similar to that on Byzantine ivory reliefs.

461   Relief of west rood-screen in Naumburg Cathedral: Christ before Pilate, by the Naumburg Master, c. 1260. Dramatic emphasis and spiritual deepening by life-like rendering of bodies and clothing.

the Pietà, Christ with S. John, the Man of Sorrows. Many of these works are in wood, which is also the material of the shrine altarpiece, an important German contribution to late Gothic art developed by the wood-carvers from the early fourteenth century on. The central part of such an altarpiece takes the form of a case containing figures or else scenes in relief. Only at high festivals was it opened and made visible to the congregation *[482]*, for on ordinary days it was covered by the outer wings, which usually had paintings or reliefs on them.

Stone – in Italy mostly marble – and wood are the most important materials of the Gothic sculptor. Wood-carvings were nearly always coloured by specialists and often gilded as well. Though by nature it contains fewer creative possibilities, ivory was popular in court art, above all that of France, where small Madonnas were made. The natural arching of the tusk was suited for the delicate curve of these figures. Finally, bronze-casting, which was being practised more extensively in Italy before this, developed into an important medium of sculptural expression in the North at the passage to the Renaissance.

EARLY GOTHIC SCULPTURE

France

Executed shortly before the mid-twelfth century, the tripartite *Porte Royale* at the west front of *Chartres Cathedral [462]* stands on the threshold of the new figuration. Even in their outward structure the three individual portals combine the old with the new. The reliefs of the slightly pointed tympana have been joined by the sculpture on the archivolts and, before the jamb columns, by statues of a kind unknown to Romanesque *[463]*. Even if there is still much about the themes that recalls older representations, as in the case of the enthroned Christ surrounded by Evangelist signs on the central tympanum, the narrating of the life of Christ in the capital zone is already freer. Particularly noticeable, the figures do not have that ecstatic quality which agitates French sculpture of the early twelfth century. The apparent stiffening of the jamb figures therefore signifies a clarification. Their bodies have an incipient roundness, their faces dawning life.

So far as we can still form a general picture of the development of French sculpture at this period (too much was destroyed in the outbreaks of iconoclasm during the Wars of Religion and the Revolution), the next decisive step is again to be seen at *Chartres*.

462 *Porte Royale on the west façade of Chartres Cathedral, c. 1145–50. Three porches in the main body. In the tympana are represented (central arch) Christ as Judge; Ascension (left) and the Virgin Enthroned (right).*

463 *Clothed figures (the Forefathers of Christ), from the right wall of the central west portal of Chartres Cathedral, c. 1145–50.*

464   *Group of the Visitation and the Prophet Daniel, from the right wall of the left north portal of Chartres Cathedral, 1205–15.*

465   *Group of the Visitation from the right wall of the central west portal of Reims Cathedral, c. 1230.*

The figures dating from soon after 1200 on the transept portals *[464]*, and even those that followed on the west front of *Amiens*, are still reserved and severe. But under the drapery with its folds like those of real fabric a naturally proportioned and securely standing body is discernible. No longer abstract presentations, the reliefs with religious subjects begin to tell a story. Those possessing the freest movement are the scenes that have more worldly subjects: the *Representations of the Months [459]* among the jamb sculptures at Amiens or the reliefs executed from 1230 in the transept porches at Chartres.

Round about the same time (*c.* 1230–60) the figures of the west portals at *Reims* were being carved. Here, as with the other big cathedrals, several – very different – masters were at work (today we can only distinguish between 'hands' as names have not come down to us) for the great task could not have been accomplished otherwise. One must bear in mind that the sculptural programmes of the big cathedrals reach right up to the topmost stories of the towers and include thousands of figures. Thus in addition to the still rather archaic-looking sculptures there, the particularly animated and inwardly agitated figures

of the *Visitation [465]* by a strongly classicizing master at Reims stand beside the delicate and slimly bending ones of the Annunciation. The graceful movement and spiritualization intimated here became a feature of the next stage in the development, shortly after the mid-thirteenth century. To it belongs the so-called *Vierge Dorée*, the Madonna of the south transept portal at Amiens *[456]*.

Further notable works of sculpture were certainly produced in France during the second half of the thirteenth and the early fourteenth century. But, as in architecture, the level of quality shown by the art of the classic cathedrals was not reached again, and, above all, no more radically new creative possibilities were discovered.

Germany

The curious situation of German art in the first half of the thirteenth century complicates the picture presented by sculpture at this period. Sculptors who had undoubtedly been trained in the great workshops of the French cathedrals, above all at Reims, worked after their return on buildings that still belonged entirely to Hohenstaufen late Romanesque. Accordingly there were at first no great figure portals in Germany. Even the extensive French programmes, at the centre of which come the Last Judgment, Christ, and the Virgin, were abridged and, through this simplification, sometimes monumentalized. Thus the *Angel Pier* in the transept of *Strasbourg Minster* (c. 1230) is a highly individual reinterpretation of the Last Judgment motif *[466]*. In general, Germans obviously preferred to bring their sculpture inside, whether into porches, as with the tower of Freiburg Minster, or right into the interior of the church. Thereby German sculpture won considerable independence even at this early period, being less subservient to architecture than the French. In addition, the much reduced programmes made it possible to achieve a more even quality, and so it is easier to recognize and isolate the special characteristics of the masters active at the different spots.

The older sculpture at Strasbourg, that of the transept (c. 1230), is distinguished by the exceptional slenderness and delicacy of the figures. Shortly afterwards there appeared also at Bamberg similar, if less

466   Angel Pier of the transept in Strasbourg Minster, c. 1230.

467   The Blessed Virgin, from the Visitation group (S. Elizabeth in the background) in Bamberg Cathedral, 1240–55.

sensitive figures, but they are distinctly Gothic, as in the case of Ecclesia and Synagoga. Near these figures more conservative men worked on the Apostles and Prophets for the screens of St George's choir, their products still full of late Romanesque linear agitation. On the other hand, the *Bamberg Virgin [467]* and St Elizabeth are, in their lively balance, German counterparts of the Reims Visitation group. The famous *Rider [468]* is among the most remarkable images of the regal and knightly lord of this period.

Undoubtedly the Naumburg Master was also trained at French cathedrals – indeed, traces of his activity in France are thought to have been detected. In the already Gothic west chancel of *Naumburg Cathedral* there stand those figures of men and women *[469]* that, carved soon after the mid-thirteenth century, presented the truest image of the chivalrous human being at the very moment when Hohenstaufen splendour passed away. Though completely idealized, they also have amazing vitality. The scenes and figures of the choir-screen are profoundly dramatic *[461, 475]*. To this phase of late Hohenstaufen early Gothic belong sculptures in the cathedrals of Meissen, Brunswick, and Magdeburg.

468　*The Bamberg Rider, in Bamberg Cathedral, 1240–5.*

469　*Ekkehard and Uta, figures of the founders in the west choir of Naumburg Cathedral, c. 1250.*

470　*Prophets, from the right wall of the central west portal of Strasbourg Minster, c. 1280. (Above.)*

Germany's one great completed portal arrangement with statues, that of the Strasbourg west front, was not built until about 1280. Much was destroyed during the French Revolution, but the elongated Prophets and the tall slender figures of maidens announce a new withdrawal disavowing all earthly things. This is characteristic of the subsequent development as far as the middle of the fourteenth century.

Italy

Whereas Spain's early Gothic sculpture closely conformed, like its architecture, to the French pattern, Italy proved its independence in this field. Sculpture was far less tied to the actual building than in other

countries. The sculptors worked here mainly on furnishings and fittings for the church, such as pulpits or bronze doors. As regards the remarkable art produced during the first half of the thirteenth century in Hohenstaufen Apulia, the scanty remains make us sure that it had strong classicizing tendencies. Italian sculpture, which in the early Middle Ages had been particularly influenced by the Byzantine aversion to reality, linked up with the antique heritage even before the other kinds of art, and thenceforth helped substantially to prepare for the Renaissance.

From the second half of the thirteenth century on, the development was sustained by sharply defined artistic personalities who are traceable in documents and whose productions show clearly recognizable individual styles. The first of these masters, Niccolò Pisano (*c.* 1225–*c.* 1280), came from Apulia to his real sphere of action, Tuscany, which now became the art centre where works foreshadowing the future were produced. On his marble pulpit of 1260 for the *Pisa Baptistry [471]*, Niccolò reveals, in a pictorial relief style, unmistakable influences from late Roman sarcophagi such as have survived at Pisa itself. He has built up his scenes monumentally and boldly, even if they are not free from all trace of uncertainty. Niccolò's son and pupil Giovanni Pisano (*c.* 1250– *c.* 1315) undoubtedly saw French models. He combined his father's simple, antique-based portrayals of situations with examples of French cathedral sculpture in scenes of dramatic intensity, as on the *pulpit in Pisa Cathedral, 1302–10 [472]*. During the rest of the fourteenth century French Gothic influence increased, most plainly on the oldest *bronze doors for the Florentine Baptistry*, which Andrea Pisano (*c.* 1290– *c.* 1350), a goldsmith by training and unrelated to his above-mentioned namesakes, executed from 1330 to 1336 *[473]*. But even here the figures under the drapery's play of line hint at a new feeling for the body, and the architecture gives the scenes a real, self-contained existence.

471 Niccolò Pisano, Nativity. Relief from a pulpit in the baptistry at Pisa, 1260.

472 Giovanni Pisano, Nativity. Relief from a pulpit in Pisa Cathedral, 1302–10.

473 Andrea Pisano, Scene from the Life of John the Baptist. Relief from the first bronze door of the baptistry in Florence, 1330–6.

In the early fourteenth century the focus of sculptural activity shifted more and more clearly to Germany. Although here too architectural sculpture remained the most important field throughout the century, it was joined by a growing number of new tasks, including the production of shrine altarpieces and devotional images, the latter enriched by new subjects such as Christ with S. John or the Pietà, in addition to the already common Madonnas and Crucifixes. Wood-carving now became as important as sculpture in stone – indeed, during the fifteenth century the most outstanding works were generally fashioned from wood.

German thought of the early fourteenth century was charged with the deep experience of mysticism, with an intense longing for God that took visible form in the art of this age [458]. Probably set up shortly before the 1322 consecration, the statues in

the chancel of Cologne Cathedral, the Apostles and Annunciation group as well as the so-called *Milan Madonna [476]*, climb from earth to heaven as slender, almost incorporeal, strongly deflecting curves. It is an upward movement already prefigured before the turn of the century in the sculpture of the west portals at Strasbourg *[470]* and Freiburg. The same spiritual intensity is expressed by the groups of *Christ with St John* at Freiburg, early fourteenth century *[474]*, the Crucifixions, the Pietàs (Erfurt, Ursuline church, *c.* 1320), and the tombstones (Archbishop Friedrich of Hohenlohe, Bamberg Cathedral, 1352) from this first half of the fourteenth century. Towards the middle of the century a certain stiffening set in, with the figures growing more compact and statuesque (Rottweil, chapel tower; related works at Schwäbisch Gmünd, Heiligkreuzkirche; and at Esslingen, Frauenkirche). The Parler style emerged, probably from the Swabian area, for example in the *chancel portals of the Heiligkreuzkirche at Schwäbisch Gmünd, c.* 1351 *[479]* and at Augsburg Cathedral, *c.* 1356, but rapidly spread to other regions (Prague, Vienna, Freiburg, Thann, Nuremburg). Concisely modelled figures clad wholly in the fashion of the times and multi-figured narrative scenes indicate a turning towards reality. The tombstones and busts that Peter

474 Group of Christ and St John, beginning of fourteenth century. Freiburg, Augustiner Museum. This is a picture subject developed under the influence of the mysticism of the Holy Communion, chiefly in the nunneries of the upper Rhine and Bodensee.

475 Weeping Madonna from the Crucifixion group on the west rood-screen of Naumburg Cathedral, c. 1260, by the Naumburg Master, trained in France. An example of the transitional style between late Hohenstaufen and early Gothic. In the inwardness of expression, the force of the gestures, and closeness to earthly reality, this work resembles contemporary [476] and earlier [464] achievements of French cathedral sculpture, although idealism rather than characterization is stressed. (Above left.)

476 The 'Milan Madonna' in Cologne Cathedral, c. 1320. The style looks forward to high Gothic. Physicality is dominated by the fine lines of the drapery. The elegant, rather precious attitude and courtly stylization show the close relationship to conventional French style. (Below left.)

477 The Krumau Madonna, c. 1400. Vienna, Kunsthistorisches Museum. An example of the so-called 'Soft Style'. A 'Beautiful Madonna' full of loveliness, grace, and flowing harmony. The clothing falls loosely to both sides. (Above right.)

478 The Dangolsheim Madonna, c. 1460–70. Formerly Staatliche Museen Berlin, Museum Dahlem, Gemäldegalerie. An example of late Gothic realism. (Below right.)

479 The Kiss of Judas and Arrest of Christ, relief from the north choir portal of the church of the Holy Cross at Schwäbisch Gmünd, after 1351. Some realistic elements (coarse forms, contemporary clothing).

Parler (1330–99) carved for Prague Cathedral (*c.* 1380) – he also did not forget to represent himself – may be regarded as the first portraits in German art.

Around 1400 the formal language became softer and more opulent. If in the early fourteenth century the fold lines were drawn almost parallel to one side, so that on the other a hollow space *[476]* was formed which towards the mid-century filled up with swag-like folds, around 1400 the rich festoons developed on both sides, curving out in softly modelled bunches of folds and piling up on the ground *[477]*. The Luxembourg centre at the court in Prague under Charles IV was superseded by a new one in Burgundy. This duchy likewise owed its existence to dynastic connexions, and the Burgundian court had an even stronger attraction for artists from different parts of Europe, above all from Flanders. The Netherlander Claus Sluter (died 1406) became the leading sculptor of this circle, and he succeeded in giving the forms of the period a human and dramatic quality free of any close relationship to architecture. He produced his most remarkable works between

480 Claus Sluter, Well of Moses in the Chartreuse of Champmol near Dijon, 1395–1406. The physiognomy and heavily formed style of the clothing show some of the crude realism of folk art.

481 Hans Multscher, Man of Sorrows on the west portal of Ulm Minster, c. 1430. Middle-class realism influenced by Burgundian models.

work was finally completing the change that had already commenced in the art of Peter Parler. With Multscher there began the succession of distinctively fashioned individual works that show, besides the general period style, the personal one of the particular artist who created them. And with Multscher there also began an art that, in painting too, no longer idealized the subjects but seized them directly in their plain humanity. It was the start of a middle-class objectivity; but the realistic representation of mother and child was elevated by the piety of the period into a credible and inspiring image of the *Mother of God* *[478]*.

The second half of the fifteenth century saw the beginning of a stylistic development that brought a renewed emphasis on more abstract tendencies. Figures were given bolder twists, as in the case of those by Nicholas Gerhaert of Leyden, who was active at Strasbourg in the sixties. Their movements look more artificial and angular, and the drapery, whose folds bunch together in crumpled clusters and eddies, breaks free to an agitation of its own. This

483   Tilman Riemenschneider, Altar of the Virgin at Creglingen, c. 1500. Expressive inwardness and craftsmanlike mastery of the material; note the realistic carving of the clothes.

482   Veit Stoss, High Altar of the Marienkirche at Cracow, 1477–89. Typical example of a late Gothic carved altar with open wings. Fully plastic, monumentally pathetic figures of the Death of the Virgin in the middle section; scenes from the Life of the Virgin at the side; Coronation of the Virgin and figures of saints at the apex.

1395 and 1406 for the Chartreuse (Carthusian monastery) of Champmol near Dijon, namely the doorway to the chapel of Philip the Bold, the so-called *Well of Moses [480]*, and parts of the Duke's tomb. Contemporary German works in a similar formal language are quieter and more intimate. Let us mention here the *Schöne Madonnen* or 'Beautiful Madonnas' *[477]* that, along with a few Pietàs, are associated with an anonymous master who probably moved shortly before 1400 from the lower Rhine to the east, where he left behind him works at Thorn, Breslau, and Krumau in Bohemia. Charm and the graceful play of line are characteristic of these sculptures.

Beside the still 'soft' figures of Master Hartmann at the west entrance of Ulm Minster stands the *Man of Sorrows [481]* attributed to Hans Multscher (c. 1400–67). Here a new and vigorous realism drives out idealized beauty. At the time when the Renaissance was getting under way in Italy, Multscher's

484   Master HL, High Altar of Breisach Minster, 1523–6. A baroque, late phase of Gothic carving. Figures and background are indeterminate.

highly expressive manner was intensified around 1480 to an amazing vehemence by artists such as Erasmus Grasser, Michael Pacher, and lastly Veit Stoss (1440/50–1533) whose *Cracow Altarpiece* is of 1477–89 *[482]*. By comparison, the large œuvre of Tilman Riemenschneider (*c.* 1460–1531), with his carved altarpieces dating from about 1500 at Rothenburg and *Creglingen [483]*, seems more sensitive and high-strung.

A final group of sculptors raised the vehemence of the late fifteenth century to wild, almost baroque swirls. In the north there were Bernt Notke, Claus Berg, and Hans Brüggemann, all of whom were also active in the neighbouring Scandinavian lands. In south-west and south Germany there were Hans Backofen and Hans Leinberger, but above all the Master HL whose *Breisach Altarpiece*, 1523–6 *[484]*, concludes the series of great shrine altarpieces that belong as much to the specifically German *Sondergotik* as do the Gothic hall churches.

Painting

Produced by the same historical agents – historical in the widest sense of political, religious, intellectual, social, and economic – the lines of development in painting followed paths on the whole very similar to those of sculpture. Nevertheless one must pay regard to certain fundamental regional shifts of accent, which to some extent were caused by the medium itself. Thus there is only stained glass in the Northern cathedrals, but in Italian churches mainly fresco painting. Making a survey is also complicated by the fact that very different techniques are embraced by the term 'painting' at this time: manuscript illumination, which continued to flourish chiefly in France and England but also in Germany during the thirteenth and fourteenth centuries; and wall-painting, though it was almost only in Italy that this found possibilities of development, since Gothic architecture had a positive aversion to walls. Other techniques increased their importance or were actually rediscovered at this period. The art of tapestry-making was revived quite widely, in particular in fourteenth-century France *[485]*, whereas in the fifteenth the focus of activity moved to the Netherlands. Stained glass is quite obviously bound up with the developments. The technique was practised earlier but could only now light up in all its richness on the great window surfaces of the cathedrals. Finally we must mention the panel picture, the painting done on a movable wooden panel. Its rise is linked with the development of the altar, which was at first a plain stone table, and then acquired in the early Middle Ages a decorative frontal for which metal-work was used as well as stone relief and textiles. In the thirteenth century, painted panels were occasionally set before the altar, for example the *Westphalian frontal* of *c.* 1250 *[499]*. More important, though, is the true altar panel, which, of Italian origin and connected in its beginnings with the Byzantine icon, stood on or behind the altar table. These panels grew increasingly conspicuous in the fourteenth century, and from them there finally developed in Germany the great shrine and winged altarpieces of the late fourteenth and fifteenth century that often combined painting with sculpture. A technical change occurred in the Netherlands during the early fifteenth century. Instead of the hitherto customary tempera colour, with its rather hard and dry effect, people began to use pigments bound in an oil medium which allowed more delicate transitions, glazes (successive transparent layers of paint), and brilliant hues.

It was painting that gave artists the opportunity to express new ideas. Sculpture renders an isolated image of man, and only in the relief, which significantly grew more and more pictorial during this period, can it show man in his environment. Painting, on the other hand, became increasingly devoted to visual detail and in the choice of scale and perspective had to decide on the relative importance of the different pictorial elements. Lastly, it also gave up the gold background for religious scenes in favour of an increasingly realistic setting. Apart from Giotto, who depicted landscape in his frescoes as early as about 1300, the extensive conquest of reality took place mainly in the panel pictures of Bohemian, Netherlandish, and south-west German painting of the second half of the fourteenth and the first half of the fifteenth century.

The various European art regions made their decisive contributions to the development of Gothic painting at different times. In the early Gothic period activity concentrated mainly on book illumination and stained glass, and here again it was from France that the most important impulses flowed. The Italian Giotto stood alone about 1300. His monumentality and his urge to conquer mass and space already pointed the way into a new age *[486]*. Initiated by the court at Prague around the middle of the fourteenth century, Bohemian painting mainly worked up foreign ideas in its pictures, combining popular piety with courtly traits and feeling its way towards reality

485   Scene from the Apocalypse, detail of a series of tapestries for Angers Cathedral, manufactured c. 1377–81 in the workshop of Nicolas Bataille at Paris, after drawings by Hennequin of Bruges. A high point of medieval tapestry-work; originally seven pieces more than 4 metres high and 24 metres long.

486   Giotto, Madonna from the Ognissanti Church, c. 1310. Florence, Uffizi. Strong closed form and heroically idealistic rendering of the main figure. Medieval 'significance proportions': the Virgin is larger than the angels and saints.

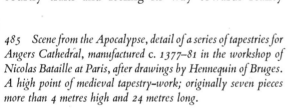

cautiously at first *[487]*. It merged towards 1400 into what is known as International Gothic, which corresponds to the Soft Style in sculpture and had a new court centre in Burgundy. Also from Burgundy came the Netherlanders who early in the fifteenth century undertook the great and courageous thrust into reality *[488]* at the same time as a few south-west German painters and the artists of the early Renaissance at Florence. In Jean Fouquet *[489]*, who about the middle of the fifteenth century occupied a place beside the outstanding Netherlandish and German painters of this age, France was affected by Netherlandish and also Italian influences. England and Spain had nothing to equal these achievements. Pictorial production certainly did not languish there, but in England the book illumination that was predominant during the thirteenth century had a strong

mutual relation with French work, while as well as absorbing French and Italian influences, the panel painting that bloomed in Spain from the fourteenth century on was fertilized in the fifteenth century chiefly by the Netherlands, whence also came much in the form of direct imports.

Mention has still to be made of a new means of expression in planar art, namely the print, which as woodcut and line-engraving on copper developed during the fifteenth century into an independent art form. Its own progressive spread played a vital part in the development of late Gothic stylistic features [514–16].

487 *The Glatz Madonna, c. 1350. Formerly Staatliche Museen Berlin, Museum Dahlem, Gemäldegalerie. German-Bohemian inwardness with overtones of the conventional French style (posture, clothing). Note the beginning of realistic detail (the lion on Solomon's throne; the donor's glove on the platform; angels behind window-shutters).*

488 *Jan van Eyck, Madonna of Chancellor Rolin, c. 1434. Paris, Louvre. Early Netherlandish realism, atmospheric landscape; figures and space unified (the kneeling donor and the Virgin are the same size).*

489 *Jean Fouquet, Madonna with Angels, mid-fifteenth century. Antwerp, Museum. Despite the crown and ceremonial chair the atmosphere is that of a bourgeois living-room. Bright side light, plastic modelling.*

MANUSCRIPT ILLUMINATION AND STAINED GLASS

Much of pictorial activity centred on book illumination, above all in early Gothic times. Previously produced only in specialized monastery scriptoria, manuscripts from the mid-thirteenth century on were also written and illustrated in secular workshops run commercially. As well as works for ecclesiastical use there now appeared richly adorned 'books of hours' for the private devotion of laymen, mostly highly placed personages in the temporal sphere.

Since the mid-thirteenth century France under Louis IX (St Louis) had been the centre of book illumination *[490]*. From here important influences were exerted on England, Spain, and, with limitations, Germany. Splendid and lavish manuscripts were produced, at times already with worldly contents: Tristan, Parsifal, the chronicle of world history, and so forth. Outstanding and famous English

490 Psalter of St Louis, c. 1260. Nahash the Ammonite threatening the Jews at Jabesh. Courtly art with a tapestry-like effect (the space of borders and tracery is identical for every picture). A flat, relief-like representation of clearly contoured forms in conventionally stylized attitudes.

491 Christ as Pantocrator, from the Holkham Bible picture book, probably second quarter of fourteenth century; London, British Museum. An outstanding example of medieval English manuscript illumination.

contributions to the art of this period were the work of Matthew Paris, who illustrated his own historical writings with delicately tinted pen and ink drawings, and the Arundel and Queen Mary's Psalters, characterized by rich borders where animals, birds, and leaves are portrayed with life-like naturalism *[491]*. The predominant religious miniatures are best described as 'chivalrous', even if chivalry played no special part in either the making or the using of these manuscripts. An affected conventionalization in standard ideal postures can be followed from the still comparatively natural figures of the thirteenth century, through the slender curvities of the early fourteenth, to the nascent realism of about 1400.

The link between bookcraft and stained glass, evident in the brilliant colours and linear compositions on illuminated pages of the thirteenth century, was replaced in the fourteenth by a growing relationship with the up-and-coming panel painting. The style now became more painterly, and, probably under Italian influence, realistic details appeared,

492   King Konradin out hawking, from the Manesse Codex (Book of Songs), c. 1300. Heidelberg, Universitätsbibliothek. A collection of middle high German songs of courtly love, named after Manesse of Zurich, who commissioned the work. Stylized indication of the coulisses.

giving evidence of man's new relation to his environment. This applies above all to Burgundian illumination of about 1400 [510], which thus became one of the foundations of fifteenth-century Netherlandish panel painting. Then with the rise of the printer's art illumination lost its earlier importance in the course of the fifteenth century.

German illumination also went through these different stylistic phases; the chivalrous idealization of the thirteenth, the spiritualized, ornamental curvilinear quality of the early fourteenth, and the incipient middle-class objectivity of the late fourteenth century. Nevertheless its general character is simpler, less contrived, and in return more profound. Here, too, the first worldly themes appeared, as in the *Manesse Codex* of *c.* 1300 [492], which describes the chivalrous life of the age of the Minnesingers, though at a time when this knightly system was already passed its political prime.

The rise of stained-glass manufacture was dependent on the development of the French cathedral

with its tendency to open up the confining walls more and more. Through the radiant windows the cathedral received its internal colour, which often also came from its painted sculptural decoration although only faint traces of colour now remain.

Chartres Cathedral has the finest and most complete surviving set of early Gothic windows. It reaches from works of the second half of the twelfth century (the three big west windows and the *Belle Verrière* in the ambulatory) to the stained glass of the mid-thirteenth. As in the case of the few Romanesque examples that still exist elsewhere, the older windows are filled by large figures or else divided up into medallions containing simple scenes drawn like miniatures. The subject-matter, like that of book illumination, includes the whole range of Christian themes. At first windows were put together from glowing bits of glass with the aid of lead strips as a fine, almost mosaic-like structure. The separate pieces later grew bigger, and the importance of the internal details applied with lead solder increased.

493   Emperor Henry II, detail of a stained-glass window in the north aisle of Strasbourg Minster, c. 1260. For the contours and inner drawing lead brushes were still used.

of years to evolve more freely, although this evolution remained tied to the historical development of particular regions even particular city-states – above all Tuscany with its great centres at Florence, Siena, and Pisa. To understand the complete reorientation that took place in Italian art towards the end of the thirteenth century one must realize to what extent many fields of the country's visual art had remained till then in the grip of Byzantine formulae. Though the revolution is also apparent in architecture and sculpture, it is no accident that it was carried out most

494 *Crucifixion, stained-glass window in the chancel of S. Dionysus at Esslingen, c. 1300. Narrative borders and vines decorate the background. A plummet was used for the inner drawing.*

The panes of the fifteenth century imitated panel painting more and more closely.

The *aisle windows of Strasbourg Cathedral* date back to the second half of the thirteenth century. They too display large figures surrounded by architectural motifs in glass. Even now, at the time of the interregnum, German kings and emperors were represented *[493]*. Then about 1300 the scenes often came to be elaborately framed by decorative accessories, as at *Esslingen*, chancel of the town church of *S. Dionysus [494]*. The slenderly curving figures reflect the general stylistic taste of this age. German windows of the fifteenth century eventually developed into a pictorial form bearing little relation to the material.

WALL AND PANEL PAINTING

Italy

The collapse of Hohenstaufen rule in the mid-thirteenth century gave Italy its first chance for hundreds

495 *Cimabue, Madonna from S. Trinità, c. 1290. Florence, Uffizi. The symmetry of the composition and golden web of the garments are in the Byzantine tradition. The work is still archaic when compared to Giotto's Ognissanti Madonna [486].*

boldly in painting, the mode of giving form least
dependent on the materials used.

Around 1300 Cimabue (*c.* 1240–1302) was still
painting his *Madonnas* entirely as queens of heaven in
the Byzantine tradition *[495]*. Yet whereas the Byzantine models continued in all the many varied repeti-
tions to be abstractive, planar renderings of the
elevated and the supernatural, one senses in Cimabue's
Madonnas, despite his adherence to traditional types,
the struggle to achieve a three-dimensional effect by
free use of line and bolder movement.

'Cimabue thought that he held the field in painting,

*496   Giotto, The Flight into Egypt, fresco in the Arena Chapel,
Padua, 1305–7. A closed composition with the figures carefully
divided. Note the clear spatial arrangement of the picture field.*

but now Giotto is acclaimed and his fame obscured',
wrote their contemporary Dante (*Purgatory*, XI,
94–96). A comparison of Cimabue's Madonna
panel with a roughly contemporary work by Giotto
(*c.* 1266–1337) makes evident the crucial difference
between the younger master and the older one who
was probably his teacher. Giotto's *Madonna [486]* is
also supernaturally enthroned as a queen of heaven

surrounded by angels, but she has a plastic and corporeal monumentality. The body is revealed – at first in its volumes rather than as an entity pulsing with life – and with its space and thus the dimension in which earthly reality has its being. Giotto composed the frescoes of the Arena Chapel at Padua (1305–7) with heroic simplicity and severity. He gave the events a landscape, as in the *Flight into Egypt [496]*, or an interior as their setting, and unlike his contemporaries and a good many younger artists did not merely suggest it with coulisse. The gold background, still a symbol of the transcendental with later artists, is for Giotto something obsolete. But the setting remains subordinated to the action, and the scenes obtain their life wholly from the drama of the figure groups. Little as Giotto's work has to do with Gothic in the narrow sense – that is, the French or German, it still clearly reflects the endeavour of this age to break free from the old bonds. Though the art of Giotto found many imitators in Italy during the fourteenth century, its true meaning was not grasped again until Masaccio at the start of the Renaissance.

A second focus of the new painting developed in a less daring stylistic trend at Siena. Here the work of Duccio (died 1319; *Maesta*, Siena, 1308–11) disengaged itself almost as much as Cimabue from tradition. Sienese painting, especially panel painting, was more strongly affected by the Gothic formal idiom – indeed, Giotto's Sienese contemporary Simone Martini (1284–1344) can in this sense be called the most Gothic of Italian painters. Though freer and more natural than those of his predecessors, his figures, such as the *Annunciation* of 1333 *[497]* are governed by a courtly, aristocratic spirit that is made manifest with extreme technical skill. Besides this, his frescoes reveal a new interest in problems concerning reality. Simone, who like Giotto became famous as a painter in his own lifetime, was summoned to the papal court at Avignon during his last years of activity, and gained thereby a direct influence on French painting and above all on Burgundian illumination.

The work of Giotto and his following on the one hand and the more Gothic art of the Sienese on the other provided the major stylistic events of Italian painting in the fourteenth century. It is true that Giotto's heroic monumentality did not reappear until the works of the early Renaissance. Even in Italy, however, Gothic tendencies remained active. During the early fifteenth century Gentile da Fabriano (*c.* 1370–1427) – *Adoration of the Kings*, 1423 *[498]* – and Pisanello (1397–1455) were painting wholly in accordance with the courtly International Gothic style of about 1400.

497 *Simone Martini, Annunciation, 1333. Florence, Uffizi. An example of the International Gothic style, with the fine lines of the Gothic. An altar composition with fields of pointed arches and decorated gables.*

498 *Gentile da Fabriano, Adoration of the Kings, 1423. Florence, Uffizi. An example of the International Soft Style, with courtly narrative and realistic observation of detail (garments, animals).*

Germany

In Germany, a continuous development of Gothic painting can only be traced from the start of the fourteenth century, and in considering it we shall keep mainly to panel pictures. There were, of course, wall-paintings too at this period (Wienhausen, early fourteenth century; Cologne Cathedral, choir-screens, mid-fourteenth century); but the body of surviving works is the outcome of chance and very incomplete, quite apart from the fact that in Germany wall-painting never played the part it did in Italy. One of Germany's oldest panel pictures, a *Westphalian altar frontal* from the mid-fourteenth century *[499]*, has already been mentioned (p. 254). While there are quite a number of links with contemporary sculpture (Bamberg) in the basic conception of this work, the jagged drapery lines still indicate its dependence on late Romanesque illumination.

A first centre of Gothic panel painting developed in the early fourteenth century at Cologne. Here there were produced in particular small devotional pictures *[500]* and winged altarpieces, whose soulful Annunciations and Crucifixions against a gold background (the symbol of a supernatural reality) fully reveal the mystical temper of this age.

Around the middle of the century, painting was concentrated in Prague and the Bohemian area. We

499   *Antependium from the Wiesenkirche at Soest, c. 1250. Formerly Staatliche Museen Berlin, Museum Dahlem, Gemäldegalerie. An example of the 'jagged style', transitional between late Romanesque and Gothic. The bodies are clearly evident beneath the clothing.*

are well informed on the architects and sculptors at the court of Prague (e.g. Peter Parler, pp. 250, 253) but know less about the painters there. Several German names referred to as being those of court painters cannot be connected with any works, and there is disagreement over the nationality of Master Theodoric, the one man whose name and œuvre are both known. It can hardly be supposed, though, that Bohemian painting was a native growth like its architecture and sculpture. In its beginnings – *Glatz Madonna [487]*, and *Hohenfurth Altarpiece [501]*, both *c.* 1350 – it still had a good deal of the early fourteenth century's depth of feeling, although many features – architecture, indication of landscape, courtly elegance – show Sienese Italian influence. Around 1365 Master Theodoric of Prague (active 1359–80) decorated the castle at Karlstein with paintings for Emperor Charles IV. His figures are heavy, and modelled to appear solid *[502]* for the first time in German painting. This painterly and corporeal style was abandoned by Bohemian painting at its next stage of development in favour of a new spirituality and almost visionary intensity in representation, as in the *Wittingau Altarpiece* of 1380 *[503]*. In northern Germany, on the other hand, the style found its imitator and chief representative in Master Bertram of Minden (*c.* 1345–1415). Bertram's pictorial world is impressive for naïve and vivid narration, as in the *Altarpiece of St Peter* of 1379 *[504]* and for an increased clarity in the setting, in the depiction, that is, of landscape and architecture.

Then, with two more north German artists, Konrad of Soest and Master Francke, the transition took place to the richer forms and more graphic rendering

500 Annunciation; a work of the Cologne school, c. 1328. Cologne, Wallraf Richartz Museum. Lyrical harmony and mystic inwardness with delicate enamel-like colouring. As in contemporary sculpture [476], stylized features and conventional gestures.

501 Annunciation from the Hohenfurth Altarpiece, c. 1350. Prague, National Museum. Expressive tenderness of the figures; the architecture and landscape coulisses are influenced by Italian examples.

502 Theodoric of Prague, Crucifixion, c. 1360. Burg Karlstein. Strong colours and large forms contribute to the expressive effect.

503 Wittingau Altarpiece, Christ on the Mount of Olives, c. 1380. Prague, National Gallery. Painterly chiaroscuro, and elements of spatial composition.

504 Master Bertram of Minden, Nativity, from the Grabow Altarpiece, 1379–83. Hamburg, Kunsthalle. The influence of Theodoric of Prague is evident in the size of the figures and the softer colours. Realistic narrative detail.

505 Konrad Witz, Annunciation, c. 1455. Nuremburg, Germanisches Museum. In place of elevated idealization the spatial coulisses have an earthly reality. (Above.)

of reality of the Soft Style. The most important representative of this trend belongs to its last phase, namely Stephan Lochner (*c.* 1410–51), who probably came from Meersburg on Lake Constance and was later active at Cologne. Executed between about 1430 and 1450, his principal works, the so-called *Kölner Dombild* showing the city's patron saints *[506]* and the *Madonna of the Rose-Garden* (Cologne), add the traditional charm of Cologne to the idealizing realism, the formal opulence, and the luminous colour that about the same time characterized Burgundian and Netherlandish painting also.

Stephan Lochner's work is free, however, from all the harshness of realism, and does not reveal the passionate interest in actuality that at this date had not only long been felt by Netherlanders but was also shared by some German painters from the south-west: Hans Multscher, Lukas Moser, and Konrad Witz. Of these, Konrad Witz (*c.* 1400–44) is certainly the boldest and most consistent *[505]*. He has set his representation of the *Miraculous Draught of Fishes*, 1444 *[507]* in a landscape that is no longer put together in the imagination out of separate motifs, but derives from the actual surroundings of Lake Constance. His interiors are rooms in the style of the period, not framing architectural coulisses.

Contemporaries and successors up to Dürer's times did not grasp the wide possibilities that the art of Konrad Witz discovered for them. In the large output of the second half of the fifteenth century, German painting lacked outstanding personalities. Moreover the diverse stylistic trends that are characteristic of painting from this period make it harder to form a general picture. One feature is common to the artistic statements of the times, namely the increasing *embourgeoisement* of religious themes. Court chivalry was now finally superseded by the ethos of the rising towns. Many of the very numerous

506 Stephen Lochner, Annunciation, from the outer wings of the Cologne Altarpiece, c. 1440. Idealizing realism of the Soft Style, full of painterly delicacy. The rendering of the material is masterly.

507 Konrad Witz, Miraculous Draught of Fishes, from the Geneva Altarpiece, 1444. Geneva Museum. First depiction of an actual landscape.

late Gothic altar panels display a sober, craftsman-like middle-class spirit. Admittedly, we again find painters who diverge from the current mean. Thus, alongside Michael Pacher (*c.* 1435–98), a wood-carver and painter from the south Tyrol who worked up north Italian ideas in pictures with complex fore-shortenings and a plastic, illusionistic mode of representation – *Altarpiece of the Church Fathers, c.* 1483 *[508]* – there is Martin Schongauer from Colmar whose pictures were to some extent produced under the impact of the Netherlander Rogier van der Weyden. Other artists of this period derive their importance less from their own works than from the fact that they were the instructors of the next generation who were far more distinguished. This applies in Nuremburg to Michael Wolgemut, from whose workshop Dürer emerged, or in Augsburg to Hans Holbein the Elder, the teacher of his son. The painters of Dürer's times were, of course, working under the direct influence of the Italian Renaissance.

508   Michael Pacher, SS. Augustine and Gregory from the Altar of the Church Fathers, c. 1483. Munich, Alte Pinakothek. Spatial illusionism and plastic modelling through strong side light.

But even in their productions, as in the whole of German art, the Gothic sense of form lived on for a long while yet.

The Low Countries

The origins of early Netherlandish painting in the fifteenth century are closely bound up with artistic activity at the Burgundian court. Formed as a French vassal state in 1363, the duchy of Burgundy included all the Netherlands in the early fifteenth century; and through its rulers' wealth and love of art it attracted eminent artists from Italy, France, and the Netherlands themselves to its court centres at Dijon and Bruges. Not only did the different tendencies of European art encounter one another there, but a late chivalrous and courtly spirit joined forces with the realistic middle-class outlook of the rising Netherlandish towns. This situation brought forth a new style whose far-reaching influence over the entire Northern area in the fifteenth century is inconceivable without the achievements of great, pioneering artistic personalities who showed the way far into the future. Of first importance to this development were the sumptuous manuscripts illuminated for the dukes and leading figures of the court. The Limbourg brothers (active by the start of the fifteenth century), who judging by their name came from the Netherlands, adorned the calendar pages of a *Book of Hours* towards 1416. They did so not only very realistically with the castles that their patron, the Duke de Berry, owned or particularly liked *[510]*, but by depicting on the same pages the life of both court and people.

The Van Eyck brothers, too, probably illustrated books like this (Turin – Milan Hours, 1415/17), in which the interiors may be regarded as direct preparations for quite a number of their later panel pictures. Beginning with the famous *Ghent Altarpiece*, completed in 1432 *[511]*, these panel works were evidently sometimes painted for new clients who soon outmatched the courts as art patrons, namely the large, rich trading cities of the southern Netherlands and their citizens.

Jan van Eyck (*c.* 1390–1441), who survived his brother Hubert (*c.* 1370–1426) by fifteen years, and to whom we must ascribe the bulk of their pictorial output, came very close to realism in his works which, built out of masses of very careful separate observations, grew into convincing wholes through his own creative power. In accordance with this natural quality, his figures move about in real interiors or landscapes, though without losing their dominant status in the picture. Thus Jan lets Chancellor and

Cardinal Rolin, who displays here the vitality of a portrait, kneel forbiddingly close in a magnificent palace room before a Madonna who by comparison looks almost like a shy woman of the middle class *[488]*. Between these two figures our eye is lead into the depths of a rich landscape. The portraits, also, are the sum of their details, yet they have a convincing unity, for example in the *Marriage of Giovanni Arnolfini and Giovanna Cenami* of 1434 *[509]*. In other panels certain passages already anticipate the painterly virtuosity of later Netherlandish still-lifes, although this does not mar the cohesion and closeness to life of the picture as a whole. This technical facility is inconceivable without the use of oil-paint, here to be observed for the first time. Jan cannot be called simply the inventor of oils, since they had long been known in connexion with the specialists who painted and gilded others' wood-carvings. But he was probably among the first who recognized the suitability of oil for panel painting, and who thereby made possible an entirely new colourfulness.

509 Jan van Eyck, Giovanni Arnolfini and his Wife, 1434. London, National Gallery. A high point of psychological portraiture. Observation of detail and control of the medium are both masterly.

510 The Limbourg brothers, calendar page of October, from the Book of Hours of the Duke de Berry, c. 1416. Chantilly, Musée Condé. The depiction of landscape and observation of nature show Netherlandish and Burgundian realism.

It is plain that Jan's contemporaries were still unable to comprehend in all their implications the solemn inevitability of his work and his vivid realism that never peters out in scenes comprising many little incidents. The art of Rogier van der Weyden (*c.* 1400–64), whose style held sway over large areas of late Gothic painting, seems more Gothic by comparison and, for all its richness of composition, more set, as in the *Deposition* of *c.* 1435 *[512]*. Rogier stylized his figures with masterly skill, both in expression and in the play of line, thereby giving far more opportunities to borrow details as formulae.

Netherlandish painting continued to develop in the direction indicated by Rogier, with individual masters standing out from the high general level of quality on account of particularly memorable achievements or for going further into points of detail. Besides Dirk Bouts and Hans Memling, let us mention here in particular Hugo van der Goes (*c.* 1440–82), whose *Portinari Altarpiece* of 1473–5 *[513]* was considered a masterpiece by his contemporaries, including even the very progressive and critical Italians. His extreme realism, as in the figures of the shepherds, is suffused with deep feeling.

A painter like Hieronymus Bosch (*c.* 1450–1510) already belongs through many of his works to the sixteenth century, even though his surreal universe of spectres is still animated by the spirit of the Middle Ages. In Netherlandish painting as in all art north of the Alps, the end of the Gothic tradition cannot be arbitrarily placed about 1500, at the point in time, that is, when the direct encounter with the Italian Renaissance began. The Gothic sense of form remained more or less visibly active until well into the sixteenth century.

511 Hubert and Jan van Eyck, Adoration of the Lamb, central section of the Ghent Altarpiece, 1426–32. Ghent, S. Bavon. A masterpiece of early Netherlandish realism.

513 Hugo van der Goes, Adoration of the Shepherds, from the Portinari Altarpiece, 1473–5. Florence, Uffizi. Expressive realism, psychological differentiation, warm colours, continuous spatial depths.

512 Rogier van der Weyden, Deposition, c. 1435. Escorial. Strong Gothic stylization despite the life-likeness.

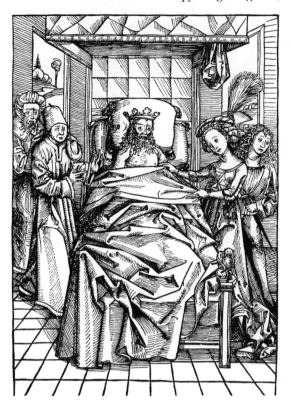

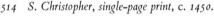

514   *S. Christopher, single-page print, c. 1450.*

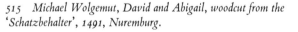

515   *Michael Wolgemut, David and Abigail, woodcut from the 'Schatzbehalter', 1491, Nuremburg.*

The need for individual, personal devotional pictures led to new artistic media: the woodcut and copper engraving. The introduction of paper manufacture in the second half of the fourteenth century created the technical prerequisites. Single-page prints [514], i.e. prints which resembled woodcuts, first appeared in Germany. These woodcuts were next carved in outline only (previously drawn by hand) and then hand-coloured as before. This technique was first extended into a series of woodcuts by Wolgemut [515] and his pupil Dürer. Carved lines remained on the blocks. In copper engraving, on the other hand, lines were carved into the plate by the graver, a technique first developed by goldsmiths around 1440. The so-called 'Master of the Playing Cards' from south-west Germany was probably the first artist to use this medium. Master ES and Martin Schongauer [516] developed it, and Albrecht Dürer [610] brought copper engraving to technical and artistic perfection.

516   *Martin Schongauer, The Temptation of S. Anthony, copper engraving, c. 1475.*

All subsequent accounts of the Renaissance as the first in the modern cycle of cultural epochs are heavily indebted to the concept evolved by Giorgio Vasari (1511–74) and embodied in his *Lives of the Most Eminent Painters, Sculptors, and Architects*, first published in Florence in 1550. This monumental work, cast in the form of a series of biographies of Italian artists, has earned for its author the title of 'father of art history', completely overshadowing his achievements as a painter and architect. But the central role attributed by Vasari to the *rinascita* or rebirth of classical antiquity is only one aspect of what is now understood by the Renaissance. For the present comprehensive definition of the epoch as a cultural and artistic unit was reached only in the nineteenth century when the form 'Renaissance', the French cognate of *rinascita*, was employed to denote the period between the Middle Ages and the Baroque, and its essential features were analysed in depth by such historians as Jakob Burckhardt.

Vasari's concept of the rebirth of 'good, ancient art' is rooted in the strong historical consciousness which had developed in the period and which had important consequences for the artist. The Renaissance represents a deliberate break with the artistic tradition of the Middle Ages, which was stigmatized as the creation of the barbarian Goths. Only a few artists from the 'Dark Ages', such as Giotto and Cimabue, could be accepted as precursors. At the same time the Italian artists carefully distinguished their work from the contemporary art of northern Europe.

In the broad context of the overall European stylistic development the Renaissance may be said to have fragmented an existing stylistic unity. The International Style, which unified the art of the European West in a splendid flowering in the years before and after 1400, was in fact only the last wave in a long succession of phenomena of pan-European scope. But the Italian artists, whose attempt to revive the art of Roman antiquity began to bear fruit about 1420, created an emphatically national style, whose first phase, the early Renaissance, was succeeded about 1500 by the high Renaissance. The Italian practice of calling centuries after their first year

expressed in hundreds (e.g. 1400=400) has led to the use of the term *Quattrocento* in the study of Italian art. The Quattrocento denotes not only the fifteenth century but also the style of the period, so that it is to all intents and purposes synonymous with 'early Renaissance'. The *Cinquecento*, however, which chronologically refers to the entire sixteenth century, is usually limited in art history to the 'high Renaissance', corresponding roughly to the first quarter of the century. This culminating stage, in which the stylistic tendencies of the age received their classic formulation, veered in the 1520s towards the anti-classic reaction of Mannerism, which brought into question the Renaissance ideal of beauty. In the years since the First World War art historians have attempted to elucidate the specific qualities and values of this hitherto neglected stylistic phase which spanned the years from the 1520s to the end of the century. The characteristics which have emerged as a result of this scholarly stock-taking have led to a decreasing use of the neutral phrase 'late Renaissance' for the period lying between the high Renaissance and the early Baroque in favour of the descriptive term Mannerism.

While the early and high Renaissance was taking shape in Italy, the other countries of Europe remained faithful to the Gothic style, which they elaborated in late forms in part characterized by national variations. With a very few exceptions, it was only at the beginning of the sixteenth century that the Renaissance began to penetrate across the Alps. The new style was disseminated by Italian emigrant artists and northern visitors returning from Italy. Only in the Mannerist phase did the rest of Europe join in concert with the Italians.

In Italy the direct contact with ancient art which was regarded as a national heritage laid the foundations for a unified and generally valid stylistic development. For this reason Italian artists had a considerable advantage over their northern colleagues, however studiously the latter might work to redress the balance. For the northerners antiquity remained a matter of academic instruction to be learned as a foreign language. Outside Italy – and even in such countries as Spain where there was a plentiful supply of antique monuments but no real awareness of them as a living part of the national heritage – the art of the sixteenth century was always dependent on the stimulus of the homeland of the new style. Only in

517 *Michelangelo, Moses, from the Tomb of Pope Julius II, 1515–16. Rome, S. Pietro in Vincoli. An over life-size marble statue. A heroically inspired representation of Renaissance man.*

France, where special conditions obtained, could a national style begin to develop on the basis of Italian models, thus laying the foundations for a further national development in the Baroque period.

Mannerism can be described as an international style only if certain essential limitations are taken into account. Unlike Gothic art, it did not achieve such universal diffusion as to make its formal language obligatory for even the humblest craftsman or mason. Especially outside Italy it was a highly sophisticated art appreciated only by a select, chiefly noble class of patrons, such as the Hapsburgs in Vienna, the Wittelsbachs in Munich, and the court circle of Emperor Rudolf II in Prague. Travelling artists, either Italians summoned from Italy or northerners who had studied there, were the purveyors of this art. They implanted it in various centres, where, however, it quickly languished and died when its creators left. Thus the steady, unified stylistic progress of Italy contrasts with a complicated pattern of stylistic borrowings in the North, a pattern which acted to dissolve older local styles without laying the foundations for a new autonomous development.

The leading characteristics of the Renaissance may now be briefly summarized. The return to models taken from the store of classical antiquity involved the resurrection of ancient architectural forms, such as the Five Orders, the use of formal motifs of ancient sculpture and painting, the reintroduction of themes and ideas from the realms of mythology and Graeco-Roman history, and lastly the revival of ancient symbolic forms (e.g. the use of the triumphal arch and the temple pediment as distinguishing features for church façades, tombs, and altar canopies). The aim was not mechanical imitation, but the acquisition of the fundamental laws that were felt to underlie antique art. Inspired by his model, the Renaissance artist sought to equal, if not surpass the ancient masters. The Renaissance was also characterized by the appearance of a new attitude towards nature, which was closely linked to the empirical orientation of contemporary science. The aid of mathematics was tirelessly invoked to provide a rational foundation for the artistic ideal of beauty. The striving for fidelity to nature, which was felt to be in harmony with the return to the antique, was not directed towards the accidental and individual but rather sought to grasp the type, the underlying idea. The basically anthropocentric attitude of the Renaissance made man 'the measure of all things'. An art of educated people required scientifically trained artists free of the anonymity of their medieval predecessors and able to move easily in the upper social strata. Renaissance artists were imbued with a faith

in the general validity of the norms of perfected beauty, together with a serenely optimistic belief in the ideal nature of the world, which reached its culmination in the phase of the high Renaissance.

Politically, fifteenth-century Italy was divided into a number of separate states, of which the most important were Venice, Milan, and Florence, the States of the Church, and the Kingdom of Naples. The Holy Roman emperors and the French kings were rivals for the hegemony of Italy and they transmitted their claims into reality through extensive military campaigns; the issue was resolved with the conquest of Rome and Florence by the troops of the Hapsburg Emperor Charles V. Although external pressures hindered the growth of political unity, they promoted the cultural self-awareness of the Italians. The cities were the centres of artistic renewal. Long after the return of the papacy from its Babylonian captivity in Avignon (1378) Rome remained relatively insignificant. In Florence, however, a prosperous middle class stood ready to support the emerging intellectual leaders of the Renaissance. Florence became the cradle of the new style. Here under the patronage of the Medici its first creations appeared and from here the style spread thoughout Italy. Around the various dynasts and the leading citizens of the republican states gathered artists and scholars as well as educated members of the families concerned. When the sovereign position of the pope was consolidated once more Rome took the leading role in cultural matters under Julius II (1503–11) and Leo X (1513–21). In its concentration of worldly power and pomp the papacy created the essential conditions for the classical phase. The papacy was the direct source of the most important commissions, which went to Bramante, Michelangelo, Raphael, and others. When however, the troops of Charles V sacked the city in 1527, the flowering of this ideal world abruptly ended. The free city-states gave way to powerful duchies and kingdoms, all dependent in one way or another on the Spanish court. The Empire, which under Charles V had seen the unification of Spain's far-flung possessions with the Hapsburg ancestral lands in Germany and the Low Countries and Burgundy, was torn by religious and social strife. The Reformation and the Wars of Religion shattered the European West. Under the influence of the Counter-Reformation, which saw the condemnation of the paganizing trend in church art by the Council of Trent (1545–63), the spiritual climate in the countries that had remained Catholic turned towards denial of the world, asceticism, and religious fervour. These characteristics were widely diffused in Mannerist art, above all in the work of the painter El Greco.

Architecture

While Gothic architecture developed independently in the cultural context of its own time, Renaissance architecture was conditioned throughout by an awareness of antiquity. The perfection of the antique was contrasted with 'barbarian' Gothic art and its example held up as an aid to end the 'darkness' of the Middle Ages. While the Gothic architect strove to dematerialize, as it were, the solidity of building structure and to soften spatial boundaries his Renaissance counterpart took inspiration from the clearly comprehensible geometric and stereometric forms that he saw in the buildings of ancient Rome. Because of their perfect regularity, the circle and square, cube, cone, and cylinder best satisfied the growing sense for the rational. The ambiguity of Gothic interpenetrations and interlacings and the consequent linear dynamism vanished before the simplicity and logical clarity of antique forms. The wall, which the northern architects had divided up to its greatest extent, recovered its full surface extension. A harmoniously ordered membering was achieved in articulating cornices, pilasters, and columns. Throughout the Quattrocento this membering remained essentially two-dimensional in character, one of the chief traits of early Renaissance architecture. With a few exceptions, a fully plastic treatment of the wall structure was achieved within the framework of the classical system of ordering of masses only in the high Renaissance.

As the architect trained his eye for mass and proportion on ancient models, he began to seek an objective understanding of the artistic process through a scientific and systematic codification of aesthetics. He no longer depended on formulas handed down as professional secrets from generation to generation in the medieval building lodges, but sought to give his practice a rational foundation within the framework of a comprehensive theoretical system. For him architecture stood in the closest possible relation to mathematics, both being rooted in demonstrable and objectively valid laws. Inasmuch as the determination of relations of mass was the central problem of architectural theory, the architect felt a strong kinship with the Neoplatonic philosophy of the period. For this mode of thought the cosmos is everywhere informed by the law of regularity which manifests the omnipotence of God. Thus the harmonious relations of mass demonstrated in the works of man are capable of reflecting the divine harmony of the universe. The most perfect forms in this sense are the circle and the square. The dome and the central-plan building were consequently regarded as symbols of the divine order of the world. The Renaissance concepts of beauty and perfection were imbued with mathematically oriented rationalism. This is clearly brought out in the definition of beauty laid down by the architect and artistic theorist Leone Battista Alberti: 'the harmony and concord of all the parts achieved in such a manner that nothing could be added or taken away or altered except for the worse'.

With regard to the Renaissance architects' approach to the antique, two points of contact may be discerned. First, there was the direct study of the surviving ancient monuments at first hand, a study that became increasingly systematic; second, the absorption of the theoretical content of ancient writings on architecture. In the first phase of the assimilation of the ancient formal repertory attention was directed towards such individual forms as capitals, cornices, and window and door mouldings. This empirical

518 Ground-plan of a church with a human figure. Turin, Biblioteca Reale, Codex Saluzzo. The Renaissance theory on proportions tried to unite the organic proportional canon of the human body with the geometrical laws of mathematics.

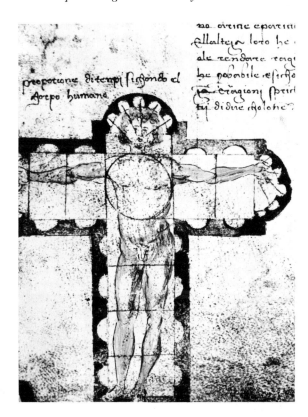

borrowing characterizes the work of the pioneer of
early Renaissance architecture Filippo Brunelleschi
(1377–1446). In the next generation, represented by
Leone Battista Alberti (1404–72), and in the third
generation, represented by Giuliano da Sangallo
(1445–1516), the study of the antique was pursued
on a broader base with more scientific methods. It is
known that in the 1430s Alberti was the first to
assemble a systematic collection of measurements of
the ancient buildings of the city of Rome. In his
rebuilding of a church in Rimini, begun in 1446,
Alberti took over details from the Augustan triumphal
arch which still stood in the town. Shortly after the
middle of the century the wall articulation of the
ancient Roman Colosseum was revived for the first
time in the loggias of the *cortile* of the Palazzo Venezia
in Rome. Great architectural complexes, such as the
thermae of Rome and the Sanctuary of Fortuna at

*519   Sebastiano Serlio, the Orders of the Columns, woodcut
from 'Sette libri d'Architettura', Venice, 1556. Illustration of the
five orders: Tuscan, Doric, Ionic, Corinthian, Composite. The
architectural tracts of the Renaissance made a decisive contribution
towards the spread of the new style. English, German, and
Netherlandish architecture in particular was planned from such
sources.*

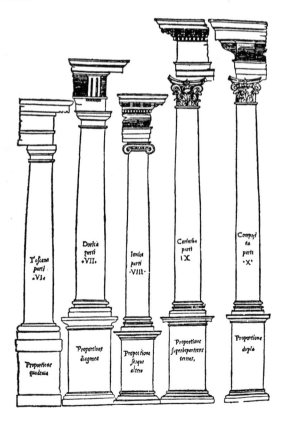

Palestrina, became the object of careful study; i
1493 the remains of Nero's Golden House wer
brought to light. This second stage of the assimilatio
of the antique was marked by a more profoun
understanding of ancient formal expression and th
integration of individual forms into larger units, suc
as triumphal arch designs. The architects' under
standing advanced from a grasp of individua
elements of vocabulary to a penetration of the funda
mental laws that informed the architecture o
antiquity.

Researches into architectural theory took as thei
starting-point the ancient authors, especially th
treatise of Vitruvius. Under the title of *De architectur
libri decem* (*Ten Books on Architecture*), this work
which was written in the time of Augustus an
rediscovered about 1415, provided a manual o
ancient architecture that discussed, in addition t
general questions of aesthetics, building types
structural methods, and machines. Since Vitruviu
text was often unclear and hard to use in actua
practice, the architects made commentaries based o
their own experience, illustrated various points o
the original, and naturally enough produced thei
own treatises (L. B. Alberti, Filarete, Francesco d
Giorgio Martini; followed in the sixteenth century b
the writings of Serlio [519], Palladio, Vignola
Scamozzi, and others).

Amongst the most important themes discussed b
the treatises is the proportioning of buildings and thei
parts. The proportional relationships of Gothi
cathedrals are independent of any measurable relatio
to man. In this sense the buildings may be said t
exist in a realm beyond human experience. By con
trast the Renaissance architect related his buildings t
the human form. This concept found support i
Vitruvius who held that the parts of the buildin
should be related to one another as the proportions o
the human body are interrelated. A proportiona
canon derived from nature and from the observatio
of the anatomical relations was inscribed, so to speak
in architecture; this procedure was not infrequentl
carried out literally, as may be seen in many drawing
of columns, capitals, and ground-plans, where an idea
human figure is introduced [518]. Architectura
theorists strove to synthesize the proportional canoi
of the human body and the regularity of basic geo
metrical forms and to create generally valid propor
tional rules. One of the best-known rules and on
which has since become a classical mode of surfac
division is the Golden Section, whereby a given lengtl
is so divided that the smaller portion is related to th
larger as the larger is to the whole length. Brunel
leschi, who rediscovered this ancient proportiona

law, employed it for the first time in his Pazzi Chapel in Florence, begun in 1430. The systematic attention to the proportioning of the whole building ensemble – plan and elevation, columns, capitals, and cornices – make the buildings of the Renaissance rationally comprehensible unities, whose inner structure can be immediately grasped by the viewer.

The early Renaissance

In 1421 Filippo Brunelleschi was commissioned to build the Medici family church, *S. Lorenzo at Florence* *[521]*. He sought to organize the plan according to a system of rational relations. Even such subordinate areas as the sacristies, which do not form part of the interior space of the church, were incorporated into this geometrical scheme. In a later building, the church of *S. Spirito*, begun in 1436, Brunelleschi achieved an even greater simplification. His plan *[520]* takes its point of departure from the square of the crossing beneath the dome, which is joined by three equal squares on the west, north, and east, while towards the south stretch the four half-squares of the nave. The individual units of the aisles, which are formed of squares whose sides are half the length of the larger ones, proceed in a continuous series around the arms of the transept and choir. These aisle squares terminate in semicircular chapel niches whose side is half as long as the aisle units. This 'square schematism' as we know it from the bay system of medieval buildings *[cf. 265]*, is here transformed in accordance with Neoplatonic thought: the total configuration of the plan is logically developed from the 'absolute' forms of the square and the circle.

520 Filippo Brunelleschi, ground-plan of S. Spirito at Florence, begun 1436. Geometric systematization developed from the square crossing.

521 Filippo Brunelleschi, S. Lorenzo at Florence, begun 1421. View in the nave facing the choir. Several details look back to the buildings of eleventh–twelfth-century Florentine 'proto-Renaissance'. The spatial effect is the same as at S. Spirito: a pillared basilica with a box-shaped nave, aisles with pilaster projections, and domed bays.

522 Leon Battista Alberti, view of the nave of S. Andrea at Mantua, begun 1472. Closed side chapels are placed on both sides of the foreground; behind is an open, well-lighted chapel. The mouthpiece of the barrel-vault is visible at the crossing.

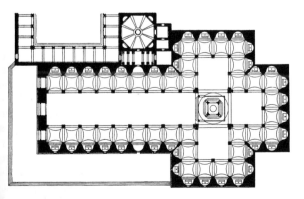

The organization of space is also dominated by the regularity of simple proportional relations. The nave, for example, is twice as high as it is wide. The transept arms are completely symmetrical: the dominance of the main choir over its neighbours, which Brunelleschi retained in S. Lorenzo, is abandoned and the altar is brought forward to the crossing, whose central position is emphasized by a dome. Standing beneath this dome, the viewer has the same image in each of the four directions: a high, chest-like form with a flat roof, round-arched arcades on slender columns, low side aisles, and a surrounding series of chapels. The unity of this scheme must have struck Brunelleschi's contemporaries as the ideal solution for a basilica.

In the second half of the fifteenth century no building reflects more accurately the progressive tendencies of the age than *S. Andrea at Mantua*, begun in 1472 *[522]*. Leone Battista Alberti (1404–72), the Venetian-born architect and artistic theorist of universal scope, designed this building two years before his death for Lodovico Gonzaga, Duke of Mantua. It cannot be established with certainty whether the dome and transept arms as executed correspond to Alberti's conception. On entering the church one discovers a wide, hall-like nave covered by a vast barrel-vault. The nave is flanked on either side by six chapels *[523]*, of which only three are significant for the interior space; the other three are closed by a wall and accessible only through small doors. The spacious wall areas in which these doors are set are framed at the sides by high pilasters. Above runs an entablature upon which the barrel-vault rests. The architectural theorist Alberti regarded this type of vaulting as the only worthy covering which could be employed beside the dome in a religious building, and for this reason he gave barrel-vaults to the open side chapels also. The alternation of the closed-square chapels and the open longitudinal ones gives rise to a rhythmical

524   Filippo Brunelleschi, view of the interior of the Pazzi chapel in S. Croce at Florence, begun 1430. An early Renaissance building with ribbed dome and antiquitizing structure of the pilasters. Note the strictly proportional relationships.

organization of the wall surfaces. This rhythmic quality affects the light sources as well; the side lights fall exclusively through the large side chapels, the smaller intervals between them remaining dark. Behind the total configuration of this church, which is without precedent apart from Alberti's own theoretical considerations, stands the continuous contact with the Roman architecture of antiquity and the intensive study of the ancient texts. It goes without saying that the proportions of the plan and elevation have been worked out to the last detail. The greatest advance from the buildings of the Brunelleschi phase lies in the recovery of the ancient feeling for space, in which the boundary is once more understood as an articulated mass. The architectural scheme of a broad nave accompanied by side chapels (rather than the traditional side aisles of the basilica) was to exercise a decisive influence beyond the limits of the Renaissance proper in Mannerist and Baroque architecture. A hundred years later when Vignola planned the mother-church of the Jesuit Order, Il Gesù in Rome

523   L. B. Alberti, ground-plan of S. Andrea of Mantua, begun 1472. The main body is a simple-naved, barrel-vaulted room with alternating open and closed side chapels.

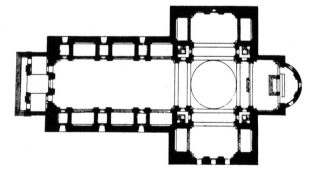

[543], he adopted the scheme of the wide nave accompanied by side chapels and thereby opened the way to such an enormous expansion of the type beyond the borders of Italy that it was able to overcome the dominance of the traditional basilican scheme.

The ideal form of Renaissance architecture upon which the Italian architectural theorists dwelt with especial predilection was the central-plan church. The fact that it could only with difficulty be accommodated to the needs of the divine service led frequently in the case of the larger congregational churches to a compromise in which the central-plan scheme was combined with the traditional longitudinal type. Even in the pure central-plan buildings the essential idea was seldom perfectly realized; the desire to emphasize the entrance interfered with

526 Donato Bramante, Tempietto in the inner courtyard of the monastery of S. Pietro in Montorio, Rome, 1502. A centralized building of the high Renaissance; the ideal realization of an architectural theory. The central point was originally conceived as a round court [535], while the walls of the present rectangular space were narrower.

525 Giuliano da Sangallo, S. Maria delle Carceri at Prato, 1485–91. A centralized building of the early Renaissance, related to Brunelleschi's Pazzi chapel [524]. For the first time in the Renaissance the Greek cross was used as the point of departure for the design. The forceful proportions already herald the high Renaissance. The exterior construction is still in the style of the early Renaissance, with coloured incrustations in the Tuscan tradition.

absolute symmetry as did the liturgical need to move the main altar from the centre to one of the walls or to a cross-arm which took the place of the choir. Owing to such limitations many designs were arrested in the planning stage and are preserved only in such sketches as those of Leonardo da Vinci *[528]*, or else were worked up as didactic material for architectural treatises. That Renaissance artists were concerned with the problem transpires from the architectural backgrounds of religious paintings and reliefs. From Ghiberti, through Mantegna and Ghirlandaio, and up to Raphael, the central-plan building constantly recurs as a symbol of absolute perfection and purity.

Various models for this architectural scheme were available to Renaissance builders; these include the rotunda of the Pantheon in Rome *[cf. 124]*, the niched halls of the imperial thermae, late antique tombs and early Christian baptismal chapels, Romanesque baptistries, and the domed cross-plan church

527   Cola da Caprarola and others, S. Maria della Consolazione at Todi, begun 1508. Influential embodiment of the high Renaissance centralized building. A large-scale development of the plan at Prato [525]. Rounded apses rather than barrel-vaulted arms connect the dome to the main body. The plastic monumentality of the construction is heightened by the free position in open landscape. On the exterior, delicate, two-storied Corinthian capitals with a mezzanine story.

528   Leonardo da Vinci, sketch with ground-plan and view of a centralized structure. Paris, Institut de France, MS. 2037. In his sketches Leonardo developed rich central-building systems from main and side chapels, apses, ambulatories, and side spaces, with a lucid overall arrangement of the central space.

of Byzantine derivation, such as St Mark's in Venice [cf. 311]. As in the case of basilicas, the first Renaissance examples are found in Florence, and once more Filippo Brunelleschi was their creator. His Old Sacristy of S. Lorenzo (1421–9) and the *Pazzi chapel* [524] adjacent to S. Croce (begun in 1430) are small, sensitively designed structures, whose central space is covered with a ribbed dome and whose walls bear membering of antique derivation. To be sure Brunelleschi had not yet arrived at a conception of space as a uniformly distributed total organism; his walls constitute a well-proportioned pattern of individual parts which are only unified by the dome above.

In the next stage of development the design of central-plan buildings depended directly upon antique prototypes. It is known, for example, that Michelozzo erected the mid-fifteenth-century rotunda which now serves as the choir of SS. Annunziata in Florence in conscious imitation of the decagonal Temple of Minerva Medica in Rome.

In the church of *S. Maria delle Carceri at Prato* [525], built in 1485–91, Giuliano da Sangallo (1445–1516) created an outstanding example of an early Renaissance central-plan building. Its plan is that of a Greek cross with equal arms. The dome-vaulted central square is surrounded on all four sides with flat-walled rectangular areas covered by barrel-vaults. As in the case of Brunelleschi's central-plan buildings the lower zone of the ribbed dome is pierced by a series of round windows which give an even flow of light in accordance with Renaissance ideals.

The central-plan scheme is achieved with a grandeur and simplicity characteristic of the high Renaissance in the church of *S. Maria della Consolazione at Todi* [527], which was begun in 1508. The central domed square is adjoined on all four sides by high and broad apses, so that over the clover-leaf plan an interior of absolute balance results, whose monumental spatial character is emphasized by an interior two-story Ionic pilaster order and an exterior Corinthian one. The efforts of Renaissance builders reached their ultimate culmination in the projects for St Peter's in Rome, which will be discussed below.

With the Renaissance, secular building acquires an importance equal to that of religious architecture and the great architects are also the creators of significant secular buildings. Besides public structures two types of buildings are of surpassing importance: the palace, which was built by noble families and wealthy citizens within the city, and the country villa, erected outside the city as a holiday residence during the heat of summer. While the palace expressed a grandeur in keeping with its owner's social position, the villa was intended to be a pleasant seat where the revived feelings of the ancients for rustic life could be enjoyed. In both types Florence was well ahead of the rest of Italy.

The Gothic town-house [cf. *439*] and the medieval castle of northern Europe [cf. *437*] develop organically from within outwards in accordance with living conditions, so that even from the exterior the main rooms are distinguishable from the more private ones. The Florentine Renaissance palace, however, is confined within the closed form of the block, with clearly demarcated stories, regularly distributed windows, and uniform room heights, without regard to the diverse uses of the rooms. Once more rational clarity characterizes the building ensemble. Within, the four sides enclose an inner *cortile* surrounded by loggias.

In the course of development a number of variations of the palace scheme appeared. Florentine city palaces continued the tradition of Tuscan town halls as represented by the Palazzo Pubblico in Siena [cf. *444*] and the Palazzo della Signoria in Florence. The Duke of Milan, however, required that his palace, the Castello Sforzesco, serve also as a fortress to dominate the unruly city. The highly cultivated Duke of Urbino built a spacious Court of the Muses which, despite its defensive exterior, effectively conveyed the free atmosphere of the worldly Quattrocento through its lively decoration, its airy loggias, and its 'hanging gardens' overlooking the Marches. The prosperous merchants of Venice, whose palaces surveyed the impressive canal water-fronts, were seized in the sixteenth century by a veritable passion for building which fundamentally altered the Venetian scene. In Rome, it was the popes and cardinals who competed with one another through their palaces and villas. Although local tradition and the wishes of the patrons were strong forces, the Florentine palaces still constituted the standard for the palace building of the Quattrocento.

In Florence the architect Michelozzo (1396–1472) began the *City Palace of the Medici* in 1444 [*530*]. He took as a starting-point the Palazzo della Signoria of a hundred years earlier; if the tower is taken away from this building a simple cube remains whose bare façade with the rough-hewn blocks of rusticated masonry repels the viewer. At this point the artistic shaping of the Palazzo Medici begins. A broad bench for the commercial clients of the Medici surrounds the whole building like a socle. The ground story, whose arches were originally open, is clad in rusticated masonry; the middle story above, which is somewhat lower, exhibits a smoother rustication, while the top story, which is lower again, is entirely

529, 530 Michelozzo di Bartolommeo, cortile surrounded by loggias, and exterior of the Palazzo Medici-Riccardi at Florence, 1444–60. Block-like form; the height of the stories is reduced. Rustic ashlar pieces cover the surface. The façade is held together by an antiquitizing cornice. After the monumental heaviness of the exterior, the cortile presents a sense of intimacy and serenity.

smooth, consisting of carefully placed ashlar blocks. The whole building mass is crowned by a strongly projecting cornice of antique type, replacing the traditional crenellation. The double-lighted arched windows of the two upper stories rest upon denticulated friezes. What appears from the exterior as the outward manifestation of the division between stories is really the line of the sills. The façade does not express the constructional reality of the building but a geometrical articulation whose proportions are determined in accordance with the harmonious divisions of surfaces and not by the structure of the building itself. All the three stories are brought into demonstrable relation through the graded diminution of height and surface roughness. As in the case of contemporary religious architecture, here also in secular building simple, rational relations are stressed. Like the basilicas of Brunelleschi, however, this palace façade is characterized by an additive mode of composition, in which the individual elements are not yet subordinated to larger principles of form as they were to be in the high Renaissance.

531 Leone Battista Alberti, Palazzo Rucellai in Florence, 1446–51. Further development of the façade formation: note the horizontal and vertical truss of pillars and ledges.

532 Raffaelo Santi (Raphael), Palazzo Vidoni-Caffarelli in Rome, c. 1515. The façade looks back to Bramante's work of the high Renaissance.

Another world opens as one passes from the entrance into the *cortile [529]*. The intimacy of the pleasant courtyard, which originally contained a fountain by Donatello, surprises after the imposing austerity of the exterior; the architect employs contrast as a means of artistic expression. The *cortile* is surrounded by airy loggias; in the middle story the connecting passages have been closed.

In palace building also Leone Battista Alberti carried the development forward. He was responsible for the design of the city palace of the Florentine merchant Giovanni Rucellai, which was built in 1446–51. The novelty of Alberti's façade of the *Palazzo Rucellai [531]* consists in his use of a more sophisticated type of rustication with smooth, regular blocks separated by grooving and especially in his revival of the three-story scheme of the Roman Colosseum, in which the capitals of the pilasters are successively Doric, Ionic, and Corinthian. This rectangular net of pilasters and cornices produces a uniform system of horizontal and vertical axial relationships.

For the second main secular architectural type, the country villa, the *Medici Villa at Poggio a Caiano*, begun in 1485, ranks as the most important example of the fifteenth century *[534]*. Its builder Giuliano da Sangallo (1445–1516) departed completely from the type of fortified country-seat hitherto dominant, in an effort to create for his patron Lorenzo il Magnifico a more suitable setting for the cultivation of the revived ancient feeling for rustic life than the older castles could provide. He linked the building to the landscape by placing the simple cube on a base consisting of an open loggia. The smooth façade is enlivened only by rhythmically placed windows, while the corners are only slightly emphasized with rusticated quoins. This simplicity sets off the temple pediment rising over the entrance hall, a feature used here for the first time in Renaissance secular architecture. This villa was greatly admired by contemporaries for its barrel-vaulted central room rising through two stories. Of especial importance for the further development of the country villa was the clear and rational organization of plan and elevation.

534 *Giuliano da Sangallo, Villa Medici (later Villa Reale) at Poggio a Caiano, begun 1485. A clear building cube over a loggia terrace, with steps in a semicircle added later.*

533 *Bartolommeo Ammanati, inner courtyard of the Palazzo Pitti in Florence, 1558–70. A typical Mannerist façade. The pillars are rusticated.*

The high Renaissance

The turn of the sixteenth century signifies a shift in stylistic orientation; for a brief period the high Renaissance raised the achievements of the early stage to classical perfection. The last decades of the fifteenth century saw an increased penetration of antique motifs and the diffusion of the new style throughout Italy. These developments favoured a diversification of the formal apparatus, leading to the danger of dissipation and misunderstanding in which the ancient forms could be employed as mere decoration. The high Renaissance, however, achieved a concentration both in the geographical and psychological sense. With a few exceptions it can be said that the master-works of the high Renaissance were created in Rome under Popes Julius II (1503–13) and Leo X (1513–21) in the first two decades of the sixteenth century. Concentration took place also in the artistic sphere. Everything petty and frivolous was rigorously excluded; the predilection for refined architectural decoration was held in check. Nothing external was to distract the attention from the primary concern of the work of art. A heightened awareness of the ideal replaced the enjoyment of the here-and-now of the earlier phase. The sense for harmony and logic went hand in hand with an aspiration towards monumental solemnity. For this reason architects concentrated on massive forms and

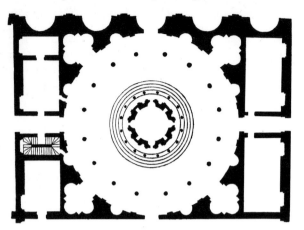

535   *Donato Bramante, ground-plan of the Tempietto with a circular court as originally planned for S. Pietro in Montorio at Rome, 1502 (after Serlio). After this project the 'Tempietto' was built in the circular form of the court as an 'island construct'.*

plastic differentiation. The process of design depended upon a spiritual discipline informing the external details and their relation to the whole. The building became a fully articulated organism; every element had a firm place within a hierarchical scheme. But within the bounds of the strictest order there flourished an enormous inner freedom. The principle of consistent design reached far enough to draw the representational arts within the framework of the architectural order.

The *Tempietto [526]* built by Donato Bramante (1444–1514) in a court adjacent to S. Pietro in Montorio at Rome offers the clearest realization of Renaissance architectural ideals. It was erected in 1502 on the site of St Peter's martyrdom. For the Renaissance the circle must have seemed the inevitable basis for such a monument and thus the Christian memorial took the form of an ancient round temple. Above a circular stepped base rose in slender austerity sixteen Tuscan columns bearing a triglyph frieze surmounted by a balustrade. The curving wall of the cella received a series of niches which are so arranged that two niches on the exterior cella wall correspond to one on the exterior *[cf. plan, 535]*. Over the balustrade rises the cylindrical drum capped by a spherical dome. The drum is articulated with alternating rectangular and curvilinear niches. The harmonious closed form of the Tempietto exists in a state of complete repose; its only decoration is the necessary architectural membering.

When Pope Julius II laid the cornerstone for one of the crossing piers of Bramante's St Peter's in Rome, patron and builder envisioned the ultimate realization

of the ideal category of the central building. But doubts soon appeared about the plan to make the most notable church in Christendom a purely central plan building. Since construction stretched over a hundred years the chief architects of the sixteenth century were able to contribute in succession to the debate. In the end the defenders of the time-honoured basilican scheme were victorious. After 1607 Carlo Maderno joined a nave and monumental façade to the central-plan building.

The basic form underlying Bramante's plan *[536]* is the Greek cross with equal arms terminating in semicircular niches. Over the crossing of the arms a spherical dome was envisaged. In the four angles between the cross-arms the motif of the domed space was to be echoed in smaller scale; finally at the corners octagonal sacristies were planned, providing massive blocks at the external extremities of the building. The whole is developed more as an abstract geometrical scheme than with a view towards unity of spatial effect. In its exterior aspect the building would have suggested a domed mountain in which the smaller volumes support and prepare for the larger ones. The interior would have been felt by the powerful Greek cross and the comparatively dark dome. The central areas of the smaller nuclei would have been experienced as autonomous spatial units subordinate to the larger one. The harmony of the whole would have depended more upon the uniform handling of independent spatial units than upon their integration into a continuous spatial whole.

536   *Donato Bramante, ground-plan of St Peter's in Rome, 1506 (after Geymüller). The form of the Greek cross with rounded arms is repeated in the four subsidiary chapels; in the diagonals are light corner spaces.*

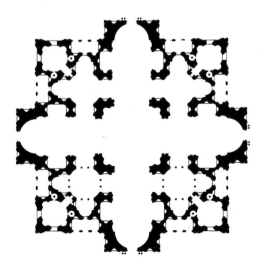

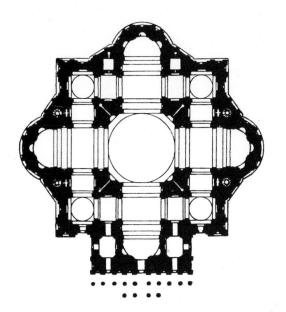

537   Michelangelo, ground-plan of St Peter's in Rome, after 1547. The spatial effect is of tautness and unity. Within the central square there is a stronger emphasis on the dome pillars.

After Bramante a number of architects, including Raphael, had a share in the varied fortunes of St Peter's. In 1547 the supervision of the building was entrusted to Michelangelo Buonarroti (1475–1564). He returned to the original idea of the central-plan scheme [537], though he did not live to achieve his new version. In conformity with the altered stylistic aspirations of the period Michelangelo intended to place before the building an imposing columnar vestibule, which would have given an emphasis to the long axis. The most salient quality of his design is the thorough simplification and tightening of the plan. The accessory domed areas have a clearer place within the overall spatial effect. Thus Michelangelo strengthened a building concept which he found in Bramante's Greek-cross scheme. This was the placement of a massive dome on four supports within a square. The impressive dome would have dominated the whole the more strongly once the accessory areas had lost their autonomy.

The complexity of the architect's challenge in central-plan sacred buildings diminished in the realm of secular architecture where the stylistic tendencies of the age could be realized more easily. We can only form an approximate idea of the important buildings of this period inasmuch as most of them have yielded to later buildings, undergone reconstruction, or remained unfinished. Bramante's own palazzo, which he erected shortly before his death in the neighbourhood of St Peter's, has been destroyed. It is known, however, that his nephew, Raphael Santi (1483–

1520), who was active as an architect as well as a painter, derived the façade of his *Palazzo Vidoni-Caffarelli [532]* from Bramante's palace. The Palazzo Vidoni-Caffarelli was subsequently made higher and wider. In all likelihood both palaces had only two stories, a socle-like ground story with heavy rustication surmounted by an upper story which translated the flat pilaster articulation of Alberti's Palazzo Rucellai *[531]* into high Renaissance terms. Paired half-columns with strongly projecting bases alternating with balustrades are realized in terms of plastic volumes, as are also the profiled window tops with their strong shadow.

The most important Roman palace of the high Renaissance is the *Palazzo Farnese [538]*, begun in 1514 by Antonio da Sangallo (1485–1546). The general scheme recalls the Florentine palace type. The façade, however, has a genuine brick wall according to Roman tradition in place of the heavy Florentine rustication; only at the corners does rustication appear in the low quoins. Strongly profiled cornices emphatically separate the stories, and upon them rest the window aediculae with their alternatingly triangular and segmental gables. The total effect is one of repose and subtle enlivenment, of powerful monumentality and aristocratic reserve. In the middle bay, which is emphasized by the rusticated portal and richer plastic quality of the middle window (both added by Michelangelo after Sangallo's death), alien elements intrude; the tight constraint of the portal area between the windows and the emphatic accent of the balcony window reveal a new way of thinking: Mannerism.

538   Antonio da Sangallo the Younger, Palazzo Farnese in Rome, begun 1514. Michelangelo designed the upper storey, after 1546.

Mannerism

The contrast of two styles in the Palazzo Farnese is indicative of the general development, for the classical style of the high Renaissance dominated the scene for only a short period. Then, in the wake of Michelangelo, new talents came to the fore, who affirmed the individual freedom of the artist instead of the Renaissance ideal of absolute objectivity. The byword of 'Michelangelo's manner' (*la maniera di Michelangelo*) served to legitimize the need to break free from the bonds of classical canons and move in the direction of a subjective, decoratively playful, and even at times absurd art. The aim of the Mannerists was not balanced harmony, but clever conceits and astonishing effects – basically non-architectural tendencies. The main representatives of Mannerist architecture were painters and sculptors by training and temperament. In the interests of originality they did not hesitate to juxtapose the most contradictory elements, to change room heights abruptly, and consciously to distort the ancient orders. Sebastiano Serlio (1475–1554) justified the bizarre effects proposed in his architectural treatise with the declaration that he had 'broken and overturned beautiful form' in order to create novelty. The spatial tendencies of Mannerism are seen at their clearest in small compressed interior units which lead the spectator into depth, and in the oppressive interiors of narrow courtyards and planned urban areas.

540   *Michelangelo, vestibule of the Biblioteca Laurenziana 1530–4. The reversal of classicist rules is evident in the arrangement of the ante-room.*

539   *Giulio Romano, Palazzo del Tè in Mantua, 1525–35. Mannerist form: the triglyphs are apparently collapsing; the quoins are of disproportionate size, and the rustication is irregular.*

The first great building enterprise which shows the move from high Renaissance to Mannerism is a creation of Raphael's pupil Giulio Romano (1499–1546). In 1525–35 he built for Duke Federico Gonzaga the *Palazzo del Tè [539]*, a suburban villa just outside the gates of Mantua. As in classical times, the wall of the inner court is articulated by an ancient order. This order, however, no longer expresses the architectural function of load and support, but rather constitutes a mere decorative overlay. Conscious bluntness and even dissonances disrupt the classical harmony. Narrow rusticated bands alternate with taller ones. Whole blocks seem to be broken off from the wall bond; the abnormally large keystone over the portal intrudes into the triangular pediment; and individual triglyph stones over the windows and niches seem to be dropping out of the row. The whole building seems to be in danger of collapse. In general, this is an example of an arbitrary and intentionally distorted composition. The artist, who could expect from his sophisticated public a real understanding of 'regular' relationships, engages in a *jeux d'esprit* in which the mind is entertained by intentional solecisms. Mannerism retains the outward appurtenances of classicism, but transforms the classic repose and balance into conscious violations of the rules in the form of tense, recherché and, indeed, dissonant combinations – a stylistic principle especially evident in the inner court of the *Palazzo Pitti* (1558–70) in Florence *[533]* by Bartolommeo Ammanati (1511–92). As in the case of the Palazzo Rucellai the three stories exhibit the so-called 'Colosseum order', in which the sequence of Tuscan, Ionic, and Corinthian forms corresponds to the classical canon. The rustication is no longer restricted to the wall surface, but spreads over the columns in a band-like decorative appliqué. The broad intervening spaces between the blocks of the two upper stories suggest that the rustication is not an integral part of the wall; it outweighs the structural elements of the wall articulation.

The great pioneer and exemplar of Mannerism was Michelangelo (1475–1564), architect, sculptor, poet, and painter all in one. With his grandiose personal style he broke free from classical idealism,

542 *Michelangelo, dome of St Peter's, Rome, after 1557. Influenced by the extra height of the dome at Florence; the dynamic flow of movement is pre-Baroque.*

541 *Filippo Brunelleschi, dome of Florence Cathedral, 1420–36. A great technical achievement of the early Renaissance, with a strong springing to the dome.*

sweeping aside its rules. Characteristic of his work are the reading room (1524–7) and vestibule (1530–4) of the *Laurentian Library [540]*, which he built adjacent to S. Lorenzo in Florence for the Medici. The staircase, which was designed by Michelangelo and executed after his death, hardly seems to fit into the high, narrow vestibule. This steep shaft-like room is followed by the long narrow reading-room, which seems to draw the visitor into its depth. Thus abrupt contrast is used as a means of stylistic expression in conscious disregard of the classical canon. In the vestibule the columns do not stand in front of the wall as they normally do, but just the reverse; the wall surfaces presses forward so that the columns are pushed back into their niches. The columns are neither supporting nor supported, for the volute consoles beneath are just as unfunctional as the columns above. Every element of the wall articulation exists as a separate entity. The wall is conceived not as an organic whole, but as an assemblage of parts in which each member retains an independent value.

543, 544 *Giacomo da Vignola, Jesuit church of Il Gesù in Rome, begun 1568. View of the interior, and engraving showing the façade (completed by Giacomo della Porta) and spatial scheme (after J. van Sandrart).*

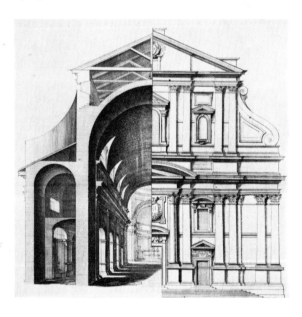

The total impression, however, is a kind of over-riding unity achieved here through a conflict and tension felt throughout.

Although the aesthetic concepts of Mannerism are fully evident in this building, Michelangelo also left a work which points beyond the Mannerist style to the Baroque, the dome of St Peter's in Rome. A hundred and fifty years before (1420–36), Brunelleschi had achieved an extraordinary technical feat in his *Dome of the Cathedral of Florence [541]*. The unusual size was determined by the plan of the existing Gothic building *[cf. 423]*. Although the dome produces a powerful effect in the interior, it assumes its true significance as the dominating central feature of the city only from the exterior. From its octagonal base it rises majestically from the surrounding half-domes, swelling into a steeply arched profile and concluding in the finial-like lantern. Profiled ribs emphasize the soaring quality. In comparison with the Florentine dome the half-sphere with which Bramante covered the Tempietto *[526]* constitutes the fulfilment of the Renaissance ideal of balanced harmony. When in 1557 Michelangelo began to crown St Peter's with a dome *[542]* he went back to that of Brunelleschi which was still basically Gothic. To be sure, Michelangelo planned not an octagon but a circle. A drum, powerfully articulated in paired columns, rises over a broad massive ring. From the attic above, the ribs rise to the lantern, which is surrounded by another ring of paired columns and decorated with volutes and candelabra. Manneristic qualities may be discerned in the double-column motif. More important, however, is the fact that the dome did not take the form of a half-sphere as Bramante intended but was strikingly elevated. Instead of the mathematically perfect but relatively relaxed form of the spherical covering appealing primarily to reason, the eye could now follow the dynamic rise of the dome. This pattern of moving energy is an important feature of the subsequent Baroque style.

Another harbinger of the Baroque in architecture is the Jesuit church of *Il Gesù in Rome [543]*, begun by Vignola (1507–73) in 1568. The Vicar-General of the Order required a wide-vaulted hall because of the more favourable acoustics for preaching; this hall disembogued in a centralized eastern section. So successful was Vignola's solution – evolved by returning to the scheme of Alberti's S. Andrea in Mantua *[523]* – that the scheme of Il Gesù was tirelessly repeated throughout Catholic Christendom. In the nave, which was accompanied by niche-like chapels instead of side aisles, paired pilasters support a broad entablature with a high attic surmounted by a barrel-vault. Interpenetrations in the vault permit the introduction of windows so that the lighting system recalls that of the basilica. If the later Baroque decoration is ignored, a rather sober, closed interior space results in accordance with the church ideal of the Counter-Reformation. This unified space receives relatively little light and the last bay lacks a window altogether, making an effective contrast with the fuller light at the crossing.

The development of the two-story façade *[544]* may also be traced back to the fifteenth century. In S. Maria Novella in Florence Alberti used volutes to mask the transition from the lower side wings to the high upper story. Although Giacomo della Porta (1540–1602), who continued the building after Vignola's death, remained on the whole faithful to the Renaissance coolness of his predecessor's design, he made a number of specific alterations. Whereas in Vignola's façade design the pilasters are arranged in regular sequence and the height of the stories is equalized, Della Porta groups the pilasters in pairs and emphasizes the lower story by giving it greater height. The central portal is strongly accented with respect to the other parts by the placement of a double gable in the cornice zone over it. Although this façade design is not yet dynamic in the Baroque sense, it contains elements which were to be important for the future.

If Florence excelled in the early Renaissance and Rome in the high Renaissance, Venice took the lead in the course of the sixteenth century. In Andrea Palladio she had an architect whose influence was to extend over a long period and far beyond the boundaries of Italy. The Renaissance reached Venice relatively late. While two Renaissance generations were at work in Florence, the Adriatic city remained true to the late Gothic style. Moreover the first buildings in the new mode show painterly display rather than structural logic or cubic monumentality. The tendency towards the painterly and the decorative may be regarded as a survival of the Byzantine heritage, always present to the Venetians in St Mark's; it may also be attributed more generally to the East where Venice had extensive trade relations. It is not surprising that in a city so dominated by particularist tendencies no building appeared which could be compared with Bramante's creations. But a local form of Mannerism did grow up; a leading example is the *Old Library of St Mark's*, 1536–53 *[545]*, across the Piazzetta from the Doge's Palace. Jacopo Sansovino (1486–1570), its builder, was a Florentine who had worked in Rome. He took his point of departure for the Library façade from the wall system of the Roman Colosseum whose arcades, preceded by columnar orders, are utilized in the two loggia-like stories. When one compares this façade with a Roman palace front of the high Renaissance *[532]*, a much richer orchestration is immediately apparent in the relief decoration at Venice. The triglyph frieze over the ground story, the rhythmically ordered balustrades of the upper story, and the entablature filled with fruit garlands and putti beneath the crowning attic bear witness to the profusion. Mannerist also and at

545 Jacopo Sansovino, *Old Library of St Mark's at Venice, 1536–53. Decorative Venetian Mannerism with an accumulation of ornamental forms.*

546 Andrea Palladio, *Villa Rotonda at Vicenza, 1550–2. The centralized structure design is here applied to a country house with a completely symmetrical ground-plan.*

Because of their absolute rationality and impressive monumentality the buildings of Andrea Palladio (1508–80) may be regarded as the culmination of the high Renaissance. Their abstract formal discipline has sometimes led to their being labelled creations of a Neoclassic mentality. Palladio, however, thanks to the eloquence and harmoniously balanced richness of his invention, stands far apart from the academically correct but bloodless design of the 'true' classicism of later periods. Nor can he be fitted into the Mannerist frame. His deep insight into the nature of ancient architecture inspired him to brilliant, thoroughly independent creations. Palladio worked partly in Venice proper, where he built churches, and partly in the Venetian terra firma, especially Vicenza, where he built palaces and villas. In the *Villa Rotonda* of 1550–52 *[546]* he realized his conception of an ancient villa in the form of a central-plan structure. A round room at the centre is the focus for a series of chambers fitted within the square building block; symmetry prevails in both the plan and the external aspect. Each of the four sides is preceded by a great flight of steps leading to a temple façade. In the correspondence of interior and exterior, and in the clear legibility of the revived antique elements, an ideal clarity of form is realized.

The church of *Il Redentore at Venice*, 1579–92 *[548]* is Palladio's contribution to the type of broad-nave church with accompanying side chapels. As in Il Gesù *[543]*, a centralized space is combined with a longitudinal area. But while Vignola strove to blend the choir and nave into a spatial unity, Palladio separated the two parts by a triumphal arch. This motif recurs before the main apse of the clover-leaf plan choir. The half-dome of the apse is supported by a semicircle of columns allowing a view into the monks' choir beyond. The nave is plastically articulated with colossal half-columns and the smooth surfaces of the undecorated vault rise over the powerful entablature. At the sides of the vault, antique thermae windows are introduced, filling the space with a bright, festive light which places the wall articulation in deep shadow. The serene authority of the spatial ensemble and the repose of its architectural elements with their finely graded proportional relations have nothing to do with the Baroque, despite their plastic weightiness. Here, as in few buildings of the later sixteenth century, the antique is present in all its purity.

As has been seen, Palladio chose ancient temple façades for his villas. For the fronts of his churches he created, in conformity with the tradition of Alberti (S. Andrea in Mantua and S. Francesco in Rimini), a complicated pattern of individual motifs of different

547   *Andrea Palladio, façade of S. Giorgio Maggiore at Venice, 1565–80. Two systems are superbly united here (two-story column with half-column; one-story order with pilasters).*

548   *Andrea Palladio, view of the interior of Il Redentore at Venice, 1576–92. View of the nave facing the choir. A variation on the type of the hall church with side chapels; plastic wall design through colossal half-columns; the centralizing eastern part is divided from the main body by triumphal arches.*

the same time typically Venetian is the crowded fullness of motifs, the accumulation of decorative accessories, the hollowing out of the wall and the definition of forms in the contrast of light and shade.

value. The façade of *S. Giorgio Maggiore* at Venice (1565–80) bears in its central portion before the nave a colossal order running over two stories, whose powerful columns stand on high bases *[547]*. The sides of the façade have a smaller order of flat pilasters, which runs straight across the colossal order. The architect has made the two systems interpenetrate. The aediculae with niches in the side zones of the smaller order are raised on pedestals to the height of the colossal column bases; conversely, the main portal in the area of the colossal order is framed by two pilasters of the smaller order. Although the contradictions of this system may be interpreted as symptomatic of Mannerism, the façade, because of its carefully controlled proportions, is characterized as a whole by harmonious clarity. Together with the cool elegance of Palladio's buildings this last quality seems to have been much appreciated. Palladianism – through the agency of the architect's treatise *Quattro libri dell'architettura*, published in 1570 and rapidly diffused throughout Europe – exercised a very strong influence on England after 1600, had an enduring effect on French architecture in the seventeenth century, and in the eighteenth century provided an important source for Neoclassicism.

In town planning the Renaissance mentality opposed arbitrary development of previous cities in favour of the ideal of systematic planning due to the same aspiration towards mathematical and rational order that informed the design of individual buildings. In the treatises, town planning and the discovery

549 Vincenzo Scamozzi, Palmanova (province of Venice), begun 1593. Radial streets stretch from the central six-cornered open place out to the nine-sided fortifications.

550 Michelangelo, the Capitol in Rome, after 1538. The layout shown in this print (after Lafréry) was changed by Giacomo della Porta's addition of a ramp after 1576.

of an ideal scheme for the whole city layout played no small role. Once more the theoreticians sought to ground their findings in the testimony of the ancient authors. Especially favoured was the star plan mentioned by Vitruvius. For modern times, however, the strategic advantages of this plan were most important; from the projecting points every part of the walls could be easily covered with artillery and musket fire. Vincenzo Scamozzi's (1552–1616) design of *Palmanova [549]* in Venetian territory was executed after 1593 in an absolutely symmetrical star shape; today it preserves the abstract scheme almost intact.

But Renaissance architects seldom had the opportunity to build a whole city according to their own conception. They usually had to come to terms with an existing cityscape and could only improve individual quarters or reshape smaller complexes. One of the outstanding urban achievements is Michelangelo's rebuilding of the *Capitol in Rome*, executed in stages beginning in 1538 *[550]*. The trapezoid piazza is enclosed on three sides by palaces planned on Michelangelo's designs and whose measurements, position, and façades were carefully calculated in relation to the whole complex. In the centre of the piazza on a gently rising oval mound stands the antique equestrian statue of Marcus Aurelius, from which radiates a star-shaped design executed in the paving. As the visitor mounted the steps he saw himself cut off from the central space and was encouraged to proceed around it – a truly Mannerist idea which only increases the effectiveness of this pioneering plan for a city square.

Painting

ITALY

Painting is the most varied of all the arts of the Renaissance. While panel- and wall-painting found a broad range of new opportunities in the secular realm, book illumination became less and less important until it virtually ceased to exist as an independent category in the sixteenth century. The graphic arts took over the function of providing book decoration.

For the Renaissance the central task of all representational art remained the imaging of the truths of the Christian faith. The whole field of religious iconography was reinterpreted in the new artistic style. At the same time there appeared previously unknown themes, such as the *Sacra Conversazione*, which shows a meditational dialogue between the enthroned Madonna and her attendant saints [551, 552]. Deferential, yet free and unconstrained, the holy figures gather round as representatives of the earthly kingdom of the Mother of God. A profound change in the attitude towards transcendental reality is evident. It is true that the Madonna as embodiment of the supramundane is substantially identical with the Queen of Heaven enthroned in majesty as she was painted by Giotto [cf. 486]. However, she has been drawn into the sphere of men, who associate themselves with her immediate company. Secularization of Christian themes is also evident in the fact that contemporary persons occur with increasing frequency as saints in religious pictures.

The development of the concept of a free humanity promoted by the humanists opened the way to the establishment of a new category of painting, portraiture. The medieval representation of man as a type was replaced by the characterization of the individual and the elaboration of unique and unrepeatable features, in not only their tangible reality but also their psychological differentiation. The older type of severe profile figure, which had been established as early as the fourteenth century in Sienese equestrian portraits, gave way in the second half of the fifteenth century to the portrait in half or three-quarter profile, to which the most significant creations of portraiture belong – the portraits of the popes by Raphael and Titian and Leonardo's enigmatic Mona Lisa.

The development of portraiture reveals a characteristic feature of Renaissance art, the search for reality. Instead of rendering the world in terms of a repertory of stereotypes, as Gothic artists had done, Renaissance artists sought to show it in its reality. Nature was the greatest teacher. In their concern with

reality artists envisioned a kind of *summa* of nature they hoped to understand nature as a spiritual o intellectual phenomenon. It is no contradiction, there fore, to say that Renaissance artists tried with all thei might to reach reality in order to elevate it to an idea sphere. The trend towards reality is common t northern and southern Europe alike – it is of out standing importance in the work of Jan van Eyc [cf. 509] and Konrad Witz [cf. 507] – the differenc being that Italian artists explored nature and it objective laws more consistently and systematically Once more the fundamentally rational basis of Renais sance art is evident. In the study of proportions th artists sought an ideal canon for the interrelation o parts of the human body; in their anatomical studie they began to penetrate the secrets of the functionin of the body with especial attention to the movemen of the limbs and the transmission of motion. Thei predilection for basic geometric and stereometri forms made them prefer elementary compositiona

551 *Andrea Mantegna, middle section of the Sacra Conver sazione from the High Altar of S. Zeno at Verona, 1457-9 Systematic combination of antique motifs. Despite the shar rendering of reality, the opulently painted architecture of th throne and playing putti effectively distance the Madonna.*

example of this being Mantegna's *Camera degli Sposi* in the Ducal Palace, Mantua, completed 1475). Colouristic perspective employs the effects of psychological distance evoked by certain colours, such as the 'near' red and the 'distant' blue. Aerial perspective, in which distant objects seem to dissolve into the general atmosphere, took its place beside linear perspective towards the end of the fifteenth century with the masterly example of Leonardo da Vinci [553]; it was to become one of the chief resources of landscape painting.

In the sixteenth century the feeling for nature led to the embryonic appearance of two new painting categories which emerged in their own right in the sixteenth century – landscape and still-life. In their pictorial backgrounds the Quattrocento painters did not try to reproduce particular landscape scenes, as Konrad Witz [cf. 507] had done in the north, but they sought an ideal, almost cosmic landscape. Giovanni Bellini, for example, came close to achieving this in his landscape backgrounds. Such artists as Leonardo da Vinci [553], Giorgione [562], and Titian

552 Piero della Francesca, Sacra Conversazione with kneeling donor, c. 1475. Milan, Brera. Monumental realism. Light proceeding from the sides illuminates the illusionistic architecture. The symmetrical structure and dignified figures help distance the scene from everyday reality.

553 Leonardo da Vinci, Madonna and Child with St Anne, c. 1503–6. Paris, Louvre. A classical 'figura pyramida' of the high Renaissance. Dark sfumato creates an aerial perspective.

schemes – the circle, the triangle, the pyramid. But in linear perspective they created an instrument which permitted the two-dimensional representation of the appearance of three-dimensional reality.

The true use of centralized perspective, whose discovery is attributed to the architect Brunelleschi, seemed to offer an objective means of evaluation for the work of art; no wonder then that it excited the greatest interest among the artists of the Renaissance, oriented as they were towards theory and experiment. The artists soon became dissatisfied with simple box-like spaces placed parallel to the picture plane in which the vanishing point lay on the middle axis. Complicated spatial forms were constructed producing diagonal spaces with eccentric vanishing points. Unusual points of view were tried out, such as the *sotto in sù* or extreme foreshortening. In ceiling paintings perspective served to give the spectator the illusion of looking directly into the sky (the earliest

[563] made the landscape a vehicle of mood so as to reflect the emotions of the spectator. Thus in the high Renaissance landscape was still linked to man. When it appears for the first time as an independent subject in the work of Polidoro da Caravaggio (1495–1546), landscape seemed justified to its creator by its connexion with ancient wall-painting, from which it also depended in the formal sense.

The stylistic advance of Renaissance painting was paralleled by an enlargement of its function and of the sociological sphere in which it flourished. Instead of being restricted to ecclesiastical and governmental use, it increasingly became the object of individual enjoyment and a magnet of the collecting impulse of powerful private purchasers from the nobility and the prosperous bourgeoisie. Paintings were especially sought for the embellishment of the *studiolo*, the gentleman's private study chamber, or of other rooms of intimate domestic character. Botticelli's *Birth of Venus* [557] or Titian's *Sacred and Profane Love* [563] are characteristic examples that suggest the preferred thematic material of this branch of painting:

554 *Parmigianino, Madonna del collo lungo, c. 1535. Florence, Uffizi. A highly artificial Mannerist composition full of contrasts (crowded and empty space; large Madonna figure/small Prophet). The Madonna is an elongated 'figura serpentinata'.*

ancient mythology, ancient history, and allegory – humanistic subject-matter opening the way to representation of the world and of man and cherishing the perfection of the nude human body as the noblest part of creation.

Pictorial allegory (from Greek *allegorein*, 'to say otherwise') was directed towards the concrete representation of abstract ideas and concepts; in practice this usually meant personifications. The allegorical message might be conveyed by single figures (e.g. Chastity, Justice, Faith), as well as by groups or scenes (e.g. the Battle of the Virtues and Vices, the Ages of Man, the Four Elements). It also penetrated into other pictorial categories, such as history painting and above all portraiture (Courage and Fortune crown the victorious general), and gave the impetus to the creation of great festive scenes of civic character – for instance the *Triumph of Venice* [567] – which closely anticipated the Baroque apotheosis. The spread of allegory was greatly assisted by love of the problematic and the desire to avoid superficial obviousness. Mannerist artists, especially, surpassed themselves in inventing complex pictorial conundrums and *jeux d'esprit* which were difficult even for contemporaries to interpret. This led to the publication of the first iconographical manual for artists at the end of the sixteenth century.

The early Renaissance

As Brunelleschi was the great pioneer in architecture, Masaccio (1401–28) was the revolutionary painter of the new style. In an age whose tone was set by the courtly elegance of Gentile da Fabriano [cf. 498], with his fluent linear melodiousness and softly glowing colour, the brief career of Masaccio brought a new seriousness into painting. While his master Masolino (1383–1447) tried to blend the polychromy of late Gothic painting with the new realistic trend, Masaccio turned back to Giotto [cf. 496], whose monumental figure style he translated into early Renaissance terms. With an equal intensity of expression, Masaccio achieved a heightened feeling for life, a more individual, often portrait-like sense of characterization, a greater fluency of gesture and movement, a more dramatic quality in the arrangement of figure groups, and an organization of pictorial space according to the laws of linear perspective.

In the same period – about 1426–7 – as he created his masterpiece, the frescoes of the church of the Carmine in Florence, Masaccio found time to embellish the church of S. Maria Novella with a *Fresco of the Trinity* [555]. This work is conceived as a kind of the Florentine monastery of S. Marco endowed by Cosimo de' Medici, represents a side of the early Renaissance in which understanding of the perspectival conception of space and grasp of realistic detail are combined with a softness and intimacy that is still medieval. The golden ground and the Gothic brilliance of colour long persisted in his work, until late in life he turned to a sober, more monumental narrative art. Close to Fra Angelico is the more worldly Fra Filippo Lippi (1406–69); in addition to frescoes, he created a number of tender *Madonna* pictures *[560]*, whose charm resides in their mundane serenity. The background of these paintings affords a glimpse into the everyday life of the contemporary bourgeoisie. The example illustrated shows a lying-in room in which the young mother attended by her servants receives a visit from neighbours. Without the transparent, perspectively rendered haloes, it would be hard to guess that the scene in the background shows the birth of Mary and that the youthful middle-class girl in the foreground is Mary herself. The observation of everyday situations and their elaboration in a religious painting are characteristic features of Quattrocento realism.

Other Florentine painters, adhering more closely to Masaccio, sought to exploit particular aspects of his art. Paolo Uccello (1397–1475) combined a passionate interest in perspective with a fable-like narrative quality. Andrea del Castagno (1423–57), who was fanatically obsessed with formal reality, rendered the corporeal appearance of a series of 'famous men' and thus created a pictorial counterpart of Donatello's sculptural realism. Finally, Domenico Veneziano (*c.* 1410–61) strove for unity of composition through light and colour.

The rapidly spreading renown of the Florentine masters of the new style caused them to be sought after throughout the Italian peninsula. Masaccio painted in Rome, Castagno travelled to Venice, and Fra Angelico together with his pupil Benozzo Gozzoli worked in Rome for Pope Nicholas V. Under the influence of these and other artists the various regions began to conform more or less closely to the Renaissance ideal, creating (from the mid-fifteenth century on) their own schools of painting, each of which shows its own characteristic and unmistakable qualities.

The Umbrian school boasted a master whose monumental realism served as a link between Masaccio and the high Renaissance, Piero della Francesca (1416–92). He worked chiefly in Urbino where Duke Federico da Montefeltro had assembled a select company of artists and savants. At the Duke's behest, Piero about 1475 painted a picture *[552]* for

555 *Masaccio, fresco of the Trinity in S. Maria Novella at Florence, c. 1426–7. Architectural painting with a central point of perspective. The donor figure is represented illusionistically 'in front of the picture surface'; the figure style is monumental.*

painted tomb chapel, whose cleverly constructed setting is so consistently executed in accordance with the laws of linear perspective that Brunelleschi's hand has been suspected in the underlying construction and the realistic details of the architecture. In a foreground plane that stands before the painted architecture two donors kneel. Behind them rise two painted pilasters flanking the central area covered by a coffered barrel-vault. At the opening, between the Virgin and St John, stands the Crucifix borne by God the Father. The living forms of the figures appeal strongly to the observer. But the realistically conceived foreground figures and the perspectively ordered space are not satisfactorily integrated; the figures do not yet enjoy the power of free movement in space that was to be, achieved later, as shown by Raphael's frescoes *[559]* where the figures fill the whole space with their life.

The Dominican monk Fra Angelico (1387–1445), who was responsible for the frescoes in the cells of

556 Domenico Ghirlandaio, Birth of the Virgin from the
fresco cycle of the Life of the Virgin in S. Maria Novella at
Florence, c. 1485–90. Realistic narrative style with portrait-like
accuracy in the rendering of reality.

557 Sandro Botticelli, Birth of Venus, c. 1485. Florence,
Uffizi. An atmospheric fairy-tale mythical representation with
composition stylized by linear definition.

the funerary chapel of S. Bernardino which shows
the donor kneeling before the Madonna accompanied
by a semicircle of saints and youthful angels – a *Sacra
Conversazione*. As with Masaccio [555] the scene
takes place before a setting of painted architecture
which continues and enlarges the real architecture.
Behind the illusionistic manipulation of fictive architecture may be discerned the intention to draw the
supersensible sphere into the real world. Still, through
the severely symmetrical composition, the solemn

monumentality of the architecture, the inner dignity
of the figures, a distance is created that clearly distinguishes the transcendent from the world of everyday reality. The hierarchical differentiation of the
figures is striking, as is the masterly handling of
colour and light, which falls from the left and is used
in a virtuoso manner to realize the spatial illusion of
the barrel-vault.

With other means, but with the same monumental
effect, Andrea Mantegna (1431–1506) was at work
in north Italy. More than any other painter of the
time he trained his eye on the remains of the antique.
This is evident both in the statue-like quality of his
figures and in the multiplicity of ancient ornaments,
sculptures, and architectural elements included in his
works. In 1457–9 Mantegna created the *main altarpiece for the Church of S. Zeno at Verona* [551]. This
work remains in place today in its original frame.
Painted pilasters and projecting plastic half-columns
divide the panel into three fields, while the continuous painted architectural coulisse, a pillared hall
resembling a peristyle, assures spatial unity. The
architectural background is constructed with perspectival exactness with a rather distant horizon, so
that the lower zone corresponding to the height of the
observer intensifies the monumental effect. The
middle field is reserved for the Madonna who is surrounded by music-playing putti. In the side fields
four saints echelon into the spatial depth. Reliefs of
antique character cover the pilasters and the entablature. The heavy fruit garlands also have prototypes
in Roman naturalistic wall decoration. The whole
composition is deeply imbued with the ancient spirit:
the ornate construction of the throne, the calm dignified pose of the Madonna, and the seriousness of the
entourage of putti. The whole is conveyed according
to a pictorial mode that presents every detail with
inexorable clarity, while at the same time adjusting
all the subsidiary and contrasting elements to the
discipline of the overall scheme.

The last decades of the fifteenth century saw the
dissipation of the active force of the painting of the
preceding years. In Florentine painting trends towards
multiplicity, decorative refinement of form, and
nervous haste of movement signal a late style, as does
the neglect of spiritual intensity. The churches receive
extensive fresco cycles in which contemporary
society is faithfully portrayed in the story of the Life
of Mary and in the legends of the lives of the saints.
Domenico Ghirlandaio's (1449–94) S. Maria Novella
frescoes (completed *c.* 1490) exemplify this varied art
of narration which commemorates the daily life and
customs of the period in loving detail. A comparison
of the *Birth of Mary* [556] with the lying-in room of

Filippo Lippi *[560]* shows the more elaborate architectural setting in which the carefully rendered reliefs and the rich ornament betray a greater mastery of ancient decorative forms. With all the emphasis on detail their clarity of composition none the less secures a monumental quality for these frescoes. They serve to demonstrate by comparison how applicable the concept of a late phase is to the crowding of motifs of a Pinturicchio or to the formal eccentricity of a Filippino Lippi. This phase finds its outstanding representative in Sandro Botticelli (1444–1510), whose work shows evident affinities for the Gothic in the linear emphasis and in the delicacy of the figures. In the *Birth of Venus [557]*, painted *c.* 1485, the nude, almost brittle figure of the goddess floats on her shell over stylized waves. The simple contour of Venus contrasts with the ornamental interlacings that encumber the figures of the wind gods and of the nymph waiting on the bank with the wind-blown cape. The *fin de siècle* quality of the underlying attitude, which leads to stylization of nature and human forms decoratively as surface filling and emotionally as lyrical story-telling, clearly reveals the painting as a creation of the late Quattrocento.

The high Renaissance

The painting of the high Renaissance should not be regarded as an immediate continuation of the artistic trends of the late fifteenth century. The works of Pinturicchio, Filippino Lippi, and Signorelli represent the conclusion of a stylistic phase rather than the beginning of a new one. It has been noted that the most salient characteristic of architecture at the beginning of the classic phase is an intense concentration; this is true of painting to an even higher degree. The additive, small-focus, and restless qualities of the declining years of the early Renaissance gave way to harmoniously balanced pictorial form in which figures and surrounding landscape or architecture are all informed by the same monumental sense. The geographic focus of high Renaissance painting was Rome where Raphael and Michelangelo created their masterpieces in glorification of the Church and the papacy.

The new style was introduced by Leonardo da Vinci (1452–1519). Owing to the experimental emphasis of his art – which caused him to leave many projects unfinished – and the ravages of time, only a

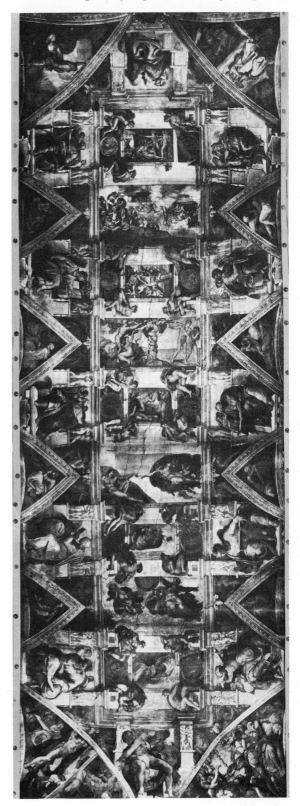

558 Michelangelo, fresco of the ceiling of the Sistine Chapel in the Vatican, 1508–12. Note the clear subordination of individual features within the overall structure.

few complete works by his hand have survived. It is difficult today to grasp the full extent of his influence. The famous *Last Supper* in Milan shows him master of a richly varied repertoire of gesture and movement, by virtue of which the rhythmically grouped Apostles seem to fill the space with overwhelming life. The painting of the *Madonna and Child with St Anne [553]*, from c. 1503–6, is impressive for figure composition and landscape alike. St Anne, the Madonna, and the Christ child form a figural pyramid. The clear, compact concentration of the figures on the picture plan contrasts with the loose sequential arrangement of earlier masters. Figures and landscape are blended into a tonal unity; they are bound together by the famous *sfumato*, a soft shadowy veil, which acts in conjunction with the suggestive use of chiaroscuro to give perspectival depth.

Pope Julius II summoned the sculptor Michelangelo (1475–1564) to Rome, entrusting him with the creation of his tomb. But Julius's interest soon shifted to a new project; he wanted the vault of the Sistine Chapel of his uncle Sixtus IV covered with a vast ceiling fresco. The execution was given to Michelangelo despite all his protests. The artist's fatiguing labours of 1508–12 produced a masterpiece *[558]* that ranks among the highest achievements of Western art. The extensive cycle of religious scenes is controlled by a painted architectural setting that provides a structural frame for the correlation of pictorial

elements of the most varied kind – the scenes of Creation and of the Fall in the middle fields, the titanic Prophets, sibyls, and giants, as well as the various painted medallions, reliefs, and sculptures. According to their relative importance and inner weight these elements are subordinated to a supple system that binds them together in a formal and intellectual order that seems both self-evident and unconstraining, and yet is decisive for every component.

The power of this striving for free ordering in the works of the high Renaissance may be sensed again a few steps away in the Vatican Stanze painted by Raphael Santi (1483–1520) and his assistants. The Camera della Segnatura (1509–11), the first room in this series, may be regarded as the pictorial counterpart of Bramante's Tempietto. The four great frescoes – see *The School of Athens [559]* – constitute high points of monumental painting in which figures and architecture are fused into a spiritual unity. The usual stiffness of ceremonial painting is totally absent. The individuals seem to move in the painted space with a perfect realization of their powers, without ever disturbing the balance and clarity of the composition. Raphael evokes an ideal world whose forms seem empirically accessible, while at the same time participating in an elevated sphere of order. It is a world that excludes ecstatic raptures as well as the constraint of a formal system.

The aspiration towards elevated idealism and dignified interpretation is equally evident in altar paintings. The theme of the Sacra Conversazione, for example, was often treated as a vision of the Madonna in Glory, as is the case with Raphael's *Madonna of Foligno* of 1511–12 in the Vatican. In a mandorla of light which illuminates the whole scene the Madonna floats down upon clouds surrounded on top by a company of child angels. The four persons in the lower zone respond to this epiphany with eloquent, expressive gestures. St Jerome recommends the suppliant donor kneeling on the right; St Francis kneeling on the left points to the viewer while directing his attention to the event above. Similarly John the Baptist looks out of the picture while he points to the Christ child. A carefully considered scheme of visual directions and gestures unites the group. Just as rich in relationships is the compositional structure of the whole painting. The triangle of the Madonna and the kneeling figures below, the vertical axis emphasized by the putto, the half-circle in the centre of the painting where the landscape links the two standing figures – these are all clearly distinguishable pictorial elements that are used not as a constricting schematism but as a freely variable means of

559   Raphael, The School of Athens, fresco in the Vatican Stanze, 1509–11. An idealizing elevation of the human form gives both figures and architecture a spiritual unity.

organization. This free linkage permits the circular composition of a roundel such as Raphael's *Madonna della Sedia [561]* of 1514–15 to be understood not as a formal abstraction, but as the living embodiment of the Renaissance ideal.

Although Rome is the centre of high Renaissance painting, Florence had important representatives of the classical style in Fra Bartolommeo and Andrea del Sarto. But the extraordinary transformation of the style into a new painterly mode took place in Venice.

Venetian painting showed a marked preference for panel and canvas paintings as the climate proved hostile to fresco. When painted cycles were required they were executed on canvas and then installed in their architectural setting. The stimulus to artistic competition with real architecture was absent. Under such conditions the individual easel painting independent of a pre-existing structural context could develop more easily and rapidly than in Florence or in Rome. To be sure, there are some autonomous paintings from the fifteenth century from these cities, but they never gained the importance with respect to monumental painting that they enjoyed in Venice.

A typical easel painting, as indicated by the measurements ($32\frac{1}{4} \times 29\frac{3}{4}$ ins.), is the *Tempest [562]* of c. 1505 by Giorgione (1478?–1510). The interpretation of the subject is disputed; some regard it as mythological legend, others as an Arcadian genre scene. What it presents to the observer is a tonally painted, masterfully composed landscape which no longer serves as background, but encloses the figures in a rhythmically unified pictorial whole. The mood informing the figures and the landscape is the same. The key to the harmony of the softly modelled forms lies in the subordination of all elements to the luminosity of colour.

The gulf that divides the high Renaissance from the fifteenth century may be appreciated by comparing Titian's (1477–1576) *Sacred and Profane Love [563]* of c. 1516 with Botticelli's *Birth of Venus [557]*. In place of a stylized fable, a 'pseudo-reality', Titian's painting presents a warm and vital world raised to festive grandeur. Colour takes on a seductive glow. The nude at the fountain's edge has a sensuous fullness unknown in the preceding century. On the other side sits a second female figure whose bodily form seems palpably present beneath the garments. Together with the putto who splashes in the water filling the antique sarcophagus the figures form a carefully composed group embedded as a self-sufficient whole in the surrounding landscape. The convincing rendering of reality is bathed in a warm light which enhances the festive ideality of the painting.

560 *Fra Filippo Lippi, circular picture (tondo) with Madonna and Child, and in the background the Birth of the Virgin, 1452. Florence, Palazzo Pitti. A genre-like realistic rendering of a religious subject. The circular form is not exploited in the composition.*

561 *Raphael, Madonna della Sedia, 1514–15. Florence, Palazzo Pitti. A classical example of a high Renaissance tondo. In this centralized composition the circular form is voluntarily accepted and conceived as both spatial and plastic.*

*562   Giorgione, The Tempest, c. 1505. Venice, Accademia.
The colourful landscape serves as an atmospheric space for the
figure groups.*

*563   Titian, Sacred and Profane Love, c. 1516. Rome, Galleria
Borghese. A painting imbued with the solemn idealism of the
high Renaissance, joy in the senses and glowing colourfulness.
Figures and landscape are smoothly integrated.*

The literary formulation of the human type of the
age is found in *Il Cortegiano* of Count Baldassare
Castiglione (written 1514, published 1528), a treatise
that glorifies the figure of the perfect courtier. The
many-sided gentleman serenely confident of his
cultivation became the model. When Raphael painted
a *Portrait of Castiglione [564]* about 1516 he designed
it in complete accord with literary ideal. All irrelevant
detail is excluded; the whole emphasis is placed upon
the eyes which look out in a cool and considered way.
Characteristically, the composition is based entirely
on forms that relate to the circle.

Mannerism

With the death of Raphael a phase of disorientation
disrupted the unfolding of the ideal world of balanced
forms. His pupils attempted no new great enterprises.
They did not attain the formal powers of their
masters. In the confusing fullness of the falling and
knotted bodies on the walls of the Sala di Costantino
in the Vatican (1517–25) one notes behind the formal
weaknesses a profound doubt of the general validity
of the artistic ideal. The subjective artificiality and the
discordant tensions of Mannerism are announced.
The chief centre of this new style was not Rome but
Florence, where the Medici reigned as Dukes of
Tuscany from 1531. Here as in the other courts of
Italy art turned towards a ceremonial style in which
the artistic frequently becomes the precious and form
is no longer felt organically and inwardly but as a
fixed formula imposed from without. Thus were
created great pictorial cycles in glorification of the
reigning houses, as well as the eagerly collected

The 'Maniera', the recherché and forced qualities of the new style, and its inner contradictions are strongly pronounced in the *Madonna with the Long Neck, c.* 1535 *[554]* by Parmigianino (1503–40). This artist, who worked in Parma in Emilia, deliberately exploited for stylistic ends the contrast between the tall statuesque Madonna and the tiny emaciated Prophet with phylactery standing beside the abruptly foreshortened row of columns. For the classical artist the need for a well-proportioned relation between the man and the columns would have been a matter of course. In theory nothing had changed in Mannerism. But this did not prevent the artist from proportioning the individual elements of the picture according to different and incommensurable standards. Another striking feature is the way in which the formal artificiality is associated with refined elegance and colouristic coolness.

As has been seen, Venice acquired its great school of painters contemporaneously with the rise of Mannerism. Although Titian continued at work straight through the period of Mannerism, hardly any traces of this style can be discerned in his work; throughout his development he remained faithful to the harmony

564 *Raphael, Portrait of Count Castiglione, c. 1516. Paris, Louvre. An exemplary representation of the aloof, self-assured courtier.*

565 *Jacopo Pontormo, Joseph in Egypt, c. 1518–19. London, National Gallery. Note the assured departure from the customary rules of composition. Despite the unity of situation, the places of events distributed round the edges of the picture show several different scenes happening simultaneously.*

princely portraits and miniatures, in which the pomp of courtly etiquette was rendered in pedantic detail. Academies came into being in which the great spirit of the classic style was reduced to a dogmatically enforced cult of rules. Inasmuch as painting was increasingly permeated by theoretical elements the main focus of interest shifted from the formal to the iconographic. The new art required a commentary to be understood.

In *Joseph in Egypt [565]*, painted by Jacopo Pontormo (1494–1557) about 1518–19, narrative unity is abandoned. In two separate places, in the lower left foreground and the upper right background, the chief events are staged simultaneously. The parallel with Gothic altar paintings is significant. In the areas between the two main events children in richly varied poses are interspersed among adults who gesticulate like actors. The uncannily floating stairs curve up to the upper staging area. The stylistic similarity to Michelangelo's vestibule of the Laurentian Library *[540]* is evident; there too the 'alienation effect' was consciously pursued.

ful repudiation of heretical intent and his claim to the right of pictorial license become a classic defence of artistic freedom. And in an ambitious allegory, such as the *Triumph of Venice* of *c.* 1580–5 *[567]*, he could unfold all the pomp of a ceremonial glorification without fear of disapproval from the authorities.

The churches of Toledo in Spain contain several of the eccentric creations of a painter whose very personal interpretation of Mannerism stands at the furthest remove from the secular attitude of the Renaissance: El Greco (1541–1613). To be sure, his manner of painting did not conceal his training in Venice, but in expression and formal construction his works belong to an altogether different world. The sensuous beauty of the human body, as it is revealed in Titian's works, was cast aside. In *The Martyrdom of St Maurice and the Theban Legion* of *c.* 1580–4 *[568]* the elongated figures seem to be imbued with the fire of inner faith; the postures show an affected and violently distorted quality. Moreover, the classical laws of composition are disregarded. The abrupt change of proportions are evidence of a lack of

566 *Tintoretto,* Rescue of the Body of St Mark, *c. 1562. Venice, Accademia. Manneristic depth in the schematically indicated architectural coulisse, and an agitated, flickering play of light.*

567 *Paolo Veronese,* Triumph of Venice, *c. 1580–5. Venice, Doge's Palace. This ceiling picture, painted on canvas, stands at the transition to Baroque ceiling decoration in its bold allegorical forms.*

of serenely self-sufficient composition. Titian, Tintoretto, and Paolo Veronese form the great triad of Venetian Cinquecento painting. In such works as the *Rescue of the Body of St Mark* of *c.* 1562 *[566]*, Tintoretto (1518–94), the chief master of Venetian Mannerism, combined the visionary dematerialization of figures and architectural forms with a clever spatial composition which takes over the hallucinatory perspectival recession effect from Mannerist architecture. At the same time light acquires an independent value as a dramatic element.

Much less affected by Mannerism was Paolo Veronese (1528–88), whose paintings are filled with opulence and ceremony. The luxurious character of his religious scenes brought him into conflict with the Counter-Reformation Church which was disturbed by the excessive worldly display. His success-

68 El Greco, The Martyrdom of St Maurice and the Theban Legion, c. 1580–4. Escorial. Individual enhancement of Manneristic formal tendencies under the influence of the Spanish Counter-Reformation.

espect for the principle of continuous unfolding of patial depth. The gestures and gazes of the four main igures, who in typically Mannerist fashion are placed off-centre on the right, do not serve to bind together he group as a whole. Over the scene of martyrdom hat is depicted in small scale in the lower left fore-ground a bundle of light rays leads to a company of gesticulating angels, behind whom the clouds open as if to disclose Heaven to the faithful. The pale flickering light becomes a symbol for the inner unrest and ascetic otherworldliness of the time. Although the work was commissioned by Philip II, it failed to please the King and was refused.

El Greco passed the rest of his life in Toledo. Here he ecstasy and intensity of his mystical experience found expression in several portraits and the superb series of the Twelve Apostles (now in the Casa del Greco).

Sculpture

ITALY

The central problem that repeatedly engaged the ingenuity of Renaissance sculptors is the separation of the figure from the bonds of the relief and of the architectural setting. Of course the niche figure and the increasingly painterly relief remained important categories for the stone-carver and bronze-worker. But the chief focus of interest had clearly shifted to free-standing sculpture in the round which occupied a position comparable to that of the central-plan structure in architecture. The Renaissance artist viewed the representation of the human nude as his highest task. The artists of the fifteenth century strove towards this end in so far as they sought to clarify the anatomy and function of the body and its relation to space.

The early Renaissance

For sculpture in the early Renaissance Florence was again the decisive centre. A number of important projects had remained incomplete in the fourteenth century: the cathedral lacked its dome and façade, the baptistry had received only one of the three planned pairs of bronze doors [cf. 473], and Or S. Michele (the oratory of the guilds whose patrons were to be shown in the tabernacles of the exterior) still awaited its sculptural embellishment. These projects were controlled by the citizens, who awarded commissions through competitions and supervised their execution. For this reason works of art were strongly linked to the civic pride of the Florentines. Also the Medici distributed some important private commissions for their city palace and country villas. A further important category was the expensive funerary monuments of the nobility and high ecclesiastics, in which decorative architectural elements were combined with rich relief decoration and free-standing sculpture. On the whole, though, the quantity and scope of great undertakings was less than in painting. But there was a flourishing production of small sculpture which was eagerly collected by private purchasers. Frequently the sculptors were also gold-smiths, who were intimately familiar with work in small format. Free from all connexion with liturgical or other high aims, medals, bronze statuettes, and objects of decorative character offered the artist opportunities to exploit mythology and history, everyday life and nature in their works; for this

569 Donatello, bronze statue of David, c. 1430. Florence, Museo Nazionale. The first free-standing sculpture of the early Renaissance. Realism is combined with the freshness and elegance of the early period.

570 Michelangelo, marble statue of David, 1501–5. Florence, Accademia. A colossal figure (three times larger than life), and an example of the heroically inspired image of man during the high Renaissance.

571 Benvenuto Cellini, bronze statue of Perseus, 1554. Florence, Loggia dei Lanzi. Manneristic over-emphasis on anatomy (muscles). Note the contrast between the coolly aloof features and the crude realism of the bleeding Medusa head.

reason these works provide a broader and more immediate conspectus of the interests and taste of the period than does larger sculpture.

On the borderline between the Gothic and the early Renaissance stands Lorenzo Ghiberti (1378–1455). In the individual forms, in the delicacy of his figures, and in the flow of the drapery he remained indebted to the linear grace of the International Style, especially in his first main work, the older pair of doors for the Baptistry of Florence, upon which he and his assistants worked for more than twenty years.

In this time he drew increasingly close to antique ideals of form, so that the Ghiberti workshop became the place of training for a number of Renaissance artists. His second pair of Baptistry doors [572], the 'Gates of Paradise' (1425–52), is much more strongly imbued with the spirit of the early Renaissance. The medieval quatrefoils in which the individual scenes of the two earlier pairs of doors were inserted, gave way to rectangular fields, whose reliefs with their airy spaciousness were constructed according to the rules of the new way of design. Their ideal architecture displays a precise knowledge of linear perspective and the figure groups show a clear understanding of the complementary relation of bodies and space. Beneath the garments which still flow in gentle swaying movements the body may be sensed as a palpable and living reality. The frames around the separate relief fields betray a familiarity with ancient sculpture, especially in the portrait-like heads projecting from the medallions.

The chief master of the incipient Renaissance is Donatello (1386–1466), who achieved pioneering solutions in a number of categories. His bronze David is the first truly free-standing sculpture in the round, his Gattamelata the first equestrian monument after the antique, and his representation of Niccolò da Uzzano the first portrait bust in the ancient sense. For the development of the niche figure and the relief he opened new paths in expressiveness and in the naturalistic elaboration of figures and drapery.

Donatello made the life-size bronze statue of David [569] about 1430, endowing a favourite motif of Renaissance sculpture, the nude human figure, with a vital sensuousness. Vasari suggests that the vibrant feeling for reality derives from a direct imitation of life. This quality is associated with a balanced ponderation which, in accordance with antique prototypes, determines the play of the limbs. Over the supporting right leg the thigh is raised up and the shoulders lowered, while the bodily parts on the side of the flexed left leg are distributed in the opposite sense. In contrapposto, the reciprocal movement of the bodily parts up and down and backwards and forwards, lies a wealth of tensions and at the same time harmoniously balanced plays of energy which are decisive henceforth for the statue.

Donatello's Cantoria or 'Singing Gallery' of 1433–9 [573] in the cathedral of Florence with its shells, rosettes, amphoras, and acanthus leaves provides a masterly ensemble of exuberant Renaissance ornament; the form of the whole is traceable to antique sarcophagi. These decorative elements, together with the glitter of the gold mosaic tesserae on the columns and in the background of the relief, form a splendid

572 *Lorenzo Ghiberti, detail from the 'Porta del Paradiso' of the Baptistry at Florence, 1425–52. Note the linear perspective of the architectural coulisses, the spatial effect, the portrait-like medallion heads, and the survival of Gothic in the fine lines of the clothing.*

573 *Donatello, Cantoria ('Singing Gallery') of Florence Cathedral, 1433–9. Florence, Cathedral Museum. Note the lively realism of the playing putti on the painterly mosaic ground, the richest decoration of the early Renaissance period.*

and colourful frame for boisterous putti, whose sequence does not stop at the paired columns but continues behind them as if on a stage. The whirling, half-naked putti are successors of the antique erotes, which – reinterpreted by the Renaissance as Christian child angels – are employed as a charming, gaily sensuous contrast to the ideality of the sacred realm. Donatello has used them here for the first time in a larger context, imparting to them in their naturalistic treatment a tense, almost coarse, corporeality. After the putto had been naturalized, so to speak, as a motif of Christian art, it became almost ubiquitous in painting and sculpture.

If one compares Donatello's *Equestrian Statue of the Condottiere Gattamelata*, 1447–53 *[574]* in Padua with the *Monument of Colleoni* begun in 1479 *[575]* by Andrea Verrocchio (1436–88) in Venice, the direction of sculptural development in the fifteenth century becomes clear. The Gattamelata radiates a self-possessed calm which recalls the balance of the antique statue of Marcus Aurelius *[cf. 125]* on the Roman Capitol. The bronze statue stands independent of any architectural setting on its high base. Horse and rider are blended into unity; they form a self-contained composition of great serenity. Verrocchio consciously departs from this serenity in his Colleoni. Everything is tenser and more momentary in effect. The horse seems more fiery, and also more restless. The twist of his head is taken up by the accentuated counter-movement of the rider, who stands stiffly upright on his stirrups. The face is forced into an expression of masterly superiority and the movements have an angular harshness. As in painting so here in sculpture

575   *Andrea Verrocchio, Equestrian Statue of the Condottiere Colleoni in Venice, 1479–88. The general stylistic trend of the late fifteenth century is evident in the increased expressiveness of the representation.*

574   *Donatello, Equestrian Statue of the Condottiere Gattamelata in Padua, 1447–53. Statuesque composure of rider and horse, forming a closely integrated unit.*

on the eve of the classic phase a certain tendency to exaggeration makes itself felt.

The stone-carvers, who like Benedetto da Maiano and Mino da Fiesole came in great numbers from the district of Florence, found a rich field of activity in the decoration of churches. To the more elaborate side of their work belongs the *Tomb of the Florentine humanist Marsuppini*, 1455 *[576]* by Desiderio da Settignano (1428–64). In structure it depends closely upon the medieval niche tomb, embellished by pilasters, entablature, and round arch of antique character. Within the niche stands the richly decorated sarcophagus, upon which the deceased rests as if asleep in his bed. Putti bearing shields and child angels supporting garlands complete the figure ensemble. In structure and decoration the Marsuppini tomb belongs to the earliest example of a category in which the Renaissance magnates intended to create a monument with a double aim – the glorification of God and the commemoration of personal fame.

scheme of folds, but only the laws of its own material weightiness. With prophetic gaze, scornful of human frailty, this Moses looks challengingly out at the world; he incarnates both the self-possessed man of the Renaissance and the historic figure of the Biblical patriarch. Antiquity and Christianity are fused here in an image of Michelangelesque *terribilità*, that super-human grandeur by which the works of the great Florentine grip the observer's attention. In the Moses he created a counterpart to the painted Prophets and sybils of the Sistine Chapel. All these forms constitute not merely examples of a particular stylistic ideal but also evidences of a personal attitude. In them the general validity of the contemporary formal language and the uniqueness of the individual creative act is reconciled.

'Il Gigante' was the name the Florentines gave to the 18-foot-high marble statue of *David [570]*, which Michelangelo began to carve in 1501 out of a block hewn some forty years before for another colossal figure. Intended to be set up in the Piazza della

576   *Desiderio da Settignano, wall tomb of Carlo Marsuppini, c. 1455. Florence, S. Croce. The exuberant decoration leaves no place uncovered. The influence of antique models such as the Ara Pacis of Augustus is evident in the fruit garlands.*

The high Renaissance

Compared with architecture and painting the high Renaissance created few works of sculpture. Two grandiose sculptural projects, both entrusted to Michelangelo, were destined to remain tragically incomplete: the facing of S. Lorenzo in Florence, where the artist envisioned a kind of *summa* of the ideals of Italian architecture and sculpture of the time, and the Tomb of Pope Julius II intended for new St Peter's, which was similarly conceived as a monumental fusion of architecture and sculpture. The figure of *Moses* (1515–16) *[517]* gives an indication of the grandeur of the second of these two projects. Work on the Julius tomb was interrupted by the Pope himself in favour of the painting of the Sistine Chapel ceiling. The muscular body of the seated figure of Moses is constructed organically in accordance with the character of the component bodily parts; the drapery follows no externally imposed abstract

577   *Michelangelo, Tomb of Duke Lorenzo de' Medici, 1530–4. Florence, S. Lorenzo, New Sacristy. A tragic solemnity characterizes this wall tomb, which looks forward to Mannerism in several details.*

Signoria, this naturalistically conceived colossus is gigantic both in size and in the psychic intensity bestowed by its creator upon a member of a super-human race of heroes. Athletic appearance and intellectual and spiritual disposition are here blended into a moral and material unity.

A few years later Michelangelo began the task of designing the *Medici tombs*, funerary monuments for the Dukes Giuliano and Lorenzo de' Medici [577], in the new sacristy of S. Lorenzo (1520–7 and 1530–4). Although this project was not brought to full completion, the two balancing groups give an effective idea of the artist's stylistic progress in the direction of Mannerism. The architectural scheme depends upon tensions comparable to those evoked in the vestibule of the Laurentian Library [540]; individual elements, such as the balusters on the crowning attic, are brought into the system contrary to all precedent. Added to this is the severity of the colouristic impression – the cool white of the marble and the neutral grey of the other walls. Girded with cuirass and helmet, the pensive, melancholically reserved figure of Lorenzo sits cramped in his narrow niche. Michelangelo is now as remote from the imperious energy of the Moses as from the Apollonian youth of the David; what remains is a deeply felt resignation. The compositional structure, a triangle composed of one seated and two reclining figures, is characterized by an unusual artistic perfection. It does not have the ease of the contemporary triangular compositions of the classical phase, but shows – flattened and extended in adherence to an almost two-dimensional concept – the Mannerist tendency towards centrifugal dissolution. All forms seem imbued with an inner fateful heaviness. This heaviness is especially evident in the two allegorical figures of Morning and Evening on the sarcophagus, where they can neither rest calmly nor slip down. The tragic tension of their expression is combined with complicated movements and a nervously projecting silhouette. In the hands of Michelangelo's Manneristic followers these last two qualities became almost a credo.

Mannerism

The most striking characteristic of Mannerist sculpture is the strong emphasis on motifs of movement. This comes to the fore in the *figura serpentinata*, the artificially twisted scheme in which classical ponderation yields to a helically ascending form. The bronze fountain figure of *Neptune* (1563–6) [578] by Giovanni da Bologna (1529–1608), an artist who contributed greatly to the development of sculpture and

578 *Giovanni da Bologna, Fountain of Neptune in the Piazza del Nettuno at Bologna, 1563–6. The outline of Mannerist sculpture is enlivened by multi-axial directions of movement. Greater mass is evident in the composition of the body, as opposed to the athletic tautness of the Renaissance [570].*

whose influence was widely felt both within and outside Italy, shows this quality. The twist of the head, the retreat of one shoulder, the extension of the arm, and the projection of one knee establish a complicated play of movement which everywhere enlivens the contour. The figure is no longer designed to be seen from one predominant view, as was the case of the block-like form of Michelangelo's David [570], but it is conceived spatially as the synthesis of an infinite number of views. The spectator must walk around it in order to experience the multiplicity of motifs and the sequence of overlappings. The development of the sculptor's art was advanced to a new stage.

The corkscrew principle could embrace whole figure groups, as in Giovanni da Bologna's marble *Rape of the Sabine Women* [579], completed in 1583. In the complicated compression of the bodies this composition is intentionally designed to be seen from many sides. The projecting angular movements and the expressive tension recall the *Colleoni* of

Verrocchio, and generally speaking there are many similarities between Mannerism and the late Quattrocento.

The juxtaposition of contrasts, not excluding dissonances, is a preferred stylistic device of Mannerism. In the *Neptune* fountain *[578]* the protagonist's sophisticated pose contrasts with the obtrusive fullness of the body, which amounts almost to a caricature of Michelangelo's *terribilità*. In another chief work of Mannerism, the *Perseus* of 1554 *[571]* by Benvenuto Cellini (1500–71) the cool perfection of form and the disinterestedness of the facial expression joins with a crude enthusiasm for realism which

579 *Giovanni da Bologna, Rape of the Sabine Women, 1583. Florence, Loggia dei Lanzi. The 'figura serpentinata' was the ideal form of Mannerism. Extravagant gestures take the place of harmonious postures.*

580 *Giacomo della Porta and Taddeo Landini, Fontana delle Tartarughe (Tortoise Fountain) in Rome, 1581–4. Note the contrast between the thin streams of water and the heavy shells.*

manifests itself in the nude, in the gushing blood and the snake hair of the Medusa head. The impression is painful, even repellent, but this evocation of contradictory feelings was consciously intended by Mannerist artists. One of the most rewarding opportunities to display contrasting effects lay in fountains. As an intentional contradiction the Mannerists first grasped the possibilities of water as an artistic element. In the Baroque *Trevi Fountain* [cf. *687*] the water flows and rushes in a rich stream over artificial rocks in a wide deep pool. Mannerists avoided such harmonious effects. Even when they were given a large basin to fill, an astonishingly small stream was designed to feed it. The *Fontana delle Tartarughe* or *Tortoise Fountain* in Rome (1581–4) *[580]* is a striking example of Mannerist aquatic display. In the middle of a shallow basin rises an architectural base with sharply cut profiles. At the corners stand four great shells heavy with water, and in the centre a swelling vase bearing a low fountain cup. Four nude boys with limbs jutting out at angles stretch like *ajouré* ornament between the upper cup and the base. With one hand they grip the curiously placed tortoises, while the other holds the dolphins that stand upon shell volutes. In thin, sharp streams the water spurts out of the cup directly into the flat basin; a second group of streams is ejaculated from the mouths of the dolphins into the shells. This contrast between the heaviness of the shells calling for a broad stream of water and the scarcity of the overflow is characteristic of the inner attitude of Mannerism.

Architecture outside Italy

FRANCE

While the development of Renaissance architecture in Italy embraced both the sacred and the secular branches, in France secular architecture, or more precisely the château, was absolutely dominant. By comparison church buildings in Renaissance forms occupy a wholly subordinate position; in plan and feeling French churches remain indebted to the Gothic until far into the sixteenth century.

The introduction of Renaissance forms was promoted by a series of military campaigns conducted in Italy by the French kings before and after the turn of the sixteenth century. Following the policy initiated under his predecessors, Francis I (1515–46) summoned a group of Italian artists and builders to his court, among them Leonardo da Vinci and Benvenuto Cellini. In the second quarter of the century a number of Italian painters, sculptors, and architects (including Rosso Fiorentino, Primaticcio, and Serlio) assisted by native artists formed the School of Fontainebleau, which as the representative of an officially supported court art exercised a wide influence outside France's borders. The still feudal crust of society, the high nobility and the wealthy bourgeoisie with the king at the head, initiated an enormous building activity, at whose centre stood the projects for the various châteaux. In the district of Paris, and especially in the hunting estates of the Loire valley, patrons vied one with another in the vastness and luxury of their new constructions. In contrast to the Italian suburban villa of this period which served only for occasional residence, the French Renaissance castles were erected as fixed country-seats and were inhabited for long stretches of time.

Unlike the Italian palazzo, the French château did not conform to any single type. In ground-plan and in the grouping of building masses considerable freedom existed, though certain stylistic uniformities that are broadly diffused can be discerned: the emphasis placed on the corners by round towers or rectangular pavilions, the heightening and differentiation of the roof zone in a lively silhouette (steep roofs of different heights, crowning turrets, decorative gables, and the so-called lucarnes, i.e. ornamental dormer windows), and the predilection for circular staircases attached like towers to the building mass. The persistence of some elements of Gothic castles emerges from a careful scrutiny of the building structure [cf. 510].

In 1519 Francis I ordered the rebuilding of the greatest of the Loire châteaux, *Chambord [581]*.

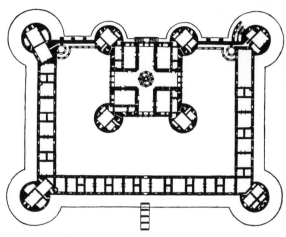

581, 582 Pierre Nepveu, called Trinqueau, Château de Chambord, begun 1519. General view and ground-plan of a gigantic, axially symmetrical design (400 rooms) with fantastic roof buildings. The style contains elements of the Gothic and upper Italian Renaissance. The square centre building has four circular corner towers and cruciform passages, in the middle of which is the circular winding staircase. A three-storied gallery leads to the side wings which flank the great inner courtyard and are single-storied in places.

Tradition has it that Leonardo da Vinci served as consultant for the design. In fact Italian influence is discernible not only in the systematization of the plan [582], but also in the block-like unification of the building mass. The new units of the sixteenth century, which show no conscious return to older building parts, all derive from a geometrically regulated plan, whose uniformity, however, is broken by the plastic accent of the traditional towers. Similarly the native tradition is evident in the roof organization and in the vertical articulation. In a view of the *court façade* [583] one easily recognizes how the thin Renaissance-like pilaster order, whose foreign and somewhat bookish quality is obvious, is spread over the façade like a network. This is co-ordinated with the vertical rows of windows, which extend above the roof-line in richly decorated aedicule windows. In the columns of the circular staircase the articulation is less oriented to the Gothic than in the case of the vertical pilasters of the façade. The detail also shows the combination of the two styles. Renaissance decoration deriving from Lombardy stands next to Gothic relics, such as the shrimp-like gable decoration and the transomed windows, whose rectangular field division seems to be incised into the surface. Even where an Italian 'corrector' sought to build in the Renaissance spirit, as did Sebastiano Serlio in the Château of Ancy-le-Franc (1546), the French drive towards vertical accenting proved inescapable.

When Henri II ascended the French throne in 1547 he named Philibert de l'Orme (*c.* 1512–70) as his chief architect; only the royal château in Paris, the Louvre, was excluded from his field of competence. For Diane de Poitiers de l'Orme built the *Chateau of Anet* (1549–52) which was largely destroyed in the French Revolution. Fortunately a drawing [584] by Jacques Androuet du Cerceau (1510–84) gives us an idea of its original arrangement. With de l'Orme and du Cerceau two artists appear who towards the middle of the sixteenth century gained prestige and influence as builders and architectural theorists. They belong to a generation which was capable of detaching itself from the immigrant Italians. Both had seen the old and the new architecture of Italy with their own eyes and possessed the theoretical equipment to overcome the mixed style of the first decades of the sixteenth century. Du Cerceau had received a lasting impression from the ancient works of architecture and from the creations of Bramante. His huge book of engravings *Les plus excellens bastiments de France* (1576–9) had an incalculable influence. De l'Orme was more effective through the numerous buildings in which he sought to turn the experiences of his Italian trip to account for the architecture of his own country. In the Château of Anet various motifs can be traced to specific Italian prototypes; thus the triumphal-arch motif was taken up in the gatehouse as well as in the middle part of the three-winged main building. But despite all his Italian studies the French elements came to the fore in the great open court and the emphasis on the vertical achieved through high windows, lucarnes, and steep chimneys. Du Cerceau's drawing also gives an idea of how gardens were conceived in the Renaissance; the great rectangle is

583 *Château de Chambord. Detail of Francis I's Staircase. The high pilasters have a certain Gothic effect as projecting supports.*

584 *Philibert de l'Orme, Château d'Anet, 1549–52. Drawing by Jacques Androuet du Cerceau in the British Museum. An example of the transition to the style of French Renaissance architecture from independently combined motifs of Italian origin (e.g. triumphal arches) and elements of the native tradition (open inner courtyard, vertical emphasis, steepled roof). A Renaissance garden design of regular proportions.*

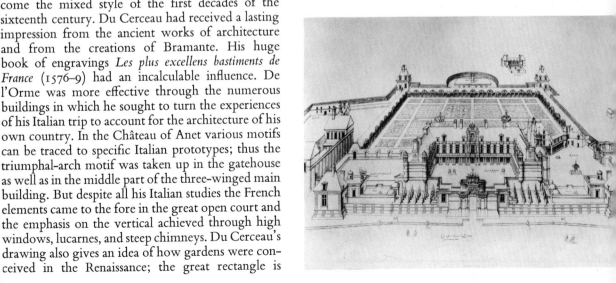

585 Pierre Lescot, west wing of the Louvre, Paris, begun in 1546. Composed harmony of the façade with various relief decoration, giving a cool and elegant overall effect.

586 Rosso Fiorentino, Francis I's Gallery in the Château de Fontainebleau, c. 1533–40. The typical style of decoration of the School of Fontainebleau, with marked Italian influences. Note the stucco ornament, painting and carved woodwork joined into a unified system of decoration, showing the first steps of scroll-work.

divided into smaller regular rectangular fields, which were planted in geometrical figures. The garden spreads out like a carpet before the château. Architecture and landscape seem almost accidentally conjoined, rather than ingeniously and consciously interrelated as in the succeeding Baroque period.

Towards the middle of the sixteenth century French architecture entered a second stylistic stage, producing new works of architecture such as the *West Wing of the Louvre in Paris [585]* begun in 1546 by Pierre Lescot (1510–78), which demonstrates more distinctly the traits of an independent national architectural style. The Gothic elements of the indigenous tradition have almost completely disappeared. The point of departure is the formal vocabulary of the Italian Renaissance now accurately understood but reinterpreted in terms of a differing stylistic ideal. French architects blended the foreign stimuli with their own artistic aspirations to achieve a marvellous transformation. Although Raphael created a plastic modelling of the wall in his Palazzo Vidoni-Caffarelli in Rome *[532]*, the articulation of Lescot's Louvre façade – even where it displays full columns – acts as a flat rationally distributed décor imposed on the surface from without. The shallow salients crowned with flat segmental arches are scarcely experienced as a plastic articulation of the architectural block, but rather as rhythmic accentuation of a wall that could be extended at will to either side. This flat serene articulation, combined with the cool elements of the individual forms, was to predominate henceforth in France. When more than a hundred years later the Roman Baroque architect Gian Lorenzo Bernini presented proposals for the enlargement of the Louvre his project came to grief precisely because of its powerful plastic configuration.

Although Lescot's Louvre façade may be appropriately compared to the stylistic stage of the Italian high Renaissance (as shown, for example, by projecting parts of the façade in which the classical triumphal-arch motif with niches between the paired columns is utilized), the *Château of Fontainebleau* was the centre of a Mannerist efflorescence. Outside of Florence no other place in the decades of the Mannerist phase showed such a strong power of stylistic creation as did the irregular château that had grown up over a period of centuries and upon which the French kings bestowed their especial affection. Two Italians belong to the most important representatives of the School of Fontainebleau: the Florentine Rosso Fiorentino (1494–1540) and Francesco Primaticcio (1505–70), who was trained in the school of Giulio Romano and thus counts as an indirect pupil of Raphael. The main focus of activity lay in the spheres of decorative and representational art. In the ornamenting of the vast château complex these artists created a decorative style that united painting and stucco sculpture in a single whole. The *Galerie François I [586]*, which Rosso Fiorentino designed in about 1533–40, is a characteristic example. With a

idth of 16 feet and a length of nearly 200 feet it
chieves a typically Mannerist effect of space. Recal-
ng for comparison Michelangelo's ceiling of the
istine Chapel *[558]* one finds in the painted articula-
on a logical ordering of complex elements: from the
cenes from Genesis in the main fields to the medal-
ions in the small accessory areas a differentiated
intellectual scheme governs the whole. In Fontaine-
leau, however, the inner tension which informs
Michelangelo's system is transformed into a kind of
precious and decorative 'neutrality', which provides
o standard of differentiation for the diverse elements.
Thus this interior reveals a tendency paralleling the
uniform flat rhythmic scheme observed in the
xterior façades of French Renaissance architecture.

SPAIN

The first signs of contact with the Renaissance here
appear in the late fifteenth century, earlier than in
France, although this influence is confined to a kind
of decorative enhancement freely spun over the
building mass (the Plateresque style). Examples of
genuine understanding of Italian formal achievements remained isolated. In church building the late
Gothic style maintained a tenacious grip. In the sixteenth century vast hall churches were built which
gradually absorbed the proportions and architectural
membering of the imported style.

The closest approach to the Italian style was
realized in works commissioned by the Emperor
Charles V (1519–58). No Spanish building has a
stronger Renaissance aspect than the Royal *Palace of
the Alhambra* in Granada *[587]*, begun in 1526. Had it
been completed it would have provided a good idea
of its model, Raphael's Villa Madama in Rome, which
was also destined to remain an unfinished fragment.
It seems that the Spanish architect Pedro Machuca
(died 1550) derived the concept of his design directly
from the workshop of Raphael and Antonio da
Sangallo the Younger. From the standpoint of Renaissance architectural theory the building counts as the
realization of a recurring dream. The plan unites two
ideal geometric forms, the circle and the square. In
reality, however, the square is slightly distorted into
a rectangle in accordance with the demands of the
site; within is inscribed the round court, bounded by
a two-story order of Tuscan and Ionic columns.
This order reveals the balanced classical spirit of the
Italian Renaissance so clearly that one's thoughts turn
to Bramante's Tempietto.

Under the influence of the Counter-Reformation,
whose ideals were energetically promoted by the

587 Pedro Machuca, Palace of Charles V at the Alhambra in
Granada, begun 1526. A circular courtyard built on the model of
Raphael's Villa Madama in Rome, in classical Renaissance style.

588 Juan Battista de Toledo and Juan de Herrera, the Escorial
near Madrid, 1563–84. Monastery and residence are united in
the dark solemnity and absence of decoration. The formal
apparatus shows transitional steps to the incipient Baroque.

ageing Charles V and his son Philip V, Spanish Renaissance architecture turned towards a severe, even
gloomy monumentality. The point of departure of
this development is the gigantic pile of the *Escorial
[588]*, begun by Philip II in 1563 as a symbol of his
concept of the office of a Christian ruler. The great
complex, incorporating a monastery church and

palace, stands isolated on a shelf-like plateau, a fitting monument to the religious zeal of its founder. The powerful building block has the aspect of a cold repellent mass of stones, broken only by the monotonous series of windows. Square towers at the four corners suggest a fortified castle. The main front, nearly 700 feet long, is articulated by three surmounting gables. Although the central gable has a strong emphasis in the colossal order extending through several stories, the uniformity of the whole is only slightly enlivened. In the stabilization which is achieved here through a sober and ascetic restriction of decoration the seeds for one aspect of the succeeding Baroque style developed. Thus the wall is enlivened not through an overlay of decoration but through the forces that seem to emerge from the mass itself. Although the façade of the Escorial is still far from this end result, it represents a necessary preparation for the process.

ENGLAND

In the sixteenth-century architecture of England, as in the other countries of Europe outside Italy, native elements interpenetrate with imported Renaissance forms. In contrast with France, however, this encounter did not lead to the synthesis of a national style. The familiar and the alien were put into a disjointed

589　Robert Smythson, Wollaton Hall in Nottinghamshire, 1580–8. The wall surfaces look back to the Perpendicular style in the lattice-work. Mannerist decorative forms are suggested by the Flemish strap-work.

but picturesque juxtaposition. The basis of the formal repertory and the architectural attitude remained the Gothic. The late Gothic Perpendicular style set the course for the entire Tudor period (1485–1603). This concept is diametrically opposed to the corporeal and plastic emphasis of the Italian Renaissance. Even when the classical orders of columns appear they are treated less as structural articulation of the wall than as a kind of barred screen, functioning often merely as an externally applied décor.

In England too the most important architectural achievements of the sixteenth century belong to the secular realm. When the Wars of the Roses had ended in the long-desired peace, the nobility could retire to the tranquillity of their country-seats without concerning themselves with military defences. Stately residences arose which on occasion accommodated the whole court entourage on its country progresses. Alongside the old nobility a new class of ambitious merchants took their place at the levers of power, seeking to display their newly acquired social status in imposing residences.

A typical example is *Wollaton Hall [589]* in Nottinghamshire built by Robert Smythson in 1580–8. The external aspect is characterized by the dissolution of the wall in great rectangular window openings which are distributed grille-wise following the lead of the Perpendicular style. The middle block which rises in the centre after the precedent of the medieval dwelling tower also has regular Gothic tracery windows. The several stories are separated by a triglyph frieze and by decorative bands. The French mansard roof is lacking; instead of the blind gables and dormer windows with the accompanying overlapping and projecting roof-lines the main building parts conclude here with a continuous balustrade. The forceful upper cornice of Italian palazzi was not adopted in the English Renaissance; moreover the cubic building units lack the massiveness of their southern counterparts. The influence of the Renaissance is most evident in the emphasis on horizontals and in the clarification of the storey zones, as well as in the symmetry of the plan. In fact the ground-plan of Wollaton Hall is new for England. It derives from a prototype in Sebastiano Serlio's architectural treatise; a square building nucleus containing the hall is flanked on either side by a somewhat longer gallery. The four corners are furnished with squat towers so that the frontal views present three planes receding into depth. Noteworthy is the exuberant use of architectural decoration deriving from the formal repertory of continental Mannerism. The majority of the ornamental forms, including the scroll- and strap-work (cf. p. 314), the cartouches and obelisks, must lacked understanding for the architectural significance of the columnar orders. They consort freely on the tower with the other ornamental elements – Gothicizing sculpture, battlements, and crocketed pinnacles.

GERMANY

The sixteenth-century architecture of Germany, together with that of the Low Countries and Scandinavia, has been characterized as a 'decorative art'. This description does in fact reveal something essential about its nature. While Italian architecture steadily developed for two centuries, the German architecture of the same period manifested no consistent evolution of style. Unlike French château architecture, in which the Italian prototypes were subjected to a thoroughgoing transformation, German building was always dependent on external stimuli. In Germany there were no universal artistic personalities such as those of the Italian Renaissance who might have brought about a national architectural style. Building activity lay in the hands of masons, stone-carvers, and joiners. Alongside these trades there slowly arose a class of educated architects free from the bonds of guild obligations, who could find a measure of social acceptance at the various courts. At the same time there came into being the officer-architect, a figure who originally functioned as a fortifications engineer with the option of supplementary duties in the field of castle architecture. Among the architects in the modern sense of the term were also Italians, though no outstanding names can be cited among them.

Apart from cases in which Italian artists undertook entirely new commissions for German patrons (i.e. Residenz in Landshut, 1536), most of the architectural forms of this period were large complexes such as fortresses and castles in which a medieval, usually Gothic core was retained and the new decorative forms imposed upon it from without. Even in new enterprises the situation was not radically different; the building remained substantially indebted to the native tradition, and even in cases where an attempt was made to come to terms with the Renaissance the structure is overlaid with decorative forms. Churches, town-houses, portals, gables, altars, tombs, pulpits, choir stalls, and furniture – even glass vessels and other objects of the minor arts – present the same characteristics. The transmission of decorative forms, which developed in great profusion from a more or less uniform repertory, occurred through the use of column books and ornamental pattern sheets. The spread of ornamental engravings, which provided a

590 Thomas Holt, 'Tower of the Five Orders' of the Bodleian Library, Oxford, 1625. Academically faithful application of a column book within an otherwise Gothic system of decoration.

have been taken from engravings, specifically from the ornamental and architectural engravings of Hans Vredeman de Vries (1527–1604), which were diffused in countless variants. Apart from direct contact with Italian art and Italian immigrant artists, the 'column books' of Serlio, the Flemish ornament engravings, and the French treatises and handbooks constitute the chief sources influential for the Renaissance architecture of Elizabethan England.

An important place belongs to the theoretical preoccupation with the five columnar orders. The North became acquainted with these through Italian publications. The main channels of transmission were the books of Serlio [519] and Vignola. The influence of these works found concrete embodiment in numerous structures, especially in towers. No architect adhered as closely to the rules as Thomas Holt in his *Tower of the Five Orders [590]* of the Bodleian Library in Oxford (1625). Tuscan, Doric, Ionic, Corinthian, and Composite are superimposed as if the illustrations of a column book were arranged one above the other. None the less the decorative system in which the elements are inserted betrays how much Holt

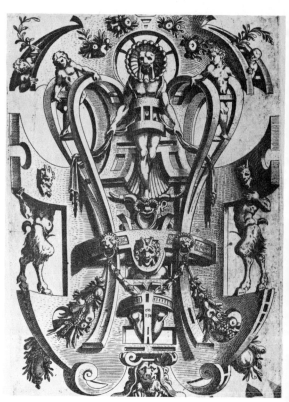

591–594 *The ornament of the early Italian Renaissance stems from two sources: Nature and the Antique. Naturalistic ornament starting with the surrounds of Ghiberti's bronze door [572] plays a noteworthy part in the decorative motifs of the fifteenth and sixteenth centuries, especially in the form of flower and fruit garlands [561, 576]. At the same time, antique ornamentation served as an influential model, first on pillar capitals, then in ribbon and wave-like motifs, in palmettes and acanthus leaves [573]. This partly abstract, partly naturalistic formal vocabulary was combined with figures (lions, centaurs, herms, etc.), a development that culminated in the antiquitizing grotesque rediscovered by Raphael. An example by A. Veneziano of about*

1520 [591] is shown upper left. The arabesque, whose symmetrical and geometrizing linear patterns should be seen as an abstraction of antique foliage shapes, has its origins in Islamic culture. The example shown upper right [592] is by Hans Rudolph Manuel Deutsch, c. 1549. France and the Netherlands during the sixteenth century contributed the scroll-work, where ribbons are looped over one another and terminate in scrolls. The example by Hans Vredeman de Vries shown lower left [593] dates from c. 1560–70. Scroll-work is often combined with metal-work, reminiscent of earlier and superseded forms. Figures such as satyrs or animal heads were often squeezed in between the spaces of these abstract forms: see the example of 1554 by Cornelius Bos [594].

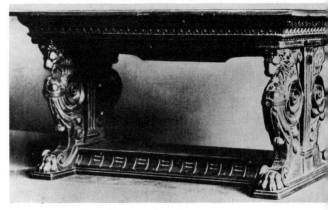

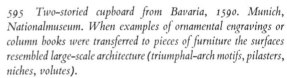

595 Two-storied cupboard from Bavaria, 1590. Munich, Nationalmuseum. When examples of ornamental engravings or column books were transferred to pieces of furniture the surfaces resembled large-scale architecture (triumphal-arch motifs, pilasters, niches, volutes).

596 Two-storied cupboard from France, second half of sixteenth century. A richly plastic composition probably taken from an ornamented engraving influenced by figural motifs: corners and centre carry herms and caryatids. Reliefs of armour and heraldic emblems cover the panels.

597 Side-table from Italy, sixteenth century. Carved volutes with lions' heads and claws support the massive table cover. The traverse and crossing plank are set between heavy covers.

598 Scissor-chair from Italy, sixteenth century. Paris, Musée de Cluny. A rounded form introduced as early as the fifteenth century. The shoulders and carved arms are all of one piece.

599 *Baccio Pontelli, inlay in the 'studiolo' of Duke Federico da Montefeltro, c. 1480. Urbino, Palazzo Ducale. The technique of inlay was practised in order to achieve painterly illusionistic effects, in the early Renaissance particularly the effect of perspective.*

600 *Living-room of the 'Seidenhof' in Zürich, 1592. Zürich, Landesmuseum. A heavily coffered ceiling, carved and inlaid walls with projecting half-columns and aediculae. Coloured tiled stove of 1620.*

601 *Evert and Jonas Wolf, Ceremonial Portal of the Golden Hall in Bückeburg Castle, 1605. Exuberant style of decoration with fine individual motifs in an overladen composition.*

mine of inspiration, was especially important. The decoration could be applied to a church façade *[602]* or a piece of furniture *[595]*. The grotesque *[591]* and the arabesque *[592]*, scroll- and strap-work *[593, 594]*, the cartouche and the obelisk, penetrate into all branches of architecture and the allied arts.

In Renaissance Italy the ornamental elements show a clear relationship to the object to which they are applied *[573, 576]*. With Mannerism, and especially in transalpine work, this unambiguous relationship begins to break down. Abstract forms appear; spatial and two-dimensional patterns combine with the human figure, stylizing it ornamentally. Although Fontainebleau set the tone for this new mode, its most intricate elaborations appeared in Germany: the *Ceremonial Portal of the Golden Hall in Bückeburg Castle [601]* is a characteristic example. The focus of the portal architecture is the cartouche on the door which displays the whole range of elements employed in the scheme as a whole. From this centre the detail spreads over the whole area, leaving no part untouched. The artist has succumbed to a true *horror*

602 *Façade of the town church of Bückeburg, 1611–15. The ground-plan is that of a late Gothic hall church. Buttressed pillars and tracery windows are covered with extravagant Mannerist ornament.*

vacui. An architectonic framework may be discerned only if the spectator succeeds in disregarding the distractions of such profusion and seeks to penetrate beneath the detail.

That this conflict between architectural core and luxuriant décor pertains not solely to exterior architecture is demonstrated by the façade of the *Town Church at Bückeburg [602],* erected between 1611 and 1615. The interior space takes the form of a three-aisled hall church in the late Gothic tradition, with only the Corinthian capitals of the round piers pointing to the Renaissance. The nave is screened off by a towerless pedimental façade, which characteristically represents the unarchitectonic, purely decorative mode of design. The window shapes and the

603, 604 *Friedrich Sustris, façade and interior of S. Michael at Munich, 1582–97. A hall church with side chapels after the model of Il Gesù in Rome. Barrel-vaulted galleries with large windows form a story above the piers. The monumental effect of the interior is not visible in the façade.*

vertical articulation correspond fairly closely to practices familiar from the Gothic. This simple scheme is overlaid in a rich decorative mantle with motifs deriving from contemporary engravings.

Three decades before (1582–97) the Jesuit church of *S. Michael* at Munich *[603, 604]* was begun. Intended as a bulwark of the Counter-Reformation, its architect, Friedrich Sustris (*c.* 1540–99), was a Fleming who had learned his trade in Italy. The destination of the church would lead one to expect a close dependence on the scheme of the Jesuit mother-church in Rome, Il Gesù *[543]*. At first glance the connexion seems self-evident: both buildings belong to the type of the barrel-vaulted, chapel-flanked unified space church. Its wall system, however, reveals an essentially different mode of structural composition. In Il Gesù the wall surfaces over the side chapels constitute the element of space; in S. Michael this function is performed by the wall piers standing perpendicular to the axis of the church. Between the piers stretch galleries, forming individual units perceptible as brightly lit barrel-vaulted upper niches; at the same time they isolate the dark side chapels below. The high vault of the nave is covered by impressive ribbed arches, whose springings provide a decisive conclusion to the enclosing character of the wall. This system, which derives in principle from the late Gothic wall-pier

church, later became dominant in south German Baroque churches.

The *façade of S. Michael [603]* shows an attempt to fuse the German gable front with Roman façade solutions. The result is obviously discordant. Compared with the logical articulation of the façade of Il Gesù *[544]*, one is confronted here with the attractive but naïve effect of joiner's architecture. The two portals, which provide a plastic accent to the otherwise rather flat façade, recall Italy. But the pilasters of the lower story lack all organizing power. They have the same additive quality as the membering of the upper stories. The idea of placing the cornice strips so that they rest only upon a single pilaster at each side makes it evident that the design of this main front is developed as the decoration of surface and not as the manifestation of architectural forces. The impression is of a drawing-board architecture projected with ruler and compass.

The conception that stems from planimetric drawing figures appears at *Freudenstadt [605]* in the guise of an extensive town-planning scheme. When

605   Heinrich Schickhardt, town plan of Freudenstadt, c. 1600. The aerial view shows the concentric right angle of the 'windmill' plan, whose corners are emphasized with higher angle buildings. In the corner in the foreground the town church was built, with rooms that separated the sexes.

Heinrich Schickhardt (1558–1634) designed this own for Protestant refugees from Austria, he placed he streets like beams on the arms of a windmill wheel radiating from the great central market-place. The middle was reserved for a square palace situated diagonally but which was never executed, while the corners of the market-place itself were emphasized with higher angle buildings, including the town hall and the church. It seems certain that the old Roman camp plan lies behind this scheme, even though the Renaissance architect has elaborated the division of the separate quarters in a different geometrical form.

In the field of secular architecture Germany is also characterized by the predominance of château or castle building. Despite some important achievements (Hartenfels Castle at Torgau, Dresden Castle, the Residenz in Munich, Aschaffenburg Castle, etc.), no generally valid national style emerged. The elements in common are confined to decoration. Even the symmetrical ordering of the ground-plan cannot be taken for granted. The various parts of Heidelberg Castle, for example, suggest an accidentally assembled group of individual buildings and not an axially determined, rationally organized system of interdependent structures. Within the complex the present cubic and closed form of the *Ottheinrichsbau [606]*, erected c. 1556–9, is less the result of architectural planning than a product of chance; the steep roof disappeared in the fire of 1689. In the articulation of the Italianizing, clearly stratified façade with its gradation of the heights of the stories, the cultural trend of the period becomes evident. For in this case, as in so many others, writings of architectural theory, pre-eminently those of Serlio, provided the impetus for the princely patron. As an educated layman he must have participated directly in the design, although the question of the architect who collaborated with him cannot be satisfactorily resolved. Perhaps no single individual was responsible. When architecture had become a humane study to be learned from books, one could leave the practical details of building to trained craftsmen and take charge of the higher aspects oneself. It is noteworthy that the façade – apart from the amateurish distortion of Renaissance elements – shows a generally Mannerist quality. Each second pilaster is omitted and replaced by a console beneath the entablature, with the result that the natural functions of load and support seem to have been disturbed. In the place of each omitted pilaster a plain unprofiled niche has been inserted into the wall. These niches shelter a carefully planned group of statues personifying the virtues and the planets. The statues were the work of a Netherlandish sculptor and the rich ornamental carving also

606 *The Ottheinrichsbau of Heidelberg Castle, c. 1556–9. In structural composition and the combination of Italian and Netherlandish effects this is one of the most successful achievements of German Renaissance castle building.*

points to the Low Countries (Cornelis Floris). By virtue of its imaginative reworking of Italian and Netherlandish materials this façade ranks as a showpiece of German Renaissance architecture, even though it proved incapable of establishing a tradition. This is accounted for to a considerable degree by the fact that the German princely courts never reached the inner understanding of artistic development that was achieved in the French royal court.

From the widest standpoint the Northern Renaissance – from Switzerland to the Netherlands and Scandinavia – may be regarded as a middle-class art. Its most extensive building projects rose amid the prosperous towns, in houses and fortifications (ramparts, town walls, gates, and towers) and public buildings (town halls, hospitals, warehouses, and stores). The point of departure was the several-storied house with a high gable. With it the new building attitude first made itself felt in the emphasis on the horizontal which was enhanced by the carving of the decorative forms into the beams of the framework. In the more imposing buildings in stone masonry the

607 *Jakob Wolff the Elder, inner courtyard of the Pellerhaus in Nuremburg, 1605. Despite the application of late Gothic tracery motifs the composition displays an understanding of Italian models.*

native type of the gabled house persisted, richly bedecked with Renaissance decoration. Strong contrasts are exhibited, characterized in the town buildings of the North Sea and the Baltic where the traditional red brick was freely combined with light stone – indicating a painterly rather than a plastic architectural feeling. In outstanding examples, such as the *Pellerhaus in Nuremburg [607]* of 1605 the townhouse reaches a level that reveals throughout the quality and spirit of the Renaissance.

THE LOW COUNTRIES

In the lower Rhine basin, in Holland, and Flanders, where Low German and French influences intermingled, the prosperous towns – Bruges and Ghent, Antwerp and Brussels – had grown into important artistic centres, whose influence radiated as far as Sweden and England. The particular predilection of the Netherlanders was for ornament; this is seen in the work of the sculptor, architect, and ornamental

engraver Cornelis Floris (1514–75). His sets of engravings poured forth from the middle of the century on, with their fanciful enhancement of the Roman grotesques *[591]*. It is noteworthy that the Floris Style shows a mixture of vegetable leaf and rinceau ornament with abstract scroll-work, where strips and ribbons are variously intertwined and rolled up at the ends like leather thongs. They stand out plastically from the background, but strap-work *[593]* – which found a wide diffusion though the pattern books of Floris's pupil Hans Vredeman de Vries (1527–1604), with their straps, ribbons, and prisms suggesting stencilled or sawed forms – remains embedded in the background. This ornamental world is frequently scattered with figural details; buffoons' masks, animal heads, and male and female busts introduce a half-surrealistic, half-demonic quality.

A favourite spot for the display of ornament is the stepped gable of the town-house. An example in Antwerp *[608]* provides a veritable catalogue of the

608 *Residential houses in Antwerp, sixteenth century. The architects covered the gables with rich decoration, as on the neighbouring town hall [609]. With a similar ground-plan to the façade elevation, the separate structures show the development of ornamentation during the sixteenth century.*

609 Cornelis Floris, Town Hall of Antwerp, 1561–5. Strongly influenced by Mannerism, and in decorative richness looking back to Flemish examples, this is a successful adaptation of the contemporary architecture of Italy.

decorative vocabulary of the sixteenth century; its material ranges from the late Gothic to *Knorpelwerk*. Not surprisingly the change is confined to the ornamental formal apparatus, while the concept underlying the structure of all these façades remains the same. In the dissolution of the wall in small glass surfaces enclosed in a trellis-like frame and in the vertical narrowness the houses seem to merge together into a single whole.

Antwerp's *Town Hall* erected in 1561–5 [609] has a special position inasmuch as its builder Cornelis Floris dispensed with excessive decoration, confining himself entirely to a sober articulation *all' antica*. The builder shows a degree of understanding for the spirit of Italian Mannerist architecture that is rare in Germanic lands. But one recognizes at first glance a hall-mark of Northern building in the high roof. The middle of the façade displays a high and narrow frontispiece, whose derivation from the gable house is evident, though its stories are composed in strict accord with Renaissance architectural theory. The carefully adjusted heights of the stories over the rusticated socle zone and the orders of the columns speak the language of the classical architecture of Italy, while the complicated system of the middle portion and the squeezing of the pilasters between the large windows, which leave insufficient wall surface in reserve, are Mannerist features. Buildings near the north German coast such as the Emden Town Hall were influenced by Floris's example in Antwerp. The use of extensive fenestration is a clue to the persistence of the Gothic tradition in this key monument of Flemish Renaissance architecture.

Painting outside Italy

GERMANY

Germany heads the section on non-Italian painting with good reason; in this field the North made its most considerable and creative contribution to the Renaissance. The 'Age of Dürer' describes a period that set in towards the turn of the sixteenth century and lasted several decades only. At this time German painting and the graphic arts enjoyed an astonishing efflorescence, only to revert, before the middle of the century, to provincial mediocrity. The situation in painting was markedly different from that in architecture, where Italian models influenced but did not transform the inner substance of art.

Albrecht Dürer (1471–1528) experienced the encounter with Italy as a personal challenge. He travelled on his own initiative to Venice (1495 and 1505), where he established friendly relations with local artists. He exchanged letters and drawings with Raphael. Like a true Renaissance artist he composed theoretical treatises in which he sought to capture his own views and those of others regarding the artistic process. His fame is founded in the first instance on his graphic work. Approximately 100 engravings and 350 woodcuts that have survived bear witness to his extraordinary achievement in raising these fields to new heights both technically and formally [610]. In his drawings, of which about 900 are preserved, he established a process that led to the autonomy of drawing as an independent branch of art. Apart from numerous studies and sketches ancillary to larger works, many sheets are known which show such self-consistent perfection that they could only have been created for their own sake. Dürer's paintings reveal his delight in rendering states of mind, his affectionate attention to detail, and his penetration of the mysteries of landscape. In a series of splendid portraits, including paintings and drawings of the artist, he succeeded in advancing beyond a faithful account of likeness to a revelation of the inner self. The two panels in Munich with *The Four Apostles* of 1526 [611] show the achievement to which he was spurred by his encounter with Italian art. Against the dark ground stand the monumental forms which Dürer in the years of religious and political turmoil of the Reformation sought to portray as 'Guides to Righteousness', as admonitory witnesses of the true faith. Even in Italy only the greatest masters could hope to realize the ideal of humanity with such consummate success. And in spiritual penetration and individual characterization Dürer seems to surpass the southern masters.

610 Albrecht Dürer, Adam and Eve, copper engraving, 1504. High technical finish. Idealized portrayal of humanity in an atmospheric landscape.

The range of intellectual and formal strength in German painting of the sixteenth century is revealed by a comparison of Dürer's work with the smaller œuvre of Matthias Grünewald (properly Mathis Neithart-Gothart, *c.* 1460?–1528). His work too shows contact with the Renaissance; indeed the *Isenheim Altarpiece* (*c.* 1515) is inconceivable without this. Although Dürer envisioned his goal as formal mastery of the pictorial world with insight into the laws of art providing the regulating force, Grünewald's work contains an almost overpowering expressiveness which often transcends the bounds of mere correctness. In a panel from the Isenheim Altarpiece, *The Hermits Anthony and Paul [612]* converse in a landscape setting that is convincingly constructed from the standpoint of linear and aerial perspective. But every element has its own expressive quality emphasizing the rusticity and poverty of hermit life. The colour, intensifying symbolic values, serves to heighten the expressive content which is here raised to a visionary level.

Another trend in German Renaissance painting is evident in the work of Albrecht Altdorfer (*c.* 1480–1538). Although Altdorfer looks back to Dürer's achievement, as the leading master of the so-called Danube school he created his own style, which displays a romantic magic reminiscent of a fairy-tale within the framework of passionate narration and dramatic use of colour and light. Carefully constructed interiors, evocative ruins, and unconstrained nature provide the backgrounds with whose help Altdorfer transposes reality into fable. With Altdorfer, landscape appears for the first time in European art as an independent branch of painting. One such example is his *Danube Landscape [613]* of *c.* 1520–5, which, omitting any figural 'extras', shows an intense feeling for nature. While landscape in sixteenth-century Italian painting was transposed into a heroic and mythological key and later endowed with cosmic aspirations, the draughtsman-like narrative style of Altdorfer dwells lovingly on every detail: the painter's brush picks out the luminosity of a patch of sunlight, the shadow of a shrub, or the curious quality of a gnarled bough. If Altdorfer frequently depicts a section of landscape, it is that he

611 Albrecht Dürer, The Four Apostles (John and Peter, Mark and Paul), 1526. Munich, Alte Pinakothek. A masterpiece of German Renaissance painting in the intensity of spiritual expression and formal enclosure.

eeks the magic of mood, the all-embracing and the inner image' rather than the monumental effect.

The last great German master of the Renaissance was Hans Holbein the Younger (1498–1543). With his death the powerful upsurge of German painting comes o an end. Holbein was trained as a painter in Augsburg nd Basle. He knew Italy. In England he became ourt painter to the King and a celebrated portraitist. His reputation still rests on his portraits today. The truth to reality he demonstrated in reproducing very detail is paralleled in the portraits produced

612 *Matthias Grünewald, The Hermits Anthony and Paul from the Isenheim Altarpiece, c. 1515. Colmar, Musée Unterinden. Emphasis on expressive shapes and colour. Late Gothic formal elements combine with those of the Renaissance.*

613 *Albrecht Altdorfer, Danube Landscape near Regensburg, c. 1520–5. Munich, Pinakothek. A fully developed landscape without figures, showing an intimate feeling for nature.*

614 *Hans Holbein the Younger, The French Ambassadors at the English Court, 1533. London, National Gallery. The portrait and surrounding details explain the whole existence of the two sitters. Despite the many details the composition is unified.*

by Italian Mannerists. But the joy in narration that he reveals in for example the double portrait of the *Ambassadors [614]* of 1533, with the varied paraphernalia of scholarship and humanistic culture, is un-Italian. The spectator is invited to read the picture at his leisure so as to acquire an objective understanding of the intellectual background of the sitters. Facial expressions have been captured with the same sharpness as the details of dress. This unfettered, unobtrusive truthfulness is combined with a formal discipline acquired from Italy to produce an indissoluble whole.

THE LOW COUNTRIES

In Netherlandish painting, the traditionally sober approach to reality was broken in the 1520s by the new impulse known as Romanism, which combined

615   *Jan Gossaert van Mabuse, Venus and Amor, 1521. Paris, Private Collection. Mabuse, the founder of Romanism, depicted the round niche and naked figure in close dependence on Italian models.*

616   *Bartholomäus Spranger, Minerva Victorious over Ignorance, 1590. Vienna, Kunsthistoriches Museum. An example of the Manneristic style north of the Alps.*

influences of Italian Renaissance art with late Gothic elements, producing a somewhat exaggerated version of early Mannerism. Although such formal innovations as perspective had hitherto served simply as an aid to the mastery of nature, in this new phase the entire Italian achievement was held up as a fashionable dogma. Northern artists schooled themselves in these examples with touching zeal, but the result was usually a kind of virtuoso quotation which lacked any understanding of the inner laws. The formal repertory opened up by Raphael and Michelangelo was systematically exploited. Familiarity with Michelangelo was facilitated by the engravings (1527) of Marcantonio Raimondi, while Raphael's work could be more simply and directly approached through his cartoons for the tapestries in the Sistine Chapel which were sent to ateliers in Brussels for execution (1516–19). In the course of the fifteenth century tapestry working in the southern Netherlands had grown into a real industry whose products, including those of Arras and Brussels, enjoyed a European fame. Although the painting of the Romanists reveals only a moderate native artistic capacity, its creators (Joos van Cleve, Jan van Scorel, Jan Gossaert or Mabuse *[615]*, Maerten van Heemskerck, etc.) contributed to the final destruction of the Gothic tradition and thus helped to prepare the way for the great age of Netherlandish painting in the seventeenth century.

A later generation of Netherlandish painters, including Adrian de Vries, Bartholomäus Spranger, and Abraham Bloemaert, who were all born about the middle of the sixteenth century, came to close terms with Florentine Mannerism. So intimate was their attachment that they have been regarded as straightforward Mannerists like Giorgio Vasari or Giovanni da Bologna. Bartholomäus Spranger (1546–1611), born in Antwerp, went to Vienna, where he served for a time as court painter to Emperor Maximilian II, and then travelled to Prague and the court of Emperor Rudolf II, with whom he was on very friendly terms. In Prague a late but unadulterated Northern Mannerist centre had grown up. Italians vied with Netherlanders and Germans trained in Italy to supply the Hradčany Palace and the

imperial *Kunstkammer* with works of sculpture, painting, and the minor arts, together with all sorts of curiosities. A revealing light is shed on the taste of Rudolf II by his systematic effort to acquire the most important works of Dürer and Pieter Bruegel the Elder. Also active at the court in Prague was the Lombard painter Giuseppe Arcimboldo (1530–93), who created his *capriccio* portraits in which the most unexpected objects were juxtaposed to create the sitter's image. Arcimboldo painted a reclining figure of Autumn composed of produce – fruits and vegetables – with the head representing the features of the Emperor himself.

Among the most important artists at the court were the painters Hans von Aachen and Bartholomäus Spranger, whose pictures teem with learned allusions. Spranger's *Minerva Victorious over Ignorance [616]* of 1590 displays the full scope of the age's interest in allegory; the compositional structure is just as complicated. The goddess takes on the twisting pose of the Mannerist *figura serpentinata*. Behind her the murky space seems to recede into an immeasurable depth. The visual directions indicated by the gazes of the figures are intentionally crossed, and every direct reference to the viewer is avoided. Light and dark alternate abruptly with little transition; the colour scheme is dominated by broken, restless, and iridescent hues.

Netherlandish painting produced one artist who

617   Pieter Bruegel the Elder, The Blind leading the Blind, 1568. Naples, Museo Nazionale. The figures reel along an inclined plane incorporated into the diagonal.

went his own way at a distance from the Romanist development of style. Pieter Bruegel the Elder (1525/30–69) was the greatest painter of the second half of the century north of the Alps. Although his works may be shown to bear a deep-seated inner affinity with Mannerism, this appears only in the most general form of his pictorial work. Bruegel, who discovered the everyday life of the peasantry as an independent artistic theme – hitherto shown only symbolically in medieval cycles of the Labours of the Months [cf. 459] – avoided borrowing Italian motifs, even though he visited Italy in 1553. His almost inexhaustible imagination was nourished by the observation of everyday life. The difference in approach to design is best exemplified in *The Netherlandish Proverbs*. The Renaissance aimed to treat composition as an organic whole even with complicated themes. Bruegel breaks this unity into a multiplicity of colour patches. Their ensemble serves to convey something of the content of the satirical scenes. This art is neither idealizing nor ingenuous; the demonic and the mischievous, the tragic and the grotesque exist in his works side by side. In the *Blind Leading the Blind [617]* of 1568 a chain of blind men follow a fellow-sufferer, who falls into a ditch. The setting, an idyllic landscape, is painted with transparent clarity in Bruegel's characteristic colour scale from brown through green to blue which was to be so influential on into the seventeenth century.

FRANCE

Painting and sculpture in France, like architecture, were closely linked to the royal court which dominated the country's political and cultural life. The stylistic development in these fields was similarly conditioned by the presence of artists summoned from Italy. Until Rosso Fiorentino (1494–1540) introduced Florentine Mannerism into France in 1530, the late Gothic style persisted, though without creative vitality. Painting was a kind of neutral territory where the new artistic attitude could penetrate without hindrance. The focus of radiation for this attitude was the Château of Fontainebleau, where Rosso worked together with Italian, Flemish, and French artists on an elaborate programme of decoration [586]. Two years after Rosso came Francesco Primaticcio (1504–50), who had collaborated with Giulio Romano in the decoration of the Palazzo del Tè in Mantua and had also been considerably influenced by Parmigianino [554]. The Italian impulse in the School of Fontainebleau was further strengthened in 1552 by the arrival of Niccolò dell' Abbate

(1509–71). Among the French members of this circle were the sculptors Goujon [627] and Pilon [626], as well as the painters Jean Cousin (father and son) and Antoine Caron. Many anonymous masters, such as the creator of the famous hunting portrait of Diane de Poitiers, worked alongside these artists.

The painter who created the *Portrait of a Young Woman at her Toilette [618]* in about 1560 is also anonymous. (This painting is ascribed by some to François Bunel the Younger, 1522–95.) In the background, partly screened off by the hanging, a servant-woman kneels rummaging in a chest, a motif deriving from Titian's work. In the foreground the sitter displays her beautiful form, bedecked with splendid jewels. A gossamer-thin veil lies around her shoulders. With an affected gesture she takes a precious ring from her jewel casket. The self-conscious elegance of her attitude, the frivolity with which she sets off her nakedness with jewels, and the mask-like stare dominating her classically chiselled, but expressionless face – especially in the mirror reflection – reveal the picture as unmistakably Manneristic and an example of the

618 *Unknown Master of the School of Fontainebleau, Young Woman at her Toilette, c. 1560. Dijon, Musée. A frivolous and precious attitude; combination of French court art and Mannerism.*

Sculpture outside Italy

The development of Renaissance sculpture outside Italy is concentrated in the German region of the Netherlands and France. Spain and England, although they produced individual works of value, do not present the same consistent evolution of style.

The last quarter of the fifteenth century and the beginning of the sixteenth saw the appearance in German-speaking countries of many talented artists, who produced the last great efflorescence of the Gothic. Where works of this type were influenced by Italian examples, they were for the most part transformed to suit the different needs of the late Gothic style. This effect is especially evident in the borrowing of Renaissance motifs of gesture and movement, which are incorporated in the turbulent profusion of the late Gothic fold style.

In the first decades of the sixteenth century, the broad stream of works stemming from the late Gothic was joined by a considerable number of others in a pure German Renaissance style. The two chief centres were the south German cities of Augsburg and Nuremburg, connected to the Mediterranean by numerous ties of trade and culture. Between 1509 and 1518 Augsburg created the first Renaissance structure of German architecture, the funerary chapel of the Fugger banking family at St Anne's. Architecturally it is a work of the transition; a Gothic basilica has been clothed in a Venetian pilaster order. This building is the setting for a group of sculptural works connected with the names of the most important representatives of the new style. Hans Daucher (1458–1538) created the free-standing 'Mercy Group' on the altar, while Sebastian Loscher (c. 1480–1538) was responsible for the two middle reliefs on the rear arcades which derive from drawings by Dürer. The organ housing was designed by the joiner, ornamental draughtsman, and sculptor Peter Flötner (1490–1546), who later became famous in Nuremburg. A monumental choir screen from the foundry of Peter Vischer the Elder (c. 1460–1529) originally stood in place of the present stone barrier; the screen was later removed to the Nuremburg Town Hall.

The most noteworthy figure in this group is Peter Vischer the Elder. He took part in the most extensive project of the period: the Monument of Emperor Maximilian I (1493–1519) in the Hofkirche in Innsbruck, which was begun in the first decade of the sixteenth century according to a programme devised by the humanist Peutinger. The fate of this project is

619 François Clouet the Younger, Equestrian Portrait of Francis I. Florence, Uffizi. Courtly portraiture to some extent influenced by Holbein, but with less psychological intensity.

French court art in which the sensuousness of the Renaissance was turned to refined eroticism.

Apart from the compact group of foreign and French Mannerists the royal court employed artists who cannot be considered members of the School of Fontainebleau, among them the court painter Jean Clouet (died 1540/1) and his son François Clouet (died 1572), who continued his father's work. Especially evident in the work of the younger Clouet is the cool objectivity of Holbein's art, but without Holbein's inner vitality. In his *Equestrian Portrait of Francis I [619]*, probably executed about 1545, horse and rider are rendered with great fidelity. The small picture plane (10⅝ × 8⅝ ins.) is fully used to represent courtly pomp, and the armour is exhibited as a masterpiece of craftsmanship. While Holbein sought to interpret the intellectual character of his sitters with the aid of the objects introduced into the picture, Clouet adheres to the letter of court ceremony. Only the small head with the calculating eyes hints that the work relates to the wily opponent of Charles V. Portrait painters drew on Holbein's example for many years, but none of them achieved the intensity with which he grasped the personality of his sitters.

characteristic of the undertakings of the Emperor. The commissions did in fact give much encouragement to German art, but energy was dissipated because of the large number of artists employed and the complexities of the iconography. The ancestors and relatives of Maximilian, including Roman emperors and Christian patron saints, were given the leading place in the Innsbruck monument. Forty over life-size statues, 32 busts, and 100 statuettes were envisioned, an ambitious scheme which could only be realized by summoning a great number of artists. When work ceased about 1550 it remained a fragment, suffering a fate similar to though less catastrophic than Michelangelo's Julius Monument. Although the majority of the executed statues derive from conventional late Gothic types, a genuine feeling for the Renaissance appears in the pair of bronze standing figures completed by Peter Vischer the Elder in 1513. The figure of *King Arthur [620]* employs the antique contrapposto with full confidence. We can see the body as a physical reality beneath the richly embellished armour. It is no exaggeration to compare Vischer's

621 *Peter Vischer the Younger, bronze plaquette with Orpheus and Eurydice, 1519. Hamburg, Museum für Kunst und Gewerbe. An example of small-scale sculpture which achieves a great effect in a tiny format.*

620 *Peter Vischer the Elder, bronze statue of King Arthur from the Tomb of Maximilian, 1513. Innsbruck, Hofkirche. An over life-size figure in an heroic, idealizing posture.*

work with the *Colleoni [575]* of Verrocchio. Both figures express the self-confidence of Renaissance man.

Vischer's atelier also produced a great number of small sculptures which were in much demand among German collectors. Medals and plaquettes, portrait busts and statuettes gave even the middle class the opportunity to display a cultivated humanistic taste. As an example of this genre which was practised in other workshops as well (e.g. by Konrad Meit from Worms, active in the Low Countries), one may cite the small plaquette ($6\frac{1}{4} \times 4\frac{1}{4}$ ins.) of *Orpheus and Eurydice [621]* executed by Peter Vischer the Younger (1487–1528) in 1519. The theme of the two nudes is splendidly realized both in the formal mastery and psychological differentiation. The inner monumentality is on the same level as comparable works of the classical art of Italy.

As in the case of painting, Northern sculpture of the second half of the sixteenth century adhered losely to the standards of Italian Mannerism, in the irst instance to the example of Giovanni da Bologna '578]. Like the painters (e.g. Bartholomäus Spranger), he sculptors of this phase were travelling court irtists, free of the narrow craft and guild restrictions hat still held for the generation at the beginning of he century. The most faithful follower of the style of Giovanni da Bologna was Adriaen de Vries (*c.* 1560–626), a pupil of the great Mannerist. De Vries became *Kammerbildhauer* to Rudolf II and executed he Mercury and Hercules Fountains in Augsburg in ι purely Mannerist style. Hubert Gerhard (*c.* 1550–620), his fellow-countryman who also worked in outh Germany, had strong links with Bologna's vorkshop, but retained much of the realism of his iomeland despite a period of study in Italy. This quality is evident in his figure of *Bavaria [622]* of 1595, intended for a fountain in the court of the Munich Residenz. Despite the richness of the siliouette the figure is built up in a series of smoothly iowing movements. The structure of the body,

623 Hubert Gerhard, bronze statue of St Michael, 1588. Munich, façade of church of S. Michael. An over life-size figure group fitted exactly into the round niche, and this in turn squeezed between two pilasters, to form a typical Mannerist ensemble.

622 Hubert Gerhard, Bavaria, 1595. Schleissheim. Note the controlled Mannerist proportions and realistic portrayal of allegorical attributes (ears of corn, barrel of beer).

however, follows the Mannerist ideal of beauty; above the broad hips the narrow shoulders are crowned by a small, delicate head.

Gerhard's greatest enterprise was the decoration of the church of S. Michael in Munich, though much of this has since been destroyed. In the central niche of the façade *[603]*, only a little above the viewpoint of the observer, stands the colossal *Statue of St Michael [623]* of 1588. Over the fiercely writhing figure of the Devil rises the powerful movement of the Archangel. The drapery flutters over his body in nervous folds and the small head with its classically chiselled features is lost in a pile of curls. All these traits belong to the Mannerist repertory.

FRANCE

The chief works of French Renaissance sculpture were produced within a relatively narrow field of endeavour; for the most part they consist of tomb

624 *Roulland Leroux and Pierre d'Aubeaux, Monument of Cardinals Georges I and Georges II d'Amboise in Rouen Cathedral, begun 1515. Two large free-standing sculptures in a background of relief and decorative forms. A combination of Gothic and Renaissance styles.*

embellishments and architectural decorations. Like the popes in Italy and the emperors in Germany, the kings of France placed particular stress on funerary monuments as the most effective means of commemorating their earthly fame. In terms of quantity, however, sculpture on buildings was a much more productive genre. This can only evoke real interest when it rises above the sphere of mere ornament, as does Jean Goujon's work for Lescot's Louvre façade *[585]*. This façade has already been mentioned as an example of the French preference for calm, severe form. A parallel trend may be observed in French sculpture. Here too cool forms are preferred and reason controls any tendency to emotional excess. The French feeling for regularity formed the basis for a characteristic national development, which is as alien to the rhetorical gestures of Italian sculpture as it is to the expressive extravagances of much German sculpture.

In the *Monument of Cardinals Georges I and Georges II d'Amboise [624]*, begun by Roulland Leroux in

Rouen Cathedral in 1515, the medieval heritage of Claus Sluter's portal sculptures for the Chartreuse of Champmol (late fourteenth century) is still effective in the two kneeling figures. As in contemporary architecture, this marble wall tomb combines a profuse array of decorative forms of the new style with elements surviving from the traditional Gothic, a characteristic situation for the early stage of the French Renaissance.

The *Monument of Francis I [625]* in the abbey church of St-Denis, the Pantheon of the French kings, represents the transition to the classical stage. The architecture of the monument, which was conceived by Philibert de l'Orme as a restatement of the medieval tomb type in the new style, is based on the triumphal-arch motif, executed with remarkable proportional subtlety. The King is shown with the same cool objectivity as in the equestrian portrait by François Clouet *[619]*.

Another calm and tranquil witness of the French classical trend is the marble monument *[626]* carved

625 *Philibert de l'Orme, Monument of Francis I, designed 1547. St-Denis, Abbey Church. Note the antique triumphal-arch motif in the middle arch of the sarcophagus. The kneeling figures on the platform are those of the King and his family.*

(1510–68). He carved the *Caryatids [627]* bearing the musicians' gallery of the great hall of the Louvre (1550–1). The delicate, richly ornamented entablature reveals a thorough knowledge of the antique. The extraordinary precision of the execution shows considerable patience. Such details demonstrate the rational order and intellectual discipline that are the motive forces of this art, so close in its spiritual attitude to the high Renaissance in Italy. But the caryatids' stance is stylized into a pose of cool classicism combining decorative elegance and idealizing elevation. The thin folds of the drapery are of a precision far removed from the Baroque and recall Greek reliefs rather than Roman art. In 1563 the Protestant Goujon found himself obliged to flee from an intolerant France and sought refuge in Catholic Bologna. Here all trace of him is lost. Italy, dedicated as it was to Mannerism, seems to have offered no opportunity for an artist who above all others personified the French spirit in the art of the sixteenth century.

627 *Jean Goujon, caryatids in the musicians' gallery of the great hall of the Louvre, 1550–1. A high point of the classical epoch of French Renaissance sculpture.*

626 Germain Pilon, The Three Graces bearing an urn containing the heart of Henri II, 1559. Paris, Louvre. A closed composition, expressing aloof spirituality and chill idealizing forms.

in 1599 by Germain Pilon (*c.* 1536–90). This work shows *The Three Graces* bearing on their heads an urn containing the heart of King Henri II. Chronologically the monument belongs to the period of Mannerist domination. But it seems inappropriate to compare this work with the creations of a Bartholomäus Spranger or a Giovanni da Bologna. Although certain relationships of detail may be discerned, the inner balance of the figures with their elegant drapery is characteristically French. The bodies seem informed by the breath of life, but the restrained spirituality avoids the impression of immediate sensuousness communicated by Italian works. An impalpable veil of inaccessibility seems to separate the observer from these figures. The French sense of form adjusts the sensuous figure to a compositional pattern.

The most important representative of the classic stage of French Renaissance sculpture is Jean Goujon

The Baroque is a dynamic art. Action and pathos, appealing to the observer's emotional participation, determine its character. Through the impassioned agitation of motifs and boldness of formal means the picture and statue draw the viewer out of his self-isolation, while architecture captivates him through a lavish profusion of squares, avenues, ramps, portals, staircases, and spatial vistas. Reception halls, garden rooms, and staircases are the most important considerations for the plan of the Baroque château. They provide a festive setting for the events in which the age reached its apogee – processions, ballets, operas, and festivals.

The Baroque love of movement expressed itself in contrasts between large and small, near and distant forms, between concave and convex, dark and light. But these contrasts were subsumed into a higher unity: synthesis is a Baroque ideal. The individual work of art almost always aspires to association with other works, and the separate branch to merge with other branches. Under the leadership of architecture, which regained the pre-eminence it had enjoyed in the Middle Ages, painting, sculpture, decoration, and garden planning were brought together. This development brought forth a new type of artist who was at once architect, painter, sculptor, and decorator. The prototype is personified by Gian Lorenzo Bernini, who became the arbiter of all artistic questions throughout Europe.

In his attempt to blur the boundary between appearance and reality the Baroque artist transcended the representation and transformation of visual truth. The means at his disposal were manifold. They included illusionistic effects in easel paintings, shifts from painting to sculpture in Baroque stucco-work, the use of natural light in sculptural ensembles, perspectival illusion in architecture, and surprising reflexion effects in Baroque gardens and mirror rooms. The goal that was sought was a heightened sense of reality in which the natural and the miraculous fuse into a great whole. This aim finds its culmination in the Baroque theatre.

628 Egid Quirin Asam, S. Georg in the choir of the monastery church of Weltenburg, 1717–21. The dragon slayer is presented dramatically, as if in a theatre. Opposing light from concealed windows creates a 'sacred sphere' and complete illusion. Twisted columns, flower garlands, and graduated profile enliven the architecture.

The term Baroque seems to result from a combination of two etymological sources, the Portuguese *baroco*, 'irregular pearl', and the Italian *barocco*, 'a type of logical syllogism'. Like the term 'Gothic', it was originally employed as a pejorative epithet in the sense of 'bizarre', or 'anarchic'. It is now used to describe the period beginning at the end of the sixteenth century and reaching into the eighteenth, when it was developed and carried over, chiefly in painting and decoration, into the Rococo. The heart of the Baroque lies in Italy and the countries influenced by it, though Baroque principles of design are none the less fundamental for the local styles of the Northern countries.

In the narrower sense, the concept of the Baroque is not applicable to all the artistic manifestations of the period. Seventeenth-century France developed a characteristic classicism, and the art of the Netherlands, North Germany, and especially England show strong classicistic leanings.

Politically and socially the age was dominated by a system of secular and ecclesiastical absolutism, whose outstanding representative was the *Roi Soleil*, Louis XIV (1638–1715). His great château at Versailles is indeed the symbol of the centralized State and could not have arisen without this concentration of power. Between four and five thousand workmen were employed on occasion at Versailles. The embodiment of power in a single individual found its justification in the doctrine of kingship by divine right; the king was God's deputy on earth. Associated with this was the ideal of the hero of classical antiquity, for Baroque culture in general was imbued with a love of allegory, a splendid intellectual manipulation of humanistic, antique, and Christian systems of ideas.

Not only the great rulers but also the numerous lesser and petty princes were inspired by the dream of absolutism, which they strove to realize in vast château layouts. This is especially true of Germany, a country which lacked a central power and was split into many small States. A new class of patrons arose among the great bourgeoisie in the Protestant Northern Netherlands, which in 1648 after its war of liberation finally consolidated its political, religious, and economic independence under a republican form of government. The Southern Netherlands remained under the rule of the Spanish monarchy, which also extended its influence from its possessions of Naples and Sicily through much of Italy. The greatest patrons were the popes, especially Paul V (1605–21), Urban VIII (1623–44), Innocent X (1644–55), and Alexander VII. Throughout most of the seventeenth century Rome remained the great European art centre, the goal of countless architects, sculptors, painters, and connoisseurs of all countries who came to study and admire – apart from the antique works – Raphael, Michelangelo, and the Rome of the popes. Artists returning to their homeland and travelling Jesuit fathers contributed to the world-wide diffusion of the Roman Baroque. The festive and triumphant qualities of this style, its intoxicating pomp and luxury, made it an effective instrument in the Jesuit propagation of the Counter-Reformation.

Although Spain was introduced to the Baroque by Italian artists of the second rank, it soon succeeded in freeing itself from this tutelage. As the royal power declined, the Spanish Golden Age, the *Siglo de Oro*, reached its zenith in poetry and painting. At the same time, and after the execution of King Charles I, England under Cromwell became the leading Protestant power of Europe.

The seventeenth-century national variants of style began to draw closer together in the century of the Enlightenment. The newly enriched bourgeoisie advanced to the foreground of patronage as the old links with the Church and the great princely courts gradually loosened.

The foundations for the Rococo were laid as early as *c.* 1700, in the late Louis Quatorze style. This was followed by the short Régence period (until *c.* 1725), by the Louis Quinze style of the 1750s, and the Louis Seize. The term Régence refers to the regency of Philippe of Orléans (1715–23) during the minority of Louis XV. The stylistic period of Louis Quinze did not last until the end of the reign in 1774, for the artistic phase known as Louis Seize begins in the last years of Louis XV's reign. The Rococo, by and large identical with the Louis Quinze, takes its name from *rocaille* (shell-work) and is purely French in origin. Rococo forms abroad, including the South German Rococo, are either direct French importations or special local variants (*Sonderrokoko*).

We may extend these stylistic terms derived from the French reigning monarchs to Europe outside France, for French art and manners were accepted in this century as models of absolute validity. While the Louis Quatorze style of Versailles was a public style in its purest form, striving towards elevation and idealization of reality, the more intimate Rococo sought to transform reality into a lyrical key. Rococo is the style of a social group and not that of a court. After the death of the aged *Roi Soleil* the creative spirit left Versailles. Paris became the political and artistic centre. Freed from the obligations of court ceremonial, idle nobles with their favourites, rich financiers, poets, philosophers, and artists flocked to the elegant salons. The smaller Parisian city palace, the *hôtel particulier*, succeeded Versailles. Here taste and fashion were decreed and the consciously modern style of the *rocaille* was formed, the elegant and playful interior decoration of a society whose whole effort was directed towards the highest refinement of the pleasures of life.

The Rococo of France manifested itself almost exclusively in secular works: in the decoration of palaces, in gardens, in portraiture, and in a kind of painting with the light and joyful character of an earthly paradise. In South Germany the originally wholly secular Rococo was allowed unhindered access to churches, thereby creating the magnificent efflorescence of late Baroque church art. In all other lands Rococo forms were restricted to the margin of the artistic stage.

629 Carlo Maderna, S. Susanna in Rome, 1596–1603. The flat, towerless church façade was already customary in Italy; the Baroque created from this an architecture of columns, pilasters, and aediculae together with triumphal arches. The balustrade is a new motif.

Architecture

ITALY

The high Baroque in Rome

The European Baroque is uniquely indebted to the city of Rome. Here, at the focus of the greatest concentration of spiritual power in the Catholic world, there arose the artistic undertakings that were to leave a decisive imprint on the architecture of the age. The strict discipline of the Church organizations, especially the Jesuit Order, made for a rapid diffusion of new ideas. The mother-church of the Jesuit Order, Il Gesù in Rome (1568–75) [cf. 543], designed by Vignola, was the prototype for countless later churches. In Il Gesù the long-standing conflict between the central and the longitudinal scheme found its resolution. The nave and the domed central structure are joined together harmoniously in one and the same building.

The elaboration of centralized motifs and the establishment of the principle of subordination replacing the earlier co-ordination were equally important for secular architecture. All rooms of the palace, which was laid out as symmetrically as possible, were related to the *salone*, the great ceremonial hall. Even more imposing were the staircases, which later in the eighteenth century as a setting for festive receptions, especially in Germany [652], provided a setting for spatial display on a vast scale. The building complex became a plastic whole, dominated by a strong central emphasis – the light-filled dome in the church, the central pavilion in the palace and castle. A continuous flow of movement gathered up all the elements of the building in a rhythm most evident in the centre.

Rome was the scene of these developments, although for the most part the architects there were

630 Pietro da Cortona, S. Maria della Pace in Rome, 1656. The façade is distinguished by flanks set back from the centre. The contrast between convexes in the tempietto-like vestibule [cf. 526] and the concaves on the wings are repeated in the upper story of the central section.

631 Francesco Borromini, S. Carlo alle Quattro Fontane, Rome. Every form is separate on the façade, begun 1667. The ground story runs in a concave–convex–concave line, thus emphasizing the centre. On the lighter upper story three concave divisions are placed together in a row.

north Italians rather than Romans. Carlo Maderna (1556–1629), who came from the Ticino, was a pioneer of forcefully articulated Baroque church façades. *S. Susanna [629]*, S. Andrea della Valle, and St Peter's exhibit fully plastic columns with strongly projecting entablatures set back at intervals producing lively contrasts of light and shadow.

The Roman Baroque was at its height between 1630 and 1670. In this period three outstanding architects shaped its development: Giovanni Lorenzo Bernini, Pietro da Cortona, and Francesco Borromini. The Cavaliere Bernini (1598–1680) was the Papal architect and personifies, both in the eyes of his Italian contemporaries and of posterity, the style of the period in its full surge of emotion and ceremony. He brought together architecture, painting, sculpture, and decoration in a homogeneous system *[632]*. With the integration of light into the architectural conception, light acquires a formal and symbolic role for the first time since the Gothic period.

Pietro da Cortona (1590–1669) from Tuscany exploited the fertile innovation of the convex-curved façade. The projecting semicircular front

632 Giovanni Lorenzo Bernini, Scala Regia of the Vatican, 1660–70. Masterly extension of the oblique ground-plan. The colonnaded main stairway tapers off into 'accelerated perspective'.

[630] of *S. Maria della Pace* (1656) forms the centre-piece of a five-cornered piazza design, foreshadowing Bernini's later envelopment of the façade of St Peter's in an elliptical colonnade. This interpenetration of free space and architecture is especially evident in palatial country-seats and their generously large gardens.

In the work of the north Italian Francesco Borromini (1599–1667), the most individual of the three great architectural geniuses active in Rome, these Baroque forms acquire their boldest and most dramatic development. The façade (begun in 1667) of the small church of *S. Carlo alle Quattro Fontane [631]*, enlivened with niches and sculptures, mirrors the effect of the complex movement of the curving elements of the interior, which Borromini had designed some thirty years before at the beginning of his career *[633, 634]*. Borromini's new architectural idiom, confused as it may appear on first acquaintance, is in fact the result of careful architectural considerations.

Tuscany maintained a very reserved attitude towards the Baroque. Venice's contribution culminates in the volute-crowned central-plan church of S. Maria della Salute (1631–56) of Baldassare Longhena (1598–1682). Genoa, with its city palaces

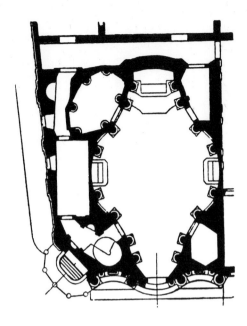

633, 634 *Francesco Borromini, view of the interior and ground-plan of S. Carlo alle Quattro Fontane, Rome, 1638–41. A combination of a longitudinal and centralized structure. Although the ground-plan is constructed geometrically from segments of an ellipse, the space seems free and open.*

635 *Filippo Juvara, Palazzo Madama at Turin, 1718–21. The French influence is evident in the flat, precisely decorated relief of the façade. The slightly projecting centre between slightly recessed walls creates an independent spatial zone.*

636 *Filippo Juvara, pilgrimage church of La Superga near Turin, 1716–31. A classicistic pillared hall with playful Rococo turrets – all the elements depend on the massive rotunda to give unity to the building. The strength of Baroque composition is still evident.*

incorporating columnar halls and broad flights of steps, developed a special form which is rather classic in detail, though its penetrations and overlappings provide a confusingly rich spatial image. In Piedmont a second important centre grew up in the wake of the fantastic creations of the Theatine father Guarino Guarini (1624–83). Guarini's central-plan churches are characterized by a complex play of geometric forms with spiralling vaults supported by a net of interlacing ribs. Clusters of light stream through great windows, recalling the effects of the Islamic mosques of Spain. In Lecce in Apulia a number of curious structures arose between 1650 and 1700, combining Spanish decorative elements with Roman Baroque forms.

Classicism in the late Baroque

In the age of the Rococo the Italian fusion of antique and Baroque monumentality remained so strong that only a few individual Rococo forms found a place for themselves. In about 1700 a classicistic trend began to assert itself amid the multiplicity of current architectural forms. At first there were only elements, individual forms culled from older styles, which were combined by the great masters in a highly original manner. Broadly

637   Luigi Vanvitelli, Palazzo Reale at Caserta, 1752–74. In the hard-edged profiles and splendour of this staircase classicism is more in evidence than Rococo. Cruciform though diagonal sources of light in the domed space.

and Austrian structures. The bright interior space of the church is developed according to a complicated central plan with a high dome and a deep columnar porch. Behind, two flanking towers with Baroque cupolas effect the transition to the dwelling blocks.

With the evident intent of surpassing Versailles, Luigi Vanvitelli (1700–73) laid out the *Royal Palace of Caserta* (begun 1752) in vast dimensions *[637]*. The square block of the palace with its 1,200 rooms is broken by four courtyards and bisected by a long open gallery leading from the street front to the garden side with its two-mile-long park. In the centre the imposing staircase with its intriguing vistas leads through ever-varied vaulted passageways which dissolve like mirrors into the distance. This highly calculated plan based on specific optical effects betrays a direct influence from stage design – the architectural schemes for stage settings which found their supreme examples in the works of the masters of the Bibiena family of Bologna and which in the eighteenth century exercised increasing ascendancy over permanent monumental architecture.

speaking the first half of the eighteenth century exhibits a tendency towards increase in scale, severe geometrization of the overall plan, and a certain stiffening of the plasticity of the high Baroque.

The spirit of the Rococo in Rome achieved momentary expression in a few works such as the elegant concave and convex sequence of the Spanish Steps (1723–5). But the only slightly later façade at S. Giovanni in Laterano (from 1732) by Alessandro Galilei (1691–1736), compared to its prototype, the façade of St Peter's in Rome, presents a stiff juxtaposition of hard stereometric forms altogether lacking the plastic vitality of the high Baroque.

The last flowering of Baroque forms in Italy took place not in the artistically exhausted setting of Rome, but in Piedmont in the works of Filippo Juvara (1678–1736). The imposing façade of his *Palazzo Madama*, 1718–21 *[635]*, employs motifs from Versailles, but the proportions are reduced and the overall effect is more tense and compact. The powerful *piano nobile* (main story) becomes the decisive element, and the horizontal extension of the composition is focused on the projecting four columns in the centre. Just outside Turin upon a steep mountain stands the majestic pilgrimage church of *La Superga*, 1716–31 *[636]*, which in its combination of church and monastery closely parallels contemporary German

SPAIN

It is difficult to speak of a specifically Spanish Baroque architecture of the seventeenth century. There was no great master and the lesser architects of the more active artistic regions of Castille, Andalusia, and Valencia were slow to advance beyond the classic sobriety of the Herrera Style *[cf. 588]* with the aid of Baroque forms taken from Italy and Flanders. Pilasters and columns acquired plastic volume, the vaults were opened up in large windows, and light and shadow contrasts were increasingly emphasized. Although progressive architects adopted the scheme of Il Gesù *[543]* in Rome for the interiors of Spanish and Portuguese churches, the façade designs show considerable uncertainty. The wall and the decoration are not unified and the surface-filling forms are only applied, a tendency typical of earlier periods of Spanish architecture. Often a two-tower façade of medieval derivation embraces a flat west front preceded by the columnar framework of the Italian two- or three-story façade.

Buildings of a specifically Spanish character appear only with José Benito Churriguera (1665–1725) and his circle. The decoration of façades *[638]* undulates in a manner recalling the Plateresque Style *[cf. 442]* in a restless overlay of columns, portals, windows, pediments, and towers. In the work of those who continued the Churriguera Style in the early eighteenth century there appears a special form of the Rococo in which the decorative again predominates. It transforms both exterior and interior walls and erects altarpieces of deceptive height employing fantastic combinations of marble, wood, stucco, and colour [639].

GERMANY

Italian influences in the early Baroque

The Thirty Years War greatly retarded the growth of the Baroque in Germany. At the very beginning of the seventeenth century there were some attempts to overcome the tendency to small-focus composition and the serial or layered scheme by introducing the Baroque principle of fusing all details into a totality of plastic monumentality. Thus in the *Augsburg Town Hall* (1615–20) by Elias Holl (1573–1646), the horizontals of the Renaissance are broken by the energetic vertical emphasis of the middle portion [640]. After the upheaval of war the power and

638 *Casas y Novoa, façade of the cathedral of Santiago y Compostela, begun 1738. The front is extended beyond the two medieval towers, and connected to them only by applied ornament. Despite the great richness, strict arrangement is evident.*

639 *L. de Apévalo and F. M. Vasquez, sacristy of the Carthusian monastery of Granada, 1727–64. As at Santiago de Compostela [638] the delicacy and lightness of space is the effect of the decoration.*

640 *Elias Holl, Augsburg Town Hall, 1615–20. A monumental, block-like structure, with a massive façade. The sides of the many-storied central portion resemble wings.*

importance of the cities and the burghers were eclipsed. The new patrons were territorial princes, especially the princes of the Church and the high nobility. Foreign architects took the lead: in the Protestant North – from Westphalia to Königsberg – the Netherlanders, in the Catholic South – from Vienna to the Lake of Constance – the Italians. The religious division into a Northern and a Southern Baroque style remained decisive for Germany right into the following period.

A sober classicism characterized the North German congregational churches. Answering to the needs of the Protestant service, a number of variants of the centrally unified spatial scheme were produced – square, elongated octagon, Greek cross, and rotunda plans [645]. In the South the type deriving from S. Michael in Munich [cf. 604] dominated, a single nave with barrel-vault. Lateral piers forming cross-walls masked off spaces for chapels, above which small galleries were sometimes disposed. The façade

641   *Agostino Barelli and Enrico Zuccalli, Theatine church in Munich, begun 1663. Erected by Barelli and Zuccalli as a hall space with side chapels and a flat transept, and decorated in white stucco by Perti, this building became a model for South German artists.*

642   *Andreas Schlüter, south front of Berlin Castle, 1698–1706. A façade solution in which both Italian influences and deliberate monumentality are evident.*

wall running in one plane was usually flanked by twin towers, a motif deriving from the Middle Ages. In the North the white unfrescoed interiors were enlivened with modest stucco ornaments. The South German church interior, however – for instance the Theatine church at Munich (begun in 1663 by Barelli and Zucalli) – displays an overflowing profusion of heavy acanthus and fruit garlands, among which play energetic Baroque putti, laden with allegorical attributes [641]. Towards the end of the seventeenth century German architects again came to the fore. They initiated a notable phase of activity running through two generations when Italian and French influences were blended with native motifs. In Austria French classicism was fused with the Italian Baroque forms of Borromini; in Berlin, Saxony, and Westphalia the classicism of Dutch buildings played a large role; from Bohemia, Guarini's curving walls and interpenetrating spatial units were brought by the Dientzenhofer family to Franconia; and in the area of the powerful princely family of the Schönborns in the Rhineland and in

643 *Jakob Prandtauer, Benedictine foundation at Melk on the Danube, 1702–16. The natural site is turned to advantage: church, imperial hall, and library are grouped in an impressive ensemble on the top of the ridge.*

644 *Johann Fischer von Erlach, Collegiate church at Salzburg, 1696–1707. The vaulting of the façade is achieved through the modelled structure; the wall elevation remains flat, anticipating the architectural features of German Rococo.*

645 *Georg Bähr, Frauenkirche at Dresden, 1726–38. A Protestant preacher's church built by the city joiner, whose daringly constructed dome rises out of the four-sided lower parts regardless of classical rules.*

Franconia, French influences remained strong. The Swabian churches adhered to the type of the wall-pier church [cf. *604*]. In Bavaria, however, the Italian and French influences were quickly assimilated and majestic building forms at times reminiscent of folk-art decoration were developed.

The outstanding masters of the early phase are in Berlin Andreas Schlüter (1660/4–1714), and in Austria Johann Fischer von Erlach (1656–1723) and Johann Lukas von Hildebrandt (1688–1745), whose work shows a transition to Rococo [*650*]. Roman grandeur is evident in the severely monumental *Berlin Castle* (1698–1706) by Schlüter, over whose classicist-ically plain socle zone a powerful colossal order rises [*642*]. In Salzburg, a little before, appeared the *Collegiate Church* (1696–1707) by Fischer von Erlach with a strongly plastic façade curving forward and flanked by lateral towers, forming a prototype for numerous other church façades [*644*] such as that of S. Charles Borromeo in Vienna, while the concave front of the Trinity Church in Salzburg is more sober.

the most impressive examples of this type of a powerful fortress-like monastery complex *[643]*. In the following period the designer's imagination turned increasingly towards the interior. Numerous churches built around 1730, especially in the South, have exterior walls and portals enlivened only with flat articulation while the interiors combine a complex variety of spatial forms with great decorative richness. The oval-plan interior, the conscious result of the longitudinal and centralized schemes, comes to the fore. In the beginning pure forms were still preferred, frequently combined in an additive manner. Soon, however, curving walls were in fashion and ceilings were opened up in illuministic vistas of the heavens. Piers were placed diagonally and spatial design disclosed complicated conjunctions of round, rectangular, and oval forms, most evident in the curves and angles of the vault zone.

The greatest master of these late Baroque spatial forms is Balthasar Neumann (1687–1753) who created his churches of *Vierzehnheiligen [648]* and

648   Balthasar Neumann, pilgrimage church of Vierzehnheiligen in upper Franconia, 1743–72. The interior has no recognizable wall; no two vaulted bays are alike. The altar of grace in the centre of the nave was designed by J. J. Küchel in 1763.

646, 647 Johann Michael Fischer, view of the interior and ground-plan of the monastery church of Rott am Inn, 1759–63. Late Rococo: the dome fresco has a circular shape; every arcade is independent, and the Rococo work is concentrated in the cartouches.

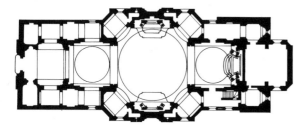

Churches and Palaces of the high and late Baroque

After 1700 Germany and Austria were infected by a veritable passion for building. Spiritual and temporal lords, great and small landed princes competed in building monasteries, castles, town palaces, and pilgrimage churches. A special characteristic of German monasteries is the linkage of residential blocks with the church building. The Benedictine foundation of *Melk* (begun 1702 by Jakob Prandtauer), rising high above the rocks of the Danube, is one of

650 Johann Lukas von Hildebrandt, Upper Belvedere in Vienna, 1721–3. The castle, built for Prince Eugène, is a combination of various pavilions. A line of buildings on similar axes is therefore avoided and instead the effect is of cheerful lightness.

649 Dominikus Zimmermann, triforia in the choir of Wies church. The whole interior space is filled with confused and blossoming Rococo forms. Ornament and architecture, sculpture and painting are hardly distinguishable.

651 Matthäus Daniel Pöppelmann, wall pavilion of the Zwinger at Dresden, 1711–22. The whole plan is conceived as a festive tilt-yard – the pavilion is one of the onlookers' areas, while some of the sculptural decoration is given over to representations of Greek divinities.

Neresheim, two high points of the South German Rococo, by exploiting the principles of spatial interpenetration developed in Bohemia. The Bavarian variants of this church architecture incline to over-emphasize decorative qualities, though here too spatial problems play a large role. In the *Wies* church of 1746–54 *[649]*, the masterpiece of Dominikus Zimmermann, the classical architectural elements – columns, capitals, entablatures – abandon all clarity of form and weightiness of mass and are drawn into the curving walls where they are overlaid with complicated ornament. Plastic and decorative motifs absorb capitals, arches, and entablatures and realize all the latest implications of the S-curve so favoured by the Rococo.

The late German Baroque, especially the church buildings of South Germany, cannot be understood as architecture alone. More than in any other period the individual arts – architecture, sculpture, and ornament – find their meaning and effect only in inter-relationship. In Johann Michael Fischer's (1691–

652   *Balthasar Neumann, staircase of Schloss Augustusburg at Brühl, 1743–8. A very simple architectonic spatial plan. The upper galleries and ingenious decoration enhance the splendour of the staircase.*

1766) late work, the church in *Rott am Inn*, 1759–63, *[646, 647]* the flow of imaginative forms begins to weaken. The centralized spatial units are no longer integrated but stand side by side in relative isolation. The ceiling frescoes have clearer divisions and the stucco ornament is confined to a few important points. A new spatial ideal heralding the rise of Neo-Classicism is announced. Castle building also enjoyed a tremendous flowering after 1700. As in France, architects erected enormous stables and orangeries for exotic plants. Architecture was set in the vegetable vastness of great garden tracts *[674]* with imposing aquatic effects. The *Zwinger* in *Dresden* (begun 1711) by Matthäus Daniel Pöppelmann (1662–1736) is the extreme example of an architecturally framed outdoor setting for festive occasions, in which the boundaries between great building complexes and decorative small-scale architecture are completely effaced *[651]*.

The example of Versailles was reinterpreted in the eighteenth century on a smaller, more human scale.

Replacing the serious and dignified colonnades, statues – niches and sculpture – bounded the portals, and gayer, more fanciful Régence and Rococo ornament enlivened windows and doors, led upwards in herm pilasters, expressed itself in the vase forms of the balustrades and deprived the flat pediments of their solemnity. A loosening of the severe rhythm of French window compositions was achieved through the insertion of the mezzanine, an inter-story with small squarish windows, between the main story and the upper zone. In the interior organization the *sala terrena* was often introduced, a grotto-like room with an earthen floor linking the gardens to the entrance vestibule. The high points of the German Baroque are the monumental staircases of castles and monasteries. Balthasar Neumann built such staircases in Würzburg, Bruchsal, and *Brühl [652]* as festive spaces of enormous proportions, in which single and double stairs connected by luxuriously appointed Rococo landings rise from the vestibule to the reception hall. Light streams through many large windows; stucco ornament, sometimes white, sometimes coloured, covers all the wall surfaces, and the ceilings display the painted worlds of allegory.

THE SOUTHERN NETHERLANDS (FLANDERS)

While the Protestant northern half of the Netherlands treated Italian forms with marked reserve, in Flanders the Roman Baroque was consciously sanctioned from the religious standpoint and was received as the Catholic style. But in practice Roman prototypes were handled in a markedly decorative fashion; individual forms were detached from their original context and the plastic elements dissolved in a painterly play of light and shade. Despite the evident enjoyment of ornaments liberally employed the Baroque organization of architecture as a rationally disposed building mass was not understood and the building forms remained essentially arrested at the Renaissance stage.

In church architecture the Jesuits set the prevailing tone; here again the majority of the buildings stand in the line of succession to the Roman mother-church of Il Gesù. At the same time, however, Gothicizing tendencies survived, as in other parts of Europe outside Italy. The *Jesuit church in Louvain* (1650–66) by Father Willem Hesius (1601–90) must be regarded as a showpiece of Flemish Baroque *[653]*. The enormous vertical of the central bay with its slender columns rises to the complex broken entablatures. As a counterweight to this bold ascent the attic is laden with heavy decoration.

653 Willem Hesius, Jesuit church of S. Michael at Louvain, 1650–66. The façade is a showpiece of Flemish Baroque: steep elevation, lively decoration; even the columns and pilasters become ornamental motifs.

654 Guild-halls in the Grand' Place at Brussels, c. 1700. An example of self-assured Brabant architecture with its enthusiasm for crude, irregular decoration. (Below.)

The effusiveness of Jesuit architecture is somewhat toned down in secular buildings, which in the guild-halls of powerful craft associations acquire a palatial luxury. The vast surfaces given to windows of the guild-halls built between 1696 and 1720 on the *Grand' Place in Brussels [654]* leave little scope for plastic façade articulation. Much more noticeable is the overflowing vitality of the rich ornament which develops in the wall parts remaining between the windows and especially in the gable zone. The realistic motifs of this ornament, with its sometimes comic sometimes spectral imagery, recalls the decoration of medieval cathedrals.

THE NORTHERN NETHERLANDS (HOLLAND)

After the predominantly Calvinist northern provinces had separated from the Catholic South (Flanders) in the Union of Utrecht (1579) the latent sobriety of the Northern Netherlands favoured the emergence of a classicistic art. This is to be distinguished from genuine classicism inasmuch as classicistic art tends to adopt and combine historical styles in a more or less eclectic fashion. The Dutch classicistic art that emerged in the first half of the seventeenth century spread outside the country's borders into North Germany, the Baltic Lands, and England.

Despite strict adherence to the principle of the plane and the exclusion of any Baroque plastic features (not a single column is used) the overall design of the *Mauritshuis* (1633–5) in The Hague by Jacob van Campen (1595–1657) still follows the Baroque principle of subordination *[655]*. The central part of the façade projects very slightly to provide a dominant motif crowned by an antique temple pediment. A colossal order of flat pilasters envelops the building on all sides. Short antiquitizing garlands placed between the windows constitute the sole plastic motif. Van Campen's second major undertaking, the *Amsterdam Town Hall*, begun in 1648 *[656]*, is the outstanding monument of Dutch classicism. Here too the centralizing scheme appears. In plan the building is a long rectangle with a central hall, expressed on the exterior by means of forceful

655   *Jacob van Campen, Mauritshuis at the Hague, 1633–5. Carefully planned proportions and strict organization contributed to the dignified impression. Elements of the Southern Baroque are avoided.*

656   *Jacob van Campen. Town Hall at Amsterdam, 1648–1700. Dutch classicism here achieves monumental expression. A broad middle section and smaller side pavilions articulate the two stories.*

projection of a rectangular central block, the corners being marked by four slightly projecting pavilions. A severe colossal order of pilasters frames the rectangular windows and the short garland motifs. The core of the building is the great hall in the centre comprising two stories, in which the fusion of architecture, sculpture, and painting creates a noteworthy example of Baroque spatial design. Following the needs of the Protestant sermon, Dutch churches developed several variations of the central-plan scheme; more complicated ground-plans appear only infrequently. The private residences were grouped in rows of several-story façades of surprising narrowness, leaving just enough room between the large high window surfaces for the ornament. Towards 1680 Holland lost its artistic independence; and French influences, in the style of Louis Quatorze, became predominant.

FRANCE

Seventeenth-century classicism

The French classical style of the seventeenth century is easily distinguishable from the contemporary Italian Baroque, even though both depend upon the classical columnar orders *[cf. 519]*. Movement and pathos were consciously avoided in favour of clarity, symmetry, and regularity – norms which were imposed throughout the country by the rules of the Académie Royale *[cf. 379]* which became the model for many of the later Academies.

The first half of the seventeenth century witnessed a continuing conflict between classical formal principles and imported Italian Baroque motifs. Under the rule of the Italian Queen Marie de Médicis, of Cardinal Richelieu and Louis XIII, the *mode italienne* reached its height. The first Parisian church after the model of Il Gesù in Rome, the Église des Carmes, was built in 1613; the two-story columnar façade of Saint-Gervais followed in 1616–21.

Château building developed in a way which was to influence all Europe. The most important French architect of the seventeenth century and also the purest representative of the incipient classical phase is François Mansart (1598–1666). His works, created mostly between 1635 and 1660, present wall designs of a sensibility so subtly developed that Italian church façades seem by comparison almost over-orchestrated. Columns appear only in comparatively outstanding spots or in a few areas where they are needed for the spatial opening up of large surfaces, as in the *Orléans wing* of the *Château of Blois*, begun in 1635 *[657]*. The walls are enlivened through subtly articulated flat layers in relief, achieved through the calculated pilasters, entablatures, and door and window frames. Mansart uses an enfilade to arrange the rooms of a château or an hôtel uniformly on an axis; this procedure was first developed in Italy.

657 *François Mansart. Orléans wing of the Château de Blois, 1635–8. Colonnades decorate the corners of the court and lead the focus away from the central portico. No overall vertical line holds the stories together.*

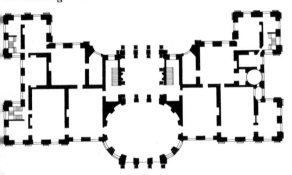

658, 659 *Louis Levau, Château de Vaux-le-Vicomte, 1657–61. Ground-plan and view from the garden. The oval of the main hall is flanked by flat corner pavilions with Gothic steepled roofs. (Left below.)*

660 *Claude Perrault, east façade of the Louvre, Paris, begun 1665. An exemplary French solution with a simple pedestal and fluted columns in the upper story placed in pairs away from the wall except at the centre. (Above.)*

661 *Louis Levau and Jules Hardouin-Mansart, garden front of Château de Versailles, 1661–84. The façade, begun by Levau and continued from 1678 on with a new plan by Hardouin-Mansart, seems block-like. The similar alignment of the axes reflects the absolutism of its creator. (Below.)*

Louis Levau (1612–70), who in contrast to Mansart enjoyed the King's favour and became court architect, created in his *Château of Vaux-le-Vicomte*, 1657–61 *[658, 659]* the prototype for most of the château plans of the seventeenth century and for a number of those of the eighteenth. Of the original layout of several wings there remains only a single broad section, bounded by four slightly projecting corner pavilions. The centre is occupied by a great ceremonial oval hall surmounted by a dome which projects into the façade overlooking the garden side. The Baroque compactness and heaviness that linger here were shortly to be loosened, in the rebuilding of Versailles, into more elegant, cubic forms.

In 1665 Louis XVI summoned Bernini, the presiding genius of the Baroque, to plan the rebuilding of the Louvre in Paris. But his designs encountered such powerful opposition that though loaded with gifts and honours, he had to withdraw without having accomplished anything substantial. Instead, the plans of the versatile physician Claude Perrault (1613–88) were executed. Perrault's *East Façade of the Louvre [660]* satisfied all the aesthetic demands of the Grand Siècle and anticipated those of the eighteenth century. The principles that were to be so important for further development were clearly enunciated for the first time: adherence to essentially pure stereometrical forms, renunciation of a dominating central feature, absolute adherence to integrity of the plane. On these lines Jules Hardouin-Mansart (1646–1708) redesigned Levau's *Garden Façade of the Château of Versailles [661]*. The serial extension of a motif emphasizing the planar quality is here pressed to an extreme. The façade, nearly 2,000 feet long, must be evaluated in connexion with the park *[673]* laid out by the brilliant André Le Nôtre (1613–1700), which stretches an enormous distance from the main building in a splendidly composed geometrical framework.

Towards the end of the age there appears a *détente* in the forms that had been adapted to the needs of a stiff and distant courtly ceremonial. New developments appeared in the decoration of interiors. The heavy marble incrustation of walls gave place to bright wood panelling, where the light gilded stucco ornament and playful putti ushered in the gaiety of the Rococo style.

Régence and Rococo

The styles following the Louis Quatorze, the Régence and Rococo which lasted from *c.* 1710/15 to 1750/60, were created by a generation which included as its

662   *Jules Hardouin-Mansart, Dôme des Invalides in Paris, 1675–1706. The smooth corners and many columns at the centre emphasize the plastic quality of the dome.*

663   *Jean Courtonne, Hôtel de Matignon in Paris, begun 1721. The Rococo town palace avoided all magnificence: the garden façade gives the effect less of distinction than of intimacy.*

main representatives Robert de Cotte (1656–1735), Germain Boffrand (1667–1754), and Jacques-Ange Gabriel (1698–1782). The revolutionary elements that they introduced are less evident in châteaux and churches than in small city palaces, hôtels, and the intimate living-rooms which were placed unobtrusively (as at Versailles) next to the great ceremonial halls of the Louis Quatorze era. Official and public pomp was balanced by the provision for intimacy and social ease. The Parisian *hôtel [663]*, with its wings grouped around a court, was now frequently reduced to a simple block in which the ends and middle sections were enlivened solely by slight forward projections and gentle curves. The heavy basement with its rusticated masonry was usually dispensed with, as were the majestic orders. There remained two stories of almost equal compositional value, covered by a flat roof. The whole is characterized by a new clarity and comprehensibility of architectural form.

In addition to their vast château complexes the great French architects of the seventeenth century created important religious architecture. The cityscape of Paris acquired new accents in the monumental domed structures, such as the church of the Sorbonne (1635–42) by Jacques Lemercier, the monastery church of Val-de-Grâce (1645–65) by François Mansart, the Église des Quatre Nations (1661) by Louis Levau, and lastly the *Invalides* (1675–1706) by Jules Hardouin-Mansart *[662]*. These buildings all represent variations of the cross-plan theme, which remained binding for Soufflot's *Panthéon [cf. 747]*. The chief façade motif is the portice, orchestrated with many colours, which are echelonned in two stories in the Invalides, lending the building plastic richness through the play of light and shadow, an effect seen at its best in the Galerie des Glaces which Mansart, as court architect to Louis XIV, inserted between the corner pavilions at Versailles.

Of great artistic importance also are the innovations in town planning. The old type of square closely hemmed in by houses was broadened out to become wide and open, giving on to radiating avenues and streets concluded perspectivally by church façades, monuments, or châteaux. When feasible the planners combined several squares into a vast continuous space in which the crossings were advantageously disguised as motifs derived from landscape architecture, such as lawns, aquatic displays, and colonnades. Squares such as the *Place de la Concorde* (begun 1757) in Paris *[665]* and the royal squares of Nancy (1753) rank among the finest achievements of European town planning.

664 *Jacques-Ange Gabriel, Petit Trianon in the park at Versailles, 1762–8. Self-assured departure from monumentality and excessive number of side structures. The crystalline structure can be taken in at a glance.*

665 *Place de la Concorde, Paris. Whereas in Italy the public squares give an impression of movement, in France flat, symmetrical walls contribute to the harmony and peace of the design. The buildings in the foreground, begun in 1757, are by Jacques-Ange Gabriel.*

ENGLAND

England had little influence in the general development of the Baroque and Rococo; it formed its characteristic mode from precedents derived from French and Dutch architecture of the seventeenth century. Parallel to the main current there ran two broad currents of provincial building: a Flemish Mannerist trend lasting until the outbreak of the Civil War in 1642, and the Gothic survival which lingered on far into this period. As early as the middle of the eighteenth century the strongly intellectual classicism of England merged into the Neo-Classicism that was to spread throughout Europe.

Palaces and country-seats for the King and the nobility, the houses of the middle classes, university buildings, and hospitals are the main types of English architecture for the period between *c.* 1630 and 1750. The prevailing church type underwent two forms of innovation directed largely by impulses from higher authorities, first after the Great Fire of London of 1666, and then again after 1711.

Inigo Jones (1573–1652) is the first English architect to contribute new and influential impulses derived from the works of Vitruvius, the monuments of the antique and especially Palladio's buildings, to a country as yet hardly touched by the spirit of the Renaissance [cf. 546]. But English Palladianism as initiated by Jones never constituted a mere literal

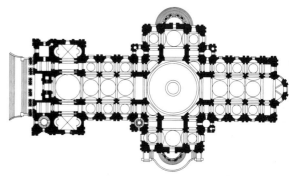

667, 668 Sir Christopher Wren, St Paul's Cathedral, London, 1675–1710. View from the west and ground-plan. Note the strong feeling for antiquity, even in the positioning of the columns at the entrance, but also the addition of fantastic elements such as the towers. The tension between classicism and Baroque is characteristic of Wren.

666 Inigo Jones, Banqueting House in London, 1611–22. Built with Palladio's example in mind, the subordination of the parts is nevertheless Jones's own achievement. Wall surfaces and trusses are both stressed.

imitation. Jones's palaces and houses present a clearly bounded cubic block, usually with two stories, each of which has its own order. As in the case of the *Banqueting House*, 1611–22 [666], the centre was frequently emphasized with columns.

During the Civil War and Protectorate (1642–60) building activity was slight and of little importance. After the Restoration of the Stuart monarchy refugees returning from the Continent brought with them the Dutch classicism which displaced Palladianism for a time. Dutch brick construction was naturalized in England and Van Campen's Mauritshuis found a wide and enthusiastic following. The town-house of the middle classes absorbed the colossal order of pilasters running through all floors, so that as in Holland and Flanders street fronts took on an energetic vertical quality recalling the Gothic.

In 1666 the Great Fire broke out in London, destroying some 13,000 houses. Sir Christopher Wren (1632–1723), who then occupied the post of Professor of Astronomy at Oxford, became the great planner and architect of the reconstruction. With almost unflagging powers of invention he created not only his masterpiece *[667, 668]*, the new building of the gutted *St Paul's Cathedral* (1675–1710), but in a very short space of time 51 new churches to replace 86

670 *Sir Christopher Wren, Royal Hospital at Chelsea, begun 1682. A practical building with a highly objective character.*

669 *Sir Christopher Wren, tower of St-Mary-le-Bow, London, 1670–5. An example of the prolific inventiveness of Wren: various towers are placed one on top of each other in almost endless succession.*

that had been burned. His breadth of culture and unprejudicial interests permitted him to produce solutions in Roman, Gothic, Dutch, or French forms according to the task at hand. The exteriors of his varied London churches are dominated by the unusual silhouettes of towers in which historical styles are mingled in the several stories. In a highly original manner rise successively rusticated bases; stories of the most diverse orders with pilasters of columns; round, square, or octagonal tempiettos; and round or pencil-like spires *[669]*.

Wren's church towers and façade for St Paul's reveal a trait that runs all through English classicism: the feeling for proportions and for interrelations of forms is restricted to the details, while the well-balanced play of forces between volumes and spaces that would bind the various parts into a whole is lacking. The great compositions of mass and space into an ensemble of the continental European Baroque and classicism were translated by the English into a simple symmetrical succession of units, as exemplified by Wren's *Chelsea Hospital [670]*.

In the period from 1710 to 1750, when the gaiety and imagination of the Rococo flourished in France and Germany, England underwent a second stage of Palladianism. In 1715–17 the architect Colin Campbell published his *Vitruvius Britannicus*, a collection of engravings with over one hundred reproductions of classical English, that is to say Palladian, buildings. About the same time appeared the first direct translation of Palladio's treatise. The so-called Palladian house introduced by Campbell *[671]*, consisting of a

671 Colin Campbell, Mereworth House, Kent, 1723. English classicism of the early eighteenth century appears impersonal, cool, the work of epigones. Mereworth is almost a copy of Palladio's Villa Rotonda.

672 John Wood the Younger, Royal Crescent in Bath, 1767–75. The combination of pleasing proportions and representative beauty became possible with the slackening of ceremony during the eighteenth century.

rectangle block with portico, flat pediment or balustrade, with or without side wings, became a favourite type for all manner of buildings. Characteristic is the increasing isolation of the individual building units, whose interrelations are restricted to those of mere symmetry, a quality in no way concealed by the sparse cool ornament. The classicistic tendency imminent in English art veered towards an historical attitude, long before this was understood on the Continent.

Artistic design was soon applied to residential blocks. The *Royal Crescent [672]* in Bath (1767–75) by John Wood the Younger, a half-circle open to gardens and sunlight, is the outstanding example of a uniformly planned living complex.

LANDSCAPE ARCHITECTURE

In the seventeenth century Italy yielded the leading place in the design of gardens and parks to France. Italy long remained faithful to the small-scale Renaissance garden with its statues, grottoes, and numerous fountains. Only towards the end of the seventeenth century under the influence of Versailles did a more generously proportioned concept of design appear, as in the gardens of Caserta and those of the Villa Pisani at Stra near Venice.

In France from the reign of Henri IV, that is from the turn of the seventeenth century, the classical garden developed not only as a setting for works of art such as sculptures and grottoes, but as an independent entity which could itself claim to be regarded as a work of art. The outlines of the new conception appeared about 1630 in the garden of the Palais du Luxembourg in Paris. The area is no longer divided in chequerboard fashion into individual parcels of equal value [cf. 584]; instead, to the right and left of a central axis stretch symmetrical ranges of lawns, flower beds, and the first bosquets, orderly free spaces surrounded by bushes and trees. The entire garden layout was ranged about a great central axis to an increasing degree; fountains, grottoes, and pavilions were ordered according to a calculated plan at the crossing points of avenues or as points of focus. Towards the middle of the century perspectival interests arose which soon led to the installation of canals, avenues, and complicated bosquet forms.

In 1661 the great landscape architect André Le Nôtre (1613–1700) began to lay out the park of *Versailles* for Louis XIV *[673]*. In a few years it became renowned and imitated among all the princely courts of Europe as a miracle of artistically shaped nature. The well-balanced disposition of terraces, avenues, trees, flower beds, and water courses, which surprised the viewer with new vistas from every standpoint, was counterpointed by the allegorical accompaniment of garden sculpture which played on the theme of Louis as the *Roi Soleil*.

The French garden changed little during the Régence and Rococo. The new fashion emanating from England disturbed neither the grand axis nor the regular plan. The two modes were often combined, so that symmetrical parts lay beside irregular ones. But grottoes, fountain niches, playful miniature architecture, and a great number of sculptures were now felt to be old-fashioned. A series of elaborated flowered parterres would be replaced by flowing lawns when patrons allowed 'Nature' freer rein.

Thus the most important innovations in garden planning proceeded not from France but from England. Together with a whole series of theoretical writings the English developed the landscape garden, which contrasted so clearly with the architectonic and symmetrical character of the French garden. Although the terms have changed, 'Nature' is still shaped artistically and artificially: watercourses thread through undulating lawn areas, little springs gurgle from piles of stones, and picturesque clusters of trees stand against the horizon. The new awareness of Chinese gardens and the Romantic enthusiasm for

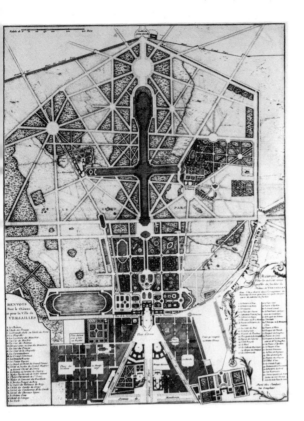

673   André Le Nôtre, Park of Versailles, 1661–8. The layout shows the geometrical character of Le Nôtre's landscape architecture. Rigid symmetry is however avoided: the ideal is to enclose and arrange nature as far as possible.

675   English Garden of the Duc de Praslin at Neuilly, 1788. The English landscape garden abandons architectural considerations. The maze leads to no final goal: it is rather an invitation to passive contemplation.

674   Garden of the Lower Belvedere in Vienna, c. 1700. The Baroque garden is always arranged as a central structure. Walls, gates, doors, and pathways surround the parterre. The garden was designed by Claude Girard, a pupil of Le Nôtre.

Roman ruins produced a whole series of historicizing garden buildings *[675]*. William Kent (1684–1748), the greatest English garden architect of the first half of the century, filled his gardens of Chiswick and Stowe with antique theatres, obelisks, Egyptian pyramids, Chinese pagodas, antique temples of the Virtues, of Venus and of Victory, pyramid tombs, Palladian bridges, a grotto of Dido, and a shepherd's hut.

In Germany too, where the model of Versailles had been received just as enthusiastically as in other countries, the English precepts in gardening began to make their way. Seventeenth-century gardens followed Italian, then French models; they were laid out geometrically, as in the case of the grandiose setting of the *Lower Belvedere in Vienna* of about 1700 *[674]*. But even before the first pure landscape garden, that of the Fürst Pückler in Wörlitz (1769), irregular tracts appeared here and there in the midst of the severe system of avenues and paths. The patrons of the Rococo, entranced by the exotic, erected their Chinese tea houses and pagodas and sought the melancholy of artificial ruins. The most fascinating examples of this kind are the park at Nymphenburg near Munich and that of Frederick the Great at Sanssouci near Berlin.

ORNAMENT

Ornament in the eighteenth century comes so much to the fore that its forms influence the major arts of painting, sculpture, and even architecture. A society that was deserting the official galleries and halls employed the new decorative style in living-rooms where it reflected the new requirement for intimacy and cultivated taste. Thus the 'petits appartements' of the great châteaux and the Parisian hôtels became hot-houses, so to speak, of the 'style moderne', which was created by such great decorative artists as Gilles-Marie Oppenord (1672–1742) and François-Antoine Vassé (1683–1736).

The heavy plastic acanthus hangings were replaced even in the late Louis Quatorze style by light, flat rinceaux. At the beginning of the Régence, about 1710/15, appeared a fine framing ribbon-work that rolled up at the ends and corners of rooms or else spanned the whole surface like a net. Fields thus bounded on the wood-revetted walls received symmetrically arranged rosettes formed from naturalistic and abstract elements, small trophies consisting of weapons, masks, and musical instruments carved in fine relief, between which pastorals and chinoiseries were sometimes placed.

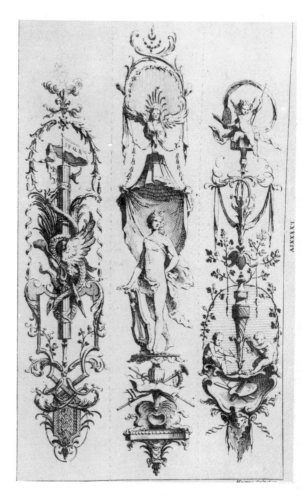

676 *Gilles-Marie Oppenord, decorative sketch, c. 1730. The ornament of the Régence shows the origin of the grotesque, but is rather lighter and more painterly. Little genre scenes, antique forms, or decorative motifs (left: a 'trophy') show the decorator's fancy.*

The *rocaille* appeared at about 1730 with the Louis Quinze style, a mixture made up of palmettes and shells swaying in S- and C-curves. Asymmetry characterizes not only individual motifs, but spreads throughout the whole decorative system. Ornaments playfully exaggerated unfold in the pattern books of famous engravers; the illusionistic border rolls over a pastoral scene, water bubbles over reedy growths, and little putti climb out of the rocky heights of shell interiors *[677]*. The *rocaille* curves about a building leading into depth with grottoes, pavilions, and fountains in a play of imagination that is no longer intellectually comprehensible. Although the in-dividual *rocaille* can produce the optical impression of a spatial entity in French interiors, it is employed on the wall as an ornament of planar character. With the exception of the traditional mirror setting over the mantelpiece, it always retains this character of a firmly bounded surface never broken by illusionistic fresco decoration on walls or ceilings.

An ornament that was so easily susceptible to irrational fancies of form did not establish itself in the land of its birth without creating, about 1750, a formidable reaction in favour of a new and clearer type of decoration. In the meantime, however, and transmitted by numerous publications, it conquered the Rhineland, Berlin, and especially Bavaria and Austria, where it appeared from 1730 in a somewhat altered form.

677 François Cuvilliés, copper engraving from the 'Phantasie-stücken', c. 1740. Rococo, beginning about 1730, became the favourite ornamental form at the middle of the century. The 'inventions' sometimes possess the character of an autonomous work of art.

678 François Cuvilliés, Amalienburg in the Nymphenburg Park near Munich, 1734–9. Notice the absence of columns or pillars. Rich ornamentation, made out of plants and details of landscape, covers the room. Mirrors blur the spatial dimensions.

The *rocaille* tends to establish itself particularly at 'boundary positions', where two different spatial elements converge: at transitions between capitals and entablature; between frame and picture; at the apex of an arch, and in the spandrels of vaults *[648]*. Sometimes frayed out like a cloud, sometimes broken up in strips, it is flaunted on altars, confession boxes, pulpits, organs, gallery railings, and on all forms of furniture *[682]*; whole architectural articulations begin to sway in *rocaille* forms. This characteristic harmony between architecture and decorative elements lends the Rococo room a unique musical quality. Alongside the precious Rococo decoration of the *Amalienburg* in the Nymphenburg Park *[678]* by François Cuvilliés (1695–1768), and in his Theatre and the Reichen Zimmer of the Residenz in Munich, we must also mention the fine decoration of the châteaux of Frederick the Great at Berlin and Potsdam (Sanssouci), where the *rocaille* is distinguished from the more exuberant and folk-like motifs of the Bavarian Rococo by its elegant and highly cultivated taste.

FURNITURE

In the art of furniture the course of change from the Renaissance to the heavy plastic forms of the Baroque did not run smoothly. In the seventeenth century

France and Holland were the leading countries. Dutch influence radiated through North Germany, England, and Scandinavia, where its austere forms were long maintained. France became the European model only towards the end of the seventeenth century; in the Rococo it clearly surpassed all other countries in taste, elegance, and refinement. About the middle of the eighteenth century the outlines of the trend to the cooler classicistic forms of the Louis Seize style appeared.

The luxury furniture for the court circle of France was designed and produced in a royal furniture factory specially set up for this purpose. The new technique of *marqueterie* recalls the *intarsia* of the Italian Renaissance. The craftsmen fitted together pieces of various woods and also brass, tin, ivory, and tortoise-shell in order to produce abstract or figural ornament. Many heavy figural bronze-gilt mountings were employed in order to heighten the effect of luxury. Craftsmen often drew their inspiration from contemporary ornament, and such engravers of ornaments as Le Pautre, Margot, Bérain, and later in the Rococo Meissonnier, Toro, and Pineau became very important for the *ébénistes*, or master cabinet-makers. The furniture by André-Charles Boulle (1642–1732), whose reputation penetrated far beyond France, reflects the general development from the heavy acanthus of the early Louis Quatorze style through the elegant leaf and flower rinceaux of the late phase *[679]* to the ribbon-work and chinoiserie of the Régence. Besides the straight-lined, flat-surfaced *marqueterie* furniture there was a rich production of

679   *André-Charles Boulle, cupboard, 1672. Ebony inlaid with copper and mother-of-pearl, and gilt fittings. A deliberately single form with harmonious proportions.*

680   *Charles Cressent, commode, mid-eighteenth century. Cressent's fame lay in his design of fittings. Note the neglect of functional qualities in the positioning of the griffin between gilded plant ornament. Every piece of furniture was to be an integral part of interior decoration.*

681   *Venetian commode, mid-eighteenth century. Venice was the single enclave of Rococo in Italy – as is particularly apparent in the production of furniture. Flower painting was applied to furniture decoration.*

682 *Melchior Kambly, writing-table, c. 1765. Kambly, one of the outstanding talents at the court of Frederick the Great, created this table for the Neue Palais at Potsdam. The Rococo found wood suitable for modelling and experimented with asymmetrical forms.*

carved chairs and cabinets with curved silhouettes and heavy plastic forms. The whole piece was frequently gilded. Charles Cressent (1685–1768) became the great rival of the elder Boulle in the Régence. His furniture abandoned heavy pomposity and corresponded to the new ideal of elegance and comfort in its curved, bulging forms. The large heavy cabinet became rarer, and the commode appeared [680], together with the corner cabinet and every imaginable kind of seat. The low, upholstered fauteuil, the sofa, and the chaise-longue appeared in this period.

Until about 1750 all types of furniture were of a decorative form. Chairs were narrow and their backs, like those of the fauteuils, were increasingly lower; they were often painted in white or golden tones. Splendid coverings of bright silk or fine embroideries with bouquets of flowers and small scenes added a tone of gay elegance. Apart from the normal veneered pieces there appeared the shining lacquer furniture influenced by the Far East, which displayed flowers in decorative vases, birds or small chinoiseries against a dark or red ground.

Italian Baroque furniture was heavier and more compressed in appearance. Only the Florentine *pietra dura* technique, a type of inlay using polished coloured stones set into the pieces and forming abstract and figural motifs, enjoyed general renown. In the Rococo, Italian furniture acquired a certain rugged quality. Venice alone created a more original style of furniture depending chiefly upon the effect of colour. In common with the rest of the furniture the heavy

bulging commode [681] and tables, often covered with marble, are brightly overpainted or lacquered and provided with painted carvings, a style of furniture that recalls Alpine folk art.

In the seventeenth century Germany presents a multiplicity of furniture styles, but most work remained strongly provincial until about 1700. The more progressive craftsmen of the North employed severe Dutch classicistic forms, which were mostly caught up in a solid bourgeois heaviness. In the South craftsmen often retained, especially for heavy cabinets, whole systems of Renaissance-like house and church façades [cf. 595] with small architectural forms.

In the second quarter of the eighteenth century a surprising efflorescence of German furniture took place. The ribbon and leaf work of the Régence soon gave way to the unsymmetrically carved *rocaille* forms in which an active overflowing imagination appeared, often to the considerable disadvantage of proportions and good taste. French ornamental prints were influential, though they were interpreted in a

683 *David Roentgen, writing-table, c. 1775. As opposed to the furniture of the preceding generation, England began to influence continental taste, as is evident in the more delicate proportions of this piece.*

684 *Style of Thomas Chippendale, chair, mid-eighteenth century. Firm construction distinguishes Chippendale from the continental furniture-makers. Note the French Rococo ornament on the borders of the supports.*

different manner in the different regions with greater or lesser originality. Elegant and tasteful *marqueterie* furniture was produced by the Roentgen family in Neuwied *[683]*. Lively Rococo forms appear in the furniture of the Neumann castles of Würzburg and Bruchsal, as well as in the Munich Residenz and at Nymphenburg. But in artistic quality, taste, and excellence all these were surpassed by the furniture of Frederick the Great in Potsdam *[682]* and Sanssouci.

In England, also, furniture-makers overcame provincial coarseness only in the eighteenth century. Dutch and French elements were utilized in accordance with the English preference for Gothic thinness, emphasized by the predilection for dark mahogany wood. Thomas Chippendale (1718–79) was famous for the furniture style named after him *[684]* in part through his own works but chiefly through his pattern book published in 1754. His designs show a certain stiffness; the famous Chippendale chairs have high backs of small, often curved styles, which run either vertically or are crossed to form geometric patterns sometimes interlocking at right angles but also forming Gothic and chinoiserie curves. Towards the middle of the eighteenth century classicistic tendencies appeared in English furniture along with lighter forms and new ornament.

Sculpture

ITALY

In the early Baroque the plastic human form began to acquire an inner agitation slowly turning towards an easier flowing movement. The garments became increasingly independent of the body and in the high Baroque actually vie in artistic value with their wearers, who are eclipsed by the voluminous expansion of the drapery. A rich movement taking its departure from the emotional content of the subject-matter unites all formal details into a great agitated arabesque. It is in the nature of high Baroque sculpture, whose chief representative is Bernini (1598–1680), that it often appeared to violate the specific qualities of the sculptural medium itself – the heaviness and the nature of the material employed, even the corporality of the human figure. A Baroque piece of sculpture is essentially a paradox.

Initially the individual figure unfolded in the plane, and consequently took full account of the effects of

685 *Giovanni Lorenzo Bernini, Ecstasy of St Theresa, 1644–7. Rome, S. Maria della Vittoria. The scene appears like a vision above the altar. Bernini carried illusionism so far that one almost forgets the medium (here white marble).*

686 *Giovanni Lorenzo Bernini, Triton Fountain in the Piazza Barberini, Rome, c. 1640. This work is built up out of dolphins' bodies, realistic mussel-shells, and the muscular Triton. Tectonic forms are absent.*

light and shadow. Later the Baroque statue was made to be seen from one or at most two points of view; only in exceptional cases was the viewer's standpoint conceived as indeterminate. General sculpture was incorporated in larger architectural contexts, e.g. niche figures in churches, the figures of an altar structure or those of a wall tomb. The free-standing public monument and the garden figure also remained oriented to the major visual directions of the architectonic scheme of the whole. The Baroque principle of mutual interpenetration meant that the effect of a figure never remained confined to the space it occupied. It needs to impinge upon the surrounding space in order to acquire its true being. Thus, for example, the gaze of Bernini's *Longinus* in St Peter's in Rome is turned upwards towards the transcendent light streaming through the dome. Only through this relation to a point of view present in space or simply imagined does the figure achieve the significance intended for it. The boldest instance of the Baroque synthesis in which architecture, sculp-

ture, painting, and light fuse into a single whole is Bernini's design *[685]* for the Cornaro Chapel with the *Ecstasy of St Theresa* (1644–7). The stage setting of the space emphasizes the pathos and ecstasy of the visionary epiphany; the scene becomes the high point of a drama witnessed by a simulated audience looking on from the side walls. The many-layered quality of the Baroque work of art is especially evident in sculpture. Thus in Bernini's *Triton Fountain* (c. 1640) the element of water and the world appropriate to it appear in several guises *[686]*. Triton, the conch-blowing son of Poseidon, was known to the Greeks as a friendly being; shells and dolphins are his attributes here. This level of meaning is combined with a broader aim of glorifying Pope Urban VIII Barberini. Thus the Triton symbolizes Papal patron-age, which is friendly and beneficial to men. To a contemporary person of humanistic education this allegorical message was understood without explana-tion, and it only required the presence of the Papal emblem of the bee to make the allusions compre-hensible.

As in the other arts a classically oriented opposition group made itself felt, best represented in Rome by the Bolognese Algardi (1602–54). Despite the drama of the event represented, Algardi's *Beheading of St John* retains its classical balance. Towards the end of the century French sculptors became increasingly prominent in Rome, while only a few Italians distinguished themselves. The best commissions went

687 *Fontana di Trevi in Rome, designed by the architect Nicola Salvi in 1732, completed by the sculptor Pietro Bracci in 1762. Palace façades, triumphal arches, and monumental fountains all in one. (Etching by Giovanni Battista Piranesi, dated 1751.)*

688 *Giacomo Serpotta, Valour, 1714–17. Palermo, Oratorio del Rosario. This cardinal virtue was personified by a richly clad young lady with a column. The painterly style of the dress reveals the influence of Bernini's elegant artistry.*

to Frenchmen such as Monnot, Legros, and Slodtz. Outstanding among the Italians about the turn of the century was Camillo Rusconi (1658–1728), whose four tabernacle figures in S. Giovanni in Laterano combine Bernini's teaching and that of the French with bulkiness that is more Netherlandish than Roman. Pietro Bracci (1700–73) is the important name of the following generation. His *Neptune* of the Fontana Trevi *[687]* directs the playful aquatic motifs with a Bernini-like richness of movement. Probably the most original Italian sculptor of the eighteenth century is the versatile Giacomo Serpotta (1656–1732.) He brought a somewhat audacious Rococo grace into religious settings as in the *Oratorio of the Rosary in S. Domenico at Palermo* (1714–17), which is entirely covered with statuettes and ornamental work *[688]*.

SPAIN

With a very few exceptions, the clergy and the guilds provided the patrons for Spanish sculptors. For both groups, however, religious works were made, since the guild members competed with one another in the commissioning of popular Passion figures, the *pasos*, for the Good Friday processions.

The free-standing figures of the saints in church interiors *[689]* – often saints of the various Orders – assume attitudes of typically Spanish nobility, to which a moderate movement of the folds confers an almost elegant note. The alert seriousness of the faces is either turned inward, as if lost in prayer, or directed with penetrating urgency on the faithful. The *pasos* figures, however, are characterized by a highly realistic conception. Through emphatic gestures, bright colours sought to make the passion of religious experience believable. The quality here lies more in emotional expression than in the artistic form.

689 *Gregorio Hernandez, St Veronica, 1614. Valladolid, Provincial Museum. While Italians and French preferred the glow of marble and bronze, Spanish artists sought for the colouring of antiquity, so as to heighten the realism of their religious images.*

religious, not least because of a new piety that was expressed in innumerable monastery and Order foundations and which exercised an appreciable influence on artistic creation. The leading artistic personality is Jacques Sarazin (1588–1660), who returned from Italy in 1628 at about the same time as the painter Simon Vouet and like him transmitted a whole repertory of Baroque forms. As early as the 1640s, however, his work developed in a classical direction comparable to that of François Mansart in architecture and Nicolas Poussin in painting. His famous *Tomb of the Prince de Condé*, 1649–63 *[691]*, and of Cardinal Bérulle (1657) are instances of an elevated classical style.

Sarazin was one of the founders of the *Académie de Peinture et de Sculpture* (established in 1684) which began by formulating canons applicable to any kind of subject-matter based on Raphael and the Antique. During the period of the Academy's greatest power the strict control of the rules had the effect of submerging the creative individuality of the artists in the

690 Narciso Tomé, 'Trasparente' in Toledo Cathedral, completed 1732. In order to focus attention on the altar in the ambulatory, the vaulting is pierced. The effect is almost surrealistic: all the figures are in deep shadows at the bottom, and are illuminated from above.

Towards the end of the seventeenth century Spanish sculpture visibly declined in significance, and this situation was prolonged throughout the eighteenth century. The individual figures served only as components of the ornamental wealth of great decorative ensembles (portal and altar walls). A brilliant example is the so-called *Trasparente* (completed 1732) by Narciso Tomé in the Cathedral of Toledo *[690]*, an altar structure towering over the observer in numerous figures and ornaments which are illuminated by a hidden source of light.

FRANCE

Unlike architecture and painting seventeenth-century French sculpture was only slightly affected by the conflict between Baroque and classical trends. The ideal of the antique was the effective standard. The sculpture of the first half of the century is essentially

691 Jacques Sarazin, Tomb of Henri II of Burgundy, Prince de Condé, 1649–63. Chantilly, Palace chapel. The features of the small girl who holds the plaque express sorrow for the departed, while she herself symbolizes the eternal youth of the life hereafter.

collective character of the organization. The single Baroque sculptor and one of the greatest sculptural geniuses of France, the southerner Pierre Puget (1620–94), came into conflict with this system. The personal idiom he had developed in Italy in contact with the works of Michelangelo and Bernini led to a vivid and expressive realism beside which the products of the academic teaching seemed pallid. In 1666 the French Academy in Rome was founded. Its scholars studied antique works by making drawings and casts of them. Many casts and originals were dispatched to Paris. But there was seldom any talk of the contemporary Baroque works of Rome.

At this time the King and the court circles patronized an artist who knew how to assimilate all the varied tendencies and doctrines of the age. François Girardon (1628–1715) remains the unsurpassed interpreter of the Grand Siècle. His works, always inspired by the Antique, by Raphael or Poussin, may be regarded as Baroque in their painterly and two-dimensional mode of presentation and in their links with a larger context. But while pathos and movement triumph in Bernini's work, here cool elegance, absolute balance, and tranquillity rule. Girardon's masterpiece, *Apollo attended by the Nymphs of the Sea Goddess Tethys* (1666–75), is characteristic of the period of Louis XIV both formally and thematically [692]. It is a genuine Baroque allegory glorifying the Sun King in the guise of Apollo, god of light, at the same time constituting a symbol for Versailles as a whole. Just as the sun god after his daily course across

693   *Jean-Baptiste Lemoyne, portrait bust of the painter Coypel, 1730. Paris, Louvre. The portrait is developed out of the Baroque clothing of the body.*

692   *François Girardon, Apollo and the Nymphs of Tethys, 1666–75. Versailles. The somewhat theatrical marble group displays in its cool, antiquitizing style the court art of Louis XIV. The 'Roi Soleil' is represented as the god attended by nymphs.*

the earth sinks into the sea in the west, taking his nightly rest with Tethys, so the King betook himself to Versailles to enjoy his leisure.

After the death in 1683 of the King's minister Colbert who had supervised artistic production, the authority of the Antique and of the old masters was brought into question for the first time. The famous dispute between the *anciens* and *modernes* signalled a loosening of the domination of the severe academic doctrine in all fields. A new age, more human and more playful, is announced in the portraits of Antoine Coysevox (1640–1720). With his graceful forms which convey youthful charm rather than princely authority he provides a transition to the new concepts of the Régence.

The silhouette of the Rococo is capricious and the elegant garments flutter restlessly, though French sculpture never goes so far as to abandon altogether the classical concept of the human body, as is sometimes the case in South Germany. In outstanding works of portraiture Jean-Baptiste Lemoyne (1704–78) returned to clay as the sculptural material, which has the advantage of permitting the modelling of the finest nuances of human character *[693]*. Lemoyne's art is *mouvementé* and elegant, and he catches in masterly fashion the fleeting quality of a look or an emotion. By comparison his contemporary Edmé Bouchardon (1698–1762) seems a full-blown reactionary. In his *Fountain of the Seasons* in the Rue de Grenelle in Paris, created after the model of the monumental Roman wall fountains, the classical spirit lives on as a counterpoise to the Rococo. For the porcelain factory of the Marquise de Pompadour, Étienne-Maurice Falconet (1716–91) created charming *bibelots*, in part after designs by Boucher *[695]*. In 1766 he was called to Russia to erect the great bronze equestrian statue of Peter the Great in St Petersburg.

The stage of Neo-Classicism imposed itself almost imperceptibly in sculpture, its chief master being the gifted Jean-Antoine Houdon (1741–1828). For him the portrait *[694]* took first place among all the genres. From an old craft tradition and a new understanding of the Antique he forged a rare combination of physiognomical precision and classical beauty.

695 *Étienne-Maurice Falconet, Allegory of the Hunt, c. 1788. Copenhagen, Private Collection. The small format and the material (burnt clay) characterize the intimate art of the Rococo.*

694 *Jean-Antoine Houdon, portrait of Voltaire, 1778. Gotha, Museum. The influence of Roman portraiture characterizes Houdon's classicism.*

GERMANY

As in other countries German Baroque sculpture was generally conceived in relation to an architectural setting. Few sculptors rose above the level of the decorative. There is often a certain carelessness of execution in their works, since they were usually meant to be seen at a distance. Germany is characterized by the long enduring and renewed dependence upon the late Gothic tradition, which is connected with the striving to present formal problems in terms of emotional expressiveness. At the beginning of the German Baroque the *Crucifixion* group (1625–30) by Georg Petel (1590/3–1633) surpasses in quality all contemporary work in the fields of architecture and painting *[696]*. The Magdalen crouches at the foot of the Cross; her Gothic garments show a pattern of sharp-edged folds revealing the figure's volume in the Baroque manner. After the middle of the century this externalized emotion becomes quieter and more inward in character. The grand gestures recur again in the late Baroque.

Around the turn of the century Andreas Schlüter (1664–1714) personified the high Baroque in Berlin. After Bernini he was the most powerful sculptural talent of international rank. Schlüter eliminated the harsh breaks and expressionist dilations of the lingering Gothic heritage. His figures acquired an intense plasticity combined with a new passion of

696   Georg Petel, St Mary Magdalen, c. 1625–30. Regensburg, Niedermünster. Richness of details and the high relief of the clothing show the expressive power of early seventeenth-century German art, before the Thirty Years War paralysed cultural development.

movement. Yet true emotional pathos is lacking; his figures retain an inner, masculine monumentality, which in the case of the *Dying Warrior* of 1696 in the Berlin Zeughaus is raised to a convincing tragic grandeur *[697]*.

The heavy forms of the *Apotheosis of Prince Eugen* *[698]* by the South German Balthasar Permoser (1651–1732), who lived for many years in Italy and after his return was employed as court sculptor in Dresden, stand much closer to the spirit of the high Baroque. The theme of glorification surrounds the figure with an extensive allegorical apparatus to make a complicated but spirited group. At the same time the arabesque-like character of the whole fore-shadows the coming Rococo.

Georg Raphael Donner of Vienna (1693–1741) represents a placid idealistic mode of the Baroque. Characteristic is his use of the matt-surfaced effects of lead, as in his masterpiece, the *Mehlmarktbrunnen* in Vienna (1737–9), whose allegorical female figures

representing the chief rivers of Austria presage Neo-Classicism *[701]*.

About 1730 the individual figure was still further absorbed into the decorative context of the interior, though garden figures by their very nature retained a certain isolation. Many sculptors, many of them simultaneously stucco-workers, were active at this time, particularly in South Germany and Austria. Their products, which were executed for interior spaces conceived almost as stages and meant to be seen at some distance, often stand on the borderline between art and decorative craft. The outstanding names are those of Egid Quirin Asam (1692–1750) of Munich *[628]*, the Mannheim court sculptor Paul Egell (1691–1752), Joseph Anton Feuchtmayer (1696–1770), who worked around the Lake of Constance *[699]*, and the Munich court sculptor Ignaz Günther (1725–75). If the leading traits of French Rococo are charm, grace, and the qualities of the individual physiognomy, in Germany, especially in the ecclesiastical art of the South, the expressive depiction

697   Andreas Schlüter, mask of a dying warrior, 1696. Berlin, Zeughaus. Here, captured in stone, is the impressive last moment of a dramatic death. Pathos, movement, and painterly surfaces are the characteristics of this sculpture.

698   Balthasar Permoser, *Apotheosis of Prince Eugen, 1718–21,* Vienna, Österreichische Galerie. An allegory of the victorious field-marshal, with highly imaginative forms and bold patterns of movement in the composition. (*Left.*)

699   Joseph Anton Feuchtmayer, altar of St John the Baptist in the pilgrimage church at Birnau, 1748–50. A side altar firmly linked to the architecture and overall decoration, made of marble stucco. The asymmetry and pieces of landscape are characteristic. (*Below left.*)

700   Ignaz Günther, *S. Mary Magdalen,* 1755. Starnberg, Städliche Heimatmuseum. The lively upper surfaces show the last refinements of Baroque sculpture. The folk art of Bavarian Rococo is also evident here. (*Below.*)

701 Georg Raphael Donner, nymphs from the Mehlmarkt-brunnen, 1737–9. Vienna, Österreichische Galerie. Lead lustre and calm delineation characterize many works by this Viennese sculptor.

of the varieties of human experience is stressed. Devotion, anguish, ecstasy, and fervour are shown in vehement gestures, in an excited fluttering of garments, in unrealistic bodily twistings, and in rolling or half-closed eyes. The manneristically attenuated saint figures of Ignaz Günther *[700]* with their small heads and brows nervously raised, are beings from a supra-sensible realm. His figures rank among the few that maintain their own identity in decorative ensembles.

THE LOW COUNTRIES

Like England, Holland produced no important native sculpture in the seventeenth century. When large sculptural undertakings were required, as in the decoration of the great hall of the Amsterdam Town Hall, Flemish artists were usually employed.

Important schools of sculptors flourished in Catholic and Baroque Flanders at this time, especially in Antwerp, Brussels, Liège, and Malines. Bernini and Rubens were taken as models and their motifs were endlessly imitated and varied. Compared with the Roman works, however, Baroque buoyancy was absent in Flanders. An earthy heaviness prevents the gestures from achieving their full scope; the bodies lack the Roman elegance. Bourgeois sedateness is not entirely concealed by the strongly *mouvementé* drapery.

Flemish sculptors were active in Amsterdam, Versailles, Paris, and Rome. François Duquesnoy (1594–1643), the most famous of these emigrants,

spent his whole creative life in Rome. The small round winged children of his funerary monuments brought him great fame there. Artus Quellin the Elder (1609–68) is the most outstanding sculptor from his workshop. Endowed with considerable decorative gifts, Quellin first worked on the churches of Antwerp. With a staff of assistants he created his masterpiece in the immense ensemble of the *Amsterdam Town Hall [702]*. Here the extravagance of the Flemish mode takes on a substantial yet delicate corporality.

702 Artus Quellin the Elder, Diana (terracotta model), 1650–7. Amsterdam, Rijksmuseum. The classical Greek pose betrays the Southern schooling of Quellin. Despite the close contact with the relief ground, the free posture shows remarkable virtuosity.

Painting

Wall and ceiling painting in Rome

The course of Italian painting in the early Baroque period was shaped by two artistic personalities who were active mainly in Rome: Michelangelo Merisi de Caravaggio (1573–1610) from the neighbourhood of Bergamo, and the Bolognese Annibale Carracci (1560–1609), whose influence was reinforced by the activity of his brothers Ludovico and Agostino. Caravaggio's art brought a revolution which effected not only Italy, but Spain, France, and the Low Countries. In contrast to the classical ideal of the high Renaissance and the elevated, often recherché world of Mannerism, Caravaggio has a compelling realism, in which coarsely literal scenes of martyrdom stand beside tender, almost lyrical depictions of genuine piety. Dispensing with the perspective depth of the picture space, he concentrates more upon the objective reality of the figures who stand out with extraordinary force against the mainly dark backgrounds [703]. A similar reaction against the preceding phase of Mannerism is evident in Annibale Carracci's depictions of daily life, and especially in

703 *Caravaggio, Calling of S. Matthew, 1601. Rome, S. Luigi dei Francesi. Features and gestures are portrayed in artificial light; the faces are plastically moulded; nothing is idealized.*

704 *Annibale Carracci, Roman river landscape with bridge, c. 1600. Formerly Staatliche Museen Berlin, Museum Dahlem, Gemäldegalerie. Carracci readily took the beauty of Italian landscape into his pictures: his figures are in complete harmony with the setting.*

705 *Pietro da Cortona, ceiling painting in the Palazzo Barberini, Rome, 1633–9. A glorification of Pope Urban VIII and his family. The tectonic is completely abandoned: the eye finds no rest in the agitated confusion of richly decorative forms and figures.*

706 *Andrea del Pozzo, ceiling fresco in S. Ignazio, Rome, 1685–8. Painted architecture creates the effect of a space opened from above, vaulted by the heavens. A triumphant example of Baroque ceiling painting.*

his landscapes filled with a freshness of classical feeling [704]; the small figure scenes that are introduced in the latter seem to be only accessories. Carracci's votive paintings with their large figures are however key examples of Baroque rhetoric; pathetic attitudes, mystical raptures, spiritual and sensual emotions characterize his sacred and profane figures alike. The divine world of his famous frescoes in the Gallery of Cardinal Farnese (1597–1604) is only a little more realistic. In Carracci's followers the borderline between the profane and the sacred was effaced, so that often no essential difference in content can be distinguished between the two.

Pietro da Cortona (1596–1669), the chief representative of high Baroque painting in Rome, created in the great *salone* of the Palazzo Barberini [705] a glorification of Pope Urban VIII (1633–9) endowed with all imaginable worldly pomp. While in the Galleria Farnese individual fresco fields were isolated like paintings on the walls by heavy stucco frames the viewer's gaze here is drawn beyond the painted framework that follows the curvature of the vault into a heaven populated with countless allegorical figures.

At the end of the century this illusionism leads to painted continuations of real architecture. With the most daring perspectival foreshortenings the Jesuit father Andrea del Pozzo of Trento (1642–1709) extended the space of *S. Ignazio* (1685–8) in Rome to a dizzying height [706]. The individual figure in a distant sky is reduced to a hardly noticeable element among the crowd of indistinct forms.

Beside the somewhat tumultuous pathos of Cortona there flourished a classicism in easel painting whose finest representatives were the Bolognese followers of the Carracci, Guido Reni (1575–1642), Domenichino (1581–1641), and Andrea Sacchi (1599–1661). Inspired by Raphael and the Antique they created a deeply poetic world; their forms are more meditative and moderate in their expression of emotional states, echoing the clarity of the classic ideal [707]. The landscape developed by Annibale Carracci enjoyed considerable importance. A tranquil, often monumental conception of nature was enlivened by

707 *Andrea Sacchi, Vision of St Romuald, c. 1640. The Vatican, Museums and Galleries. Dramatic accents are avoided. The painter looked for Renaissance models in formal composition, though the illumination and flaky painting are Baroque.*

idyllic pastoral scenes or by saints manifesting a more intimate, more strongly inward world of faith.

In Venice the colouristic tradition was continued in the seventeenth century by three painters, Domenico Feti (1588/9–1624), Johann Liss (*c.* 1597–1629), a German by birth, and Bernardo Strozzi (1581–1647). In Bologna the influence of the *Accademia degli Incamminati* remained all-powerful, dominating the whole century, but without providing any essential impetus for further development. In Naples late Baroque tendencies appeared relatively early.

The late Baroque in Venice

In the second decade of the eighteenth century Venice eclipsed all other art centres. Italian Baroque painting, which elsewhere was already on the verge of succumbing to a dry Neo-Classicism, here attained a late and brilliant flowering. The first important

708 Giovanni Battista Piazzetta, Beach Idyll, c. 1740. Cologne, Wallraf Richartz Museum. Thundery light gives Venetian painting its individual charm together with glaring contrasts of light and shade and the shimmer of clothing.

709 Giovanni Battista Tiepolo, Sacrifice of Iphigenia, 1737. Vicenza, Villa Valmarana. The last triumph of Baroque fresco painting. This is not only festive interior decoration but an intensification of meaning of antique material.

figure is Giovanni Battista Piazzetta (1683–1754), whose plastic earthy forms stand out from pools of darkness produced by the bright lights that pick them out [708]. A palette varying from cool to warm in a brownish-red key began to brighten in his late period, when besides the altar paintings with their ascending zigzag compositions there appeared small idyllic Rococo scenes in a rustic and naïve vein corresponding to the taste of the time.

From Piazzetta's atelier there came the presiding genius of the Venetian late Baroque, Giovanni Battista Tiepolo (1696–1770). He moved from the dark-toned chiaroscuro of his master towards uniformly bright cool tones which in their transparency, their refined juxtapositions of bright blue, rose, bright yellow, silver-grey with honey-yellow and coffee-brown produce a delight in colour that is altogether independent of the objective content. Tiepolo's chief works appeared on the walls and ceilings of Venetian churches and palaces and in the Palladian villas of the Venetian mainland, but

710 *Francesco Guardi, Rio dei Mendicanti, c. 1776. Bergamo, Accademia Carrara. Guardi portrays more than a topographically faithful 'vedute'. He captures the painterly atmosphere of his native Venice in sympathetic, brilliantly coloured details.*

also in the Würzburg Residenz and the Royal Palace in Madrid, where he painted the *Triumph of the Spanish Monarchy* in the last eight years of his life. Tiepolo is the last great representative of illusionistic wall-painting. In the Palazzo Labia (1757) in Venice and in the smaller rooms of the *Villa Valmarana* (1737) near Vicenza the actual spatial boundaries disappear *[709]*. Colossal and fantastic façade walls yield to vistas of loggias and harbours with tantalizing immediacy, a hand moves around a painted column and the clouds seem to scurry through the sky towards Iphigenia who lies extended over the altar of sacrifice. The world of the Baroque approached its end in Tiepolo. Although his painted trains of nobles, his scenes of gods and heroes lacked nothing of the old brilliance, pomp, and grandeur and still exhibited bravura mastery of all artistic means, and though Baroque directness, pathos, and breadth of gesture were still felt to be fundamental, they clearly yielded to a theatrical element and to a *grandezza* that belonged only to the moment.

Beside the great decorative painting of the Venetian eighteenth century there flourished a quieter and more intimate genre, the painting of *vedute* or city views. Palace façades shimmering in the sunlight, the breadth of St Mark's Square, the picturesque domes of St Mark's and other churches, the still water of the lagoon – all this was exploited for painting. Small colourful figures teem in this dream-like setting or else glide in gondolas over blue-green waters with a careful brush and almost pedantic exactness. Antonio Canaletto (1697–1768) defined every architectural detail in his city scenes, whose topographical exactness is softened by a warm tranquil light. Less correct and orderly, less objective, and consequently of enhanced colouristic beauty are the *vedute [710]* of Francesco Guardi (1712–93), which seem to capture more of the essential mood of Venice.

SPAIN

Until about 1627, the year in which Velazquez was called to the court in Madrid, early Baroque painting

711 *Francesco de Zurbarán, St Francis, c. 1658–60. Munich, Alte Pinakothek. The Saint, painted with light from the side and tactile immediacy, is contrasted with the dark sky. Religious intensity characterizes one aspect of Spanish Baroque art.*

A deeply religious painter is the Sevillian Francisco de Zurbarán (1598–1664), who in contrast to the court painter Velazquez painted chiefly for small monasteries and churches. Something of the monastic severity of cloistered life penetrated into his work *[711]*. The cool yet forceful colours portray monumentally conceived saints imbued with great inner power and devotion while the harsh chiaroscuro creates an atmosphere of mystical transport.

The external circumstances that formed the background of another Sevillian painter, Diego Velazquez (1599–1660), are essentially different. Working at the court of Madrid from 1627 onwards he soon became court painter to Philip IV, accompanying him on journeys and military campaigns and occupying important posts in the ceremonial, architectural, and administrative organization. His pictures have a more worldly character, which makes him something of a phenomenon among Spanish painters. With a few exceptions he was concerned with purely secular painting. Like his contemporaries he began with a naturalism deriving from Caravaggio. But he soon began to depart from this uncompromising objectivity

712 *Diego Velazquez, the Court Dwarf Sebastian de Mora, 1643–4. Madrid, Prado. Despite the realism, costume and colour give the figure a heightened value and melancholy force.*

713 *Diego Velazquez, the Infanta Margarita Teresa, c. 1654. Madrid, Prado. In this portrait of a child naïve charm is balanced by the life-like posture, full of painterly refinement, especially in the depiction of material contrasts.*

lay chiefly in the hands of Italian immigrants. The great Spanish painters of the *Siglo de Oro* flourished until about 1692, when Luca Giordano, again an Italian, took the leading role at the court. He was followed by a number of compatriots, the most important of whom, Tiepolo, witnessed the end of the age. In the short span of sixty-five years five great painters, Ribalta, Ribera, Zurbarán, Velazquez, and Murillo created a pictorial world of incomparable grandeur, characterized by extraordinary dignity and beauty, by penetrating realism and psychological profundity, which spread the fame of Spanish Baroque painting throughout the world.

Although Spain as a purely Catholic country was closely linked to Italy, it never accepted the full Roman Baroque. In Spain emotional expression seems less artificial; more genuine and even ardent expressions of feeling avoid the pathetic. Men and saints are endowed with the same seriousness. The worlds of religious sentiment and real experience flow together inasmuch as they share the same modes of representation. Biblical scenes lack nothing in religious character even when they are presented with the most striking naturalistic detail.

714 *Bartolomé Esteban Murillo, Family Scene, c. 1660. Private Collection. The wall is the only spatial indication. Emphasis is concentrated only on the incidental attitudes of the subjects and their prosaic actions. An unartificial genre picture of considerable importance and effectiveness.*

with its strong contrasts of light and shade in order to construct his paintings upon careful gradations and the interplay of calm bright colour surfaces [712]. The exceptional seriousness of the children's faces of his later court portraits [713], the small slender bodies in their gorgeous robes of carefully chosen colours show a complete departure from the imposing princely portrait as it was practised by Italian and French artists.

The reputation of Bartolomé Esteban Murillo (1618–82) has proved unstable. Passionately admired in the eighteenth and nineteenth century when he was compared with Titian and Rubens, he later came to be regarded as a superficial sentimentalist who painted saccharine Madonnas and endearing little beggar children. But his *œuvre* also includes Biblical scenes, episodes from saints' lives, portraits, and carefully observed depictions of different social milieux [714]. Everything seems to be captured without effort, well balanced, and with a fine feeling for the arrangement of space and the delineation of inward differences.

FLANDERS

Peter Paul Rubens (1577–1648), who in his lifetime was heaped with honours as a painter, architect, decorator, diplomat, and talented man of the world, is not only the greatest figure of seventeenth-century

Flemish art but its absolute master. Up to the Impressionists he influenced generation after generation of European painters. For his ecclesiastical and princely patrons he created a world of exalted pathos, in which saints, gods, princes, heroes, commoners, and beggars unite to form triumphal images of creation. Rubens is the only painter resident in the North who mastered Baroque forms and themes in a well-nigh universal manner. What distinguishes him from the Italian painters is the native predilection of the Flemings for the pulsating phenomena of earthly life. Painted with the greatest virtuosity and often transcending the limitations of the format, his compositions never degenerate into a false pathos. Content and representation form a convincing and indivisible unity in his work. The strongest overall movement combines easily with the physical dynamism of the individual figures, and this quality endows his portraits also with their great immediacy. The consonance of all the pictorial elements is extraordinary – form, colour, and the chiaroscuro that conditions them both. Especially in landscapes where an uneventful, entirely undramatic scene is unfolded, the play of relationships between various pictorial elements evokes spiritual qualities. Thus the tension of a clearing storm is stamped on the image of the landscape [715]; the disquieting darkness of the wood contrasts with the pleasant variety of the open area. An over-arching rainbow serves as a natural device to unify the composition.

715 *Peter Paul Rubens, Landscape with Rainbow, c. 1635. Munich, Alte Pinakothek. Thunder and sunshine, dark wood and open field, dry hay and water make up the bold and lively contrasts. There is no attempt at topography, as in Dutch painting.*

None of his countless followers reached Rubens's universality. Most confined themselves to special branches of painting – still-life, portraiture, or other genres. Out of his rich and vital style of portraiture his urbane pupil Anthony van Dyck (1599–1641) tailored a courtly and elegant variant *[716]*. Van Dyck always placed special emphasis upon the elevated social standing of the sitter as expressed by his dress, attitude, and gestures. Combined with his uncommonly effective colour, these qualities made Van Dyck the most sought-after portraitist of the most fashionable European courts. Of special importance is his lasting influence on the portrait painting of England, where he worked as an honoured court painter in the last nine years of his life.

The lesser masters usually cultivated special areas. The animal and flower painters of the Rubens workshop and the genre painters, such as David Teniers

716 *Anthony van Dyck, Marchesa Elena Grimaldi, c. 1625. Washington, National Gallery. As a privileged portraitist of distinguished society Van Dyck depicts people not simply as they are, but rather as their background affects them. The page and the columns heighten the dignity of the sitter.*

717 *Adriaen Brouwer, Boors carousing, c. 1630. Munich, Alte Pinakothek. The assured depiction of the peasants at play is as distinctive of this painter as the lively illumination and concise detail.*

the Younger (1610–90), painted daily life and commerce, popular festivals, coarse behaviour, sickness, and misery in the tradition of Pieter Bruegel the Elder. Adriaen Brouwer (1605–38), a pupil of Frans Hals, became the most important painter of the lower strata of society *[717]*. The peasants who play cards, dice, and smoke are his tragicomic heroes. His small, miniature-like panels are master-works of painterly observation, presented in an uncommonly open mode of representation.

HOLLAND

The greatest fame of Dutch painting is associated with the name of Rembrandt Harmensz van Rijn (1606–69). The mysterious light effects of his early paintings betray Caravaggio's influence, although Rembrandt never visited Italy. He derived these features from the circle of 'Utrecht Caravaggisti', to which the painters Gerard Honthorst and Hendrick Terbrugghen belonged. Rembrandt's Amsterdam teacher Pieter Lastman passed on his Italian training.

718 *Jacob van Ruysdael, Egmond am Zee, 1655. Glasgow, Art Gallery. Portrait-like fidelity and yet a special feeling for the Dutch village scene. The Dutch painters of the seventeenth century first discovered such peaceful beauty.*

719 *Willem Claesz Heda, Still-life, 1650. Haarlem, Frans Hals Museum. The picture comprises objects on which the painter could exercise his virtuosity and colouring to record the fullness of life and yet portray an allegory of the transitory.*

In contrast to the worldliness of this artist Rembrandt sought from the very beginning – especially in Biblical scenes – to concentrate on the significance of the event while intensifying the humanity of his figures. He pursued this aim with single-minded earnestness. His wilfulness and shy, passionate temperament are evident in his early self-portraits. Rembrandt's middle period shows him more open to the world. His position was recognized and as the leading portrait painter of Amsterdam he was over-burdened with commissions. From this period comes

his *Self-portrait with Saskia* (c. 1634) showing the artist as a man of the world with a proud, extravagant attitude [720]. A warm brownish green forms the basic tone of this luscious painting, brilliant in every detail. Later – the so-called *Night Watch* signifies the critical shift – there appears the lonely, brooding master who has turned away from the public taste. Alone and impoverished Rembrandt created his powerful late works in which everything spectacular and ornate yield to a kind of ultimate seriousness and spirituality. His interpretation of Bible stories departs more strongly from tradition. He is concerned exclusively with the inner substance of the event. Details become less important and the warm-gold colour tones indicate not material preciousness but become the vehicle of spiritual expression [721].

As in Flanders the broad streams of Dutch painting consisted of a countless number of lesser masters. Being largely involved in the happenings of every-day life, they specialized in individual branches of painting. Adrian van Ostade, Jan Steen, and Pieter de Hooch painted genre scenes. Willem C. Heda [719] and Willem Kalf confined themselves to the

720 *Rembrandt, Self-Portrait with Saskia, c. 1634. Dresden, Gemäldegalerie. From the happiest period of Rembrandt's life. The position of the two figures is most unusual for a portrait.*

the paintings of Frans Hals and Jan Vermeer of Delft.

The importance of Frans Hals (*c.* 1580–1666) as a portrait painter transcended his native region. He knew how to heighten the appearance of his sitters through proud and audacious attitudes; at the same time he created colour structures of highly autonomous character. His tight and vehement brush strokes served to characterize physiognomy by simultaneously opening up structure and costume in an almost impressionistic fashion *[722]*. Close social integration is revealed by his group portraits which represent guilds, charitable organizations, and superintendents in lively, sharp characterizations.

A profound light-filled stillness pervades the paintings of Jan Vermeer of Delft (1632–75). The scholar at his desk, the maid washing in the kitchen, the woman sewing, all find themselves in a state of motionlessness which seems strangely related to the world of lifeless objects. A carefully adjusted colourism of jewel-like limpidity gives his work an extraordinary brilliance *[723]*.

721   Rembrandt, *Return of the Prodigal Son, 1668–9. Leningrad, Hermitage. One of the last works of the master, in which every gesture is imbued with the spiritual: the laying on of hands, the inclination of a head, and the features. All circumstantial details are sunk in shadows.*

722   *Frans Hals, Portrait of a Man, c. 1650. London, National Gallery. Note the heavy volumes of the figure clothed in black; collar and gloves are light, white touches.*

still-life; the members of the Van de Velde family were active as marine painters; Paulus Potter and Melchior d'Hondecoeter produced animal pieces; Pieter Sanredam and Emanuel de Witte depicted church interiors. Out of this enormous production Dutch landscape painting rose to European prominence. The works of Jacob van Ruysdael (1628–82) and of Meindert Hobbema convey through their simple but grandiose conceptions an idea of the high seriousness ascribed to this subject *[718]*. Although landscape was usually fixed to topographical exactness it still bore a hint of the religious spirit; a dying tree by Hobbema is a *vanitas* symbol, a cross on a rock turns a waterfall into the symbol of the Church.

The Protestant States General did not wish to imitate such Baroque themes of the South as the Triumph of the Church, Lives of the Gods, or Glorification of Rulers. Artists worked at refining an independent, bourgeois culture. How far within these limits art could become a powerful and noble work of the human spirit is shown especially by

the work of the numerous still-life painters whose themes of everyday life found their way into the living-rooms of the burghers.

After the war Johann Heinrich Schönfeld (1609–82) returned from Italy to South Germany where he transmitted the message of the Italian Baroque. But the vitality of Schönfeld's forms seems more subdued in Germany and are characterized by a landscape filled with light which dissolves into the distance in a colourful haze *[724]*. Generally speaking the range of painting in the second half of the century is uneven and the artists oscillated between Netherlandish and Italian influences, between the examples of Rubens, Rembrandt, and Van Dyck and those of Caravaggio and Cortona.

A factor restricting the creation of a genuine German style was the territorial fragmentation of the country with the consequent absence of any great power capable of centralizing artistic and scientific effort. It is indicative that the only really gifted high

724 Johann Heinrich Schönfeld, Halt for a Gift, 1655–60. Vienna, Kunsthistorisches Museum. The group is built up in chiaroscuro. A melancholy memento of the 'Wanderjahre' in Italy.

723 Jan Vermeer of Delft, Woman Reading a Letter, c. 1657. Dresden, Gemäldegalerie. The shiny silk curtains, the dull reflecting windowpane, the loose structure of the tapestry, the clear silhouette of the woman in front of the wall, are all combined in the manner of a still-life.

By the end of the century all the great masters were dead. Throughout the eighteenth century Holland's native artistic expression was subdued by the influence of France.

GERMANY

As in architecture and sculpture, the Thirty Years War in the first half of the seventeenth century had a paralysing effect on painting so that the level of achievement usually remained very provincial. For the most part German painters went abroad, since commissions by the Church and the nobility were not forthcoming. From the hand of Joachim von Sandrart (1608–88), the many-sided and much-travelled author of the *Teutschen Akademie* (a collection of artists' biographies on the model of Vasari), comes a portrait of a burgomaster which shows the somewhat stiff *grandezza* by which artists strove to equal the Italians, but more especially the formal Netherlandish portraiture. Netherlandish influence also lies behind

725 Michael Willmann, *Lamentation of the Virgin*, c. 1700.
*Munich, Alte Pinakothek. Strong light streaming from the side
raise the bodies of Christ and Mary out of the darkness; only
St John remains in shadow. Note the agitated brush strokes.*

court painter in Berlin, Antoine Pesne (1683–1757)
came from Paris, while the Bavarian court painter
George Desmarées (1697–1776) was from Sweden.
Trained in the great artistic centres of Europe, both
brought the refined international portraiture of the
Rococo to Germany. Anton Raffael Mengs (1728–
79), the only German whose fame was European,
lived in Rome and later in Madrid. Mengs's efforts in
the field of artistic theory were of more importance
than his painting, which soon turned into tepid
Neo-Classicism. With his *Gedanken über die Schönheit
und den Geschmack in der Malerei* he sought to
resuscitate a new classicism on the antique model.

The most gifted painters of the eighteenth century
devoted themselves not to easel paintings but to the
new decorative undertakings of wall and ceiling
painting. They were the great decorators of the
festive halls and *Kaisersälen*, of staircases, libraries,
monasteries, and churches. Especially in South
Germany and Austria they developed an illusionistic
fresco painting of considerable distinction. For the
outstanding masters – Daniel Gran (1694–1757), Paul
Troger (1698–1762), Franz Anton Maulbertsch
(1724–96) in Austria; and Cosmas Damian Asam
(1686–1739), Johann Baptist Zimmermann (1680–
1758), Matthäus Günther (1705–88), and Januarius
Zick (1732–97) amongst others in South Germany,
where there was a crowd of such talents – the
isolated painting served only for sketches and
modelli. The decorative painter of the Rococo was

Baroque painter, Michael Willmann (1630–1706),
worked on the periphery of the country, in Bohemia
and Silesia. His almost exclusively religious paintings
are works of touching pathos *[725]*, in which holy
figures and landscape are blended in a visionary play
of colour, light, and shadows. Apart from Rembrandt
Rubens's influence always stands behind such works,
but Willmann's forms have nothing of that master's
directness and enjoyment of earthly things. With
their sharp contrasts of light and shadow they seem
like uncomposed ciphers for a supra-terrestrial event.
In the *Lamentation of the Virgin* every movement and
dramatic element has been eliminated; the darkness
devours the glowing colours of the main figures.

In the period in which the great achievements of
German poetry, music, and philosophy surpassed
those of all other European countries, easel painting
did not develop beyond the level of a craft produced
by individual small masters. As in the Netherlands
each artist concentrated upon a particular domain,
among which only portraiture attained a certain
degree of quality. Characteristically the two portrait-
ists most in demand were foreigners: the Prussian

726 Franz Anton Maulbertsch, *Coriolanus before Rome*,
c. 1790. *Stuttgart, Württembergische Staatsgalerie. Like
Hogarth, Goya, and Tiepolo's sons Maulbertsch too showed a
preference for caricature in his late period. Note the large,
agitated composition and the jewel-like application of paint.*

preoccupied by new concerns. Inasmuch as his work was always tied to architecture he had to take account not only of the spectator's standpoint and of the spatial and vaulting forms, but also of the plastic and colouristic ensemble and of the directions of light. The example of Rome, in this case Pozzo's ceiling of S. Ignazio [cf. 706] again pointed the way. Thus the earlier buildings continued to link the real architectural setting to the painted one. Variations and innovations soon appeared. Asam portrayed secular scenes in the heavens and reserved the vaulting zones for his visions. Zimmermann renounced the architectural coulisses and displayed on his ceilings earthly landscapes on the borders of heaven. Gran and Troger began their light-filled skies right at the edge of the vault. The high point and conclusion of this flowering of German-Austrian ceiling painting was provided by Maulbertsch. His ceilings show pure glowing colours. *Mouvementé* figures picked out with pale light convey the transcendental leanings of this master's imagination [726]. In Maulbertsch's late works, as in those of Zick, there begins the shift to Neo-Classicism.

FRANCE

The seventeenth-century French conflict between Baroque and classical tendencies made itself felt in

727   Simon Vouet, Allegory of Peace, c. 1630–40. Chatsworth, Devonshire Collection. A spirited composition, in which the loosely draped materials betray the Italian training of the artist.

728   Nicolas Poussin, Arcadian Shepherds, c. 1639. Paris, Louvre. Baroque pathos is here achieved through strict ordering. The figures, in classical postures, are gathered round a monument inscribed 'Et in Arcadia ego'. An elegy of the transitoriness of life.

painting throughout the century. In 1627 Simon Vouet (1590–1649) returned from Italy and started a school which stamped the whole production of painting of the Paris court school for some time with Baroque forms [727]. But even Vouet's own buoyant draperies and his theatrical architectural backgrounds retain a mysterious quality of classical restraint.

Almost contemporary with Vouet were two painters who, in the select company of such architects as Mansart and Levau and such poets as Corneille and Racine, produced between 1640 and 1660 works that rank among the masterpieces of French classical culture. These artists are Nicolas Poussin (1593–1665) and Claude Lorrain (1600–82). Both spent most of their creative lives in Rome where they could exercise their artistic freedom untrammelled by the powerful State machinery of the French Academy. Poussin became the most profound representative of a classical ideal that has continued to project its influence down to our own day. His pictorial forms [728], which are constructed upon underlying geometrical schemata, show an absolute equipoise of formal means. A feeling for mass and weight akin to that of classical Greek art imbues all forms, architectural settings, and landscapes. Everything transitory or episodic is raised to the ideal plane of a super-individual, Arcadian sphere of timelessness. Poussin's countryman in Rome, Claude Lorrain, evolved a type of landscape painting in which the Roman Campagna and an imaginative architecture of

729   Claude Lorrain, The Dismissal of Hagar, 1668. Munich,
Alte Pinakothek. As in a theatrical set, the temple coulisses are a
foil for the wide landscape in the background. The Biblical event
is portrayed in a simple, almost story-like manner.

antique palaces and temples is poetically transposed
into a dream-like evocation of mood *[729]*. Claude's
pictures never constitute an attempt at objective
depiction of nature as is the case with Dutch painters.
They are ideal landscapes, shaped with subtle
rationalism and suffused with a transfiguring light,
with vistas through temple steps, along majestic
façades and over sparkling waters into a light-filled
distance. Turner, Corot, and nineteenth-century
landscape painting as a whole are the heirs of Claude.

In France itself there developed a more strongly
realistic painting, whose spiritual affinities with the
Jansenists of Port-Royal are especially evident in the
work of Philippe de Champaigne (1602–74). His
sober portraits rendered in the smallest detail are
master-works of the art of psychological representation, while his religious pictures, characterized by an
extraordinary restraint of emotional expression, strike
modern observers as among the most convincing
examples of religious feeling that the age produced.
The Lorrainer Georges de la Tour (1593–1652)
achieved a very personal interpretation of Caravaggio's realism in which he places forms of statuesque
stillness in settings defined by carefully calculated
light effects. His scenes from the lives of the Saints set
in a peasant-like but still somewhat idealized milieu
acquire a strongly mystical flavour through the
candlelight effects *[730]*. A similarly realistic depiction
of human circumstances was pursued by the three
Le Nain brothers, who with their genre scenes of
Netherlandizing character introduced a more lively

note into the rather idealistically oriented pictorial
themes of the French seventeenth century.

The leading and typical representative of the court
art under Louis XIV is Vouet's pupil Charles Le Brun
(1619–90), the great artistic orchestrator of Versailles
and other buildings for the King and the nobility.
His talents lay pre-eminently in the realm of the
decorative; he had remarkable ability to invent and
carry through decorative ensembles of enormous
extent. Endowed with a uniform and majestic pathos,
his paintings cover galleries and ceilings of the royal
châteaux. As the first director of the *Académie des
Beaux-Arts* he strove to codify Poussin's classical
mode of painting and theories into an inexhaustible
repertory for French artists, thereby limiting the
individual artist's scope for personal development.

In the painting of the Régence and Rococo the
manly and heroic ideal of the Louis Quatorze style
gave way to a rather feminine sentimentality.
Royalty and nobility no longer controlled taste so
exclusively as before; the prosperous bourgeoisie
began to take its place. The intellectual and artistic
élite gathered in the salons presided over by society
ladies, private circles where questions of taste were
arbitrated seriously; sometimes not so seriously. In
conformity with this larger public and its new
requirements the themes of painting shifted; they
became more trivial, charming, and pointed, or else
poetic, sentimental, and playful. The theme of
amorous dalliance appeared in endless variations.
The *fête galante* theme is essentially Rococo; a park

730   Georges de la Tour, The Birth, c. 1645. Rennes, Musée.
As an exponent of the style of Caravaggio, the painter makes the
centre of the picture the source of light, which heightens the
spiritual effect of the figures and objects.

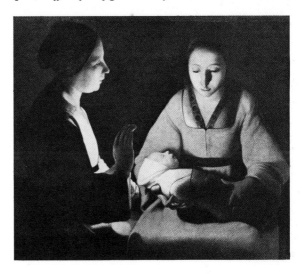

731 *Antoine Watteau, 'La Gamme d'Amour'. London, National Gallery. Note the theatrical dress of the men and the scintillating texture, which lends more freedom to the lyrical expressiveness of the theme.*

732 *François Boucher, The Bath of Diana, 1742. Paris, Louvre. Classical mythology is only a pretext for the playful Rococo. Here the goddess appears before the chase, as a sympathetic Goddess of Love. The lightly coloured painting seeks to emulate porcelain.*

landscape losing itself in a misty distance in which tender couples promenade blissfully in the shade of statues of Cupid, the Nymphs, and Venus. Luxurious costumes borrowed from the world of the theatre clothe the figures who converse in a carefully arranged natural setting. At the same time, in France as elsewhere, there flourishes the vein of fashionable international portraiture.

An important asset of French eighteenth-century painting is its superb use of colour. With ease and assurance artists deployed cool, light tones – grey, blue, green, pink, and bright yellow – in the most delicate transitions. The almost doll-like and relatively unadventurous portraits achieved an indefinable charm through the careful depiction of such softly shimmering materials as silk, satin, taffeta, and velvet and through the powdered hair framing the rosy faces. The expressive possibilities of white were discovered, and it was employed with subtle transitions to grey, light blue, soft green, and violet. When the Venetian Rosalba Carriera (1675–1757) brought her art of pastel to Paris about 1720 the innovation was received with great enthusiasm and soon became the rage of the fashionable world. The light, sketchy technique of chalk drawing with its effects of striking luminosity exercised a genuine fascination over contemporaries, especially in Germany.

The most important painter of the Régence and probably the greatest of the entire century was Antoine Watteau (1684–1721) from Valenciennes, the creator of the *fêtes galantes [731]*. But the themes that were repeated so insipidly by Watteau's numerous followers always kept a dream-like freshness and depth in the master's own work. Seldom has an artist been so successful in capturing the spirit of his time. It is not surprising to find that he had close links with the theatre. Over and over again Watteau painted the stock figures of the Italian and French comedy and something of the transitory and insubstantial world of the stage transpires in the gentle melancholy of many of his paintings.

François Boucher (1703–70), the renowned protégé of the Marquise de Pompadour, has taken his place in history as the painter of a frivolous and fickle society *[732]*. His ingenious Rococo ladies and the feminine elegance of his male portraits are certainly engaging, but all his brilliance of technique cannot disguise the superficiality of much of his work. His landscapes, somewhat unconvincingly furnished with brooks, rocks, abandoned mills, and little bridges, show a genuine painterly charm in their delicate blue-green and silver-grey tonalities.

In many respects Jean-Baptiste Siméon Chardin (1699–1779) stands outside the mainstream. He

733 *Jean-Baptiste Siméon Chardin, Still-life, c. 1760. Paris, Louvre. The magic of Chardin's art lies in nuance. His finely calculated arrangement and careful painting raise everyday objects to the level of poetry and art.*

734 *Jean-Honoré Fragonard, The Lecture (drawing), 1760–70. Paris, Louvre. The lightness of touch of the Louis XV period is seen at its best in this freely composed sketch.*

shares a fine sense of colour harmony with his contemporaries, but his pictorial world stands far apart from the fashionable trends of the period. Stimulated by Dutch and Flemish painting, he sought out the simplest subjects in the daily life of the street, the kitchen, and the family circle. The world he cultivated was the tranquil, the inconspicuous, and the unheroic. Chardin gave an intense reality to his subjects through a careful use of light, warm tones [733]. In this respect he foreshadows the realism of nineteenth-century painting.

Jean-Honoré Fragonard (1732–1806), who outlived his own time and died forgotten in the Napoleonic era, is the last and perhaps most brilliant master of the Rococo. Fragonard's virtuosity is especially evident in the scintillating facility of his brush-work and in the boldness and delicacy of his colour harmonies. He is a master of ebullient, sketchy drawings, which can stand beside those of Watteau among the best produced in the French eighteenth century [734].

ENGLAND

English painting of the seventeenth century and eighteenth century followed a course all its own in which the continental Baroque and Rococo found only occasional distant echoes. Religious painting played an insignificant role. The painters worked chiefly on commissions from the King, the nobility, and the gentry. Although the subject-matter is secular inasmuch as portraiture and landscape are the leading branches, the Baroque world of allegories, allusions, and personifications was never naturalized in England. It is not surprising that the aristocratically muted splendour of a Van Dyck exercised a lasting influence in English painting, while Rubens's paintings in the Banqueting House were almost ignored.

Sir Peter Lely (1618–80) adhered closely to Van Dyck's example. Lely, born Peter van der Faes, studied in Haarlem before he came to the English court on Van Dyck's death. He continued to paint during the Commonwealth, and at the Restoration embarked on his career as a portraitist that was to bring him a knighthood and a reputation as Van Dyck's legitimate successor. With Lely the dominance of English portraiture in the grand manner begins, a dominance that was not to be ended until the establishment of romantic landscape painting at the end of the eighteenth century. Lely's portraits of members of the royal family and the nobility [735] are proper, impersonal likenesses, whose effectiveness lies in the masterful handling of silken garments. His colour tonalities have the dull warmth that was to be predominant in English painting for a considerable period. The change in background is significant for the future: the conventional apparatus of columns and draperies is either replaced by a varied landscape or is shifted to the margin of the picture so that the vista into nature remains open. A certain concern with Baroque movement is shown by the inexhaustible wealth of poses, though these are often stylized in a stiff and unconvincing manner. The 'Windsor Beauties' of Charles II's court (now in the Royal Collection) and the twelve 'Admirals' (now in the National Maritime Museum) represent the outstanding examples of Lely's art.

The intellectual, rather sardonic figure of William Hogarth (1697–1764) had little following in his own day. His portraits *[736]*, especially those of his later years, display a simple, touching humanity and are

736 *William Hogarth, The Painter's Servants, 1755–60. London, Tate Gallery. A composition put together out of individual studies. Perhaps a 'pièce d'occasion', but typical of this self-conscious and critical period, when the single idea was thought more important than the ordering of the whole.*

735 *Sir Peter Lely, Henry Sidney Earl of Romney, c. 1650. Private Collection. The painter followed the fashion of his times when he portrayed the young nobleman in the costume of the hunter Adonis. The pose is deliberate, and the effect resembles salon painting. The landscape affords a clear contrast to the sitter.*

outstanding for painterly quality as well. He began by painting conversation pieces and small groups, but it was the 'Beggar's Opera' that first established his name. This, and the subsequent series of engravings, provide an extreme contrast to contemporary 'fêtes galantes'. Hogarth created a literary genre that became very popular during the second half of the eighteenth century, and was later adopted in France by Greuze. Besides his socially moralizing caricatures, he also invented the 'conversation piece', portraiture for a middle-class clientele in which several members of a family or a group of friends are shown either in an interior or in the open air.

In 1753 Sir Joshua Reynolds (1723–91) returned from Italy and quickly obtained the success that had been denied to Hogarth. Reynolds's adroit combination of rank and individuality were well attuned to the English inclination toward social differentiation and the strong individualism that had become important at this time. He knew just how to soften English reserve with a touch of Baroque movement *[737]* which finds its echo in landscape, light, and shadow so that the effects of the sitter and the background are mutually reinforcing. Reynolds carried on the tradition of Van Dyck in his depiction of aristocratic bearing and his treatment of precious stuff or fabrics. He became the close friend of Goldsmith and Dr Johnson, Garrick and Burke, and through his learning and his own personality very considerably raised the status of the artist in England. He determined to use the Royal Academy to create a British School of History Painters, and his own works, regularly exhibited there, were either formal history paintings or portraits in the historical manner. His great authority and influence in the second half of the eighteenth century are not least attributable to his *Discourses* delivered before the Academy in which his grand style found a theoretical and programmatic apology recalling the continental Baroque.

Richard Wilson (1713–82), another English painter in Rome, confined himself to pure landscape painting. The hills and lakes of the countryside around Rome and the green plains of England are always presented by Wilson with a certain classical Roman clarity blended with a personal melancholy, heralding the coming of the ideal landscape of the romantic painters. There is no link here with the gay Arcadias of Rococo landscape painting. Thomas Gainsborough (1727–88) is the only English painter who may be usefully compared to the Rococo *[738]*. Untouched by Italy, he developed his art in contact with the

738 Thomas Gainsborough, The Painter's Daughters chasing a Butterfly, c. 1758. London, National Gallery. The motif effortlessly follows the facial features and gestures, almost impressionistic in their naturalism.

737 Sir Joshua Reynolds, Lord Heathfield, 1788. London, National Gallery. Still no breach with the expressive Baroque standing portrait, but note the more natural posture and the close relationship to the landscape in the background.

French Rococo and Dutch landscape painting. With a light, often rather free brush technique he captured the subtle nuances of atmospheric colour and light. Landscape and figure painting were of almost equal value to him, yet in typical Rococo fashion he preferred the female portrait. His likenesses of women, though not to be compared with Venus or the Nymphs as in France, display an extraordinary feminine grace and even show an occasional touch of coquetry, while his portraits of children are of a freshness and purity that has probably never been surpassed. All his life Gainsborough considered landscape his true *métier*, but it was portraits that he painted for a living. Nine years in Bath established his reputation, and in 1774 he moved to London and set himself up as Reynolds's rival. As a portraitist of society, he was at least the equal of Reynolds, and the ease with which he could render aristocratic reserve, as in the famous portrait of Mrs Siddons, is most noticeable. His landscapes, idealized and Arcadian as they often were, introduced a new richness of colour to English painting in this genre, and his later scenes were much influenced by Rubens. Constable, who is considered in the following chapter, turned back to the Dutch for his models.

The Nineteenth Century

Towards the middle of the nineteenth century the history of European art entered a new phase. The cycle of epochal styles embracing all realms of artistic creation seemed to be played out and the age of the *Gesamtkunstwerk* over. The concept of the past implicit in the rising historicism led to uncertainty about contemporary creativity. Historicism demonstrated that every style belonged to the age that had produced it, but it hesitated to grant the right of the present to evolve new forms not based on historical precedent. The artist was faced with the problem of choice of styles. Should he give his allegiance to one or the other of the historical styles or was it better to cast off the burden of the past, to stand on one's own feet and forge a contemporary style to meet contemporary needs? Out of this dilemma arose the divided consciousness that afflicted the art of the nineteenth century. Artistic creation was split into two camps in fierce conflict with one another. One side insisted on the absolute value of some epoch of the past and imitated variously the antique, the Renaissance, or the Gothic; the other strove to tackle artistic problems with new expressive means informed by an awareness of the present.

Any account of the stylistic development of the period must come to terms with this basic split. Chronologically the break appeared in the middle of the eighteenth century. At this time the reception of the historical styles began. About 1750 Horace Walpole started the construction of his country-house of Strawberry Hill in an early version of the Gothic revival style *[741]*. Soufflot, who had given a lecture on the Gothic as early as 1741, began the classicistic church of Ste-Geneviève (now the Panthéon) in Paris in 1757 *[747]*. Attachments to the Gothic and the antique appeared side by side, sometimes in the person of a single architect. The source is the freedom of choice that permitted the artist to select among a number of stylistic formulas *[740]*. The eclecticism of patrons induced architects to

assemble three-dimensional 'illustrations' of the historical styles which in their ensemble provided a kind of museum of architecture and styles. The English garden provided a welcome setting for these exhibits. In 1758 in a park near Birmingham James Stuart built a Doric temple in immediate proximity to a Gothic revival gatehouse, both structures being commissioned at the same time by the patron. The renewal of antique architectural forms proceeded along with art-historical publications, among which Johann Joachim Winckelmann's *Geschichte der Kunst des Altertums* (1763) was pre-eminent. By this means an archaeological storehouse upon which the architects were to draw was established.

A few years after the renewal of the Gothic and the antique another direction of discovery was opened up whose exponents did not acknowledge the tutelage of previous styles. In 1777 Abraham Darby erected a cast-iron bridge over the Severn near Coalbrookdale *[753]*, in which iron was first employed for a large-scale work of public utility. Works such as this constitute the decisive beginnings of the powerful development of a new functional architecture adapted to meet the needs of the advancing industrial revolution. But close inspection shows that the new iron architects did not scorn to dress up their works in a decorative overlay of historical derivation.

Henceforth architecture presents two different streams of development: the idealistic architecture of historicism and the realistic construction of the engineer. 'Idealistic' here means that the architect working with historically given forms employed them to encase the constructional core of his building in an impressive aesthetic facing so that the objective needs of the project yielded first place to the preoccupation with decoration. 'Realistic' means that the architect was aware of constructional principles and did not hesitate to make them evident in the work. The consciousness of the present in the building of the engineers expressed itself in the use of new 'artificial' materials – iron, glass, concrete – created by industrial processes. The new materials were a great stimulus in the development of adequate constructional principles. These meant a departure from the closed mass of the building entity in favour of steel-frame construction, which posed for the builder the problem of developing a new beauty of form appropriate to the material and constructional

739 Paul Cézanne, La Carrière Bibémus, c. 1900. Zürich, Collection Bührle. This representation of a quarry belongs to the late landscapes, in which Cézanne's stylistic innovations are especially clear.

740   Sir John Soane, sketch for a church in three different styles. From the second half of the eighteenth century historical consciousness confronted the artist with a choice of styles.

requirements. For some time the course of the new engineering building ran unnoticed or ignored beside traditional architecture, which being regarded throughout the nineteenth century as the only really respectable architecture was favoured by taste-makers in official and intellectual circles.

Towards the end of the eighteenth century a similar process occurred in painting. It was evident that the compositional formulas of the Baroque and Rococo had lost their efficacy. Artists appeared who were no longer concerned with the modulated harmony of form, which seemed to them empty, hollow, and conventional. The work of William Hogarth [cf. *736*] shows precociously the conflict between representative formalism of historical derivation and the spontaneous rendering of reality, between the idealized and documentary modes. A decade before, the history painter James Thornhill had questioned whether a history painting should be executed in accordance with the facts of the event or whether these should rather be embellished and allegorized. At the end of the eighteenth century this conflict was decided by David [*761*] and Goya [*764*] in favour of the depiction of reality. They created new pictorial forms that allowed reality to be presented more directly and plainly than heretofore. Although just as in architecture the conflict between 'history' and 'life' was first resolved in the nineteenth century in favour of 'life' (i.e. the present), the split continued to run through the period.

The situation in sculpture was similar, though the scope of its achievement was narrower. The smooth tranquil formalism of Neo-Classic sculpture embodied all the forces that strove towards the antique ideal. Passionate figures captured in active attitudes appear only when the artist preferred vitality to the formulas of the classic style.

Painting and sculpture parallel architecture in carrying out the split between idealistic and realistic form. The idealistic trends adhered closely to approved prototypes from the past; they inclined to finished forms that betrayed nothing of the process of creation just as the historically oriented architectural styles concealed the underlying construction. The realistic trends permitted the viewer to participate, so to speak, in the artist's process of design. Instead of concealing the artistic handwriting they displayed it as a part of the work of art, just as in architecture the engineers not only revealed their constructional methods but endowed them with positive value.

ARCHITECTURE

Neo-Gothic

An overall view of the Gothic revival in Europe shows the following development. At first the outstanding feature was the discovery of archaeological details and pious imitation of them; ultimately, at the turn of the nineteenth and twentieth century, architects concentrated upon the renewal and further development of the Gothic principles of design, leaving the preoccupation with 'correctness' to one

741   Horace Walpole, Neo-Gothic room at Strawberry Hill, Twickenham, c. 1750. A decorative application of Gothic architectural form without any genuine understanding of its structural necessity.

side. It can be affirmed that the encounter with the style showed an increasing depth and intensity – beginning in superficial copying and ending in personal creation from the repertory of possibilities inherent in the Gothic idea. Gaudí's church of the Sagrada Familia in Barcelona *[744]* is the supreme example of the concluding stage of this process.

The Gothic revival was diffused in the eighteenth century from England. Although England with its Palladian classicism *[cf. 666]* revered the antique while the Baroque dominated the Continent, in landscape design *[cf. 675]* it created the basis for an anti-classical trend which was ultimately to develop into Romanticism. English landscape artists broke with the severe, linear regularity of the Italian and French garden and preferred a variety of points of view, a looser grouping of trees, and the opening of nature into space without measurable limits. The predilection for the picturesque, the irregular, and the 'unspoiled' favoured the rediscovery of the Gothic. It must also be remembered that in England the Gothic revival follows almost directly upon the last manifestations of the Gothic survival, though the protagonists of the new trend sought to achieve a more accurate and detailed imitation. In the beginning the knowledge required was not available, and the feeling for the unity of style had not yet developed. Delight in picturesque detail was the keynote; people were enthusiastic about pointed arches and concentrated their attention on the smaller decorative motifs *[741]*. Pinnacles, tracery, and rib-vaults were carefully reproduced in colourful and *mouvementé* settings. The impression of the whole was disregarded in favour of striking effects. The emphasis upon playful decorative motifs may be connected to the fact that the Gothic revival overlaps the Rococo chronologically. The contemporary fashion for chinoiserie is also indicative; its advocates found common ground with the Gothicists in their delight in bizarreries and irregularities. In the following decades the Gothic came increasingly to be regarded as the very embodiment of the principle of organic growth untrammelled by any system. These qualities were contrasted with the smoothness and equipoise of the antique. Especially in Germany, where the Gothic revival made its entry in 1773 in the *Gothic House [742] of the park at Wörlitz*, the concept of the style was intensified in the direction of the primeval, powerful, and elementary in disregard of all rules. Goethe's rhapsodic evocation of the Cathedral of Strasbourg *[cf. 407]* (*Von deutscher Baukunst*, 1773) added a new element to these ideas that foreshadowed the Romantic interpretation of the Gothic. Besides its 'characteristic' traits (it is 'more felt than measured'),

742 *Friedrich Wilhelm von Ermannsdorff, 'Gothic House' in the Park at Wörlitz, 1773. A small Neo-Gothic garden palace in an 'English' park: architecture and garden design emphasize the painterly irregular, and organic.*

743 *Friedrich Schmidt, Town Hall in Vienna, begun 1873. An example of a building complex whose many-sided functions aimed to overcome the architecture of historical styles. The different Gothic styles are here placed one on top of the other.*

744   Antoni Gaudí, church of the Sagrada Familia in Barcelona, 1883–1926. A fantastic Neo-Gothic building designed to create a completely plastic form from natural shapes.

Goethe exalted the Gothic as an expression of the Germanic spirit. In German Romanticism this last response was to receive new emphasis and the Gothic became a symbol of patriotic feeling. The pious sentiments evoked by the Gothic were important not only for the religious realm, but equally for the feeling for the national past, which was now seen in a transfigured light. This vision of history regarded the Gothic as a symbol of wholeness – that is, of unalloyed faith, of the organic hierarchic ordering of life, and so on – contrasting it to the 'pastiches' of the imitators of the antique, whose forms were decried as being 'thought rather than felt'. During the struggle against French hegemony the Gothic was exalted as the German national style, with the result that soon non-religious elements were added to its stock in the form of new architectural themes. Numerous projects sought to embody architecturally the dream of national unity in the form of a Gothic national monument. From the complex of the organic and

the original, new concepts of value were evolved in the 1830s. The Gothic came to be regarded not merely as the only sincerely religious style of building, but also as the touchstone of craftsmanlike excellence and honesty. This concept arose in England and led, towards the middle of the century, to the reform movement headed by William Morris which sought to renew the minor arts in terms of the ideal of truth to materials.

Among the most important aspects of architectural practice of the second third of the century is the appearance of new categories of secular building. Besides the church and the commemorative monument (e.g. Schinkel's cast-iron monument for the War of Liberation, 1821) there appeared vast museum and administrative structures. Once more England took the lead with the Houses of Parliament in London by Charles Barry and Augustus W. N. Pugin, begun in 1835. This development may be said to be concluded with Friedrich Schmidt's *Town Hall in Vienna*, begun in 1873 *[743]*. For these secular works the formal repertory of ecclesiastical Gothic was inadequate and medieval secular building was resorted to as a secondary source. The development of the Neo-Gothic administrative centre shows this tendency as the original source, as the country-seat or the artificial ruin became increasingly obscured in the extensive new layouts with their many courts and wings corresponding to the complex needs of modern government.

If we leave the romantic and picturesque interpretation of the Gothic and turn to the structural and functional one, we find that this had its roots in the extensive campaigns of reconstruction of historic monuments. The preoccupation with a style purified as far as possible from later accretions lead to the study of the means of construction. Herein lies the difference from another, literary and sentimental interpretation of the Gothic style that – 'more felt than measured' – used its formal idiom as the starting-point for a roving imagination, endorsing Ruskin's conviction that decoration was the most important part of architecture.

France, the original homeland of the Gothic, pioneered in the sober inventory of its structural forms. Through his restorations and theoretical writings Eugène Viollet-le-Duc (1814–79) laid the foundations. His example decisively influenced the Catalan architect Antoni Gaudí (1852–1926) in his renewal of the Gothic 'from within'. When he began to erect the *Church of the Sagrada Familia* in 1883 *[744]*, he undertook to go beyond the Gothic: 'The Gothic is noble, but imperfect, a beginning that the lamentable Renaissance cut short too soon. Today we must

745 William Richard Lethaby, Brockhampton Church, 1900–2. The point of departure is not the direct application of Gothic details but the effort to carry out the laws of Gothic structure.

and France. In England William Richard Lethaby (1857–1931) distinguished a 'hard' and a 'soft' Victorian architecture. He opted for the hard type, that is for truth to materials. Along these lines he built the *Church in Brockhampton* in 1900–2 *[745]*, whose simple spatial articulation foreshadows the later Gothic interpretation of Expressionism. Anatole de Baudot (1834–1915) built the *Church of St-Jean-de-Montmartre [746]* in Paris from 1894 to 1902. Here he employed the newest discoveries of reinforced concrete construction, especially the grid system invented by Hennebique in 1892. Baudot's church is the first monumental structure in which reinforced concrete plays a dominant role. As a pupil of Viollet-de-Duc the architect had direct access to a synthesis of Gothic skeleton construction employing the most up-to-date technical means of the period. He treated the material with undisguised frankness, achieving structural boldness through a spatially

746 Anatole de Baudot, St-Jean-de-Montmartre in Paris, 1894–1902. An interpretation of Gothic scaffolding with the most up-to-date technical means: the pillars and rib-vaulting are of steel and concrete.

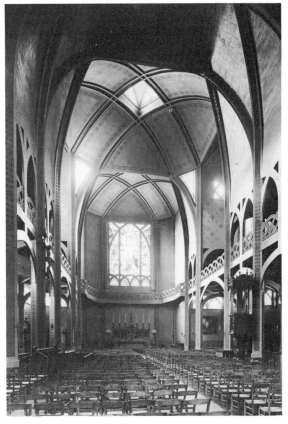

not imitate or copy the Gothic, we must continue it by returning to the phase before the late Gothic.' Gaudí concentrated upon the vaulting and the ground-plan. The latter was not to be subordinated to a schema but must appear the result of growth. The qualities of the organic should be seen not only in details but in the 'growth' of the building mass and its elements. The wall and roof zones should inter-penetrate and the towers should evolve organically from the nave and aisles. Gaudí regarded the Gothic buttresses as crutches and tried to solve the problem of the relief of stress by means of oblique supports suggesting trees. In this way he contrived a scaffold-like system of support that in architectural ingenuity rivalled the diagonal dynamism of contemporary steel structures *[759, 760]*. Gaudí's style with its orientation towards natural forms constitutes a link between the Gothic revival and Art Nouveau *[806]*.

Similar efforts to understand Gothic in the structural sense appeared at the same time in England

staggered arrangement. In this work of Baudot two nineteenth-century trends meet: steel and reinforced concrete construction, which could be described as the modern counterpart to the Gothic skeleton method, and the structural Gothic revival, which finally encounters the new building materials.

Neo-Classicism in France and Germany

In contrast to the Gothic revival, the renewal of Mediterranean styles (antique, Renaissance) reached its creative apogee not at the end of the century, but at its beginning. As the nineteenth century advanced, more superficial and theatrical forms came to the fore. Scale increased to the point of colossal pomposity, and the decorative forms inclined to material prettiness and luxury [752]. This development gradually embraced all styles dependent on the antique orders. Beside the Greek appeared Roman architecture; the early Christian basilica was re-modelled, then the Byzantine and Romanesque styles, toward the middle of the century the Renaissance, and finally in the period after the Franco–Prussian War the Baroque. The Gothic revival had its adherents among those who wished to entrust the creative process to the irrational forces of the imagination. Classicistic trends were effective where the measured was preferred to the felt, and the clearly

748   Claude-Nicolas Ledoux, Barrière de la Villette in Paris, 1784–9. The wall mass is emphasized in strong and single geometrical forms. The functional building (Customs House) becomes a monument.

747   Germain Soufflot, Ste-Geneviève (now the Panthéon) in Paris, 1757–90. A closed, block-like classical body built on a single geometrical design. Despite the gigantic proportions the effect of antique and Renaissance motifs is successful.

delimited to the unpredictably dynamic. The Gothic camp maintained that 'All beautiful forms are derived from curves' (Ruskin). Classicism responded with its vocabulary of elementary stereometric forms – the cube, the cone, the cylinder, and the pyramid. It was the manner of classicism to place its faith in the primary and the elementary. Architects of this trend built in large masses – in contrast to the Gothic revival which was led historically to the concept of the space frame. The closed block form was most impressive in the first decades, when it was manifested in lapidary, smooth wall surfaces [749]; later it turned to a complicated layering of surfaces.

A severe articulation of vast building units was successfully carried out by Germain Soufflot (1713–80) on the exterior of his *Church of Ste-Geneviève* in Paris, begun in 1757 [747]. Roman and Renaissance prototypes conditioned the concept, while Wren's St Paul's Cathedral in London [cf. 667] stands as godparent. The building underwent varied fortunes which show how church building lost its central role in architecture at this time. After the outbreak of the Revolution Ste-Geneviève became a temple of the hero cult and was proclaimed the Pantheon of the Nation. This infiltration of non-ecclesiastical claims was paralleled by a notable uncertainty regarding tradition, so that when the Church of La Madeleine in Paris was erected in the form of an ancient temple, nobody was surprised when Napoleon conceived a project to turn it into a 'Temple de la Gloire'.

Two architects of the generation following Soufflot, Claude-Nicolas Ledoux (1736–1806) and

Étienne-Louis Boullée (1728–99) treated the antique model in even more severe fashion. They favoured the Doric column, emphasizing the massive stoniness of the structure. Practical considerations were of secondary importance; instead everything was accentuated that might convey the serious, symbolic character of a monument. These men, who left many projects though they executed little, have been dubbed revolutionary architects. This designation is justified. if the Revolution of 1789 is understood in its broadest cultural and social sense. The drive towards social improvement was also present in the architects. Ledoux designed the plan of an ideal city which was intended to guarantee the happiness and concord of a morally purified society. Among his few executed buildings the incompletely preserved *Paris Customs House* (1784–9) gives the best idea of his style *[748]*.

Similar characteristics are found at about the same time, though untouched by French influences, in the work of John Soane (1753–1837: Rotunda of the Bank of England, begun 1788), while somewhat later Friedrich Gilly (1772–1800), after a stay in Paris, brought the new mode to Berlin. At his early death this architect left two grandiose projects which were never to be executed: a design for a monument to Frederick the Great, in which the kernel of the idea of the later Valhalla can be discerned, and a plan of 1800 for a *National Theatre in Berlin [749]*. The new building problem of the theatre was prophetically resolved in this project. The exterior masses reflect the interior disposition of the building: the half cylinder corresponds to the spectators' area, the dominating block to the stage. The overlapping layers of the several units are presented in sparely articulated, unbroken surfaces.

Karl Friedrich Schinkel's (1781–1841) extensive life work depends upon the example of his teacher Gilly. His vision embraced both the antique and Gothic worlds. Like Soane he provided a choice between the two styles in one of his church projects. His moderate historicism did not exclude the idea that 'function is the principle of all building'. He did not envision a merely archaeological interpretation of the antique, but sought to grasp its 'spiritual principle' at the same time 'enlarging it to meet the needs of our new world epoch'. Through this insight he succeeded in forming his work upon a sober utilitarian mould (Bauakademie in Berlin, begun 1832). His mature classical works include the Altes Museum (1822–8) in Berlin. Along with the theatre the museum belongs to the most important categories of the high-minded architecture of improvement of the early nineteenth century. Schinkel's Museum endowed a cultural centre with a sacred dignity and sublimity.

749 *Friedrich Gilly, sketch for a National Theatre in Berlin, 1800. A solution whose single geometric design looks forward to future developments. Single parts (foyer, auditorium, stage) are evident on the exterior.*

750 *Karl Friedrich Schinkel, Perspective Drawing of the Great Hall in the Antonin Hunting Box. An important example of German classicism, where the fitments give the building an antique character.*

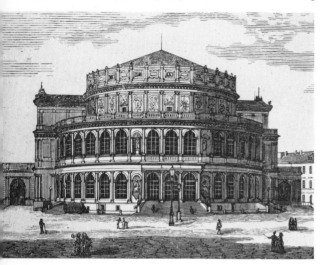

751 Gottfried Semper, Opera house in Dresden, 1838–41 (from a contemporary print). The functional design is here realized in connexion with Florentine Renaissance forms.

752 Charles Garnier, Staircase of the Paris Opéra, 1861–74. Magnificence and pomp are the characteristics of later nineteenth-century architecture.

At the beginning of the second decade of the nineteenth century the horizon widened to include early Christian and Byzantine building, which formed the basis for Ludwig Persius's (1803–45) *Rundbogenstil*, and the Renaissance. Within a development that inclined more and more to a 'masked ball of styles', and which did not shrink from actual copies (cf. Munich's Feldherrnhalle, a replica of the Florentine Loggia dei Lanzi), the work of Gottfried Semper (1803–79) shows an effort to attain a rational point of view within the context of historically oriented architecture. In his theatre and museum buildings he strove to reach a logical articulation of elements. Examples are the *Opera House* (first version, 1838–41) *[751]* and the Gemäldegalerie (1843) in Dresden.

The last third of the century was dominated by a magniloquent architecture of display, whose exponents used antique forms to achieve showy, bombastic effects. The *Staircase of the Opéra in Paris* (1861–74) by Charles Garnier (1825–98) is perhaps the most characteristic example of this architecture of prestige *[752]*.

Iron, steel, and glass structures

Iron was first used as a building material in England, the country that had reached the most advanced stage of industrialization in the eighteenth century. The material basis for this was laid when the industrial production of iron began in the middle of the century.

The first phase of the use of the new material comprised arch and suspension bridges, and roof and dome structures for buildings of several stories. In 1777 Abraham Darby began the *arch bridge near Coalbrookdale* which was finished after two years' work *[753]*. The width of the span was 100 feet. In 1793–6 Burdon executed the Sunderland Bridge after plans of Thomas Paine with a span of 235 feet. The Pont des Arts in Paris was built in 1803. In this connexion several important suspension bridges should be mentioned. In 1819 Samuel Brown erected an iron-chain bridge over the Tweed near Berwick with a span of 435 feet. The Conway Castle Bridge in Wales, built at about the same time by Thomas Telford, was about 25 feet shorter. In 1836 I. K. Brunel began the Clifton Bridge in Bristol. The gatehouses of these iron bridges were executed in stone with the monumentality of Greek or Egyptian pylons.

The first cast-iron framework for a large-scale building appeared as early as 1796 in a flax mill in Shrewsbury. Iron roof constructions appeared even earlier. In 1780 the Grand Salon of the Louvre was provided with a cast-iron roof frame, in 1787 followed the Théâtre-Français, and in 1824 the British Museum. The dome of the Paris Halle au Blé (1809–11) showed cast-iron ribs of 130 feet span; the barrel-vault covering of the Viennese Diana Baths had a span of 62 feet.

Although at first iron was only used sporadically in the first half of the nineteenth century, and was rarely displayed in visually prominent spots, the theoretical speculations of architects already took it into consideration. The conservative wing treated the possibility of these new structural procedures becoming truly architectural with undisguised scepticism. Since iron construction was characterized by purely functional attitudes, in the view of its critics it adhered to an inadequate concept. Schinkel himself expressed this in a piece of self-criticism. When he 'developed the whole conception for a particular work from its immediate and trivial function alone . . . there appeared something that was dry, rigid, and lacking in freedom, altogether excluding two essential components, the historical and the poetic'.

Passionate arguments were soon put forward in favour of the possibilities of the new materials against these doubts about the poetic expressiveness of pure construction, doubts which were evinced when iron was declared to be brutal and ugly. The discussion of the pros and cons of aesthetic conviction reached its point of greatest intensity about the middle of the nineteenth century when practice entered decisively into the conflict of theories. John Ruskin in his *The Seven Lamps of Architecture* of 1849 decreed that 'True architecture cannot endure iron as a structural material', whence it followed that the iron halls of the railway station were for Ruskin excluded from the realm of architecture. In 1846 the German archaeologist Karl Boetticher explained why it was wrong to rely upon the model of the historical styles. These were past and done with and consequently not susceptible to further perfection. He stated his conviction that 'another art in which another static principle sets the standard will emerge from the womb of time'. Another material would replace the traditional building elements with others in conformity with a new principle of creative energy. Iron was predestined 'to serve as the basis for the roofing system of the building style of the coming age'. Boetticher stipulated that one must drop the mask of style and start again with fundamentals. This requirement recalls the anti-traditionalism manifested at the same time in the realistic painting of Courbet, whose aim was to rehabilitate the 'process of painting'. A few years after Boetticher Théophile Gautier

753 *Abraham Darby, cast-iron bridge over the Severn at Coalbrookdale, 1777–9. The closed wall mass of earlier bridges is abandoned through the transparent construction in the new material iron.*

754 *K. L. Althans, Foundry in Sayn (Rhineland), 1824–30. An early example of a hall with inner supports made from iron. The design of the gabled front is no imitation of Gothic tracery-work, but the result of constructional necessities. The building is still strengthened by walls on its longer sides.*

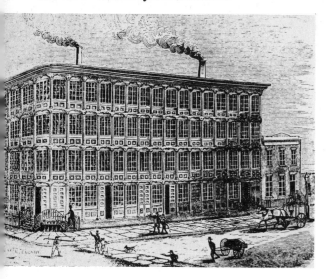

755   *James Bogardus, cast-iron factory in New York, 1848. The outer walls are of prefabricated cast iron (Renaissance-style columns), with glass panes between. A step to modern skeleton-type building.*

756   *Jules Saulnier, the Menier Chocolate Factory at Noisiel-sur-Marne, 1871. The bearing function of the exterior wall is here assumed by the interior iron framework.*

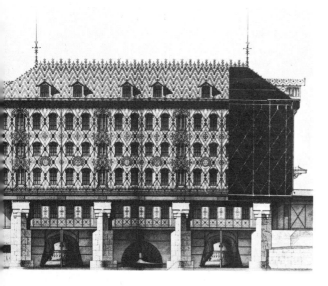

wrote: 'At the same time an architecture of our own can be created using the new means furnished by the new industry. The use of cast iron permits and requires many new forms, as can be seen in railway stations, suspension bridges, and in the vaults of winter gardens' (1850). The 'process of replacement of existing artistic types' (Semper) which could no

longer be ignored by the middle of the century found its ultimate source in the growth of industry. This process was also to make the building engineer the spokesman for the future.

Some of the most important pioneer works of the new way of building appeared in these years. In 1843–50 Henri Labrouste (1801–75) erected the reading room of the Bibliothèque Sainte-Geneviève in Paris. In 1845 Burton and Turner began the Palm House in Kew Gardens [757]. In 1848 James Bogardus built a cast-iron factory in New York [755]. In 1851 the Crystal Palace [758] arose under Joseph Paxton's direction. Three years afterwards I. K. Brunel and M. D. Wyatt built the hall of Paddington Station in London. In 1858 Labrouste began the great reading room of the Bibliothèque Nationale in Paris. At this time there also appeared an important technical advance in the making of steel, for in 1855 Henry Bessemer discovered his process. Ingot steel could now be mass produced at economical prices.

The buildings that appeared in the mid-century manifest the structural possibilities and limits which the new materials offered the builder. Iron is more a constructional than a building material; its inherent qualities are more suited to a frame of girders than to the closed plastic mass of stone building. It is no accident that its use in buildings of several stories extended only gradually from the interior to the exterior. The first cast-iron frameworks were used on the inside of buildings where dividing walls are dispensed with, as for example in the flax mill of Shrewsbury where the exterior is built of bricks. The effort to give a tectonic and formal expression to the iron on the exterior had to find a *modus vivendi* with a material whose flatness would complement the skeletal characters of the iron frame. Glass was available for this purpose.

Far-reaching aesthetic consequences were to result from this process. An early example is the *Foundry in Sayn*, Germany (begun 1824), by K. L. Althans [754]. The gabled front of three-aisled building clearly displays the bowed lines of force of the construction. In 1848 James Bogardus (1800–74) applied the skeleton construction for the first time to a traditional building unit. Although his *cast-iron factory [755]* used prefabricated, standardized elements, outwardly it conformed to the type of the Italian Renaissance palace. Bogardus did not hide his satisfaction at being the first to have cast the ancient decorative forms in iron. More important than this compromise with the historical styles is the fact that glass became the element that ordered and unified the exterior. A further consequence of this way of building was the reversal of traditional practices, that is, the exterior wall was structurally devalued in favour of the supporting interior framework. In the building for a *chocolate factory [756] in Noisiel-sur-Marne* (1871) Jules Saulnier realized a new principle of construction. The whole load was borne by the iron skeleton and the exterior wall became a 'curtain' composed of a network of iron lozenges. The fields of this show screen were decoratively filled with bright tiles. This association of the traditional surface decoration with iron slabs again reveals the conflict observed in James Bogardus's factory with its Renaissance columns.

Striking contradictions are evident in many railway stations of the middle of the century, e.g. Paddington Station and King's Cross Station (1851–2) in London and the Gare de l'Est (begun 1847) in Paris. The street fronts were conceived as great masses of masonry. The ostentatious grandeur of their historical forms concealed the halls with their bold use of iron construction.

England produced the first buildings in which the builders entirely escaped from the convention of the interposed façade, exploiting the inherent qualities of iron for structure and style alike. These were the *Palm House* (1845–7) *in Kew Gardens [757]* by Decimus Burton and Richard Turner and the *Crystal Palace [758]* built in 1851 by Joseph Paxton (1803–65). Although for practical reasons office and factory buildings [755, 756] often adhered to the vertical wall treatment derived from architecture in stone (from which the later skeleton construction of the American skyscraper [797] was to develop), new categories of building, such as the greenhouse or the exhibition hall, exploited the novel expressive possibilities of iron, including the curving exterior wall. Structural

758 *Joseph Paxton, Crystal Palace in London, 1851. The first application of prefabricated parts (iron and glass) in Europe. Advantages: less time taken in erection; actual building can be done by unskilled labour; transparency.*

means which the architecture of mass had confined to the vaulting zone were extended to the entire building.

The *Crystal Palace* was erected in the space of a few months to serve as an exhibition hall for the first world's fair. The surprisingly short construction time was made possible by the first use in Europe of prefabricated building elements which were assembled on the site. Construction with prefabricated parts led the architect to the principle of standardization. Paxton turned the inherent limitations of his method to great advantage, notably in the monumentalization achieved through the clear linear organization and simple articulation of the gigantic structure. But the Crystal Palace made no new contribution to the problem of vaulting. The supports were placed close together and the widest span was 75 feet. Apart from its enormous dimensions – the whole structure was nearly 2,000 feet long – what made the building a world sensation and the triumphant symbol of the industrial age was its almost lyrical character. This was brought about through the spatial experience proper to the glass house. Never before had an interior space conveyed such an impression of boundlessness and infinity. There were no partition walls to block the observer's gaze which was permitted to sweep the flowing spatial complex in all directions. Contemporary visitors spoke with enthusiasm of the disappearance of barriers between interior and exterior and of the apparent dissolution of material

757 *Decimus Burton and Richard Turner, Palm House at Kew, 1845–7. The truss of iron supports and the inlaid glass frames make a building structure of curved walls.*

substance in the atmosphere, an effect the Impressionists later sought to convey in painting.

In the second half of the century England yielded the leading place in iron construction to France. Horeau, Flachat, and Baltard did important pioneer work when the erection of the great market halls was undertaken around the middle of the century; Labrouste's achievement with his two library halls was outstanding. The two high points of nineteenth-century steel construction arose on the grounds of the Paris World's Fair of 1889: the *Hall of Machines* by Dutert and Contamin *[759]* and the *Eiffel Tower* *[760]* named after its builder Gustave Eiffel (1832–1923).

The *Hall of Machines* was 1,400 feet long and its span of 380 feet ranked as a new achievement in vaulting technique. The two builders used a structural procedure that not only dispensed with the distinction between load and support, but ignored all known rules of statics. The construction depended upon three-joint fittings that permitted the transmission of

760   Gustave Eiffel, the Eiffel Tower in Paris, 1889. Symbol of the new technical possibilities opened up by overcoming the heaviness and mass of stone structures.

759   Ferdinand Dutert and Contamin, Hall of Machines for the Paris World Exhibition, 1889. A 'single space' measuring 115 metres in breadth, with arches resting apparently without weight on their feet.

stress at the apex and at the ground through joints. In this way the traditional distinction between post and lintel was abolished and the structure rose in a continuous curve from the floor to the apex of the vault.

The main attraction of the World's Fair was the 1,000-foot tall *Eiffel Tower [760]*. Since this was intended as a symbol rather than a functional building the inherent tendency of iron construction to turn the building from a closed mass to an open skeleton could be pressed to its ultimate conclusion unhindered by practical considerations. At first controversial, the tower was soon regarded as an emblem of a technological optimism apparently on the threshold of unprecedented discoveries.

With these achievements European iron architecture reached a stylistic high point. The central focus of further development, however, was not the problem of the great hall, but the cellular construction of business and office buildings. In the last decade of the nineteenth century the initiative for the solution of this problem in terms of skeleton construction passed to the so-called Chicago School *[797]*. This development heralded the twentieth century more effectively than the works of Eiffel, Dutert, and Contamin. In France itself this shift was completed with the help of a new building material, reinforced concrete, which gradually displaced iron *[746]*.

Looking back over a hundred years of steel construction one can affirm that the growth of the builder's self-awareness paralleled his increasing mastery of technical means. Construction gradually began to dominate the whole building, though at first it had to fight the compromise with historical forms. The aesthetic possibilities proper to steel construction lie in the recognition of the linear, unplastic character of the individual elements, the emphasis on the dynamic framework of the total conception, and in the contrapuntal use of glass as a transparent spatial boundary. Technically and formally this signifies the unification of the building elements in accordance with the dictates of prefabrication procedures. The beauty of steel construction lies not in artistically 'interesting' features used for their own sake but in the intelligent disposition of standardized details.

PAINTING

Neo-Classicism to Impressionism

The art of painting, like architecture, underwent a fragmentation into opposing trends, but its development is more complicated. This is due to the fact that the formal contrasts do not always correspond to differences in content. Broadly speaking the two poles of stylistic contrast were the linear and the painterly modes. Content was split between past and present, history and life. The use of the contour line made for closed static form, favouring history and figure painting; the major use of colour unconstrained by linear boundaries was best suited to boundless and open forms, to atmospheric free space. As a rule the conservative trends, especially Neo-Classicism, adhered to a strictly defining line in their historical and mythological scenes *[761, 762]*. With the Romantics, Realists, and Impressionists, however, painterly handling often went hand in hand with the representation of contemporary themes *[767, 769, 778–81]*. A more careful examination shows that there were many exceptions to these parallels; thus for example there was a painterly and a linear romanticism, the first in France *[767]*, the

761 *Jacques-Louis David, The Oath of the Horatii, 1784–5. Paris, Louvre. A key work of classicism: severe composition in cool colours and clearly defined spatial stage, filled with moral pathos.*

second in Germany *[765]*, as well as a painterly and linear late Neo-Classicism *[777, 775]*. The rendering of simple, everyday reality sometimes made for atmospheric dissolution *[770]*, conveying the charm of the spontaneous and the momentary, and sometimes lent itself to a linear and calculated illusion of material substance *[773]*, where the laborious exactness radiates something of the timeless and unchanging. Only at the beginning of the last third of the nineteenth century was the combined triumph of colouristic form and contemporary content evident in Impressionism. The linear and conservative talents were almost everywhere eclipsed.

Jacques-Louis David's (1748–1828) *Oath of the Horatii [761]* was recognized by contemporaries as the programme picture of Neo-Classicism. The revolutionary significance of the picture is evident if one compares its sober idiom with the playful charm of the *galant* painting of the French Rococo. David arranged his compositions for clear comprehensibility so that nothing ambiguous remained. A comparison with Boucher or Fragonard *[cf. 734]* brings out David's combination of brutal factualism with archaic severity. These effects were achieved by means that were to become characteristic for Neo-Classicism: the arrangement of the figures parallel to the picture plane corresponding to the architecture; the astute draughtsmanlike characterization contrasting with

762 *William Blake, Nebuchadnezzar, 1795. London, Tate Gallery. Colour print drawing; an example of Blake's highly individual vision and his nonconformist religious imagination.*

He relied less upon the world of sense experience than upon his imaginative powers. To be sure he favoured linear contours ('The work of art becomes more perfect as the line is firmer, sharper and more wiry'), though he refused to pay homage to the antique models: 'Greek form is mathematical form, Gothic form is living form.' The formal idiom Blake developed from these postulates *[762]* shows the following characteristics: the forms are stylized into linear patterns, their linearism avoids the impression of plastic volume, and their rhythm blends into a sinuous display of organic energy. In this way Romanticism escaped the severely delimited, 'Greek' linearism of the classicists. Blake was wholly unconcerned with fashion and portrait painting. He stayed alive by working as a publisher's engraver, and between whiles wrote the Songs of Innocence and of Experience (1789 and 1794) and various 'Prophetic Books', in which the engraved text is surrounded by

763 *Samuel Palmer, Coming home from Evening Church, 1830. London, Tate Gallery. Tempera painting. A work that conveys a sense both of tranquillity and profuse richness.*

the painterly chiaroscuro of the Baroque; and the avoidance of complicated spatial overlappings. The carefully calculated pictorial composition is supported by cool, rational use of colour. Pictorial form and content pay tribute to ancient Rome; at the same time they express the moral pathos which was to be one of the components of the revolutionary mentality. In David's painting the artistic shift heralds the political upheaval; it witnesses the importance of content, moral seriousness and humanity.

David's Neo-Classicism evolved its vital power of conviction from a penetrating vision of reality stylized in heroic gestures. In portraiture his realism was unfettered, while in his later history paintings – David was court painter to Napoleon – the original tautness was sacrificed to academic finesse. The revolutionary became a conservative classicist, who was to be challenged by the upsurge of French romantics at the end of the second decade of the nineteenth century.

Romanticism had made its appearance earlier beyond the borders of France. Its cultural roots lay in England and Germany in the rediscovery of Shakespeare and the Gothic, and in the cult of original genius and imagination of the Sturm und Drang movement. It is characteristic of the stylistic situation about 1800 that the Romantic School used means which – albeit somewhat differently conceived – were also those of Neo-Classicism. An example is the work of William Blake (1757–1827).

his hand-coloured illustrations. *Nebuchadnezzar [762]* is a work that shows Blake's personal and non-conformist religious attitude at its most inward and subjective. The tortured battle of the soul is here contrasted with the animality of the body and the indifference of nature. Blake expressed the visionary, supramundane trend of Romanticism with the lack of restraint characteristic of strong individuality. His followers, chief among them Samuel Palmer (1805–81) and Edward Calvert (1799–1883), were most influenced by his engravings of pastoral scenes. Palmer's work *[763]* shows the magnificent intensity of his visions of the Kentish countryside. After seven years of fervour and artistic genius he lapsed into conventionality and an Anglo–Italianate style.

Francisco de Goya (1746–1828) brought the straightforward pictorial analysis of reality into relation with a world beyond the rational order. His powers of invention embraced the realm of the terrible and the absurd, but he found his subject-matter in reality, as in the *Raging Madness [764].* What is surprising and unsettling in this work is its unclear presentation of space. Once again there is a shallow area of action, a small platform menaced by shadows, discontinuities, and gaps. The architecture emphasizes the general uneasiness. The chiaroscuro lacks the emphatic, activating role it had in Baroque painting, serving instead to create an oppressive and disturbing effect. Goya rejected the compositional patterns accepted since the Renaissance. The direct-ness of his arrangement has been heightened, but at the same time it has also become dissonant. The painting is free of any poetic transfiguration or idealization in the sense of the Baroque allegory, but it also avoids the Neo-Classical tendency to harmonic balance. Breaking with the traditional canon of beauty, Goya was the first cultivator of the demonic and the ugly in modern times. Ruled by instinct, his figures are heaped together disconsolately, their gestures raw and awkward.

'The artist's feeling is his law.' This was how Caspar David Friedrich (1774–1840) put the credo of the new subjectivism. Friedrich belonged to the idealistic side of Romanticism. His recommendation to 'Close your bodily eye so that you may see your picture with your spiritual eye' sounds like an echo of Blake, but Friedrich's painting followed a different road from that of his English contemporary. Like Blake he began by rejecting academic rules, virtuoso brushwork, and the hollow pathos that turned the picture into an 'old-clothes shop', 'where a great deal lies tumbled and heaped together, but nothing goes together'. Out of this rejection Friedrich created a pictorial mode of his own with spatial breadth and

764   Francisco de Goya, Raging Madness, from the 'Proverbios', c. 1816–24. Goya's hatred of and fascination with the irrational and bestial in man is fully expressed in this copper engraving.

stillness as the dominating characteristics. Man must again experience his isolation and insignificance in the encounter with nature. Nature is no longer man's opponent, but the symbol of change and transience. Friedrich strove towards a poetic trans-formation of the world of perception, that is towards natural truth of a higher, no longer merely illustra-tional kind. His *œuvre* constitutes the purest and most exalted embodiment of the contemplative land-scape painting of Romanticism. His figures, placed tentatively and expectantly in nature's vastness, are emblems of self-absorbed reverie. His reverence of nature is the expression of a subjective feeling which became intensified in the course of the nineteenth century so as to become a kind of substitute religion.

Friedrich's severe and unconstrained poetry consti-tutes a high point of Romantic painting in Germany. His observation of nature was directed beyond the material substance of familiar things towards remote dimensions of the vastness of space. His lapidary composition employs axes that are spatially creative; frequently the horizontal expresses the uniform and the unbounded which always remains the same, whereas the verticals – men, trees, church ruins, sailing ships – represent the effort of the individual to maintain himself against boundlessness. Friedrich succeeded in grasping the mysterious more deeply and universally than his contemporaries of the Nazarene group. The Romanticism of the Nazarenes is narrower, though for this reason it corresponded more closely to the taste of the time. This artistic association originated in Vienna in 1809, in which

765   Peter von Cornelius, Kriemhild sees Siegfried's corpse. Drawing, 1811. Frankfurt am Main, Städelsches Kunstinstitut. A fine drawing technique used for a historical narrative representation.

year its two founders, the painters Overbeck and Pforr, settled in Rome, where they were joined by Cornelius and Schnorr von Carolsfeld. Living in a monastery, they strove to practise the ideal of a religious way of life. In a moral and artistic context they harked back to the example of the 'ancient holy art' of the Middle Ages. They found their artistic ideals in Dürer and the Italian Quattrocento painters (e.g. Perugino). Their aim was a 'neo-German religious and patriotic art', a painting of noble and pious uplift. Their choice of material focused upon the unusual and the fabulous: legends *[765]* and myths, old folk-songs, and a nature bestrewn with venerable monuments of the past. Thus they adhered to the poetic medievalism of wish-fulfilment conjured up by Novalis in his essay 'Die Christenheit und Europa' (1799). The bravura handling of the brush and the surface polish taught in the academies were eschewed in favour of a sober drawing style based upon Dürer. The aim was a simple, straightforward formal idiom. These considerations reduced colour to a mere secondary role with no part to play

in the development of form. Local colour alone was permitted, unsubordinated to any overall unifying tonality. This gives their pictures an impression of disconcerting variety of hue. Peter von Cornelius (1783–1867) went so far as to describe the brush as the enemy of painting. His severe draughtsmanship developed from archaizing beginnings to a more buoyant, mellifluous pathos *[765]*, which opened the way to later academic painting with its heroic but desiccated stylistic ideal.

In the decades of the *Vormärz* and Biedermeier, German Romanticism turned towards a kind of reportage of experience with contemplative overtones. The reserved tenderness of the Nazarenes was exploited for sentimental and anecdotal effects, and the elevated nature mysticism of Friedrich was adapted to an idyll containing the germ of the later 'bower sentimentality'. The painters followed life values that exalted security. The genre-like repertory of subjects dealt chiefly with the family and marriage, children and old people. The central theme is an unruffled and sheltered life set apart from awareness of contemporary problems.

In France Romanticism appeared later and followed other paths. Its attitude was not exclusively contemplative and hostile to the present, but favoured a direct rendering of life, human passions, and dramatically heightened action. The development of French painting grew out of the circle of the dominating figure of David. His late academic style was decisive for his pupil J.-A.-D. Ingres (1780–1867). Ingres's inclination toward the sober characterization of reality conflicted with an unrestrained admiration for the plastic ideal of the antique. His beginnings belong to a romantically exalted linear style of refined elegance. Ingres's uncorruptible sense for reality found its appropriate field of action in portraiture; in his history paintings he was often hampered by an attachment to a pedantic and detailed literalism. The nude human form gave him an escape from the dead pedantry his conscientiousness required, where he could devote himself to a bent for ornamental beauty of line *[776]*.

Ingres's formal ideal insisted upon the primacy of line over colour. He thought that clouds and smoke must be reduced to line. Every form must be a closed, self-contained entity. Colour must emphasize material substance and corporeal volume. Tranquillity, harmony, and balance are the highest qualities of a composition. This cool and uncomplicated artistic ideal, which Ingres, as director of the French Academy in Rome from 1834, could expound from a position of high authority, was to be transmitted by a great number of pupils, becoming one of the main sources of the academic history painting of the nineteenth century, where it soon degenerated into the lifeless perfection of the epigones.

In the disciplined and closed formal idiom of David and Ingres, Neo-Classicism's characteristic tendency to doctrinaire arrogance is evident; the Neo-Classicists thought they had reached a final synthesis of style valid for all times. This dogma provoked the opposition of the Romanticists. For Géricault and Delacroix, their spokesmen, the forms of Ingres were not perfect but lifeless. They sought different means of design: the observer was to be introduced into the arcana of the act of creation itself. Painting was to proceed from colour, conceived less as an expression of static, immobile order, than as the vehicle of dynamic forces, human passions, and vast natural processes. Active forms were preferred to smooth and tranquil ones, contours were opened out and the brushwork was emphasized as a formal counterpart of creative passion. The Romantic also harked back to historical precedents, not from the antique or the Gothic, but from the more congenial painting of the Baroque era. Théodore Géricault (1791–1824), whose *Raft of the 'Medusa' [766]* signalled the Romantic breakthrough in the Salon of 1819, was influenced by David's pupil Gros, who was also an admirer of Rubens. Eugène Delacroix (1798–1863) also derived his colourism and his compositional canon from the sixteenth-century Venetians and the seventeenth-century Flemings. Diagonal axes, dramatic chiaroscuro, and stormy entanglements of bodies bear witness to this affinity *[767]*. Notwithstanding these historical relationships the Romanticism of Géricault and Delacroix followed a more revolutionary, militant path. It dazzled a new generation weary of tradition and anxious to free itself of dogmatism whether political or artistic. After Géricault's early death (1824) Delacroix was regarded as the standard-bearer of the Romantic movement. With his polar opposite Ingres he dominated the field of French nineteenth-century painting. If one looks beyond the formal and thematic contrasts, however, it is evident that both painters remained in the tradition of literary and allegorical painting. Their central concern was with monumental composition and with large-scale figure painting in the line descending from the Renaissance.

Outside the bounds of this prestigious category of painting lay the modest beginnings of a development concerned not with men in action, but chiefly with processes of nature. A new and unprejudiced experience of nature was announced, which often drew upon scientific findings in forming its attitudes. The concern of this landscape painting to render an

766 Théodore Géricault, *The Raft of the 'Medusa', 1819. Paris, Louvre. The raft with fifteen survivors of the 'Medusa', sunk in 1816, is depicted in a realistic and dramatic composition whose dynamism harks back to the Baroque.*

767 Eugène Delacroix, *The Massacre of Chios, 1824. Paris, Louvre. A scene from the Greek War of Liberation against the Turks. A dramatic and monumental composition which has Baroque overtones in the structure, figures, and colour.*

768　*John Constable, Clouds over Trees, c. 1821. London, Victoria and Albert Museum. An example of international Pre-Impressionism: landscape painting as spontaneous representation of an incidental segment of nature.*

769　*Camille Corot, Le quai des Pâquis, 1841. Geneva, Musée d'Art et d'Histoire. A light-filled, delicately idealized atmospheric landscape with a clear pictorial structure.*

impression as directly and immediately as possible eventually became one of the leading artistic aims of the century and a stimulus to its greatest talents.

In contrast to the painters of ideas, who created their intellectual world chiefly under the inspiration of literary sources [761, 762], the new landscape painters took reality as they found it. They did not seek after significant motifs, but painted unlikely looking ordinary scenes, for art, as they firmly held, could be found 'under every hedge' (Constable). This is the difference between Dutch and English landscape in the seventeenth century and eighteenth century, which fitted the impressions derived from nature into a compositionally closed image of the world. In the nineteenth century the accent was placed upon a small section of reality, with its unimportant detail and transitory light effects. With John Constable (1776–1837) light and clouds are the real themes, captured in an extremely painterly design and a free brush style [768]. Since the appearance of clouds was perpetually changing, the brushwork became hurried and more open and acquired a propensity for suggestive improvisation. This heralds the Impressionism of the second half of the century. This Pre-Impressionism is a European phenomenon. As early as *c.* 1806 one finds studies of clouds alone by Caspar David Friedrich, and in the twenties and thirties by Goethe, Blechen, Stifter, Wasmann, and Delacroix. Pre-Impressionism was often linked to naturalistic detail, and often with Romantic tendencies towards evocation of mood. Under the influence of the Dutch, especially Ruisdael, the Barbizon School painters Rousseau, Millet, and Dupré opted for a subdued, pastoral image of nature, in which the dense clusters of trees give the tone. Drawn to classical form by his experience of Italy and the example of Claude Lorrain, Camille Corot (1796–1875) developed independently a softer, gently idealizing rendering of nature. His pictures create the impression of a relaxed casualness, but they are executed with carefully placed pictorial axes, producing a kind of floating balance [769]. Corot disregarded topographical exactitude, letting details be absorbed in a light-filled whole.

It is characteristic of the nineteenth century that the positivistic craving for reality was manifested by many painters away from the public eye, or else lost its freshness in the process of turning the sketch into a finished picture. Delacroix and Constable are examples of this. It was the same with Adolph von Menzel (1815–1905) whose Proto-Impressionist works are cast in the shade by his enormous production of patriotic pictures. His *Balcony Room* [770] belongs among the best examples of the coloured light poetry

770 Adolph von Menzel, The Balcony Room, 1845. Berlin, Staatliche Museen, National-Galerie. Early impressionistic study of a detail of reality, defined by light and colour.

of the first half of the century. The subject is in conformity with the taste for comfortable and familiar domesticity, but it is stripped of sentimental prettiness and turned into an achievement in colour and light. The intimate relaxation of the interior decoration is in keeping with the bold yet unobtrusive choice of the scene. Everything in this room – window, curtain, mirror, chair, and empty wall – serves as a pretext for light effects.

Towards the middle of the century the new feeling for factuality – increasingly motivated by scientific positivism – penetrated into figure painting, creating a new sphere of subject-matter unexplored by Romanticism and Neo-Classicism. The working man was now paintable. One of the pioneers of this new realism, which sought to finally liberate the world of facts from the idealizing grip of the imagination, is Gustave Courbet (1819–77). He painted men, nature, and animals with an instinctive, provocative bluntness; his fanatical insistence upon life embraced the ugly and the ordinary *[771]*. His colourful handling of material substance consciously avoided any idealization, and the harshly delineated details left no place for transfiguring light. When the jury of the official Paris Salon of 1855 rejected his pictures,

Courbet presented his own show under the programmatic emblem of *Le Réalisme*. The thickness and heaviness of his painting formed one of the foundations for the inception of Impressionism a little later.

When some of Courbet's paintings were exhibited in Munich in 1869 his eye for everyday detail and his tonal painting influenced by Rembrandt, Hals, and Velazquez created a sensation among the young painters anxious to emancipate themselves from history painting in the wake of the Nazarenes. Wilhelm Leibl (1844–1900) adhered to Courbet's precedent, though he soon replaced the proletarian milieu with peasant simplicity and detachment from civilization *[773]*. This reverent idealization was rooted in the characteristic German Romantic avoidance of social conflicts and striving for 'inwardness'. Leibl's work affects a careful brushwork based upon the old masters in an effort to immortalize every detail of reality.

The danger of naturalism's being overwhelmed in a welter of detail was countered by Honoré Daumier (1810–79) in France. As a caricaturist he learned to heighten reality and to simplify it meaningfully. This comprehensive power gives his pictures an epic monumentality, which stands between Romanticism and Expressionism *[772]*. Daumier's social pathos is deeper than Courbet's, for it is not directed towards factual truth but towards sympathy with the human condition.

771 Gustave Courbet, The Corn Riddler, 1854. Nantes, Museum. Social pathos and the striving for a clear conception of reality led Courbet to the working-class milieu, which he faithfully interpreted in every detail.

772   Honoré Daumier, Third-Class Carriage, c. 1862. New York, Metropolitan Museum of Art. The realistic situation is raised through expressive features and bold play of light to an interpretation of the meaning of human existence.

773   Wilhelm Leibl, Three Women at Village Church, 1882. Hamburg, Kunsthalle. Leibl's realism turned him towards peasants' surroundings, which he idealized by choice of theme and the technique of the old masters.

England's share in the figure painting of the middle of the century is noteworthy. In 1848 Dante Gabriel Rossetti, Holman Hunt, and John Millais founded the Pre-Raphaelite Brotherhood. Their anti-academic artistic stance was modelled upon that of the Nazarenes, and like the earlier movement it turned to the more outspoken and uncomplicated feeling for nature of the Italian painters before the time of Raphael. Line was primary, colour being subordinated to it. The choice of subject-matter was varied; the painters took into consideration the men of the great cities, the workers and transients, but were also concerned with religious themes [774], together with medieval legends and hero epics. Stylistically the Pre-Raphaelites stood close to the chaste Romanticism of the Nazarenes, the social documents of humanity of the middle of the century, and the late Romantic literary painting of the second half of the century. Their involvement with the revival of crafts inspired by William Morris belongs to the prehistory of Art Nouveau.

The literary painting of the second half of the century continued the premises of Romantic and

774   Dante Gabriel Rossetti, Ecce Ancilla Domini, 1850. London, Tate Gallery. The Pre-Raphaelite Brotherhood sought to combine beauty of line, decorative effect, and closeness to nature.

775 *Puvis de Chavannes, Antique Vision, 1855. Lyons, Musée des Beaux-Arts. Antiquitizing monumental painting with balanced structure and delicate colouring.*

Neo-Classic idealism together with their formal conflict, the opposition of line and colour. Cornelius and Ingres died in 1867 – the latter finished his *Turkish Bath [776]* four years before his death; Delacroix died in 1863. Literary painting continued to enjoy the support of official patronage. Antique ideas of value are central to the paintings and fresco cycles of Puvis de Chavannes (1824–98). He depicts a noble, dignified humanity. The epic form has a cool simplicity, employing Arcadian landscape motifs in a broadly scaled articulation and preferring, in emulation of classicism, the arrangement of the figures parallel to the picture plane. Action and conflict were avoided in favour of restful tranquillity.

In German-speaking countries this literary painting was represented by Anselm Feuerbach, Hans von Marées (1837–87), and the Swiss Arnold Boecklin (1827–1901). Feuerbach's enthusiasm for antiquity conflicted with the naturalistic illusionism of his personal style. This conflict is also evident in the works of Boecklin. He combined the often sentimental allegory of his pictorial ideas with a hard and dry naturalism, often following an inclination to general stylization. Hans von Marées drew upon a much stronger native capacity for design *[777]*. Antiquity helped him to fight his way through the jungle of historical knowledge to a rounded and satisfying vision of organic wholeness. He formed his figure paintings from summarily articulated colour masses. Although his colourism is indebted to the

dark tones of the studio and the contrasting effects of Romanticism, he had the extraordinarily bold intention of elevating colour to a primary role of forming the basis for the whole painting.

Impressionism was radically opposed to the conservative attitudes of literary painting. This movement transferred the act of painting out of the studio into the open air. The Impressionists preferred actual events to the literary ones. The spontaneously captured 'slice of reality' was more in accord with their aims than carefully composed, recherché, and dignified themes. Their painterly vision accepted the world with all its accidental, casual, or transitory attractions. What interested the Impressionists in the forms of appearance was, in contrast to the naturalism of Courbet which served as their point of departure, not the physical structure and the material qualities as shown by local colour, but the texture of appearance as it is given for every object through light. Their aim was a subtly differentiated web of colour saturated by light. The historical antecedents lie in the Pre-Impressionism of the first half of the century *[768]*. Use of bright colours had been previously recommended by Delacroix: 'The enemy of all painting is grey – in nature there are only coloured reflections. . . .' The Impressionists excluded all dark tones from their palette; they painted even the shadows in colour. The name of the group, originally coined by critics

776 *Jean-Auguste-Dominique Ingres, The Turkish Bath, 1863. Paris, Louvre. The linear precisions of technique and the plastically modelled illumination create a cool but sensuous atmosphere.*

777 Hans von Marées, The Golden Age II, 1879–85. Munich, Neue Staatsgalerie. A portrayal of humanity full of statuesque idealism. The pictorial space is built up of modulated tonal values.

the charm of the countryside around Paris. The greatest source of provocation lay in their handling of colour. Out of Delacroix's procedure of the rapid brush fleck they created a new technique. Draughtsmanship and the closed outline were suppressed. In place of these stabilizing elements in the pictorial structure the observer's eye encountered a loose pattern of colour patches. This fluttering restlessness permitted objects to fuse into one another, effacing the boundaries between foreground and background, between things and the shadows they cast. Such an elementary, flowing, and dematerializing mode of painting caused confusion among the public inasmuch as the painters proceeded to treat colour unmixed in short comma-like brush strokes, leaving the optical mixture to the observer.

The Impressionists sought to approach physical reality as closely as possible. They took their easels out of doors, surrendering themselves to the influence of fleeting effects of light. This striving for eyewitness reportage reinforced the central role given to colour; this alone was to be the transmitter of external reality. But apart from its primary importance as the vehicle of visual description colour became a powerful force in its own right. Colour stood for light. The coloured atmosphere is the all-embracing element by virtue of which the fluid object of uncertain contour is absorbed into the whole.

as a nickname, derived from a picture exhibited by Claude Monet (1840–1926) in 1874 with the title 'Impression – Sunrise'. The core of the group consisted of a circle of friends formed in the Parisian ateliers in 1862, including Auguste Renoir (1841–1919), Sisley, Monet, Bazille, Cézanne, and Pissarro. In 1874 Edgar Degas (1834–1917) joined them. The intellectual leader of the group was Edouard Manet (1832–83), who however never took part in the group exhibitions (1874–86). Monet, who fled to London to escape the Franco–Prussian War in 1870, was uninhibited by the everyday world of conventions. Manet, on the other hand, stayed behind in Paris and was generally regarded as a rebel at the time of the Commune riotings, despite his steadfast adherence to bourgeois ideals and standards.

What irritated the public in the Impressionist pictures [778–81] was precisely their historical achievement – the discovery of a new immediate way of seeing and of representing the phenomena of sense experience. They mirrored the multiplicity of a great city: they discovered the pulsing life of the great boulevards, the holiday mood of outdoor cafés, and

778 Edouard Manet, Horse Race in the Bois de Boulogne, 1872. New York, Collection J. H. Whitney. A rendering of the 'fleeting moment' (the action and apparently casual detail) through the spontaneous method of painting.

779 *Auguste Renoir, The Seine at Argenteuil, 1873. Portland (Oregon), Portland Art Museum. The Impressionists sought 'to depict natural objects not in their physical sense but to resolve them into colour, to evoke sun, light, and air'.*

780 *Claude Monet, Breakfast in the Garden, 1872–4. Paris, Louvre. The 'Impressionist' painting is comprised of particles of pigment, which fuse together to make an atmosphere of colour.*

781 *Edgar Degas, Le Café-Concert, 1876–7. Lyons, Musée des Beaux-Arts. Degas preferred man rather than nature as his subject. He portrays his characters from exciting side-views and fascinating effects of light.*

SCULPTURE

Neo-Classicism to Impressionism

The development of sculpture from the end of the eighteenth century until the end of the nineteenth century paralleled that of painting in the same period, though the sculptor lacked the opportunity to express himself in the same range of formal and thematic possibilities. His sphere of artistic activity was narrower and the leading place belongs to the painters of the period. This is a result of a historical process beginning in the Renaissance that involved artists increasingly with the problem of the reproduction of the phenomenal world. From this point of view the range of reality accessible to the painter is much broader than that available to the sculptor. The latter was restricted to two vehicles of expression: figures of men and animals. As the twentieth century has shown, there were indeed ways of inventively enlarging this sphere of forms, for example one could translate the human figure into the realm of the idol and the demon and so create a kind of mixed class. But this path was closed to the nineteenth century, for it contradicted the fundamental artistic dictate of the age, the striving towards reality.

The art of sculpture is of only sporadic importance in the nineteenth century. It lacked not only individual talents, but also a continuous development. One cannot help feeling that sculpture is largely outside the main lines of development. The sustained and systematic exploration of reality lay in the hands of the painters. They succeeded in translating material substance into colour and atmosphere; in this the sculptors could only play a secondary role.

Like painting, nineteenth-century sculpture lost its relationship to architecture and was left to its own resources. This isolation was only slightly mitigated by the commissioning of some large-scale monuments with a plethora of figures. The loss of the architectural context ultimately drove sculptors to the cultivation of the statuette. As Baudelaire observed in his essay 'Why Sculpture is Boring' (1847), bourgeois taste did not hesitate to turn medieval kings' monuments into cigar-boxes and Florentine bronzes into trinkets for personal adornment.

The predilection for the dainty, playful, and sentimental which was already evident in Neo-Classicism and which became a matter of mass production in the Romantic era was the counterpart of the opposed trend to the theatrical and the colossal. Melodramatic traits are already evident in the Neo-Classical figure group, as shown by Canova's Tomb of the Archduchess Christine in Vienna; later the treatment became more dramatic and calculated. Neo-Classic sculptors found that the funerary monument was a category especially congenial to their elegiac spirit, and later the tomb commemorating great men and outstanding human achievements became the central concern of official sculpture. Sculpture became an instrument of the propaganda of national patriotism. The 'Religion of Great Men' founded by Rousseau and romanticized by Carlyle was proclaimed by figures in squares and broad avenues, and places of pilgrimage in parks and the open country. If one surveys the means of expression

782   *Antonio Canova, Pauline Bonaparte Borghese, 1808. Rome, Galleria Borghese. Neo-Classicism was modelled on Roman examples. Despite exact observation of detail the pose seems to possess a timeless quality.*

that characterized this sector of sculpture its exaggeration and showy aggrandizement become obvious. Beginning with the antique and ending with the Neo-Baroque, stylistic history was recapitulated. The Neo-Classicism of the beginning of the century is disciplined and reserved; the Neo-Baroque monumental style with its many figures is confusingly complex and luxurious, the total effect additive rather than synthetic.

An examination of the great mass of sculptural production of the period shows two main branches of development: a classicistic trend, employing tranquil forms and smooth surfaces, and a Romantic trend, which treated the representational mass not as a symbol of the unchanging, but as a moving, pulsating document of human transience. In the first case one finds reticent immobility and aristocratic chasteness; in the second, creatures who breathe and participate in life.

The Neo-Classicism of Antonio Canova (1757–1822) depended upon Roman prototypes. His cult of the great man, amply encouraged by the currents of the Napoleonic era, was permeated by a dislike of the present. Greatness and timelessness did not seem possible in contemporary costume, an expression of 'corrupted taste'. For this reason he represented Washington as a Roman general and the Emperor Napoleon as a nude heroic youth. But this rejection of the profane dress of contemporary times was not the expression of an attitude that despised imitation of nature and factual reality. Canova was attracted to physiognomic and corporeal detail, which he strove to capture with a deceptive accuracy without departing from the bounds of the classical ideal of beauty. Apart from his busts, the outstanding witness of this is the reclining *Pauline Bonaparte Borghese [782]*. The figure is adjusted to the obligatory Neo-Classical dictate of parallel planes, which in the case of sculpture is suited only to frontal presentation. The attitude is sophisticated and also provocatively unveiled in the fullest sense of the word. The gaze, directed into the distance, bars the possibility of direct access. The figure lies in a calculated pose upon a series of cushions, the tense bulkiness of which contrasts with the slender smoothness of the body. The material qualities are presented completely and illusionistically in a way that would only be possible within the limits of a naturalism controlled by Neo-Classic discipline.

783 Gottfried Schadow, Two Princesses, 1795. Berlin, Staatliche Museen, National-Galerie. In the unforced, natural nobility and the differentiation of character, this marble group shows the life-like classicism of Schadow.

784 Bengt Erland Fogelberg, The God Thor, c. 1840. Stockholm, Nationalmuseum. Plaster study. Fogelberg worked in Rome in the circle surrounding Thorwaldsen. This powerful evocation of the ancient Nordic god is tempered with a restrained classicism.

In Germany Neo-Classicism was represented by Gottfried Schadow (1764–1850). His relation to life was warmer and more direct than that of Canova, whom Schadow knew in Rome. His art drew more upon the vitality of the Baroque tradition, endowing the best of his figures with an unpretentious natural charm and grace *[783]*.

The Neo-Classic trend soon attracted an international following. Here one should mention the Dane Thorwaldsen, the Swede Fogelberg *[784]*, the Frenchman David d'Angers, the Austrian Zauner, and the Germans Dannecker, Schwanthaler, Rauch, and Rietschel. The influence of the last-named stretched into the second half of the century, whose didactic and heavy-handed style he heralded (e.g. in the Monument of Luther and the Reformation, Worms, 1858).

As at the beginning of the century the Neo-Classicism of the century's end once again showed itself capable of pointing the way to a quieting and

785 *François Rude, La Marseillaise, 1832–6. Paris, Arc de Triomphe. As opposed to statuesque classicism, Rude creates an agitated composition full of dynamism, with Baroque trends.*

purification of style. Adolf von Hildebrand (1847–1921) undertook the role that fell to his friend Hans von Marées in painting [777]. Hildebrand preferred tectonic relationships and simple contours. He was thus opposed both to the formal anarchy of the theatrical monumental style and to Rodin's 'subjective arbitrariness', though his own work lacked inspiration. While Hildebrand was searching for an enlightened 'style of being', the line of development of Romantic sculptors running from Rude to Rodin and Rosso, aimed at a style of movement and action. This trend was oriented toward painterly form and worked with the means of formal fusion and blending; its forms press out into space or open themselves to it. The bodily mass is not closed and immobile as in the works of the Neo-Classicists, but mined with hollows and declivities. One can speak of an open form corresponding to the open brushwork of the painters which served to make the process of creation visible on the canvas (e.g. the Impressionists).

The Romantic trend found its main representatives in France. Its first great exponent was François Rude (1784–1855), whose masterpiece was the colossal relief of the *Departure of the Volunteers of 1792* on the Arc de Triomphe in Paris (1832–6), commonly known as *La Marseillaise* [785]. The elegant aristocratic image Canova had created for a Napoleonic heroic age was supplemented by Rude along popular and democratic lines. He glorified the

elemental awakening personified by the people. The over life-size relief is a compact group resolved to common action and exhorted by a fierce goddess of battle. Within the closed whole one finds harsh and vehement gestures and complicated overlappings. The aim is not clarity of the individual form but interaction of all forms.

In the dramatic massing and staggering of Rude's figures one can discern Baroque stylistic characteristics. These come increasingly to the fore in the second half of the century when sculpture had entered into a late Romantic phase. A representative example of this tendency is the group of the *Dance* which Jean-Baptiste Carpeaux (1827–75) created in 1869 for the *Façade of the Paris Opéra* [786]. This too represents a signal for an awakening, but not of a war-like kind. Dionysiac love of life fills the space with energetic, bounding rhythm. Light and shadows enliven the interstices between the figures. The joyful light-heartedness of this group recalls the world of the Rococo with its tender playful accents.

786 *Jean-Baptiste Carpeaux, La Danse, 1869. Paris, Façade de l'Opéra. Carpeaux heightens the Baroque pathos of Romantic French sculpture to a buoyant, joyful vitality.*

787 Honoré Daumier, Ratapoil, 1850. Cologne, Wallraf Richartz Museum. The ridges and bulges of the plastic mass gives this bronze an expressive energy. Note the elements of caricature in features and expression.

Apart from its public stylistic development Romantic sculpture had a more intimate aspect manifested in works of small format. This was represented by Jean-Pierre Dantan, Daumier, and later Degas. Dantan created a great number of small portrait busts and statuettes which reveal the unmistakable accents of caricature. The devices of disproportionate exaggeration constitute the sculptural principle of these figures. Honoré Daumier (1810–79) travelled farther along this path. For him the human figure became an image of overpowering energy, which from its seat within the body overflowed on to the surface. Daumier's tempestuous idiom found contemporary costume congenial. In the statue of *Ratapoil* the clothing is caught up in the serpentine movement of the body *[787]*, so that it seems to fuse with it. The rat-catcher of Bonapartism has become a timeless figure of the twilight man. The sculptures of Edgar Degas (1834–1917) show the transition from the Romantic statuette to the Impressionist study of movement. This is the logical consequence of the path pursued by Daumier; since life manifests itself in constant change it is best captured in the figure observed in the act of movement.

Auguste Rodin (1840–1917) embodied the highest achievement of the Romantic stream of sculpture. He combined the Impressionist and Baroque stylistic impulses of the second half of the century. His art embraced the whole span of plastic possibilities open to his age, from intimate improvisation of movement to heroic pathos. The hall-mark of his work is a transitory restlessness. None of his figures may be said to exist for its own sake, but each is absorbed into a larger rhythm, exposed to space or transfixed in the material out of which it is formed. What stormy paths this flowing world of expressiveness could lead to is demonstrated by Rodin's masterwork *[788]*, the *Gate of Hell* begun in 1880. Beside the acknowledged gains of this type of design – above all its plastic fusion and spatial openness – it is not hard to discern its inherent dangers. It is not that the 'painterly' dissolution seems misleading, nor the disappearance

788 Auguste Rodin, The Gate of Hell (detail), begun 1880. Zürich, Kunsthaus. Impressionistic formlessness and the joining together of figures and space are combined with a dynamic flow of movement.

789 Medardo Rosso, Yvette Guilbert. Rome, Galleria Nazionale d'Arte Moderna. A 'realistic' representation with manneristic traits. The Futurists regarded Rosso as a precursor of 'dynamism' in sculpture.

of firm and bounded elements, but rather one objects to a dubious dalliance with obvious effects. Rodin's claim that sculpture could compete with the theatre often played him false. This is the other side of his unconstrained dynamism; the inclination towards *chic* arrangement and pathetic gesticulation.

Rodin's artistic procedure of evoking form from chaos as a dramatic, Promethean experience owed much to the work of Medardo Rosso (1858–1928). Rodin's summary figures with their effacement of formal boundaries were probably suggested by Impressionism (he also followed them in the fusion of the figures with space), but he ultimately arrived at a Romantic symbolism of the transitory *[789]*.

Rodin and Rosso are the stylistic end products of the spontaneous, expansive treatment of form developed in the nineteenth century. Their art caused a reaction among contemporaries, first with Hildebrand, then later in the more effective example of Maillol. These two sculptors adopted a composed and undramatic form that withdrew from space into the security of the block *[792]*.

In 1886 the last group exhibition of the Impressionists took place. Beside the well-known names of artists previously represented there appeared a new figure, Georges Seurat (1859–91). His painting of 1885, *A Sunday Afternoon on the Grande Jatte [790]* (an island in the Seine on the outskirts of Paris) caused a scandal. This work seemed to contain an answer to the critical epilogue on Impressionism Zola had published in 1880. He wrote: 'The real misfortune is that none of the artists of this group has realized powerfully and definitively the new means of expression that they all show here and there in their works. They are all forerunners. The real genius has not yet appeared. We can see and approve of their intentions, but we look in vain for the new masterpiece.'

Although this criticism may be refuted, it still gives insight into the hopes that Impressionism had left unfulfilled in the circles sympathetic to it. The freer brushwork of the artists brought them under suspicion of a sketchy looseness; the coloured dissolution of the contour was regarded as a premonitory sign of a more general disintegration. Artistic circles were also infected by a desire for a new approach. The limited production of Seurat's short creative life must be understood in this context. He represents an attempt to monumentalize Impressionism through a methodical reworking of its basic principles, in order to advance beyond it. The rapid, restless brush stroke was systematized. Instead of the flickering hooks and commas the painting displays a uniform surface treatment made up of points of colour of equal size. Seurat's Pointillism or Divisionism favoured the transformation of the picture surface into a unified field of forces. In the history of painting this meant a further advance along the road to the autonomy of the artist's means of design where the colour patch ultimately becomes an independent unit detached from the object in nature. The unmixed application of dot-like colour cells produced a continuous web of elementary contrasts. It must be remembered, however, that this impression of textual completeness is effective for the observer only when he has found the proper distance from which to view the painting. The screen of the surface then yields a pictorial image. This technique transforms the vibrant restlessness of Impressionism into its opposite. If the stroke is suited to a dynamic tendency, the point is conducive to a static one. A uniform diffusion of points is not 'directed', but constitutes a network of relationships radiating in all directions. The everyday scene takes on a measure of dignity and classical immortality.

In the 1880s, which have been termed the crisis years of Impressionism, Paul Gauguin and Paul Cézanne also developed the foundations of new systems of painting. With Seurat they shared a common aspiration towards a closed type of pictorial construction. The road to this led by way of a new emphasis on volumes and a simplification of spatial relationships. In 1888 Gauguin (1848–1903), for a time a fellow-traveller with the Impressionists, developed in collaboration with Émile Bernard the aesthetic foundations of Synthetism. Later visits to the islands of the Pacific Ocean strengthened his feeling for simple and primitive forms with mythical overtones *[791]*. Like Seurat he saw painting's task as the effort to render spiritual states through colour and line. A particular type of line should evoke sorrow, another joy. Line and colour should produce a 'magical harmony' that conveys the 'music of the picture'. In contrast to the Divisionist technique of Seurat Gauguin was accustomed to surround his figures with an even, steadily flowing contour; this procedure is sometimes termed 'Cloisonnism' after the cloisonné enamel technique. Since the inner modelling of the figures was neglected in favour of a flat application of colour there could be no illusion of volume. Spatial illusionism was consequently avoided, inasmuch as neither light and shadow nor perspective lines were admitted to give the effect of recession in depth. The result was a powerful emphasis on the integrity of the picture plane. Gauguin himself recognized that this procedure reinforced the autonomy of the formal structure: 'Before you know what the picture represents, your attention is immediately captured by the magical harmony of the colours.' A painter from Gauguin's circle, Maurice Denis, evolved the famous definition: 'One must bear firmly in mind that before a painting is a charger, a nude, or an anecdote, it is a surface covered with colours arranged in a certain order.'

In 1890, when these words were written, Paul Cézanne (1839–1906) was creating his mature works. Before he found his own way he had also explored the possibilities offered by Impressionism. He wanted to 'realize' the world, to render visible its elementary structure, not by reproduction but by evocation. He wanted to 'think with the eyes'. From his schooling with the Impressionists he retained a faith in colour as the symbol of the spiritual world. Hence the deeply perceptive application his work reveals. He seems to delineate harmonies parallel to those of nature.

It was Cézanne's pioneer historical achievement to have legitimatized the autonomy of the painter's process of design. For him the picture begins not with

790 *Georges Seurat, A Sunday Afternoon on the Grande Jatte, 1885. Chicago, The Art Institute. The Pointillist Seurat aimed to overcome the Impressionist depiction of the momentary through strengthening the picture in a new arrangement of the surface, which he built up out of clusters of coloured points covering every inch of the canvas.*

791 *Paul Gauguin, The Gold of their Bodies, 1901. Paris, Louvre. A departure from the spatial and illusionistic rendering of reality. The surface-like painting leads to an emphasis on pictorial planes: the figures are built out of broad forms without inner drawing, and are articulated by dark lines.*

792 *Aristide Maillol, The Three Graces. London, Tate Gallery. Maillol was at first attracted to Impressionism, but later reacted and turned to classical idealizing sculpture.*

the natural prototype, but with the pictorial elements. In this way he achieved an original expression mirroring the act of painting itself. The painting became an autonomous entity whose true existence lay in a realism different from the prototypes provided by sense data. It is not surprising therefore that Cézanne suppressed the spatial system of linear perspective, for he was concerned not with the adventitious 'slice of reality' but with an immutable 'purely painterly truth of things'. Kandinsky has best described Cézanne's achievement. 'What is represented is not a man, an apple, or a tree. All these things are employed by Cézanne to create an internally resonant object, called a painting' (1912).

Seurat, Gauguin, and Cézanne followed different paths in a common effort to capture a vision of the world free of the quotidian and ephemeral qualities exalted by the Impressionists. Stylistically they all show a certain inclination to archaizing forms, especially in the case of Gauguin who felt the need to immerse himself in an exotic setting. The importance of the picture plane was most consistently explored by Cézanne; his tectonic construction was opposed to

the isolating contour method of Gauguin, for he employed a graduated colour modulation that knits the whole picture surface into a seamless whole.

The trend towards the lasting and the stable, towards firm form, is also evident in sculpture. The source of the shift lies not in a latent classicism, such as that manifested by Hildebrand's somewhat enervated art, but in the vigour provided by a fresh, primary formal impulse. Only in the last decade of the century did Aristide Maillol (1861–1944), after a gradual development from ornamental charm to corporeal vitality, succeed in overcoming the excited, Romantic gesticulation of Rodin and Rosso *[788, 789]*. Instead of a spatially ramified, inconstant formal complex, he tightened up the surfaces and concentrated on a palpable block form. A carefully meditated relationship to archaic forms is also evident here *[792]*.

Up to this point reactions to Impressionism have been considered which arose out of the principles of the movement itself. Van Gogh, Toulouse-Lautrec, Munch, and Ensor all exaggerated Impressionist methods. In the work of these artists, three of whom are not French, the style was prepared that was later to be named 'Expressionism'. It is characteristic of these four pioneers that they could no longer participate in the balanced outlook on man's environment shared by the Impressionists.

Impressionism shows a joyful attitude towards the things of this world; Expressionism emphasizes the obsessive and demonic, the indissoluble conflicts of man in an often hostile, usually overpowering environment. The formal idiom was also affected by this shift of focus. Balanced and harmonious methods of design were discarded and the composition was filled with restless, disturbing elements. The attention of the observer is sometimes captured by drastic means. An emblematic clarity is found in the poster which becomes important at the end of the nineteenth century, particularly in the work of Toulouse-Lautrec *[793]*. The treatment of line tends to be summary and almost hectic; colour contrasts are pressed to violent dissonances since they are meant to shock. Exaggerated and violent effects are often cultivated. The unattractive appearance of man is meant to bring out his all-too-human qualities. The handling of paint represents a rejection of the soft and supple brush stroke of the Impressionists. The pictures were not meant to be seen as 'fine painting', but to communicate human truths. The handling might be characterized as abrupt, uncontrolled, and sometimes careless, though formal components, in particular the emphasis on outline, look forward to a new spontaneity of expression.

so that it acquires a psychic dimension; they move from the sphere of the eyes to that of the nerves. Henri de Toulouse-Lautrec (1864–1901) took his cue from Degas's sardonic interpretations of the diversions of great city life. His art depends upon an astonishing sureness of line, due in part to his study of Japanese prints. The economy of the characterization makes the Impressionist mode seem loose and indulgent by comparison. The colour is calculated and caustic. Toulouse-Lautrec also knew how to handle line ornamentally and in this respect his work shades over into Art Nouveau, as in his lithographs and posters.

The Norwegian Edvard Munch (1863–1944) came to Paris for the first time in 1889 when he became acquainted with the work of Gauguin and Van Gogh. His first show was held in Berlin in 1892 and caused such a scandal in the art world that it quickly closed. In general his imagination can be described as heavy-handed and his handling as viscous. Munch was in close touch with Strindberg and the Symbolist movement in literature *[795]*. The sombre visions of his 'inner landscape' comprise situations that reveal man's helplessness before his fate: loneliness, death, the battle of the sexes, temptation, and jealousy. Form moves towards monumental condensation. The typical aspects of a landscape, a tree and a man are emphasized by the oppressive contours. The empty space in which the bulky figures seem to have grown

793 Henri de Toulouse-Lautrec. Jane Avril, poster lithograph, 1893. The momentary is captured in this early Expressionistic composition. Foreshortening and flakes of colour with bizarre ornamental contours characterize the pictorial effect.

794 Vincent Van Gogh, Cornfield, 1889. Otterlo, Rijks-museum Kröller-Müller. The short, agitated brush strokes become an expressive element in the picture, in which all visible objects are filled with a dramatic vitality.

The Dutchman Vincent Van Gogh (1853–90) came to Paris in 1886, the year of the last Impressionist Exhibition. Although he practised Pointillism for a time, contact with Gauguin accelerated the emergence of the visionary powers that drove him to a restless exploration of his inner being. He too wished to express the spiritual through colour, to capture 'the fearful passions of men with red and green'. While Cézanne deprived line of any active role in pictorial construction, Van Gogh used it as an intense vehicle of expression. He draws with colour; the whole picture surface is covered with short powerful brush strokes which combine to form a flickering ensemble *[794]*. Even inanimate objects seem endowed with life. A powerful subjective sympathy is conveyed by the emphasis on the perspective axis.

There are a number of significant parallels between what Van Gogh and what Toulouse-Lautrec created out of Impressionism. They both show a heightening, or more accurately an exaggeration of visual sensitivity

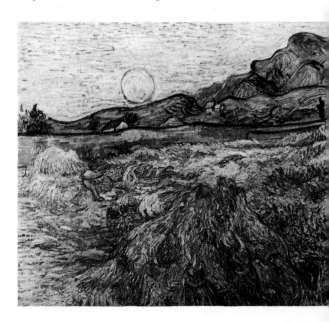

795   *Edvard Munch, Madonna, coloured lithograph, 1895. The pessimistic outlook of Munch is shown in composition and in details: from the threatening, dark, empty surrounding space the figure achieves a symbolic quality.*

796   *James Ensor, The Intrigue, 1911. Paris, Collection A. Croquez. Pessimism here contains unreal elements: grinning, contorted masks in flickering forms and colours become a symbol of oppression.*

becomes itself an element of expression. The line of the brush proceeds in slow billowing curves. All these characteristics show the melancholy and pessimistic element of Expressionism in its full form.

The last two decades of the nineteenth century were the most fruitful period of the work of the Belgian James Ensor (1860–1949). His early works show a feeling for the atmosphere of Realism. At the beginning of the eighties, however, his palette brightened up and masks and lemurs began to make their appearance in bourgeois interiors. Ensor made his mark with a highly personal view of composite creatures. Although his works recall the fantastic art of earlier centuries (Bosch, Bruegel, Callot), their menacing aggressiveness reveals a more uncompromisingly despairing image of the human predicament. Hysteria and pretence rule man's existence; none can make himself understood by another *[796]*. The evocation of the absurd foreshadows Surrealism. Ensor's caustic and ironic view of life is supported by his formal idiom. The line is stiff, angular, and drastically clumsy; the composition is restricted to an artless and lapidary presentation recalling popular prints; colour inclines to bright hues and harsh contrasts revealed by a pallid light.

All the painters treated in this section contributed to the achievements of Impressionism and Realism. They find their own paths in the need for a symbolic deepening of content. This need became more insistent in the last two decades of the nineteenth century. In 1890 Oscar Wilde wrote that 'All art is at once surface and symbol.' His words herald symbolic transformation, free play of artistic imagination, emancipation of experience, and the pronounced autonomy of the work of art. Compared with these demands, the straightforward, relatively naïve lyricism of the Impressionists appears ordinary and 'superficial'. Artists came to reject the unique, momentary occurrence in favour of the search for significant content and the eternal validity of the symbol.

THE BREAKTHROUGH TO MODERN ARCHITECTURE

The last two decades of the nineteenth century were also of great importance for architecture. As in paintings, the foundations were laid for a new attitude towards architecture. While in France two high points of engineer building appeared in the hall and the monumental symbol *[759, 760]* builders in the United States created a new category to answer the needs of great cities, the office skyscraper. At the same time they found new solutions to a problem that had occupied architects since the Renaissance, the single-family house surrounded by a garden. In the 1880s, while eclecticism and historicism still reigned in Europe, decisive advances took place in the Chicago School that only became known to European architects around the turn of the century.

The strongest personality of the Chicago School was the architect and theorist Louis Sullivan (1856–1924). He denounced the eclectic practice of masking buildings with an ornamental façade. Such screens bore no genuine relation to the interior of the building and falsified its conception. Sullivan wanted to build from within once more. For him construction was not something to be ashamed of, but the essential core of the building. Moreover he held that the exterior should merge with the interior of the building to form an indissoluble unity, and that nothing should be merely applied. Every building must constitute an unmistakable organic whole, where nothing can be added or taken away. This holistic design procedure was expressed by Sullivan in a lapidary saying: 'Form follows function.' Every part should reflect the role appropriate to it. It is not surprising that such a functionalism should seek to restrict the place of architectural decoration. 'With regard to the aesthetic aspects it would be very much to our advantage if we refrained from any use of ornament for a period of years, so that our attention could be entirely concentrated upon the buildings whose nakedness is pleasing' (1892).

In realizing his ideas Sullivan turned to steel skeleton construction. A forerunner of this technique was the grid construction in cast iron familiar in the United States from the middle of the century [755]. When Sullivan built the Guaranty Trust Building in Buffalo [797] in 1895, the steel skeleton method had the advantage of a decade of use, for William Le Baron Jenney had begun his Home Insurance Building in Chicago as early as 1883. The exterior of this building still displays historicist tendencies. Sullivan relegated these to the past. The Buffalo skyscraper united the characteristic constructional transparency of the skeleton building with new expressive qualities. Sullivan required that a skyscraper be 'a unity from bottom to top without a single aberrant line'. His functionalism looks forward to the constructions of Gropius or Le Corbusier.

It is noteworthy that Sullivan gave new accounts to the relation between wall mass and windows. The window is no longer carved out of the background of the wall like a 'figure', but the two are now interrelated. Since the mass lost its heaviness it could be structurally activated so that it no longer formed a spatial barrier.

797 *Louis Sullivan, Guaranty Trust Building in Buffalo, 1895. The new function of the high building led its revolutionary solutions by the 'Chicago School'. The structure forms, both inside and out, an organic, functional whole.*

The trend towards simplification is unmistakable in the Chicago School. Since all spatial cells serve the same practical purpose the office building lent itself to a uniformly articulated surface pattern. This surface treatment could be described as an architectural counterpart of Divisionism. The architect could balance the tendency to repetitiveness by emphasizing the individuality of the building.

If the business and office buildings followed the dictates of unity, architectural variety was preserved in individual residences. The skyscraper, a closed, self-sufficient whole, is the conscious symbol of the great city, while the detached dwelling-house lies in the realm of nature, linking man and the elements. This comparison illuminates the role of Frank Lloyd Wright (1869–1959) in domestic architecture. Although he came out of Sullivan's office, he soon turned his back on the building concerns of the megalopolis. The proud verticalism of the skyscraper was opposed by horizontalism of his country-houses. From his teacher Wright derived his awareness of the organic, which he understood in a much more comprehensive sense. For him it no longer meant simply that the individual building should form a whole, but that it must also attain an overall unity of design with its surroundings. This expansive attitude broke down the barrier between architecture and nature. In his houses Wright preferred to use the organic materials of nature (wood and stone), in accordance with his Romantic concept of the sheltering quality of architecture. In order to make the interaction of man's creation and nature visible he employed the open ground-plan [798, 799]. This type of plan derives from English houses in the provinces; it occasionally occurs in Neo-Classicism where it is used as a 'painterly' architectural motif

798, 799 Frank Lloyd Wright, Willits House in Highland Park near Chicago, 1902. Ground-plan of the ground story and view of exterior. The organic building of the residential dwelling leads to an 'open ground-plan' which reaches out into space.

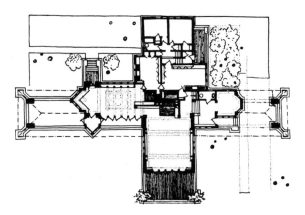

(e.g. Schinkel). It was fruitful for the future development in that it led to the dissolution of the solidity of the façade and the shaping of the building from within. Wright adapted this idea of Sullivan's to the single-family house. He freed himself from the superficial devices of prestige formulas and assembled spatial cells according to living needs, instead of forcing them into the mould of a previously given ground-plan scheme. Thus he created a complex form stretching in every direction into space. In the interior of the house Wright eliminated useless spatial barriers. Great windows facilitated access to the outside, while heavy protecting roofs emphasized the intimate character of the interior. In this way a gradual cohesion is created: the resident is sheltered in a house that in turn is organically related to nature.

At first the American development went unnoticed in Europe. Adolf Loos (1870–1933) seems to be the only architect before the turn of the century to have seen these buildings with his own eyes. When he came back to Vienna in 1896 after several years' stay in the United States he devoted himself to the rationalistic principles of the Americans. Here he saw an opportunity to restore an ethical dimension to building. The rejection of any kind of decoration announced in his essay 'Ornament and Crime' (1908) went far beyond Sullivan. One of his earliest works, the Goldmann Store in Vienna in 1898, exhibited the rectangular purism of the Americans with a consistency that was unique in Europe. The individualist achievement of Loos was at first little regarded, for the reform he advocated encountered a powerful opponent whose dominance extended throughout Europe: Art Nouveau.

JUGENDSTIL AND ART NOUVEAU

Art Nouveau was a European phenomenon. It began about 1890, reached its peak at the turn of the century and came to an end only a few years later. As it spread from England into Belgium, Germany, France, and Austria, eclecticism went out of fashion. The weapon employed in the struggle against the architecture of historicism was ornament – not a historical but a dynamic and organic ornament that was capable of expressing a new and original feeling for form. The advocates of Art Nouveau understood the term 'organic' somewhat differently from Sullivan and Wright. It is true that Sullivan's work shows luxuriant ornamental inventions which come close to the flowing line of Art Nouveau, but the ornament does not penetrate into the tectonic framework of the building mass. It remains confined to certain areas and is fundamentally inessential. But for Art Nouveau ornament is the indispensable element. It is conceived as the vital source and elementary impulse of formal creativity. There are two characteristics of ornament that explain its leading role in Art Nouveau: its adaptability which could lead to ever-new transformations – especially mixed formations – of abstract forms and references to objects, and its dynamism that flows over boundaries, binding together a variety of objects into a synthesis.

This aptitude for synthesis and fusion explains the key role attributed to ornament in the context of the formal idiom of the Art Nouveau style. Ornament had the task of providing a common denominator for all the arts. This is one of the main aims of the Art Nouveau – to create a 'Gesamtkunstwerk' with means appropriate to the contemporary situation. The great artistic achievements of the nineteenth century had been in a certain sense isolated attempts; the unity of the arts had been lost. The great painters did not concern themselves with the development of architecture, and the architect was accustomed to ignore the 'lesser arts' of painting and sculpture. The negative aspects of this development were first suspected in England, where industrialization had progressed furthest and had consequently created the most evident disturbances in taste. An empty pathos of overcharged forms and bowdlerized versions of historical styles were offered to the public. When the Great Exhibition of 1851 revealed the shockingly low level of the modern 'taste industry', critical voices were raised. William Morris and John Ruskin devoted strenuous effort to the renewal of the decorative arts. Since Morris saw the source of formal decadence in industrialization, he turned back to craft production. In 1861 he started a firm for crafts and interior decoration in which he secured the collaboration of the Pre-Raphaelite painters (Madox Brown, Rossetti, Burne-Jones). Morris's concern was with simple forms and truth to materials.

Art Nouveau found a guiding spirit in Morris. He too had the aim of overcoming the isolation of the arts and of reuniting artistic activity with life so that it might take its place at the centre of a new attitude towards culture. Ceasing to devote all his talents to the easel painting, the artist should provide beautiful forms for man's everyday needs. The manifesto of the Vienna Secession of 1897 reads: 'We turn to all of you without distinction of position or means. We recognize no difference between "fine art" and the "minor arts", between art for the poor and art for the rich. Art is the property of everyone.' This striving for synthesis by abolishing formal distinctions and social barriers found its true vehicle in ornament. Ornament is pure form and as such the second voice of the arts such as architecture and decoration communicate no conceptual content. Owing to its capacity for transformation it is also able to penetrate painting and sculpture, that is to ornamentalize the representational. Art Nouveau ornament took full advantage of these possibilities. The ornamental structure harmonized fabric patterns with house façades, door-knockers with bookbindings, the smallest with the largest, the intimate with the public style. Everything fused, the boundaries between things disappeared and one thing turned into another. In this the characteristic tendency of the age was expressed, the predilection for the unstable and wayward in form. Although it is true that the linear 'signature' of Art Nouveau, the whiplash line, has a history going back to Blake *[762]* and the 'rocaille' of the eighteenth century *[677]*, the first true manifestations of the style occurred at the beginning of the 1880s in a book-jacket by Mackmurdo (1883) and glass by Gallé (from 1884). The

800 Louis Comfort Tiffany and Emile Gallé, stem glasses, candelabra, and cups, c. 1900. New York, Collection Edgar Kauffmann, Junior. Art Nouveau aimed to complete the process of organic growth.

801   Hector Guimard, Métro station in Paris, c. 1900. Organic forms become ornament and, combined with construction, make a bizarre picture.

fragile, intimate form of these first beginnings is non-tectonic, one suited to surface ornament or for decorative objects. This situation continued for several years, until Art Nouveau penetrated architecture. At first artists concentrated upon the small forms so as to demonstrate a creative spontaneity. The creative act was to be revealed in the finished object. Form is not something rigid and final, but a phase that an artist like Louis Comfort Tiffany (1848–1933) selects out of the many possibilities and infinite processes of transformation *[800]*. Behind the

802   Henry van de Velde, writing-table, 1899. Even the furniture of Art Nouveau was to appear 'organic'. Dome-like supports and curved arms take the place of a rectangular frame.

artistic form stands the model of nature – but not as finished form to be imitated, but as growth, the source of energy. August Endell (1871–1925) defined line as a force: 'It takes its force from the energy of those that have drawn it.' In this the Art Nouveau artist believed himself bound to organic nature: his task was to combine his energy with the natural beauty proper to every growing, developing movement of life. The artist raises the organic to the plane of the fantastic, as in Hector Guimard's (1867–1942) plant-like entrances to the *Paris Métro* of about 1900 *[801]*. Where the object is not susceptible to linear treatment the mass is reduced to soft curves. An example is the *desk* of 1899 by Henry van de Velde (1863–1957). The right angle is largely displaced by bulging and curved forms; the constructed object passes for a growing thing *[802]*.

At the beginning of the 1890s the small forms tested in the decorative arts entered architecture. Characteristically, they at first occupied zones that were suited to their linear dynamism. As early as 1885–9 the Güel House in Barcelona by Antoni Gaudí (1852–1926) showed a curvilinear screen on its portal; similarly, yet in a more dissolved and asymmetrical manner Guimard designed the entrance to the Castel Béranger in Paris (1894–8). The most important building of this phase is the *Tassel House [803]* erected in Brussels in 1892–3 by Victor Horta (1861–1947). The exterior of this building is severe; only the balcony grille shows vegetable interlace. The staircase is pure Art Nouveau. Horta used iron not as a decorative surface silhouette but as a tectonic element. From the slender columns lines extrude which are continued in the ceiling construction and in the painted ornament. Floors, steps, landings, lighting fixtures, and ceilings create a linear unity from the curved lines and surfaces. The limits between bearing and supporting elements are effaced and the impression of organic growth displaces the traditional concept of architecture as rational construction. Horta's staircase influenced August Endell's design of the *Elvira Photographic Studio [804]* in Munich (1897–8). The façade wall is dominated by a bizarre motif of Far Eastern inspiration.

The high point of Art Nouveau inventiveness was reached in the work of the Catalan architect Antoni Gaudí (1852–1926). In 1905–7 Gaudí built the Batlló House and about 1910 there followed the Mila House, both in Barcelona. The design of the façade discards the traditional distinction between wall and openings. The wall is not a two-dimensional surface, but a plastic entity. The wall and the opening are indissolubly interwoven and unfold in spatial expansiveness. The recollection of an anatomical skeleton

803 *Victor Horta, staircase and entrance to the Tassel House in Brussels, 1892–3. Art Nouveau ornament covers the entire interior of the living-room, even the tectonic members and the foot-stools, walls, and ceiling.*

804 *August Endell, The Elvira Photo Studio in Munich, 1897–8. Monumental ornament becomes applied to the façade surfaces as a conveyor of linear energy. The differentiated relief structure is in strong contrast with the contours of door and window sections. (Above right.)*

805 *Antoni Gaudí, living-room in the Batlló House at Barcelona, 1905–7. The interior is composed of rounded forms right up to the ceiling, combining all parts (window, door, corner cupboard, bench) into one whole. (Right.)*

suggests itself to the spectator. Gaudí's work belongs to organic architecture in the literal sense. There are hardly any flat surfaces; everything is treated in terms of swellings, bumps, and curves. Similarly the right angle is virtually excluded. Everything seems to be poured from a crucible; nowhere are there visible seams, joints, or corners. In the ground-plan and in the interior design *[805]* Gaudí again shows the predilection of Art Nouveau for synthesis and fusion. He softens rigid formal boundaries. The rooms seem

806   *Charles Voysey, living-room in 'The Orchard House', Chorley Wood, 1900. The interior and furniture were to be 'organic', not in the sense of an expressive overriding of all the elements, but in their purposefulness, their functional necessity.*

807   *Charles Rennie Mackintosh, main entrance of the north façade of the Glasgow Art School, 1897–9. Assured asymmetry and contrasts give the building a fine monumentality.*

to develop in accordance with a particular principle of growth. Their extension does not adhere to any axial scheme. The result is a labyrinthine whole. Windows and doors proceed in soft curves. The furniture seems to merge with the walls. Spatial boundaries are fluid and within the rooms the division between wall and ceiling is absent.

In contrast to Gaudí's Baroque exuberance which reveals no underlying geometrical basis, the English variant of Art Nouveau depends upon the principle of the right angle. Its hall-mark is the severe, vertically extended element. Unlike the Spaniard Gaudí the English and Scottish designers adhered to the method of understatement. This artistic attitude was not unresponsive to practical needs. People wished to live in beautiful, but also comfortable surroundings. From this point of view Charles Annesley Voysey (1857–1941) ranks as the renewer of the English domestic style. In this he drew upon the country farmhouse of the seventeenth century, though he avoided imitating historical forms. The ground-plan is closed or L-shaped, the building mass is horizontally developed, and the roof and chimney give it weight and security. The interior was sparsely decorated, the space was intended to be bright and friendly, and the furniture was not to obstruct. With such interior designs as that of 'The Orchard House' *[806]* Voysey exercised a restraining influence on the Viennese Art Nouveau that centred on Hoffmann and Olbrich.

An even stronger influence upon Vienna was the work of the Scot Charles Rennie Mackintosh (1868–1928). His masterpiece as an architect is the Glasgow Art School of 1897–9 *[807]*. The main façade of the long building is asymmetrically organized in a double fashion. The entrance does indeed mark the true centre, but to its right lie four window bays, to its left only three. The entrance zone is also asymmetrically disposed. Its plastic, Romanesquoid forms contrast with the great flanking window surfaces. If one isolated the entrance from these it would appear as an extrusive formation which has nothing to do with the rest of the architecture of the building. Cubic forms contrast with soft, curving ones; the latter appear submerged and weighted down, the former emphasize the verticals with a fortress-like severity. The whole is organized with many surprises. The tower and the slit in the wall belong to a repertory of harshly carved forms. Their verticalism crowns the oriel windows, leading to the little balcony above and continuing in the ground-floor windows. The double window in the first floor stands abruptly next to the oriel windows. Two aspects of Art Nouveau are evident here: asymmetry and surprise effects.

penetrating into the roof zone are a surprising motif which Hoffmann derived from the English country-house. The way in which the ornamental strips are led along the corners of the blocks mitigates the tectonic character of the building and recalls fine furniture. The interior is also dominated by slender, right-angle forms. The interior decoration was the work of the Wiener Werkstätte, founded by Hoffmann in 1903. The marble-faced dining-room is revetted on three sides by a mosaic by Gustave Klimt in which the figures are embedded in a delicate ornament. In this room the Art Nouveau aspiration to the 'Gesamt-kunstwerk' found a worthy outlet.

Painting and sculpture, though comparatively marginal to its stylistic impulse, were also affected by the Art Nouveau idiom. The tendency towards rounded linearism may be observed in Gauguin, Toulouse-Lautrec, and Munch *[791, 793, 795]*. The human figure of the Art Nouveau is lanky and long-limbed, and resembles those of Blake *[762]*. Affected gestures emphasize the delicate fragility of the body and its contours have a subtle linearism, often brittle in the Gothic manner and then again swooping in rich curves. The ornamental transformation favoured surprising taperings and interlacings. Composition translated space into linear energies, proceeding from the pictorial centre to the edges and playing off empty areas against crowded ones. The human body was transformed into a kind of vegetable entity. From this eccentric attitude stemmed the figures from which

808 Joseph Maria Olbrich, Exhibition Building of the Vienna Secession, 1898–9. The temple-like structure is composed from simple cube forms.

In 1898 Joseph Olbrich (1867–1908) erected the Exhibition Building of the Vienna Secession *[808]*. This symmetrically organized, block-towered edifice has the character of an architectural monument. Dignity and sacred ceremony are embodied in this temple of art. The severe cube is crowned by an uncommonly light motif deriving from the local Baroque tradition; between the four pylons rises an *ajouré* dome made up of bronze laurel leaves. Flat ornament has become spatial ornament.

The masterpiece of the Viennese Art Nouveau is the Palais Stoclet in Brussels, built by Josef Hoffmann (1870–1956) in 1905–11 *[809]*. Mackintosh's influence is unmistakable, but it is stripped of the ascetic, bizarre severity and transposed with a light hand into a brilliant and festive *mise en scène*. The open juxta-positions of form continue in the garden. Flower beds, hedges, and pools are placed and framed in a similar manner to that of the walls clad in white marble. The overall layout emphasizes the asymmetrical basic concept. Empty surfaces are confronted with great windows. The windows of the second story

809 Josef Hoffmann, Palais Stoclet in Brussels, 1905–11. The English influence is evident, though marble-faced walls and more massive forms are the distinguishing features here.

810 Gustav Klimt, Portrait of Frau A. Block-Bauer, 1907. Vienna, Österreichische Galerie des 19. und 20. Jahrhunderts. The asymmetrical structure shows complete disregard for the spatial and physical. The clothing is stylized and over-refined.

Gustav Klimt a few years later was to construct his pictures *[810]*. A small-focus, excitedly colourful mosaic of ornamental motifs filled the picture plane. Almost unnoticed, a part of the ornamental field forms a contour from which gradually arms, fingers, shoulders, and a face detach themselves. The head, at the edge of the picture, floats in a sea of artificial forms. Through this conception of painting Klimt could consistently carry out the process of dissolving the closed easel painting in his wall decorations and it is as a designer for the applied arts that he is best known.

Art Nouveau painting, however, gave no new impulse to point the way to the future development of the easel picture. The artistic attitude was embodied not in the isolated aesthetic entity, but in the 'Gesamtkunstwerk'. With its retreat about the middle of the first decade of the nineteenth century a dialogue came to an end and the innovators of painting turned back to the most powerful of the 'conquerors' of Impressionism, first to Van Gogh and Gauguin, then to Cézanne.

The Twentieth Century

FAUVISM, EXPRESSIONISM, CUBISM

In 1901 a great Van Gogh memorial exhibition was held in Paris. Two years later, just after the artist's death, Gauguin's work was shown at the new Salon d'Automne, one of whose founders was Henri Matisse. In 1905 this Salon saw the appearance of a group of young painters, who were dubbed collectively 'Les Fauves' (the wild beasts) by a critic. The group included Matisse, Rouault, Vlaminck, Derain, Dufy, and Braque. At about the same time the original nucleus of Expressionist painting was formed in Germany. In 1905 a Van Gogh exhibition was held in Dresden and in the same year four architecture students who had been painting on the side founded the Brücke group (Kirchner, Heckel, Schmidt-Rottluff, and Bleyl). In 1906 Nolde and Pechstein joined them.

In an extended sense Fauvism and the Brücke can be described as the true Art Nouveau style in painting. These two artistic movements brought about a radical renewal, beside which the actual Art Nouveau appears as a cultivated, aesthetically refined dead end. The strengthening of form and the revivification of content are connected to the vehement and deeply-felt gestures of Van Gogh in which life itself seemed to 'stammer forth' (Vlaminck), and to the full, saturated colours of Gauguin. When Gauguin called himself a barbarian, he referred to the sources from which he derived many important hints for the tightening and broadening of form: the art of the traditional cultures of Oceania and Africa, which were later discovered and collected by members of the Fauve and Brücke groups. The coarse, anti-classical and anti-academic elementary idiom of the statuettes and masks fascinated a generation of artists who felt alienated from the concept of the beautiful in its accepted European connotation. Matisse put it this way: 'Fauvism broke the tyranny of Divisionism. It was no longer possible to live in a commonplace household, the household of a provincial aunt. We broke a path in the wilderness so as to create new means that saved the spirit from suffocation. Here we encountered Gauguin and Van Gogh. These are the original ideas: structures and coloured surfaces. The search is for the strongest effects of colour – the material is indifferent.' Nolde acknowledges an instinctive sense of design: 'I want my work to grow out of the material. There are no fixed aesthetic rules. The artist follows his instincts when he creates his work. He himself is astonished by it, and others with him.' Painting became *doing* in the strongest sense of the word. This ideal, and a struggle for unconstrained truthfulness, also determined the choice of subject-matter. The German and French Expressionists of the first decade of the century did not enter into an assured, unexplored world. They undertook rather to expose the human condition. For them nature and man no longer constituted particular motifs, but the heightening of the individual instance into a symbol. For this reason art announced a spontaneous and direct message 'from me to you' (Kokoschka). 'Life' was placed above 'art'. Everything living was right – as had already been proclaimed by the Romantics. This truth must humble art; in its name careful painting and the idealizing canons of beauty were cast aside, together with everything smooth and perfect. Instead, powerful and vehement means were preferred.

Within these generalizations we may distinguish several national and personal differences in painting. Despite its radicalism the agitated idiom of Maurice de Vlaminck (1876–1958) remained indebted to the surface rhythms of Van Gogh *[811]*. The Germans inclined to broken contours recalling woodcuts *[813]*, as well as to Baroque formal exuberance *[814]*. In France Henri Matisse (1869–1954), the leader of the Fauves, soon set himself the goal of a balanced formal structure. In the search for 'purity of means' he arrived, as in *Luxe, Calme et Volupté* of 1905, at a

812 *Henri Matisse, Luxe, Calme et Volupté, 1905. Copenhagen, Statens Museum for Kunst. A calm, objective formal language is evident in this composition. The 'expressiveness' in the movements of the clearly contoured figures is less an emotional than an integrating element in the pictorial structure.*

811 *Maurice de Vlaminck, Country Party, 1905. Paris, Private Collection. Art Nouveau aesthetics was opposed to the forceful forms of the 'Fauves'. The figures are embedded in the highly expressive pictorial rhythm.*

cool, flat mode of composition in which curvilinear rhythms provide the decisive factor *[812]*.

Expressionism is characterized by a neglect of detail for the sake of overall form and concentration on the totality of the image rather than the individual status of the formal components. 'The force of the expression springs from the coloured surface as a whole', wrote Matisse. What were the Expressionists' favourite themes? Both French and Germans chose extreme situations: sometimes paradisiacal nudity *[812]*, sometimes the pervasive pandemonium of a great city *[813]*. Primitive man is one of its leading images: another is the man condemned by bourgeois society to an uprooted and marginal existence: the streetwalker, the clown, the actor.

The events of 1905 in Paris and Dresden opened the way to the twentieth century. Sculpture was also affected by this new orientation; it looked again to

813 Ernst Ludwig Kirchner, *Five Women on the Street*, 1913. *Cologne, Wallraf Richartz Museum. The Expressionist painters of 'Die Brücke' show a preference for a structure resembling woodcuts.*

814 Emil Nolde, *Maria Aegyptica, left wing of a triptych*, 1912. *Hamburg, Kunsthalle. Grotesque figures in crude colour and formal contrasts give the religious theme disturbing overtones.*

classical gestures. Maillol's ideal of the body concentrated in a column or block served as a point of departure. The play of limbs, which had no significance for Maillol's art, was rediscovered. The body was studied in terms of plant-like growth or tectonic patterns.

Henri Matisse played an important pioneer role in sculpture too. He replaced the tranquil mass by flowing, twisting energy. The limbs become supple, elastic vehicles of the lines of force [815]. Since the distinction between torso and limbs, between 'trunk' and 'branches' disappears, the uniform character of the whole triumphs over the difference between the individual formal components. As in painting, the spectator's attention is fixed upon the whole rather than upon the parts.

With this important step Matisse emphasized the autonomy of artistic invention as against the point of departure for the design, the 'anatomical' man. This implied the especially significant step of claiming the freedom of action for the sculptor that the painters had gradually conquered since Impressionism. Thus the claim of the sculptor to impress upon his objects departures from reality entered on a new, more radical phase.

No less significant is the introduction of the spatial factor. Just as in painting from the time of Seurat, Gauguin, Van Gogh, and Cézanne the coloured surface was activated into a textural unity so that one could no longer distinguish between 'figure' and its 'setting' or 'background' inasmuch as the coloured and formal arrangement of all the components is endowed with the same intensity, so one can say of Matisse's *Serpentine* that the hollows are no longer mere interspaces. Rather mass and space, positive and negative form enter into a mutual relationship based upon equal rights. Space is not a filling or background but a fully co-ordinated formal component.

The German sculptor Wilhelm Lehmbruck (1881–1919), who was decisively influenced by several years' stay in France, also subordinated the physical relationships of man to the concern for the dialogue between space and mass. His concept of man is not a vegetable but a tectonic one. The limbs are turned into a system of spatial clasps [816]. The whole body is conceived in term of links and linear paths.

The Rumanian Constantin Brancusi (1876–1957) went the furthest along the road to the autonomy of the sculptural image. Rodin and Maillol were his starting-points. His results, however, exclude any direct comparison with his contemporaries. Coming to Paris in 1904 he soon decided to reject the furrowed surface treatment of Rodin. In his tightening,

816 *Wilhelm Lehmbruck, The Fallen, 1915–16. Stuttgart, Collection Lehmbruck. The body is full of physical expressiveness. The hollowed space created by the lines of the figure contributes to the overall effect.*

817 *Constantin Brancusi, Maiastra, 1912. Venice, Collection Peggy Guggenheim. The bird features in a native saga cycle of the Rumanian artist; here it becomes a spirited symbol of personal meaning. Note the strongly unified forms; the material is polished bronze.*

815 *Henri Matisse, La Serpentine, 1909. New York, Museum of Modern Art. The formal inventiveness explored by painters after Cézanne was carried over into sculpture and lead to the deformation of reality.*

polishing, and stretching of the limbs he had other aims than those of Maillol. He was interested not in a general feeling for the body but in a shapely beauty which excluded any identification with the human condition. He envisioned this beauty with an idol-like severity and remoteness. Sculptural invention thus entered into an area hitherto regarded as the domain of Neo-Classicism – the careful treatment of materials, worked so as to produce effects of preciosity. The craft perfection was not, however, subordinated to an external cult of beauty, but imbued with an intellectual content, that of the immaculate regarded as a metaphor of perfection. Sublimation of the material and spiritualization of content are inseparable in Brancusi. It should be noted that the volumes do not exclude space, which serves to dematerialize the masses. Space is captured in the reflexions visible on the smooth figures whose surfaces act as a kind of space trap. Space streams from all sides into the object, which retains its character as a segment of infinity *[817]*.

In 1907 a Cézanne memorial exhibition was held
in Paris. This was just in time to serve as a stimulus
and support for a new departure in painting, the
beginning of Cubism. Pablo Picasso (born 1881) and
Georges Braque (1882–1963), the two first Cubists,
took up the problem Cézanne had posed for himself
and whose methodical examination had been postponed by the Fauves – the striving for an enhanced
reality and density of form. Seen from a broader
context one can discern here a desire to reconcile
realism with idealism. Since this ambitious programme was not pursued methodically, sometimes
realistic features come to the fore and sometimes
idealistic ones. The effort maintained in early Cubism
to achieve a more factual reality was directed against
the illusionism of traditional painting. Picasso stated:
'In a picture of Raphael's it is impossible to measure
the distance from the end of the nose to the mouth.
I want to paint pictures in which this is possible.'
The artist was no longer to 'hoodwink' the observer.
This attitude tended towards factual reportage and

*818   Georges Braque, Houses at L'Estaque, 1908. Berne,
Kunstmuseum. As early as Cézanne inner rules are evident in
Cubist constructs. The group of houses here is composed out of
crystalline cubic forms.*

*819   Pablo Picasso, The Aficionado, 1912. Basle, Kunstmuseum.
Analytical Cubism resolves outlines and inner drawing of real
events into tiny detailed facets, in order to convey a total picture
of the many different aspects from which an object can be viewed.*

careful documentation. When carried into practice as
in Picasso's *Aficionado [819]* it confuses the observer
who has not had a chance to become familiar with
the conventions of this mode of vision. At the same
time the paradoxical character of this rendering of
reality is evident. The artist is interested in the
distance from the end of the nose to the mouth only
in so far as this gives him the excuse to carry through
a reorganization of the stereotyped concept of the
human face and fill it with a new reality. This
requirement also permits the combination of several
different views of an object into a complex whole.
The painter gives up his fixed standpoint and instead
'circulates' about his model so as to grasp it in its
totality. He protests against the 'slice of reality'
provided by central perspective in which the painter
selects a particular aspect out of the multitude of
possible views. Early Cubism, however, wished to
express the coexistence of several views of a head or a
still-life and this led to a definite break with perspectival space. The artist concentrated upon the affirmation

of corporeal reality. Men, things, and landscape are contoured in hard and angular fashion; the colour range shrinks to brown, grey, green, and ochre, as in *Houses at L'Estaque [818]* by Georges Braque. Here one finds compact blocks consisting of recurring basic forms that emphasize the tight, taut, and cubic.

Analytic Cubism (1909–11) organizes these basic forms in a transparent framework of lines *[819]*. The previously closed figure is opened and comes to terms with its setting, which now penetrates into the broken inner form. This produces a fluctuating interaction of bars, bows, facets, and corners constituting an autonomous pictorial geometry. The pictorial surface no longer admits of a distinction between figure and ground; it is rather a formal field of force. The objective starting-point is thus tectonically 'coded'. What the painting loses in objective readability it gains in density of form.

The later development of Braque, Picasso, and Gris sought to create in Synthetic Cubism (from 1912) a new encounter with the world of experience. The autonomous means of design were again directed towards the object without losing their own character. This shift from one function to another is clearly evident in the *Still-life with Guitar* of 1915 *[820]*, by Juan Gris (1887–1927). The curves delimiting the musical instrument have also an independent function

821 *Pablo Picasso, Bottle, Glass and Newspaper, 1912. Paris, Private Collection. Cubist compositions were made of 'papier collé', which enriched the formal texture with objects of everyday life. These fragments of reality contained a new, almost magical power within the picture.*

820 *Juan Gris, Still-life with Guitar, 1915. Otterlo, Rijksmuseum Kröller-Müller. The independent formal particles combine in Synthetic Cubism; the object becomes autonomous and unambiguous.*

in a system that partitions the picture surface. The middle sheet of music is part of an irregular pentagon whose upper part is arbitrarily contoured so that it follows no objective outline. The object turns into an embracing shape (the pentagon) for which there is a compositional justification, but no excuse in reality. In Synthetic Cubism things are once more readable and even where they appear fragmented it is only to enter into a larger formal organization. The course of the contours is more tranquil than in the analytic phase and the splintering gives way to a clearly stratified formal scheme, but the object still retains its transparency. The picture became a kind of 'coloured surface architecture' (Gris). An especially striking way of heightening the factual character of the picture without falling into traditional illusionism is represented by the *papier-collé* (glued-paper) technique *[821]*, to which the Cubists turned in 1912. Since the artists introduced newspaper clippings and fabrics to their formal structure this consequently acquired the character of tangible material substance; it is as if the artist wanted to satirize *trompe l'œil* painting. These fragments of reality have not merely the function of testifying to a banal, unvarnished reality, but are also to be interpreted as pure form and composition elements as if to affirm that painting does not aim at imitation, but represents an autonomous artistic reality.

Cubism succeeded in formulating two points of view in which future development was to be polarized. Malevitch and Mondrian carried the idealistic tendencies of Analytic Cubism to the point where every reminiscence of the external world is banished from the formal structure and this is proclaimed as 'pure painting' (Apollinaire) *[823]*. Both were to make the passage to pure geometric form in opposition to the means of Cubism and sought to refine from these means all hint of the world of object. The more realistic trend led from the collages of the Cubists to the conjurations of the Dadaists' glued and nailed composite pictures *[839]*.

The turning-point signified by Cubism is reflected in its immediate effects. It displaced the two principles upon which European painting had rested since the Renaissance. Since the time of the introduction of central perspective, pictorial space and the space of experience enjoyed a mutual interrelationship. Space provided an intellectual and physical medium binding together all the elements of the painting. This continuity among the illusionistic components found a material counterpart in the homogeneous surface of the picture. The surface of a medieval painting has a discontinuous character; it falls into disparate zones (e.g. figural representation, decorative gold ground, inlaid precious stones, narrative scrolls). In the Renaissance the surface was unified; the entire picture became exclusively 'painting' and the whole work was entrusted to the brush as the symbol of the subjective sense of design. Henceforth the rectangle of the easel painting was the ideal plane; it represented the results of a uniform manual act of design informing every single area of the picture.

The Cubists rejected these principles. The figures were segmented and deprived of their organic integrity; instead of the continuous medium of space one finds an interlacing of separate spatial zones. In the collage the formerly homogeneous surface is made heterogeneous through the added parts. These are characteristics which emphasize the creative will of the artist, and testify to his claim to be an originator. The act of design becomes independent of perceived reality.

FROM CUBISM TO ABSTRACT ART

The formal achievements of the Cubists fell upon fertile soil. The aspect which related to the manifestation of 'total' reality was carried further by the Italian Futurists (Balla, Boccioni, Carrà, Russolo, and Severini). While the Cubists fitted their multiple views into a framework of static units, the Futurists gave the whole composition the effect of movement. Not a situation, but a process, a sequence of events seemed to Umberto Boccioni (1882–1916) a proper subject for painting. From this attitude came the need to give the content a temporal dimension. The moment of sense perception was woven into a field of association, whose Symbolist origin may be detected in the titles of the paintings themselves (*The City Rises; Recollections of a Night*). Bergson's support was appealed to ('Perception is nothing but an occasion for recollection'). Pictures should be 'dynamic hieroglyphs' from the past and the present *[822]*. The Futurists opened and fractured fixed forms; they multiplied boundaries and made them seem transparent. They were especially fond of diagonals and spirals.

In contrast to this dynamic interpretation of Cubist formal elements, which evokes a plethora of motifs from the external world, the Dutchman Piet Mondrian (1872–1944) followed a path leading to a static concept of painting. He succeeded in creating a

822 Umberto Boccioni, Farewell, 1911. New York, Private Collection. The Futurists opened up a new pictorial dimension: movement. The composition abandoned the tectonics of Cubism and exploited dynamic accents with spiritual expressiveness.

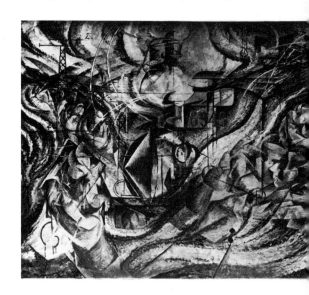

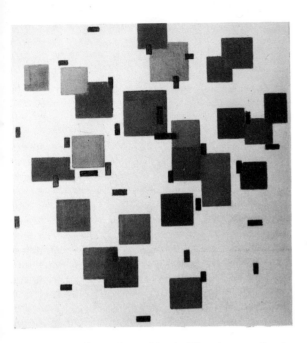

823 Piet Mondrian, Composition in Blue A, 1917. Otterlo, Rijksmuseum Kröller-Müller. No objects intervene in the harmony of this piece. Rectangles of various size show a geometric progression in pictorial terms.

style of his own, Neo-Plasticism. Mondrian methodically dissected the complex formal components of Cubist painting. His elimination of diagonals and curves left only right-angled conjunctions of verticals and horizontals [823]. Thus he achieved a kind of 'visual' representation of logic, where the objective forms are untouched by subjective emotion. His painting pressed the geometrical factors of the Cubist painting to their ultimate consequences inasmuch as he excluded any reference to concrete reality. The painting became a harmonic structure and an object existing in its own right.

With some simplification one can describe the 'pure painting' which Mondrian elaborated between 1911 and 1914 as 'Apollonian'. Its 'classical' aspect was foiled by the contemporaneous work of Wassily Kandinsky (1866–1944), which may be regarded as essentially romantic. His style depends not upon the crystalline tendencies of Cubism, but stems from an intensely colouristic Fauvism with roots in Art Nouveau and the late Impressionism of Monet – that is in the direction of open, molten, and dissolved form. In Munich in 1911 Kandinsky and Franz Marc (1880–1916) founded the artistic group 'Der Blaue Reiter'. In 1910 the discovery that the object spoiled his pictures led Kandinsky to decide to create the first consciously non-objective painting. This work –

like others produced a little later [824] – shows a kind of dialogue between nervous and flowing colour skeins, line clusters, and darting strokes. In contrast to Mondrian, Kandinsky emphasizes the subjective, tragic, and transient. With this elemental harmony of design the artist opened the way to unsuspected areas of spontaneity. Like Delacroix, Seurat, and Gauguin before him Kandinsky recognized that certain colours and forms evoked particular responses in the observer. Hence he concluded that objective content was superfluous and embarked upon the autonomous development and ordering of pictorial means. Kandinsky prophesied that 'in time it will become possible for us to speak through purely artistic means; then it will be superfluous to introduce forms from the external world into the internal discourse'. The object was treated as an intrusive element. The aestheticism of the late nineteenth century had affirmed that 'all art constantly aspires towards the condition of music' (Walter Pater).

Kandinsky and Mondrian opened the way to non-objective design, often loosely designated 'abstract', at the same time indicating the two polar extremes between which it was to move: vital spontaneity, and the painting of geometrical meditation. This revolution in painting corresponds to Brancusi's

824 Wassily Kandinsky, Composition 7 (Sketch 1), 1913. Berne, Private Collection. Kandinsky too practised a style of painting free of objects after the stark colourism of the Fauves, though his works contain an expressive dynamism of their own.

achievement in sculpture *[817]*. The comparison is of course valid only for the inner tendencies and not for the formal results. Brancusi made the sculptural object fully autonomous. The Cubist achievements – formal crystallization and stratification – are also significant for sculpture, for they offered a chance to resume with a new radicalism the dialogue between figure and space posited by Matisse *[815]*. Boccioni *[822]* played an especially important role in this. His 'Manifesto of Futurist Sculpture' (1912) praises Rosso *[789]* as the only sculptor who succeeded in bringing sculpture into contact with surrounding space. This is also his own aim: 'We proclaim the absolute and complete abolition of the definite linear boundary; we proclaim the abolition of self-contained sculpture. We break the image up and set it into space. We treat the surrounding space as part of the sculpture itself.' Furthermore Boccioni spoke in favour of the use of new, 'modern' materials (glass, iron, leather, etc.). At the same time Alexander Archipenko (born 1887) held that when sculpture was autonomous it was open to any material.

825 Alexander Archipenko, Boxing Match, 1913. Vienna, Museum des 20. Jahrhunderts. The hollowed space takes on an autonomous form in the composition.

Archipenko experimented with *sculpto-peinture*, an attempt to join painting with the relief that was intended as a protest against the illusionism of the ideal picture plane.

Here again one finds a formal characteristic which is evident in the development of painting as early as Impressionism. Figure and ground, figure and surrounding space are with increasing consistency endowed with an equal formal intensity. This has the important consequence that the world of objects in a picture loses its position of prominence and superiority in isolation from the rest of the formal structure. For sculpture this means that figure and surrounding space are equivalent. This insight gave Archipenko the starting-point for his formal results; he opened the volumes of his forms, consciously contrasted the convex with the concave, and endowed the 'interspace' (the open form) with positive value *[825]*. Boccioni had similar intentions in breaking up the figure and displacing it into surrounding space. Both artists depend upon the advances made in Cubism. Moreover one can connect their efforts to incorporate new materials with Kandinsky, who declared in 1912 that the present has the spiritual freedom to employ 'any material from the hardest to the merely two-dimensional [abstract] as a form element'.

What was happening in architecture in that revolutionary decade of painting and sculpture from 1906 (when Picasso began the first early Cubist painting, *Les Demoiselles d'Avignon*) to World War I? Are there buildings that exhibit principles of design comparable to those of Cubism, Futurism and geometrical Purism (Mondrian)? These principles are the opening and perforation (or segmentation) of the closed unit; the mutual interpenetration of mass and surrounding space; and the manifestation of the lines of force of the formal framework. This produces a multi-axial space and, especially in Cubism, the complex superimposition of formal units, so that the painting, ceasing to be a juxtaposition of separate forms, becomes a transparent oscillation of many elements.

In 1903 Auguste Perret (1874–1954) built a house in the rue Franklin in Paris *[826, 827]*. The street front closely recalls the *cour d'honneur* scheme of French châteaux. It has five bays which alternately advance and retreat. The 'abbreviated' *cour d'honneur* acts like a façade which opens to disclose a view into the inner workings of the construction. Thus the balconies are not expansions into free space but incisions in which the exterior folds into the interior space. The staggering of the building mass is expressed in clefts and bucklings. The verticals are continuous, but the viewer from the street can see no consistent horizontal.

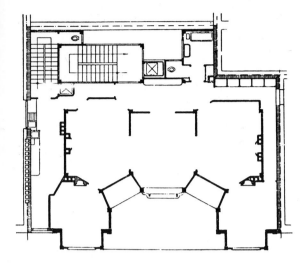

826, 827 Auguste Perret, residential block in the rue Franklin, Paris, 1903. Ground-plan and façade. In the sloping walls of the façade the balconies form a bridge between inner and outer space. Steel and concrete construction enables a freer arrangement of rooms in the interior.

He sees a broken line which manifests itself in different ways: sometimes it is a flat band, sometimes the outer edge of the balcony. These optical displacements suggest that the five windows of a story are placed at three different heights. Here, as well as in the interpenetration of exterior and interior space, one can see a principle that is related to Cubism. The construction of the house uses the reinforced concrete that had

been invented and developed in France. The supports of the construction are visible on the exterior. The texture of the façade is heterogeneous like a Cubist collage. The two outer bays are the most richly decorated, the windows are framed by panels of leaf ornament surrounded in turn by flat bands. In the middle the fine revetment disappears, disclosing the naked structure of support to the viewer. The façade is stripped bare. The plan *[826]* of the house shows that the small number of vertical supports gave the architect great freedom in the organization of interior space. Here also one finds a staggered arrangement of rooms. Since the interior walls are adjustable and can be freely disposed, the monotonous succession of closed spatial cells is avoided, permitting an interpenetration of parts within the larger spatial complex. An additive grouping yields to a staggered effect. Although in this respect Perret's house reveals a parallel with the spatial labyrinths of Art Nouveau, it belongs more to the early twentieth century than to the end of the nineteenth century by virtue of its constructional realism.

A turning away from the organically oriented linearism of Art Nouveau is first evident among its Austrian adherents. About 1900 there was a shift to the square and the rectangle. The right angle and the open spatial differentiation of the Palais Stoclet by Josef Hoffmann *[809]* do indeed show an early 'Cubistic' tendency, but the stylistic connexion with Art Nouveau remains valid. The longing for an aesthetic synthesis of the arts must be seen in the larger context of the *fin de siècle*, where the attractive was preferred to the functional. In this sense the Wiener Werkstätte founded by Hoffmann in 1903 should be distinguished from the more methodical approach of the Deutscher Werkbund (1907). While the Viennese strove for luxurious craft-work, the Germans tried to evolve the design of practical objects in conformity with the nature of the machine so as to resolve the conflict between individual and industrial production that had bedevilled Morris. Here lie the beginnings of modern industrial design. One of its pioneers was Peter Behrens (1868–1940), who was preparing bottles for mass production as early as 1898. In 1906 the AEG (German General Electrical Company) appointed him as an artistic adviser. In this capacity he laid the foundations for rational industrial design. His designs range from industrial articles (lamps, ventilators, etc.) to packing and advertising (prospectuses, trade marks). The AEG also employed Behrens as an architect. In 1908–9 he built the firm's *Turbine Erection Hall* in Berlin *[828]*. Attracted by a powerful symbol of energy, he felt impelled to dramatic intensification. Constructional needs were

828   *Peter Behrens, AEG Turbine Erection Hall in Berlin, 1908–9.*

829   *Hans Poelzig. Water-tower in Poznan, 1911.*

Both buildings show the Expressionist components of German architecture. Behrens contrasts the horizontal layers of the corners with the delicate structure of the windows. The broken contour of the gable gives the structure a powerful expression. Poelzig builds his water-tower out of a three-storied base that resembles a prism. The functional architecture takes on the character of a monument.

sacrificed to expressive effects. This monumental treatment of service structures is also characteristic of the industrial buildings of Hans Poelzig (1869–1936). His concern with industrial building rested on the understanding that only in this category of building did the architect have the freedom to work with undecorated functional forms. An example is the *water-tower* he built in Poznan in 1911. The steel construction was made visible; the expressive values which point towards a monumental 'Cubism' derive from the rhythmic organization of the building mass which almost achieves the status of a monument *[829]*.

What these buildings lost in rejecting decorative forms had to be made up in the proportion and precision of the execution. A sober, severe beauty of material was produced that was far more functionally oriented than in Art Nouveau. This attitude is summed up by Otto Wagner's (1841–1918) statement that 'nothing that is not useful can be beautiful' (1896). He realized this functionalist credo in 1905 in the main hall of the Vienna Postal Savings Building. The right angle dominates in this room. The wall masses contrast with the thin membranes of the glass roof. This unsentimental juxtaposition of heterogeneous materials recalls the montage techniques of the Cubists.

Wagner contributed nothing to the solution of the problem of the opening out of the ground-plan. (The open ground-plan corresponded to the breaking of closed outlines of figures and objects in Cubist painting.) Perret's attempt to open the closed cube was of limited scope, since the building in the rue Franklin *[827]* was hemmed in on either side by other structures. The free play with loosely arranged blocks, as carried out under the inspiration of the Anglo-American country-house in such buildings as Hoffmann's Palais Stoclet, was neither possible nor desirable in this restricted space. The principle developed by the English and Americans of combining the different spatial cells in a kind of domino arrangement – recalling Mondrian's organization of two-dimensional surfaces *[823]* – was especially suited to the horizontal loosening up of the building mass. In Vienna Adolf Loos (1870–1933) followed another path. He retained the closed rectangle of the ground-plan, and decided to differentiate the building in the vertical sense, to shift the 'opening out' from the plan to the elevation. In his *Haus Scheu in Vienna [830]* of 1912 each story has a different plan; the ground story has the largest area, the second story the smallest. Thus he created, doubtless under the influence of the Mediterranean terrace house, the stepped building block. What is noticeable from the very first is the absence of any articulated façade. The building block is no longer a closed unit framed vertically at the sides by quoins and horizontally by ground and roof lines. Part of the old cube – the two 'steps' – has been cut out by the architect. The interpenetration of mass and space is unmistakable.

The concept of a revolutionary ground-plan appears in Loos's work about 1919 and is first realized in the Rufer House of 1922. In this building Loos breaks with the custom of placing all the rooms of a story upon the same level. In any two adjacent rooms that he built one was always higher than the other. The interior walls are largely abolished and short stairs connect the rooms. In this fashion two great spatial units flow into a continuum. Thus Loos transferred the principle of interlocking units from surfaces to space. In the 1920s Le Corbusier, apparently acting independently of Loos, used this principle even more consistently. He inserted two overlapping single-storied rooms in a greater room, raising the height of two stories.

However strongly this type of construction inclined to the differentiation of the interior it always remained a *built* architecture; space was manifested as hollow form and not as a substance transformed by lines of force. Moreover this spatial design did not express the intimate character of the family house, but appeared in public building projects, in great dimensions. In the later nineteenth century large spaces were covered with steel construction [759]. If reinforced concrete was to be used for works of this type it was first necessary to develop a constructional form which was also aesthetically satisfying. This occurred when architects learned to build bearing structures consisting of shells and pleated units, a type of building that permitted them to cover broad spaces with a minimum expense for materials. An early example of the agitated spatial pathos of this constructional trend is the *Jahrhunderthalle* in Breslau [831] built by the architect Max Berg (born 1870) and the engineer Trauer in 1912–13. The dome, which rests upon four pendentives, is made up of 32 ribs in reinforced concrete. In the formal management of the space, curved lines and surfaces dominate. In this way the impression of elastic tension and dynamic action is created. The linear paths of force present many overlappings to the eye. The construction gives the impression of a flowing, whirling movement. If one experiences this characteristic as the painter Lothar Schreyer did, one cannot help comparing it with the cosmic fantasies of the Futurists (e.g. with the painting *Mercury Passes the Sun* by Balla): 'It seemed to me as if the cosmos opened and disclosed the ordering of the paths of the stars and a vision into the Empyrean.'

830 Adolf Loos, Haus Scheu in Vienna, 1912. A building block where space and weight interpenetrate. There is no special emphasis on the façade; and decoration is avoided.

By and large, however, the interest of the Futurists was directed not towards cosmic forces but to the activities of the great city scene. In this they demonstrated an awareness of the present that did not shrink from comparing the Victory of Samothrace unfavourably to a motor car. The theme of city traffic occurs again and again in Futurist painting. The architect Antonio Sant'Elia (1888–1916), who joined

831 Max Berg and the engineer Trauer, Jahrhunderthalle in Breslau, 1912–13. An early attempt to form a large space out of steel and concrete, as had been achieved in iron. The bold rimmed dome conveys a feeling of new, dynamic space.

the Futurists in 1914, gave the central position in his city projects to traffic as the social manifestation of the abstraction 'movement'. In his 'Manifesto of Futurist Architecture' he demanded an unqualified adherence to modern building materials (iron, concrete, glass). The architect must build in full awareness of the present and master all the mechanical sciences. The Futurist living block became a gigantic machine, the street a ship's dock. The relation to the machine was conceived as a principle of the highest value. In this Sant'Elia spoke in favour of unceasing creative renewal and rejected any museum-like fossilization of the cityscape, in much the same way as the Futurist painters called for the destruction of museums of fine arts. The lifetime of a house would be shorter than that of a man. In this stipulation the cult of movement united with the enthusiasm for unceasing change. Sant'Elia's projects, whose execution was prevented by his early death in World War I, seem to embody this radical programme only in part. They constitute almost megalomaniac architectural visions of a never-ending metropolis. In this total architecture the individual complex merges with the 'layout' *[832]*. Building masses and traffic installations (bridges, streets, and lifts) form an indissoluble complex in which the dynamic elements dominate. The staggering and mutual interpenetration of space and mass are no longer achieved in the individual building but in the larger context of town planning.

833   *Walter Gropius and Adolf Meyer, Fagus Factory in Alfeld a.d. Leine, 1911. A transparent glass and steel construction. Exterior walls are completely resolved into glass surfaces between the masonry supports.*

832   Antonio Sant' Elia, sketch for the 'città futurista', 1914. Plan for a central traffic station in Milan, with several traffic levels between high buildings, and an airfield in the background.

Overlappings and complementary penetrations suggest that no single entity can be understood in its own right but only within the many-layered spatial axes of the whole complex, the 'layout'. The design principle of step arrangement, which was being explored by Loos at about the same time in the residential house *[830]*, was understood dynamically by Sant'Elia and utilized for the separation of several levels of traffic. His projects are concerned with one of the most important tasks confronting the architect's integrating powers in the twentieth century: the synthesis of enclosing architecture (i.e. residential or communal buildings) with traffic architecture.

The way in which Sant'Elia expanded the single building into the infinite architectural layout shows that he grasped the ultimate consequences of the open ground-plan. This gives his projects the quality of a labyrinthine vision. His contemporaries proceeded more modestly. Between 1911 and 1914 Walter Gropius (born 1883) and Adolf Meyer (1881–1929) erected a *shoe last factory* in Alfeld an der Leine *[833]*.

Architectural critics have described the Fagus Factory as a synthesis of contemporary industrial building. The task permitted the architects to carry through an entirely novel solution of the relations between block and mass, and between interior and exterior space. Like Loos, Gropius selected the right angle as the basic form but used it differently. Gropius's work differs from the emotionally accented industrial building of his teacher Behrens *[828]* in its cool, functional understatement. Without staggering the ground-plan or stepping the elevation he was able to open out the building block by simply making it transparent. The layout of the interior was freely exhibited. The relation of glass to supports is so conceived that the windows do not suggest clefts in the wall. Rather the character of the whole wall is a glazed surface. The small wall supports have the effect of vertical accents. The glass windows stretching through all the stories without interruption depend upon a steel framework; they have no bearing function. In this way the construction is stripped bare and the bearing and filling elements are visibly differentiated. A kind of formal polyvalence becomes evident; a single glass window of a story belongs to the context of both the horizontal and the vertical window strips. The lightening and de-materialization of the building mass is promoted by the absence of corner supports; the angles of the buildings are virtually suppressed. The rooms lying immediately behind the glass wall have the quality of both exterior and interior space. This means that the observer perceives the constituent cells at the same time as the building block itself. In this way the sum of the constructive – or in the painters' terminology, Cubist or Purist – architectural experience of the period before 1914 was drawn up.

ART BETWEEN THE WARS

Constructivism, Suprematism, and De Stijl

World War I exposed bourgeois and national values as masks for the pursuit of political and commercial power. All traditional forms of artistic and social life were affected by the resulting loss of confidence. But while it is true that the political uneasiness affecting victor and vanquished alike left its mark on the artistic symbols that embellished outmoded social structures, the first impulses for criticism and renewal came from the arts themselves.

It is revealing to examine the role played by the easel painting in this situation. Its connexion with bourgeois and liberal artistic requirements is obvious.

It corresponds to the aesthetic lip-service paid to art as the ennobled reflection of life, while refusing it the right to try to change or improve existing conditions. This kind of taste transferred the work of art into a kind of consecrated realm, valuing the creative achievement primarily as the expression of isolated genius. In so far as it acted in accordance with the principles of *laissez faire* and disregarded planning and co-ordination, easel painting was granted immunity from social obligations. Every attempt to fuse the individual branches of art into a common idiom necessarily implied a criticism of the preferential treatment accorded to the easel painting. Efforts in this direction had already appeared in Art Nouveau, and they came to the fore again in three artistic movements – Constructivism, De Stijl, and the Bauhaus – whose beginnings lay in the shadow of World War I.

These new movements were distinguished from Art Nouveau by a sober attitude towards problems, the renunciation of emotional accents, and by the striving for a contemporary attitude towards the artistic process directed by reason rather than feeling. It is no accident that these aspirations made themselves felt in Russia, Germany, and the Netherlands, countries placed on the borders of Mediterranean culture where the Renaissance aesthetic could be overcome more easily. The artistic and philosophical aims show Protestant and in fact Puritanical features. Artists wished to serve the common good, armed themselves against extra-artistic suggestion, and condemned unrestrained expression of feeling.

On the eve of the war Vladimir Tatlin (born 1885) and Alexander Rodchenko (born 1891) came together in Russia. From this meeting emerged the Constructivism that later after the October Revolution was able to exercise a considerable influence with the approval of the new political authorities. Entirely independent contributions to this renewal were made by the two brothers Naum Gabo (born 1890) and Antoine Pevsner (1886–1963) with their 'Realistic Manifesto', and by Malevitch with the proclamation of Suprematism. On the basis of a geometrical formal scheme these artists devoted themselves to a severe asceticism that reaches its extreme point in a painting by Kasimir Malevitch (1878–1935) showing a white square on a white ground. This meditative purification recalls the cult of icons. At the same time, however, the reliefs and spatial structures of the Constructivists show their concern with the material realities of a technological age. Glass and iron took the place of bronze and marble, while the sculptural image frequently left its base to float and move.

Much more methodical was the renewal of all areas of design undertaken by Mondrian and Theo van Doesburg when they founded the De Stijl movement in the Netherlands in 1917. Here too asceticism was practised; the right angle and the three primary colours constituted the whole formal repertory. The easel painting was no longer considered an isolated wall decoration but a component of a larger whole. The members of De Stijl sought formal equivalents for the 'harmonious balance of life'. This idealistic and Utopian aspect took its purest form in Mondrian's 'icons'; but it was expressed also in the more everyday guise of typography and the poster and it gave a new impulse to architecture. The building block was opened out; it was no longer 'walled in', but articulated plastically and differentiated through the application of colour.

These constructive tendencies were concentrated and pedagogically reworked in the Bauhaus which was founded by Walter Gropius in 1919 in Weimar. Among others Klee, Kandinsky, Schlemmer, Feininger, Moholy-Nagy, and later Mies van der Rohe worked here. The Bauhaus Manifesto proclaimed: 'There is no essential difference between the artist and the craftsman. The artist is the craftsman intensified. . . . Together we will conceive and create the new building of the future in which all will be fused in a single image: architecture and sculpture and painting. . . .'

What had been undertaken in Russia, the Netherlands, and Germany was directed towards two ends. Art must once again become a vital factor in human civilization, must allow itself to be shaped by the industrial influences on modern daily life. Second, the art work must constitute an independent reality no longer as illusionistic appearance but as a fact 'no less important than the fact of nature itself' (Malevitch). With complete consistency the artists propagated the concept of 'concrete art' (Van Doesburg), which describes this factuality better than the word abstract. The Renaissance had separated painting and sculpture from architecture as distinct media. This division now collapsed. Formal analysis confirms this fact by identifying structural characteristics that run through all categories of art. In place of the closed corporeal mass there appears an open and transparent assemblage of elements. The components that make up the formal unit do not fuse together, but remain visibly independent and apparently separable. The quality of transparency is realized in architecture through an increasing use of glass. The building elements seem mounted or assembled together. Although every part retains its formal independence in the face of the demands of

834   Gerrit Thomas Rietveld, Schröder House in Utrecht, 1924. An exciting combination of horizontals and verticals, massive and fenestrated surfaces of a varied height.

835, 836   Ludwig Mies van der Rohe, German pavilion at the International Exhibition in Barcelona, 1929. Ground plan and view of exterior. A flat roof is carried by chrome and steel supports. The wall partitions are of glass so arranged as to form a 'flowing' space.

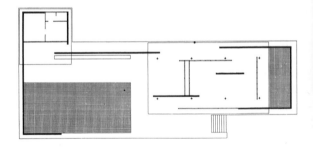

function, the result is not a mere additive combination, but an entity composed of calculated interpenetrations and overlappings. In other words the formal elements – such as the vertical slab of the balcony of the *Schröder House* in Utrecht (1924) by Gerrit Thomas Rietveld *[834]* – fit into the context of several functional systems. The same is true of the partitions that replace the walls in the *Barcelona Pavilion* (1929) by Ludwig Mies van der Rohe (born 1886): they belong to several spatial complexes *[836]*. Forms disregard functional boundaries and often exceed them *[835]*. This is a principle of design used by the 'constructive' artist in protest against the total domination of logical functionalism. 'The elements should produce forms, but without sacrificing their own nature. They must be true to themselves' (Klee, 1920).

This maxim is also valid for painting. The architect opens out the plan on all sides and the painter no longer proceeds from a previously selected dominant feature (an object or a human figure), but brings elements together in which figures ultimately find their proper place. These 'figures' show the same structural characteristics as works of architecture and sculpture, though occasionally the more capricious possibilities of improvisation are exploited *[842]*.

Dadaism and Surrealism

The opposition to traditional artistic attitudes and their bourgeois prestige symbol, the easel painting, was not confined to the Constructivist movements. This is the central theme for the contemporary protest of the Dadaists and Surrealists. Art would no longer serve as a justification for the bourgeois 'life lie'. Its new tasks were ridicule and exposure, illumination of reality and exploration of existence. Paralleling the Constructivists these artists wished to merge the art work with 'life', to rip away the barriers separating the art work from the everyday object and finally to create a reality that would be more complete and – while still replete with unresolved conflicts and contradictions – also truer, more down-to-earth and realistic than the partial world of appearance presented by the existing easel painting. In this way a feeling for life was expressed that aimed at 'resolving the formerly contradictory requirements of dream and reality into an absolute reality, a sur-reality' (Breton).

Dada was founded in Zürich in 1916 by Ball, Hülsenbeck, Arp, Tzara, and Janco. The name Dada was discovered by a chance procedure: a knife was inserted between the pages of a dictionary and the word 'dada', which in French means a child's horse,

837 *Giorgio de Chirico, The Poet's Joys, 1913. New York, Museum of Modern Art. Chirico's 'metaphysical painting absolves figures and surrounding space from their customary relationship and combines apparently opposed areas of reality'.*

was found. In the struggle against the 'dictatorship of the drawers of the brain' (Arp) accident was exalted as the embodiment of a new realm of unrestricted freedom; with its help the artists hoped to explore the area of the primitive, the wondrous, and the mysterious. 'Dada was a kind of nihilism, a way of escaping from a state of mind . . . and of getting rid of clichés, of becoming free' (Marcel Duchamp). Among the clichés are to be included the commonplaces by which our understanding orients itself to

838 *Max Ernst, Woman, Grey and Blue, 1923–4. New York, Museum of Modern Art. Veristic Surrealism transforms precisely rendered fragments of reality into fantastic, ambiguous juxtapositions.*

All these efforts clearly lie in a narrow border zone separating the intentionally inartistic registration of reality *[840]* from its artistic transformation. One can speak of a new 'realism' which borrows directly from profane reality. The Surrealists also acknowledged the total and unrestricted documentation of reality. They built upon the ideas and achievements of the Dadaists but were more concerned with literary and philosophical explanations. At the same time they tackled the delicate problem of delimiting the zones of the unconscious with the instruments of consciousness. Taking their statements literally – the 'First Manifesto' was published in 1924 by André Breton – the Surrealists aimed at the abolition of creativity. The artist noted the insignificance of the aesthetic and moral façade of civilization before the overwhelming power of irrational forces of life, but at the same time he was prepared to utilize these forces – madness, ecstasy, dreams, and the libido – to make a fantastic

840   Marcel Duchamp, Bottle stand, 1914. Duchamp made the 'ready-made' functional object a 'work of art' as a social provocation. This was also an enterprising discovery of the poetic potentialities of the 'everyday' object.

839   Kurt Schwitters, montage relief, 1923. Private Collection. The 'objet trouvé' (ticket, splinter of wood, pasteboard, cloak-room number) contains its own 'value', and at the same time introduces a new order in an 'object-free' composition.

reality. If this system of understanding is discarded, new and unsuspected insights into reality will be gained. This conviction also informs the contemporary 'metaphysical painting' of Giorgio de Chirico (born 1880). Chirico was occupied with 'the enigma of things which we find unimportant . . . so as to live in the world as if in a gigantic museum full of rarities' *[838]*. Similarly, about 1914 Marcel Duchamp (born 1887) discovered that it sufficed to displace a familiar object from its conventional setting to evoke the poetic mysteriousness of the world of things *[840]*. The found object ('objet trouvé') required no artistic working or reshaping to communicate its poetic content. Another individualist, Kurt Schwitters (1887–1948), developed a kind of matter painting taking the Cubist collage as his point of departure *[839]*: 'Rubbish painting *[Merzmalerei]* employs not only colour and canvas, the brush and the palette, but all materials perceived by the eye and all necessary tools. In this it is inessential whether the materials employed are already shaped for any particular end. A child's wagon wheel, wire-netting, twine, or cotton-wool are on an equal plane with colour.'

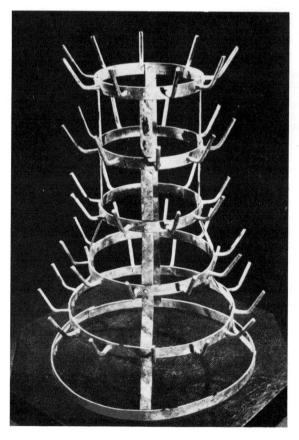

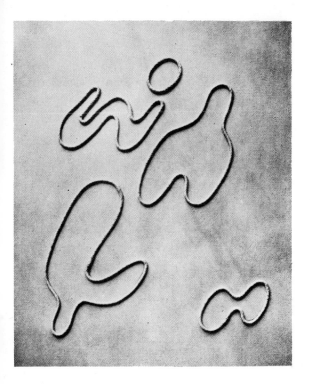

841 Hans Arp, Composed Object, string relief, 1928. Zürich,
Collection Giedion-Welcker. A rhythmically grouped vegetative
form. Arp 'returns to creatures and objects their mythical,
fundamental existence'.

Giacometti, González, and Calder can be included.
Alberto Giacometti (born 1901) devoted himself to
the discovery of sculptural images whose strange,
often sardonic attraction points to the realm of
experience indicated by the words idol, fetish, and
magic. About 1930 Julio González (1876–1942)
began to make masks and figures out of iron rods
and plates. To the principle of assemblage of heterogeneous parts he added the technique of welding.
His flat elements show the influence of the oscillating
faceted forms of the Cubists. But they soon yield to
linear material from which González obtained
mocking and spectral effects. With these 'spatial
drawings' in the last two decades of his life González
became the model for most of the artists concerned
with the linear possibilities of iron. Alexander Calder
(born 1898) originated the mobile sculpture.
About 1930 he began to construct movable constructions from rods, wires, and metal sheets. At first
a motor provided movement, but later Calder turned
to organic forms. The constructions became 'growing
things' whose parts moved about and in their floating

842 Paul Klee, The Step, 1923. Berne, Private Collection.
In Klee's symbolic language the 'letters', here the abbreviations
for eyes and feet, form the bridge to the objective world of
experience.

world of forms *[838]*. If one overlooks this dilemma,
which in any case lies outside the bounds of art-
historical analysis, one can divide the artistic manifestations of Surrealism into two groups. The first
gives the laws of chance the essential role in the
formal process, avoiding the demand of representation of objects. The artist goes back to a pre-objective
elementary realm of formal design using an unpredictably wandering line and spots of colour. This
freedom unconstrained by the claims of objects with
a seemingly abandoned pictorial means was pursued
by Hans Arp *[841]*, André Masson, Joan Miró, and
Paul Klee (the last in a particular group of works
admired by the Surrealists). These artists make the
forms and materials 'speak', directing this expression
towards basic organic forms and demonic images of
fantasy. Their playful and often child-like improvisa-
tions must be distinguished from the rather sombre
and literary dream and fantasy images produced by
another wing of Surrealism. To this belongs much of
the work of Max Ernst *[838]*, Salvador Dali, Magritte,
Delvaux and, as a pioneer, Chirico. Similarly
unorthodox and opposed to traditional forms is
Surrealistic sculpture, among whose representatives

and turning, rising and falling formed ever new groupings. As in the case of Arp, a joy in the accidental led to happy results.

In content and form the works of both the Dadaists and the Surrealists are informed by the same criterion of ambiguity. In cases where an elementary and summary idiom was employed this ambiguity is based on the circumstance that primeval forms, being relatively undifferentiated, invite various interpretations *[841]*. Thus the less a form is polished and articulated the more the observer can read into it. His attempts at interpretation proceed in various directions, deciding sometimes for this, sometimes for that context. Veristic Surrealism is ambiguous in a different way *[838]*. The image is rather exact in its correspondence to reality and the painter employs illusionistic techniques (modelling of figures, perspective) but this suggestion of reality in the representation serves to evoke a profoundly 'unreal' world for which our reason provides no key. The observer suspects that behind the literal meaning of the represented objects the true meaning is hidden. Enigmatic and unstable connexions are suggested, permitting a multitude of interpretative possibilities. The criterion of ambiguity also affects the 'matter' paintings inasmuch as the material (e.g. a piece of string) simultaneously 'means' itself and points beyond *[841]*. Already in 1912 Kandinsky recognized that 'Line is a thing which also has a practical and useful sense, like a chair . . .', from which statement the converse was inferred, and objects were made to take the place of a design device. This means that the bottle stand *[840]* loses its practical function to become a sculptural image. The assemblages of Kurt Schwitters (1887–1948) pose a choice between seeing the work as a piece of depicted reality or as an ambiguous formal constellation *[839]*.

The characteristic of ambiguity is supplemented by that of heterogeneity. The art work should retain something of the non-logical contradictions of existence. Clever conjunctions emphasize the predominance of the absurd. The intention is to show that beyond the signposts of reason apparently stable reality suddenly shifts into a romantic and fantastic world in which all things are interrelated.

On the formal plane heterogeneity implies the association of different materials and the conjunction of different methods of design, and sometimes the introduction of real objects in the ideal picture plane, as this had already been developed in Cubist experiments.

These are the chief means used by the Dadaists and Surrealists to take possession of a territory previously occupied by fantastic art, allegory, rebus figures, and

843   Oskar Kokoschka, *The Elbe near Dresden (Neustadt I)*, *1919. Chicago, Art Institute (Winterbottom Collection). Kokoschka uses bright, broad flakes of colour to make a tapestry-like composition; his Expressionistic pathos stands in the tradition of the Baroque.*

844   Max Beckmann, *Night, 1918–19. Düsseldorf, Kunst-sammlung Nordrhein-Westfalen. In this nightmarish scene of torture, which seems to jump out of the picture space, the artist represents the experience of war and the inescapable fate of human existence.*

satire. Ambiguity affects not only form and meaning, but is also reflected in the social attitudes of the two movements. Anti-bourgeois in their militant stance, the artists sought to satisfy their anarchic bent in an association with the politics of the Left, and gave a Marxist justification to their revolutionary longings. If one separates from the political and didactic goals the poetic and fantastic core, it is evident that the latter could not satisfy popular requirements. The public of the Surrealists was an intellectual *élite;* the patrons of the anti-bourgeois came from the wealthy aristocracy. Only in the areas of advertising and window decoration was Surrealism later to enjoy a certain popularization. Constructivists, Dadaists, and Surrealists strove in different ways to create a new foundation for artistic activity. Thus they often reached points of agreement, as always happens when groups realize that they have a common enemy. These points of agreement were found in the decision to free painting from the conventions of the easel canvas and to dissolve the links of sculpture with the human figure. This expansive attitude opened many new creative possibilities, but at the same time contained an element of renunciation: any dealings with the world of perception were excluded. But it was just in such dealings, independently of the radically new positions, that a large part of the art of the period between the wars found its scope. The easel painting and the technique of oil painting were restored to their rights. Hand in hand with the appeal

846   Marc Chagall, Paris through the Window, 1913. New York, Solomon R. Guggenheim Museum. Note the close interrelationship between exterior and interior; the contrasts between large and small forms and variety of textures.

845   Pablo Picasso, Bathing Women on the Beach, 1929. New York, Museum of Modern Art (Mrs Simon Guggenheim Fund). Towards the end of the 1920s Picasso combined Cubist and Surrealist elements in fantastic, organic, and technical forms.

to the traditional tasks of art to bear witness to man and his environment went an attraction to traditional prototypes. Thus Oskar Kokoschka (born 1886) returns to the pathos of the Baroque *[843]*; Max Beckmann (1884–1950) suggests the anatomical violence of the German late Gothic *[844]*, and the artists who gathered under the banner of the 'Neue Sachlichkeit' (New Objectivity) have their prototype in the severe adherence to reality of the age of Dürer. In a broad context this subjective realism stands in the general line of pre-war Expressionism. Since the artist was a participant in his environment, many aspects of the earlier movement were retained. One was the emphasis on the dark side of existence, the unredeemed emptiness in which civilized life is conducted. Age-old symbolic situations were represented in which masks, streetwalkers, and the circus play a prominent part. The other trend was directed to the colourful and organic panoply of the world, a pagan affirmation of life. A painting by Kokoschka called *The Pagans* shows a naked pair of figures. In this vital work man seems to live a prelapsarian existence in full accord with nature. But with Beckmann man is burdened with distrust, anguish, and despair. Somewhere between these two extremes lies the work of certain painters settled in France (Matisse, Modigliani, Chagall *[846]*, and Soutine).

847 *Georges Braque, Still-life with Newspaper, 1929. Washington, National Gallery of Art (Chester Dale Collection). Braque creates a metamorphosis of objects from his Cubist aesthetic.*

The situation is somewhat different with those artists who continued along the lines of Cubism. Picasso, Braque, and Léger provide examples. In Picasso's work an expressive demonism comes to the fore [845]. Braque continued to cultivate the sheltered world of the still-life [847]. In the 1920s Fernand Léger (1881–1955), who had begun by translating the Cubist vocabulary into cylindrical 'building stones', worked towards a stable, monumental figure painting, that submitted men and things to a common geometric treatment. Volumes and surfaces were brought into harmony [848]. The intellectual concept lies close to that of the fresco.

What are the Cubist preconceptions upon which these painters based their idiom? Most important is the radical liberation of line and colour from any obligation to represent objective reality. Line took on a primarily pictorial meaning and only secondarily (and then only in some instances) an objective meaning. This implied, for example, that coloured fields could run straight across different complexes of objects [845], so that line can suggest a rhythmical interweaving of images that does indeed recall the contours of objects, while unfolding its own life. This gives men as well as lifeless objects a common background of metamorphosis.

This method of design is related to Paul Klee's (1879–1940) way of retaining the autonomy and

transparency of elements, while at the same time arriving at a figural invention [842], though Klee abandons reference to the world of experience in favour of a series of 'form letters' free of visual impressions. With Picasso and Braque, however, distortion is employed so that reference to familiar objects is immediately invoked. This gives their art a certain human quality and connects them with the more conservative tendencies of the period between the wars. On the other hand it should not be forgotten that the fantastic and monstrous vein discovered by Picasso links him with the spectral images of the Surrealists. (Picasso also sometimes participated in Surrealist exhibitions.)

Placing the national variants discussed here in their European context, the following pattern emerges. In terms of content the scope of painting embraces all traditional pictorial categories: the figure composition (often allegorical), the nude, the landscape, the still-life, the individual and group portrait. Features of the genre picture are also revived. The interpretation of reality is sometimes oriented towards criticism of the age and of society, and sometimes towards fantastic wish-fulfilment. The figure of man, sometimes contemporary, sometimes mythical, again acquires a dominant role; the human condition receives a new emphasis. The formal possibilities are full of nuances; their boundaries lie sometimes in the exaggeration and dramatization of subjective handwriting [843], sometimes in a sober

848 *Fernand Léger, The Great Parade, 1945. New York, Solomon R. Guggenheim Museum. Léger's figures achieve a certain lightness and agility despite their massive, robot-like forms on this canvas (approx. 10 × 13 feet), which shows a happy juxtaposition of the human and mechanical.*

FROM WORLD WAR II TO THE PRESENT

Architecture

Since the end of World War II architects have been presented with new tasks of enormous scope. These include the rebuilding of the destroyed European cities, an opportunity that was seldom utilized properly (an exception is Rotterdam); the design of cultural and commercial complexes (civic centres, universities, supermarkets); and the founding of new capitals in Asia (Chandigarh by Le Corbusier) and in South America (Brasilia). These are projects in the grand manner and which often confronted the architects with the problem of dealing with vast dimensions. It was understandable, therefore, that they approached these tasks through the principle of co-ordination. The need to shape and control great complexes made the meticulous building of the 1920s and 1930s seem puny by comparison. This is clearly shown in the fusion that began to develop between the traditional enclosing or sheltering

849   Jacques Lipchitz, Mother and Child, 1929–30. From the block-like verticality of his early Cubist works Lipchitz produces huge, primitive volumes, whose transformation serves to heighten the expression.

850   Ludwig Mies van der Rohe, Seagram Building in New York, 1953. A rectangular tower, with a bronze profile that strengthens the height of this skyscraper.

hardening *[844]*. The latter is dominated by a precise, uncompromising fanaticism for the object, the former by a colourful exuberance expressing the joy of the senses. Similarly the post-Cubist situation tends to two extremes: in Braque *[847]*, the saturation and polishing of the formal idiom; in Picasso *[845]*, trenchant sharpness. A qualified return to the view-. point of natural experience of the world is a general characteristic of the formal attitude. Men and things regain their integral terrestrial character and the heavy, massive, and pressing take their place once more.

Sculpture, which parallels these trends in painting, returns to the human figure without rejecting the possibilities explored in the metamorphic tendency. Thus one finds fabulous creatures recalling the composite monsters of ancient mythology. Henri Laurens and Jacques Lipchitz (born 1891) represent at its most impressive the concern for organic and expressive intensification of corporeal volumes *[849]* by their concern for openwork structures.

851 Pier Luigi Nervi and Annibale Vitellozzi, Palazzo dello Sport in Rome, 1956–7. The curved surfaces of this steel construction and the broad covering roofs with their walls are diametrically opposed to the 'architecture of the right angle'.

852 Alvar Aalto, cultural centre in Helsinki, 1955–8. The organic and plastic form of the construction reaches out into space with its swinging curves. Colourful clinker bricks enliven the exterior wall.

architecture (including cultural, residential, and factory buildings) and traffic architecture (motorways, bridges, airports), leading the architect into realms of landscape and spatial planning. On the town-planning level this interplay is expressed on the one hand in the combination of different building types in overall schemes, and on the other in an increasing structural differentiation. These are indications that the creative and artistic values of the idiom of the 'new building' developed in the 1920s by Gropius, Le Corbusier, and Mies van der Rohe were now being re-examined. The need to think in terms of town planning forced the architect to adjust formal accents to present problems. This seems to have led to a differentiation of architectural symbolic forms. In the process the strict functionalism of the right angle lost considerable ground. Creative thought turned more and more to a new interpretation of the concept of organic architecture. The situation recalls the end of the nineteenth century when Wright turned away from the architectural model of the Chicago School, the skyscraper, and set up the ideal of the house in nature against the mass architecture of the great cities. In the meantime Mies van der Rohe developed the tall building (with which he was concerned since 1919) to a point of structural refinement in which the three factors of fulfilment of function, standardized production, and formal invention were fused into a classic solution *[850]*. In this way a certain finality was achieved in the course of the development of this type of building.

The most evident characteristic of the cellular mode of building is the severe system of perpendicular and vertical lines. Technical and practical considerations (mass production and population increases) especially favour this procedure where it is necessary to concentrate large numbers of people (office and dwelling blocks). From the town-planning point of view there is an increase in the amount of traffic facilities and green areas. On the other hand it must be admitted that the rectangular schematism becomes more and more the instrument of an anonymous functional architecture. The formal asceticism of this practical building contrasts with a group of monumental projects set by unique and unrepeatable conditions. These include especially churches, theatres, concert buildings, assembly halls, transport buildings, and sports facilities. In the solution of these problems architects of the post-war period have turned increasingly to free, organic, and plastic forms. The pioneering role of Wright was recognized and in the Guggenheim Museum in New York (1947–59) with its almost sculptural conception Wright himself made a contribution to the new architecture. Gaudí's

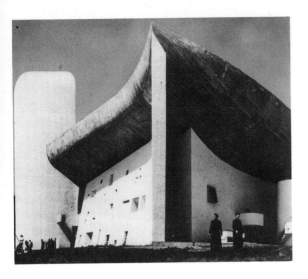

1927–34 the roof of his Library in Viipuri shows a clear rejection of the right angle – a solution that finds a sculptural parallel in the work of Hans Arp *[841]*. Through the use of flowing curves Aalto was later able to open up the building block *[852]* and to place it in a landscape setting.

Among the most daring and at the same time most convincing achievements of plastic architecture are the post-war buildings of Le Corbusier (born 1887), including the *Unité d'Habitation* in Marseille (1947–52), the *pilgrimage church [853]* at Ronchamp (1950–4), and the buildings at Chandigarh. Spatial and building interest no longer focused upon the light and graceful, nor did it seek the effects of floating or the spatial possibilities of vast halls. The material was no longer suppressed but exhibited in all its massive heaviness. This building mode has led

853 Le Corbusier, pilgrimage church of Notre-Dame-du-Haut at Ronchamp, 1950–4. 'Architecture is the accurate and wonderful play of forms in light' (Le Corbusier) – here applied to the vault surfaces and plastic form.

854 Ludwig Mies van der Rohe, Barcelona chair, 1929. An example of classic elegance still unsurpassed today, of mathematically precise form and subtle contrasts of material (chromium, steel, and leather).

855 Hans J. Wegner, armchair, 1949. An example of the Scandinavian-inspired direction of modern furniture: note the plastic modelling and the harmonious combination of materials (teak wood and wicker-work).

856 Charles Eames, chair, 1952. Filigrain metal rods that support an upholstered wire basket express the modern ideal of visual weightlessness and lend an aesthetic element to the technical form.

achievement too *[744, 805]* was rediscovered. Another link with the past was provided by engineering structures like those created by Pier Luigi Nervi (born 1891) for sports facilities (Florence Stadium; 1930–2) and airport hangars (1939). With the use of the shell construction of curved planes, reinforced concrete could be turned to the purpose of a strongly plastic idiom *[851]*. The real pioneer of organic architecture is the Finn Alvar Aalto. As early as

to the 'new brutalism' (Kenzo Tange in Japan). This should be distinguished from a structural elegance, especially cultivated in Italy and Latin America, that has tried to adapt thin-wall shell construction to large hall buildings (Niemeyer, Candela, Castiglioni).

The design tendencies noted for architecture appear also in the furniture of our century. Functionalism and plastic form *[856]*, steel *[854]* and artificial materials together with traditional materials such as wood and leather comprise the range of possibilities. In furniture and interior decoration national variations (e.g. Italian or Scandinavian) can be more easily discerned than in architecture.

Sculpture

The importance of sculpture has steadily increased in the two decades since 1945. Sculpture moved from the interior to the open air. Sculptural development became independent of that of painting and advanced further along the path indicated for it at the turn of the century. The formal poles are mass and space, concentrated thickening and linear aspiration, to which is added a new element, movement – largely in dependence upon Calder. In objective sculpture

858 *Fritz Wotruba, large recumbent figure, 1951. The process of working directly in the material (stone) is to be turned to a self-imposed 'limitation and narrowing of the image through clarity and lucidity', according to the sculptor.*

the emphasis lay upon the human figure, and symbolic meanings were explored in free inventive forms. The material possibilities of sculpture underwent an important expansion through the increased use of iron (González was the pioneer in this). The reciprocal effects of the new iron techniques upon form were not neglected.

It is difficult to find a common denominator for the sculptural image of man. Employing Surrealist reminiscences, sculptors enlarged the sphere of action to include conglomerate images made of junk or organic 'objets trouvés' (Dubuffet). This is connected with an increasing tendency to Baroque exuberance and playful treatment of inchoate material.

A tragic, distorted image of man appears in the work of Alberto Giacometti (born 1901) and Germaine Richier (1904–59). From about the middle of the century Giacometti has concentrated upon the human figure. His figures seem to shrink from the consuming forces of space. The physical mass of the figures appears to have undergone a drastic shrinkage *[857]*. Giacometti returns to Rodin by continuing the disembodiment and linearization on the one hand, and on the other by dealing with 'fallen' man. The fragile antennae of these bodies have a twofold significance: they constitute rough signposts of a labyrinth and at the same time represent those caught up in it. It is not surprising that literary and philosophical existentialism (Genet, Sartre) has recognized the kinship of these works. Fritz Wotruba (born 1907) shows a stony block treatment of the figure mass emphasizing the element of weight *[858]*. His development is an example of a characteristic feature of the twentieth century. The block discards

857 *Alberto Giacometti, Forest, 1950. A bronze group of stick-like forms which seem to find no relationship to each other despite their juxtaposition.*

859   Henry Moore, recumbent figure, 1953–4. Plastic forms and hollow spaces, which offer various views from the various sides of the bronze figure, create an organic and dynamic resemblance to material creation.

860   Naum Gabo, construction in space, 1954–7. Rotterdam, Bijenkorf Store. A piece of constructionist sculpture, with a transparent scaffolding of mathematical precision which surrounds the nucleus.

its geometric sharpness; it seems to have 'grown'. As in architecture, where curved forms displaced flat surfaces, sculptors came to prefer the organic. It is regarded as the dark source in which form and vitality have their common origin. The life-work of Henry Moore (born 1898), on the whole eclectically oriented, moves about this focus. The flowing form enlivened by curved surfaces is the symbol of a burgeoning, twisting vitality *[859]*. Here Moore uses the hole as a metaphor pointing sometimes to security and sometimes to the mysterious.

The gigantic metal monument created by Naum Gabo (born 1890) for a Rotterdam store may be regarded as the constructive paraphrase for the theme 'interior and exterior form' *[860]*. Transparency and multi-axiality – the two postulates that separate Constructivism from the traditional sculpture of mass – appear here in a web of vibrating curves.

Painting

The post-war development of painting depends upon the achievements of the pioneer movements. Cubism, Expressionism, and Surrealism are its chief begetters. The European scene immediately after 1945 was dominated by offshoots of Cubism with their centre in Paris. Linear lattice-work and coloured cell structures gave the pictorial composition a geometrical yet mysterious dignity (Manessier, Vieira da Silva, Bazaine, etc.). At the same time the great masters demonstrated the possibility of bringing the Cubist concept up to date. Nicolas de Staël (1914–55) arrived at another interpretation of Cubism. The composition draws its firmness and tension from the blocks of colour. The colour, endowed with a new freedom and immediacy, suggests flatness and depth, near and far, and the light evokes both the abiding and the transient. The painting attains that mysterious point of ambivalence that Cézanne had first demonstrated; every colour cell is capable of being simultaneously pure painting and the embodiment of objective content *[861]*.

The calm and tranquil handling of this painting contrasts with currents preferring a conflict of forces and a rapid brush stroke. They hark back to the Picasso of the 1930s, the Kandinsky of 1912, the psychic automatism of the Surrealists, and the symbolic writing of Klee *[824, 842]*. This trend has been given various labels among which the following are the most common: tachism (from French *tache*, 'spot'), *art informel*, action painting, lyrical abstraction, and abstract expressionism. This turn to dynamic and open form appears in Hartung and Wols,

861   *Nicolas de Staël, Figure on the beach, 1952. Basle,*
E. Beyeler. The scraped colour surface constitutes a pictorial
language where forms and objects coexist.

two Germans living in Paris, and the American
Pollock.

In 1912, at the very time when Kandinsky began to
limit and codify his effervescent world of forms *[824]*,
Hans Hartung (born 1904) began to explore further
in the area of elementary shapes. He slowly evolved a
vocabulary of non-objective pictorial signs, through
which he created a new area of communication with
the observer. This painting is no longer concerned
with treating perceived content, no longer with the
process of 'abstraction', but with the communication
of experiences and impressions, which are more
comprehensive than optical sense data *[862]*.
Elementary situations of the human condition are
explored. This means either that the painter proceeds
from the sum of his experiences and memories
(Hartung) or that, like Wols who sought to exclude
any recollection from painting, he requires from the
painting the answer that he seeks. In the latter case
the painting does not record occurrences or feelings,
but manifests an experience which is only achieved in
the act of creation. Interpretation seems to be
conducted along the path of empathy. In Hartung
the elastic tension and sure ductus of line combines

with an aristocratic and idealistic outlook in which
light struggles with dark. The more violent work of
Wols (1913–51) suggests an act of demonic evocation
descending into chaos *[863]*. In close or more distant
relation to Hartung stand the paintings of Soulages,
Mathieu, Schneider, Kline, and Vedova.

The less a painting conforms to a preconceived
idea the more it becomes the record of an act. As a
result the means and methods of painting alter. This
is most evident in the work of the American Jackson
Pollock (1912–56) who, influenced by European
Surrealism (Masson, Ernst, Miró) and Picasso,
decided about 1947 to abandon the composed
rectangle of easel painting and to create a porous,
active texture through his drip method *[864]*. The
labyrinthine web of colour records the course of the
act of painting. Pollock's gigantic canvases constitute
the very stuff of physical dynamism. His whole
concern was to produce a tightly meshed pictorial
surface in which everything chaotic and accidental is
absorbed in an all-embracing vitality. He is perhaps
the most important of a group of American painters
who gave a great impulse to the post-war development (Tobey, Rothko, de Kooning, Francis, Still).

A third important branch of the post-war painting
seeks a renewed encounter with the object. It
recapitulates the Expressionist experiences of the first
half of the century. Ensor, Nolde, and Picasso *[796,
814, 845]*, and the drawings of children and the insane
were significant once more. The new image of man
draws its demonic force from a radical ugliness. The
beginnings lie in the grotesque primitivism *[865]* of
Jean Dubuffet (born 1901) who shortly after the war
began to protest against the aestheticism of 'bonne
peinture'. A little later the COBRA group appeared

862   *Hans Hartung, T. 1948–9, 1948. Paris, Collection Hardy.*
A 'psychographic' picture drawing, a spontaneous record of the
fundamental conditions of human existence.

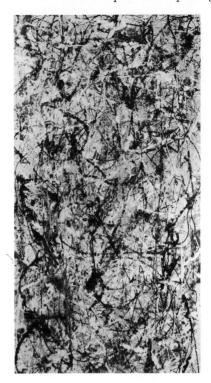

863   Wols, Composition, 1947. Hamburg, Kunsthalle. Wols's works, usually small scale, tend towards a representation of recollected images and are composed by 'psychic automation', the experience and registration of forms being simultaneous. (Above.)

864   Jackson Pollock, Cathedral, 1947. Dallas, Texas, Museum of Fine Arts (Bernard J. Reis Foundation). An 'action painting' in huge format composed of dripped and superimposed oils. (Above right.)

865   Jean Dubuffet, Antonin Artaud aux Houppes, 1947. Chicago, Collection Neumann. Such caricature portraits are 'determined by the idea that he who paints the essential needs to avoid the incidental in a portrait' (Dubuffet). (Right.)

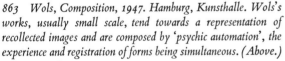

(Appel, Constant, Jorn, Alechinsky, etc.), which derives its demonic figures in part from the world of Northern mythology.

More recently under the catchword of 'pop art' a certain return to the fetishism of the Dadaists has come to the fore (Rauschenberg, Tinguely, Spoerri, etc.). Observing the post-war development as a whole, it seems comparable to the situation between 1910 and 1914. Then too geometrical calculation, turbulent gesticulation, expressionistic distortion, and the Dadaist cult of materials stood side by side. The situation is similar today, but the radicalism is more pronounced and the formal procedures are more sophisticated and self-conscious.

BIBLIOGRAPHY

General References

STYLE

G. Semper, *Der Stil in den bildenden Künsten*, 2 vols., Munich, 1860–3.

A. Riegl, *Stilfragen*, Berlin, 1893.

M. J. Friedländer, *On Art and Connoisseurship*, London, 1942.

E. Panofsky, *Meaning in the Visual Arts*, New York, 1955.

H. Focillon, *The Life of Forms in Art*, New York, 1957.

W. Weisbach, *Stilbegriffe und Stilphänomene*, Vienna, 1957.

E. H. Gombrich, *Art and Illusion*, London, 1960.

R. Bernheimer, *The Nature of Representation*, New York, 1961.

HISTORIES AND HANDBOOKS OF ART

Histoire de l'art depuis les premiers temps chrétiens jusqu'à nos jours (ed. A. Michel), 8 vols. in 17, Paris, 1905–29.

Handbuch der Kunstwissenschaft, 27 vols., Berlin-Neubabelsberg, 1913–30.

Propyläen-Kunstgeschichte, 24 vols., Berlin, 1923–35.

Summa Artis (ed. M. B. Cossío and J. Pijoán), Bilbao, Madrid, 1931– .

E. H. Gombrich, *The Story of Art*, London, 1950.

Pelican History of Art (ed. N. Pevsner), Harmondsworth, 1953– .

D. M. Robb and J. J. Garrison, *Art in the Western World*, 3rd ed., New York, 1953.

Encyclopedia of World Art, London, New York, 1959–

H. W. and D. J. Janson, *A History of Art*, London, 1962.

WORKS PERTAINING TO ARTISTIC CATEGORIES

Architecture

G. Dehio and G. von Bezold, *Die kirchliche Baukunst des Abendlandes*, Stuttgart, 1887–1901.

Wasmuths Lexikon der Baukunst, 5 vols., Berlin, 1929–37.

N. Pevsner, *An Outline of European Architecture*, 6th ed. (Jubilee), Harmondsworth, 1960.

H. A. Millon, *Key Monuments of the History of Architecture*, New York, 1964.

Town Planning

A. E. Brinckmann, *Stadtbaukunst*, Berlin, 1920.

P. Lavedan, *Histoire de l'urbanisme*, 3 vols., Paris, 1926–52.

L. Mumford, *The City in History*, London, 1961.

Gardens

M. L. Gothein, *A History of Garden Art*, 2 vols., London, 1928.

Sculpture

G. H. Chase and C. R. Post, *A History of Sculpture*, New York, London, 1924.

Les sculpteurs célèbres (ed. P. Francastel), Paris, 1954.

H. Read, *The Art of Sculpture*, New York, Paris, 1956.

Painting

D. M. Robb, *The Harper History of Painting*, New York, 1951.

H. W. and D. J. Janson, *The Picture History of Painting*, London, New York, 1957.

Minor Arts

A. Feulner, *Kunstgeschichte des Möbels*, Berlin, 1927.

H. Havard, *Dictionnaire de l'ameublement et de la décoration depuis le XIIIe siècle jusqu'à nos jours*, 4 vols., Paris, 1928–35.

Geschichte des Kunstgewerbes aller Zeiten und Völker (ed. H. T. Bossert), 6 vols., Berlin, 1929–35.

J. Evans, *Pattern: A Study of Ornament in Western Europe from 1180 to 1900*, 2 vols., Oxford, 1931.

WORKS PERTAINING TO INDIVIDUAL COUNTRIES

England

The Oxford History of English Art (ed. T. S. R. Boase), Oxford, 1949– .

N. Pevsner, *The Englishness of English Art*, London, 1956.

France

J. Evans, *Art in Medieval France, 987–1498*, London, New York, 1948.

P. Lavedan, *French Architecture*, Harmondsworth, 1956.

Germany

G. Dehio, *Geschichte der deutschen Kunst*, 4 vols. and plates, 4th ed., Berlin, Leipzig, 1930–4.

Bruckmanns deutsche Kunstgeschichte, 6 vols., Munich, 1942–56.

Italy

A. Venturi, *Storia dell'arte italiana*, 11 vols. in 25, Milan, 1901–40.

R. van Marle, *The Development of the Italian Schools of Painting*, 19 vols., The Hague, 1928–38.

P. Toesca, *Storia dell'arte italiana*, 2 vols. in 3, Turin, 1927–51.

Low Countries

M. J. Friedländer, *Die altniederländische Malerei*, 14 vols., Berlin, 1924–37.

H. E. van Gelder and J. Duverger, *Kunstgeschiedenis der Nederlanden van de middeleeuwen tot onze tijd*, 2 vols., Utrecht, 1954–5.

Spain

J. de Lozoya, *Historia del arte hispánico*, 5 vols., Barcelona, 1931–49.

Ars Hispaniae, Madrid, 1947–

F. Jiménez-Placer and A. Cirici Pellicer, *Historia del arte espanol*, 2 vols., Barcelona, 1955.

References for Specific Periods

ANTIQUITY

General

M. Swindler, *Ancient Painting*, New Haven, 1929.

D. S. Robertson, *A Handbook of Greek and Roman Architecture*, 2nd ed., Cambridge, 1943.

P. Ducati, *L'Arte classica*, rev. ed., Turin, 1944.

G. Rodenwaldt, *Die Kunst der Antike*, 4th ed., Berlin, 1944.

Enciclopedia dell'Arte Antica, Rome, 1958–

G. von Kaschnitz-Weinberg, *Strukturgeschichte der mittelmeerischen Kunst*, Berlin, 1964.

R. L. Scranton, *Aesthetic Aspects of Ancient Art*, Chicago, 1964.

GREEK ART

General

J. D. Beazley and B. Ashmole, *Greek Sculpture and Painting to the End of the Hellenistic Period*, Cambridge, 1932.

G. M. A. Richter, *Archaic Greek Art against Its Historical Background*, New York, 1949.

S. Marinatos, *Crete and Mycenae*, London, 1960.

F. Matz, *Crete and Early Greece*, London, 1961.

G. M. A. Richter, *A Handbook of Greek Art*, 3rd ed., London, 1963.

J. Boardman, *Greek Art*, London, 1964.

P. Demargne, *Aegean Art*, London, 1964.

Architecture

W. B. Dinsmoor, *The Architecture of Ancient Greece*, London, New York, 1950.

A. W. Lawrence, *Greek Architecture*, Harmondsworth, 1957.

R. L. Scranton, *Greek Architecture*, New York, London, 1962.

V. Scully, *The Earth, the Temple and the Gods*, New Haven, London, 1962.

Sculpture

C. Picard, *Manuel d'archéologie grecque: La sculpture*, 4 vols., Paris, 1935–63.

G. Lippold, *Die griechische Plastik* (*Handbuch der Archäologie*, III, 1), Munich, 1950.

G. M. A. Richter, *The Sculpture and Sculptors of the Greeks*, rev. ed., New Haven, New York, 1950.

R. Lullies, *Greek Sculpture*, rev. ed., London, 1960.

G. M. A. Richter, *Kouroi*, 2nd ed., London, 1960.

M. Bieber, *The Sculpture of the Hellenistic Age*, 2nd ed., New York, 1961.

Painting

E. Pfuhl, *Malerei und Zeichnung der Griechen*, 3 vols., Munich, 1923.

E. Buschor, *Griechische Vasen*, Munich, 1940.

A. Rumpf, *Malerei und Zeichnung* (*Handbuch der Archäologie*, IV, 1), Munich, 1953.

M. Robertson, *Greek Painting*, Geneva, 1959.

R. M. Cook, *Greek Painted Pottery*, London, Chicago, 1960.

P. E. Arias, *A History of Greek Vase Painting*, London, 1962.

ETRUSCAN ART

M. Pallottino, *Etruscan Painting*, Geneva, 1953.

P. J. Riis, *An Introduction to Etruscan Art*, Copenhagen, 1953.

E. Richardson, *The Etruscans; Their Art and Civilization*, Chicago, London, 1964.

ROMAN ART

General

F. Wickhoff, *Roman Art*, London, New York, 1900.

E. Strong, *Art in Ancient Rome*, 2 vols., New York, 1928.

H. Koch, *Römische Kunst*, 2nd ed., Weimar, 1949.

H. Kähler, *Rom und seine Welt*, 2 vols., Munich, 1958.

H. Kähler, *Rome and Her Empire*, London, 1963.

G. M. A. Hanfmann, *Roman Art*, London, 1964.

M. Wheeler, *Roman Art and Architecture*, London, 1964.

Architecture

L. Crema, *L'architettura romana*, Turin, 1959.

A. Boethius, *The Golden House of Nero*, Ann Arbor, Mich., 1960.

F. E. Brown, *Roman Architecture*, New York, London, 1962.

Sculpture

E. Strong, *La scultura romana*, 2 vols., Florence, 1923–6.

B. Schweitzer, *Die Bildniskunst der römischen Republik*, Leipzig, Weimar, 1948.

D. E. Strong, *Roman Imperial Sculpture*, London, 1961.

Painting

A. Maiuri, *Roman Painting*, Geneva, 1953.

L. Curtius, *Die Wandmalerei Pompejis*, 2nd ed., Darmstadt, 1960.

EARLY CHRISTIAN ART

General

O. Wulff, *Altchristliche und byzantinische Kunst*, vol. I, Berlin, 1914.

C. R. Morey, *Early Christian Art*, 2nd ed., Princeton, 1953.

A. Rumpf, *Stilphasen der spätantiken Kunst; Ein Versuch*, Cologne, Opladen, 1957.

W. F. Volbach, *Early Christian Art*, London, 1961.

Architecture

F. W. Deichmann, *Frühchristliche Kirchen in Rom*, Basle, 1948.

W. L. MacDonald, *Early Christian and Byzantine Architecture*, New York, London, 1961.

Sculpture

J. Wilpert, *I sarcofagi cristiani antichi*, 5 vols., Rome, 1929–36.

H. P. L'Orange, *Studien zur Geschichte des spätantiken Porträts*, Oslo, 1933.

F. Gerke, *Christus in der spätantike Plastik*, 3rd ed., Mainz, 1948.

W. F. Volbach, *Elfenbeinarbeiten der Spätantike und des frühen Mittelalters*, 2nd ed., Mainz, 1952.

J. Natanson, *Early Christian Ivories*, London, 1953.

Painting

J. Wilpert, *Die Malereien der Katakomben Roms*, 2 vols., Freiburg in Breisgau, 1903.

J. Wilpert, *Die römischen Mosaiken und Malereien der kirchlichen Bauten vom IV. bis XIII. Jahrhundert*, 4 vols., Freiburg in Breisgau, 1916.

M. van Berchem and E. Clouzot, *Mosaïques chrétiennes du IVe au Xe siècle*, Geneva, 1924.

A. Grabar and C. Nordenfalk, *Early Medieval Painting from the Fourth to the Eleventh Century*, London, 1957.

H. P. L'Orange and P. J. Nordhagen, *Mosaik von der Antike bis zum Mittelalter*, Munich, 1960.

BYZANTINE ART

General

O. M. Dalton, *Byzantine Art and Archaeology*, Oxford, 1911.

O. Wulff, *Altchristliche und byzantinische Kunst*, vol. II, Berlin, 1916.

D. Talbot Rice, *Art of Byzantium*, London, 1959.

J. Beckwith, *The Art of Constantinople*, London, 1961.

Architecture

A. van Millingen, *Byzantine Churches in Constantinople*, London, 1912.

Painting and Sculpture

A. Goldschmidt and K. Weitzmann, *Die byzantinischen Elfenbeinskulpturen des X.-XIII. Jahrhunderts*, 2 vols., Berlin, 1930–4.

E. Diez and O. Demus, *Byzantine Mosaics in Greece: Hosios Lucas and Daphni*, Cambridge, Mass., 1931.

O. Demus, *The Mosaics of Norman Sicily*, London, 1949.

O. Demus, *Byzantine Mosaic Decoration*, 2nd ed., London, 1953.

A. Grabar, *Byzantine Painting*, Geneva, 1953.

W. Felicetti-Liebenfels, *Geschichte der byzantinischen Ikonenmalerei*, Olten, Lausanne, 1956.

A. Grabar and M. Chatzidakis, *Greece: Byzantine Mosaics*, Greenwich, Conn., 1960.

Russia

I. E. Grabar, V. N. Lazarev and V. S. Kemenev, *Geschichte der Russischen Kunst*, vols. 1–2, Dresden, 1957.

G. H. Hamilton, *The Art and Architecture of Russia*, Harmondsworth, 1954.

ART OF THE MIGRATION PERIOD

B. Salin, *Die altgermanische Thierornamentik*, Stockholm, 1904.

A. Riegl, *Die spätrömische Kunstindustrie*, 2nd ed., Vienna, 1927.

N. Åberg, *The Occident and the Orient in the Art of the Seventh Century*, 3 vols., Stockholm, 1943–7.

T. D. Kendrick, *Late Saxon and Viking Art*, London, 1949.

W. Holmqvist, *Germanic Art*, Stockholm, 1955.

F. Henry, *L'art irlandais*, 3 vols., La-Pierre-qui-Vire, 1963–4.

EARLY MEDIEVAL AND ROMANESQUE ART

General

M. Hauttmann, *Die Kunst des frühen Mittelalters*, Berlin, 1921.

J. Hubert, *L'art preroman*, Paris, 1938.

C. R. Morey, *Medieval Art*, New York, 1942.

H. Jantzen, *Ottonische Kunst*, Munich, 1947.

H. Swarzenski, *Monuments of Romanesque Art*, London, Chicago, 1954.

H. Focillon, *The Art of the West in the Middle Ages: I, Romanesque Art*, London, 1963.

P. E. Schramm and F. Mütherich, *Denkmale der deutschen Könige und Kaiser*, Munich, 1963.

J. Beckwith, *Early Medieval Art*, London, 1964.

Architecture

P. Frankl, *Die frühmittelalterliche und romanische Baukunst*, Berlin, 1926.

G. T. Rivoira, *Lombardic Architecture*, 2 vols., rev. ed., Oxford, 1933.

E. Lehmann, *Der frühe deutsche Kirchenbau*, 2nd ed., Berlin, 1949.

L. Grodecki, *Au seuil de l'art roman: L'architecture ottonienne*, Paris, 1958.

K. J. Conant, *Carolingian and Romanesque Architecture, 800–1200*, Harmondsworth, 1959.

H. Saalman, *Medieval Architecture*, New York, London, 1962.

Sculpture

A. Goldschmidt, *Die Elfenbeinskulpturen*, 4 vols., Berlin, 1914–26.

A. K. Porter, *Romanesque Sculpture of the Pilgrimage Roads*, 10 vols., Boston, 1923.

E. Panofsky, *Die deutsche Plastik des elften bis dreizehnten Jahrhunderts*, Munich, 1924.
A. K. Porter, *Spanish Romanesque Sculpture*, 2 vols., Paris, 1928.
A. Haseloff, *Preromanesque Sculpture in Italy*, Florence, 1930.
P. Deschamps, *French Romanesque Sculpture*, Florence, 1930.
H. Focillon, *L'art des sculpteurs romains*, Paris, 1931.
G. H. Crichton, *Romanesque Sculpture in Italy*, London, 1954.

Painting

A. Goldschmidt, *German Illumination*, 2 vols., New York, Paris, 1928.
A. Boeckler, *Abendländische Miniaturen bis zum Ausgang der romanischen Zeit*, Berlin, Leipzig, 1930.
E. W. Anthony, *Romanesque Frescoes*, Princeton, 1951.
P. Deschamps and M. Thibout, *La peinture murale en France: Le haut moyen âge et l'époque romane*, Paris, 1951.
R. Oertel, *Die Frühzeit der italienischen Malerei*, Stuttgart, 1953.
A. Grabar and C. Nordenfalk, *Romanesque Painting*, London, 1958.
J. Porcher, *French Miniatures*, London, 1960.

GOTHIC
General

H. Karlinger, *Die Kunst der Gotik*, 2nd ed., Berlin, 1934.
P. Frankl, *The Gothic: Literary Sources and Interpretations through Eight Centuries*, Princeton, 1960.
H. Focillon, *The Art of the West in the Middle Ages:* vol. II, *Gothic Art*, London, 1963.

Architecture

E. Gall, *Die gotische Baukunst in Frankreich und Deutschland*, I, Leipzig, 1925.
R. de Lasteyrie, *L'architecture religieuse en France à l'époque gothique*, 2 vols., Paris, 1926–7.
J. Harvey, *The Gothic World, 1100–1600*, London, 1950.
E. Panofsky, *Gothic Architecture and Scholasticism*, Latrobe, Pa., 1951.
O. von Simson, *The Gothic Cathedral*, New York, 1956.
P. Frankl, *Gothic Architecture*, Harmondsworth, 1962.

Sculpture

H. Jantzen, *Deutsche Bildhauer des XIII. Jahrhunderts*, Leipzig, 1925.
M. Aubert, *French Gothic Sculpture, 1140–1225*, New York, Florence, 1929.
P. Vitry, *French Gothic Sculpture, 1226–70*, New York, Florence, 1929.
A. Gardner, *English Medieval Sculpture*, 2nd ed., Cambridge, 1951.
J. Pope-Hennessy, *Italian Gothic Sculpture*, London, 1955.
E. Mâle, *The Gothic Image: Religious Art in France of the Thirteenth Century*, New York, 1957 (reprint of 1913 ed.).
W. Vöge, *Bildhauer des Mittelalters*, Berlin, 1958.

Painting

A. Stange, *Deutsche Malerie der Gotik*, 11 vols., Berlin, Munich, 1934–61.
G. Ring, *A Century of French Painting, 1400–1500*, London, 1949.
E. Panofsky, *Early Netherlandish Painting*, 2 vols., Cambridge, Mass., 1953.
J. Dupont and C. Gnudi, *Gothic Painting*, Geneva, 1954.
M. Aubert and A. Chastel, *Le vitrail français*, Paris, 1958.
P. Deschamps and M. Thibout, *La peinture murale en France au début de l'époque gothique (1180–1380)*, Paris, 1963.

RENAISSANCE AND MANNERISM
General

O. Benesch, *The Art of the Renaissance in Northern Europe*, Cambridge, Mass., 1945.
W. Paatz, *Die Kunst der Renaissance in Italien*, Stuttgart, 1953.
H. Wölfflin, *Classic Art*, London, 1953.
E. Panofsky, *Renaissance and Renascences in Western Art*, Stockholm, 1960.
A. Chastel, *The Age of Humanism: Europe, 1480–1530*, London, 1963.
P. and L. Murray, *The Art of the Renaissance*, London, 1963.
F. Württenberger, *Mannerism*, London, 1963.

Architecture

L. Hautecoeur, *Histoire de l'architecture classique en France*, vol. I, Paris, 1943.
B. Lowry, *Renaissance Architecture*, New York, London, 1962.
P. Murray, *The Architecture of the Italian Renaissance*, London, 1963.
R. Wittkower, *Architectural Principles in the Age of Humanism*, 3rd ed., London, 1963.

Sculpture

W. Pinder, *Die deutsche Plastik vom ausgehenden Mittelalters bis zum Ende der Renaissance*, 2 vols., Berlin, 1924–9.
G. Weise, *Die Plastik der Renaissance und des Frühbarock im nördlichen Spanien*, 2 vols., Tübingen, 1957–9.
J. Pope-Hennessy, *Italian Renaissance Sculpture*, London, 1958.
T. Müller, *Deutsche Plastik der Renaissance*, Königstein im Taunus, 1963.
J. Pope-Hennessy, *Italian High Renaissance and Baroque Sculpture*, 3 vols., London, 1963.

Painting

H. Voss, *Die Malerei der Spätrenaissance in Rom und Florenz*, 2 vols., Berlin, 1920.
B. Berenson, *The Italian Painters of the Renaissance*, London, 1952.
S. Béguin, *L'école de Fontainebleau*, Paris, 1960.
E. De Wald, *Italian Painting, 1200–1600*, New York, 1961.
S. Freedberg, *Painting of the High Renaissance in Rome and Florence*, 2 vols., Cambridge, Mass., 1961.

BAROQUE

General

W. Weisbach, *Der Barock als Kunst der Gegenreformation*, Berlin, 1921.
W. Weisbach, *Die Kunst des Barock in Italien, Frankreich, Deutschland und Spanien*, Berlin, 1924.
F. Kimball, *The Creation of the Rococo*, Philadelphia, 1943.
A. Blunt, *Art and Architecture in France, 1500–1700*, Harmondsworth, 1954.
R. Wittkower, *Art and Architecture in Italy, 1600–1750*, Harmondsworth, 1958.
G. Kubler and M. Soria, *Art and Architecture in Spain and Portugal and their American Dominions, 1500–1800*, Harmondsworth, 1959.
H. Gerson and E. H. ter Kuile, *Art and Architecture in Belgium, 1600–1800*, Harmondsworth, 1960.
A. Schönberger and H. Soehner, *The Age of Rococo*, London, New York, 1960.

Architecture

A. E. Brinckmann, *Die Baukunst des 17. und 18. Jahrhunderts*, 2 vols., Berlin, 1915–19.
H. Sedlmayr, *Österreichische Barockarchitektur, 1690–1740*, Vienna, 1930.
N. Lieb, *Barockkirchen zwischen Donau und Alpen*, Munich, 1953.
J. Bourke, *Baroque Churches of Central Europe*, 2nd ed., London, 1962.
H. A. Millon, *Baroque and Rococo Architecture*, New York, London, 1963.
J. Summerson, *Architecture in Britain, 1530–1830*, 4th ed., Harmondsworth, 1963.
H. Wölfflin, *Renaissance and Baroque*, London, 1964.

Sculpture

A. E. Brinckmann, *Barockskulptur*, Berlin, 1917.
A. E. Brinckmann, *Barock-Bozzetti*, 4 vols., Frankfurt am Main, 1923–5.
R. Wittkower, *Gian Lorenzo Bernini, the Sculptor of the Roman Baroque*, London, 1955.
I. Faldi, *La scultura barocca in Italia*, Milan, 1958.
A. Schönberger, *Deutsche Plastik des Barock*, Königstein im Taunus, 1963.
M. Whinney, *Sculpture in Britain, 1530–1830*, Harmondsworth, 1964.

Painting

M. J. Friedländer, *Die niederländischen Malerei des 17. Jahrhunderts*, Berlin, 1923.
H. Voss, *Die Malerei des Barock in Rom*, Berlin, 1925.
W. Drost, *Barockmalerei in den germanischen Ländern*, Berlin, 1926.
N. Pevsner and O. Grautoff, *Barockmalerei in den romanischen Ländern*, Berlin, 1928.
W. Weisbach, *Die französische Malerei des 17. Jahrhunderts*, Berlin, 1932.

W. Bernt, *Die niederländischen Malerei des 17. Jahrhunderts*, 3 vols., Munich, 1948.
H. Tintelnot, *Die barocke Freskomalerei in Deutschland*, Munich, 1951.
E. Waterhouse, *Painting in Britain, 1530–1790*, Harmondsworth, 1953.
M. Levey, *Painting in Eighteenth Century Venice*, London, 1959.

NINETEENTH AND TWENTIETH CENTURIES

General

G. Pauli, *Die Kunst des Klassizismus und der Romantik*, Berlin, 1925.
S. T. Madsen, *Sources of Art Nouveau*, Oslo, New York, 1956.
M. Brion, *Romantic Art*, London, 1960.
J. Cassou, É. Langui and N. Pevsner, *The Sources of Modern Art*, London, 1962.
R. Rosenblum, *Cubism and Twentieth-Century Art*, New York, 1961.
R. Schmutzler, *Art Nouveau*, London, 1964.

Architecture

B. Zevi, *Storia dell'architettura moderna*, Turin, 1950.
S. Giedion, *Space, Time and Architecture*, 3rd ed., Cambridge, Mass., 1954.
J. Joedicke, *A History of Modern Architecture*, New York, 1959.
R. Banham, *Theory and Design in the First Machine Age*, London, 1960.
Encyclopedia of Modern Architecture (ed. G. Hatje), London, 1963.
H.-R. Hitchcock, *Architecture: Nineteenth and Twentieth Centuries*. 2nd ed., Harmondsworth, 1963.

Sculpture

A. C. Ritchie, *Sculpture of the Twentieth Century*, New York, 1952.
W. Hofmann, *Die Plastik des 20. Jahrhunderts*, Frankfurt am Main, 1958.
M. Seuphor, *The Sculptor of this Century*, New York, 1960.
C. Giedion-Welcker, *Contemporary Sculpture: An Evolution in Volume and Space*, New York, London, 1961.
Dictionary of Modern Sculpture (ed. R. Maillard), London, 1962.
H. Read, *A Concise History of Modern Sculpture*, London, 1964.

Painting

A. Barr, *Cubism and Abstract Art*, New York, 1936.
W. Friedländer, *David to Delacroix*, Cambridge, Mass., 1952.
J. Rewald, *The History of Impressionism*, 2nd ed., New York, 1955.
J. Rewald, *Postimpressionism from Van Gogh to Gauguin*, New York, 1956.

Dictionary of Abstract Painting (ed. M. Seuphor), London, New York, 1957.

B. S. Myers, *Expressionism*, New York, London, 1957.

P. Selz, *German Expressionist Painting*, Berkeley, Los Angeles, 1957.

W. Verkauf, *Dada: Monograph of a Movement*, London, 1957.

J. Golding, *Cubism*, London, 1959.

J. Leymarie, *Fauvism*, Geneva, 1959.

W. Haftmann, *Painting in the Twentieth Century*, 2 vols., London, 1960.

M. Jean, *History of Surrealist Painting*, London, 1960.

F. Novotny, *Painting and Sculpture in Europe, 1780–1880*, Harmondsworth, 1960.

W. Hofmann, *Art in the Nineteenth Century*, London, 1961.

ACKNOWLEDGEMENTS

A. C. L., Brussels 446, 489, 511, 796
Acta Archaeologica III, Copenhagen 1932 (Photo Paul Sandberg) 193
Aerofilms and Aero Pictorial Ltd, London 390, 436, 549
Alinari, Florence 86, 87, 90, 102, 103, 109, 114, 117, 119, 123, 125, 129, 145, 153, 177, 179, 303, 306, 307, 313, 315, 316, 317, 318, 325, 336, 338, 401, 421, 425, 435, 443, 444, 457, 460, 473, 486, 495, 496, 497, 498, 513, 521, 522, 525, 529, 533, 534, 539, 540, 545, 546, 548, 552, 555, 557, 560, 561, 563, 567, 570, 571, 573, 575, 576, 627, 631, 632, 635, 637, 686, 705, 707, 782
Anderson, Rome 83, 92, 116, 140, 147, 150, 151, 178, 305, 309, 310, 319, 328, 337, 471, 524, 526, 527, 530, 531, 532, 538, 542, 543, 547, 551, 554, 556, 562, 569, 572, 574, 578, 579, 580, 599, 629, 630, 685, 688, 703, 706
Annan, Glasgow 807
Antikvarisk Topografiska Arkivei, Stockholm 200
Archaeological Museum, Istanbul 79, 84, 202
The Architectural Review, London (Photo Dell and Wainwright) 758
Archives Photographiques, Paris 245, 367, 456, 459, 488, 528, 553, 564, 692, 693, 731
The Art Institute of Chicago, Chicago 790, 843
ATA, Stockholm 185, 200
Lala Aufsberg, Sonthofen im Allgäu 400, 424, 463, 628
Louis Baumgartner, St Gall 238
Max Baur, Aschau/Chiemgau 645
Otto Bayer, Vienna 458
Bayerische Staatsbibliothek, Munich 248
Bayerische Staatsgemäldesammlungen, Munich 508, 611, 613, 711, 715, 717, 729, 777
Bayerisches Landesamt für Denkmalpflege, Munich 350
Bayerisches Nationalmuseum, Munich 595, 695
Beratungsstelle für Stahlverwendung, Düsseldorf 753
Rudolf Berliner, 'Ornamentale Vorlage-Blätter', Leipzig, 1925 591, 592, 593, 594, 675, 676
Berne, Kunstmuseum 818
E. Beyeler, Basle 861
Biblioteca Apostolica Vaticana, Rome 173
Biblioteca Palatina, Parma (photo Tosi) 175
Biblioteca Reale, Turin 518
Bibliothèque Nationale, Paris 170, 171, 183, 490
Bildarchiv Foto Marburg 13, 15, 19, 29, 30, 34, 36, 45, 46, 47, 50, 54, 56, 62, 64, 69, 71, 76, 77, 78, 96, 104, 106, 115, 118, 120, 124, 127, 130, 146, 232, 242, 246, 247, 252, 253, 254, 255, 321, 329, 340, 341, 346, 347, 348, 353, 403, 405, 439, 455, 461, 465, 466, 470, 482, 506, 517, 577, 622, 623, 624, 644, 651, 652, 665, 697, 721, 786, 804, 809, 828
Bórd Fáilte Éireann 199

Editions Braun, Mulhouse 231, 349
Ann Bredol-Lepper, Aachen 212
Brenwasser, New York 778
British Museum, London II, 27, 63, 80, 196, 241, 491, 584, 764
Brogi, Florence 304, 327, 472
Albrecht Brugger Luftbild, Stuttgart Airport (by permission of the Baden-Württemberg Ministry of the Interior, no. 2/7753) 605
Photo Bulloz, Paris 110, 732, 760
Bundesdenkmalamt, Vienna 355
Burlington Fine Arts Club, London, 'Catalogue of an Exhibition of Art of the Dark Ages in Europe', London 190
Cabinet des Médailles, Paris 191
J. Camponogara, Industrie Photo, Lyons 776, 781
Carvajol, Valladolid 689
Cassou, Langui, Pevsner 'Durchbruch zum zwanzigsten Jahrhundert', Munich 745
Wilhelm Castelli, Lübeck 409, 410
Central Press Photos Ltd 667
Chevojou, Paris 91, 746, 759
Photo Cichy 112
Prof. K. H. Clasen, Berlin-Grünau 438
Compagnie Aérienne Française, Suresnes (Seine) 445
Corpus Christi College, Cambridge IV
Cramers Kunstanstalt KG., Dortmund 602
Cuatro Hermanos, Madrid 568
Tošo Dabac, Zagreb (Hans Reich Verlag, Munich, 'Terra Magica-Fresken und Ikonen') 180
Dallas Museum of Fine Arts, Dallas (Texas) 864
Danish National Museum, Copenhagen 188, 189
O. Demus, 'Byzantine Mosaic Decoration', London 1948 182
Deutsche Fotothek, Dresden 233, 433, 723
Deutsche Kunstverlag GmbH., Munich and Berlin 742
Deutsches Archäologisches Institut, Athens 31, 39, 48, 75 (photo E. M. Czako) 26, 33, 37
Deutsches Archäologisches Institut, Madrid 221, 222, 223
Deutsches Archäologisches Institut, Rome 49, 68, 85, 108, 113, 131, 194
Devonshire Collection, Chatsworth (with permission of the Trustees of the Chatsworth Settlement) 727
E. Diez—O. Demus, 'Byzantine Mosaics in Greece, Hosios Lukas and Daphni', Cambridge (Mass.) 1931 174
Doeser Fotos, Holland 655, 834
Walter Dräyer, Zurich 107, 788
Robert Durandaud, Paris 447
Dyckerhoff & Widmann Archiv, Munich 831

Foto Eidenbenz, Basle 485
'The Encyclopedia of Architecture' (F. A. Praeger, New York) 680
Charles Fellmann, Colmar 612
Herbert Felton 416
A. Feulner, 'Kunstgeschichte des Möbels', Berlin 1927 682, 683
Fotocielo, Rome 312
Paul Frankl, 'Die frühmittelalterliche und romanische Baukunst' 216, 266, 290
Alison Frantz, Athens 162, 163
Dagobert Frey, 'Englisches Wesen im Spiegel seiner Kunst', Stuttgart and Berlin 740
Gabinetto Fotografico della Soprintendenza alle Gallerie, Florence 619
Gabinetto Fotografico Nazionale, Rome 28, 149, 335, 339
Galleria Nazionale, Naples 617
Galleria Nazionale d'Arte Moderna Arte Contemporanea, Rome, 789
'Gallia', XIIe Supplément, 1958 186
Photo-Atelier Gerlach, Vienna 830
Germanisches Nationalmuseum, Nuremberg 192, 505
Otto Gerson Gallery 849
G. Gherardi–A. Fiorelli, Rome 851
Giraudon, Paris 275, 287, 510, 625, 691
Glasgow Art Gallery and Museum, Glasgow, 718
Grabar, Lazarev, Kemenev, 'Geschichte der Russischen Kunst' II, Dresden 1957 165
The Green Studio Ltd., Dublin 237
Kurt Grimm, Thorn 432
Heikki Havas, Helsinki 852
Lucien Hervé, Paris 827
Esbjørn Hiort, 'Modern Danish Furniture', Copenhagen 853
Hirmer Verlag, Munich 1, 3, 6, 7, 8, 9, 10, 12, 17, 40, 41, 42, 51, 53, 57, 58, 60, 67, 70, 73, 132, 133, 141, 152, 164, 166, 168, 169, 172, 176, 181, 646, 648, 699; illustration from 'Frühchristliche Kunst': 148; plans and drawings from 'Kreta und das mykenische Hellas': 5; 'Griechische Tempel und Heiligtümer': 24, 25, 38, 43, 44, 66, 97; 'Frühchristliche Kunst': 134, 135, 137, 139, 154, 155; 'Kunst aus Byzanz': 161
Henry-Russel Hitchcock, 'Architecture: Nineteenth and Twentieth Centuries', Penguin Books, Ltd, London 1958 748, 757
Werner Hofmann, 'Das Irdische Paradies', Munich 767
Hubmann, Vienna 853
Jos. Jeiter, Hadamar/Nassau 217
H. Kähler, 'Rom und seine Welt', Munich 122
A. F. Kersting, London 121, 126, 224, 225, 293, 294, 296, 302, 306, 308, 324, 331, 357, 358, 385, 388, 391, 392, 393, 402, 418, 419, 441, 541, 589, 590, 609, 636, 638, 653, 656, 666, 670, 671, 672, 747
Kestner-Museum, Hanover 448
Erich Klatt, 'Die Konstruktion alter Möbel', Stuttgart 323
Felix Klee, Berne 824, 842
Kleinhempel Fotowerkstätten, Hamburg 504, 773, 814, 863
Ernst Kloss, 'Michael Willmann', Breslau 725
Adalbert Komers-Lindenbach, Vienna 825

Kubler/Soria, 'Art and Architecture in Spain and Portugal, 1500–1800', Penguin Books Ltd, London 714
Kunstgeschichtliche Bildstelle der Humboldt-Universität, Berlin 363, 434
Kunstgewerbemuseum, Zurich (photo Walter Binder) 795, 803
Kunsthistorisches Museum, Vienna 616, 724
Landesbibliothek, Darmstadt 244
Landesbildstelle Baden, Karlsruhe 484
Landesbildstelle, Hanover 234, 601
Landesbildstelle, Salzburg (photo Puschej) 431
Landesbildstelle Württemberg, Stuttgart 269, 454, 474, 479, 483, 494
Landesdenkmalamt Westfalen-Lippe, Münster 271, 430
Liverpool City Museum, Liverpool 197
Marlborough Fine Art Ltd, London 859
M.A.S., Barcelona 301, 361, 397, 442, 587, 588, 639, 690, 744, 805
Paul Mayen, New York 800
Metropolitan Museum of Art (bequest of Mrs H. O. Havemeyer), New York 772
Willi Moegle, Stuttgart, 816
Fritz Monshouwer, Rotterdam 860
Werner Moser, Zurich 799
Musée d'Art et d'Histoire, Geneva 507, 769
Musée des Arts Décoratifs, Paris 450, 679, 681
Musée des Beaux-Arts, Nantes 771
Musées Nationaux, Versailles 626, 728, 733, 761, 780, 791
Museo Nazionale, Rome 195
Museo del Prado, Madrid 712
Museum der Stadt Ulm 449
Museum des 20. Jahrhunderts, Vienna 802
Museum für Kunst und Gewerbe, Hamburg 621
Museum of Art, São Paulo VIII
Museum of Modern Art, New York (photo Sunami) 815, 837, 838, 845; (photo George Barrows) 855
Narodni Galerie V, Prague (photo Vlad. Fyman) 501, 503
National Buildings Record, London 297, 298, 396, 415, 669
National Gallery, London 509, 565, 614, 722, 731, 737, 738
National Gallery of Art, Washington D.C. 716; VII (Chester Dale Collection), 847
Nationalmuseum, Stockholm 784
National Museum of Ireland, Dublin 199
National Portrait Gallery, London 735, 737
Detlef Michael Noack 329
Öffentliche Kunstsammlung, Basle 819
Österreichische Galerie, Vienna 698, 810
Österreichische Nationalbibliothek, Vienna 167, 198, 362; (photo Otto Schmidt, Vienna) 743, 751
Pär Olsén, 'Die Saxe von Valsgärde', Acta Musei Antiquitatum, Uppsala 204, 205
N. Pevsner, 'Europäische Architektur', Munich 741
Artur Pfan, Mannheim-Fendenheim 263
Phaidon Press, London 721
Portland Art Museum (photo Condit) 779
R. Remy Studio, Dijon 618
Eduard Renner, Frankfurt am Main 272

Hans Retzlaff, Tann/Rhön 258

Rheinisches Bildarchiv, Cologne 239, 249, 250, 342, 343, 351, 500, 708, 787, 813

Rheinisches Landesmuseum, Bonn 187

E. Richter, Rome 59

Rijksmuseum, Amsterdam 702

Rijksmuseum Kröller-Müller, Otterlo 794, 820, 823

Photo Rossi, Venice 566

J. P. Rossignol 821

Fotoatelier Rossmann, Innsbruck 620

Jean Roubier, Paris 215, 228, 229, 230, 256, 259, 276, 279, 280, 282, 283, 285, 286, 289, 291, 292, 332, 224, 354, 359, 365, 366, 368, 380, 382, 384, 398, 414, 420, 462, 464, 480, 585, 608, 654, 662, 664

B. Salin, 'Die altergermanische Thierornamentik' 206

M. Sauvage, 'Vlaminck', Geneva 811

Oscar Savio, Rome 550

Dr Arthur Schlegel, Munich 603, 604, 641, 696

Schlossmuseum Gotha, Schloss Friedenstein 694

Erica Schmidt 268

Helga Schmidt-Glassner, Stuttgart 219, 220, 257, 262, 264, 274, 322, 344, 358, 404, 407, 408, 426, 429, 467, 468, 469, 475, 476, 481, 606, 640, 642, 643, 649, 650, 657, 678

Schmölz und Ulrich KG., Cologne 273

Anton Schroll & Co., Vienna 701

Schweizerisches Landesmuseum, Zurich 203, 600

Walter Scott, Bradford 417

Photo Edwin Smith 757

Societé Française du Microfilm, Paris 675

Solomon R. Guggenheim Museum, New York 846, 848

J. Sommer, Starnberg/See (Oberbayern) 700

Photo Sphinx, Athens 100

Staatliche Antikensammlungen, Munich (photo C. H. Krüger-Moessner) 16; (Photo Reproduktionsanstalt Franz Kauffmann) 89

Staatliche Bibliothek, Bamberg 243

Staatliche Bildstelle, Munich/Berlin 607

Staatliche Graphische Sammlung, Munich 610

Staatliche Kunstsammlungen, Dresden 720

Staatliche Landesbildstelle Hessen, Frankfurt am Main 260

Staatliche Museen zu Berlin: Antikensammlung 2, 72, 93, 94; Nationalgalerie 783

Staatsgalerie Stuttgart 687, 726

Stadtbibliothek Trier 211

Städelsches Kunstinstitut, Frankfurt am Main 765

Statens Museum for Kunst, Copenhagen 812

Stiftung Preussischer Kulturbesitz, Nationalgalerie Berlin 478, 704, 770

Dr Franz Stoedtner, Düsseldorf 240, 752, 801, 829

Robert Th. Stoll, 'Van Gogh, Gauguin, Cézanne', Zurich 739

Ezra Stoller Associates, Rye, N.Y. 850

Tate Gallery, London 736, 762, 763, 774, 792

Editions Pierre Tisné, Paris 862

Universitet i Bergen, Årbok, 1955, Histor.—antikvarisk rekke no. 3 207

Universitetes Oldsaksamling, Oslo 208

Universiteitsbibliotek, Utrecht III

USIS, Bad Godesberg 797

Vatican, Archivio Fotografico 88, 101, 558, 559

Verein Deutscher Eisenhüttenfachleute, Bildarchiv Stahleisen, Düsseldorf 754

Victoria and Albert Museum, London 684, 768

Roger-Viollet, Paris 95, 143, 281, 288, 330, 333, 335, 383, 386, 581, 583, 586, 659, 660, 661, 663, 766, 775, 785

Verlag Ernst Wasmuth, Tübingen 449, 450, 451, 452, 596, 597, 598

Photo-Wehmeyer, Hildesheim 251

Walter Wellek 858

Peter Witte, Spich über Troisdorf 844

Württembergisches Landesmuseum, Stuttgart 201, 210

Zeitschrift für Württembergische Landesgeschichte, Stuttgart, 209

Zentralinstitut für Kunstgeschichte, Munich 270